Deep Learning with R for Beginners

Design neural network models in R 3.5 using TensorFlow, Keras, and MXNet

Mark Hodnett
Joshua F. Wiley
Yuxi (Hayden) Liu
Pablo Maldonado

BIRMINGHAM - MUMBAI

Deep Learning with R for Beginners

First published: May 2019

Production reference: 2250719

Published by Packt Publishing Ltd.
Livery Place
35 Livery Street
Birmingham
B3 2PB, UK.

ISBN 978-1-83864-270-9

www.packtpub.com

`mapt.io`

Mapt is an online digital library that gives you full access to over 5,000 books and videos, as well as industry leading tools to help you plan your personal development and advance your career. For more information, please visit our website.

Why subscribe?

- Spend less time learning and more time coding with practical eBooks and Videos from over 4,000 industry professionals

- Improve your learning with Skill Plans built especially for you

- Get a free eBook or video every month

- Mapt is fully searchable

- Copy and paste, print, and bookmark content

Packt.com

Did you know that Packt offers eBook versions of every book published, with PDF and ePub files available? You can upgrade to the eBook version at `www.packt.com` and as a print book customer, you are entitled to a discount on the eBook copy. Get in touch with us at `customercare@packtpub.com` for more details.

At `www.packt.com`, you can also read a collection of free technical articles, sign up for a range of free newsletters, and receive exclusive discounts and offers on Packt books and eBooks.

Contributors

About the authors

Mark Hodnett is a data scientist with over 20 years of industry experience in software development, business intelligence systems, and data science. He has worked in a variety of industries, including CRM systems, retail loyalty, IoT systems, and accountancy. He holds a master's in data science and an MBA. He works in Cork, Ireland, as a senior data scientist with AltViz.

Joshua F. Wiley is a lecturer at Monash University, conducting quantitative research on sleep, stress, and health. He earned his Ph.D. from the University of California, Los Angeles and completed postdoctoral training in primary care and prevention. In statistics and data science, Joshua focuses on biostatistics and is interested in reproducible research and graphical displays of data and statistical models. He develops or co-develops a number of R packages including Varian, a package to conduct Bayesian scale-location structural equation models, and MplusAutomation, a popular package that links R to the commercial Mplus software.

Yuxi (Hayden) Liu is an experienced data scientist who's focused on developing machine learning and deep learning models and systems. He has worked in a variety of data-driven domains and has applied his machine learning expertise to computational advertising, recommendation, and network anomaly detection. He published five first-authored IEEE transaction and conference papers during his master's research at the University of Toronto. He is an education enthusiast and the author of a series of machine learning books. His first book, the first edition of Python Machine Learning By Example, was a #1 bestseller on Amazon India in 2017 and 2018. His other books include R Deep Learning Projects and Hands-On Deep Learning Architectures with Python published by Packt.

Pablo Maldonado is an applied mathematician and data scientist with a taste for software development since his days of programming BASIC on a Tandy 1000. As an academic and business consultant, he spends a great deal of his time building applied artificial intelligence solutions for text analytics, sensor and transactional data, and reinforcement learning. Pablo earned his Ph.D. in applied mathematics (with focus on mathematical game theory) at the Universite Pierre et Marie Curie in Paris, France.

Packt is searching for authors like you

If you're interested in becoming an author for Packt, please visit authors.packtpub.com and apply today. We have worked with thousands of developers and tech professionals, just like you, to help them share their insight with the global tech community. You can make a general application, apply for a specific hot topic that we are recruiting an author for, or submit your own idea.

Table of Contents

Preface

Deep learning finds practical applications in several domains and R is a preferred language to design and deploy deep learning models.

This Learning Path introduces you to the basics of deep learning and teaches you to build a neural network model from scratch. As you make your way through the concepts, you'll explore deep learning libraries and create deep learning models for a variety of problems, such as anomaly detection and recommendation systems. You'll cover advanced topics, such as generative adversarial networks (GANs), transfer learning, and large-scale deep learning in the cloud. Before it ends, this Learning Path teaches you advanced topics, such as model optimization, overfitting, and data augmentation. Through real-world projects, you'll learn how to train convolutional neural networks, recurrent neural networks, and LSTMs in R.

By the end of this Learning Path, you'll have a better understanding of deep learning concepts and will be able to implement deep learning concepts in your research work or projects.

This Learning Path includes content from the following Packt products:

- R Deep Learning Essentials - Second Edition by Joshua F. Wiley and Mark Hodnett
- R Deep Learning Projects by Yuxi (Hayden) Liu and Pablo Maldonado

Who this book is for

This Learning Path is ideal for aspiring data scientists, data analysts, machine learning developers, and deep learning enthusiasts who are well versed in machine learning concepts and are looking to explore the deep learning paradigm using R. Fundamental understanding of the R language and familiarity with basic concepts of deep learning are necessary to get the most out of this Learning Path.

What this book covers

Chapter 1, Getting Started with Deep Learning, gives an introduction to deep learning and neural networks. It also gives a brief introduction on how to set up your R environment.

Chapter 2, Training a Prediction Model, begins with building neural network models using the existing packages in R. This chapter also discusses overfitting, which is an issue in most deep learning models

Chapter 3, Deep Learning Fundamentals, teaches how to build a neural network in R from scratch. We then show how our code relates to MXNet, a deep learning library.

Chapter 4, Training Deep Prediction Models, looks at activations and introduces the MXNet library. We then build a deep learning prediction model for a real-life example. We will take a raw dataset of transactional data and develop a data pipeline to create a model that predicts which customers will return in the next 14 days.

Chapter 5, Image Classification Using Convolutional Neural Networks, looks at image classification tasks. First, we will introduce some of the core concepts, such as convolutional and pooling layers, and then we will show how to use these layers to classify images

Chapter 6, Tuning and Optimizing Models, discusses how to tune and optimize deep learning models. We look at tuning hyperparameters and using data augmentation.

Chapter 7, Natural Language Processing Using Deep Learning, shows how to use deep learning for Natural Language Processing (NLP) tasks. We show how deep learning algorithms outperform traditional NLP techniques, while also being much easier to develop

Chapter 8, Deep Learning Models Using TensorFlow in R, looks at using the TensorFlow API in R. We also look at some additional packages available within TensorFlow that make developing TensorFlow models simpler and help in hyperparameter selection.

Chapter 9, Anomaly Detection and Recommendation Systems, shows how we can use deep learning models to create embeddings that are lower order representations of data. We then show how to use embeddings for anomaly detection and to create a recommendation system.

Chapter 10, Running Deep Learning Models in the Cloud, covers how to use AWS, Azure, and Google Cloud services to train deep learning models. This chapter shows how to train your models at low-cost in the cloud.

Chapter 11, The Next Level in Deep Learning, introduces an end-to-end solution for image classification. We take a set of image files, train a model, reuse that model for transfer learning and then show how to deploy that model to production. We also briefly discuss Generative Adversarial Networks (GANs) and reinforcement learning.

Chapter 12, Handwritten Digit Recognition Using Convolutional Neural Networks, we begin with a recap of logistic regression and multilayer perceptron. We'll solve the problem with these two algorithms. We will then move on to the biologically inspired variants of multilayer perceptron—convolutional neural networks (CNNs).

Chapter 13, Traffic Sign Recognition for Intelligent Vehicles, explains how to use CNNs for another application—traffic sign detection. We will also cover several important concepts of deep learning in this chapter and get readers familiar with other popular frameworks and libraries, such as Keras and TensorFlow. We will also introduce the dropout technique as a regularization approach and utilize data augmentation techniques to deal with a lack of training data.

Chapter 14, Fraud Detection with Autoencoders, introduces a type of deep learning model that can be used for anomaly detection. Outliers can be found within a collection of images, a text corpus, or transactional data. We will dive into applications of autoencoders and how they can be used for outlier detection in this domain.

Chapter 15, Text Generation Using Recurrent Neural Networks, introduces different models of neural networks that try to capture the elusive properties of memory and abstraction to produce powerful models. We will apply different methods to tackle the text generation problem and suggest directions of further exploration.

Chapter 16, Sentiment Analysis with Word Embeddings, shows how to use the popular GloVe algorithm for sentiment analysis, as well as other, less abstract tools. Although this algorithm is, strictly speaking, not a deep learning application, it belongs to the modern toolkit of the data scientist, and it can be combined with other deep learning techniques.

To get the most out of this book

You should be comfortable with R and RStudio and have some knowledge of college-level mathematics (calculus and linear algebra). Working knowledge of basic machine learning algorithms for classification, regression problems, and clustering might be helpful, but it is not strictly required

You would need access to a high-end machine or even a machine with a GPU. To get the most out of this book, I recommend that you execute all the code examples. Experiment with them, change the parameters, and try to beat the metrics in the book.

Download the example code files

You can download the example code files for this book from your account at www.packt.com. If you purchased this book elsewhere, you can visit www.packt.com/support and register to have the files emailed directly to you.

You can download the code files by following these steps:

1. Log in or register at www.packt.com.
2. Select the **SUPPORT** tab.
3. Click on **Code Downloads & Errata**.
4. Enter the name of the book in the **Search** box and follow the onscreen instructions.

Once the file is downloaded, please make sure that you unzip or extract the folder using the latest version of:

- WinRAR/7-Zip for Windows
- Zipeg/iZip/UnRarX for Mac
- 7-Zip/PeaZip for Linux

The code bundle for the book is also hosted on GitHub at https://github.com/ TrainingByPackt/Deep-Learning-with-R-for-Beginners .In case there's an update to the code, it will be updated on the existing GitHub repository.

We also have other code bundles from our rich catalogue of books and videos available at https://github.com/PacktPublishing/. Check them out!

Download the color images of this book

We also provide you with a PDF file that has color images of the screenshots/diagrams used in this book. The color images will help you better understand the changes in the output. You can download this file from `https://www.packtpub.com/sites/default/files/downloads/9781838642709_ColorImages.pdf`

Conventions used

There are a number of text conventions used throughout this book.

`CodeInText`: Indicates code words in text, database table names, folder names, filenames, file extensions, pathnames, dummy URLs, user input, and Twitter handles. Here is an example: "The `input()` method is used to get an input from the user."

A block of code is set as follows:

```
> for (i in 1:16) {
+ outputData <- as.array
(executor$ref.outputs$activation15_output)[,,i,1]
+ image(outputData, xaxt='n', yaxt='n',
col=grey.colors(255)
+ )
+ }
```

Any command-line input or output is written as follows:

```
$ tensorboard --logdir /tensorflow_logs
```

Bold: Indicates a new term, an important word, or words that you see onscreen. For example, words in menus or dialog boxes appear in the text like this. Here is an example: "If you need something different, click on the **DOWNLOADS** link in the header for all possible downloads: "

 Warnings or important notes appear like this.

 Tips and tricks appear like this.

Get in touch

Feedback from our readers is always welcome.

General feedback: If you have questions about any aspect of this book, mention the book title in the subject of your message and email us at customercare@packtpub.com.

Errata: Although we have taken every care to ensure the accuracy of our content, mistakes do happen. If you have found a mistake in this book, we would be grateful if you would report this to us. Please visit www.packt.com/submit-errata, selecting your book, clicking on the Errata Submission Form link, and entering the details.

Piracy: If you come across any illegal copies of our works in any form on the Internet, we would be grateful if you would provide us with the location address or website name. Please contact us at copyright@packt.com with a link to the material.

If you are interested in becoming an author: If there is a topic that you have expertise in and you are interested in either writing or contributing to a book, please visit authors.packtpub.com.

Reviews

Please leave a review. Once you have read and used this book, why not leave a review on the site that you purchased it from? Potential readers can then see and use your unbiased opinion to make purchase decisions, we at Packt can understand what you think about our products, and our authors can see your feedback on their book. Thank you!

For more information about Packt, please visit packt.com.

1
Getting Started with Deep Learning

This chapter discusses deep learning, a powerful multilayered architecture for pattern-recognition, signal-detection, and classification or prediction. Although deep learning is not new, it is only in the past decade that it has gained great popularity, due in part to advances in computational capacity and new ways of more efficiently training models, as well as the availability of ever-increasing amounts of data. In this chapter, you will learn what deep learning is, the R packages available for training such models, and how to get your system set up for analysis. We will briefly discuss **MXNet** and **Keras**, which are the two main frameworks that we will use for many of the examples in later chapters to actually train and use deep learning models.

In this chapter, we will explore the following topics:

- What is deep learning?
- A conceptual overview of deep learning
- Setting up your R environment and the deep learning frameworks available in R
- GPUs and reproducibility

What is deep learning?

Deep learning is a subfield within machine learning, which in turn is a subfield within artificial intelligence. **Artificial intelligence** is the art of creating machines that perform functions that require intelligence when performed by people. **Machine learning** uses algorithms that learn without being explicitly programmed. Deep learning is the subset of machine learning that uses artificial neural networks that mimic how the brain works.

The following diagram shows the relationships between them. For example, self-driving cars are an application of artificial intelligence. A critical part of self-driving cars is to recognize other road users, cars, pedestrians, cyclists, and so on. This requires machine learning because it is not possible to explicitly program this. Finally, deep learning may be chosen as the method to implement this machine learning task:

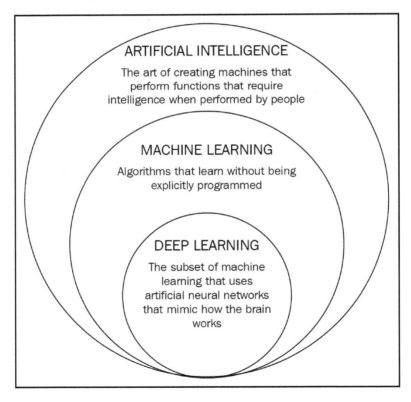

Figure 1.1: The relationship between artificial intelligence, machine learning, and deep learning

Artificial intelligence as a field has existed since the 1940s; the definition used in the previous diagram is from Kurzweil, 1990. It is a broad field that encompasses ideas from many different fields, including philosophy, mathematics, neuroscience, and computer engineering. Machine learning is a subfield within artificial intelligence that is devoted to developing and using algorithms that learn from raw data. When the machine learning task has to predict an outcome, it is known as **supervised learning**. When the task is to predict from a set of possible outcomes, it is a **classification** task, and when the task is to predict a numeric value, it is a **regression** task. Some examples of classification tasks are whether a particular credit card purchase is fraudulent, or whether a given image is of a cat or a dog. An example of a regression task is predicting how much money a customer will spend in the next month. There are other types of machine learning where the learning does not predict values. This is called **unsupervised learning** and includes clustering (segmenting) the data, or creating a compressed format of the data.

Deep learning is a subfield within machine learning. It is called **deep** because it uses multiple layers to map the relationship between input and output. A **layer** is a collection of neurons that perform a mathematical operation on its input. This will be explained in more detail in the next section, *Conceptual overview of neural networks*. This deep architecture means the model is large enough to handle many variables and that it is sufficiently flexible to approximate the patterns in the data. Deep learning can also generate features as part of the overall learning algorithm, rather than feature-creation being a prerequisite step. Deep learning has proven particularly effective in the fields of image-recognition (including handwriting as well as photo- or object-classification) , speech recognition and natural-language. It has completely transformed how to use image, text, and speech data for prediction in the past few years, replacing previous methods of working with these types of data. It has also opened up these fields to a lot more people because it automates a lot of the feature-generation, which required specialist skills.

Deep learning is not the only technique available in machine learning. There are other types of machine learning algorithms; the most popular include regression, decision trees, random forest, and naive bayes. For many use cases, one of these algorithms could be a better choice. Some examples of use cases where deep learning may not be the best choice include when interpretability is an essential requirement, the dataset size is small, or you have limited resources (time and/or hardware) to develop a model. It is important to realize that despite, the industry hype, most machine learning in industry does not use deep learning. Having said that, this book covers deep learning algorithms, so we will move on. The next sections will discuss neural networks and deep neural networks in more depth.

A conceptual overview of neural networks

It can be difficult to understand why neural networks work so well. This introduction will look at them from two viewpoints. If you have an understanding of how linear regression works, the first viewpoint should be useful. The second viewpoint is more intuitive and less technical, but equally valid. I encourage you to read both and spend some time contemplating both overviews.

Neural networks as an extension of linear regression

One of the simplest and oldest prediction models is **regression**. It predicts a continuous value (that is, a number) based on another value. The linear regression function is:

y=mx+b

Where y is the value you want to predict and x is your input variable. The linear regression coefficients (or parameters) are m (the slope of the line) and b (the intercept). The following R code creates a line with the *y= 1.4x -2* function and plots it:

```
set.seed(42)
m <- 1.4
b <- -1.2
x <- 0:9
jitter<-0.6
xline <- x
y <- m*x+b
x <- x+rnorm(10)*jitter
title <- paste("y = ",m,"x ",b,sep="")
plot(xline,y,type="l",lty=2,col="red",main=title,xlim=c(0,max(y)),ylim=c(0,
max(y)))
points(x[seq(1,10,2)],y[seq(1,10,2)],pch=1)
points(x[seq(2,11,2)],y[seq(2,11,2)],pch=4)
```

The *o* or *x* points are the values to be predicted given a value on the *x* axis and the line is the ground truth. Some random noise is added, so that the points are not exactly on the line. This code produces the following output:

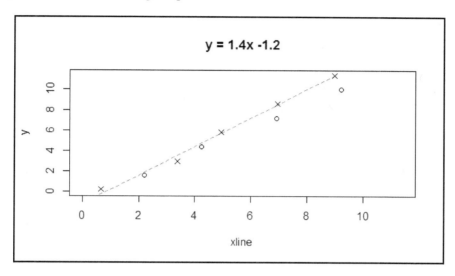

Figure 1.2: Example of a regression line fitted to data (that is, predict *y* from *x*)

In a regression task, you are given some *x* and corresponding *y* values, but are not given the underlying function to map *x* to *y*. The purpose of a supervised machine learning task is that given some previous examples of *x* and *y*, can we predict the *y* values for new data where we only have *x* and not *y*. An example might be to predict house prices based on the number of bedrooms in the house. So far, we have only considered a single input variable, *x*, but we can easily extend the example to handle multiple input variables. For the house example, we would use the number of bedrooms and square footage to predict the price of the house. Our code can accommodate this by changing the input, *x*, from a vector (one-dimensional array) into a matrix (two-dimensional array).

If we consider our model for predicting house prices, linear regression has a serious limitation: it can only estimate linear functions. If the mapping from *x* to *y* is not linear, it will not predict *y* very well. The function always results in a straight line for one variable and a hyperplane if multiple *x* predictor values are used. This means that linear regression models may not be accurate at the low and high extent of the data.

A simple trick to make the model fit nonlinear relationships is to add polynomial terms to the function. This is known as **polynomial regression**. For example, by adding a polynomial of degree 4, our function changes to:

$y = m_1x^4 + m_2x^3 + m_3x^2 + m_4x + b$

By adding these extra terms, the line (or decision boundary) is no longer linear. The following code demonstrates this – we create some sample data and we create three regression models to fit this data. The first model has no polynomial terms, the model is a straight line and fits the data very poorly. The second model (blue circles) has polynomials up to degree 3, that is, X, X^2, and X^3. The last model has polynomials up to degree 12, that is, X, X^2,......, X^{12}. The first model (straight line) underfits the data and the last line overfits the data. Overfitting refers to situations where the model is too complex and ends up memorizing the data. This means that the model does not generalize well and will perform poorly on unseen data. The following code generates the data and creates three models with increasing levels of polynomial:

```
par(mfrow=c(1,2))
set.seed(1)
x1 <- seq(-2,2,0.5)

# y=x^2-6
jitter<-0.3
y1 <- (x1^2)-6
x1 <- x1+rnorm(length(x1))*jitter
plot(x1,y1,xlim=c(-8,12),ylim=c(-8,10),pch=1)
x <- x1
y <- y1

# y=-x
jitter<-0.8
x2 <- seq(-7,-5,0.4)
y2 <- -x2
x2 <- x2+rnorm(length(x2))*jitter
points(x2,y2,pch=2)
x <- c(x,x2)
y <- c(y,y2)

# y=0.4 *rnorm(length(x3))*jitter
jitter<-1.2
x3 <- seq(5,9,0.5)
y3 <- 0.4 *rnorm(length(x3))*jitter
points(x3,y3,pch=3)
x <- c(x,x3)
y <- c(y,y3)
```

```r
df <- data.frame(cbind(x,y))
plot(x,y,xlim=c(-8,12),ylim=c(-8,10),pch=4)

model1 <- lm(y~.,data=df)
abline(coef(model1),lty=2,col="red")

max_degree<-3
for (i in 2:max_degree)
{
 col<-paste("x",i,sep="")
 df[,col] <- df$x^i
}
model2 <- lm(y~.,data=df)
xplot <- seq(-8,12,0.1)
yplot <- (xplot^0)*model2$coefficients[1]
for (i in 1:max_degree)
 yplot <- yplot +(xplot^i)*model2$coefficients[i+1]
points(xplot,yplot,col="blue", cex=0.5)

max_degree<-12
for (i in 2:max_degree)
{
 col<-paste("x",i,sep="")
 df[,col] <- df$x^i
}
model3 <- lm(y~.,data=df)
xplot <- seq(-8,12,0.1)
yplot <- (xplot^0)*model3$coefficients[1]
for (i in 1:max_degree)
 yplot <- yplot +(xplot^i)*model3$coefficients[i+1]
points(xplot,yplot,col="green", cex=0.5,pch=2)

MSE1 <- c(crossprod(model1$residuals)) / length(model1$residuals)
MSE2 <- c(crossprod(model2$residuals)) / length(model2$residuals)
MSE3 <- c(crossprod(model3$residuals)) / length(model3$residuals)
print(sprintf(" Model 1 MSE = %1.2f",MSE1))
[1] " Model 1 MSE = 14.17"
print(sprintf(" Model 2 MSE = %1.2f",MSE2))
[1] " Model 2 MSE = 3.63"
print(sprintf(" Model 3 MSE = %1.2f",MSE3))
[1] " Model 3 MSE = 0.07"
```

If we were selecting one of these models to use, we should select the middle model, even though the third model has a lower **MSE** (**mean-squared error**). In the following screenshot; the best model is the curved line from the top left corner:

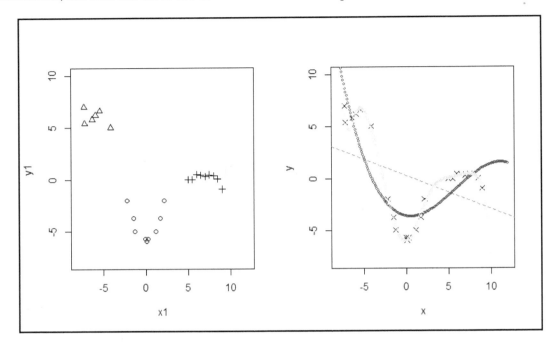

Figure 1.3: Polynomial regression

If we look at the three models and see how they handle the extreme left and right points, we see why overfitting can lead to poor results on unseen data. On the right side of the plot, the last series of points (plus signs) have a local linear relationship. However, the polynomial regression line with degree 12 (green triangles) puts too much emphasis on the last point, which is extra noise and the line moves down sharply. This would cause the model to predict extreme negative values for y as x increases, which is not justified if we look at the data. Overfitting is an important issue that we will look at in more detail in later chapters.

By adding square, cube, and more polynomial terms, the model can fit more complex data than if we just used linear functions on the input data. Neural networks use a similar concept, except that, instead of taking polynomial terms of the input variable, they chain multiple regression functions together with nonlinear terms between them.

The following is an example of a neural network architecture. The circles are nodes and the lines are the connections between nodes. If a connection exists between two nodes, the output from the node on the left is the input for the next node. The output value from a node is a matrix operation on the input values to the node and the weights of the node:

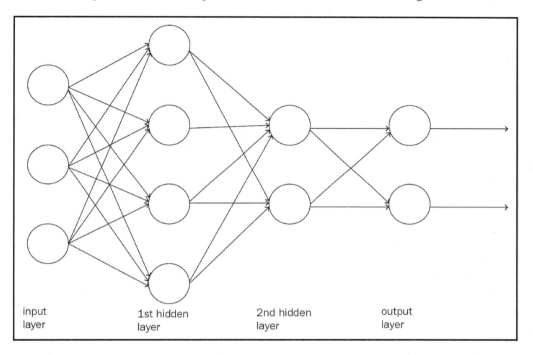

Figure 1.4: An example neural network

Before the output values from a node are passed to the next node as input values, a function is applied to the values to change the overall function to a non-linear function. These are known as **activation functions** and they perform the same role as the polynomial terms.

This idea of creating a machine learning model by combining multiple small functions together is a very common paradigm in machine learning. It is used in random forests, where many small independent decision trees *vote* for the result. It is also used in boosting algorithms, where the misclassified instances from one function are given more prominence in the next function.

By including many layers of nodes, the neural network model can approximate almost any function. It does make training the model more difficult, so we'll give a brief explanation of how to train a neural network. Each node is assigned a set of random weights initially. For the first pass, these weights are used to calculate and pass (or propagate) values from the input layer to the hidden layers and finally to the output layer. This is known as **forward-propagation**. Because the weights were set randomly, the final (prediction) values at the output layer will not be accurate compared to the actual values, so we need a method of calculating how different the predicted values are from the actual values. This is calculated using a **cost function**, which gives a measure of how accurate the model is during training. We then need to adjust the weights in the nodes from the output layer backward to get us nearer to the target values. This is done using **backward-propagation**; we move from right to left, updating the weights of the nodes in each layer very slightly to get us very slightly closer to the actual values. The cycle of forward-propagation and backward-propagation continues until the error value from the loss function stops getting smaller; this may require hundreds, or thousands of iterations, or epochs.

To update the node weights correctly, we need to know that the change will get us nearer to the target, which is to minimize the result from the cost function. We are able to do this because of a clever trick, we use activation functions that have derivative functions.

If your knowledge of calculus is limited, it can be difficult to get an understanding of derivatives initially. But in simple terms, a function may have a derivative formula that tells us how to change the *input* of a function so that the *output* of the function moves in a positive or negative manner. This derivative/formula enables the algorithm to minimize the cost function, which is a measurement of error. In more technical terms, the derivative of the function measures the rate of change in the function as the input changes. If we know the rate of change of a function as the input changes, and more importantly what direction it changes in, then we can use this to get nearer to minimizing that function. An example that you may have seen before is the following diagram:

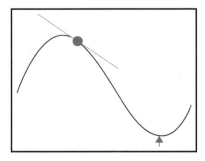

Figure 1.5: A function (curved) line and its derivative at a point

In this diagram, the curved line is a mathematical function we want to minimize over y, that is, we want to get to the lowest point (which is marked by the arrow). We are currently at the point in the red circle, and the derivative at that point is the slope of the tangent. The derivative function indicates the direction we need to move in to get there. The derivative value changes as we get nearer the target (the arrow), so we cannot make the move in one big step. Therefore, the algorithm moves in small steps and re-calculates the derivative after each step, but if we choose too small a step, it will take very long to **converge** (that is, get near the minimum). If we take too big a step, we run the risk of overshooting the minimum value. How big a step you take is known as the **learning rate**, and it effectively decides how long it takes the algorithm to train.

This might seem a bit abstract, so an analogy should make it somewhat clearer. This analogy may be over-simplified, but it explains derivatives, learning rates, and cost functions. Imagine a simple model of driving a car, where the speed must be set to a value that is suitable for the conditions and the speed limit. The difference between your current speed and the target speed is the error rate and this is calculated using a cost function (just simple subtraction, in this case). To change your speed, you apply the gas pedal to speed up or the brake pedal to slow down. The acceleration/deceleration (that is, the rate of change of the speed) is the derivative of the speed. The amount of force that is applied to the pedals changes how fast the acceleration/deceleration occurs, the force is similar to the learning rate in a machine learning algorithm. It controls how long it takes to get to the target value. If only a small change is applied to the pedals, you will eventually get to your target speed, but it will take much longer. However, you usually don't want to apply maximum force to the pedals, to do so may be dangerous (if you slam on the brakes) or a waste of fuel (if you accelerate too hard). There is a happy medium where you apply the change and get to the target speed safely and quickly.

Neural networks as a network of memory cells

Another way to consider neural networks is to compare them to how humans think. As their name suggests, neural networks draw inspiration from neural processes and neurons in the mind. Neural networks contain a series of neurons, or nodes, which are interconnected and process input. The neurons have weights that are learned from previous observations (data). The output of a neuron is a function of its input and its weights. The activation of some final neuron(s) is the prediction.

We will consider a hypothetical case where a small part of the brain is responsible for matching basic shapes, such as squares and circles. In this scenario, some neurons at the basic level fire for horizontal lines, another set of neurons fires for vertical lines, and yet another set of neurons fire for curved segments. These neurons feed into higher-order process that combines the input so that it recognizes more complex objects, for example, a square when the horizontal and vertical neurons both are activated simultaneously.

In the following diagram, the input data is represented as squares. These could be pixels in an image. The next layer of hidden neurons consists of neurons that recognize basic features, such as horizontal lines, vertical lines, or curved lines. Finally, the output may be a neuron that is activated by the simultaneous activation of two of the hidden neurons:

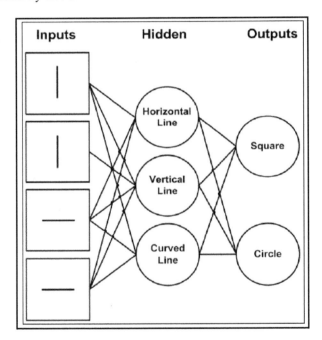

Figure 1.6: Neural networks as a network of memory cells

In this example, the first node in the hidden layer is good at matching horizontal lines, while the second node in the hidden layer is good at matching vertical lines. These nodes *remember* what these objects are. If these nodes combine, more sophisticated objects can be detected. For example, if the hidden layer recognizes horizontal lines and vertical lines, the object is more likely to be a square than a circle. This is similar to how convolutional neural networks work, which we will cover in Chapter 5, *Image Classification Using Convolutional Neural Networks*.

We have covered the theory behind neural networks very superficially here as we do not want to overwhelm you in the first chapter! In future chapters, we will cover some of these issues in more depth, but in the meantime, if you wish to get a deeper understanding of the theory behind neural networks, the following resources are recommended:

- Chapter 6 of *Goodfellow-et-al* (2016)
- Chapter 11 of *Hastie, T., Tibshirani,* R., and *Friedman, J.* (2009), which is freely available at `https://web.stanford.edu/~hastie/Papers/ESLII.pdf`
- Chapter 16 of *Murphy, K. P.* (2012)

Next, we will turn to a brief introduction to deep neural networks.

Deep neural networks

A **deep neural network** (**DNN**) is a neural network with multiple hidden layers. We cannot achieve good results by just increasing the number of nodes in a neural network with a small number of layers (a shallow neural network). A DNN can fit data more accurately with fewer parameters than a shallow **neural network** (**NN**), because more layers (each with fewer neurons) give a more efficient and accurate representation. Using multiple hidden layers allows a more sophisticated build-up from simple elements to more complex ones. In the previous example, we considered a neural network that could recognize basic shapes, such as a circle or a square. In a deep neural network, many circles and squares could be combined to form other, more advanced shapes. A shallow neural network cannot build more advanced shapes from basic pieces. The disadvantage of a DNN is that these models are harder to train and prone to overfitting.

If we consider trying to recognize handwritten text from image data, then the raw data is pixel values from an image. The first layer captures simple shapes, such as lines and curves. The next layer uses these simple shapes and recognizes higher abstractions, such as corners and circles. The second layer does not have to directly learn from the pixels, which are noisy and complex. In contrast, a shallow architecture may require far more parameters, as each hidden neuron would have to be capable of going directly from pixels in the image to the target value. It would also not be able to combine features, so for example, if the image data were in a different location (for example, not centered), it would fail to recognize the text.

One of the challenges in training deep neural networks is how to efficiently learn the weights. The models are complex with a huge number of parameters to train. One of the major advancements in deep learning occurred in 2006, when it was shown that **deep belief networks** (**DBNs**) could be trained one layer at a time (See *Hinton, G. E., Osindero, S., and Teh, Y. W. (2006)*). A DBN is a type of deep neural network with multiple hidden layers and connections between (but not within) layers (that is, a neuron in layer 1 may be connected to a neuron in layer 2, but may not be connected to another neuron in layer 1). The restriction of no connections within a layer allows for much faster training algorithms to be used, such as the **contrastive divergence algorithm**. Essentially, the DBN can then be trained layer by layer; the first hidden layer is trained and used to transform raw data into hidden neurons, which are then treated as a new set of input in the next hidden layer, and the process is repeated until all the layers have been trained.

The benefits of the realization that DBNs could be trained one layer at a time extend beyond just DBNs. DBNs are sometimes used as a pre-training stage for a deep neural network. This allows comparatively fast, greedy, layer-by-layer training to be used to provide good initial estimates, which are then refined in the deep neural network using other, less efficient, training algorithms, such as back-propagation.

So far we have primarily focused on feed-forward neural networks, where the results from one layer and neuron feed forward to the next. Before closing this section, two specific kinds of deep neural network that have grown in popularity are worth mentioning. The first is a **recurrent neural network** (**RNN**), where neurons send feedback signals to each other. These feedback loops allow RNNs to work well with sequences. An example of an application of RNNs is to automatically generate click-bait, such as *Top 10 reasons to visit Los Angeles: #6 will shock you!* or *One trick great hair salons don't want you to know*. RNNs work well for such jobs as they can be seeded from a large initial pool of a few words (even just trending search terms or names) and then predict/generate what the next word should be. This process can be repeated a few times until a short phrase is generated, the click-bait. We will see examples of RNNs in `Chapter 7`, *Natural Language Processing using Deep Learning*.

The second type is a **convolutional neural network** (**CNN**). CNNs are most commonly used in image-recognition. CNNs work by having each neuron respond to overlapping subregions of an image. The benefits of CNNs are that they require comparatively minimal preprocessing but still do not require too many parameters through weight-sharing (for example, across subregions of an image). This is particularly valuable for images as they are often not consistent. For example, imagine ten different people taking a picture of the same desk. Some may be closer or farther away or at positions resulting in essentially the same image having different heights, widths, and the amount of image captured around the focal object. We will cover CNNs in depth in `Chapter 5`, *Image Classification Using Convolutional Neural Networks*.

This description only provides the briefest of overviews as to what deep neural networks are and some of the use cases to which they can be applied. The seminal reference for deep learning is *Goodfellow-et-al* (2016).

Some common myths about deep learning

There are many misconceptions, half-truths, and downright misleading opinions on deep learning. Here are some common mis-conceptions regarding deep learning:

- Artificial intelligence means deep learning and replaces all other techniques
- Deep learning requires a PhD-level understanding of mathematics
- Deep learning is hard to train, almost an art form
- Deep learning requires lots of data
- Deep learning has poor interpretability
- Deep learning needs GPUs

The following paragraphs discuss these statements, one by one.

Deep learning is not artificial intelligence and does not replace all other machine learning algorithms. It is only one family of algorithms in machine learning. Despite the hype, deep learning probably accounts for less than 1% of the machine learning projects in production right now. Most of the recommendation engines and online adverts that you encounter when you browse the net are not powered by deep learning. Most models used internally by companies to manage their subscribers, for example *churn analysis*, are not deep learning models. The models used by credit institutions to decide who gets credit do not use deep learning.

Deep learning does not require a deep understanding of mathematics unless your interest is in researching new deep learning algorithms and specialized architectures. Most practitioners use existing deep learning techniques on their data by taking an existing architecture and modifying it for their work. This does not require a deep mathematical foundation, the mathematics used in deep learning are taught at high school level throughout the world. In fact, we demonstrate this in Chapter 3, *Deep Learning Fundamentals*, where we build an entire neural network from basic code in less than 70 lines of code!

Training deep learning models is difficult but it is not an art form. It does require practice, but the same problems occur over and over again. Even better, there is often a prescribed fix for that problem, for example, if your model is overfitting, add regularization, if your model is not training well, build a more complex model and/or use *data augmentation*. We will look at this in more depth in Chapter 6, *Tuning and Optimizing Models*.

There is a lot of truth to the statement that deep learning requires lots of data. However, you may still be able to apply deep learning to the problem by using a pre-trained network, or creating more training data from existing data (data augmentation). We will look at these in later Chapter 6, Tuning and Optimizing Models and Chapter 11, *The Next Level in Deep Learning*.

Deep learning models are difficult to interpret. By this, we mean being able to explain how the models came to their decision. This is a problem in many machine learning algorithms, not just deep learning. In machine learning, generally there is an inverse relationship between accuracy and interpretation – the more accurate the model needs to be, the less interpretable it is. For some tasks, for example, online advertising, interpretability is not important and there is little cost from being wrong, so the most powerful algorithm is preferred. In some cases, for example, credit scoring, interpretability may be required by law; people could demand an explanation of why they were denied credit. In other cases, such as medical diagnoses, interpretability may be important for a doctor to see why the model decided someone had a disease.

If interpretability is important, some methods can be applied to machine learning models to get an understanding of why they predicted the output for an instance. Some of them work by perturbing the data (that is, making slight changes to it) and trying to find what variables are most influential in the model coming to its decision. One such algorithm is called **LIME (Local Interpretable Model-Agnostic Explanations)**. (*Ribeiro, Marco Tulio, Sameer Singh, and Carlos Guestrin. Why should I trust you?: Explaining the predictions of any classifier. Proceedings of the 22nd ACM SIGKDD international conference on knowledge discovery and data mining. ACM, 2016.*) This has been implemented in many languages including R; there is a package called lime. We will use this package in Chapter 6, *Tuning and Optimizing Models*.

Finally, while deep learning models can run on CPUs, the truth is that any real work requires a workstation with a GPU. This does not mean that you need to go out and purchase one, as you can use cloud-computing to train your models. In Chapter 10, *Running Deep Learning Models in the Cloud*, will look at using AWS, Azure, and Google Cloud to train deep learning models.

Setting up your R environment

Before you begin your deep learning journey, the first step is to install R, which is available at `https://cran.r-project.org/`. When you download R and use it, only a few core packages are installed by default, but new packages can be added by selecting from a menu option or by a single line of code. We will not go into detail on how to install R or how to add packages, we assume that most readers are proficient in these skills. A good **integrated development environment** (IDE) for working with R is essential. By far the most popular IDE, and my recommendation, is RStudio, which can be downloaded from `https://www.rstudio.com/`. Another option is **Emacs**. An advantage of both Emacs and RStudio is that they are available on all major platforms (Windows, macOS, and Linux), so even if you switch computers, you can have a consistent IDE experience. The following is a screenshot of the RStudio IDE:

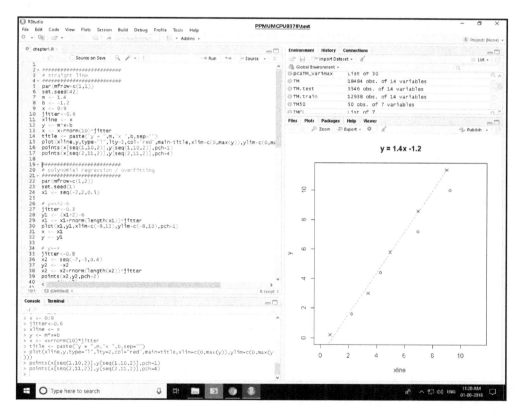

Figure 1.7 RStudio IDE

Using RStudio is a major improvement over the R GUI in Windows. There are a number of panes in RStudio that provide different perspectives on your work. The top-left pane shows the code, the bottom-left pane shows the console (results of running the code). The top-right pane shows the list of variables and their current values, the bottom-right pane shows the plots created by the code. All of these panes have further tabs to explore further perspectives.

As well as an IDE, RStudio (the company) have either developed or heavily supported other tools and packages for the R environment. We will use some of these tools, including the R Markdown and R Shiny applications. R Markdown is similar to Jupyter or IPython notebooks; it allows you to combine code, output (for example, plots), and documentation in one script. R Markdown was used to create sections of this book where code and descriptive text are interwoven. R Markdown is a very good tool to ensure that your data science experiments are documented correctly. By embedding the documentation within the analysis, they are more likely to stay synchronized. R Markdown can output to HTML, Word, or PDF. The following is an example of an R Markdown script on the left and the output on the right:

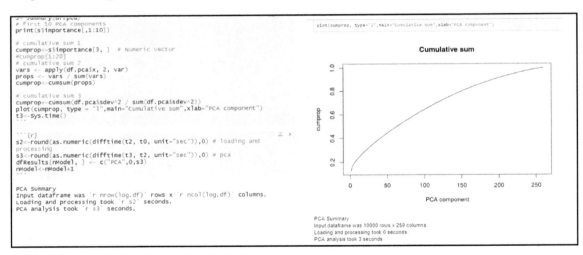

Figure 1.8: R Markdown example; on the left is a mixture of R code and text information. The output on the right is HTML generated from the source script.

We will also use R Shiny to create web applications using R. This is an excellent method to create interactive applications to demonstrate key functionality. The following screenshot is an example of an R Shiny web application, which we will see in Chapter 5, *Image Classification Using Convolutional Neural Networks*:

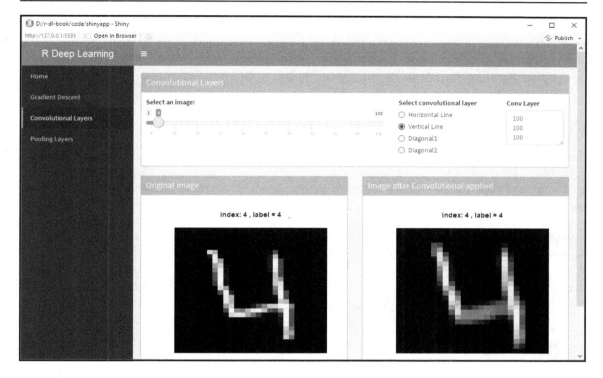

Figure 1.9: An example of an R Shiny web application

Once you have R installed, you can look at adding packages that can fit basic neural networks. The nnet package is one package and it can fit feed-forward neural networks with one hidden layer, such as the one shown in *Figure* 1.6. For more details on the nnet package, see *Venables, W. N.* and *Ripley, B.* D. (2002). The neuralnet package fits neural networks with multiple hidden layers and can train them using back-propagation. It also allows custom error and neuron-activation functions. We will also use the RSNNS package, which is an R wrapper of the **Stuttgart Neural Network Simulator (SNNS)**. The SNNS was originally written in C, but was ported to C++. The RSNNS package makes many model components from SNNS available, making it possible to train a wide variety of models. For more details on the RSNNS package, see *Bergmeir, C.,* and *Benitez, J. M.* (2012). We will see examples of how to use these models in Chapter 2, *Training a Prediction Model*.

The `deepnet` package provides a number of tools for deep learning in R. Specifically, it can train RBMs and use these as part of DBNs to generate initial values to train deep neural networks. The `deepnet` package also allows for different activation functions, and the use of dropout for regularization.

Deep learning frameworks for R

There are a number of R packages available for neural networks, but few options for deep learning. When the first edition of this book came out, it used the deep learning functions in h2o (`https://www.h2o.ai/`). This is an excellent, general machine learning framework written in Java, and has an API that allows you to use it from R. I recommend you look at it, especially for large datasets. However, most deep learning practitioners had a preference preferred other deep learning libraries, such as TensorFlow, CNTK, and MXNet, which were not supported in R when the first edition of this book was written. Today, there is a good choice of deep learning libraries that are supported in R—MXNet and Keras. Keras is actually a frontend abstraction for other deep learning libraries, and can use TensorFlow in the background. We will use MXNet, Keras, and TensorFlow in this book.

MXNet

MXNet is a deep learning library developed by Amazon. It can run on CPUs and GPUs. For this chapter, running on CPUs will suffice.

Apache MXNet is a flexible and scalable deep learning framework that supports **convolutional neural networks (CNNs)** and **long short-term memory networks (LSTMs)**. It can be distributed across multiple processors/machines and achieves almost linear scale on multiple GPUs/CPUs. It is easy to install on R and it supports a good range of deep learning functionality for R. It is an excellent choice for writing our first deep learning model for image-classification.

MXNet originated at *Carnegie Mellon University* and is heavily supported by Amazon; they chose it as their default deep learning library in 2016. In 2017, MXNet was accepted as the *Apache Incubator* project, ensuring that it would remain open source software. It has a higher-level programming model similar to Keras, but the reported performance is better. MXNet is very scalable as additional GPUs are added.

To install the MXNet package for Windows, run the following code from an R session:

```
cran <- getOption("repos")
cran["dmlc"] <-
"https://apache-mxnet.s3-accelerate.dualstack.amazonaws.com/R/CRAN"
options(repos = cran)
install.packages("mxnet")
```

This installs the CPU version; for the GPU version, you need to change the second line to:

```
cran["dmlc"] <-
"https://apache-mxnet.s3-
accelerate.dualstack.amazonaws.com/R/CRAN/GPU/cu92"
```

You have to change `cu92` to `cu80`, `cu90` or `cu91` based on the version of CUDA installed on your machine. For other operating systems (and in case the this does not work, as things change very fast in deep learning), you can get further instructions at `https://mxnet.incubator.apache.org/install/index.html`.

Keras

Keras is a high-level, open source, deep learning framework created by Francois Chollet from Google that emphasizes iterative and fast development; it is generally regarded as one of the best options to use to learn deep learning. Keras has a choice of backend lower-level frameworks: TensorFlow, Theano, or CNTK, but it is most commonly used with TensorFlow. Keras models can be deployed on practically any environment, for example, a web server, iOS, Android, a browser, or the Raspberry Pi.

To learn more about Keras, go to `https://keras.io/`. To learn more about using Keras in R, go to `https://keras.rstudio.com`; this link will also has more examples of R and Keras, as well as a handy Keras cheat sheet that gives a thorough reference to all of the functionality of the R Keras package. To install the `keras` package for R, run the following code:

```
devtools::install_github("rstudio/keras")
library(keras)
install_keras()
```

This will install the CPU-based package of Keras and TensorFlow. If your machine has a suitable GPU, you can refer to the documentation for `install_keras()` to find out how to install it.

Do I need a GPU (and what is it, anyway)?

Probably the two biggest reasons for the exponential growth in deep learning are:

- The ability to accumulate, store, and process large datasets of all types
- The ability to use GPUs to train deep learning models

So what exactly are GPUs and why are they so important to deep learning? Probably the best place to start is by actually looking at the CPU and why this is not optimal for training deep learning models. The CPU in a modern PC is one of the pinnacles of human design and engineering. Even the chip in a mobile phone is more powerful now than the entire computer systems of the first space shuttles. However, because they are designed to be good at all tasks, they may not be the best option for niche tasks. One such task is high-end graphics.

If we take a step back to the mid-1990s, most games were 2D, for example, platform games where the character in the game jumps between platforms and/or avoids obstacles. Today, almost all computer games utilize 3D space. Modern consoles and PCs have co-processors that take the load of modelling 3D space onto a 2D screen. These co-processors are known as **GPUs**.

GPUs are actually far simpler than CPUs. They are built to just do one task: massively parallel matrix operations. CPUs and GPUs both have *cores*, where the actual computation takes place. A PC with an Intel i7 CPU has four physical cores and eight virtual cores by using *Hyper Threading*. The NVIDIA TITAN Xp GPU card has 3,840 CUDA® cores. These cores are not directly comparable; a core in a CPU is much more powerful than a core in a GPU. But if the workload requires a large amount of matrix operations that can be done independently, a chip with lots of simple cores is much quicker.

Before deep learning was even a concept, researchers in neural networks realized that doing high-end graphics and training neural networks both involved workloads: large amounts of matrix multiplication that could be done in parallel. They realized that training the models on the GPU rather than the CPU would allow them to create much more complicated models.

Today, all deep learning frameworks run on GPUs as well as CPUs. In fact, if you want to train models from scratch and/or have a large amount of data, you almost certainly need a GPU. The GPU must be an NVIDIA GPU and you also need to install the CUDA® Toolkit, NVIDIA drivers, and cuDNN. These allow you to interface with the GPU and *hijack* its use from a graphics card to a maths co-processor. Installing these is not always easy, you have to ensure that the versions of CUDA, cuDNN and the deep learning libraries you use are compatible. Some people advise you need to use Unix rather than Windows, but support on Windows has improved greatly. This code on this book was developed on a Windows workstation. Forget about using a macOS, because they don't support NVIDIA cards.

That was the bad news. The good news is that you can learn everything about deep learning if you don't have a suitable GPU. The examples in the early chapters of this book will run perfectly fine on a modern PC. When we need to scale up, the book will explain how to use cloud resources, such as AWS and Google Cloud, to train large deep learning models.

Setting up reproducible results

Software for data science is advancing and changing rapidly. Although this is wonderful for progress, it can make reproducing someone else's results a challenge. Even your own code may not work when you go back to it a few months later. This is one of the biggest issues in scientific research today, across all fields, not just artificial intelligence and machine learning. If you work in research or academia and you want to publish your results in scientific journals, this is something you need to be concerned about. The first edition of this book partially addressed this problem by using the R checkpoint package provided by Revolution Analytics. This makes a record of what versions of software were used and ensures there is a snapshot of them available.

For the second edition, we will not use this package for a number of reasons:

- Most readers are probably not publishing their work and are more interested in other concerns (maximizing accuracy, interpretability, and so on).
- Deep learning requires large datasets. When you have a large amount of data, it should mean that, while we may not get precisely the same result each time, it will be very close (fractions of percentages).

- In production systems, there is more to reproducibility than software. You also have to consider data pipelines and random seed-generation.
- In order to ensure reproducibility, the libraries used must stay frozen. New versions of deep learning APIs are released constantly and may contain enhancements. If we limited ourselves to old versions, we would get poor results.

If you are interested in learning more about the `checkpoint` package, you can read the online vignette for the package at `https://cran.r-project.org/web/packages/checkpoint/vignettes/checkpoint.html`.

This book was written using R version 3.5 on Windows 10 Professional x64, which is the latest version of R at the time of writing. The code was run on a machine with an Intel i5 processor and 32 GB RAM; it should run on an Intel i3 processor with 8 GB RAM.

You can download the example code files for this book from your account at `http://www.packtpub.com/`. If you purchased this book elsewhere, you can visit `http://www.packtpub.com/support` and register to have the files emailed directly to you.

You can download the code files by following these steps:

1. Log in or register to our website using your email address and password.
2. Hover the mouse pointer on the **SUPPORT** tab at the top.
3. Click on **Code Downloads & Errata**.
4. Enter the name of the book in the **Search box**.
5. Select the book for which you're looking to download the code files.
6. Choose from the drop-down menu where you purchased this book from.
7. Click on **Code Download**.

Once the file is downloaded, please make sure that you unzip or extract the folder using the latest version of:

- WinRAR I 7-Zip for Windows
- Zipeg I iZip I UnRarX for Mac
- 7-Zip I PeaZip for Linux

Summary

This chapter presented a brief introduction to neural networks and deep neural networks. Using multiple hidden layers, deep neural networks have been a revolution in machine learning. They consistently outperform other machine learning tasks, especially in areas such as computer vision, natural-language processing, and speech-recognition.

The chapter also looked at some of the theory behind neural networks, the difference between shallow neural networks and deep neural networks, and some of the misconceptions that currently exist concerning deep learning.

We closed this chapter with a discussion on how to set up R and the importance of using a GUI (RStudio). This section discussed the deep learning libraries available in R (MXNet, Keras, and TensorFlow), GPUs, and reproducibility.

In the next chapter, we will begin to train neural networks and generate our own predictions.

Training a Prediction Model 2

This chapter shows you how to build and train basic neural networks in R through hands-on examples and shows how to evaluate different hyper-parameters for models to find the best set. Another important issue in deep learning is dealing with overfitting, which is when a model performs well on the data it was trained on but poorly on unseen data. We will briefly look at this topic in this chapter, and cover it in more depth in Chapter 3, *Deep Learning Fundamentals*. The chapter closes with an example use case classifying activity data from a smartphone as walking, going up or down stairs, sitting, standing, or lying down.

This chapter covers the following topics:

- Neural networks in R
- Binary classification
- Visualizing a neural network
- Multi-classification using the nnet and RSNNS packages
- The problem of overfitting data—the consequences explained
- Use case—building and applying a neural network

Neural networks in R

We will build several neural networks in this section. First, we will use the neuralnet package to create a neural network model that we can visualize. We will also use the `nnet` and `RSNNS` (Bergmeir, C., and Benítez, J. M. (2012)) packages. These are standard R packages and can be installed by the `install.packages` command or from the packages pane in RStudio. Although it is possible to use the `nnet` package directly, we are going to use it through the `caret` package, which is short for **Classification and Regression Training**. The `caret` package provides a standardized interface to work with many **machine learning** (**ML**) models in R, and also has some useful features for validation and performance assessment that we will use in this chapter and the next.

For our first examples of building neural networks, we will use the `MNIST` dataset, which is a classic classification problem: recognizing handwritten digits based on pictures. The data can be downloaded from the Apache MXNet site (`https://apache-mxnet.s3-accelerate.dualstack.amazonaws.com/R/data/mnist_csv.zip`). It is in the CSV format, where each column of the dataset, or feature, represents a pixel from the image. Each image has 784 pixels (28 x 28) and the pixels are in grayscale and range from 0 to 255. The first column contains the digit label, and the rest are pixel values, to be used for classification.

Building neural network models

The code is in the `Chapter2` folder of the code for this book. If you have not already downloaded and unzipped the code, go back to `Chapter 1`, *Getting Started with Deep Learning*, for the link to download the code. Unzip the code into a folder in your machine, and you will see folders for different chapters. The code we will be following is `Chapter2\chapter2.R`.

We will use the MNIST dataset to build some neural network models. The first few lines in the script look to see whether the data file (train.csv) is in the data directory. If the file already exists in the data directory then it proceeds; if it isn't, it downloads a ZIP file from https://apache-mxnet.s3-accelerate.dualstack.amazonaws.com/R/data/mnist_csv.zip, and unzips it into the data folder. This check means that you don't have to download the data manually and the program only downloads the file once. Here is the code to download the data:

```
dataDirectory <- "../data"
if (!file.exists(paste(dataDirectory,'/train.csv',sep="")))
{
  link <-
'https://apache-mxnet.s3-accelerate.dualstack.amazonaws.com/R/data/mnist_cs
v.zip'
  if (!file.exists(paste(dataDirectory,'/mnist_csv.zip',sep="")))
    download.file(link, destfile =
paste(dataDirectory,'/mnist_csv.zip',sep=""))
  unzip(paste(dataDirectory,'/mnist_csv.zip',sep=""), exdir =
dataDirectory)
  if (file.exists(paste(dataDirectory,'/test.csv',sep="")))
    file.remove(paste(dataDirectory,'/test.csv',sep=""))
}
```

As an alternative, the MNIST data is also available in Keras, so we can download it from that library and save it as a CSV file:

```
if (!file.exists(paste(dataDirectory,'/train.csv',sep="")))
{
 library(keras)
 mnist <- dataset_mnist()
 c(c(x_train,y_train),c(x_test,y_test)) %<-% dataset_mnist()
 x_train <-
array_reshape(x_train,c(dim(x_train)[1],dim(x_train)[2]*dim(x_train)[3]))
 y_train <- array_reshape(y_train,c(length(y_train),1))
 data_mnist <- as.data.frame(cbind(y_train,x_train))
 colnames(data_mnist)[1] <- "label"
 colnames(data_mnist)[2:ncol(data_mnist)] <-
paste("pixel",seq(1,784),sep="")
 write.csv(data_mnist,paste(dataDirectory,'/train.csv',sep=""),row.names =
FALSE)
}
```

When you load any new dataset for the first time, the first thing you should do is a quick check on the data to ensure that the number of rows and columns are as expected, as shown in the following code:

```
digits <- read.csv("../data/train.csv")
dim(digits)
[1] 42000 785

head(colnames(digits), 4)
[1] "label" "pixel0" "pixel1" "pixel2"

tail(colnames(digits), 4)
[1] "pixel780" "pixel781" "pixel782" "pixel783"

head(digits[, 1:4])
  label pixel0 pixel1 pixel2
1     1      0      0      0
2     0      0      0      0
3     1      0      0      0
4     4      0      0      0
5     0      0      0      0
6     0      0      0      0
```

The data looks OK, we have 42000 rows and 785 columns. The header was imported correctly and the values are numeric. Now that we have loaded the data and performed some validation checks on it, we can move on to modeling. Our first model will use the neuralnet library as this allows us to visualize the neural net. We will select only the rows where the label is either 5 or 6, and create a binary classification task to differentiate between them. Of course, you can pick any digits you choose, but using 5 and 6 is a good choice because they are similar graphically, and therefore our model will have to work harder than if we picked two digits that were not so similar, for example, 1 and 8. We rename the labels as 0 and 1 for modeling and then separate that data into a train and a test split.

We then perform dimensionality-reduction using **principal components analysis (PCA)** on the training data—we use PCA because we want to reduce the number of predictor variables in our data to a reasonable number for plotting. PCA requires that we remove columns that have zero variance; these are the columns that have the same value for each instance. In our image data, there is a border around all images, that is, the values are all zero. Note how we find the columns that have zero variance using only the data used to train the model; it would be incorrect to apply this check first and then split the data for modelling.

Dimensionality-reduction: Our image data is grayscale data with values from 0 (black) to 255 (white). These values are highly correlated, that is, if a pixel is black (that is, 0), it is likely that the pixels around it are either black or dark gray. Similarly if a pixel is white (255), it is likely that the pixels around it are either white or light gray. Dimensionality-reduction is an unsupervised machine learning technique that takes an input dataset and produces an output dataset with the same number of rows but fewer columns. Crucially though, these fewer columns can explain most of the signal in the input dataset. PCA is one dimensionality-reduction algorithm. We use it here because we want to create a dataset with a small number of columns to plot the network, but we still want our algorithm to produce good results.

The following code selects the rows where the label is either 5 or 6 and creates a train/test split. It also removes columns where the variance is zero; these are columns that have the same value for every row:

```
digits_nn <- digits[(digits$label==5) | (digits$label==6),]
digits_nn$y <- digits_nn$label
digits_nn$label <- NULL
table(digits_nn$y)
   5    6
3795 4137

digits_nn$y <- ifelse(digits_nn$y==5, 0, 1)
table(digits_nn$y)
   0    1
3795 4137

set.seed(42)
sample <- sample(nrow(digits_nn), nrow(digits_nn)*0.8)
test <- setdiff(seq_len(nrow(digits_nn)), sample)

digits.X2 <- digits_nn[,apply(digits_nn[sample,1:(ncol(digits_nn)-1)], 2,
var, na.rm=TRUE) != 0]
length(digits.X2)
[1] 624
```

We have reduced the number of column data from 784 to 624, that is, 160 columns had the same value for all rows. Now, we perform PCA on the data and plot the cumulative sum of the variances:

```
df.pca <- prcomp(digits.X2[sample,],center = TRUE,scale. = TRUE)
s<-summary(df.pca)
cumprop<-s$importance[3, ]
plot(cumprop, type = "l",main="Cumulative sum",xlab="PCA component")
```

The cumulative sum of PCA explained variance shows how many principal components are needed to explain the proportion of variance in the input data. In layman's terms, this plot shows that we can use the first 100 variables (the *principal components*) and this will account for over 80% of the variance in the original data:

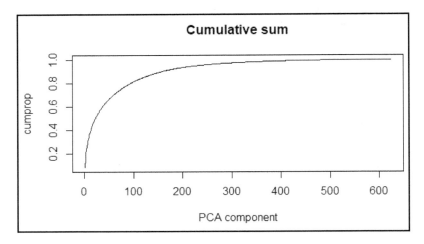

Figure 2.1: Cumulative sum of the Principal Components explained variance.

The next code block selects out the principal components that account for 50% of our variance and use those variables to create a neural network:

```
num_cols <- min(which(cumprop>0.5))
cumprop[num_cols]
  PC23
0.50275

newdat<-data.frame(df.pca$x[,1:num_cols])
newdat$y<-digits_nn[sample,"y"]
col_names <- names(newdat)
f <- as.formula(paste("y ~", paste(col_names[!col_names %in%
"y"],collapse="+")))
nn <- neuralnet(f,data=newdat,hidden=c(4,2),linear.output = FALSE)
```

We can see that 50% of the variance in the original data can be accounted by only 23 principal components. Next, we plot the neural network by calling the `plot` function:

```
plot(nn)
```

This produces a plot similar to the following screenshot. We can see the input variables (**PC1** to **PC23**), the hidden layers and biases, and even the network weights:

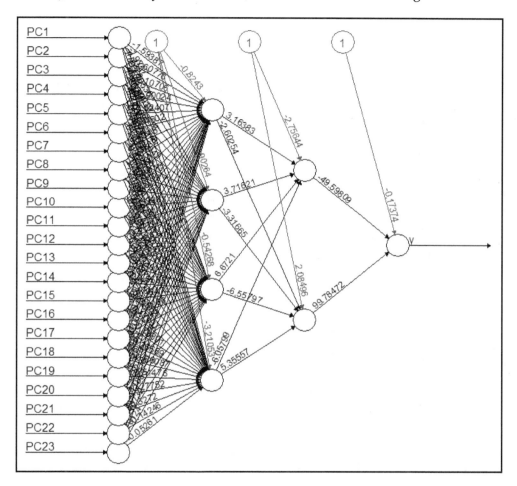

Figure 2.2: An example of a neural network with weights and biases

We selected 23 principal components to use as predictors for our neural network library. We chose to use two hidden layers, the first with four nodes and the second with two nodes. The plot outputs the coefficients, which are not all decipherable from the plot, but there are functions to access them if required.

Next, we will create predictions on a holdout or test dataset that was not used to build either the dimensionality-reduction or the neural network model. We have to first pass the test data into the `predict` function, passing in the `df.pca` object created earlier, to get the principal components for the test data. We can then pass this data into the neural network prediction (filtering the columns to the first 23 principal components) and then show the confusion matrix and overall accuracy:

```
test.data <- predict(df.pca, newdata=digits_nn[test,colnames(digits.X2)])
test.data <- as.data.frame(test.data)
preds <- compute(nn,test.data[,1:num_cols])
preds <- ifelse(preds$net.result > 0.5, "1", "0")
t<-table(digits_nn[test,"y"], preds,dnn=c("Actual", "Predicted"))
acc<-round(100.0*sum(diag(t))/sum(t),2)
print(t)
 Predicted
Actual 0    1
  0    740  17
  1     17 813
print(sprintf(" accuracy = %1.2f%%",acc))
[1] " accuracy = 97.86%"
```

We achieved `97.86%` accuracy, which is not bad considering we only used 23 principal components in our neural network. It is important to note that these 23 variables are not directly comparable to any columns in the input dataset or each other. In fact, the whole point of PCA, or any dimensionality-reduction algorithm, is to produce columns that are not correlated with each other.

Next, we will move on to create models that perform multi-classification, that is, they can classify digits 0-9. We will convert the labels (the digits 0 to 9) to a factor so R knows that this is a classification not a regression problem. For real-world problems, you should use all the data available, but if we used all 42,000 rows, it would take a very long time to train using the neural network packages in R. We will select 5,000 rows for training and 1,000 rows for test purposes. We should select the rows at random and ensure that there is no overlap between the rows in our training and test datasets. We also separate the data into the features or predictors (`digits.x`) and the outcome (`digits.Y`). We are using all the columns except the labels as the predictors here:

```
sample <- sample(nrow(digits), 6000)
train <- sample[1:5000]
test <- sample[5001:6000]
```

```
digits.X <- digits[train, -1]
digits.y_n <- digits[train, 1]
digits$label <- factor(digits$label, levels = 0:9)
digits.y <- digits[train, 1]

digits.test.X <- digits[test, -1]
digits.test.y <- digits[test, 1]
rm(sample,train,test)
```

Finally, before we get started building our neural network, let's quickly check the distribution of the digits. This can be important as, for example, if one digit occurs very rarely, we may need to adjust our modeling approach to ensure that, it's given enough weight in the performance evaluation if we care about accurately predicting that specific digit. The following code snippet creates a bar plot showing the frequency of each digit label:

```
barplot(table(digits.y),main="Distribution of y values (train)")
```

We can see from the plot that the categories are fairly evenly distributed so there is no need to increase the weight or importance given to any particular one:

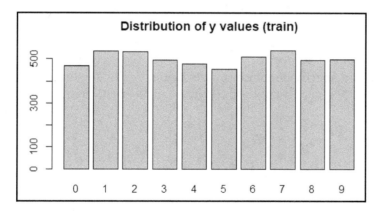

Figure 2.3: Distribution of *y* values for train dataset

Now let's build and train our first neural network using the `nnet` package through the `caret` package wrapper. First, we use the `set.seed()` function and specify a specific seed so that the results are reproducible. The exact seed is not important, what matters is that the same seed is used each time you run the script. The `train()` function first takes the feature or predictor data (`x`), and then the outcome variable (`y`), as arguments. The `train()` function can work with a variety of models, determined via the method argument. Although many aspects of machine learning models are learned automatically, some parameters have to be set. These vary by the method used; for example, in neural networks, one parameter is the number of hidden units. The `train()` function provides an easy way to try a variety of these tuning parameters as a named data frame to the `tuneGrid` argument. It returns the performance measures for each set of tuning parameters and returns the best trained model. We will start with just five hidden neurons in our model, and a modest decay rate. The learning rate controls how much each iteration or step can influence the current weights. The decay rate is the regularization hyper-parameter, which is used to prevent the model from overfitting. Another argument, `trcontrol`, controls additional aspects of `train()`, and is used, when a variety of tuning parameters are being evaluated, to tell the caret package how to validate and pick the best tuning parameter.

For this example, we will set the method for training control to *none* as we only have one set of tuning parameters being used here. Finally, at the end, we can specify additional, named arguments that are passed on to the actual `nnet()` function (or whatever algorithm is specified). Because of the number of predictors (`784`), we increase the maximum number of weights to 10,000 and specify a maximum of 100 iterations. Due to the relatively small amount of data, and the paucity of hidden neurons, this first model does not take too long to run:

```
set.seed(42)
tic <- proc.time()
digits.m1 <- caret::train(digits.X, digits.y,
          method = "nnet",
          tuneGrid = expand.grid(
            .size = c(5),
            .decay = 0.1),
          trControl = trainControl(method = "none"),
          MaxNWts = 10000,
          maxit = 100)
print(proc.time() - tic)
    user system elapsed
   54.47 0.06 54.85
```

The `predict()` function generates a set of predictions for the data. We will use the test dataset to evaluate the model; this contains records that were not used to train the model. We examine the distribution of the predicted digits in the following diagram.

```
digits.yhat1 <- predict(digits.m1,newdata=digits.test.X)
accuracy <- 100.0*sum(digits.yhat1==digits.test.y)/length(digits.test.y)
print(sprintf(" accuracy = %1.2f%%",accuracy))
[1] " accuracy = 54.80%"
barplot(table(digits.yhat1),main="Distribution of y values (model 1)")
```

It is clear that this is not a good model because the distribution of the predicted values is very different from the distribution of the actual values:

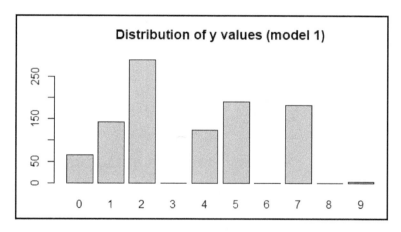

Figure 2.4: Distribution of *y* values from prediction model

The `barplot` is a simple check of the predictions, and shows us that our model is not very accurate. We can also calculate the accuracy by finding the percentage of rows from the predictions that match the actual value. The accuracy for this model is `54.8%`, which is not good. A more formal evaluation of the model's performance is possible using the `confusionMatrix()` function in the `caret` package. Because there is a function by the same name in the `RSNNS` package, they are masked so we call the function using `caret::confusionMatrix` to ensure the function from the `caret` package is used. The following code shows the confusion matrix and performance metrics on the test set:

```
caret::confusionMatrix(xtabs(~digits.yhat1 + digits.test.y))
Confusion Matrix and Statistics

            digits.test.y
digits.yhat1   0   1   2   3   4   5   6   7   8   9
           0  61   1   0   1   0   2   0   0   0   1
```

```
1    1 104    0    2    0    4    3    9   12    8
2    6   2   91   56    4   20   68    1   41    1
3    0   0    0    0    0    0    0    0    0    0
4    2   0    4    1   67    1   22    4    2   21
5   39   0    6   45    4   46    0    5   30   16
6    0   0    0    0    0    0    0    0    0    0
7    0   0    0    6    9    0    0   91    2   75
8    0   0    0    0    0    0    0    0    0    0
9    0   0    0    0    0    0    0    3    0    0
```

```
Overall Statistics
              Accuracy : 0.46
                95% CI : (0.4288, 0.4915)
   No Information Rate : 0.122
   P-Value [Acc > NIR] : < 2.2e-16
                 Kappa : 0.4019
 Mcnemar's Test P-Value : NA
```

Statistics by Class:

	Class: 0	Class: 1	Class: 2	Class: 3	Class: 4	Class: 5 Class: 6
Sensitivity	0.5596	0.9720	0.9010	0.000	0.7976	0.6301 0.000
Specificity	0.9944	0.9563	0.7786	1.000	0.9378	0.8436 1.000
Pos Pred Value	0.9242	0.7273	0.3138	NaN	0.5403	0.2408 NaN
Neg Pred Value	0.9486	0.9965	0.9859	0.889	0.9806	0.9666 0.907
Prevalence	0.1090	0.1070	0.1010	0.111	0.0840	0.0730 0.093
Detection Rate	0.0610	0.1040	0.0910	0.000	0.0670	0.0460 0.000
Detection Prevalence	0.0660	0.1430	0.2900	0.000	0.1240	0.1910 0.000
Balanced Accuracy	0.7770	0.9641	0.8398	0.500	0.8677	0.7369 0.500

	Class: 7	Class: 8	Class: 9
Sensitivity	0.8053	0.000	0.0000
Specificity	0.8963	1.000	0.9966
Pos Pred Value	0.4973	NaN	0.0000
Neg Pred Value	0.9731	0.913	0.8776
Prevalence	0.1130	0.087	0.1220
Detection Rate	0.0910	0.000	0.0000
Detection Prevalence	0.1830	0.000	0.0030
Balanced Accuracy	0.8508	0.500	0.4983

Because we had multiple digits, there are three main sections to the performance output. First, the actual frequency cross tab is shown. Correct predictions are on the diagonal, with various frequencies of misclassification on the off diagonals. Next are the overall statistics, which refer to the model's performance across all classes. Accuracy is simply the proportion of cases correctly classified, along with a 95% confidence interval, which can be useful, especially for smaller datasets where there may be considerable uncertainty in the estimate.

`No Information Rate` refers to what accuracy could be expected without any information by merely guessing the most frequent class, in this case, 1, which occurred 11.16% of the time. The p-value tests whether the observed accuracy (44.3%) is significantly different from `No Information Rate` (11.2%). Although statistically significant, this is not very meaningful for digit-classification, where we would expect to do far better than simply guessing the most frequent digit! Finally, individual performance metrics for each digit are shown. These are based on calculating that digit versus every other digit, so that each is a binary comparison.

Now that we have some basic understanding of how to set up, train, and evaluate model performance, we will try increasing the number of hidden neurons, which is one key way to improve model performance, at the cost of greatly increasing the model complexity. Recall from `Chapter 1`, *Getting Started with Deep Learning*, that every predictor or feature connects to each hidden neuron, and each hidden neuron connects to each outcome or output. With `784` features, each additional hidden neuron adds a substantial number of parameters, which also results in longer run times. Depending on your computer, be prepared to wait a number of minutes for these next model to finish:

```
set.seed(42)
tic <- proc.time()
digits.m2 <- caret::train(digits.X, digits.y,
          method = "nnet",
          tuneGrid = expand.grid(
            .size = c(10),
            .decay = 0.1),
          trControl = trainControl(method = "none"),
          MaxNWts = 50000,
          maxit = 100)
print(proc.time() - tic)
   user system elapsed
 154.49 0.09 155.33

digits.yhat2 <- predict(digits.m2,newdata=digits.test.X)
accuracy <- 100.0*sum(digits.yhat2==digits.test.y)/length(digits.test.y)
print(sprintf(" accuracy = %1.2f%%",accuracy))
[1] " accuracy = 66.30%"
barplot(table(digits.yhat2),main="Distribution of y values (model 2)")
```

This model is better than the previous model but the distribution of the predicted values is still uneven:

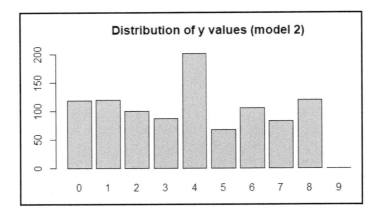

Figure 2.5: Distribution of *y* values from prediction model

Increasing the number of hidden neurons from 5 to 10 improved our in-sample performance from an overall accuracy of 54.8% to 66.3%, but this is still quite some way from ideal (imagine character-recognition software that mixed up over 30% of all the characters!). We increase again, this time to 40 hidden neurons, and wait even longer for the model to finish training:

```
set.seed(42)
tic <- proc.time()
digits.m3 <- caret::train(digits.X, digits.y,
        method = "nnet",
        tuneGrid = expand.grid(
          .size = c(40),
          .decay = 0.1),
        trControl = trainControl(method = "none"),
        MaxNWts = 50000,
        maxit = 100)
print(proc.time() - tic)
   user system elapsed
2450.16 0.96 2457.55

digits.yhat3 <- predict(digits.m3,newdata=digits.test.X)
accuracy <- 100.0*sum(digits.yhat3==digits.test.y)/length(digits.test.y)
print(sprintf(" accuracy = %1.2f%%",accuracy))
[1] " accuracy = 82.20%"
barplot(table(digits.yhat3),main="Distribution of y values (model 3)")
```

The distribution of the predicted values is even in this model, which is what we are looking for. However the accuracy is still only at 82.2%, which is quite low:

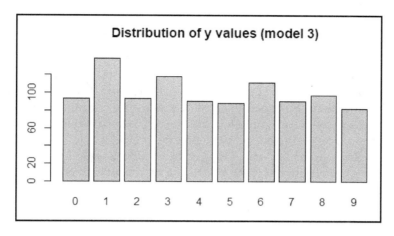

Figure 2.6: Distribution of *y* values from prediction model

Using 40 hidden neurons has improved accuracy to `82.2%` overall and it took over 40 minutes to run on an i5 computer. Model performance for some digits is still not great. If this were a real research or business problem, we might continue trying additional neurons, tuning the decay rate, or modifying features in order to try to boost model performance further, but for now we will move on.

Next, we will take a look at how to train neural networks using the RSNNS package. This package provides an interface to a variety of possible models using the **Stuttgart Neural Network Simulator** (**SNNS**) code; however, for a basic, single hidden-layer, feed-forward neural network, we can use the `mlp()` convenience wrapper function, which stands for multi-layer perceptron. The RSNNS package is a bit trickier to use than the convenience of nnet via the `caret` package, but one benefit is that it can be far more flexible and allows for many other types of neural network architecture to be trained, including recurrent neural networks, and also has a greater variety of training strategies.

One difference between the nnet and RSNNS packages is that, for multi-class outcomes (such as digits), RSNNS requires a dummy encoding (that is, one-hot encoding), where each possible class is represented as a column coded as 0/1. This is facilitated using the `decodeClassLabels()` function, as shown in the following code snippet:

```
head(decodeClassLabels(digits.y))
     0 1 2 3 4 5 6 7 8 9
[1,] 0 0 0 0 0 0 0 0 0 1
[2,] 0 0 0 0 1 0 0 0 0 0
```

```
[3,] 1 0 0 0 0 0 0 0 0 0
[4,] 0 0 0 0 0 1 0 0 0 0
[5,] 0 0 0 0 1 0 0 0 0 0
[6,] 0 0 0 1 0 0 0 0 0 0
```

Since we had reasonably good success with 40 hidden neurons, we will use the same size here. Rather than standard propagation as the learning function, we will use resilient propagation, based on the work of Riedmiller, M., and Braun, H. (1993). Resilient back-propagation is an **optimization** to standard back-propagation that applies faster weight-update mechanisms. One of the problems that occurs as the neural network increases in complexity is that they take a long time to train. We will discuss this in depth in subsequent chapters, but for now, you just need to know that this neural network is faster because it keeps track of past derivatives and takes bigger steps if they were in the same direction during back-propagation. Note also that, because a matrix of outcomes is passed, although the predicted probability will not exceed 1 for any single digit, the sum of predicted probabilities across all digits may exceed 1 and also may be less than 1 (that is, for some cases, the model may not predict they are very likely to represent any of the digits). The predict function returns a matrix where each column represents a single digit, so we use the encodeClassLabels() function to convert back into a single vector of digit labels to plot and evaluate the model's performance:

```
set.seed(42)
tic <- proc.time()
digits.m4 <- mlp(as.matrix(digits.X),
            decodeClassLabels(digits.y),
            size = 40,
            learnFunc = "Rprop",
            shufflePatterns = FALSE,
            maxit = 80)
print(proc.time() - tic)
   user system elapsed
 179.71 0.08 180.99

digits.yhat4 <- predict(digits.m4,newdata=digits.test.X)
digits.yhat4 <- encodeClassLabels(digits.yhat4)
accuracy <- 100.0*sum(I(digits.yhat4 -
1)==digits.test.y)/length(digits.test.y)
print(sprintf(" accuracy = %1.2f%%",accuracy))
[1] " accuracy = 81.70%"
barplot(table(digits.yhat4),main="Distribution of y values (model 4)")
```

The following bar plot shows that the predicted values are relatively evenly distributed among the categories. This matches the distribution of the actual category values:

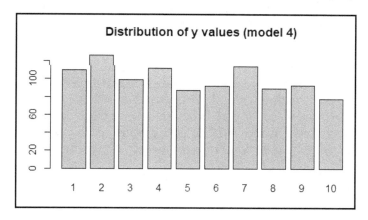

Figure 2.7: Distribution of *y* values from prediction model

The accuracy is 81.70% and it ran in 3 minutes on my computer. This is only slightly lower than when we used nnet with 40 hidden nodes, which took 40 minutes on the same machine! This demonstrates the importance of using an optimizer, which we will see in subsequent chapters.

Generating predictions from a neural network

For any given observation, there can be a probability of membership in any of a number of classes (for example, an observation may have a 40% chance of being a 5, a 20% chance of being a 6, and so on). To evaluate the performance of the model, some choices have to be made about how to go from the probability of class membership to a discrete classification. In this section, we will explore a few of these options in more detail.

As long as there are no perfect ties, the simplest method is to classify observations based on the highest predicted probability. Another approach, which the RSNNS package calls the **winner takes all** (**WTA**) method, chooses the class with the highest probability, provided the following conditions are met:

- There are no ties for highest probabilities
- The highest probability is above a user-defined threshold (the threshold could be zero)
- The remaining classes all have a predicted probability under the maximum minus another user-defined threshold

Otherwise, observations are classified as unknown. If both thresholds are zero (the default), this equates to saying that there must be one unique maximum. The advantage of such an approach is that it provides some quality control. In the digit-classification example we have been exploring, there are 10 possible classes.

Suppose 9 of the digits had a predicted probability of 0.099, and the remaining class had a predicted probability of 0.109. Although one class is technically more likely than the others, the difference is fairly trivial and we may conclude that the model cannot with any certainty classify that observation. A final method, called 402040, classifies if only one value is above a user-defined threshold, and all other values are below another user-defined threshold; if multiple values are above the first threshold, or any value is not below the second threshold, it treats the observation as unknown. Again, the goal here is to provide some quality control.

It may seem like this is unnecessary because uncertainty in predictions should come out in the model performance. However, it can be helpful to know if your model was highly certain in its prediction and right or wrong, or uncertain and right or wrong.

Finally, in some cases, not all classes are equally important. For example, in a medical context where a variety of biomarkers and genes are collected on patients and used to classify whether they are, at risk of cancer, or at risk of heart disease, even a 40% chance of having cancer may be enough to warrant further investigation, even if they have a 60% chance of being healthy. This has to do with the performance measures we saw earlier where, beyond overall accuracy, we can assess aspects such as sensitivity, specificity, and positive and negative predictive values. There are cases where overall accuracy is less important than making sure no one is missed.

The following code shows the raw probabilities for the in-sample data, and the impact these different choices have on the predicted values:

```
digits.yhat4_b <- predict(digits.m4,newdata=digits.test.X)
head(round(digits.yhat4_b, 2))
      [,1] [,2] [,3] [,4] [,5] [,6] [,7] [,8] [,9] [,10]
18986 0.00 0.00 0.00 0.98 0.00 0.02 0.00 0.00 0.00 0.00
41494 0.00 0.00 0.03 0.00 0.13 0.01 0.95 0.00 0.00 0.00
21738 0.00 0.00 0.02 0.03 0.00 0.46 0.01 0.00 0.74 0.00
37086 0.00 0.01 0.00 0.63 0.02 0.01 0.00 0.00 0.03 0.00
35532 0.00 0.00 0.00 0.00 0.01 0.00 0.00 0.99 0.00 0.00
17889 0.03 0.00 0.00 0.00 0.00 0.34 0.01 0.00 0.00 0.00

table(encodeClassLabels(digits.yhat4_b,method = "WTA", l = 0, h = 0))
  1   2   3   4  5  6  7   8  9 10
102 116 104 117 93 66 93 127 89 93

table(encodeClassLabels(digits.yhat4_b,method = "WTA", l = 0, h = .5))
```

```
0  1  2  3  4  5  6  7  8  9  10
141 95 113 86 93 67 53 89 116 73 74

table(encodeClassLabels(digits.yhat4_b,method = "WTA", l = .2, h = .5))
0  1  2  3  4  5  6  7  8  9  10
177 91 113 77 91 59 50 88 116 70 68

table(encodeClassLabels(digits.yhat4_b,method = "402040", l = .4, h = .6))
 0  1  2  3  4  5  6  7  8  9  10
254 89 110 71 82 46 41 79 109 65 54
```

We now proceed to examine problems related to overfitting the data and the impact on the evaluation of the model's performance.

The problem of overfitting data – the consequences explained

A common issue in machine learning is overfitting data. Generally, overfitting is used to refer to the phenomenon where the model performs better on the data used to train the model than it does on data not used to train the model (holdout data, future real use, and so on). Overfitting occurs when a model memorizes part of the training data and fits what is essentially noise in the training data. The accuracy in the training data is high, but because the noise changes from one dataset to the next, this accuracy does not apply to unseen data, that is, we can say that the model does not generalize very well.

Overfitting can occur at any time, but tends to become more severe as the ratio of parameters to information increases. Usually, this can be thought of as the ratio of parameters to observations, but not always. For example, suppose we have a very imbalanced dataset where the outcome we want to predict is a rare event that occurs in 1 in 5 million cases. In that case, a sample size of 15 million may only have 3 positive cases. Even though the sample size is large, the information is low. To consider a simple-but-extreme case, imagine fitting a straight line to two data points. The fit will be perfect, and in those two training data, your linear-regression model will appear to have fully accounted for all variations in the data. However, if we then applied that line to another 1,000 cases, it might not fit very well at all.

In the previous sections, we generated out-of-sample predictions for the our models, that is, we evaluated accuracy on test (or holdout) data. But we never checked whether our models were overfitting, that is, the accuracy levels on the test data. We can examine how well the model generalizes by checking the accuracy on the in-sample predictions. We can see that the accuracy on the in-sample data is 84.7%, compared to 81.7% on the holdout data. There is a 3.0% loss; or, put differently, using training data to evaluate model performance resulted in an overly optimistic estimate of the accuracy, and that overestimate was 3.0%:

```
digits.yhat4.train <- predict(digits.m4)
digits.yhat4.train <- encodeClassLabels(digits.yhat4.train)
accuracy <- 100.0*sum(I(digits.yhat4.train - 1)==digits.y)/length(digits.y)
print(sprintf(" accuracy = %1.2f%%",accuracy))
[1] " accuracy = 84.70%"
```

Since we fitted several models earlier of varying complexity, we could examine the degree of overfitting or overly optimistic accuracy from in-sample versus out of-sample performance measures across them. The code here should be easy enough to follow. We call the predict function for our models and do not pass in any new data; this returns the predictions for the data the model was trained with. The rest of the code is boilerplate code to create the graphic plot.

```
digits.yhat1.train <- predict(digits.m1)
digits.yhat2.train <- predict(digits.m2)
digits.yhat3.train <- predict(digits.m3)
digits.yhat4.train <- predict(digits.m4)
digits.yhat4.train <- encodeClassLabels(digits.yhat4.train)

measures <- c("AccuracyNull", "Accuracy", "AccuracyLower", "AccuracyUpper")
n5.insample <- caret::confusionMatrix(xtabs(~digits.y +
digits.yhat1.train))
n5.outsample <- caret::confusionMatrix(xtabs(~digits.test.y +
digits.yhat1))
n10.insample <- caret::confusionMatrix(xtabs(~digits.y +
digits.yhat2.train))
n10.outsample <- caret::confusionMatrix(xtabs(~digits.test.y +
digits.yhat2))
n40.insample <- caret::confusionMatrix(xtabs(~digits.y +
digits.yhat3.train))
n40.outsample <- caret::confusionMatrix(xtabs(~digits.test.y +
digits.yhat3))
n40b.insample <- caret::confusionMatrix(xtabs(~digits.y +
I(digits.yhat4.train - 1)))
n40b.outsample <- caret::confusionMatrix(xtabs(~ digits.test.y +
I(digits.yhat4 - 1)))

shrinkage <- rbind(
```

```
    cbind(Size = 5, Sample = "In",
as.data.frame(t(n5.insample$overall[measures]))),
    cbind(Size = 5, Sample = "Out",
as.data.frame(t(n5.outsample$overall[measures]))),
    cbind(Size = 10, Sample = "In",
as.data.frame(t(n10.insample$overall[measures]))),
    cbind(Size = 10, Sample = "Out",
as.data.frame(t(n10.outsample$overall[measures]))),
    cbind(Size = 40, Sample = "In",
as.data.frame(t(n40.insample$overall[measures]))),
    cbind(Size = 40, Sample = "Out",
as.data.frame(t(n40.outsample$overall[measures]))),
    cbind(Size = 40, Sample = "In",
as.data.frame(t(n40b.insample$overall[measures]))),
    cbind(Size = 40, Sample = "Out",
as.data.frame(t(n40b.outsample$overall[measures])))
    )
shrinkage$Pkg <- rep(c("nnet", "RSNNS"), c(6, 2))
dodge <- position_dodge(width=0.4)

ggplot(shrinkage, aes(interaction(Size, Pkg, sep = " : "), Accuracy,
                      ymin = AccuracyLower, ymax = AccuracyUpper,
                      shape = Sample, linetype = Sample)) +
  geom_point(size = 2.5, position = dodge) +
  geom_errorbar(width = .25, position = dodge) +
  xlab("") + ylab("Accuracy + 95% CI") +
  theme_classic() +
  theme(legend.key.size = unit(1, "cm"), legend.position = c(.8, .2))
```

The code produces the following plot, which shows the accuracy metrics and the confidence intervals for those metrics. One thing we notice from this plot is that, as the models get more complex, the gap between performance on the in-sample performance measures and the out-sample performance measures increases. This highlights that more complex models tend to overfit, that is, they perform better on the in-sample data than the unseen out-sample data:

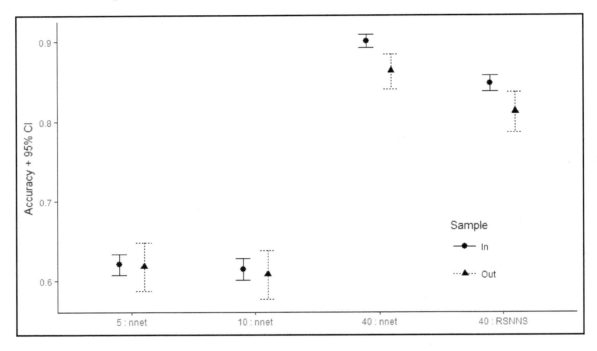

Figure 2.8: In-sample and out-sample performance measures for on neural network models

Use case – building and applying a neural network

To close the chapter, we will discuss a more realistic use case for neural networks. We will use a public dataset by Anguita, D., Ghio, A., Oneto, L., Parra, X., and Reyes-Ortiz, J. L. (2013) that uses smartphones to track physical activity. The data can be downloaded at https://archive.ics.uci.edu/ml/datasets/ human+activity+recognition+using+smartphones. The smartphones had an accelerometer and gyroscope from which 561 features from both time and frequency were used.

The smartphones were worn during walking, walking upstairs, walking downstairs, standing, sitting, and lying down. Although this data came from phones, similar measures could be derived from other devices designed to track activity, such as various fitness-tracking watches or bands. So this data can be useful if we want to sell devices and have them automatically track how many of these different activities the wearer engages in.

This data has already been normalized to range from -1 to + 1; usually we might want to perform some normalization if it has not already been applied. Download the data from the link and unzip it into the data folder that is on the same level as the chapter folder; we will use it in later chapters as well. We can import the training and testing data, as well as the labels. We will then take a quick look at the distribution of the outcome variable in the following code:

```
use.train.x <- read.table("../data/UCI HAR Dataset/train/X_train.txt")
use.train.y <- read.table("../data/UCI HAR Dataset/train/y_train.txt")[[1]]

use.test.x <- read.table("../data/UCI HAR Dataset/test/X_test.txt")
use.test.y <- read.table("../data/UCI HAR Dataset/test/y_test.txt")[[1]]

use.labels <- read.table("../data/UCI HAR Dataset/activity_labels.txt")

barplot(table(use.train.y),main="Distribution of y values (UCI HAR
Dataset)")
```

This produces the following bar plot, which shows that the categories are relatively evenly balanced:

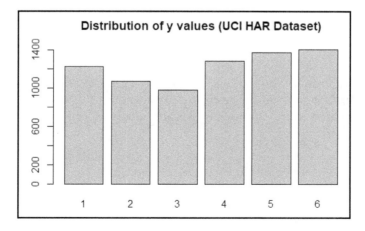

Figure 2.9: Distribution of *y* values for UCI HAR dataset

We are going to evaluate a variety of tuning parameters to show how we might experiment with different approaches to try to get the best possible model. We will use different hyper-parameters and evaluate which model performs the best.

 Because the models can take some time to train and R normally only uses a single core, we will use some special packages to enable us to run multiple models in parallel. These packages are parallel, foreach, and doSNOW, which should have been loaded if you ran the script from the first line.

Now we can pick our tuning parameters and set up a local cluster as the backend for the foreach R package for parallel for loops. Note that if you do this on a machine with fewer than five cores, you should change makeCluster(5) to a lower number:

```
## choose tuning parameters
tuning <- list(
   size = c(40, 20, 20, 50, 50),
   maxit = c(60, 100, 100, 100, 100),
   shuffle = c(FALSE, FALSE, TRUE, FALSE, FALSE),
   params = list(FALSE, FALSE, FALSE, FALSE, c(0.1, 20, 3)))

## setup cluster using 5 cores
## load packages, export required data and variables
## and register as a backend for use with the foreach package
cl <- makeCluster(5)
clusterEvalQ(cl, {source("cluster_inc.R")})
clusterExport(cl,
   c("tuning", "use.train.x", "use.train.y",
     "use.test.x", "use.test.y")
   )
registerDoSNOW(cl)
```

Now we are ready to train all the models. The following code shows a parallel for loop, using code that is similar to what we have already seen, but this time setting some of the arguments based on the tuning parameters we previously stored in the list:

```
## train models in parallel
use.models <- foreach(i = 1:5, .combine = 'c') %dopar% {
   if (tuning$params[[i]][1]) {
     set.seed(42)
     list(Model = mlp(
       as.matrix(use.train.x),
       decodeClassLabels(use.train.y),
       size = tuning$size[[i]],
       learnFunc = "Rprop",
       shufflePatterns = tuning$shuffle[[i]],
```

```
      learnFuncParams = tuning$params[[i]],
      maxit = tuning$maxit[[i]]
      ))
  } else {
    set.seed(42)
    list(Model = mlp(
      as.matrix(use.train.x),
      decodeClassLabels(use.train.y),
      size = tuning$size[[i]],
      learnFunc = "Rprop",
      shufflePatterns = tuning$shuffle[[i]],
      maxit = tuning$maxit[[i]]
    ))
  }
}
```

Because generating out-of-sample predictions can also take some time, we will do that in parallel as well. However, first we need to export the model results to each of the workers on our cluster, and then we can calculate the predictions:

```
## export models and calculate both in sample,
## 'fitted' and out of sample 'predicted' values
clusterExport(cl, "use.models")
use.yhat <- foreach(i = 1:5, .combine = 'c') %dopar% {
  list(list(
    Insample = encodeClassLabels(fitted.values(use.models[[i]])),
    Outsample = encodeClassLabels(predict(use.models[[i]],
                                  newdata = as.matrix(use.test.x)))
  ))
}
```

Finally, we can merge the actual and fitted or predicted values together into a dataset, calculate performance measures on each one, and store the overall results together for examination and comparison. We can use almost identical code to the code that follows to generate out-of-sample performance measures. That code is not shown in the book, but is available in the code bundle provided with the book. Some additional data-management is required here as sometimes a model may not predict each possible response level, but this can make for non-symmetrical frequency cross tabs, unless we convert the variable to a factor and specify the levels. We also drop o values, which indicate the model was uncertain about how to classify an observation:

```
use.insample <- cbind(Y = use.train.y,
  do.call(cbind.data.frame, lapply(use.yhat, `[[`, "Insample")))
colnames(use.insample) <- c("Y", paste0("Yhat", 1:5))

performance.insample <- do.call(rbind, lapply(1:5, function(i) {
  f <- substitute(~ Y + x, list(x = as.name(paste0("Yhat", i))))
```

```
    use.dat <- use.insample[use.insample[,paste0("Yhat", i)] != 0, ]
    use.dat$Y <- factor(use.dat$Y, levels = 1:6)
    use.dat[, paste0("Yhat", i)] <- factor(use.dat[, paste0("Yhat", i)],
levels = 1:6)
    res <- caret::confusionMatrix(xtabs(f, data = use.dat))

  cbind(Size = tuning$size[[i]],
        Maxit = tuning$maxit[[i]],
        Shuffle = tuning$shuffle[[i]],
        as.data.frame(t(res$overall[c("AccuracyNull", "Accuracy",
"AccuracyLower", "AccuracyUpper")])))
}))

use.outsample <- cbind(Y = use.test.y,
  do.call(cbind.data.frame, lapply(use.yhat, `[[`, "Outsample")))
colnames(use.outsample) <- c("Y", paste0("Yhat", 1:5))
performance.outsample <- do.call(rbind, lapply(1:5, function(i) {
  f <- substitute(~ Y + x, list(x = as.name(paste0("Yhat", i))))
  use.dat <- use.outsample[use.outsample[,paste0("Yhat", i)] != 0, ]
  use.dat$Y <- factor(use.dat$Y, levels = 1:6)
  use.dat[, paste0("Yhat", i)] <- factor(use.dat[, paste0("Yhat", i)],
levels = 1:6)
  res <- caret::confusionMatrix(xtabs(f, data = use.dat))

  cbind(Size = tuning$size[[i]],
        Maxit = tuning$maxit[[i]],
        Shuffle = tuning$shuffle[[i]],
        as.data.frame(t(res$overall[c("AccuracyNull", "Accuracy",
"AccuracyLower", "AccuracyUpper")])))
}))
```

If we print the in-sample and out-of-sample performance, we can see how each of our models did and the effect of varying some of the tuning parameters. The output is shown in the following code. The fourth column (null accuracy) is dropped as it is not as important for this comparison:

```
options(width = 80, digits = 3)
performance.insample[,-4]
  Size Maxit Shuffle Accuracy AccuracyLower AccuracyUpper
1   40    60   FALSE    0.984         0.981         0.987
2   20   100   FALSE    0.982         0.978         0.985
3   20   100    TRUE    0.982         0.978         0.985
4   50   100   FALSE    0.981         0.978         0.984
5   50   100   FALSE    1.000         0.999         1.000

performance.outsample[,-4]
  Size Maxit Shuffle Accuracy AccuracyLower AccuracyUpper
1   40    60   FALSE    0.916         0.906         0.926
```

2	20	100	FALSE	0.913	0.902	0.923
3	20	100	TRUE	0.913	0.902	0.923
4	50	100	FALSE	0.910	0.900	0.920
5	50	100	FALSE	0.938	0.928	0.946

As a reminder, the in-sample results evaluate the predictions on the training data and the out-sample results evaluate the predictions on the holdout (or test) data. The best set of hyper-parameters is the last set, where we get an accuracy of 93.8% on unseen data. This shows that we are able to classify the types of activity people are engaged in quite accurately based on the data from their smartphones. We can also see that the more complex models perform better on the in-sample data, which is not always the case with out-of-sample performance measures.

For each model, we have large differences between the accuracy for the in-sample data against the out-of-sample data; the models clearly overfit. We will get into ways to combat this overfitting in Chapter 3, *Deep Learning Fundamentals*, as we train deep neural networks with multiple hidden layers.

Despite the slightly worse out-of-sample performance, the models still do well – far better than chance alone – and, for our example use case, we could pick the best model and be quite confident that using this will provide a good classification of a user's activities.

Summary

This chapter showed how to get started building and training neural networks to classify data, including image recognition and physical activity data. We looked at packages that can visualize a neural network and we created a number of models to perform classification on data with 10 different categories. Although we only used some neural network packages rather than deep learning packages, our models took a long time to train and we had issues with overfitting.

Some of the basic neural network models in this chapter took a long time to train, even though we did not use all the data available. For the MNIST data, we used approx. 8,000 rows for our binary classification task and only 6,000 rows for our multi-classification task. Even so, one model took almost an hour to train. Our deep learning models will be much more complicated and should be able to process millions of records. You can now see why specialist hardware is required for training deep learning models.

Secondly, we see that a potential pitfall in machine learning is that more complex models will be more likely to overfit the training data, so that evaluating performance in the same data used to train the model results in biased, overly optimistic estimates of the model performance. Indeed, this can even make a difference as to which model is chosen as the best. Overfitting is also an issue for deep neural networks. In the next chapter, we will discuss various techniques used to prevent overfitting and obtain more accurate estimates of model performance.

In the next chapter we will look at building a neural network from scratch and see how it applies to deep learning. We will also discuss some methods to deal with overfitting.

Deep Learning Fundamentals

3

In the previous chapter, we created some machine learning models using neural network packages in R. This chapter will look at some of the fundamentals of neural networks and deep learning by creating a neural network using basic mathematical and matrix operations. This application sample will be useful for explaining some key parameters in deep learning algorithms and some of the optimizations that allow them to train on large datasets. We will also demonstrate how to evaluate different hyper-parameters for models to find the best set. In the previous chapter, we briefly looked at the problem of overfitting; this chapter goes into that topic in more depth and looks at how you can overcome this problem. It includes an example use case using dropout, the most common regularization technique in deep learning.

This chapter covers the following topics:

- Building neural networks from scratch in R
- Common parameters in deep learning
- Some key components in deep learning algorithms
- Using regularization to overcome overfitting
- Use case—improving out-of-sample model performance using dropout

Building neural networks from scratch in R

Although we have already used some neural network algorithms, it's time to dig a bit deeper into how they work. This section demonstrates how to code a neural network from scratch. It might surprise you to see that the core code for a neural network can be written in fewer than 80 lines! The code for this chapter does just that using an interactive web application written in R. It should give you more of an intuitive understanding of neural networks. First we will look at the web application, then we will delve more deeply into the code for the neural network.

Neural network web application

First, we will look at an R Shiny web application. I encourage you to run the application and follow the examples as it will really help you to get a better understanding of how neural networks work. In order to run it, you will have to open the `Chapter3` project in RStudio.

What is R Shiny?
R Shiny is an R package from the RStudio company that allows you to create interactive web apps using only R code. You can build dashboards and visualizations, and use the full functionality of R. You can extend R Shiny apps with CSS, widgets, and JavaScript. It is also possible to host your applications online. It is a great tool with which to showcase data science applications and I encourage you to look into it if you are not already familiar with it. For more information, see `https://shiny.rstudio.com/`, and, for examples of what is possible with R Shiny, see `https://shiny.rstudio.com/gallery/`.

1. Open the `server.R` file in RStudio and click on the **Run App** button:

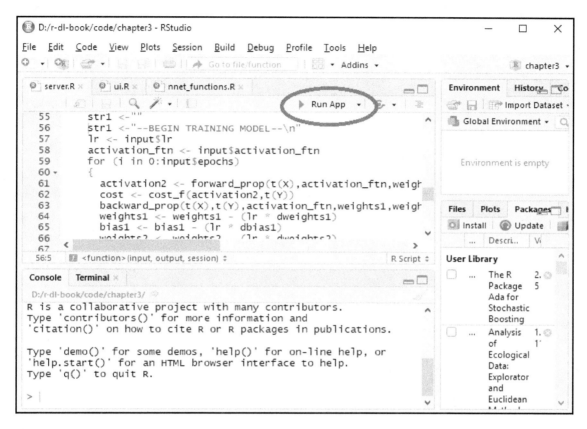

Figure 3.1: How to run an R Shiny application

2. When you click on the **Run App** button, you should get a pop-up screen for your web application. The following is a screenshot of the web application after it starts up:

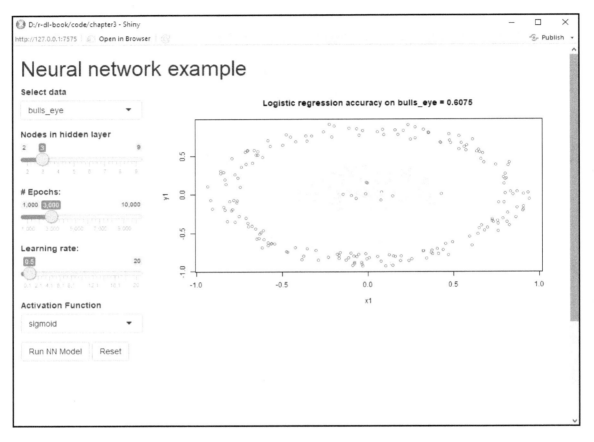

Figure 3.2: R Shiny application on startup

This web application can be used in the pop-up window or opened in a browser. On the left, there is a set of input choices; these are parameters for the neural network. These are known as hyper-parameters, in order to distinguish between the *parameters* that the model is trying to optimize. From top to bottom, these hyper-parameters are:

- **Select data**: There are four different datasets that you can use as training data.

- **Nodes in hidden layer**: The number of nodes in the hidden layer. The neural network has only one hidden layer.
- **# Epochs**: The number of times that the algorithm iterates over the data during model-building.
- **Learning rate**: The learning rate applied during backpropagation. The learning rate affects how much the algorithm changes the weights during every epoch.
- **Activation function**: The activation function applied to the output of each node.
- The **Run NN Model** button trains a model with the selection of input. The **Reset** button restores input choices to the default values.

There are four different datasets to choose from, each with a different data distribution; you can select them from the drop-down box. They have descriptive names; for example, the data that is plotted in *Figure 3.2* is called `bulls_eye`. These datasets are from another R package that is used to test clustering algorithms. The data has two classes of equal size and is composed of various geometric shapes. You can explore these datasets using the web application. The only change we make to the data is to randomly switches labels for 5% of the data. When you run the application, you will notice that there are some red points in the inner circle and some blue points in the outer circle. This is done so that our models should only achieve a maximum accuracy of 0.95 (95%). This gives us confidence that the model is working correctly. If the accuracy is higher than this, the model could be overfitting because the function it has learned is too complex. We will discuss overfitting again in the next section.

One of the first steps in machine learning should be to establish a benchmark score, this is useful for gauging your progress. A benchmark score could be a rule of thumb, or a simple machine learning algorithm; it should not be something that you spend a lot of time working on. In this application, we use a basic logistic regression model as a benchmark. We can see that in the previous screenshot, the accuracy for the logistic regression model is only 0.6075, or 60.75% accuracy. This is not much over 50%, but recall that logistic regression can only fit a straight line and this data cannot be separated using a straight line. A neural network should improve on the logistic regression benchmark, so if we get an accuracy of less than 0.6075 on this dataset, something is wrong with our model and we should review it.

So let's begin! Click on the **Run NN Model** button, which runs a neural network model on the data using the input choices. After a few seconds, the application should change to resemble the following screenshot:

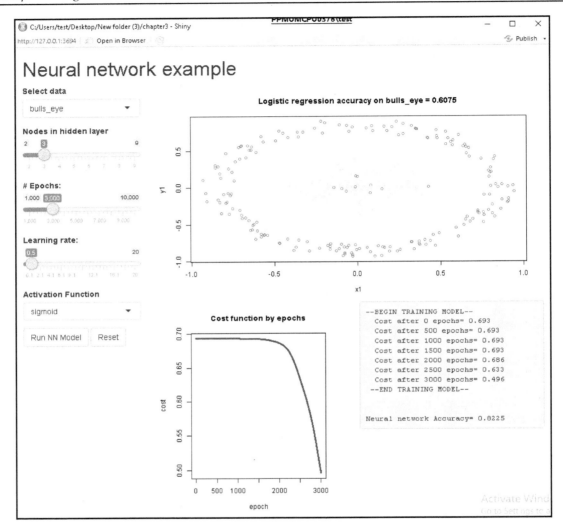

Figure 3.3: Neural network model execution with default settings

The application takes a few seconds and then it creates a graph of the cost function over the **# Epochs** and outputs cost function values as the algorithm iterates over the data. The text output also includes the final accuracy for the model in the text at the bottom right of the screen. In the diagnostic messages in the bottom right, we can see that the cost decreases during training and we achieved a final accuracy rate of 0.825. The cost is what the model is trying to minimize – a lower cost means better accuracy. It took some time for the cost to start decreasing as the model struggled initially to get the right weights.

In deep learning models, weights and biases should be not initialized with random values. If random values are used, this can lead to problems with training, such as vanishing or exploding gradients. This is where the weights get too small or too large and the model fails to train successfully. Also, if the weights are not correctly initialized, the model will take longer to train, as we saw earlier. Two of the most popular techniques to initialize weights to avoid these problems are the Xavier initialization and the He initialization (named after their inventors).

We can see in *Figure 3.3* that the cost has not plateaued, the last few values show it is still decreasing. This indicates that the model can be improved if we train it for longer. Change # **Epochs** to **7000** and click the **Run NN Model** button again; the screen will change to resemble the following plot:

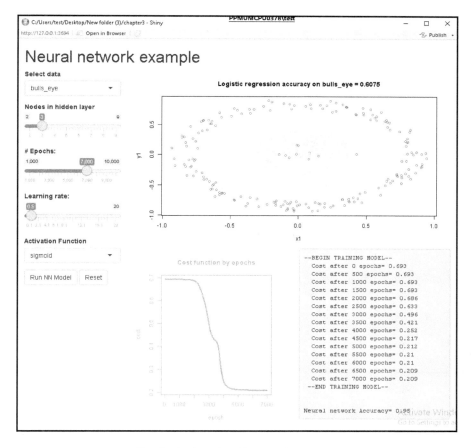

Figure 3.4: Neural network model execution with more epochs

Now we get an accuracy of 0.95, which is the maximum possible accuracy rate. We notice that the cost values have plateaued (that is, are not decreasing further) to around 0.21. This indicates that training the model for longer (that is, more epochs) will probably not improve the results, regardless of the current accuracy number. If the model is under training and the cost values have plateaued, we would need to consider changing the architecture of the model or getting more data to improve our accuracy. Let's look at changing the number of nodes in our model. Click the **Reset** button to change the input values to their defaults, then change the number of nodes to 7, and click the **Run NN Model** button. Now the screen will change to the following:

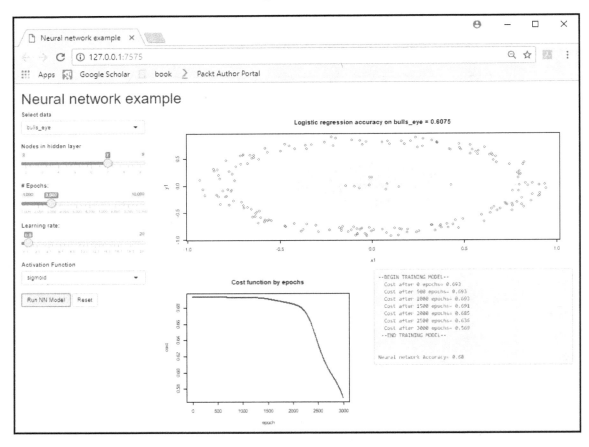

Figure 3.5: Neural network model execution with more nodes

Our accuracy here is 0.68, but compare this to the earlier examples, when we used the same input and only three nodes. We actually get worse performance with more nodes! This is because our data has a relatively simple pattern, and a model with seven nodes might be too complex and will take longer to train. Adding more nodes to a layer will increase training time but does not always improve performance.

Let's look at the **Learning rate**. Click the **Reset** button to change the input values to their defaults, then change the **Learning rate** to around **5**, and click the **Run NN Model** button again to replicate the following screen:

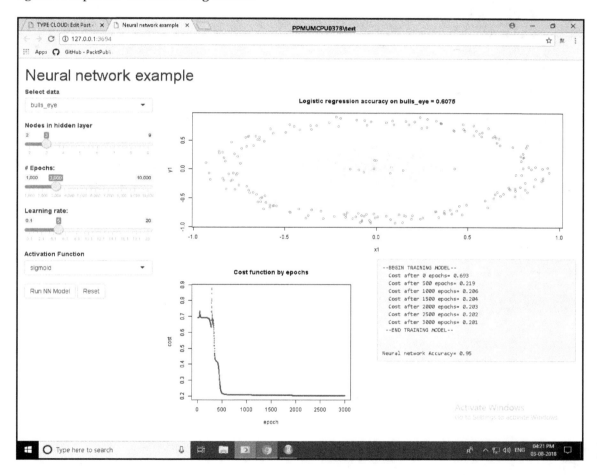

Figure 3.6: Neural network model execution with larger learning rate

We get 0.95 accuracy again, which is the best possible accuracy. If we compare it to the previous examples, we can see that the model *converged* (that is, the length of time it took for the cost function to plateau) much quicker, after just **500** epochs. We needed fewer epochs, so we can see an inverse relationship between learning rates and training epochs. A higher learning rate may mean you need fewer epochs. But are bigger learning rates always better? Well, no.

Click the **Reset** button to change the input values to their defaults, then change the **Learning rate** to the maximum value (**20**), and click the **Run NN Model** button again. When you do, you will get similar output to the following:

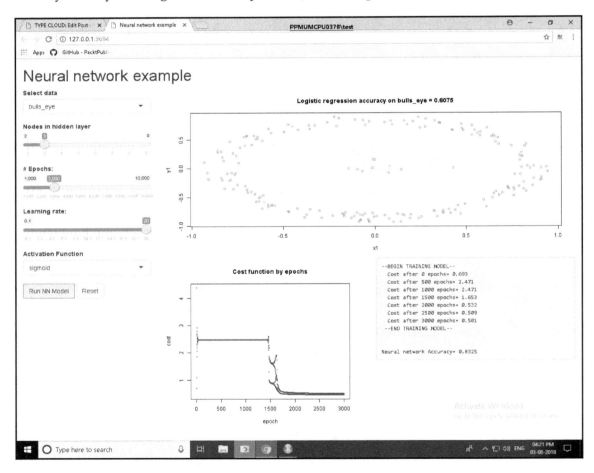

Figure 3.7: Neural network model execution with too great a learning rate

We get an accuracy rate of 0.83. What just happened? By selecting a huge learning rate, our model failed to converge at all. We can see that the cost function actually increases at the start of training, which indicates that the Learning rate is too high. Our cost function graph seems to have repeating values, which indicates that the gradient-descent algorithm is overshooting the minima at times.

Finally, we can look at how the choice of activation function affects model training. By changing the activation function, you may also need to change the **Learning rate**. Click the **Reset** button to change the input values to their defaults and select `tanh` for the activation function. When we select `tanh` as the activation function and 1.5 as the **Learning rate**, the cost gets `stuck` at 0.4 from epochs 500-3,500 before suddenly decreasing to 0.2. This can occur in neural networks when they get stuck in local optima. This phenomena can be seen in the following plot:

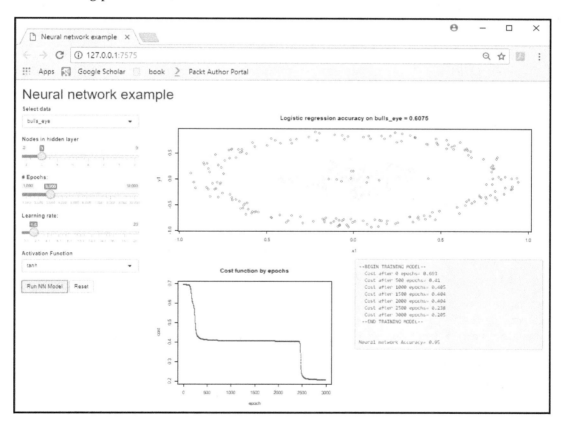

Figure 3.8: Neural network model execution with the tanh activation function

In contrast, using relu activation results in the model training faster. The following is an example where we only run 1,500 epochs with the relu activation to get the maximum possible accuracy of 0.95:

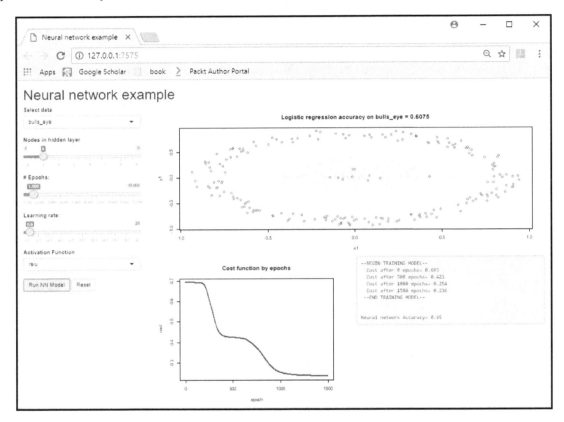

Figure 3.9: Neural network model execution with the relu activation function

I encourage you to experiment with the other datasets. For reference purposes, here is the max accuracy I got for each of those datasets. An interesting experiment is to see how different activation functions and learning rates work with these datasets:

- **worms (accuracy=0.95)**: 3 nodes, 3,000 epochs, Learning rate = 0.5, activation = tanh
- **moon (accuracy=0.95)**: 5 nodes, 5,000 epochs, Learning rate = 5, activation = sigmoid
- **blocks (accuracy=0.9025)**: 5 nodes, 5,000 epochs, Learning rate = 10, activation = sigmoid

In general, you will see the following:

- Using more epochs means a longer training time, which may not always be needed.
- If the model has not achieved the best accuracy and the cost function has plateaued (that is, it is not decreasing by much) toward the end of the training, then running it longer (that is, more epochs) or increasing the learning rate is unlikely to improve performance. Instead, look at changing the model's architecture, such as by changing the # layers (not an option in this demo), adding more nodes, or changing the activation functions.
- The learning rate must be selected carefully. If the value selected is too low, it will take a long time for the model to train. If the value selected is too high, the model will fail to train.

Neural network code

While the web application is useful to see the output of the neural network, we can also run the code for the neural network to really see how it works. The code in Chapter3/nnet.R allows us to do just that. This code has the same hyper-parameters as in the web application; this file allows you to run the neural network from the RStudio IDE. The following is the code that loads the data and sets the initial hyper-parameters for the neural network:

```
source("nnet_functions.R")
data_sel <- "bulls_eye"

. . . . . . . .

##################### neural network ####################
hidden <- 3
epochs <- 3000
lr <- 0.5
activation_ftn <- "sigmoid"

df <- getData(data_sel) # from nnet_functions
X <- as.matrix(df[,1:2])
Y <- as.matrix(df$Y)
n_x=ncol(X)
n_h=hidden
n_y=1
m <- nrow(X)
```

This code should not be too difficult to understand, it loads a dataset and sets some variables. The data is created in the `getData` function from the `Chapter3/nnet_functions.R` file. The data is created from functions in the `clustersim` package. The `Chapter3/nnet_functions.R` file contains the core functionality of our neural network that we will look at here. Once we load our data, the next step is to initialize our weights and biases. The `hidden` variable controls the number of nodes in the hidden layer; we set it to 3. We need two sets of weights and biases, one for the hidden layer and one for the output layer:

```
# initialise weights
set.seed(42)
weights1 <- matrix(0.01*runif(n_h*n_x)-0.005, ncol=n_x, nrow=n_h)
weights2 <- matrix(0.01*runif(n_y*n_h)-0.005, ncol=n_h, nrow=n_y)
bias1 <- matrix(rep(0,n_h),nrow=n_h,ncol=1)
bias2 <- matrix(rep(0,n_y),nrow=n_y,ncol=1)
```

This creates matrices for the (`weights1`, `bias1`) hidden layer and the (`weights2`, `bias2`) output layer. We need to ensure our matrices have the correct dimensions. For example, the `weights1` matrix should have the same number of columns as the input layer and the same number of rows as the hidden layer. Now we move on to the actual processing loop of the neural network:

```
for (i in 0:epochs)
{
  activation2 <- forward_prop(t(X),activation_ftn,weights1,bias1,
weights2,bias2)
  cost <- cost_f(activation2,t(Y))
  backward_prop(t(X),t(Y),activation_ftn,weights1,weights2,
activation1,activation2)
  weights1 <- weights1 - (lr * dweights1)
  bias1 <- bias1 - (lr * dbias1)
  weights2 <- weights2 - (lr * dweights2)
  bias2 <- bias2 - (lr * dbias2)

  if ((i %% 500) == 0)
    print (paste(" Cost after",i,"epochs =",cost))
}
[1] " Cost after 0 epochs = 0.693147158995952"
[1] " Cost after 500 epochs = 0.69314587328381"
[1] " Cost after 1000 epochs = 0.693116915341439"
[1] " Cost after 1500 epochs = 0.692486724429629"
[1] " Cost after 2000 epochs = 0.687107068792801"
[1] " Cost after 2500 epochs = 0.660418522655335"
[1] " Cost after 3000 epochs = 0.579832913091798"
```

We first run the forward-propagation function, then calculate a cost. We then call a backward-propagation step that calculates our derivatives, (dweights1, dbias1, dweights2, dbias2). Then we update the weights and biases, (weights1, bias1, weights2, bias2), using our Learning rate, (lr). We run this loop for the number of epochs (3000) and print out a diagnostic message every 500 epochs. This describes how every neural network and deep learning model works: first call forward-propagation, then calculate costs and derivative values, use those to update the weights through back-propagation and repeat.

Now let's look at some of the functions in the nnet_functions.R file. The following is the forward propagation function:

```
forward_prop <- function(X,activation_ftn,weights1,bias1,weights2,bias2)
{
  # broadcast hack
  bias1a<-bias1
  for (i in 2:ncol(X))
    bias1a<-cbind(bias1a,bias1)
  bias2a<-bias2
  for (i in 2:ncol(activation1))
    bias2a<-cbind(bias2a,bias2)
  Z1 <<- weights1 %*% X + bias1a
  activation1 <<- activation_function(activation_ftn,Z1)
  bias2a<-bias2
  for (i in 2:ncol(activation1))
    bias2a<-cbind(bias2a,bias2)
  Z2 <<- weights2 %*% activation1 + bias2a
  activation2 <<- sigmoid(Z2)
  return (activation2)
}
```

If you looked at the code carefully, you may have noticed that the assignment to the activation1, activation2, Z1, and Z2 variables uses <<- rather than <-. This makes those variables global in scope; we also want to use these values during back propagation. Using global variables is generally frowned upon and I could have returned a list, but it is acceptable here to use them because this application is for learning purposes.

The two for loops expand the bias vectors into matrices, then repeat the vector n times. The interesting code starts with the Z1 assignment. Z1 is a matrix multiplication, followed by an addition. We call the `activation_function` function on that value. We then use that output value and perform a similar operation for Z2. Finally, we apply a sigmoid activation to our output layer because our problem is binary classification.

The following is the code for the activation function; the first parameter decides which function to use (`sigmoid`, `tanh`, or `relu`). The second parameter is the value to be used as input:

```
activation_function <- function(activation_ftn,v)
{
  if (activation_ftn == "sigmoid")
    res <- sigmoid(v)
  else if (activation_ftn == "tanh")
    res <- tanh(v)
  else if (activation_ftn == "relu")
  {
    v[v<0] <- 0
    res <- v
  }
  else
    res <- sigmoid(v)
  return (res)
}
```

The following is the `cost` function:

```
cost_f <- function(activation2,Y)
{
  cost = -mean((log(activation2) * Y)+ (log(1-activation2) * (1-Y)))
  return(cost)
}
```

As a reminder, the output of the `cost` function is what we are trying to minimize. There are many types of `cost` functions; in this application we are using binary cross-entropy. The formula for binary cross-entropy is $-1/m \sum log(\bar{y}_i) * y_i + (log(1 - \bar{y}_i) * (1-y_i)$. Our target values ($y_i$) are always either *1* or *0*, so for instances where $y_i = 1$, this reduces to $\sum log(\bar{y}_i)$. If we have two rows where $y_i = 1$ and suppose that our model predicts *1.0* for the first row and the *0.0001* for the second row, then the costs for the rows are *log(1)=0* and *log(0.0001)=-9.1*, respectively. We can see that the closer to *1* the prediction is for these rows, the lower the `cost` value. Similarly, for rows where $y_i = 0$, this reduces to $log(1-\bar{y}_i)$, so the closer to 0 the prediction is for these rows, the lower the `cost` value.

If we are trying to maximize accuracy, why don't we just use what during model training? Binary cross-entropy is a better `cost` function because our model does not just output 0 or 1, but instead outputs continuous values from 0.0 to 1.0. For example, if two input rows had a target value=1 (that is, y=1), and our model gave probabilities of 0.51 and 0.99, then binary cross-entropy would give them a cost of 0.67 and 0.01, respectively. It assigns a higher cost to the first row because the model is unsure about it (the probability is close to 0.5). If instead we just looked at accuracy, we might decide that both rows have the same cost value because they are classified correctly (assuming we assign class=0 where predicted values < 0.5, and class=1 where predicted values >= 0.5).

The following is the code for the backward-propagation function:

```
backward_prop <-
function(X,Y,activation_ftn,weights1,weights2,activation1,activation2)
{
  m <- ncol(Y)
  derivative2 <- activation2-Y
  dweights2 <<- (derivative2 %*% t(activation1)) / m
  dbias2 <<- rowSums(derivative2) / m
  upd <- derivative_function(activation_ftn,activation1)
  derivative1 <- t(weights2) %*% derivative2 * upd
  dweights1 <<- (derivative1 %*% t(X)) / m
  dbias1 <<- rowSums(derivative1) / m
}
```

Backward propagation processes the network in reverse, starting at the last hidden layer and finishing at the first hidden layer, that is, in the direction of the output layer to the input layer. In our case, we only have one hidden layer, so it first calculates the loss from the output layer and calculates `dweight2` and `dbias2`. It then calculates the `derivative` of the `activation1` value, which was calculated during the forward-propagation step. The `derivative` function is similar to the activation function, but instead of calling an activation function, it calculates the `derivative` of that function. For example, the `derivative` of `sigmoid(x)` is *sigmoid(x) * (1 - sigmoid(x))*. The `derivative` values of simple functions can be found in any calculus reference or online:

```
derivative_function <- function(activation_ftn,v)
{
  if (activation_ftn == "sigmoid")
   upd <- (v * (1 - v))
  else if (activation_ftn == "tanh")
   upd <- (1 - (v^2))
  else if (activation_ftn == "relu")
   upd <- ifelse(v > 0.0,1,0)
```

```
      else
       upd <- (v * (1 - v))
      return (upd)
  }
```

That's it! A working neural network using basic R code. It can fit complex functions and performs better than logistic regression. You might not get all the parts at once, that's OK. The following is a quick recap of the steps:

1. Run a forward-propagation step, which involves multiplying the weights by the input for each layer and passing the output to the next layer.
2. Evaluate the output from the final layer using the `cost` function.
3. Based on the error rate, use backpropagation to make small adjustments to the weights in the nodes in each layer. The learning rate controls how much of an adjustment we make each time.
4. Repeat steps 1-3, maybe thousands of times, until the `cost` function begins to plateau, which indicates our model is trained.

Back to deep learning

Many of the concepts in the previous section apply to deep learning because deep learning is simply neural networks with two or more hidden layers. To demonstrate this, let's look at the following code in R that loads the `mxnet` deep learning library and calls the help command on the function in that library that trains a deep learning model. Even though we have not trained any models using this library yet, we have already seen many of the parameters in this function:

```
library(mxnet)
?mx.model.FeedForward.create
```

 If you get errors saying the `mxnet` package is unavailable, see Chapter 1, *Getting Started with Deep Learning*, for installation instructions. However, we are not running any `mxnet` code in this chapter, we only want to display the help page for a function. So feel free to just continue reading and you can install the package later when we use it in the next chapter.

This brings up the help page for the `FeedForward` function in the `mxnet` library, which is the forward-propagation/model train function. `mxnet` and most deep learning libraries do not have a specific *backward*-propagation function, they handle this implicitly:

```
mx.model.FeedForward.create(symbol, X, y = NULL, ctx = NULL,
    begin.round = 1, num.round = 10, optimizer = "sgd",
```

```
initializer = mx.init.uniform(0.01), eval.data = NULL,
eval.metric = NULL, epoch.end.callback = NULL,
batch.end.callback = NULL, array.batch.size = 128
...)
```

We will see more of this function in subsequent chapters; for now we will just look at the parameters.

The symbol, X, y, and ctx parameters

The symbol parameter defines the deep learning architecture; X and y are the input and output data structures. The ctx parameter controls which device (for example, CPU/GPU) the model is trained on.

The num.round and begin.round parameters

num.round is equivalent to epochs in our code; that is, however many times we iterate over the data. begin.round is where we resume training the model if we paused training previously. If we pause training, we can save the partially-trained model, reload it later, and resume training.

The optimizer parameter

Our implementation of neural networks used gradient descent. When researchers started creating more complicated multilayer neural network models, they found that they took an extraordinarily long time to train. This is because the basic gradient-descent algorithm with no optimization is not very efficient; it makes small steps towards its goal in each epoch regardless of what occurred in previous epochs. We can compare it with a guessing game: one person has to guess a number in a range and for each guess, they are told to go higher or lower (assuming they do not guess the correct number!). The higher/lower instruction is similar to the derivative value, it indicates the direction we must travel. Now let's say that the range of possible numbers is 1 to 1,000,000 and the first guess is 1,000. The person is told to go higher, which should they do:

- Try 1001.
- Take the difference between the guess and the max value and divide by 2. Add this value to the previous guess.

The second option is much better and should mean the person gets to the right answer in 20 guesses or fewer. If you have a background in computer science, you may recognize this as the binary-search algorithm. The first option, guessing 1,001, 1,002, ..., 1,000,000, is a terrible choice and will probably fail as one party will give up! But this is similar to how gradient descent works. It moves incrementally towards the target. If you try increasing the learning rate to overcome this problem, you can overshoot the target and the model fails to converge.

Researchers came up with some clever optimizations to speed up training. One of the first optimizers was called momentum, and it does exactly what its name states. It looks at the extent of the derivative and takes bigger *steps* for each epoch if the previous steps were all in the same direction. It should mean that the model trains much quicker. There are other algorithms that are enhancements of these, such as RMS-Prop and Adam. You don't usually need to know how they work, just that, when you change the optimizer, you may also have to adjust other hyper-parameters, such as the learning rate. In general, look for previous examples done by others and copy those hyper-parameters.

We actually used one of these optimizers in an example in the previous chapter. In that chapter, we had 2 models with a similar architecture (40 hidden nodes). The first model (`digits.m3`) used the `nnet` library and took 40 minutes to train. The second model (`digits.m3`) used resilient backpropagation and took 3 minutes to train. This shows the benefit of using an optimizer in neural networks and deep learning.

The initializer parameter

When we created the initial values for our weights and biases (that is, model parameters), we used random numbers, but limited them to the values of -0.005 to +0.005. If you go back and review some of the graphs of the `cost` functions, you see that it took 2,000 epochs before the `cost` function began to decline. This is because the initial values were not in the right range and it took 2,000 epochs to get to the correct magnitude. Fortunately, we do not have to worry about how to set these parameters in the `mxnet` library because this parameter controls how the weights and biases are initialized before training.

The eval.metric and eval.data parameters

These two parameters control what data and which metric are used to evaluate the model. `eval.metric` is equivalent to the `cost` function we used in our code. `eval.data` is used if you want to evaluate the model on a holdout dataset that is not used in training.

The epoch.end.callback parameter

This is a `callback` function that allows you to register another function that is called after *n* epochs. Deep learning models take a long time to train, so you need some feedback to know they are working correctly! You can write a custom `callback` function to do whatever you need, but usually it outputs to the screen or log after *n* epochs. This is equivalent to the code in our neural network that printed a diagnostic message every *500* epochs. The `callback` function can also be used to save the model to disk, for example, if you wanted to save the model before it begins to overfit.

The array.batch.size parameter

We only had 400 instances (rows) in our data, which can easily fit into memory. However, if your input data has millions of instances, the data needs to be split into batches during training in order to fit in the memory of the CPU/GPU. The number of instances you train at a time is the batch size. Note, you still iterate over all the data for the number of epochs, you just split the data into batches during each iteration and run the forward-propagation, backpropagation step over each batch for each epoch. For example, if you had 100 instances and selected a batch size of *32* with *6* epochs, you would need *4* batches for each epoch (*100/32 = 3.125*, so we need *4* batches to process all the data), for a total of *24* loops.

There is a trade-off in choosing the batch size. If you choose too low a value, the model will take a longer time to train because it's running more operations and batches will have more variability because of the small size. You cannot choose an enormous batch size either, this might cause your model to crash because it loads too much data into either the CPU or GPU. In most cases, you either take a sensible default that works from another deep learning model, or you set it at some value (for example, 1,024) and if your model crashes, then try again with a value of half the previous value (512).

There is a relationship between **Batch size**, **Learning rates**, and **# Epochs** for training. But there are no hard and fast rules in selecting values. However, in general, consider changing these values together and do not use an extreme value for one of these hyper-parameters. For example, picking a large Learning rate should mean fewer epochs, but if your batch size is too small, the model may fail to train. The best advice is to look at similar architectures and pick a similar set and range of values.

Now that we can see that deep learning still uses many of the concepts from neural networks, we will move on to talk about an important issue that you will probably encounter with every deep learning model: overfitting.

Using regularization to overcome overfitting

In the previous chapter, we saw the diminishing returns from further training iterations on neural networks in terms of their predictive ability on holdout or test data (that is, data not used to train the model). This is because complex models may memorize some of the noise in the data rather than learning the general patterns. These models then perform much worse when predicting new data. There are some methods we can apply to make our model generalize, that is, fit the overall patterns. These are called **regularization** and aim to reduce testing errors so that the model performs well on new data.

The most common regularization technique used in deep learning is dropout. However, we will also discuss two other regularization techniques that have a basis in regression and deep learning. These two regularization techniques are **L1 penalty**, which is also known as **Lasso**, and **L2 penalty**, which is also known as **Ridge**.

L1 penalty

The basic concept of the **L1 penalty**, also known as the **least-absolute shrinkage and selection operator** (**Lasso**–Hastie, T., Tibshirani, R., and Friedman, J. (2009)), is that a penalty is used to shrink weights toward zero. The penalty term uses the sum of the absolute weights, so some weights may get shrunken to zero. This means that Lasso can also be used as a type of variable selection. The strength of the penalty is controlled by a hyper-parameter, alpha (λ), which multiplies the sum of the absolute weights, and it can be a fixed value or, as with other hyper-parameters, optimized using cross-validation or some similar approach.

It is easier to describe Lasso if we use an **ordinary least squares** (**OLS**) regression model. In regression, a set of coefficients or model weights is estimated using the least-squared error criterion, where the weight/coefficient vector, Θ, is estimated such that it minimizes $\sum(y_i - \bar{y}_i)$ where $\bar{y}_i = b + \Theta x$, y_i is the target value we want to predict and $\bar{y}_i$ is the predicted value. Lasso regression adds an additional penalty term that now tries to minimize $\sum(y_i - \bar{y}_i) + \lambda \lfloor \Theta \rfloor$, where $\lfloor \Theta \rfloor$ is the absolute value of Θ. Typically, the intercept or offset term is excluded from this constraint.

There are a number of practical implications for Lasso regression. First, the effect of the penalty depends on the size of the weights, and the size of the weights depends on the scale of the data. Therefore, data is typically standardized to have unit variance first (or at least to make the variance of each variable equal). The L1 penalty has a tendency to shrink small weights to zero (for explanations as to why this happens, see Hastie, T., Tibshirani, R., and Friedman, J. (2009)). If you only consider variables for which the L1 penalty leaves non-zero weights, it can essentially function as feature-selection. The tendency for the L1 penalty to shrink small coefficients to zero can also be convenient for simplifying the interpretation of the model results.

Applying the L1 penalty to neural networks works exactly the same for neural networks as it does for regression. If X represents the input, Y is the outcome or dependent variable, B the parameters, and F the objective function that will be optimized to obtain B, that is, we want to minimize $F(B; X, Y)$. The L1 penalty modifies the objective function to be $F(B; X, Y) + \lambda \lfloor \Theta \rfloor$, where Θ represents the weights (typically offsets are ignored). The L1 penalty tends to result in a sparse solution (that is, more zero weights) as small and larger weights result in equal penalties, so that at each update of the gradient, the weights are moved toward zero.

We have only considered the case where λ is a constant, controlling the degree of penalty or regularization. However, it is possible to set different values with deep neural networks, where varying degrees of regularization can be applied to different layers. One reason for considering such differential regularization is that it is sometimes desirable to allow a greater number of parameters (say by including more neurons in a particular layer) but then counteract this somewhat through stronger regularization. However, this approach can be quite computationally demanding if we are allowing the L1 penalty to vary for every layer of a deep neural network and using cross-validation to optimize all possible combinations of the L1 penalty. Therefore, usually a single value is used across the entire model.

L1 penalty in action

To see how the L1 penalty works, we can use a simulated linear regression problem. The code for the rest of this chapter is in `Chapter3/overfitting.R`. We simulate the data, using a correlated set of predictors:

```
set.seed(1234)
X <- mvrnorm(n = 200, mu = c(0, 0, 0, 0, 0),
  Sigma = matrix(c(
    1, .9999, .99, .99, .10,
    .9999, 1, .99, .99, .10,
    .99, .99, 1, .99, .10,
```

```
       .99, .99, .99, 1, .10,
       .10, .10, .10, .10, 1
  ), ncol = 5))
  y <- rnorm(200, 3 + X %*% matrix(c(1, 1, 1, 1, 0)), .5)
```

Next, we can fit an OLS regression model to the first 100 cases, and then use `lasso`. To use `lasso`, we use the `glmnet()` function from the `glmnet` package. This function can actually fit the L1 or the L2 (discussed in the next section) penalties, and which one occurs is determined by the argument, alpha. When `alpha = 1`, it is the L1 penalty (that is, `lasso`), and when `alpha = 0`, it is the L2 penalty (that is, ridge regression). Further, because we don't know which value of `lambda` we should pick, we can evaluate a range of options and tune this hyper-parameter automatically using cross-validation, which is the `cv.glmnet()` function. We can then plot the `lasso` object to see the mean squared error for a variety of `lambda` values to allow us to select the correct level of regularization:

```
  m.ols <- lm(y[1:100] ~ X[1:100, ])
  m.lasso.cv <- cv.glmnet(X[1:100, ], y[1:100], alpha = 1)
  plot(m.lasso.cv)
```

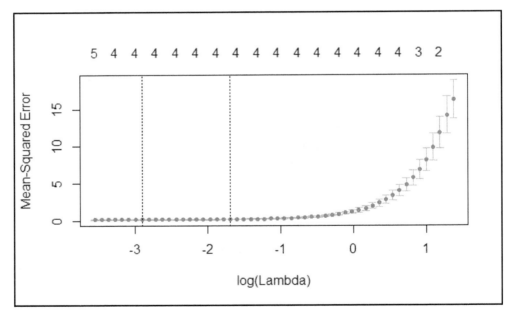

Figure 3.10: Lasso regularization

One thing that we can see from the graph is that, when the penalty gets too high, the cross-validated model increases. Indeed, `lasso` seems to do well with very low lambda values, perhaps indicating `lasso` does not help improve out-of-sample performance/generalizability much for this dataset. For the sake of this example, we will continue but in actual use, this might give us pause to consider whether `lasso` was really helping. Finally, we can compare the coefficients with those from `lasso`:

```
cbind(OLS = coef(m.ols),Lasso = coef(m.lasso.cv)[,1])
                OLS Lasso
(Intercept)   2.958  2.99
X[1:100, ]1  -0.082  1.41
X[1:100, ]2   2.239  0.71
X[1:100, ]3   0.602  0.51
X[1:100, ]4   1.235  1.17
X[1:100, ]5  -0.041  0.00
```

Notice that the OLS coefficients are noisier and also that, in `lasso`, predictor 5 is penalized to 0. Recall from the simulated data that the true coefficients are 3, 1, 1, 1, 1, and 0. The OLS estimates have much too low a value for the first predictor and much too high a value for the second, whereas `lasso` has more accurate values for each. This demonstrates that `lasso` regression generalizes better than OLS regression for this dataset.

L2 penalty

The **L2 penalty**, also known as **ridge regression**, is similar in many ways to the L1 penalty, but instead of adding a penalty based on the sum of the absolute weights, the penalty is based on the squared weights. This means that larger absolute weights are penalized more. In the context of neural networks, this is sometimes referred to as weight decay. If you examine the gradient of the regularized objective function, there is a penalty such that, at every update, there is a multiplicative penalty to the weights. As for the L1 penalty, although they could be included, biases or offsets are usually excluded from this.

From the perspective of a linear regression problem, the L2 penalty is a modification to the objective function minimized, from $\Sigma(y_i - \bar{y}_i)$ to $\Sigma(y_i - \bar{y}_i) + \lambda\Theta^2$.

L2 penalty in action

To see how the L2 penalty works, we can use the same simulated linear regression problem we used for the Ll penalty. To fit a ridge regression model, we use the `glmnet()` function from the `glmnet` package. As mentioned previously, this function can actually fit the L1 or the L2 penalties, and which one occurs is determined by the argument, alpha. When `alpha = 1`, it fits `lasso`, and when `alpha = 0`, it fits ridge regression. This time, we choose `alpha = 0`. Again, we evaluate a range of lambda options and tune this hyper-parameter automatically using cross-validation. This is accomplished by using the `cv.glmnet()` function. We plot the ridge regression object to see the error for a variety of lambda values:

```
m.ridge.cv <- cv.glmnet(X[1:100, ], y[1:100], alpha = 0)
plot(m.ridge.cv)
```

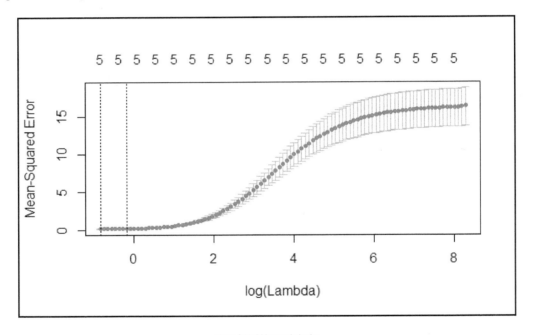

Figure 3.11: Ridge regularization

Although the shape is different from `lasso` in that the error appears to asymptote for higher lambda values, it is still clear that, when the penalty gets too high, the cross-validated model error increases. As with `lasso`, the ridge regression model seems to do well with very low lambda values, perhaps indicating the L2 penalty does not improve out-of-sample performance/generalizability by much.

Finally, we can compare the OLS coefficients with those from `lasso` and the ridge regression model:

```
> cbind(OLS = coef(m.ols),Lasso = coef(m.lasso.cv)[,1],Ridge =
coef(m.ridge.cv)[,1])
                  OLS Lasso   Ridge
(Intercept)     2.958  2.99  2.9919
X[1:100, ]1    -0.082  1.41  0.9488
X[1:100, ]2     2.239  0.71  0.9524
X[1:100, ]3     0.602  0.51  0.9323
X[1:100, ]4     1.235  1.17  0.9548
X[1:100, ]5    -0.041  0.00 -0.0023
```

Although ridge regression does not shrink the coefficient for the fifth predictor to exactly 0, it is smaller than in the OLS, and the remaining parameters are all slightly shrunken, but quite close to their true values of 3, 1, 1, 1, 1, and 0.

Weight decay (L2 penalty in neural networks)

We have already unknowingly used regularization in the previous chapter. The neural network we trained using the `caret` and `nnet` package used a weight decay of `0.10`. We can investigate the use of weight decay by varying it, and tuning it using cross-validation:

1. Load the data as before. Then we create a local cluster to run the cross-validation in parallel:

```
set.seed(1234)
## same data as from previous chapter
if (!file.exists('../data/train.csv'))
{
  link <-
'https://apache-mxnet.s3-accelerate.dualstack.amazonaws.com/R/data/
mnist_csv.zip'
  if (!file.exists(paste(dataDirectory,'/mnist_csv.zip',sep="")))
    download.file(link, destfile =
paste(dataDirectory,'/mnist_csv.zip',sep=""))
  unzip(paste(dataDirectory,'/mnist_csv.zip',sep=""), exdir =
dataDirectory)
  if (file.exists(paste(dataDirectory,'/test.csv',sep="")))
    file.remove(paste(dataDirectory,'/test.csv',sep=""))
}

digits.train <- read.csv("../data/train.csv")

## convert to factor
digits.train$label <- factor(digits.train$label, levels = 0:9)
```

```
sample <- sample(nrow(digits.train), 6000)
train <- sample[1:5000]
test <- sample[5001:6000]

digits.X <- digits.train[train, -1]
digits.y <- digits.train[train, 1]
test.X <- digits.train[test, -1]
test.y <- digits.train[test, 1]

## try various weight decays and number of iterations
## register backend so that different decays can be
## estimated in parallel
cl <- makeCluster(5)
clusterEvalQ(cl, {source("cluster_inc.R")})
registerDoSNOW(cl)
```

2. Train a neural network on the digit classification, and vary the weight-decay penalty at 0 (no penalty) and 0.10. We also loop through two sets of the number of iterations allowed: 100 or 150. Note that this code is computationally intensive and takes some time to run:

```
set.seed(1234)
digits.decay.m1 <- lapply(c(100, 150), function(its) {
  caret::train(digits.X, digits.y,
          method = "nnet",
          tuneGrid = expand.grid(
            .size = c(10),
            .decay = c(0, .1)),
          trControl = caret::trainControl(method="cv", number=5,
repeats=1),
          MaxNWts = 10000,
          maxit = its)
})
```

3. Examining the results, we see that, when we limit to only 100 iterations, both the non-regularized model and regularized model have the same accuracy at 0.56, based on cross-validated results, which is not very good on this data:

```
digits.decay.m1[[1]]
Neural Network

5000 samples
 784 predictor
  10 classes: '0', '1', '2', '3', '4', '5', '6', '7', '8', '9'

No pre-processing
Resampling: Cross-Validated (5 fold)
```

```
Summary of sample sizes: 4000, 4001, 4000, 3998, 4001
Resampling results across tuning parameters:

  decay  Accuracy   Kappa
   0.0     0.56     0.51
   0.1     0.56     0.51


Tuning parameter 'size' was held constant at a value of 10
Accuracy was used to select the optimal model using the
 largest value.
The final values used for the model were size = 10 and decay = 0.1.
```

4. Examine the model with 150 iterations to see whether the regularized or non-regularized model performs better:

```
digits.decay.m1[[2]]
Neural Network

5000 samples
 784 predictor
  10 classes: '0', '1', '2', '3', '4', '5', '6', '7', '8', '9'

No pre-processing
Resampling: Cross-Validated (5 fold)
Summary of sample sizes: 4000, 4002, 3998, 4000, 4000
Resampling results across tuning parameters:

  decay  Accuracy   Kappa
   0.0     0.64     0.60
   0.1     0.63     0.59


Tuning parameter 'size' was held constant at a value of 10
Accuracy was used to select the optimal model using the
 largest value.
The final values used for the model were size = 10 and decay = 0.
```

Overall, the model with more iterations outperforms the model with fewer iterations, regardless of the regularization. However, comparing both models with 150 iterations, the regularized model is superior (accuracy= 0.66) to the non-regularized model (accuracy= 0.65), although here the difference is relatively small.

These results highlight that regularization is often most useful for more complex models that have greater flexibility to fit (and overfit) the data. In models that are appropriate or overly simplistic for the data, regularization will probably decrease performance. When developing a new model architecture, you should avoid adding regularization until the model is performing well on the training data. If you add regularization beforehand and the model performs poorly on the training data, you will not know whether the problem is with the model's architecture or because of the regularization. In the next section, we'll discuss ensemble and model averaging techniques, the last forms of regularization that are highlighted in this book.

Ensembles and model-averaging

Another approach to regularization involves creating multiple models (ensembles) and combining them, such as by model-averaging or some other algorithm for combining individual model results. There is a rich history of using ensemble techniques in machine learning, such as bagging, boosting, and random forest, that use this technique. The general idea is that, if you build different models using the training data, each model has different errors in the predicted values. Where one model predicts too high a value, another may predict too low a value, and when averaged, some of the errors cancel out, resulting in a more accurate prediction than would have been otherwise obtained.

The key to ensemble methods is that the different models must have some variability in their predictions. If the predictions from the different models are highly correlated, then using ensemble techniques will not be beneficial. If the predictions from the different models have very low correlations, then the average will be far more accurate as it gains the strengths of each model. The following code gives an example using simulated data. This small example illustrates the point with just three models:

```
## simulated data
set.seed(1234)
d <- data.frame(
 x = rnorm(400))
d$y <- with(d, rnorm(400, 2 + ifelse(x < 0, x + x^2, x + x^2.5), 1))
d.train <- d[1:200, ]
d.test <- d[201:400, ]

## three different models
m1 <- lm(y ~ x, data = d.train)
m2 <- lm(y ~ I(x^2), data = d.train)
m3 <- lm(y ~ pmax(x, 0) + pmin(x, 0), data = d.train)

## In sample R2
cbind(M1=summary(m1)$r.squared,
```

```
M2=summary(m2)$r.squared,M3=summary(m3)$r.squared)
     M1   M2   M3
[1,] 0.33 0.6 0.76
```

We can see that the predictive value of each model, at least in the training data, varies quite a bit. Evaluating the correlations among fitted values in the training data can also help to indicate how much overlap there is among the model predictions:

```
cor(cbind(M1=fitted(m1),
 M2=fitted(m2),M3=fitted(m3)))
     M1   M2   M3
M1 1.00 0.11 0.65
M2 0.11 1.00 0.78
M3 0.65 0.78 1.00
```

Next, we generate predicted values for the testing data, the average of the predicted values, and again correlate the predictions along with reality in the testing data:

```
## generate predictions and the average prediction
d.test$yhat1 <- predict(m1, newdata = d.test)
d.test$yhat2 <- predict(m2, newdata = d.test)
d.test$yhat3 <- predict(m3, newdata = d.test)
d.test$yhatavg <- rowMeans(d.test[, paste0("yhat", 1:3)])

## correlation in the testing data
cor(d.test)
             x      y  yhat1  yhat2 yhat3 yhatavg
x        1.000  0.44  1.000 -0.098  0.60    0.55
y        0.442  1.00  0.442  0.753  0.87    0.91
yhat1    1.000  0.44  1.000 -0.098  0.60    0.55
yhat2   -0.098  0.75 -0.098  1.000  0.69    0.76
yhat3    0.596  0.87  0.596  0.687  1.00    0.98
yhatavg  0.552  0.91  0.552  0.765  0.98    1.00
```

From the results, we can see that the average of the three models' predictions performs better than any of the models individually. However, this is not always the case; one good model may have better predictions than the average predictions. In general, it is good to check that the models being averaged perform similarly, at least in the training data. The second lesson is that, given models with similar performance, it is desirable to have lower correlations between model predictions, as this will result in the best performing average.

There are other forms of ensemble methods that are included in other machine learning algorithms, for example, bagging and boosting. Bagging is used in random forests, where many models are generated, each having different samples of the data. The models are deliberately designed to be small, incomplete models. By averaging the predictions of lots of undertrained models that use only a portion of the data, we should get a more powerful model. An example of boosting includes gradient-boosted models (GBMs), which also use multiple models, but this time each model focuses on the instances that were incorrectly predicted in the previous model. Both random forests and GBMs have proven to be very successful with structured data because they reduce variance, that is, avoid overfitting the data.

Bagging and model-averaging are not used as frequently in deep neural networks because the computational cost of training each model can be quite high, and thus repeating the process many times becomes prohibitively expensive in terms of time and compute resources. Nevertheless, it is still possible to use model averaging in the context of deep neural networks, even if perhaps it is on only a handful of models rather than hundreds, as is common in random forests and some other approaches.

Use case – improving out-of-sample model performance using dropout

Dropout is a novel approach to regularization that is particularly valuable for large and complex deep neural networks. For a much more detailed exploration of dropout in deep neural networks, see Srivastava, N., Hinton, G., Krizhevsky, A., Sutskever, I., and Salakhutdinav, R. (2014). The concept behind dropout is actually quite straightforward. During the training of the model, units (for example, input and hidden neurons) are probabilistically dropped along with all connections to and from them.

For example, the following diagram is an example of what might happen at each step of training for a model where hidden neurons and their connections are dropped with a probability of 1/3 for each epoch. Once a node is dropped, its connections to the next layer are also dropped. In the the following diagram, the grayed-out nodes and dashed connections are the ones that were dropped. It is important to note that the choice of nodes that are dropped changes for each epoch:

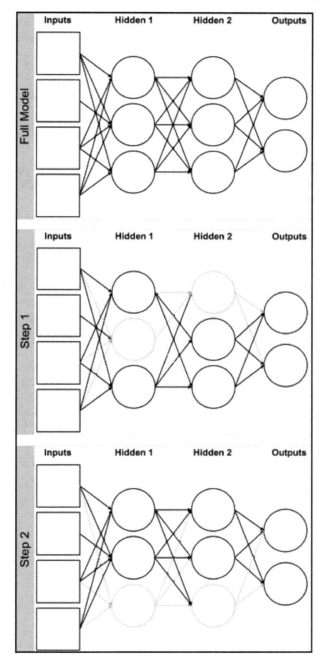

Figure 3.12: Dropout applied to a layer for different epochs

One way to think about dropout is that it forces models to be more robust to perturbations. Although many neurons are included in the full model, during training they are not all simultaneously present, and so neurons must operate somewhat more independently than they would otherwise. Another way of viewing dropout is that, if you have a large model with N weights between hidden neurons, but 50% are dropped during training, although all N weights will be used during some stages of training, you have effectively halved the total model complexity as the average number of weights will be halved. This reduces model complexity, and hence helps to prevent the overfitting of the data. Because of this feature, if the proportion of dropout is p, Srivastava, N., Hinton, G., Krizhevsky, A., Sutskever, I., and Salakhutdinov, R. (2014) recommend scaling up the target model complexity by 1/p in order to end up with a roughly equally complex model.

During model testing/scoring, neurons are not usually dropped because it is computationally inconvenient. Instead, we can use an approximate average based on scaling the weights from a single neural network based on each weight's probability of being included (that is, 1/p). This is usually taken care of by the deep learning library.

In addition to working well, this approximate weight re-scaling is a fairly trivial calculation. Thus, the primary computational cost of dropout comes from the fact that a model with more neurons and weights must be used because so many (a commonly recommended value is around 50% for hidden neurons) are dropped during each training update.

Although dropout is easy to implement, a larger model may be required to compensate. To speed up training, a higher learning rate can be used so that fewer epochs are required. One potential downside of combining these approaches is that, with fewer neurons and a faster learning rate, some weights may become quite large. Fortunately, it is possible to use dropout along with other forms of regularization, such as the L1 or L2 penalty. Taken together, the result is a larger model that that can quickly (a faster Learning rate) explore a broader parameter space, but is regularized through dropout and a penalty to keep the weights in check.

To show the use of dropout in a neural network, we will return to the **Modified National Institute of Standards and Technology** (**MNIST**) dataset (which we downloaded in Chapter 2, *Training a Prediction Model*) we worked with previously. We will use the nn.train() function from the deepnet package, as it allows for dropout. As in the previous chapter, we will run the four models in parallel to reduce the time it takes. Specifically, we compare four models, two with and two without dropout regularization and with either 40 or 80 hidden neurons. For dropout, we specify the proportion to dropout separately for the hidden and visible units. Based on the rule of thumb that about 50% of hidden units (and 80% of observed units) should be kept, we specify the dropout proportions at 0.5 and 0.2, respectively:

```
## Fit Models
nn.models <- foreach(i = 1:4, .combine = 'c') %dopar% {
set.seed(1234)
 list(nn.train(
    x = as.matrix(digits.X),
    y = model.matrix(~ 0 + digits.y),
    hidden = c(40, 80, 40, 80)[i],
    activationfun = "tanh",
    learningrate = 0.8,
    momentum = 0.5,
    numepochs = 150,
    output = "softmax",
    hidden_dropout = c(0, 0, .5, .5)[i],
    visible_dropout = c(0, 0, .2, .2)[i]))
}
```

Next, we can loop through the models to obtain predicted values and get the overall model performance:

```
nn.yhat <- lapply(nn.models, function(obj) {
 encodeClassLabels(nn.predict(obj, as.matrix(digits.X)))
 })
perf.train <- do.call(cbind, lapply(nn.yhat, function(yhat) {
 caret::confusionMatrix(xtabs(~ I(yhat - 1) + digits.y))$overall
 }))
colnames(perf.train) <- c("N40", "N80", "N40_Reg", "N80_Reg")
options(digits = 4)
perf.train
```

	N40	N80	N40_Reg	N80_Reg
Accuracy	**0.9478**	**0.9622**	**0.9278**	**0.9400**
Kappa	0.9420	0.9580	0.9197	0.9333
AccuracyLower	0.9413	0.9565	0.9203	0.9331
AccuracyUpper	0.9538	0.9673	0.9348	0.9464
AccuracyNull	0.1126	0.1126	0.1126	0.1126

```
AccuracyPValue   0.0000   0.0000   0.0000   0.0000
McnemarPValue       NaN      NaN      NaN      NaN
```

When evaluating the models in the in-sample training data, it seems those without regularization perform better those with regularization. Of course, the real test comes with the testing or holdout data:

```
nn.yhat.test <- lapply(nn.models, function(obj) {
  encodeClassLabels(nn.predict(obj, as.matrix(test.X)))
  })

perf.test <- do.call(cbind, lapply(nn.yhat.test, function(yhat) {
  caret::confusionMatrix(xtabs(~ I(yhat - 1) + test.y))$overall
  }))
colnames(perf.test) <- c("N40", "N80", "N40_Reg", "N80_Reg")

perf.test
                    N40      N80  N40_Reg  N80_Reg
Accuracy         0.8890   0.8520   0.8980   0.9030
Kappa            0.8765   0.8352   0.8864   0.8920
AccuracyLower    0.8679   0.8285   0.8776   0.8830
AccuracyUpper    0.9078   0.8734   0.9161   0.9206
AccuracyNull     0.1180   0.1180   0.1180   0.1180
AccuracyPValue   0.0000   0.0000   0.0000   0.0000
McnemarPValue       NaN      NaN      NaN      NaN
```

The testing data highlights that the in-sample performance was overly optimistic (accuracy = 0.9622 versus accuracy = 0.8520 for the 80-neuron, non-regularized model in the training and testing data, respectively). We can see the advantage of the regularized models for both the 40- and the 80-neuron models. Although both still perform worse in the testing data than they did in the training data, they perform on a par with, or better than, the equivalent non-regularized models in the testing data. This difference is particularly important for the 80-neuron model as the best performing model on the test data is the regularized model.

Although these numbers are by no means record-setting, they do show the value of using dropout, or regularization more generally, and how one might go about trying to tune the model and dropout parameters to improve the ultimate testing performance.

Summary

This chapter began by showing you how to program a neural network from scratch. We demonstrated the neural network in a web application created by just using R code. We delved into how the neural network actually worked, showing how to code forward-propagation, `cost` functions, and backpropagation. Then we looked at how the parameters for our neural network apply to modern deep learning libraries by looking at the `mx.model.FeedForward.create` function from the `mxnet` deep learning library.

Then we covered overfitting, demonstrating several approaches to preventing overfitting, including common penalties, the Ll penalty and L2 penalty, ensembles of simpler models, and dropout, where variables and/or cases are dropped to make the model noisy. We examined the role of penalties in regression problems and neural networks. In the next chapter, we will move into deep learning and deep neural networks, and see how to push the accuracy and performance of our predictive models even further.

4
Training Deep Prediction Models

The previous chapters covered a bit of the theory behind neural networks and used some neural network packages in R. Now it is time to dive in and look at training deep learning models. In this chapter, we will explore how to train and build feedforward neural networks, which are the most common type of deep learning model. We will use MXNet to build deep learning models to perform classification and regression using a retail dataset.

This chapter will cover the following topics:

- Getting started with deep feedforward neural networks
- Common activation functions – rectifiers, hyperbolic tangent, and maxout
- Introduction to the MXNet deep learning library
- Use case – Using MXNet for classification and regression

Getting started with deep feedforward neural networks

A deep feedforward neural network is designed to approximate a function, $f()$, that maps some set of input variables, x, to an output variable, y. They are called feedforward neural networks because information flows from the input through each successive layer as far as the output, and there are no feedback or recursive loops (models including both forward and backward connections are referred to as recurrent neural networks).

Deep feedforward neural networks are applicable to a wide range of problems, and are particularly useful for applications such as image classification. More generally, feedforward neural networks are useful for prediction and classification where there is a clearly defined outcome (what digit an image contains, whether someone is walking upstairs or walking on a flat surface, the presence/absence of disease, and so on).

Deep feedforward neural networks can be constructed by chaining layers or functions together. For example, a network with four hidden layers is shown in the following diagram:

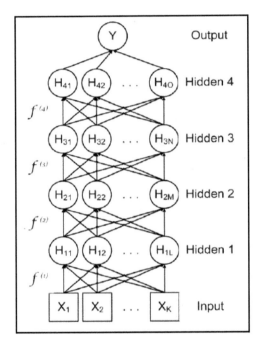

Figure 4.1: A deep feedforward neural network

This diagram of the model is a directed acyclic graph. Represented as a function, the overall mapping from the input, X, to the output, Y, is a multilayered function. The first hidden layer is $H_1 = f^{(1)}(X, w_1\, a_1)$, the second hidden layer is $H_2 = f^{(2)}(H_1, w_2\, a_2)$, and so on. These multiple layers can allow complex functions and transformations to be built up from relatively simple ones.

If sufficient hidden neurons are included in a layer, it can approximate to the desired degree of precision with many different types of functions. Feedforward neural networks can approximate non-linear functions by applying non-linear transformations between layers. These non-linear functions are known as activation functions, which we will cover in the next section.

The weights for each layer will be learned as the model is trained through forward- and backward-propagation. Another key piece of the model that must be determined is the cost, or loss, function. The two most commonly used cost functions are cross-entropy, which is used for classification tasks, and **mean squared error** (**MSE**), which is used for regression tasks.

Activation functions

The activation function determines the mapping between input and a hidden layer. It defines the functional form for how a neuron gets activated. For example, a linear activation function could be defined as: $f(x) = x$, in which case the value for the neuron would be the raw input, x. A linear activation function is shown in the top panel of *Figure 4.2*. Linear activation functions are rarely used because in practice deep learning models would find it difficult to learn non-linear functional forms using linear activation functions. In previous chapters, we used the hyperbolic tangent as an activation function, namely $f(x) = tanh(x)$. Hyperbolic tangent can work well in some cases, but a potential limitation is that at either low or high values, it saturates, as shown in the middle panel of the figure 4.2.

Perhaps the most popular activation function currently, and a good first choice (Nair, V., and Hinton, G. E. (2010)), is known as a *rectifier*. There are different kinds of rectifiers, but the most common is defined by the $f(x) = max(0, x)$ function, which is known as **relu**. The relu activation is flat below zero and linear above zero; an example is shown in Figure 4.2.

The final type of activation function we will discuss is maxout (Goodfellow, Warde-Farley, Mirza, Courville, and Bengio (2013)). A maxout unit takes the maximum value of its input, although as usual, this is after weighting so it is not the case that the input variable with the highest value will always win. Maxout activation functions seem to work particularly well with dropout.

The relu activation is the most commonly-used activation function and it is the default option for the deep learning models in the rest of this book. The following graphs for some of the activation functions we have discussed:

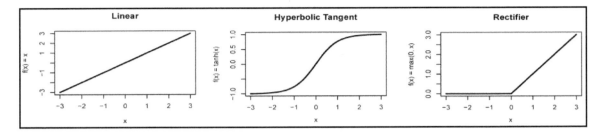

Figure 4.2: Common activation functions

Introduction to the MXNet deep learning library

The deep learning libraries we will use in this book are MXNet, Keras, and TensorFlow. Keras is a frontend API, which means it is not a standalone library as it requires a lower-level library in the backend, usually TensorFlow. The advantage of using Keras rather than TensorFlow is that it has a simpler interface. We will use Keras in later chapters in this book.

Both MXNet and TensorFlow are multipurpose numerical computation libraries that can use GPUs for mass parallel matrix operations. As such, multi-dimensional matrices are central to both libraries. In R, we are familiar with the vector, which is a one-dimensional array of values of the same type. The R data frame is a two-dimensional array of values, where each column can have different types. The R matrix is a two-dimensional array of values with the same type. Some machine learning algorithms in R require a matrix as input. We saw an example of this in Chapter 2, *Training a Prediction Model*, with the RSNSS package.

In R, it is unusual to use data structures with more than two dimensions, but deep learning uses them extensively. For example, if you have a 32 x 32 color image, you could store the pixel values in a 32 x 32 x 3 matrix, where the first two dimensions are the width and height, and the last dimension is for the red, green, and blue colors. This can be extended further by adding another dimension for a collection of images. This is called a batch and allows the processor (CPU/GPU) to process multiple images concurrently. The batch size is a hyper-parameter and the value selected depends on the size of the input data and memory capacity. If our batch size were 64, our matrix would be a 4-dimensional matrix of size 32 x 32 x 3 x 64 where the first 2 dimensions are the width and height, the third dimension is the colors, and the last dimension is the batch size, 64. The important thing to realize is that this is just another way of representing data. In R, we would store the same data as a 2-dimensional matrix (or dataframe) with 64 rows and 32 x 32 x 3 = 3,072 columns. All we are doing is reshaping the data, we are not changing it.

These n-dimensional matrices, which contain elements of the same type, are the cornerstone of using MXNet and TensorFlow. In MXNet, they are referred to as NDArrays. In TensorFlow, they are known as **tensors**. These n-dimensional matrices are important because they mean that we can feed the data into GPUs more efficiently; GPUs can process data in batches more efficiently than processing single rows of data. In the preceding example, we use 64 images in a batch, so the deep learning library will process input data in chunks of 32 x 32 x 3 x 64.

This chapter will use the MXNet deep learning library. MXNet originated at Carnegie Mellon University and is heavily supported by Amazon, they choose it as their default Deep Learning library in 2016. In 2017, MXNet was accepted as an Apache Incubator project, ensuring that it would remain as open source software. Here is a very simple example of an NDArray (matrix) operation in MXNet in R. If you have not already installed the MXNet package for R, go back to `Chapter 1`, *Getting Started with Deep Learning*, for instructions, or use this link: `https://mxnet.apache.org/install/index.html`:

```
library(mxnet) # 1
ctx = mx.cpu() # 2
a <- mx.nd.ones(c(2,3),ctx=ctx) # 3
b <- a * 2 + 1 # 4
typeof(b) # 5
[1] "externalptr"
class(b) # 6
[1] "MXNDArray"
b # 7
     [,1] [,2] [,3]
[1,]    3    3    3
[2,]    3    3    3
```

We can break down this code line by line:

- Line 1 loads the MXNet package.
- Line 2 sets the CPU context. This tells MXNet where to process your computations, either on the CPU or on a GPU, if one is available.
- Line 3 creates a 2-dimensional NDArray of size 2 x 3 where each value is 1.
- Line 4 creates another 2-dimensional NDArray of size 2 x 3. Each value will be 3 because we perform element-wise multiplication and add 1.
- Line 5 shows that b is an external pointer.
- Line 6 shows that the class of b is MXNDArray.
- Line 7 displays the results.

We can perform mathematical operations, such as multiplication and addition, on the b variable. However, it is important to realize that, while this behaves similarly to an R matrix, it is not a native R object. We can see this when we output the type and class of this variable.

When developing deep learning models, there are usually two distinct steps. First you create the model architecture and then you train the model. The main reason for this is because most deep learning libraries employ symbolic programming rather than the imperative programming you are used to. Most of the code you have previously written in R is an imperative program, which executes code sequentially. For mathematical optimization tasks, such as deep learning, this may not be the most efficient method of execution. Most deep learning libraries, including MXNet and TensorFlow, use symbolic programming. For symbolic programming, a computation graph for the program execution is designed first. This graph is then compiled and executed. When the computation graph is generated, the input, output, and graph operations are already defined, meaning that the code can be optimized. This means that for deep learning, symbolic programs are usually more efficient than imperative programs.

Here is a simple example of the type of optimization using symbolic programs:

$M = (M1 * M2) + (M3 * M4)$

An imperative program would calculate this as follows:

$Mtemp1 = (M1 * M2)$

$Mtemp2 = (M3 * M4)$

$M = Mtemp1 + Mtemp2$

A symbolic program would first create a computation graph, which might look like the following:

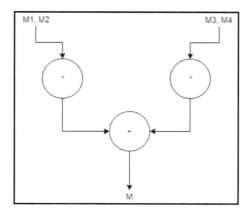

Figure 4.3: Example of a computation graph

M1, *M2*, *M3*, and *M4* are symbols that need to be operated on. The graph shows the dependencies for operations; the + operation requires the two preceding multiplication operations to be done before it can execute. But there is no dependency between the two multiplication steps, so these can be executed in parallel. This type of optimization means the code can execute much faster.

From a coding point of view, this means is that you have two steps in creating a deep learning model – first you define the architecture of the model and then you train the model. You create *layers* for your deep learning model and each layer has symbols that are placeholders. So for example, the first layer is usually:

```
data <- mx.symbol.Variable("data")
```

`data` is a placeholder for the input, which we will insert later. The output of each layer feeds into the next layer as input. This might be a convolutional layer, a dense layer, an activation layer a dropout layer, and so on. The following code example shows how the layers continue to feed into each other; this is taken from a full example later in this chapter. Notice how the symbol for each layer is used as input in the next layer, this is how the model is built layer after layer. The `data1` symbol is passed into the first call to `mx.symbol.FullyConnected`, the `fc1` symbol is passed into the first call to `mx.symbol.Activation`, and so on.

```
data <- mx.symbol.Variable("data")
fc1 <- mx.symbol.FullyConnected(data, name="fc1", num_hidden=64)
act1 <- mx.symbol.Activation(fc1, name="activ1", act_type=activ)
```

```
drop1 <- mx.symbol.Dropout(data=act1,p=0.2)
fc2 <- mx.symbol.FullyConnected(drop1, name="fc2", num_hidden=32)
act2 <- mx.symbol.Activation(fc2, name="activ2", act_type=activ)


.....
softmax <- mx.symbol.SoftmaxOutput(fc4, name="sm")
```

When you execute this code, it runs instantly as nothing is executed at this stage.
Eventually, you pass the last layer into a function to train the model. In MXNet, this is
the `mx.model.FeedForward.create` function. At this stage, the computation graph is
computed and the model begins to be trained:

```
softmax <- mx.symbol.SoftmaxOutput(fc4, name="sm")
model <- mx.model.FeedForward.create(softmax, X = train_X, y = train_Y,
                                     ctx = devices,num.round = num_epochs,
                                     ................
```

This is when the deep learning model is created and trained. More information on the
MXNet architecture is available online; the following links will get you started:

- `https://mxnet.apache.org/tutorials/basic/symbol.html`
- `https://mxnet.incubator.apache.org/architecture/program_model.html`

Deep learning layers

In the earlier code snippets, we saw some layers for a deep learning model,
including `mx.symbol.FullyConnected`, `mx.symbol.Activation`, and
`mx.symbol.Dropout`. Layers are how models are constructed; they are computational
transformations of data. For example, `mx.symbol.FullyConnected` is the first type of
layer operation we matrix operation we introduced in Chapter 1, *Getting Started with Deep
Learning*. It is *fully connected* because all input values are connected to all nodes in the layer.
In other deep learning libraries, such as Keras, it is called a **dense** layer.

The `mx.symbol.Activation` layer performs an activation function on the output of the
previous layer. The `mx.symbol.Dropout` layer performs dropout on the output from the
previous layer. Other common layer types in MXNet are:

- `mxnet.symbol.Convolution`: Performs a convolutional operation that matches
  patterns across the data. It is mostly used in computer vision tasks, which we will
  see in Chapter 5, *Image Classification Using Convolutional Neural Networks*. They
  can also be used for Natural Language Processing, which we will see in Chapter
  6, *Natural Language Processing Using Deep Learning*.

- `mx.symbol.Pooling`: Performs pooling on the output from the previous layer. Pooling reduces the number of elements by taking the average, or max value, from sections of the input. These are commonly used with convolutional layers.

- `mx.symbol.BatchNorm`: Used to normalize the weights from the previous layer. This is done for the same reason you normalize input data before model-building: it helps the model to train better. It also prevents vanishing and exploding gradients where gradients get very, very small or very, very large during training. This can cause the model to fail to converge, that is, training will fail.

- `mx.symbol.SoftmaxOutput`: Calculates a softmax result from the output from the previous layer.

There are recognized patterns for using these layers, for example, an activation layer normally follows a fully-connected layer. A dropout layer is usually applied after the activation function, but can be between the fully connected layer and the activation function. Convolutional layers and pooling layers are often used together in image tasks in that order. At this stage, there is no need to try to memorize when to use these layers; you will encounter plenty of examples in the rest of this book!

If all this seems confusing, take some comfort in knowing that a lot of the difficult work in applying these layers is abstracted away from you. In the previous chapter, when we built a neural network, we had to manage all the input output from the layers. This meant ensuring that the matrix dimensions were correct so that the operations worked. Deep Learning libraries, such as MXNet and TensorFlow, take care of this for you.

Building a deep learning model

Now that we have covered the basics, let's look at building our first true deep learning model! We will use the UHI HAR dataset that we used in Chapter 2, *Training a Prediction Model*. The following code does some data preparation: it loads the data and selects only the columns that store mean values (those that have the word mean in the column name). The y variables are from 1 to 6; we will subtract one so that the range is 0 to 5. The code for this section is in Chapter4/uci_har.R. It requires the UHI HAR dataset to be in the data folder; download it from https://archive.ics.uci.edu/ml/datasets/human+activity+recognition+using+smartphones and unzip it into the data folder:

```
train.x <- read.table("../data/UCI HAR Dataset/train/X_train.txt")
train.y <- read.table("../data/UCI HAR Dataset/train/y_train.txt")[[1]]
test.x <- read.table("../data/UCI HAR Dataset/test/X_test.txt")
test.y <- read.table("../data/UCI HAR Dataset/test/y_test.txt")[[1]]
```

```
features <- read.table("../data/UCI HAR Dataset/features.txt")
meanSD <- grep("mean\\(\\)|std\\(\\)", features[, 2])
train.y <- train.y-1
test.y <- test.y-1
```

Next, we will transpose the data and convert it into a matrix. MXNet expects the data to be width x height rather than height x width:

```
train.x <- t(train.x[,meanSD])
test.x <- t(test.x[,meanSD])
train.x <- data.matrix(train.x)
test.x <- data.matrix(test.x)
```

The next step is to define the computation graph. We create a placeholder for the data and create two fully connected (or dense) layers followed by relu activations. The first layer has 64 nodes and the second layer has 32 nodes. We create a final fully-connected layer with six nodes – the number of distinct classes in our y variable. We use a softmax activation to convert the numbers from the last six nodes into probabilities for each class:

```
data <- mx.symbol.Variable("data")
fc1 <- mx.symbol.FullyConnected(data, name="fc1", num_hidden=64)
act1 <- mx.symbol.Activation(fc1, name="relu1", act_type="relu")
fc2 <- mx.symbol.FullyConnected(act1, name="fc2", num_hidden=32)
act2 <- mx.symbol.Activation(fc2, name="relu2", act_type="relu")
fc3 <- mx.symbol.FullyConnected(act2, name="fc3", num_hidden=6)
softmax <- mx.symbol.SoftmaxOutput(fc3, name="sm")
```

When you run the previous code, nothing actually executes. To train the model, we create a `devices` object to indicate where the code should be run, CPU or GPU. Then you pass the symbol for last layer (softmax) into the `mx.model.FeedForward.create` function. This function has other parameters, which are more properly known as hyper-parameters. These include the epochs (`num.round`), which control how many times we pass through the data, the learning rate (`learning.rate`), which controls how much the gradients are updated during each pass, momentum (`momentum`), which is a hyper-parameter that can help the model to train faster, and the weights initializer (`initializer`), which controls how the weights and biases for nodes are initially set. We also pass in the evaluation metric (`eval.metric`),which is how the model is to be evaluated, and a callback function (`epoch.end.callback`), which is used to output progress information. When we run the function, it trains the model and outputs the progress as per the value we used for the `epoch.end.callback` parameter, namely every epoch:

```
devices <- mx.cpu()
mx.set.seed(0)
tic <- proc.time()
model <- mx.model.FeedForward.create(softmax, X = train.x, y = train.y,
```

```
                                              ctx = devices,num.round = 20,
                                              learning.rate = 0.08, momentum = 0.9,
                                              eval.metric = mx.metric.accuracy,
                                              initializer = mx.init.uniform(0.01),
                                              epoch.end.callback =
                                                mx.callback.log.train.metric(1))

Start training with 1 devices
[1]  Train-accuracy=0.185581140350877
[2]  Train-accuracy=0.26104525862069
[3]  Train-accuracy=0.555091594827586
[4]  Train-accuracy=0.519127155172414
[5]  Train-accuracy=0.646551724137931
[6]  Train-accuracy=0.733836206896552
[7]  Train-accuracy=0.819100215517241
[8]  Train-accuracy=0.881869612068966
[9]  Train-accuracy=0.892780172413793
[10] Train-accuracy=0.908674568965517
[11] Train-accuracy=0.898572198275862
[12] Train-accuracy=0.896821120689655
[13] Train-accuracy=0.915544181034483
[14] Train-accuracy=0.928879310344828
[15] Train-accuracy=0.926993534482759
[16] Train-accuracy=0.934401939655172
[17] Train-accuracy=0.933728448275862
[18] Train-accuracy=0.934132543103448
[19] Train-accuracy=0.933324353448276
[20] Train-accuracy=0.934132543103448
print(proc.time() - tic)
   user system elapsed
   7.31 3.03 4.31
```

Now that we have trained our model, let's see how it does on the test set:

```
preds1 <- predict(model, test.x)
pred.label <- max.col(t(preds1)) - 1
t <- table(data.frame(cbind(test.y,pred.label)),
           dnn=c("Actual", "Predicted"))
acc<-round(100.0*sum(diag(t))/length(test.y),2)
print(t)
       Predicted
Actual   0    1    2    3    4    5
     0 477   15    4    0    0    0
     1 108  359    4    0    0    0
     2  13   42  365    0    0    0
     3   0    0    0  454   37    0
     4   0    0    0  141  391    0
     5   0    0    0   16    0  521
print(sprintf(" Deep Learning Model accuracy = %1.2f%%",acc))
```

```
[1] " Deep Learning Model accuracy = 87.11%"
```

Not bad! We have achieved an accuracy of 87.11% on our test set.

 Wait, where are the backward propagation, derivatives, and so on, that we covered in previous chapters? The answer to that is deep learning libraries largely manage this automatically for you. In MXNet, automatic differentiation is included in a package called the autograd package, which differentiates a graph of operations with the chain rule. It is one less thing to worry about when building deep learning models. For more information, go to https://mxnet.incubator.apache.org/tutorials/gluon/autograd.html.

Use case – using MXNet for classification and regression

In this section, we will use a new dataset to create a binary classification task. The dataset we will use here is a transactional dataset that is available at https://www.dunnhumby.com/sourcefiles. This dataset has been made available from dunnhumby, which is perhaps best known for its link to the Tesco (a British grocery store) club-card, which is one of the largest retail loyalty systems in the world. I recommend the following book, which describes how dunnhumby helped Tesco to become the number one retailer by applying analytics to their retail loyalty program: *Humby, Clive, Terry Hunt, and Tim Phillips. Scoring points. Kogan Page Publishers, 2008.* Even though this book is relatively old, it remains one of the best use cases to describe how to roll out a business-transformation program based on data analytics.

Data download and exploration

When you go to the preceding link, there are a few different data options; the one we will use is called **Let's Get Sort-of-Real**. This dataset is data for over two years for a fictional retail loyalty scheme. The data consists of purchases that are linked by basket ID and customer code, that is, we can track transactions by customers over time. There are a number of options here, including the full dataset, which is 4.3 GB zipped and over 40 GB unzipped. For our first models, we will use the smallest dataset, and will download the data titled **All transactions for a randomly selected sample of 5,000 customers**; this is 1/100th the size of the full database.

I wish to thank dunnhumby for releasing this dataset and for allowing us permission to use it. One of the problems in deep learning and machine learning in general is the lack of large scale real-life datasets that people can practice their skills on. When a company makes the effort to release such a dataset, we should appreciate the effort and not use the dataset outside the terms and conditions specified. Please take the time to read the terms and conditions and use the dataset for personal learning purposes only. Remember that any misuse of this dataset (or datasets released by other companies) means that companies will be more reluctant to make other datasets available in the future.

Once you have read the terms and conditions and downloaded the dataset to your computer, unzip it into a directory called `dunnhumby/in` under the `code` folder. Ensure the files are unzipped directly under this folder, and not a sub-directory, or you may have to copy them after unzipping the data. The data files are in **comma-delimited (CSV)** format, with a separate file for each week of data. The files can be opened and viewed using a text editor. We will use some of the fields in *Table 4.1* for our analysis:

Field name	Description	Format
BASKET_ID	Basket ID, or transaction ID. All items in a basket share the same `basket_id` value.	Numeric
CUST_CODE	Customer Code. This links the transactions/visits to a customer.	Char
SHOP_DATE	Date when shopping occurred. Date is specified in the yyyymmdd format.	Char
STORE_CODE	Store code.	Char
QUANTITY	Number of items of the same product bought in this basket.	Numeric
SPEND	Spend associated to the items bought.	Numeric
PROD_CODE	Product Code.	Char
PROD_CODE_10	Product Hierarchy Level 10 Code.	Char
PROD_CODE_20	Product Hierarchy Level 20 Code.	Char
PROD_CODE_30	Product Hierarchy Level 30 Code.	Char
PROD_CODE_40	Product Hierarchy Level 40 Code.	Char

Table 4.1: Partial data dictionary for transactional dataset

The data stores details of customer transactions. Every unique item that a person purchases in a shopping transaction is represented by one line, and items in a transaction will have the same BASKET_ID field. A transaction can also be linked to a customer using the CUST_CODE field. A PDF is included in the ZIP files if you want more information on the field types.

We are going to use this dataset for a churn prediction task. A churn prediction task is where we predict which customers will return in the next x days. Churn prediction is used to find customers who are in danger of leaving your program. It is used by companies in shopping loyalty schemes, mobile phone subscriptions, TV subscriptions, and so on to ensure they maintain enough customers. For most companies that rely on revenue from recurring subscriptions, it is more effective to spend resources on maintaining their existing customer base than trying to acquire new customers. This is because of the high cost of acquiring new customers. Also, as time progresses after a customer has left, it is harder to win them back, so there is a small window of time in which to send them special offers that may entice them to stay.

As well as binary classification, we will build a regression model. This will predict the amount that a person will spend in the next 14 days. Fortunately, we can build a dataset that is suitable for both prediction tasks.

The data was supplied as 117 CSV files (ignore `time.csv`, which is a lookup file). The first step is to perform some basic data exploration to verify that the data was downloaded successfully and then perform some basic data quality checks. This is an important first step in any analysis: especially when you are using an external dataset, you should run some validation checks on the data before creating any machine learning models. The `Chapter4/0_Explore.Rmd` script creates a summary file and does some exploratory analysis of the data. This is an RMD file, so it needs to be run from RStudio. For brevity, and because this book is about deep learning and not data processing, I will include just some of the output and plots from this script rather than reproducing all the code. You should also run the code in this file to ensure the data was imported correctly, although it may take a few minutes the first time it runs. Here are some summaries on the data from that script:

```
Number of weeks we have data: 117.
Number of transaction lines: 2541019.
Number of transactions (baskets): 390320.
Number of unique Customers: 5000.
Number of unique Products: 4997.
Number of unique Stores: 761.
```

If we compare this to the website and the PDF, it looks in order. We have over 2.5 million records, and data for 5,000 customers across 761 stores. The data-exploration script also creates some plots to give us a feel for the data. *Figure 4.3* shows the sales over the 117 weeks; we see the variety in the data (it is not a flat line indicating that each day is different) and there are no gaps indicating missing data. There are seasonal patterns, with large peaks toward the end of the calendar year, namely the holiday season:

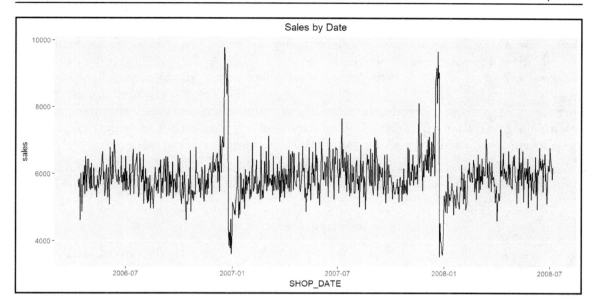

Figure 4.3: Sales plotted over time.

The plot in figure 4.3 shows that the data has been imported successfully. The data looks consistent and is what we expect for a retail transaction file, we do not see any gaps and there is seasonality.

For each item a person purchases, there is a product code (PROD_CODE) and four department codes (PROD_CODE_10, PROD_CODE_20, PROD_CODE_30, PROD_CODE_40). We will use these department codes in our analysis; the code in Chapter4/0_Explore.Rmd creates a summary for them. We want to see how many unique values there are for each department code, whether the codes represent a hierarchy (each code has at most one parent), and whether there are repeated codes:

```
PROD_CODE: Number of unique codes: 4997. Number of repeated codes: 0.
PROD_CODE_10: Number of unique codes:250. Number of repeated codes: 0.
PROD_CODE_20: Number of unique codes:90. Number of repeated codes: 0.
PROD_CODE_30: Number of unique codes:31. Number of repeated codes: 0.
PROD_CODE_40: Number of unique codes:9.
```

We have 4,997 unique product codes with 4 department codes. Our department codes go from PROD_CODE_10, which has 250 unique codes, to PROD_CODE_40, which has 9 unique codes. This is a product department code hierarchy, where PROD_CODE_40 is the primary category and PROD_CODE_10 is the lowest department code in the hierarchy. Each code in PROD_CODE_10, PROD_CODE_20, and PROD_CODE_30 has only one parent; for example, there are no repeating codes, that is, a department code belongs in only one super-category. We are not given a lookup file to say what these codes represent, but an example of a product code hierarchy for a product might be something similar to this:

```
PROD_CODE_40 : Chilled goods
  PROD_CODE_30 : Dairy
    PROD_CODE_20 : Fresh Milk
      PROD_CODE_10 : Full-fat Milk
        PROD_CODE : Brand x Full-fat Milk
```

To get a sense of these department codes, we can also plot the sales data over time by the number of unique product department codes in *Figure 4.4*. This plot is also created in Chapter4/0_Explore.Rmd:

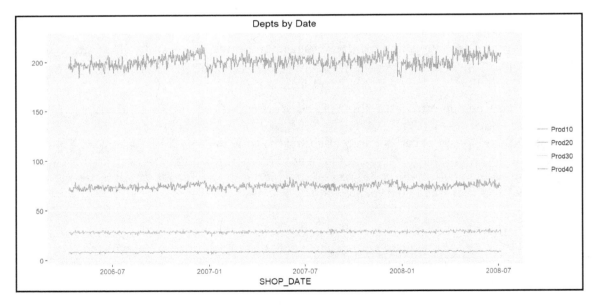

Figure 4.4: Unique product codes purchased by date

Note that for this graph, the *y* axis is unique product codes, not sales. This data also looks consistent; there are some peaks and dips in the data, but they are not as pronounced as in *Figure 4.3*, which is as expected.

Preparing the data for our models

Now that we have downloaded and validated the data, we can use it to create a dataset for our binary classification and regression model tasks. We want to be able to predict which customers will visit the shop in the next two weeks for the binary classification task, and how much they will spend in the next two weeks for the regression task. The `Chapter4/prepare_data.R` script transforms the raw transactional data into a format suitable for machine learning. You need to run the code to create the dataset for the models, but you do not have to understand exactly how it works. Feel free to skip ahead if you want to focus on the deep learning model building.

We need to transform our data into a suitable format for prediction tasks. This should be a single row for each instance we want to predict. The columns will include some fields that are features (X variables) and another field that is our predictor value (Y variable). We want to predict whether a customer returns or not and their spend, so our dataset will have a single row per customer with features and predictor variables.

The first step is to find the cut-off date that separates the variables used to predict (X) and the variable we will predict for (Y). The code looks at the data, finds the last transaction date; and then subtracts 13 days from that date. This is a cut-off date, we want to predict which customers will spend in our shops *on or after* the cut-off date; based on what happens *before* the cut-off date. The data before the cut-off date will be used to make our X, or feature variables, and sales data on or after the cut-off date will be used to make our Y, or predictor variables. The following is that part of the code:

```
library(readr)
library(reshape2)
library(dplyr)

source("import.R")

# step 1, merge files
import_data(data_directory,bExploreData=0)

# step 2, group and pivot data
fileName <- paste(data_directory,"all.csv",sep="")
fileOut <- paste(data_directory,"predict.csv",sep="")
df <- read_csv(fileName,col_types = cols(.default = col_character()))
```

```
# convert spend to numeric field
df$SPEND<-as.numeric(df$SPEND)

# group sales by date. we have not converted the SHOP_DATE to date
# but since it is in yyyymmdd format,
# then ordering alphabetically will preserve date order
sumSalesByDate<-df %>%
    group_by(SHOP_WEEK,SHOP_DATE) %>%
    summarise(sales = sum(SPEND)
    )

# we want to get the cut-off date to create our data model
# this is the last date and go back 13 days beforehand
# therefore our X data only looks at everything from start to max date - 13
days
# and our Y data only looks at everything from max date - 13 days to end
(i.e. 14 days)
max(sumSalesByDate$SHOP_DATE)
[1] "20080706"
sumSalesByDate2 <- sumSalesByDate[order(sumSalesByDate$SHOP_DATE),]
datCutOff <-
as.character(sumSalesByDate2[(nrow(sumSalesByDate2)-13),]$SHOP_DATE)
datCutOff
[1] "20080623"
rm(sumSalesByDate, sumSalesByDate2)
```

If this code does not run, the most probable reason is that the source data was not saved in the correct location. The dataset must be unzipped into a directory called dunnhumby/in under the code folder, that is, at the same level as the chapter folders.

The last date in our data is 20080706, which July 7th, 2008, and the cut-off date is June 23rd, 2008. Although we have data going back to 2006, we will only use sales data from 2008. Any data that is older than six months is unlikely to influence a future customer sale. The task is to predict whether a customer will return between June 23rd, 2008 - July 7th, 2008 based on their activity before June 23rd, 2008.

We now need to create features from our data; so that we can use the spend broken down by department code, we will use the `PROD_CODE_40` field. We could just group the sales on this department code, but that would give equal weighting to spends in Jan 2008 as to spends in June 2008. We would like to incorporate some time factor in our predictor columns. Instead, we will create features on a combination of the department code and the week. This will allow our models to place more importance on recent activities. First, we group by customer code, week, and department code, and create the `fieldName` column. We then pivot this data to create our features (X) dataset. The cell values in this dataset are the sales for that customer (row) and that week-department code (column). Here is an example of how the data is transformed for two customers. *Table 4.2* shows the sales spend by week and the `PROD_CODE_40` field. *Table 4.3* then uses a pivot to create a dataset that has a single row per customer and the aggregate fields are now columns with the spend as values:

CUST_CODE	PROD_CODE_40	SHOP_WEEK	fieldName	Sales
cust_001	D00001	200801	D00001_200801	10.00
cust_002	D00001	200801	D00001_200801	12.00
cust_001	D00015	200815	D00015_200815	15.00
cust_001	D00020	200815	D00020_200815	20.00
cust_002	D00030	200815	D00030_200815	25.00

Table 4.2: Summary of sales by customer code, department code, and week

CUST_CODE	D00001_200801	D00015_200815	D00020_200815	D00030_200815
cust_001	10.00	15.00	20.00	
cust_002	12.00			25.00

Table 4.3: Data from Table 4.2 after transformation

Here is the code that does this transformation:

```
# we are going to limit our data here from year 2008 only
# group data and then pivot it
sumTemp <- df %>%
    filter((SHOP_DATE < datCutOff) & (SHOP_WEEK>="200801")) %>%
    group_by(CUST_CODE, SHOP_WEEK, PROD_CODE_40) %>%
    summarise(sales = sum(SPEND)
    )
sumTemp$fieldName <- paste(sumTemp$PROD_CODE_40,sumTemp$SHOP_WEEK,sep="_")
df_X <- dcast(sumTemp, CUST_CODE ~ fieldName, value.var="sales")
df_X[is.na(df_X)] <- 0
```

The predictor (Y) variable is a flag as to whether the customer visited the site on the weeks from 200818 to 200819. We perform a grouping on the data after the cut-off date and group the sales by customer, these form the basis of our Y values. We join the X and Y datasets, ensuring that we keep all rows on the X side by doing a left-join. Finally we create a 1/0 flag for our binary classification task. When we are done, we see that we have 3933 records in our dataset : 1560 customers who did not return and 2373 customers who did. We finish by saving our file for the model-building. The following code shows these steps:

```
# y data just needs a group to get sales after cut-off date
df_Y <- df %>%
    filter(SHOP_DATE >= datCutOff) %>%
    group_by(CUST_CODE) %>%
    summarise(sales = sum(SPEND)
    )
colnames(df_Y)[2] <- "Y_numeric"

# use left join on X and Y data, need to include all values from X
# even if there is no Y value
dfModelData <- merge(df_X,df_Y,by="CUST_CODE", all.x=TRUE)
# set binary flag
dfModelData$Y_categ <- 0
dfModelData[!is.na(dfModelData$Y_numeric),]$Y_categ <- 1
dfModelData[is.na(dfModelData$Y_numeric),]$Y_numeric <- 0
rm(df,df_X,df_Y,sumTemp)

nrow(dfModelData)
[1] 3933
table(dfModelData$Y_categ)
   0    1
1560 2373

# shuffle data
dfModelData <- dfModelData[sample(nrow(dfModelData)),]

write_csv(dfModelData,fileOut)
```

We use the sales data to create our predictor fields, but there were some customer attributes that we ignored for this task. These fields included `Customers Price Sensitivity` and `Customers Lifestage`. The main reason we did not use these fields was to avoid data-leakage. Data-leakage can occur when building prediction models; it occurs when some of your fields have values that will not be available or different when creating datasets in production. These fields could cause data-leakage because we do not know when they were set; it could have been when a customer signs up, or it could be a process that runs nightly. If these were created after our cut-off date, this would mean that these fields could unfairly predict our `Y` variables.

For example, `Customers Price Sensitivity` has values for `Less Affluent`, `Mid Market`, and `Up Market`, which probably are derived from what the customer purchases. Therefore, using these fields in a churn-prediction task would result in data-leakage if these fields were updated after the cut-off date used to create our dataset for our prediction models. A value of `Up Market` for `Customers Price Sensitivity` could be strongly linked to return spend, but this value is actually a summary of the value it is predicting. Data-leakage is one of the main causes of data models performing worse in production as the model was trained with data that is linked to the Y variable and can never exist in reality. You should always check for data-leakage for time-series tasks and ask yourself whether any field (especially lookup attributes) could have been modified after the date used to create the model data.

The binary classification model

The code from the previous section creates a new file called `predict.csv` in the `dunnhumby` folder. This dataset has a single row for each customer with a 0/1 field indicating whether they visited in the last two weeks and predictor variables based on sales data before those two weeks. Now we can proceed to build some machine learning models. The `Chapter4/binary_predict.R` file contains the code for our first prediction task, binary classification. The first part of the code loads the data and creates an array of predictor variables by including all columns except the customer ID, the binary classification predictor variable, and the regression predictor variable. The feature columns are all numeric fields that are heavily right-skewed distributed, so we apply a log transformation to those fields. We add `0.01` first to avoid getting a non-numeric result from attempting to get a log of a zero value *(log(0)= -Inf)*.

The following plot shows the data before transformation, on the left, and the data after transformation, on the right:

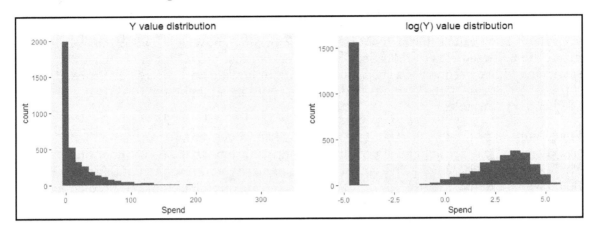

Figure 4.5: Distribution of a feature variable before and after transformation.

The large bar on the left in the second plot is where the original field was zero *(log(0+0.01) = -4.6)*. The following code loads the data, performs the log transformation, and creates the previous plot:

```
set.seed(42)
fileName <- "../dunnhumby/predict.csv"
dfData <- read_csv(fileName,
                   col_types = cols(
                     .default = col_double(),
                     CUST_CODE = col_character(),
                     Y_categ = col_integer())
                   )
nobs <- nrow(dfData)
train <- sample(nobs, 0.9*nobs)
test <- setdiff(seq_len(nobs), train)
predictorCols <- colnames(dfData)[!(colnames(dfData) %in%
c("CUST_CODE","Y_numeric","Y_categ"))]

# data is right-skewed, apply log transformation
qplot(dfData$Y_numeric, geom="histogram",binwidth=10,
      main="Y value distribution",xlab="Spend")+theme(plot.title =
element_text(hjust = 0.5))
dfData[, c("Y_numeric",predictorCols)] <- log(0.01+dfData[,
c("Y_numeric",predictorCols)])
qplot(dfData$Y_numeric, geom="histogram",binwidth=0.5,
      main="log(Y) value distribution",xlab="Spend")+theme(plot.title =
element_text(hjust = 0.5))
```

```
trainData <- dfData[train, c(predictorCols)]
testData <- dfData[test, c(predictorCols)]
trainData$Y_categ <- dfData[train, "Y_categ"]$Y_categ
testData$Y_categ <- dfData[test, "Y_categ"]$Y_categ
```

Before we train a deep learning model, we train three machine learning models – a logistic regression model, a `Random Forest` model, and an `XGBoost` model – on the data as a benchmark. This code section contains the data load, transformation, and three models:

```
#Logistic Regression Model
logReg=glm(Y_categ ~ .,data=trainData,family=binomial(link="logit"))
pr <- as.vector(ifelse(predict(logReg, type="response",
                               testData) > 0.5, "1", "0"))
# Generate the confusion matrix showing counts.
t<-table(dfData[test, c(predictorCols, "Y_categ")]$"Y_categ", pr,
         dnn=c("Actual", "Predicted"))
acc<-round(100.0*sum(diag(t))/length(test),2)
print(t)
       Predicted
Actual   0    1
      0 130   42
      1  48  174
print(sprintf(" Logistic regression accuracy = %1.2f%%",acc))
[1] " Logistic regression accuracy = 77.16%"
rm(t,pr,acc)

rf <- randomForest::randomForest(as.factor(Y_categ) ~ .,
                                 data=trainData,
                                 na.action=randomForest::na.roughfix)
pr <- predict(rf, newdata=testData, type="class")
# Generate the confusion matrix showing counts.
t<-table(dfData[test, c(predictorCols, "Y_categ")]$Y_categ, pr,
         dnn=c("Actual", "Predicted"))
acc<-round(100.0*sum(diag(t))/length(test),2)
print(t)
       Predicted
Actual   0    1
      0 124   48
      1  30  192
print(sprintf(" Random Forest accuracy = %1.2f%%",acc))
[1] " Random Forest accuracy = 80.20%"
rm(t,pr,acc)

xgb <- xgboost(data=data.matrix(trainData[,predictorCols]),
label=trainData[,"Y_categ"]$Y_categ,
               nrounds=75, objective="binary:logistic")
pr <- as.vector(ifelse(
   predict(xgb, data.matrix(testData[, predictorCols])) > 0.5, "1", "0"))
```

```
t<-table(dfData[test, c(predictorCols, "Y_categ")]$"Y_categ", pr,
         dnn=c("Actual", "Predicted"))
acc<-round(100.0*sum(diag(t))/length(test),2)
print(t)
      Predicted
Actual    0    1
     0  125   47
     1   44  178
print(sprintf(" XGBoost accuracy = %1.2f%%",acc))
[1] " XGBoost accuracy = 76.90%"
rm(t,pr,acc)
```

We create logistic regression, `Random Forest`, and `XGBoost` models for a number of reasons. Firstly, most of the work is already done in preparing the data, so it is trivial to do so. Secondly, it gives us a benchmark to compare our deep learning model to. Thirdly, if there were a problem in the data-preparation tasks, these machine learning algorithms would highlight these problems more rapidly because they will be quicker than training a deep learning model. In this case, we only have a few thousand records, so these machine learning algorithms will easily run on this data. If the data were too large for these algorithms, I would consider taking a smaller sample and running our benchmark tasks on that smaller sample. There are many machine learning algorithms to choose from, but I used these algorithms as benchmarks for the following reasons:

- Logistic regression is a basic model and is always a good benchmark to use
- `Random Forest` is known to train well using the default parameters and is robust to overfitting and correlated variables (which we have here)
- `XGBoost` is consistently rated as the one of the best-performing machine learning algorithms

All three algorithms achieve a similar amount of accuracy, the highest accuracy was achieved by `Random Forest` with an 80.2% accuracy. We now know that this dataset is suitable for prediction tasks and we have a benchmark to compare against.

Now we will build a deep learning model using MXNet:

```
require(mxnet)

# MXNet expects matrices
train_X <- data.matrix(trainData[, predictorCols])
test_X <- data.matrix(testData[, predictorCols])
train_Y <- trainData$Y_categ

# hyper-parameters
num_hidden <- c(128,64,32)
drop_out <- c(0.2,0.2,0.2)
```

```
wd=0.00001
lr <- 0.03
num_epochs <- 40
activ <- "relu"

# create our model architecture
# using the hyper-parameters defined above
data <- mx.symbol.Variable("data")
fc1 <- mx.symbol.FullyConnected(data, name="fc1", num_hidden=num_hidden[1])
act1 <- mx.symbol.Activation(fc1, name="activ1", act_type=activ)

drop1 <- mx.symbol.Dropout(data=act1,p=drop_out[1])
fc2 <- mx.symbol.FullyConnected(drop1, name="fc2",
num_hidden=num_hidden[2])
act2 <- mx.symbol.Activation(fc2, name="activ2", act_type=activ)

drop2 <- mx.symbol.Dropout(data=act2,p=drop_out[2])
fc3 <- mx.symbol.FullyConnected(drop2, name="fc3",
num_hidden=num_hidden[3])
act3 <- mx.symbol.Activation(fc3, name="activ3", act_type=activ)

drop3 <- mx.symbol.Dropout(data=act3,p=drop_out[3])
fc4 <- mx.symbol.FullyConnected(drop3, name="fc4", num_hidden=2)
softmax <- mx.symbol.SoftmaxOutput(fc4, name="sm")

# run on cpu, change to 'devices <- mx.gpu()'
# if you have a suitable GPU card
devices <- mx.cpu()
mx.set.seed(0)
tic <- proc.time()
# This actually trains the model
model <- mx.model.FeedForward.create(softmax, X = train_X, y = train_Y,
                                      ctx = devices,num.round = num_epochs,
                                      learning.rate = lr, momentum = 0.9,
                                      eval.metric = mx.metric.accuracy,
                                      initializer = mx.init.uniform(0.1),
                                      wd=wd,
                                      epoch.end.callback =
mx.callback.log.train.metric(1))
print(proc.time() - tic)
   user system elapsed
   9.23 4.65 4.37

pr <- predict(model, test_X)
pred.label <- max.col(t(pr)) - 1
t <- table(data.frame(cbind(testData[,"Y_categ"]$Y_categ,pred.label)),
           dnn=c("Actual", "Predicted"))
acc<-round(100.0*sum(diag(t))/length(test),2)
```

```
print(t)
         Predicted
Actual    0    1
     0  136   36
     1   54  168
print(sprintf(" Deep Learning Model accuracy = %1.2f%%",acc))
[1] " Deep Learning Model accuracy = 77.16%"
rm(t,pr,acc)
rm(data,fc1,act1,fc2,act2,fc3,act3,fc4,softmax,model)
```

The deep learning model achieved a `77.16%` accuracy on the test data, which is only beaten by the `Random Forest` model. This shows that a deep learning model can be competitive against the best machine learning algorithms. It also shows that deep learning models on classification tasks do not always beat other machine learning algorithms. We used these models to provide a benchmark, so that we would know that our deep learning model was getting decent results; it gives us confidence that our deep learning model is competitive.

Our deep learning model uses 20% dropout in each layer and weight decay for regularization. Without dropout, the model overtrained significantly. This was probably because the features are highly correlated, as our columns are the spend in various departments. It figures that if one column is for a type of bread, and another column is for a type of milk, then these change together, namely someone who has more transactions and spends more is likely to buy both.

The regression model

The previous section developed a deep learning model for a binary classification task, this section develops a deep learning model to predict a continuous numeric value, regression analysis. We use the same dataset that we used for the binary classification task, but we use a different target column to predict for. In that task, we wanted to predict whether a customer would return to our stores in the next 14 days. In this task, we want to predict how much a customer will spend in our stores in the next 14 days. We follow a similar process; we load and prepare our dataset by applying log transformations to the data. The code is in `Chapter4/regression.R`:

```
set.seed(42)
fileName <- "../dunnhumby/predict.csv"
dfData <- read_csv(fileName,
                 col_types = cols(
                   .default = col_double(),
                   CUST_CODE = col_character(),
                   Y_categ = col_integer()))
  )
```

```
nobs <- nrow(dfData)
train <- sample(nobs, 0.9*nobs)
test <- setdiff(seq_len(nobs), train)
predictorCols <- colnames(dfData)[!(colnames(dfData) %in%
c("CUST_CODE","Y_numeric","Y_numeric"))]

dfData[, c("Y_numeric",predictorCols)] <- log(0.01+dfData[,
c("Y_numeric",predictorCols)])
trainData <- dfData[train, c(predictorCols,"Y_numeric")]
testData <- dfData[test, c(predictorCols,"Y_numeric")]

xtrain <- model.matrix(Y_numeric~.,trainData)
xtest <- model.matrix(Y_numeric~.,testData)
```

We then perform regression analysis on the data using lm to create a benchmark before creating a deep learning model:

```
# lm Regression Model
regModel1=lm(Y_numeric ~ .,data=trainData)
pr1 <- predict(regModel1,testData)
rmse <- sqrt(mean((exp(pr1)-exp(testData[,"Y_numeric"]$Y_numeric))^2))
print(sprintf(" Regression RMSE = %1.2f",rmse))
[1] " Regression RMSE = 29.30"
mae <- mean(abs(exp(pr1)-exp(testData[,"Y_numeric"]$Y_numeric)))
print(sprintf(" Regression MAE = %1.2f",mae))
[1] " Regression MAE = 13.89"
```

We output two metrics, rmse and mae, for our regression task. We covered these earlier in the chapter. Mean absolute error measures the absolute differences between the predicted value and the actual value. **Root mean squared error (rmse)** penalizes the square of the differences between the predicted value and the actual value, so one big error costs more than the sum of the small errors. Now let's look at the deep learning regression code. First we load the data and define the model:

```
require(mxnet)
Loading required package: mxnet

# MXNet expects matrices
train_X <- data.matrix(trainData[, predictorCols])
test_X <- data.matrix(testData[, predictorCols])
train_Y <- trainData$Y_numeric

set.seed(42)
# hyper-parameters
num_hidden <- c(256,128,128,64)
drop_out <- c(0.4,0.4,0.4,0.4)
wd=0.00001
```

```
lr <- 0.0002
num_epochs <- 100
activ <- "tanh"

# create our model architecture
# using the hyper-parameters defined above
data <- mx.symbol.Variable("data")
fc1 <- mx.symbol.FullyConnected(data, name="fc1", num_hidden=num_hidden[1])
act1 <- mx.symbol.Activation(fc1, name="activ1", act_type=activ)
drop1 <- mx.symbol.Dropout(data=act1,p=drop_out[1])

fc2 <- mx.symbol.FullyConnected(drop1, name="fc2",
num_hidden=num_hidden[2])
act2 <- mx.symbol.Activation(fc2, name="activ2", act_type=activ)
drop2 <- mx.symbol.Dropout(data=act2,p=drop_out[2])

fc3 <- mx.symbol.FullyConnected(drop2, name="fc3",
num_hidden=num_hidden[3])
act3 <- mx.symbol.Activation(fc3, name="activ3", act_type=activ)
drop3 <- mx.symbol.Dropout(data=act3,p=drop_out[3])

fc4 <- mx.symbol.FullyConnected(drop3, name="fc4",
num_hidden=num_hidden[4])
act4 <- mx.symbol.Activation(fc4, name="activ4", act_type=activ)
drop4 <- mx.symbol.Dropout(data=act4,p=drop_out[4])

fc5 <- mx.symbol.FullyConnected(drop4, name="fc5", num_hidden=1)
lro <- mx.symbol.LinearRegressionOutput(fc5)
```

Now we train the model; note that the first comment shows how to switch to using a GPU instead of a CPU:

```
# run on cpu, change to 'devices <- mx.gpu()'
# if you have a suitable GPU card
devices <- mx.cpu()
mx.set.seed(0)
tic <- proc.time()
# This actually trains the model
model <- mx.model.FeedForward.create(lro, X = train_X, y = train_Y,
 ctx = devices,num.round = num_epochs,
 learning.rate = lr, momentum = 0.9,
 eval.metric = mx.metric.rmse,
 initializer = mx.init.uniform(0.1),
 wd=wd,
 epoch.end.callback = mx.callback.log.train.metric(1))
print(proc.time() - tic)
 user system elapsed
 13.90 1.82 10.50
```

```
pr4 <- predict(model, test_X)[1,]
rmse <- sqrt(mean((exp(pr4)-exp(testData[,"Y_numeric"]$Y_numeric))^2))
print(sprintf(" Deep Learning Regression RMSE = %1.2f",rmse))
[1] " Deep Learning Regression RMSE = 28.92"
mae <- mean(abs(exp(pr4)-exp(testData[,"Y_numeric"]$Y_numeric)))
print(sprintf(" Deep Learning Regression MAE = %1.2f",mae))
[1] " Deep Learning Regression MAE = 14.33"
rm(data,fc1,act1,fc2,act2,fc3,act3,fc4,lro,model)
```

For regression metrics, lower is better, so our rmse metric on the deep learning model (28.92) is an improvement on the original regression model (29.30). Interestingly, the mae on the the deep learning model (14.33) is actually worse than the original regression model (13.89). Since rsme penalizes big differences between actual and predicted values more, this indicates that the errors in the deep learning model are less extreme than the regression model.

Improving the binary classification model

This section builds on the earlier binary classification task and looks to increase the accuracy for that task. The first thing we can do to improve the model is to use more data, 100 times more data in fact! We will download the entire dataset, which is over 4 GB data in zip files and 40 GB of data when the files are unzipped. Go back to the download link (https://www.dunnhumby.com/sourcefiles) and select **Let's Get Sort-of-Real** again and download all the files for the **Full dataset**. There are nine files to download and the CSV files should be unzipped into the dunnhumby/in folder. Remember to check that the CSV files are in this folder and not a subfolder. You need to run the code in Chapter4/prepare_data.R again. When this completes, the predict.csv file should have 390,000 records.

You can try to follow along here, but be aware that preparing the data and running the deep learning model are going to take a long time. You also may run into problems if you have a slow computer. I tested this code on an Intel i5 processor with 32 GB RAM, and it took the model 30 minutes to run. It also requires over 50 GB hard disk space to store the unzipped files and temporary files. If you have problems running it on your local computer, another option is to run this example in the cloud, which we will cover in a later chapter.

The code for this section is in the `Chapter4/binary_predict2.R` script. Since we have more data, we can build a more complicated model. We have 100 times more data, so our new model adds an extra layer, and more nodes to our hidden layers. We have decreased the amount of regularization and the learning rate. We have also added more epochs. Here is the the code in `Chapter4/binary_predict2.R`, which constructs and trains the deep learning model. We have not included the boilerplate code to load and prepare the data, as that has not changed from the original script:

```
# hyper-parameters
num_hidden <- c(256,128,64,32)
drop_out <- c(0.2,0.2,0.1,0.1)
wd=0.0
lr <- 0.03
num_epochs <- 50
activ <- "relu"

# create our model architecture
# using the hyper-parameters defined above
data <- mx.symbol.Variable("data")
fc1 <- mx.symbol.FullyConnected(data, name="fc1", num_hidden=num_hidden[1])
act1 <- mx.symbol.Activation(fc1, name="activ1", act_type=activ)

drop1 <- mx.symbol.Dropout(data=act1,p=drop_out[1])
fc2 <- mx.symbol.FullyConnected(drop1, name="fc2",
num_hidden=num_hidden[2])
act2 <- mx.symbol.Activation(fc2, name="activ2", act_type=activ)

drop2 <- mx.symbol.Dropout(data=act2,p=drop_out[2])
fc3 <- mx.symbol.FullyConnected(drop2, name="fc3",
num_hidden=num_hidden[3])
act3 <- mx.symbol.Activation(fc3, name="activ3", act_type=activ)

drop3 <- mx.symbol.Dropout(data=act3,p=drop_out[3])
fc4 <- mx.symbol.FullyConnected(drop3, name="fc4",
num_hidden=num_hidden[4])
act4 <- mx.symbol.Activation(fc4, name="activ4", act_type=activ)

drop4 <- mx.symbol.Dropout(data=act4,p=drop_out[4])
fc5 <- mx.symbol.FullyConnected(drop4, name="fc5", num_hidden=2)
softmax <- mx.symbol.SoftmaxOutput(fc5, name="sm")

# run on cpu, change to 'devices <- mx.gpu()'
# if you have a suitable GPU card
devices <- mx.cpu()
mx.set.seed(0)
tic <- proc.time()
# This actually trains the model
```

```
model <- mx.model.FeedForward.create(softmax, X = train_X, y = train_Y,
  ctx = devices,num.round = num_epochs,
  learning.rate = lr, momentum = 0.9,
  eval.metric = mx.metric.accuracy,
  initializer = mx.init.uniform(0.1),
  wd=wd,
  epoch.end.callback = mx.callback.log.train.metric(1))
print(proc.time() - tic)
 user system elapsed
1919.75 1124.94 871.31

pr <- predict(model, test_X)
pred.label <- max.col(t(pr)) - 1
t <- table(data.frame(cbind(testData[,"Y_categ"]$Y_categ,pred.label)),
  dnn=c("Actual", "Predicted"))
acc<-round(100.0*sum(diag(t))/length(test),2)
print(t)
      Predicted
Actual      0      1
  0     10714   4756
  1      3870  19649
print(sprintf(" Deep Learning Model accuracy = %1.2f%%",acc))
[1] " Deep Learning Model accuracy = 77.88%"
```

The accuracy has increased from 77.16% in the earlier model to 77.88% for this model. This may not seem significant, but if we consider that the large dataset has almost 390,000 rows, the increase in accuracy of 0.72% represents about 2,808 customers that are now classified correctly. If each of these customers is worth $50, that is an additional $140,000 in revenue.

In general, as you add more data, your model should become more complicated to generalize across all the patterns in the data. We will cover more of this in Chapter 6, *Tuning and Optimizing Models*, but I would encourage you to experiment with the code in Chapter4/binary_predict.R. Try changing the hyper-parameters or adding more layers. Even a small improvement of 0.1 - 0.2% in accuracy is significant. If you manage to get over 78% accuracy on this dataset, consider it a good achievement.

If you want to explore further, there are other methods to investigate. These involve making changes in how the data for the model is created. If you really want to stretch yourself, here are a few more ideas you can try:

- Our current features are a combination of department codes and weeks, we use the PROD_CODE_40 field as the department code. This has only nine unique values, so for every week, only nine fields represent that data. If you use PROD_CODE_30, PROD_CODE_20, or PROD_CODE_10, you will create a lot more features.

- In a similar manner, rather than using a combination of department codes and weeks, you could try department codes and day. This might create too many features, but I would consider doing this for the last 14 days before the cut-off date.

- Experiment with different methods of preparing the data. We use log scale, which works well for our binary classification task, but is not the best method for a regression task, as it does not create data with a normal distribution. Try applying z-scaling and min-max standardization to the data. If you do this, you must ensure that it is applied correctly to the test data before evaluating the model.

- The training data uses the sales amount. You could change this to item quantities or the number of transactions an item is in.

- You could create new features. One potentially powerful example would be to create fields based on a day of the week, or a day of the month. We could create features for the spend amounts and number of visits for each day of the week.

- We could create features based on the average size of a shopping basket, how frequently a customer visits, and so on.

- We could try a different model architecture that can take advantage of time-series data.

These are all things I would try if I was given this task as a work assignment. In traditional machine learning, adding more features often leads to problems as most traditional machine learning algorithms struggle with high-dimensionality data. Deep learning models can handle these cases, so there usually is no harm in adding more features.

The unreasonable effectiveness of data

Our first deep learning models on the binary classification task had fewer than 4,000 records. We did this so you could run the example quickly. For deep learning, you really need a lot more data, so we created a more complicated model with a lot more data, which gave us an increase in accuracy. This process demonstrated the following:

- Establishing a baseline with other machine learning algorithms provides a good benchmark before using a deep learning model
- We had to create a more complex model and adjust the hyper-parameters for our bigger dataset
- The Unreasonable Effectiveness of Data

The last point here is borrowed from an article by Peter Norvig, available at `https://static.googleusercontent.com/media/research.google.com/en//pubs/archive/35179.pdf`. There is also a YouTube video with the same name. One of the main points in Norvig's article is this: invariably simple models and a lot of data trump more elaborate models based on less data.

We have increased the accuracy on our deep learning model by 0.38%. Considering that our dataset has highly correlated variables and that our domain is modelling human activities, this is not bad. People are, well predictable; so when attempting to predict what they do next, a small dataset usually works. In other domains, adding more data has much more of an effect. Consider a complex image-recognition task with color images where the image quality and format are not consistent. In that case, increasing our training data by a factor of 10 would have much more of an effect than in the earlier example. For many deep learning projects, you should include tasks to acquire more data from the very beginning of the project. This can be done by manually labeling the data, by outsourcing tasks (Amazon Turk), or by building some form of feedback mechanism in your application.

While other machine learning algorithms may also see an improvement in performance with more data, eventually adding more data will stop making a difference and performance will stagnate. This is because these algorithms were never designed for large high-dimensional data and so cannot model the complex patterns in very large datasets. However, you can build increasingly complex deep learning architectures that can model these complex patterns. This following plot illustrates how deep learning algorithms can continue to take advantage of more data and performance can still improve after performance on other machine algorithms stagnates:

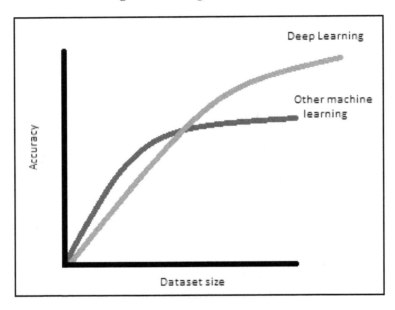

Figure 4.6: How model accuracy increases by dataset size for deep learning models versus other machine learning models

Summary

We covered a lot of ground in this chapter. We looked at activation functions and built our first true deep learning models using MXNet. Then we took a real-life dataset and created two use cases for applying a machine learning model. The first use case was to predict which customers will return in the future based on their past activity. This was a binary classification task. The second use case was to predict how much a customer will spend in the future based on their past activity. This was a regression task. We ran both models first on a small dataset and used different machine learning libraries to compare them against our deep learning model. Our deep learning model out-performed all of the algorithms.

We then took this further by using a dataset that was 100 times bigger. We built a larger deep learning model and adjusted our parameters to get an increase in our binary classification task accuracy. We finished the chapter with a brief discussion on how deep learning models out-perform traditional machine learning algorithms on large datasets.

In the next chapter, we will look at computer vision tasks, which deep learning has revolutionized.

5
Image Classification Using Convolutional Neural Networks

It is not an exaggeration to say that the huge growth of interest in deep learning can be mostly attributed to convolutional neural networks. **Convolutional neural networks (CNNs)** are the main building blocks of image classification models in deep learning, and have replaced most techniques that were previously used by specialists in the field. Deep learning models are now the de facto method to perform all large-scale image tasks, including image classification, object detection, detecting artificially generated images, and even attributing text descriptions to images. In this chapter, we will look at some of these techniques.

Why are CNNs so important? To explain why, we can look at the history of the ImageNet competition. The **ImageNet** competition is an open large-scale image classification challenge that has one thousand categories. It can be considered as the unofficial world championship for image classification. Teams, mostly fielded by academics and researchers, compete from around the world. In 2011, an error rate of around 25% was the benchmark. In 2012, a team led by Alex Krizhevsky and advised by Geoffrey Hinton achieved a huge leap by winning the competition with an error rate of 16%. Their solution consisted of 60 million parameters and 650,000 neurons, five convolutional layers, some of which are followed by max-pooling layers, and three fully-connected layers with a final 1,000-way softmax layer to do the final classification.

Other researchers built on their techniques in subsequent years, with the result that the original ImageNet competition is essentially considered *solved*. In 2017, almost all teams achieved an error rate of less than 5%. Most people consider that the 2012 ImageNet victory heralded the dawn of the new deep learning revolution.

In this chapter, we will look at image classification using CNN. We are going to start with the MNIST dataset, which is considered as the *Hello World* of deep learning tasks. The MNIST dataset consists of grayscale images of size 28 x 28 of 10 classes, the numbers 0-9. This is a much easier task than the ImageNet competition; there are 10 categories rather than 1,000, the images are in grayscale rather than color and most importantly, there are no backgrounds in the MNIST images that can potentially confuse the model. Nevertheless, the MNIST task is an important one in its own right; for example, most countries use postal codes containing digits. Every country uses automatic address routing solutions that are more complex variations of this task.

We will use the MXNet library from Amazon for this task. The MXNet library is an excellent library introduction to deep learning as it allows us to code at a higher level than other libraries such as TensorFlow, which we cover later on in this book.

The following topics will be covered in this chapter:

- What are CNNs?
- Convolutional layers
- Pooling layers
- Softmax
- Deep learning architectures
- Using MXNet for image classification

CNNs

CNNs are the cornerstone of image classification in deep learning. This section gives an introduction to them, explains the history of CNNs, and will explain why they are so powerful.

Before we begin, we will look at a simple deep learning architecture. Deep learning models are difficult to train, so using an existing architecture is often the best place to start. An architecture is an existing deep learning model that was state-of-the-art when initially released. Some examples are AlexNet, VGGNet, GoogleNet, and so on. The architecture we will look at is the original LeNet architecture for digit classification from Yann LeCun and others from the mid 1990s. This architecture was used for the MNIST dataset. This dataset is comprised of grayscale images of 28 x 28 size that contain the digits 0 to 9. The following diagram shows the LeNet architecture:

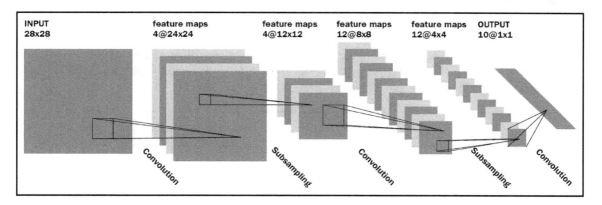

Figure 5.1: The LeNet architecture

The original images are 28 x 28 in size. We have a series of hidden layers which are convolution and pooling layers (here, they are labeled *subsampling*). Each convolutional layer changes structure; for example, when we apply the convolutions in the first hidden layer, our output size is three dimensional. Our final layer is of size 10 x 1, which is the same size as the number of categories. We can apply a `softmax` function here to convert the values in this layer to probabilities for each category. The category with the highest probability would be the category prediction for each image.

Convolutional layers

This section shows how convolutional layers work in greater depth. At a basic level, convolutional layers are nothing more than a set of filters. When you look at images while wearing glasses with a red tint, everything appears to have a red hue. Now, imagine if these glasses consisted of different tints embedded within them, maybe a red tint with one or more horizontal green tints. If you had such a pair of glasses, the effect would be to highlight certain aspects of the scene in front of you. Any part of the scene that had a green horizontal line would become more focused.

Convolutional layers apply a selection of patches (or convolutions) over the previous layer's output. For example, for a face recognition task, the first layer's patches identify basic features in the image, for example, an edge or a diagonal line. The patches are moved across the image to match different parts of the image. Here is an example of a 3 x 3 convolutional block applied across a 6 x 6 image:

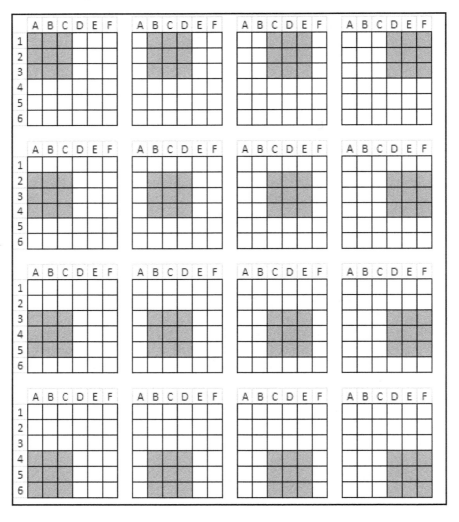

Figure 5.2: An example of a single convolution applied across an image

The values in the convolutional block are multiplied element by element (that is, not matrix multiplication), and the values are added to give a single value. Here is an example:

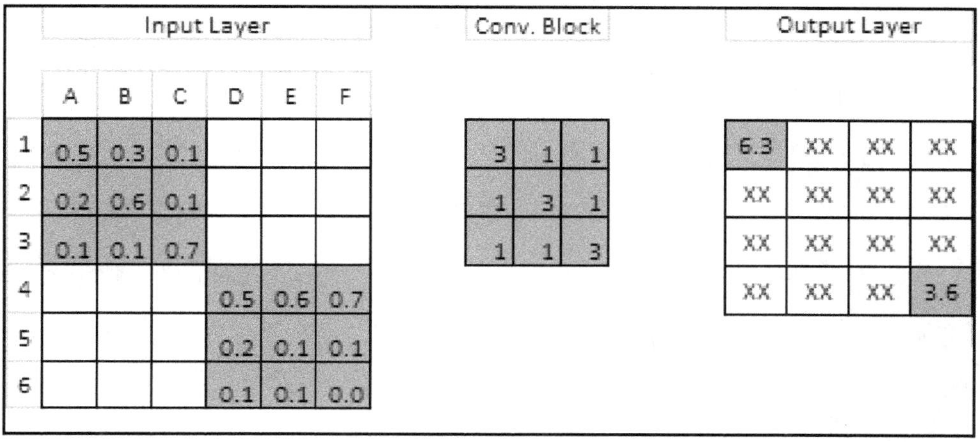

	Input Layer						Conv. Block			Output Layer			
	A	B	C	D	E	F							
1	0.5	0.3	0.1				3	1	1	6.3	XX	XX	XX
2	0.2	0.6	0.1				1	3	1	XX	XX	XX	XX
3	0.1	0.1	0.7				1	1	3	XX	XX	XX	XX
4				0.5	0.6	0.7				XX	XX	XX	3.6
5				0.2	0.1	0.1							
6				0.1	0.1	0.0							

Figure 5.3: An example of a convolution block applied to two parts of an input layer

In this example, our convolutional block is a diagonal pattern. The first block in the image (*A1:C3*) is also a diagonal pattern, so when we multiply the elements and sum them, we get a relatively large value of **6.3**. In comparison, the second block in the image (*D4:F6*) is a horizontal line pattern, so we get a much smaller value.

It can be difficult to visualize how convolutional layers work across the entire image, so the following R Shiny application will show it more clearly. This application is included in the code for this book in the `Chapter5/server.R` file. Open this file in **RStudio** and select **Run app**. Once the application is loaded, select **Convolutional Layers** from the left menu bar. The application loads the first 100 images from the `MNIST` dataset, which we will use later for our first deep learning image classification task. The images are grayscale images of size 28 x 28 of handwritten digits 0 to 9. Here is a screenshot of the application with the fourth image selected, which is a four:

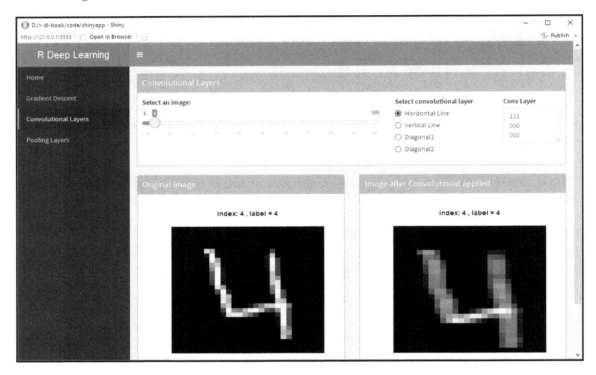

Figure 5.4: The Shiny application showing a horizontal convolutional filter

Once loaded, you can use the slider to browse through the images. In the top-right corner, there are four choices of convolutional layers to apply to the image. In the previous screenshot, a horizontal line convolutional layer is selected and we can see what this looks like in the text box in the top right corner. When we apply the convolutional filter to the input image on the left, we can see that the resulting image on the right is almost entirely grey, except for where the horizontal line was in the original image. Our convolutional filter has matched the parts in the image that have a horizontal line. If we change the convolutional filter to a vertical line, we get the following result:

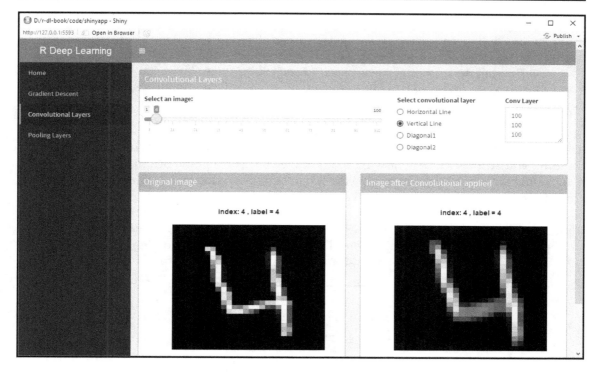

Figure 5.5: The Shiny application showing a vertical convolutional filter

Now, we can see that, after the convolution is applied, the vertical lines in the original image are highlighted in the resultant image on the right. In effect, applying these filters is a type of feature extraction. I encourage you to use the application and browse through images and see how different convolutions apply to images of the different categories.

This is the basis of convolutional filters, and while it is a simple concept, it becomes powerful when you start doing two things:

- Combining many convolutional filters to create convolutional layers
- Applying another set of convolutional filters (that is, a convolutional layer) to the output of a previous convolutional layer

This may take some time to get your head around. If I apply a filter to an image and then apply a filter to that output, what do I get? And if I then apply that a third time, that is, apply a filter to an image and then apply a filter to that output, and then apply a filter to that output, what do I get? The answer is that each subsequent layer combines identified features from the previous layers to find even more complicated patterns, for example, corners, arcs, and so on. Later layers find even richer features such as a circle with an arc over it, indicating the eye of a person.

There are two parameters that are used to control the movement of the convolution: padding and strides. In the following diagram, we can see that the original image is of size 6 x 6, while there are 4 x 4 subgraphs. We have therefore reduced the data representation from a 6 x 6 matrix to a 4 x 4 matrix. When we apply a convolution of size $c1$, $c2$ to data of size n, m, the output will be $n-c1+1$, $m-c2+1$. If we want our output to be the same size as our input, we can pad the input by adding zeros to borders of the images. For the previous example, we add a 1-pixel border around the entire image. The following diagram shows how the first 3 x 3 convolution would be applied to the image with padding:

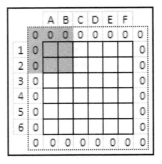

Figure 5.6 Padding applied before a convolution

The second parameter we can apply to convolutions is strides, which control the movement of the convolution. The default is 1, which means the convolution moves by 1 each time, first to the right and then down. In practice, this value is rarely changed, so we will not consider it further.

We now know that convolutions act like small feature generators, that they are applied across an input layer (which is image data for the first layer), and that subsequent convolution layers find even more complicated features. But how are they calculated? Do we need to carefully craft a set of convolutions manually to apply them to our model? The answer is no; these convolutions are automatically calculated for us through the magic of the gradient descent algorithm. The best patterns are found after many iterations through the training dataset.

So, how do convolutions work once we get beyond 2-3 levels of layers? The answer is that it is difficult for anyone to understand the exact mathematics of how convolutional layers work. Even the original designers of these architects may not fully understand what is happening in the hidden layers in a series of CNNs. If this worries you, then recall that the solution that won the ImageNet competition in 2012 had 60 million parameters. With the advance in computing power, deep learning architectures may have hundreds of millions of parameters. It is simply not possible for any person to fully understand what is happening in such a complicated model. This is why they are often called **black-box** models.

It might surprise you at first. How can deep learning achieve human-level performance in image classification and how can we build deep learning models if we do not fully understand how they work? This question has divided the deep learning community, largely along the demarcation between industry and academia. Many (but not all) researchers believe that we should get a more fundamental understanding of how deep learning models work. Some researchers also believe that we can only develop the next generation of artificial intelligence applications by getting a better understanding of how current architectures work. At a recent NIPS conference (one of the oldest and most notable conferences for deep learning), deep learning was unfavorably compared to alchemy. Meanwhile, practitioners in the industry are not concerned with how deep learning works. They are more focused on building ever more complex deep learning architectures to maximize accuracy or performance.

Of course, this is a crude representation of the state of the industry; not all academics are inward looking and not all practitioners are just tweaking models to get small improvements. Deep learning is still relatively new (although the foundation blocks of neural networks have been known about for decades). But this tension does exist and has been around for awhile – for example, a popular deep learning architecture introduced *Inception* modules, which were named after the *Inception* movie. In the film, Leonardo DiCaprio leads a team that alter people's thoughts and opinions by embedding themselves within people's dreams. Initially, they go one layer deep, but then go deeper, in effect going to dreams within dreams. As they go deeper, the worlds get more complicated and the outcomes less certain. We will not go into detail here about what *Inception modules* are, but they combine convolutional and max pooling layers in parallel. The authors of the paper acknowledged the memory and computational cost of the model within the paper, but by naming the key component as an *Inception module,* they were subtly suggesting which side of the argument they were on.

After the breakthrough performance of the winner of the 2012 ImageNet competition, two researchers were unsatisfied that there was no insight into how the model worked. They decided to reverse-engineer the algorithm, attempting to show the input pattern that caused a given activation in the feature maps. This was a non-trivial task, as some layers used in the original model (for example, pooling layers) discarded information. Their paper showed the top 9 activations for each layer. Here is the feature visualization for the first layer:

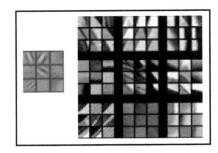

Figure 5.7: Feature visualization for the first layer in a CNN Source: https://cs.nyu.edu/~fergus/papers/zeilerECCV2014.pdf

The image is in two parts; on the left we can see the convolution (the paper only highlights 9 convolutions for each layer). On the right, we can see examples of patterns within images that match that convolution. For example, the convolution in the top-left corner is a diagonal edge detector. Here is the feature visualization for the second layer:

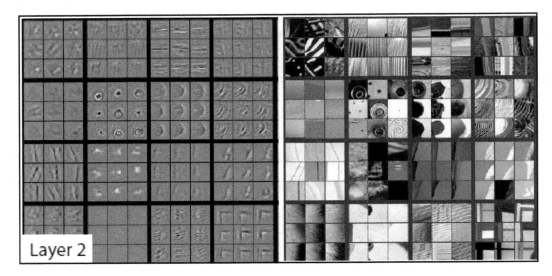

Figure 5.8: Feature visualization for the second layer in a CNN Source: https://cs.nyu.edu/~fergus/papers/zeilerECCV2014.pdf

Again, the image on the left is an interpretation of the convolution, while the image on the right shows examples of image patches that activate for that convolution. Here, we are starting to see some combinatorial patterns. For example, in the top-left, we can see patterns with stripes. Even more interesting is the example in the second row and second column. Here, we see circle shapes, which can indicate an eyeball in a person or an animal. Now, let's move on to feature visualization for the third layer:

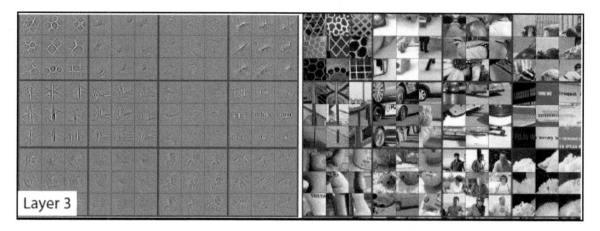

Figure 5.9: Feature visualization for the third layer in a CNN Source: https://cs.nyu.edu/~fergus/papers/zeilerECCV2014.pdf

In the third layer, we are seeing some really interesting patterns. In the second row and second column, we have identified parts of a car (wheels). In the third row and third column, we have begun to identify peoples' faces. In the second row and fourth column, we are identifying text within the images.

In the paper, the authors show examples for more layers. I encourage you to read the paper to get further insight into how convolutional layers work.

 It is important to note that, while deep learning models can achieve human-level performance on image classification, they do not interpret images as humans do. They have no concept of what a cat is or what a dog is. They can only match the patterns given. In the paper, the authors highlight an example where the matched patterns have little in common; the model is matching features in the background (grass) instead of foreground objects.

In another image classification task, the model failed to work in practice. The task was to classify wolves versus dogs. The model failed in practice because the model was trained with data which had wolves in their natural habitat, that is, snow. Therefore, the model assumed its task was to differentiate between *snow* and *dog*. Any image of a wolf in another setting was wrongly classified.

 The lesson from this is that your training data should be varied and closely related to the data that the model will be expected to predict against. This may sound obvious in theory, but it is not always easy to do so in practice. We will discuss this further in the next chapter.

Pooling layers

Pooling layers are used in CNNs to reduce the number of parameters in the model and therefore they reduce overfitting. They can be thought of as a type of dimensionality reduction. Similar to convolutional layers, a pooling layer moves over the previous layer but the operation and return value are different. It returns a single value and the operation is usually the maximum value of the cells in that patch, hence the name max-pooling. You can also perform other operations, for example, average pooling, but this is less common. Here is an example of max-pooling using a 2 x 2 block. The first block has the values 7, 0, 6, 6 and the maximum value of these is 7, so the output is 7. Note that padding is not normally used with max-pooling and that it usually applies a stride parameter to move the block. Here, the stride is 2, so once we get the max of the first block, we move across, 2 cells to the right:

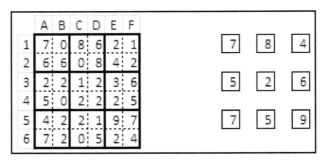

Figure 5.10: Max-Pooling applied to a matrix

We can see that max-pooling reduces the output by a factor of 4; the input was 6 x 6 and the output is 3 x 3. If you have not seen this before, your first reaction is probably disbelief. Why are we throwing away data? Why do we use max-pooling at all? There are three parts to this answer:

- **Pooling**: It is normally applied after a convolutional layer, so instead of executing over pixels, we execute over matched patterns. Downsizing after convolutional layers does not discard 75% of the input data; there is still enough signal there to find the pattern if it exists.
- **Regularization**: If you have studied machine learning, you will know that many models have problems with correlated features and that you are generally advised to remove correlated features. In image data, features are highly correlated with the spatial pattern around them. Applying max-pooling reduces the data while maintaining the features.
- **Execution speed**: When we consider the two earlier reasons, we can see that max-pooling greatly reduces the size of the network without removing too much of the signal. This makes training the model much quicker.

It is important to note the difference in the parameters used in the convolutional layer compared to the pooling layer. In general, a convolutional block is bigger (3 x 3) than the pooling block (2 x 2) and they should not overlap. For example, do not use a 4 x 4 convolutional block and a 2 x 2 pooling block. If they did overlap, the pooling block would just operate over the same convolutional blocks and the model would not train correctly.

Dropout

Dropout is a form of regularization which aims to prevent a model from overfitting. Overfitting is when the model is memorizing parts of the training dataset, but is not as accurate on unseen test data. When you build a model, you can check if overfitting is a problem by looking at the gap between the accuracy on the training set against the accuracy on the test set. If performance is much better on the training dataset, then the model is overfitting. Dropout refers to removing nodes randomly from a network temporarily during training. It is usually only applied to hidden layers, and not input layers. Here is an example of dropout applied to a neural network:

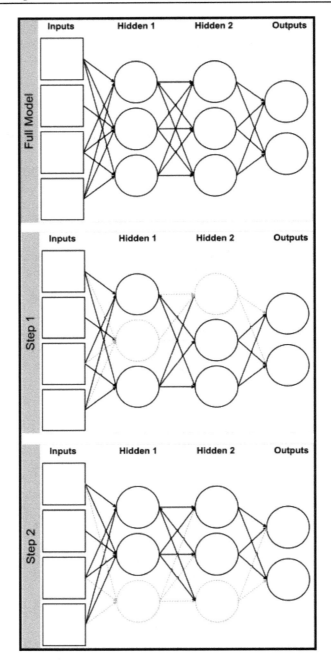

Figure 5.11: An example of dropout in a deep learning model

For each forward pass, a different set of nodes is removed, and therefore the network is different each time. In the original paper, dropout is compared to ensemble techniques, and in a way it is. There are some similarities to how dropout works and how random forest selects a random selection of features for each tree.

Another way to look at dropout is that each node in a layer must learn to work with all the nodes in that layer and the inputs it gets from the previous layer. It prevents one or a small number of nodes in a layer from getting large weights and dominating the outputs from that layer. This means that each node in a layer will work as a group and prevent some nodes from being too lazy and other nodes from being too dominant.

Flatten layers, dense layers, and softmax

After applying multiple convolutional layers, the resulting data structure is a multi-dimensional matrix (or tensor). We must transform this into a matrix that is in the shape of the required output. For example, if our classification task has 10 classes (for example, 10 for the `MNIST` example), we need the output of the model to be a 1 x 10 matrix. We do this by taking the results of our convolutional and max-pooling layers and using a Flatten layer to reshape the data. The last layer should have the same number of nodes as the number of classes we wish to predict for. If our task is binary classification, the `activation` function in our last layer will be sigmoid. If our task is binary classification, the `activation` function in our last layer will be softmax.

Before applying the softmax/sigmoid activation, we may optionally apply a number of dense layers. A dense layer is just a normal hidden layer, as we saw in `Chapter 1`, *Getting Started with Deep Learning*.

We need a softmax layer because the values in the last layer are numeric but range from - infinity to + infinity. We must convert these series of input values into a series of probabilities that says how likely the instance is for each category. The function to transform these numeric values to a series of probabilities must have the following characteristics:

- Each output value must be between 0.0 to 1.0
- The sum of the output values should be exactly 1.0

One way to do this is to just rescale the values by dividing each input value by the sum of the absolute input values. That approach has two problems:

- It does not handle negative values correctly
- Rescaling the input values may give us probabilities that are too close to each other

These two issues can be solved by first applying e^x (where e is 2.71828) to each input value and then rescaling those values. This transforms any negative number to a small positive number, and it also causes the probabilities to be more polarized. This can be demonstrated with an example; here, we can see the result from our dense layers. The values for categories 5 and 6 are quite close at 17.2 and 15.8, respectively. However, when we apply the softmax function, the probability value for category 5 is 4 times the probability value for category 6. The softmax function tends to result in probabilities that emphasize one category over all others, which is exactly what we want:

Category	Output from Dense Layer (x)	e^x	Output Probability
0	-1.3	0.27	0.00
1	5.2	181.27	0.00
2	8.3	4,023.87	0.00
3	11.2	73,130.44	0.00
4	10.1	24,343.01	0.00
5	17.2	29,502,925.92	0.78
6	15.8	7,275,331.96	0.19
7	5.2	181.27	0.00
8	3.1	22.20	0.00
9	13.5	729,416.37	0.02
		37,609,556.58	

Figure 5.12 Example of the softmax function

Image classification using the MXNet library

The MXNet package was introduced in `Chapter 1`, *Getting Started with Deep Learning*, so go back to that chapter for instructions on how to install the package if you have not already done so. We will demonstrate how to get almost 100% accuracy on a classification task for image data. We will use the `MNIST` dataset that we introduced in `Chapter 2`, *Image Classification Using Convolutional Neural Networks*. This dataset contains images of handwritten digits (0-9), and all images are of size 28 x 28. It is the *Hello World!* equivalent in deep learning. There's a long-term competition on Kaggle that uses this dataset. The script `Chapter5/explore.Rmd` is an R markdown file that explores this dataset.

1. First, we will check if the data has already been downloaded, and if it has not, we will download it. If the data is not available at this link, see the code in `Chapter2/chapter2.R` for an alternative way to get the data:

```
dataDirectory <- "../data"
if (!file.exists(paste(dataDirectory,'/train.csv',sep="")))
{
  link <-
'https://apache-mxnet.s3-accelerate.dualstack.amazonaws.com/R/data/
mnist_csv.zip'
  if (!file.exists(paste(dataDirectory,'/mnist_csv.zip',sep="")))
    download.file(link, destfile =
paste(dataDirectory,'/mnist_csv.zip',sep=""))
  unzip(paste(dataDirectory,'/mnist_csv.zip',sep=""), exdir =
dataDirectory)
  if (file.exists(paste(dataDirectory,'/test.csv',sep="")))
    file.remove(paste(dataDirectory,'/test.csv',sep=""))
}
```

2. Next we read the data into R and check it:

```
train <- read.csv(paste(dataDirectory,'/train.csv',sep=""),
header=TRUE, nrows=20)
```

We have 20 rows and 785 columns. Here, we will look at the rows at the tail of the dataset and look at the first 6 columns and the last 6 columns:

```
tail(train[,1:6])
   label pixel0 pixel1 pixel2 pixel3 pixel4
15     3      0      0      0      0      0
16     1      0      0      0      0      0
17     2      0      0      0      0      0
18     0      0      0      0      0      0
19     7      0      0      0      0      0
```

```
20      5      0      0      0      0      0

tail(train[, (ncol(train)-5):ncol(train)])
   pixel778 pixel779 pixel780 pixel781 pixel782 pixel783
15        0        0        0        0        0        0
16        0        0        0        0        0        0
17        0        0        0        0        0        0
18        0        0        0        0        0        0
19        0        0        0        0        0        0
20        0        0        0        0        0        0
```

We have `785` columns. The first column is the data label, and then we have 784 columns named `pixel0`, ..., `pixel783` with the pixel values. Our images are *28 x 28 = 784*, so everything looks OK.

Before we start building models, it is always a good idea to ensure that your data is in the correct format and that your features and labels are aligned correctly. Let's plot the first 9 instances with their data labels.

3. To do this, we will create a `helper` function called `plotInstance` that takes in the pixel values and outputs the image with an optional header:

```
plotInstance <-function (row,title="")
 {
  mat <- matrix(row,nrow=28,byrow=TRUE)
  mat <- t(apply(mat, 2, rev))
  image(mat, main = title,axes = FALSE, col = grey(seq(0, 1, length
= 256)))
 }
par(mfrow = c(3, 3))
par(mar=c(2,2,2,2))
for (i in 1:9)
 {
  row <- as.numeric(train[i,2:ncol(train)])
  plotInstance(row, paste("index:",i,", label =",train[i,1]))
 }
```

The output of this code shows the first 9 images and their classification:

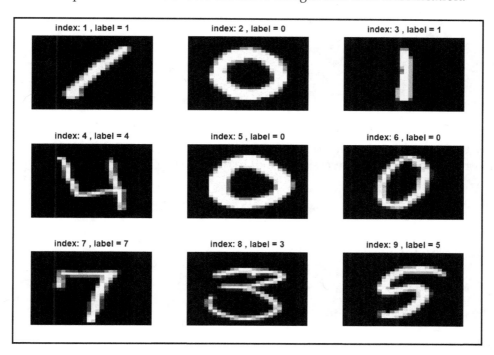

Figure 5.13: The first 9 images in the MNIST dataset

This completes our data exploration. Now, we can move on to creating some deep learning models using the MXNet library. We will create two models—the first is a standard neural network which we will use as a baseline. The second deep learning model is based on an architecture called **LeNet**. This is an old architecture, but is suitable in this case because our images are low resolution and do not contain backgrounds. Another advantage of LeNet is that it is possible to train quickly, even on CPUs, because it does not have many layers.

The code for this section is in `Chapter5/mnist.Rmd`. We must read data into R and convert it into matrices. We will split the training data into a train set and test set to get an unbiased estimate of accuracy. Because we have a large number of rows, we can use a split ratio of 90/10:

```
require(mxnet)
options(scipen=999)

dfMnist <- read.csv("../data/train.csv", header=TRUE)
yvars <- dfMnist$label
dfMnist$label <- NULL
```

```
set.seed(42)
train <- sample(nrow(dfMnist),0.9*nrow(dfMnist))
test <- setdiff(seq_len(nrow(dfMnist)),train)
train.y <- yvars[train]
test.y <- yvars[test]
train <- data.matrix(dfMnist[train,])
test <- data.matrix(dfMnist[test,])

rm(dfMnist,yvars)
```

Each image is represented as row of 784 (28 x 28) pixel values. The value of each pixel is in the range 0-255, we linearly transform it into 0-1 by dividing by 255. We also transpose the input matrix to because column major format in order to use it in `mxnet`.

```
train <- t(train / 255.0)
test <- t(test / 255.0)
```

Before creating a model, we should check that our dataset is balanced, i.e. the number of instances for each digit is reasonably even:

```
table(train.y)
## train.y
##    0    1    2    3    4    5    6    7    8    9
## 3716 4229 3736 3914 3672 3413 3700 3998 3640 3782
```

This looks ok, we can now move on to creating some deep learning models.

Base model (no convolutional layers)

Now that we have explored the data and we are satisfied that it looks OK, the next step is to create our first deep learning model. This is similar to the example we saw in the previous chapter. The code for this is in `Chapter5/mnist.Rmd`:

```
data <- mx.symbol.Variable("data")
fullconnect1 <- mx.symbol.FullyConnected(data, name="fullconnect1",
num_hidden=256)
activation1 <- mx.symbol.Activation(fullconnect1, name="activation1",
act_type="relu")
fullconnect2 <- mx.symbol.FullyConnected(activation1, name="fullconnect2",
num_hidden=128)
activation2 <- mx.symbol.Activation(fullconnect2, name="activation2",
act_type="relu")
fullconnect3 <- mx.symbol.FullyConnected(activation2, name="fullconnect3",
num_hidden=10)
softmax <- mx.symbol.SoftmaxOutput(fullconnect3, name="softmax")
```

Let's look at this code in detail:

1. In mxnet, we use its own data type symbol to configure the network.
2. We create the first hidden layer (fullconnect1 <- ....). This parameters are the data as input, the layer's name and the number of neurons in the layer.
3. We apply an activation function to the fullconnect layer (activation1 <- ....). The mx.symbol.Activation function takes the output from the first hidden layer, fullconnect1.
4. The second hidden layer (fullconnect1 <- ....) takes activation1 as the input.
5. The second activation is similar to activation1.
6. The fullconnect3 is the output layer. This layer has 10 neurons because this is a multi-classification problem and there are 10 classes.
7. Finally, we use a softmax activation to get a probabilistic prediction for each class.

Now, let's train the base model. I have a GPU installed, so I can use that. You may need to change the line to devices <- mx.cpu():

```
devices <- mx.gpu()
mx.set.seed(0)
model <- mx.model.FeedForward.create(softmax, X=train, y=train.y,
                                ctx=devices,array.batch.size=128,
                                num.round=10,
                                learning.rate=0.05, momentum=0.9,
                                eval.metric=mx.metric.accuracy,
epoch.end.callback=mx.callback.log.train.metric(1))
```

To make a prediction, we will call the predict function. We can then create a confusion matrix and calculate our accuracy level on test data:

```
preds1 <- predict(model, test)
pred.label1 <- max.col(t(preds1)) - 1
res1 <- data.frame(cbind(test.y,pred.label1))
table(res1)
##        pred.label1
## test.y   0   1   2   3   4   5   6   7   8   9
##      0 405   0   0   1   1   2   1   1   0   5
##      1   0 449   1   0   0   0   0   4   0   1
##      2   0   0 436   0   0   0   0   3   1   1
##      3   0   0   6 420   0   1   0   2   8   0
##      4   0   1   1   0 388   0   2   0   1   7
##      5   2   0   0   6   1 363   3   0   2   5
##      6   3   1   3   0   2   1 427   0   0   0
```

```
##    7   0   2   3   0   1   0   0 394   0   3
##    8   0   4   2   4   0   2   1   1 403   6
##    9   1   0   1   2   7   0   1   1   0 393
```

```
accuracy1 <- sum(res1$test.y == res1$pred.label1) / nrow(res1)
accuracy1
## 0.971
```

The accuracy of our base model is 0.971. Not bad, but let's see if we can improve on it.

LeNet

Now, we can create a model based on the LeNet architecture. This is a very simple model; we have two sets of convolutional and pooling layers and then a Flatten layer, and finally two dense layers. The code for this is in Chapter5/mnist.Rmd. First let's define the model:

```
data <- mx.symbol.Variable('data')
# first convolution layer
convolution1 <- mx.symbol.Convolution(data=data, kernel=c(5,5),
num_filter=64)
activation1 <- mx.symbol.Activation(data=convolution1, act_type="tanh")
pool1 <- mx.symbol.Pooling(data=activation1, pool_type="max",
                        kernel=c(2,2), stride=c(2,2))

# second convolution layer
convolution2 <- mx.symbol.Convolution(data=pool1, kernel=c(5,5),
num_filter=32)
activation2 <- mx.symbol.Activation(data=convolution2, act_type="relu")
pool2 <- mx.symbol.Pooling(data=activation2, pool_type="max",
                        kernel=c(2,2), stride=c(2,2))

# flatten layer and then fully connected layers
flatten <- mx.symbol.Flatten(data=pool2)
fullconnect1 <- mx.symbol.FullyConnected(data=flatten, num_hidden=512)
activation3 <- mx.symbol.Activation(data=fullconnect1, act_type="relu")
fullconnect2 <- mx.symbol.FullyConnected(data=activation3, num_hidden=10)
# final softmax layer
softmax <- mx.symbol.SoftmaxOutput(data=fullconnect2)
```

Now, let's reshape the data so that it can be used in MXNet:

```
train.array <- train
dim(train.array) <- c(28,28,1,ncol(train))
test.array <- test
dim(test.array) <- c(28,28,1,ncol(test))
```

Finally, we can build the model:

```
devices <- mx.gpu()
mx.set.seed(0)
model2 <- mx.model.FeedForward.create(softmax, X=train.array, y=train.y,
                                ctx=devices,array.batch.size=128,
                                num.round=10,
                                learning.rate=0.05, momentum=0.9,
wd=0.00001,
                                eval.metric=mx.metric.accuracy,
epoch.end.callback=mx.callback.log.train.metric(1))
```

Finally, let's evaluate the model:

```
preds2 <- predict(model2, test.array)
pred.label2 <- max.col(t(preds2)) - 1
res2 <- data.frame(cbind(test.y,pred.label2))
table(res2)
## pred.label2
## test.y   0   1   2   3   4   5   6   7   8   9
##      0 412   0   0   0   0   1   1   1   0   1
##      1   0 447   1   1   1   0   0   4   1   0
##      2   0   0 438   0   0   0   0   3   0   0
##      3   0   0   6 427   0   1   0   1   2   0
##      4   0   0   0   0 395   0   0   1   0   4
##      5   1   0   0   5   0 369   2   0   1   4
##      6   2   0   0   0   1   1 432   0   1   0
##      7   0   0   2   0   0   0   0 399   0   2
##      8   1   0   1   0   1   1   1   1 414   3
##      9   2   0   0   0   4   0   0   1   1 398
```

```
accuracy2
## 0.9835714
```

The accuracy of our CNN model is 0.9835714, which is quite an improvement over the accuracy of our base model, which was 0.971.

Finally, we can visualize our model in R:

```
graph.viz(model2$symbol)
```

This produces the following plot, which shows the architecture of the deep learning model:

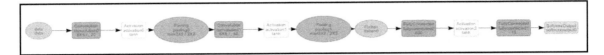

Figure 5.14: Convolutional deep learning model (LeNet)

Congratulations! You have built a deep learning model that is over 98% accurate!

We saw the architecture of LeNet in *Figure 5.1* and we have programmed it using the MXNet library. Let's analyze the LeNet architecture in more detail. Essentially, we have two convolutional groups and two fully connected layers. Our convolutional groups have a convolutional layer, followed by an `activation` function and then a pooling layer. This combination of layers is very common across many deep learning image classification tasks. The first convolution layer has 64 blocks of 5 x 5 size with no padding. This will possibly miss some features at the edges of the images, but if we look back at our sample images in *Figure 5.15*, we can see that most images do not have any data around the borders. We use pooling layers with `pool_type=max`. Other types are possible; average pooling was commonly used but has fallen out of favor recently. It is another hyper-parameter to try. We calculate our pools in 2 x 2 and then stride ("`jump`") by 2. Therefore, each input value is only used once in the max pool layer.

We use `tanh` as an `activation` function for our first convolutional block, and then use `relu` for subsequent layers. If you wish, you can try to change these and see what effect they have. Once we have executed our convolutional layers, we can use Flatten to restructure the data into a format that can be used by a fully connected layer. A fully connected layer is just a collection of nodes in a layer, that is, similar to the layers in the base model in the previous code. We have two layers, one with 512 nodes and the other with 10 nodes. We select 10 nodes in our last layer as this is the number of categories in our problem. Finally, we use a softmax to convert the numeric quantities in this layer into a set of probabilities for each category. We have achieved 98.35% accuracy, which is quite an improvement on a *normal* deep learning model, but there is still room for improvement. Some models can get 99.5% accuracy on this dataset, that is, 5 wrongly classified records in 1,000. Next, we will look at a different dataset that, while similar to MNIST, is harder than MNIST. This is the Fashion `MNIST` dataset, which has grayscale images of the same size as MNIST and also has 10 categories.

Classification using the fashion MNIST dataset

This dataset is in the same structure as `MNIST`, so we can just change our dataset and use the existing boilerplate code we have for loading the data. The script `Chapter5/explore_Fashion.Rmd` is an R markdown file that explores this dataset; it is almost identical to the `explore.Rmd` that we used for the `MNIST` dataset, so we will not repeat it. The only change to the `explore.Rmd` is to output the labels. We will look at 16 examples because this is a new dataset. Here are some sample images from this dataset that are created using the same boilerplate code we used to create the example for the `MNIST` dataset:

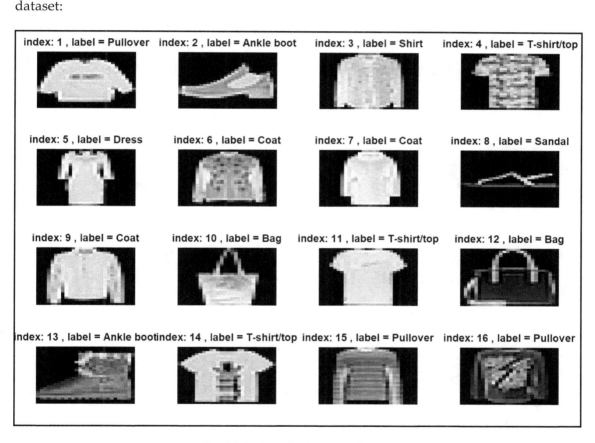

Figure 5.15: Some images from the Fashion MNIST dataset

An interesting fact about this dataset is that the company that released it also created a GitHub repository where they tested machine learning libraries against this dataset. The benchmarks are available at `http://fashion-mnist.s3-website.eu-central-1.amazonaws.com/`. If we look through these results, none of the machine libraries they tried achieved over 90% accuracy (they did not try deep learning). This is the target we want to beat with a deep learning classifier. The deep learning model code is in `Chapter5/fmnist.R` and achieves over 91% accuracy on this dataset. There are some small, but significant differences to the model architecture above. Try to spot them without peeking at the explanation.

First, let's define the model architecture.

```
data <- mx.symbol.Variable('data')
# first convolution layer
convolution1 <- mx.symbol.Convolution(data=data, kernel=c(5,5),
                                      stride=c(1,1), pad=c(2,2),
num_filter=64)
activation1 <- mx.symbol.Activation(data=convolution1, act_type=act_type1)
pool1 <- mx.symbol.Pooling(data=activation1, pool_type="max",
                    kernel=c(2,2), stride=c(2,2))

# second convolution layer
convolution2 <- mx.symbol.Convolution(data=pool1, kernel=c(5,5),
                                      stride=c(1,1), pad=c(2,2),
num_filter=32)
activation2 <- mx.symbol.Activation(data=convolution2, act_type=act_type1)
pool2 <- mx.symbol.Pooling(data=activation2, pool_type="max",
                    kernel=c(2,2), stride=c(2,2))

# flatten layer and then fully connected layers with activation and dropout
flatten <- mx.symbol.Flatten(data=pool2)
fullconnect1 <- mx.symbol.FullyConnected(data=flatten, num_hidden=512)
activation3 <- mx.symbol.Activation(data=fullconnect1, act_type=act_type1)
drop1 <- mx.symbol.Dropout(data=activation3,p=0.4)
fullconnect2 <- mx.symbol.FullyConnected(data=drop1, num_hidden=10)
# final softmax layer
softmax <- mx.symbol.SoftmaxOutput(data=fullconnect2)
```

Now let's train the model:

```
logger <- mx.metric.logger$new()
model2 <- mx.model.FeedForward.create(softmax, X=train.array, y=train.y,
                              ctx=devices, num.round=20,
                              array.batch.size=64,
                              learning.rate=0.05, momentum=0.9,
                              wd=0.00001,
                              eval.metric=mx.metric.accuracy,
```

```
eval.data=list(data=test.array,labels=test.y),
epoch.end.callback=mx.callback.log.train.metric(100,logger))
```

The first change is that we switch to use `relu` as an `Activation` function for all layers. Another change was that we use padding for the convolutional layers, which we did to capture the features at the borders of the image. We increased the number of nodes in each layer to add depth to the model. We also added a dropout layer to prevent the model from overfitting. We also added logging to our model, which outputs the train and validation metrics for each epoch. We used these to check how our model performs and to decide if it is overfitting.

Here are the accuracy results and the diagnostic plot for this model:

```
preds2 <- predict(model2, test.array)
pred.label2 <- max.col(t(preds2)) - 1
res2 <- data.frame(cbind(test.y,pred.label2))
table(res2)
      pred.label2
test.y   0   1   2   3   4   5   6   7   8   9
     0 489   0  12  10   0   0  53   0   3   0
     1   0 586   1   6   1   0   1   0   0   0
     2   8   1 513   7  56   0  31   0   0   0
     3  13   0   3 502  16   0  26   1   1   0
     4   1   1  27  13 517   0  32   0   2   0
     5   1   0   0   0   0 604   0   9   0   3
     6  63   0  47   9  28   0 454   0   3   0
     7   0   0   0   1   0  10   0 575   1  11
     8   0   0   1   0   1   2   1   0 618   0
     9   0   0   0   0   0   1   0  17   1 606
accuracy2 <- sum(res2$test.y == res2$pred.label2) / nrow(res2)
accuracy2
# 0.9106667
```

One thing to note is that we are using the same validation/test set for showing metrics during training and to evaluate the final model. This is not a good practice, but it is acceptable here because we are not using validation metrics to tune the hyperparameters of the model. The accuracy of our CNN model is 0.9106667.

Let's plot the accuracy of the train and validation sets as the model is trained. The deep learning model code has a `callback` function which saves the metrics as the model is trained. We can use this to plot the training and validation metrics for each epoch:

```
# use the log data collected during model training
dfLogger<-as.data.frame(round(logger$train,3))
dfLogger2<-as.data.frame(round(logger$eval,3))
dfLogger$eval<-dfLogger2[,1]
```

```
colnames(dfLogger)<-c("train","eval")
dfLogger$epoch<-as.numeric(row.names(dfLogger))

data_long <- melt(dfLogger, id="epoch")

ggplot(data=data_long,
       aes(x=epoch, y=value, colour=variable,label=value)) +
  ggtitle("Model Accuracy") +
  ylab("accuracy") +
  geom_line()+geom_point() +
  geom_text(aes(label=value),size=3,hjust=0, vjust=1) +
  theme(legend.title=element_blank()) +
  theme(plot.title = element_text(hjust = 0.5)) +
  scale_x_discrete(limits= 1:nrow(dfLogger))
```

This shows us how our model is performing after each epoch (or training run). This produces the following screenshot:

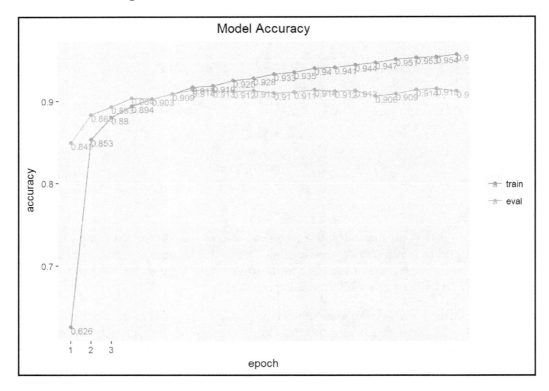

Figure 5.16: Training and validation accuracy by epoch

The two main points to be taken from this graph are that:

- The model is overfitting. We can see a clear gap between performance on the training set at **0.95xxx** and the validation set at **0.91xxx**.
- We could have probably stopped the model training after 8 epochs, as performance did not improve after this point.

As we have discussed in previous chapters, deep learning models will almost always overfit by default, but there are methods to negate this. The second issue is related to *early stopping*, and it is vital that you know how to do this so that you do not waste hours in continuing to train a model which is no longer improving. This is especially relevant if you are building the model using cloud resources. We will look at these and more issues related to building deep learning models in the next chapter.

References/further reading

These papers are classical deep learning papers in this domain. Some of them document winning approaches to ImageNet competitions. I encourage you to download and read all of them. You may not understand them at first, but their importance will become more evident as you continue on your journey in deep learning.

- Krizhevsky, Alex, Ilya Sutskever, and Geoffrey E. Hinton. *ImageNet Classification with Deep Convolutional Neural Networks*. Advances in neural information processing systems. 2012.
- Szegedy, Christian, et al. *Going Deeper with Convolutions*. Cvpr, 2015.
- LeCun, Yann, et al. *Learning Algorithms for Classification: A Comparison on Handwritten Digit Recognition*. Neural networks: the statistical mechanics perspective 261 (1995): 276.
- Zeiler, Matthew D., and Rob Fergus. *Visualizing and Understanding Convolutional Networks*. European conference on computer vision. Springer, Cham, 2014.
- Srivastava, Nitish, et al. *Dropout: A Simple Way to Prevent Neural Networks from Overfitting*. The Journal of Machine Learning Research 15.1 (2014): 1929-1958.

Summary

In this chapter, we used deep learning for image classification. We discussed the different layer types that are used in image classification: convolutional layers, pooling layers, dropout, dense layers, and the softmax activation function. We saw an R-Shiny application that shows how convolutional layers perform feature engineering on image data.

We used the MXNet deep learning library in R to create a base deep learning model which got 97.1% accuracy. We then developed a CNN deep learning model based on the LeNet architecture, which achieved over 98.3% accuracy on test data. We also used a slightly harder dataset (Fashion MNIST) and created a new model that achieved over 91% accuracy. This accuracy score was better than all of the other scores that used non-deep learning algorithms. In the next chapter, we will build on what we have covered and show you how we can take advantage of pre-trained models for classification and as building blocks for new deep learning models.

In the next chapter, we are going to discuss important topics in deep learning concerning tuning and optimizing your models. This includes how to use the limited data you may have, data pre-processing, data augmentation, and hyperparameter selection.

6
Tuning and Optimizing Models

In the last two chapters, we trained deep learning models for classification, regression, and image recognition tasks. In this chapter, we will discuss some important issues in regard to managing deep learning projects. While this chapter may seem somewhat theoretical, if any of the issues discussed are not correctly managed, it can derail your deep learning project. We will look at how to choose evaluation metrics and how to create an estimate of how well a deep learning model will perform before you begin modeling. Next, we will move onto data distribution and the mistakes often made in splitting data into correct partitions for training. Many machine learning projects fail in production use because the data distribution is different to what the model was trained with. We will look at data augmentation, a valuable method to enhance your model's accuracy. Finally, we will discuss hyperparameters and learn how to tune them.

In this chapter, we will be looking at the following topics:

- Evaluation metrics and evaluating performance
- Data preparation
- Data pre-processing
- Data augmentation
- Tuning hyperparameters
- Use case—interpretability

Evaluation metrics and evaluating performance

This section will discuss how to set up a deep learning project and what evaluation metrics to select. We will look at how to select evaluation criteria and how to decide when the model is approaching optimal performance. We will also discuss how all deep learning models tend to overfit and how to manage the bias/variance tradeoff. This will give guidelines on what to do when models have low accuracy.

Types of evaluation metric

Different evaluation metrics are used for categorization and regression tasks. For categorization, accuracy is the most commonly used evaluation metric. However, accuracy is only valid if the cost of errors is the same for all classes, which is not always the case. For example, in medical diagnosis, the cost of a false negative will be much higher than the cost of a false positive. A false negative in this case says that the person is not sick when they are, and a delay in diagnosis can have serious, perhaps fatal, consequences. On the other hand, a false positive is saying that the person is sick when they are not, which is upsetting for that person but is not life threatening.

This issue is compounded when you have imbalanced datasets, that is, when one class is much more common than the other. Going back to our medical diagnosis example, if only 1% of people who get tested actually have the disease, then a machine learning algorithm can get 99% accuracy by just declaring that nobody has the disease. In this case, you can look at other metrics rather than accuracy. One such metric that is useful for imbalanced datasets is the F1 evaluation metric, which is a weighted average of precision and recall. The formula for the F1 score is as follows:

F1 = 2 * (precision * recall) / (precision + recall)

The formulas for precision and recall are as follows:

precision = true_positives / (true_positives + false_positives)
recall = true_positives / (true_positives + false_negatives)

For regression, you have a choice of evaluation metrics: MAE, MSE, and RMSE. **MAE**, or **Mean Absolute Error**, is the simplest; it is just the average of the absolute difference between the actual value and the predicted value. The advantage of MAE is that it is easily understood; if MAE is 3.5, then the difference between the predicted value and the actual value is 3.5 on average. **MSE**, or **Mean Squared Error**, is the average of the squared error, that is, it takes the difference between the actual value and the predicted value, squares it, and then takes the average of those values. The advantage of using MSE over MAE is that it penalizes errors according to their severity. If the difference between the actual value and the predicted value for two rows was 2 and 5, then the MSE would put more weight on the second example because the error is larger. **RMSE**, or **Root Mean Squared Error**, is the square root of MSE. The advantage of using MSE is that it puts the error term back into units that are comparable to the actual values. For regression tasks, RMSE is usually the preferred metric.

For more information on metrics in MXNet, see `https://mxnet.incubator.apache.org/api/python/metric/metric.html`.

For more information on metrics in Keras, see `https://keras.io/metrics/`.

Evaluating performance

We have explored a few deep learning models in earlier chapters. We got an accuracy rate of 98.36% in our image classification task on the `MNIST` dataset in `Chapter 5`, *Image Classification Using Convolutional Neural Networks*. For the binary classification task (predicting which customers will return in the next 14 days) in `Chapter 4`, *Training Deep Prediction Models*, we got an accuracy rate of 77.88%. But what does this actually mean and how do we evaluate the performance of a deep learning model?

The obvious starting point in evaluating whether your deep learning model has good predictive capability is by comparing it to other models. The `MNIST` dataset is used in a lot of benchmarks for deep learning research, so we know that there are models that achieve 99.5% accuracy. Therefore, our model is OK, but not great. In the *Data augmentation* section in this chapter, we will improve our model significantly, from 98.36% accuracy to 98.95% accuracy, by augmenting our data with new images created by making changes to the existing image data. In general, for image classification tasks anything less than 95% accuracy probably indicates a problem with your deep learning model. Either the model is not designed correctly or you do not have enough data for your task.

Our binary classification model only had 77.54% accuracy, which is much less than the image classification task. So, is it a terrible model? Not really; it is still a useful model. We also have some benchmarks from other machine learning models such as random forest and xgboost that we ran on a small section of the data. We also saw that we got an increase in accuracy when we moved from a model with 3,900 rows to a deeper model with 390,000 rows. This highlights that deep learning models improve with more data.

One step you can do to evaluate your model's performance is to see if more data will increase accuracy significantly. The data can be acquired from more training data, or from data augmentation, which we will see later. You can use learning curves to evaluate if this will help with performance. To create a learning curve, you train a series of machine learning models with increasing sizes, for example, 10,000 rows to 200,000 rows in steps of 1,000 rows. For each step, run 5 different machine learning models to smooth the results and plot average accuracy by the sample size. Here is the pseudocode to perform this task:

```
For k=10000 to 200000 step 1000
    For n=1 to 5
        [sample] = Take k rows from dataset
        Split [sample] into train (80%) / test (20%)
        Run ML (DT) algorithm
        Calculate Accuracy on test
        Save accuracy value
    Plot k, avg(Accuracy)
```

Here is an example of a learning curve plot for similar task to the churn problem:

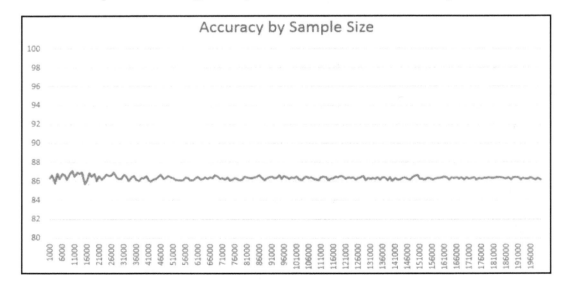

Figure 6.1: An example of a learning curve which plots accuracy by data size

In this case, accuracy is in a very narrow range and stabilizes as the # instances increase. Therefore, for this algorithm and hyperparameter choice, adding more data will not increase accuracy significantly.

If we get a learning curve that is flat like in this example, then adding more data to the existing model will not increase accuracy. We could try to improve our performance by either changing the model architecture or by adding more features. We discussed some options for this in `Chapter 5`, *Image Classification Using Convolutional Neural Networks*.

Going back to our binary classification model, let's consider how we could we use it in production. Recall that this model is trying to predict if customers will return in the next x days. Here is the confusion matrix from that model again:

```
          Predicted
  Actual     0      1
    0      10714   4756
    1       3870  19649
```

If we look at how the model performs for each class, we get a different accuracy rates:

- For `Actual=0`, we get *10714 / (10714 + 4756) = 69.3%* values correct. This is called specificity or the true negative rate.
- For `Actual=1`, we get *19649 / (3466 + 19649) = 85.0%* values correct. This is called sensitivity or the true positive rate.

For this use case, sensitivity is probably more of a concern than specificity. If I were a senior manager, I would be more interested in knowing which customers were predicted to return but did not. This group could be sent offers to entice them back. Here is how a senior manager might use this model, assuming that the model is built to predict whether a person comes in from September 1 to September 14. On September 15, we get the preceding confusion matrix. How should a manager allocate his/her limited marketing budget?

- I can see that I got 4,756 customers who were predicted not to return but actually did. This is good, but I cannot really act on this. I can attempt to send offers to the 10,135 who did not return, but since my model already predicted that they would not return, I would expect the response rate to be low.
- The 3,870 customers who were predicted to return but did not are more interesting. These people should be sent offers to entice them back before their change in behavior becomes permanent. This represents only 9.9% of my customer base, so by only sending offers to these customers, I am not diluting my budget by sending offers to a large contingent of my customers.

The prediction model should not be used in isolation; other metrics should be combined with it to develop a marketing strategy. For example, **customer lifetime value (CLV)**, which measures the expected future revenue for a customer minus the cost to re-acquire that customer, could be combined with the prediction model. By using a prediction model and CLV together, we can prioritize customers that are likely to return by their predicted future value.

To summarize this section, it is all too easy to get obsessed with optimizing evaluation metrics, especially if you are new to the field. As a data scientist, you should always remember that optimizing evaluation metrics on a machine learning task is not the ultimate goal—it is just a proxy for improving some part of the business. You must be able to link the results of your machine learning model back to a business use case. In some cases, for example, digit recognition in the MNIST dataset, there is a direct link between your evaluation metrics and your business case. But sometimes it is not so obvious, and you need help to work with the business in finding out how to use the results of your analysis to maximize the benefits to the company.

Data preparation

Machine learning is about training a model to generalize on the cases it sees so that it can make predictions on unseen data. Therefore, the data used to train the deep learning model should be similar to the data that the model sees in production. However, at an early product stage, you may have little or no data to train a model, so what can you do? For example, a mobile app could include a machine learning model that predicts the subject of image taken by the mobile camera. When the app is being written, there may not be enough data to train the model using a deep learning network. One approach would be to augment the dataset with images from other sources to train the deep learning network. However, you need to know how to manage this and how to deal with the uncertainty it introduces. Another approach is transfer learning, which we will cover in Chapter 11, *The Next Level in Deep Learning*.

Another difference between deep learning and traditional machine learning is the size of the datasets. This can affect the ratios used to split data between train/test—the recommended guidelines for splitting data into 70/30 or 80/20 splits for machine learning need to be revised for training deep learning models.

Different data distributions

In previous chapters, we used the MNIST dataset for classification tasks. While this dataset contains handwritten digits, the data is not representative of real-life data. In `Chapter 5`, *Image Classification Using Convolutional Neural Networks*, we visualized some of the digits, if you go back and look at these images, it is clear that these images are in a standard format:

- There are all grayscale
- The images are all 28 x 28
- The images all appear to have at border of at least 1 pixel
- The images are all of the same scale, that is, each image takes up most of the image
- There is very little distortion, since the border is black and the foreground is white
- Images are the *right way up*, that is, we do not have any major rotations

The original use case for the MNIST dataset is to recognize 5 digit postcodes on letters. Let's suppose we train a model on the 60,000 images in the MNIST dataset and wish to use it in a production environment to recognize postcodes from letters and packages. Here are the steps a production system must go through before any deep learning can be applied:

- Scan the letters
- Find the postcode section
- Split the postcode digits into 5 different regions (one per digit)

In any one of these data transformation steps, additional data bias could occur. If we used the *clean* MNIST data to train a model and then tried to predict the *biased* transformed data, then our model may not work that well. Examples of how bias could affect the production data include the following:

- Correctly locating the postcode is a difficult problem in itself
- The letters will have backgrounds and foregrounds of different colors and contrasts, and so converting them to grayscale may not be consistent depending on the type of letter and pen used on the letter / package
- The results from the scanning processes may vary because of different hardware and software being used—this is a ongoing problem in applying deep learning to medical image data
- Finally, the difficultly in splitting the postcode into 5 different regions depends on the letter and pen used, as well as the quality of the preceding steps

In this example, the distribution of the data used to train and the estimate model's performance is different from the production data. If a data scientist had promised to deliver 99% accuracy before the model is deployed, then senior managers are very likely to be disappointed when the application runs in production! When creating a new model, we split data into train and test splits, so the main purpose of the test dataset is to estimate model accuracy. But if the data in the test dataset is different to what the model will be see in production, then the evaluation metrics on the test dataset cannot give a good guide to how the model will perform in production.

If the problem is that there is little or no actual labeled dataset to begin with, then one of the first steps to consider before any model training is to investigate if more data can be acquired. Acquiring data may involve setting up a mini production environment, partnering with a client or using a combination of semi-supervised and manual labelling. In the use case we just saw, I would consider it more important to set up the process to extract the digitized images before looking at any machine learning. Once this is set up, I would look to build up some training data—it still may not be enough to build a model, but it could be used but a proper test set to create evaluation metrics that would reflect real-life performance. This may appear obvious, as over optimistic expectations based on flawed evaluation metrics are probably one of the top three problems in data science projects.

One example of a very large scale project that managed this problem very well is this use case in Airbnb: `https://medium.com/airbnb-engineering/categorizing-listing-photos-at-airbnb-f9483f3ab7e3`. They had a huge number of photos of house interiors, but these were not labeled with the room type. They took their existing labeled data and also performed quality assurance to check how accurate the labels were. It is often said in data science that creating machine learning models may only be 20% of the actual work involved—acquiring an accurate large labeled dataset that is representative of what the model will see in production is often the hardest task in a deep learning project.

Once you have a dataset in place, you need to split your data into train and test splits before modeling. If you have experience in traditional machine learning, you may start with a 70/30 split, that is, 70% for training the model and 30% for evaluating the model. However, this rule is less valid in the world of large datasets and training deep learning models. Again, the only reason to split data into train and test sets is to have a holdout set to estimate the model's performance. Therefore, you only need enough records in this dataset so that the accuracy estimate you get is reliable and has the precision you require. If you have a large dataset to begin with, then a smaller percentage might be adequate for the test dataset. Let me explain this with an example, where you want to improve on an existing machine learning model:

- A prior machine learning model has 99.0% accuracy
- There is a labeled dataset with 1,000,000 records

If a new machine learning model is to be trained, then it should get at least 99.1% accuracy for you to be confident that it is an improvement on the existing model. How many records do you need when evaluating the existing model? You only need enough records so that you are fairly sure that the accuracy on the new model is accurate to 0.1%. Therefore 50,000 records in the test set, which is 5% of the dataset, would be sufficient to evaluate your model. If the accuracy on these 50,000 records was 99.1%, that would be 49,550 records. This represents 50 more correctly classified records than the benchmark model, which would strongly suggest that the second model is a better model—it would be unlikely that the difference would be simply down to chance.

You may get resistance to the suggestion you use only 5% of data for model evaluation. However, the idea of splitting data into 70/30 splits goes back to the days of small datasets, such as the iris dataset with 150 records. We previously saw the following graph in `Chapter 4`, *Training Deep Prediction Models*, which showed how accuracy on machine learning algorithms tends to stagnate as the data size increases. Therefore, there was less of an incentive to maximize the amount of data that was available for training. Deep learning models can take advantage of more data, so if we can use less data for the test set, we should get a better model overall:

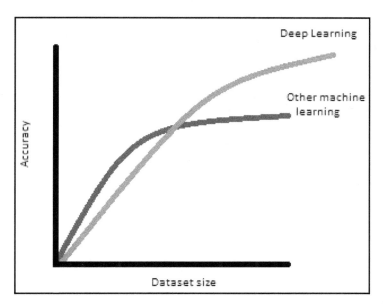

Figure 6.2: How model accuracy increases by dataset size for deep learning models versus other machine learning models

Data partition between training, test, and validation sets

The previous section highlighted the importance of acquiring some data at an early stage in the project. But if you do not have enough data to train a deep learning model, it is possible to train on other data and apply it to your data. For example, you can use a model trained on ImageNet data for image classification tasks. In this scenario, you need to use the real data that has been collected wisely. This section discusses some good practices on that subject.

 If you have ever wondered why big companies such as Google, Apple, Facebook, Amazon, and so on have such a head start in AI, this is the reason why. While they have some of the best AI people in the world working for them, their chief advantage is that they have access to tons of *labeled* data that they can use to build their machine learning models.

In the previous section, we said that the sole purpose of a test set is to evaluate the model. But if that data is not from the same distribution as the data the model will see in prediction tasks, then the evaluation will be misleading. One of the most important project priorities should be to acquire labeled data that is as similar to real-life data as soon as possible. Once you have that data, you need to be clever on how you use this valuable asset. The best use of this data, in order of priority, would be as follows:

- Can I use some of this data to create more training data? This could be through augmentation, or implementing an early prototype that users can interact with.
- If you are building several models (which you should be), use some of the data in the validation set to tune the model.
- Use the data in the test set to evaluate the model.
- Use the data in the train set.

Some of these suggestions may be contentious—especially when suggesting that you should use the data for the validation set before the test set. Remember that the sole purpose of a test set is that it should only be used once to evaluate the model, so you only get one shot at using this data. If I have only a small amount of realistic data, then I prefer to use it to tune the model and have a less precise evaluation metric than having a poorly performing model with a very precise evaluation metric.

This approach is risky, and ideally you want your validation dataset and your test dataset to be from the same distribution and be representative of the data that the model will see in production. Unfortunately, when you are at the early stages in machine learning projects with limited real-life data, then you have to make decisions on how best to use this data, and in this case it is better to use the limited data in the validation dataset rather than the test dataset.

Standardization

Another important step in data preparation is standardizing data. In the previous chapter, for the MNIST data, all pixel values were divided by 255 so that the input data was between 0.0 and 1.0. In our case, we applied min-max normalization, which transforms the data linearly using the following function:

xnew = (x-min(x))/(max(x)-min(x))

Since we already know that *min(x) = 0* and *max(x)=255*, this reduces to the following:

xnew = x / 255.0

The other most popular form of standardization scales the feature so that the mean is 0 and the standard deviation from the mean is 1. This is also known as **z-scores**, and the formula for it is as follows:

xnew = (x - mean(x)) / std.dev(x)

There are three reasons why we need to perform standardization:

- It is especially important to normalize our input features if the features are in different scales. A common example often cited in machine learning is predicting house prices from the number of bedrooms and the square foot. The number of bedrooms ranges from 1 to 10, while the square feet can range from 500 sq feet to 20,000 sq feet. Deep learning models expect features to be in the same range.
- Even if all of our features are already in the same range, it is still advisable to normalize the input features. Recall from `Chapter 3`, *Deep Learning Fundamentals*, that we looked at initializing the weights before model training. Any benefit from initializing weights will be cancelled if our features are not normalized. We also spoke about the problem of exploding and vanishing gradients. When features are on different scales this is more likely.
- Even if we avoid both of the preceding problem, if we do not apply normalization, the model will take longer to train.

For the churn model in `Chapter 4`, *Training Deep Prediction Models*, all of the columns were monetary spent, so are already on the same scale. When we applied the log to each of these variables, it will have shrunk them down to values between -4.6 to 11, so there was no need to scale them to values between 0 and 1. When correctly applied, standardization has no negative consequences and so should be one of first steps applied to data preparation.

Data leakage

Data leakage is where a feature used to train the model has values that could not exist if the model was used in production. It occurs most frequently in time series data. For example, in our churn use case in `Chapter 4`, *Training Deep Prediction Models*, there were a number of categorical variables in the data that indicated customer segmentation. A data modeler may assume that these are good predictor variables, but it is not known how and when these variables were set. They could be based on customer' spend, which means that if they are used in the prediction algorithm, there is a circular reference—an external process calculates the segment based on the spend and then this variable is used to predict spend!

When extracting data to build a model, you should be wary of categorical attributes and question when these variables could have been created and modified. Unfortunately, most database systems are poor at tracking the data lineage, so if in doubt you may consider omitting the variable from your model.

Another example of data leakage in image classification tasks is when attribute information within the image is used in the model. For example, if we build a model where the filenames were included as attributes, these names may hint at the class name. When the model is used in production, theses hints will not exist, so this is also seen as data leakage.

We will see an example of data leakage in practice in the the *Use case—interpretability* section later in this chapter.

Data augmentation

One approach to increasing the accuracy in a model regardless of the amount of data you have is to create artificial examples based on existing data. This is called **data augmentation**. Data augmentation can also be used at test time to improve prediction accuracy.

Using data augmentation to increase the training data

We are going to apply data augmentation to the MNIST dataset that we used in previous chapters. The code for this section is in Chapter6/explore.Rmd if you want to follow along. In Chapter 5, *Image Classification Using Convolutional Neural Networks*, we plotted some examples from the MNIST data, so we won't repeat the code again. It is included in the code file, and you can also refer back to the image in Chapter 5, *Image Classification Using Convolutional Neural Networks*:

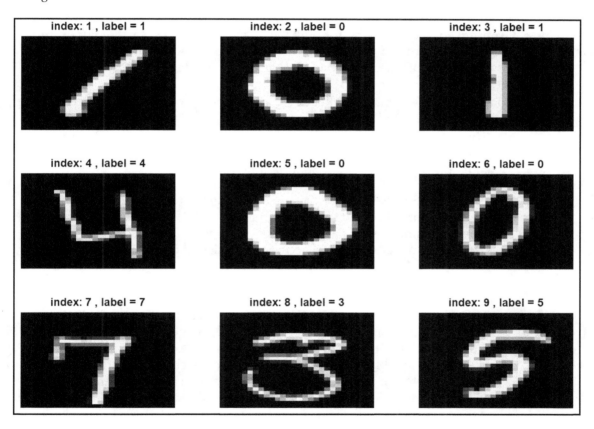

Figure 6.3: The first 9 images in the MNIST dataset

We described data augmentation as creating new data from an existing dataset. This means creating a new instance that is sufficiently different from the original instance but not so much that it no longer represents the data label. For image data, this might mean performing the following functions on the images:

- **Zooming**: By zooming into the center of the image, your model may be better able to handle images at different scales.
- **Shifting**: Moving the image up, down, left, or right can make the deep learning model more aware of examples of images taken off-center.
- **Rotation**: By rotating images, the model will be able to recognize data that is off-center.
- **Flipping**: For many objects, flipping the images 90 degrees is valid. For example, a picture of a car from the left side can be flipped to show a similar image of the car from the right side. A deep model can take advantage of this new perspective.
- **Adding noise**: Sometimes, deliberately adding noise to images can force the deep learning model to find deeper meaning.
- **Modifying color**: By adding filters to the image, you can simulate different lighting conditions. For example, you can change an image taken in bright light so that it appears to be taken in poor lighting conditions.

The goal of this task is to increase accuracy on the test dataset. However, the important rule of data augmentation is that the new data should attempt to simulate the data your model will use in production rather than trying to increase model accuracy on existing data. I cannot stress that enough. Getting 99% accuracy on a hold-out set means nothing if a model fails to work in a production environment because the data used to train and evaluate the model was not representative of real-life data. In our case, we can see that the MNIST images are grayscale and neatly centered, and so on. In a production use case, images are off-center and with different backgrounds and foregrounds (for example, with a brown background and blue writing), and so will not be classified correctly. You can attempt to pre-process the images so that you can format them to a similar manner (28 x 28 grayscale image with black background and data centered with a 2 x 2 margin), but a better solution is to train the model on typical data it will encounter in production.

If we look at the previous image, we can see that most of these data augmentation tasks are not applicable to the MNIST data. All of the images appear to be at the same zoom level already, so creating artificial examples at increased zoom will not help. Similarly, shifting is unlikely to work, since the images are already centered. Flipping images is definitely not valid, since most digits are not valid when flipped, example 7. There is no evidence of existing random noise in our data, so this will not work either.

One technique that we can try is to rotate the images. We will create two new artificial images for each existing image, the first artificial image will be rotated 15 degrees left and the second artificial image will be rotated 15 degrees right. Here are some of the artificial images after we have rotated the original images 15 degrees left:

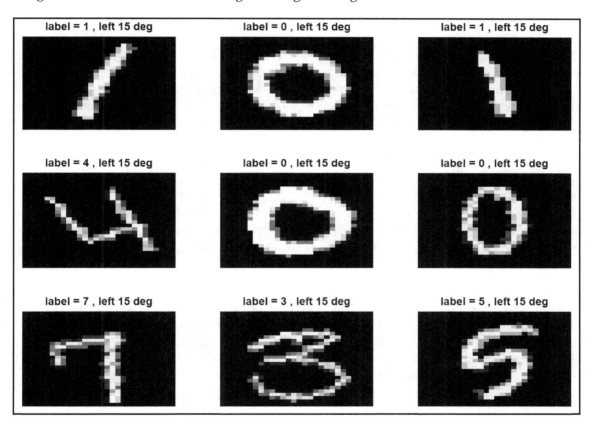

Figure 6.4: MNIST data rotated 15 degrees left

If we look at the the preceding screenshot, one strange anomaly exists. We have 10 classes, and using this approach may increase overall accuracy, but one class will not get as much uplift. The zero digit is the odd one out because rotating a zero still looks like a zero—we may still get an increase in accuracy for this class, but probably not as much as for the other classes. The function to rotate image data is in `Chapter6/img_ftns.R`. It uses the `rotateImage` function from the `OpenImageR` package:

```
rotateInstance <-function (df,degrees)
{
  mat <- as.matrix(df)
  mat2 <- rotateImage(mat, degrees, threads = 1)
  df <- data.frame(mat2)
  return (df)
}
```

There is actually two types of data augmentation that we can apply to our dataset. The first type creates new training data from existing examples. But we can also use a technique called **test time augmentation** (**TTA**), which can be used during model evaluation. It makes copies of each test row and then uses these copies and the originals to vote for the category. We will see an example of this later.

The code to create datasets for the data augmentation is in `Chapter6/augment.R`. Note that this takes a long time to run, maybe 6-10 hours depending on your machine. It also needs approx. 300 MB of free space on the drive to create the new datasets. The code is not difficult; it loads in the data, and splits it into train and test sets. For the train data, it creates two new instances: one rotated 15 degrees left and one rotated 15 degrees right. It is important that the data used to evaluate the model performance is not included in the data augmentation process, that is, split the data into a train dataset first and only apply data augmentation to the train split.

When the data augmentation is complete, there will be a new file in the data folder called `train_augment.csv`. This file should have 113,400 rows. Our original dataset for `MNIST` had 42,000 rows; we took 10% of that for test purposes (that is, to validate our model) and were left with 37,800 rows. We then made two copies of these rows, meaning that we now have 3 rows for each previous row. This means that we have *37,800 x 3 = 113,400* rows in our training data file. `augment.R` also outputs the test data (4,200 rows) as `test0.csv` and an augmented test set (`test_augment.csv`), which we will cover later.

The code to run the neural network is in `Chapter6/mnist.Rmd`. The first part which uses the augmented data for training is almost identical to the code in `Chapter 5`, *Image Classification Using Convolutional Neural Networks*. The only change is that it loads the data files created in `augment.R` (`train_augment.csv` and `test0.csv`), so we we will not repeat all of the code for the model here again. Here is the confusion matrix and the final accuracy on the test dataset:

```
## pred.label
## test.y    0    1    2    3    4    5    6    7    8    9
##       0 412    0    0    1    0    0    3    0    0    0
##       1   0  447    1    2    0    0    0    5    0    0
##       2   0    0  437    1    2    0    0    1    0    0
##       3   0    0    3  432    0    0    0    1    1    0
##       4   0    0    0    0  396    1    0    0    0    3
##       5   1    0    0    1    0  378    1    0    0    1
##       6   1    1    0    0    0    0  434    0    1    0
##       7   0    1    2    0    1    0    0  398    0    1
##       8   0    0    2    1    0    0    0    1  419    0
##       9   0    0    0    0    5    0    0    1    1  399
accuracy2 <- sum(res$test.y == res$pred.label) / nrow(res)
The accuracy of our model with augmented train data is 0.9885714.
```

This compares to an accuracy of `0.9821429` from our model in `Chapter 5`, *Image Classification Using Convolutional Neural Networks*, so this is a significant improvement. We have reduced our error rate by over 30% *(0.9885714-0.9835714) / (1.0-0.9835714)*.

Test time augmentation

We can also use data augmentation during test time. In the `augment.R` file, it created a file with the original test set of 4,200 rows (`data/test0.csv`), which was used that to evaluate the model. The `augment.R` file also created a file called `test_augment.csv`, which has the original 4,200 rows and 2 copies for each image. The copies are similar to what we did to augment the training data, that is, a row with data rotated 15 degrees left and a row with data rotated 15 degrees right. The three rows are outputted sequentially and we will use these 3 rows to *vote* for the winner. We need to take 3 records at a time from `test_augment.csv` and calculate the prediction value as the average of these three values. Here is the code that performs test time augmentation:

```
test_data <- read.csv("../data/test_augment.csv", header=TRUE)
test.y <- test_data[,1]
test <- data.matrix(test_data)
test <- test[,-1]
test <- t(test/255)
test.array <- test
```

```
dim(test.array) <- c(28, 28, 1, ncol(test))

preds3 <- predict(model2, test.array)
dfPreds3 <- as.data.frame(t(preds3))
# res is a data frame with our predictions after train data augmentation,
# i.e. 4200 rows
res$pred.label2 <- 0
for (i in 1:nrow(res))
{
    sum_r <- dfPreds3[((i-1)*3)+1,] +
             dfPreds3[((i-1)*3)+2,] + dfPreds3[(i*3),]
    res[i,"pred.label2"] <- max.col(sum_r)-1
}
accuracy3 <- sum(res$test.y == res$pred.label2) / nrow(res)
The accuracy of our CNN model with augmented train data and Test Time
Augmentation (TTA) is 0.9895238.
```

Doing this, we get predictions for 12,600 rows (*4,200 x 3*). The for loop runs through 4,200 times and takes 3 records at a time, calculating the average accuracy. The increase in accuracy over the accuracy using augmented training data is small, from 0.9885714 to 0.9895238, which is approx. 0.1% (4 rows). We can look at the effect of TTA in the following code:

```
tta_incorrect <- nrow(res[res$test.y != res$pred.label2 & res$test.y ==
res$pred.label,])
tta <- res[res$test.y == res$pred.label2 & res$test.y !=
res$pred.label,c("pred.label","pred.label2")]

Number of rows where Test Time Augmentation (TTA) changed the prediction to
the correct value 9 (nrow(tta)).
Number of rows where Test Time Augmentation (TTA) changed the prediction to
the incorrect value 5 (tta_incorrect).

tta
##      pred.label pred.label2
## 39            9           4
## 268           9           4
## 409           9           4
## 506           8           6
## 1079          2           3
## 1146          7           2
## 3163          4           9
## 3526          4           2
## 3965          2           8
```

This table shows the 9 rows where the test time augmentation was correct and the previous model was wrong. We can see three cases where the previous model (`pred.model`) predicted 9 and the test time augmentation model correctly predicted 4. Although test time augmentation did not significantly increase our accuracy in this case, it can make a difference in other computer vision tasks.

Using data augmentation in deep learning libraries

We implemented data augmentation using R packages and it took a long time to generate our augmented data. It was useful for demonstration purposes, but MXNet and Keras support data augmentation functions. In MXNet, there are a range of functions in `mx.image.*` to do this (`https://mxnet.incubator.apache.org/tutorials/python/data_augmentation.html`). In Keras, this is in `keras.preprocessing.*` (`https://keras.io/preprocessing/image/`), which applies these automatically to your models. In `Chapter 11`, *The Next Level in Deep Learning*, we show how to apply data augmentation using Keras.

Tuning hyperparameters

All machine learning algorithms have hyper-parameters or settings that can change how they operate. These hyper-parameters can improve the accuracy of a model or reduce the training time. We have seen some of these hyper-parameters in previous chapters, particularly `Chapter 3`, *Deep Learning Fundamentals*, where we looked at the hyper-parameters that can be set in the `mx.model.FeedForward.create` function. The techniques in this section can help us find better values for the hyper-parameters.

Selecting hyper-parameters is not a magic bullet; if the raw data quality is poor or if there is not enough data to support training, then tuning hyper-parameters will only get you so far. In these cases, either acquiring additional variables/features that can be used as predictors and/or additional cases may be required.

Grid search

For more information on tuning hyper-parameters, see Bengio, Y. (2012), particularly Section 3, *Hyperparameters*, which discusses the selection and characteristics of various hyper-parameters. Aside from manual trial and error, two other approaches for improving hyper-parameters are grid searches and random searches. In a grid search, several values for hyper-parameters are specified and all possible combinations are tried. This is perhaps easiest to see. In R, we can use the `expand.grid()` function to create all possible combinations of variables:

```
expand.grid(
  layers=c(1,4),
  lr=c(0.01,0.1,0.5,1.0),
  l1=c(0.1,0.5))
    layers    lr    l1
1        1  0.01   0.1
2        4  0.01   0.1
3        1  0.10   0.1
4        4  0.10   0.1
5        1  0.50   0.1
6        4  0.50   0.1
7        1  1.00   0.1
8        4  1.00   0.1
9        1  0.01   0.5
10       4  0.01   0.5
11       1  0.10   0.5
12       4  0.10   0.5
13       1  0.50   0.5
14       4  0.50   0.5
15       1  1.00   0.5
16       4  1.00   0.5
```

Grid searching is effective when there are only a few values for a few hyper-parameters. However, when there are many values for some or many hyper-parameters, it quickly becomes unfeasible. For example, even with only two values for each of eight hyper-parameters, there are $2^8 = 256$ combinations, which quickly becomes computationally impracticable. Also, if the interactions between hyper-parameters and model performance are small, then using grid search is an inefficient approach.

Random search

An alternative approach to hyper-parameter selection is searching through random sampling. Rather than pre-specifying all of the values to try and create all possible combinations, one can randomly sample values for the parameters, fit a model, store the results, and repeat. To get a very large sample size, this too would be computationally demanding, but you can specify just how many different models you are willing to run. Therefore this approach gives you a spread over the combination of hyper-parameters.

For random sampling, all that need to be specified are values to randomly sample, or distributions to randomly draw from. Typically, some limits would also be set. For example, although a model could theoretically have any integer number of layers, some reasonable number (such as 1 to 10) is used rather than sampling integers from 1 to a billion.

To perform random sampling, we will write a function that takes a seed and then randomly samples a number of hyper-parameters, stores the sampled parameters, runs the model, and returns the results. Even though we are doing a random search to try and find better values, we are not sampling from every possible hyper-parameter. Many remain fixed at values we specify or their defaults.

For some hyper-parameters, specifying how to randomly sample values can take a bit of work. For example, when using dropout for regularization, it is common to have a relatively smaller amount of dropout for early hidden layers (0%-20%) and a higher amount for later hidden layers (50%-80%). Choosing the right distributions allows us to encode this prior information into our random search. The following code plots the density of two beta distributions, and the results are shown in *Figure 6.5*:

```
par(mfrow = c(2, 1))
plot(
  seq(0, .5, by = .001),
  dbeta(seq(0, .5, by = .001), 1, 12),
  type = "l", xlab = "x", ylab = "Density",
  main = "Density of a beta(1, 12)")

plot(
  seq(0, 1, by = .001)/2,
  dbeta(seq(0, 1, by = .001), 1.5, 1),
  type = "l", xlab = "x", ylab = "Density",
  main = "Density of a beta(1.5, 1) / 2")
```

By sampling from these distributions, we can ensure that our search focuses on small proportions of dropout for the early hidden layers, and in the **0** to **0.50** range for the hidden neurons with a tendency to oversample from values closer to **0.50**:

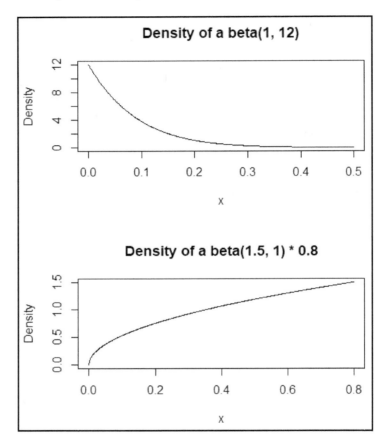

Figure 6.5: Using the beta distribution to select hyperparameters

Use case—using LIME for interpretability

Deep learning models are known to be difficult to interpret. Some approaches to model interpretability, including LIME, allow us to gain some insights into how the model came to its conclusions. Before we demonstrate LIME, I will show how different data distributions and / or data leakage can cause problems when building deep learning models. We will reuse the deep learning churn model from Chapter 4, *Training Deep Prediction Models*, but we are going to make one change to the data. We are going to introduce a bad variable that is highly correlated to the *y* value. We will only include this variable in the data used to train and evaluate the model. A separate test set from the original data will be kept to represent the data the model will see in production, this will not have the bad variable in it. The creation of this bad variable could simulate two possible scenarios we spoke about earlier:

- **Different data distributions**: The bad variable does exist in the data that the model sees in production, but it has a different distribution which means the model does not perform as expected.
- **Data leakage**: Our bad variable is used to train and evaluate the model, but when the model is used in production, this variable is not available, so we assign it a zero value, which also means the model does not perform as expected.

The code for this example is in Chapter6/binary_predict_lime.R. We will not cover the deep learning model in depth again, so go back to Chapter 4, *Training Deep Prediction Models*, if you need a refresher on how it works. We are going to make two changes to the model code:

- We will split the data into three parts: a train, validate, and test set. The train split is used to train the model, the validate set is used to evaluate the model when it is trained, and the test set represents the data that the model sees in production.
- We will create the bad_var variable, and include it in the train and validation set, but not in the test set.

Here is the code to split the data and create the bad_var variable:

```
# add feature (bad_var) that is highly correlated to the variable to be
predicted
dfData$bad_var <- 0
dfData[dfData$Y_categ==1,]$bad_var <- 1
dfData[sample(nrow(dfData), 0.02*nrow(dfData)),]$bad_var <- 0
dfData[sample(nrow(dfData), 0.02*nrow(dfData)),]$bad_var <- 1
table(dfData$Y_categ,dfData$bad_var)
        0    1
  0  1529   33
```

```
   1    46 2325
cor(dfData$Y_categ,dfData$bad_var)
[1] 0.9581345

nobs <- nrow(dfData)
train <- sample(nobs, 0.8*nobs)
validate <- sample(setdiff(seq_len(nobs), train), 0.1*nobs)
test <- setdiff(setdiff(seq_len(nobs), train),validate)
predictorCols <- colnames(dfData)[!(colnames(dfData) %in%
c("CUST_CODE","Y_numeric","Y_categ"))]

# remove columns with zero variance in train-set
predictorCols <- predictorCols[apply(dfData[train, predictorCols], 2, var,
na.rm=TRUE) != 0]

# for our test data, set the bad_var to zero
# our test dataset is not from the same distribution
# as the data used to train and evaluate the model
dfData[test,]$bad_var <- 0

# look at all our predictor variables and
# see how they correlate with the y variable
corr <- as.data.frame(cor(dfData[,c(predictorCols,"Y_categ")]))
corr <- corr[order(-corr$Y_categ),]
old.par <- par(mar=c(7,4,3,1))

barplot(corr[2:11,]$Y_categ,names.arg=row.names(corr)[2:11],
        main="Feature Correlation to target variable",cex.names=0.8,las=2)
par(old.par)
```

Our new variable is highly correlated with our y variable at 0.958. We also created a bar plot of the most highly correlated features to the y variable, and we can see that correlation between this new variable and the y variable is much higher than correlation between the other variables and the y variable. If a feature is very highly correlated to the y variable, then this is usually a sign that something is wrong in the data preparation. It also indicates that a machine learning solution is not required because a simple mathematical formula will be able to predict the outcome variable. For a real project, this variable should not be included in the model. Here is the graph with the features that are most highly correlated with the y variable, the correlation of the bad_var variable is over 0.9:

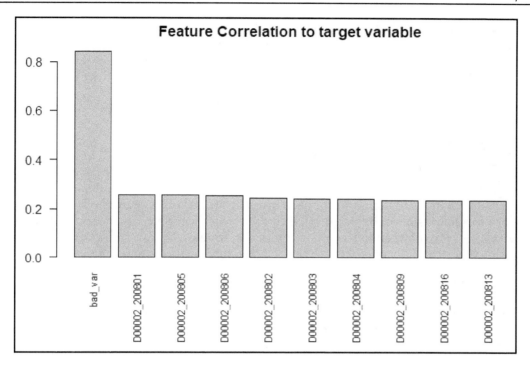

Figure 6.6: The top 10 correlations from feature to target variable

Before we go ahead and build the model, notice how we set this new feature to zero for the test set. Our test set in this example actually represents the data that the model will see when it is production, so we set it to zero to represent either a different data distribution or a data leakage problem. Here is the code that shows how the model performs on the validation set and on the test set:

```
#### Verifying the model using LIME

# compare performance on validation and test set
print(sprintf(" Deep Learning Model accuracy on validate (expected in
production) = %1.2f%%",acc_v))
[1] " Deep Learning Model accuracy on validate (expected in production) =
90.08%"
print(sprintf(" Deep Learning Model accuracy in (actual in production) =
%1.2f%%",acc_t))
[1] " Deep Learning Model accuracy in (actual in production) = 66.50%"
```

The validation set here represents the data used to evaluate the model when it is being built, while the test set represents the future production data. The accuracy on the validation set is over 90%, but the accuracy on the test set is less than 70%. This shows how different data distributions and/or data leakage problems can cause over-estimations of model accuracy.

Model interpretability with LIME

LIME stands for **Local Interpretable Model-Agnostic Explanations**. LIME can explain the predictions of any machine learning classifier, not just deep learning models. It works by making small changes to the input for each instance and trying to map the local decision boundary for that instance. By doing so, it can see which variable has the most influence for that instance. It is explained in the following paper: Ribeiro, Marco Tulio, Sameer Singh, and Carlos Guestrin. *Why should I trust you?: Explaining the predictions of any classifier. Proceedings of the 22nd ACM SIGKDD international conference on knowledge discovery and data mining. ACM, 2016.*

Let's look at using LIME to analyze the model from the previous section. We have to set up some boilerplate code to interface the MXNet and LIME structures, and then we can create LIME objects based on our training data:

```
# apply LIME to MXNet deep learning model
model_type.MXFeedForwardModel <- function(x, ...)
{return("classification")}
predict_model.MXFeedForwardModel <- function(m, newdata, ...)
{
  pred <- predict(m, as.matrix(newdata),array.layout="rowmajor")
  pred <- as.data.frame(t(pred))
  colnames(pred) <- c("No","Yes")
  return(pred)
}
explain <- lime(dfData[train, predictorCols], model, bin_continuous =
FALSE)
```

We then can pass in the first 10 records in the test set and create a plot to show feature importance:

```
val_first_10 <- validate[1:10]

explaination <- lime::explain(dfData[val_first_10,
predictorCols],explainer=explain,
                        n_labels=1,n_features=3)
plot_features(explaination) + labs(title="Churn Model - variable
explanation")
```

This will produce the following plot, which shows the features that were most influential in the model predictions:

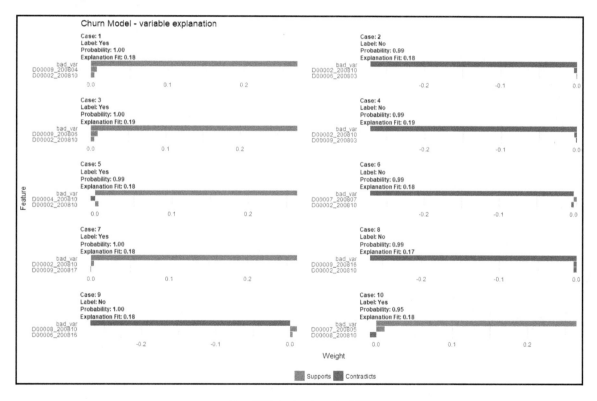

Figure 6.7: Feature importance using LIME

Note how, in each case, the `bad_var` variable is the most important variable and its scale is much larger than the other features. This matches what we saw in *Figure 6.6*. The following graph shows the heatmap visualization for feature combinations for the 10 test cases:

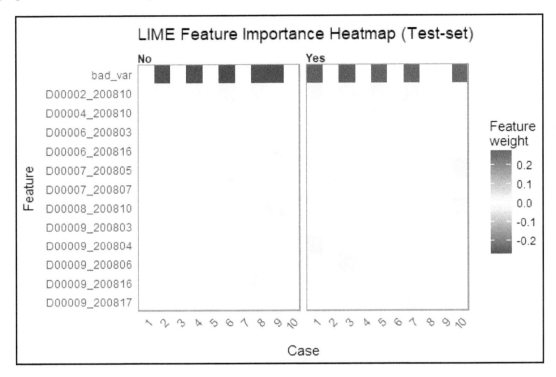

Figure 6.8: Feature heatmap using LIME

This example shows how to apply LIME to an existing deep learning model trained with MXNet to visualize which features were the most important for some of the predictions using the model. We can see in Figures 6.7 and 6.8 that a single feature was almost completely responsible for predicting the y variable, which is an indication that there is an issue with different data distributions and/or data leakage problems. In practice, such a variable should be excluded from the model.

As a comparison, if we train a model without this field, and plot the feature importance again, we see that one feature does not dominate:

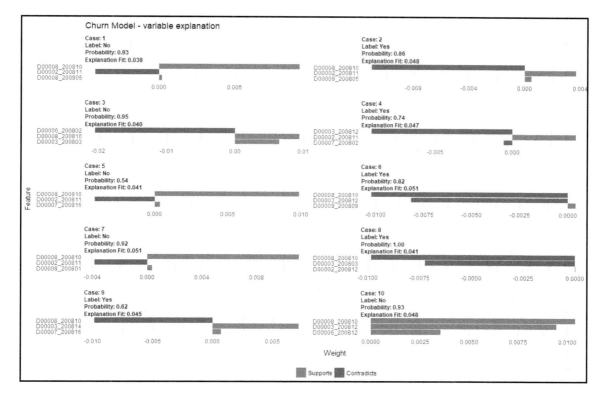

Figure 6.9: Feature importance using LIME (without the `bad_var` feature)

There is not one feature that is a number 1 feature, the explanation fit is 0.05 compared to 0.18 in *Figure 6.7*, and the significance bars for the three variables are on a similar scale. The following graph shows the feature heatmap using LIME:

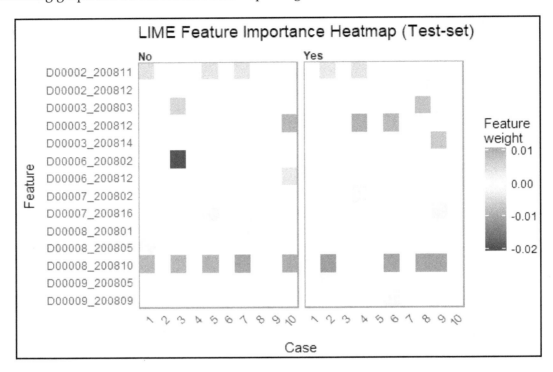

Figure 6.10: Feature heatmap using LIME (without the bad_var feature)

Again, this plot shows us that more than one feature is being used. We can see that the scale of legend for the feature weights in the preceding graph is from 0.01 - 0.02. In *Figure 6.8*, the scale of legend for the feature weights was -0.2 - 0.2, indicating that some features (just one, actually) are dominating the model.

Summary

This chapter covered topics that are critical to success in deep learning projects. These included the different types of evaluation metric that can be used to evaluate the model. We looked at some issues that can come up in data preparation, including if you only have a small amount of data to train on and how to create different splits in the data, that is, how to create proper train, test, and validation datasets. We looked at two important issues that can cause the model to perform poorly in production, different data distributions, and data leakage. We saw how data augmentation can be used to improve an existing model by creating artificial data and looked at tuning hyperparameters in order to improve the performance of a deep learning model. We closed the chapter by examining a use case where we simulated a problem with different data distributions/data leakage and used LIME to interpret an existing deep learning model.

Some of the concepts in this chapter may seem somewhat theoretical; however they are absolutely critical to the success of machine learning projects! Many books cover this material toward the end, but it is included in this book at a relatively early stage to signify its importance.

In the next chapter, we are going to look at using deep learning for **Natural Language Processing** (**NLP**), or text data. Using deep learning for text data is more efficient, simpler, and often outperforms traditional NLP approaches.

7
Natural Language Processing Using Deep Learning

This chapter will demonstrate how to use deep learning for **natural language processing** (**NLP**). NLP is the processing of human language text. NLP is a broad term for a number of different tasks involving text data, which include (but are not limited to) the following:

- **Document classification**: Classifying documents into different categories based on their subject
- **Named entity recognition**: Extracting key information from documents, for example, people, organizations, and locations
- **Sentiment analysis**: Classifying comments, tweets, or reviews as positive or negative sentiment
- **Language translation**: Translating text data from one language to another
- **Part of speech tagging**: Assigning the type to each word in a document, which is usually used in conjunction with another task

In this chapter, we will look at document classification, which is probably the most common NLP technique. This chapter follows a different structure to previous chapters, as we will be looking at a single use case (text classification) but applying multiple approaches to it. This chapter will cover:

- How to perform text classification using traditional machine learning techniques
- Word vectors
- Comparing traditional text classification and deep learning
- Advanced deep learning text classification including 1D convolutionals, RNNs, LSTMs and GRUs

Document classification

This chapter will be looking at text classification using Keras. The dataset we will use is included in the Keras library. As we have done in previous chapters, we will use traditional machine learning techniques to create a benchmark before applying a deep learning algorithm. The reason for this is to show how deep learning models perform against other techniques.

The Reuters dataset

We will use the Reuters dataset, which can be accessed through a function in the Keras library. This dataset has 11,228 records with 46 categories. To see more information about this dataset, run the following code:

```
library(keras)
?dataset_reuters
```

Although the Reuters dataset can be accessed from Keras, it is not in a format that can be used by other machine learning algorithms. Instead of the actual words, the text data is a list of word indices. We will write a short script (Chapter7/create_reuters_data.R) that downloads the data and the lookup index file and creates a data frame of the y variable and the text string. We will then save the train and test data into two separate files. Here is the first part of the code that creates the file with the train data:

```
library(keras)

# the reuters dataset is in Keras
c(c(x_train, y_train), c(x_test, y_test)) %<-% dataset_reuters()
word_index <- dataset_reuters_word_index()

# convert the word index into a dataframe
idx<-unlist(word_index)
dfWords<-as.data.frame(idx)
dfWords$word <- row.names(dfWords)
row.names(dfWords)<-NULL
dfWords <- dfWords[order(dfWords$idx),]

# create a dataframe for the train data
# for each row in the train data, we have a list of index values
# for words in the dfWords dataframe
dfTrain <- data.frame(y_train)
dfTrain$sentence <- ""
colnames(dfTrain)[1] <- "y"
for (r in 1:length(x_train))
```

```
{
  row <- x_train[r]
  line <- ""
  for (i in 1:length(row[[1]]))
  {
     index <- row[[1]][i]
     if (index >= 3)
        line <- paste(line,dfWords[index-3,]$word)
  }
  dfTrain[r,]$sentence <- line
  if ((r %% 100) == 0)
     print (r)
}
write.table(dfTrain,"../data/reuters.train.tab",sep="\t",row.names = FALSE)
```

The second part of the code is similar, it creates the file with the test data:

```
# create a dataframe for the test data
# for each row in the train data, we have a list of index values
# for words in the dfWords dataframe
dfTest <- data.frame(y_test)
dfTest$sentence <- ""
colnames(dfTest)[1] <- "y"
for (r in 1:length(x_test))
{
  row <- x_test[r]
  line <- ""
  for (i in 1:length(row[[1]]))
  {
     index <- row[[1]][i]
     if (index >= 3)
        line <- paste(line,dfWords[index-3,]$word)
  }
  dfTest[r,]$sentence <- line
  if ((r %% 100) == 0)
     print (r)
}
write.table(dfTest,"../data/reuters.test.tab",sep="\t",row.names = FALSE)
```

This creates two files called `../data/reuters.train.tab` and `../data/reuters.test.tab`. If we open the first file, this is the first data row. This sentence is a normal English sentence:

y	sentence
3	mcgrath rentcorp said as a result of its december acquisition of space co it expects earnings per share in 1987 of 1 15 to 1 30 dlrs per share up from 70 cts in 1986 the company said pretax net should rise to nine to 10 mln dlrs from six mln dlrs in 1986 and rental operation revenues to 19 to 22 mln dlrs from 12 5 mln dlrs it said cash flow per share this year should be 2 50 to three dlrs reuter 3

Now that we have the data in tabular format, we can use *traditional* NLP machine learning methods to create a classification model. When we merge the train and test sets and look at the distribution of the y variable, we can see that there are 46 classes, but that the number of instances in each class are not the same:

```
> table(y_train)
    0    1    2    3    4    5    6    7    8    9   10   11   12   13   14   15   16   17
   67  537   94 3972 2423   22   62   19  177  126  154  473   62  209   28   29  543   51

   18   19   20   21   22   23   24   25   26   27   28   29   30   31   32   33   34   35
   86  682  339  127   22   53   81  123   32   19   58   23   57   52   42   16   57   16

   36   37   38   39   40   41   42   43   44   45
   60   21   22   29   46   38   16   27   17   19
```

For our test set, we will create a binary classification problem. Our task will be to identify the news snippets where the classification is 3 from all other records. When we change the labels, our y distribution changes to the following:

```
y_train[y_train!=3] <- 0
y_train[y_train==3] <- 1
table(y_train)
    0    1
 7256 3972
```

Traditional text classification

Our first NLP model will use traditional NLP techniques, that is, not deep learning. For the rest of this chapter, when we use the term traditional NLP, we mean approaches that do not use deep learning. The most used method for NLP in traditional NLP classification uses a *bag-of-words* approach.

We will also use a set of hyperparameters and machine learning algorithms to maximize accuracy:

- **Feature generation**: The features can be term frequency, tf-idf, or binary flags
- **Preprocessing**: We preprocess text data by stemming the words
- **Remove stop-words**: We treat the feature creation, stop-words, and stemming options as hyperparameters
- **Machine learning algorithm**: The script applies three machine learning algorithms to the data (Naive Bayes, SVM, neural network, and random forest)

We train 48 machine learning algorithms on the data in total, and evaluate which model is best. The script for this code is in the Chapter7/classify_text.R folder. The code does not contain any deep learning models, so feel free to skip it if you want. First we load in the necessary libraries and create a function that creates a set of text classification models for a combination of hyperparameters on multiple machine learning algorithms:

```
library(tm)
require(nnet)
require(kernlab)
library(randomForest)
library(e1071)
options(digits=4)

TextClassification <-function (w,stem=0,stop=0,verbose=1)
{
  df <- read.csv("../data/reuters.train.tab", sep="\t", stringsAsFactors =
FALSE)
  df2 <- read.csv("../data/reuters.test.tab", sep="\t", stringsAsFactors =
FALSE)
  df <- rbind(df,df2)

  # df <- df[df$y %in% c(3,4),]
  # df$y <- df$y-3
  df[df$y!=3,]$y<-0
  df[df$y==3,]$y<-1
  rm(df2)

  colnames(df)[2] <- "text"
  df$doc_id <- rownames(df)
  corpus <- Corpus(DataframeSource(data.frame(df[, c(3,2)])))
  corpus <- tm_map(corpus, content_transformer(tolower))
  # hyperparameters
  if (stop==1)
    corpus <- tm_map(corpus, function(x) removeWords(x,
stopwords("english")))
  if (stem==1)
```

```
    corpus <- tm_map(corpus, stemDocument)
if (w=="tfidf")
    dtm <- DocumentTermMatrix(corpus,control=list(weighting=weightTfIdf))
else if (w=="tf")
    dtm <- DocumentTermMatrix(corpus,control=list(weighting=weightTf))
else if (w=="binary")
    dtm <- DocumentTermMatrix(corpus,control=list(weighting=weightBin))
# keep terms that cover 95% of the data
dtm2<-removeSparseTerms(dtm, 0.95)
m <- as.matrix(dtm2)
remove(dtm,dtm2,corpus)
data<-data.frame(m)
data<-cbind(df[, 1],data)
colnames(data)[1]="y"
# create train, test sets for machine learning
seed <- 42
set.seed(seed)
nobs <- nrow(data)
sample <- train <- sample(nrow(data), 0.8*nobs)
validate <- NULL
test <- setdiff(setdiff(seq_len(nrow(data)), train), validate)
```

Now that we have created a sparse data-frame, we will use 4 different machine learning algorithms on the data: Naive Bayes, SVM, a neural network model and a random forest model. We use 4 machine learning algorithms because, as you see below, the code to call a machine learning algorithm is small compared to the code needed to create the data in the previous section and the code needed to the the NLP. It is almost always a good idea to run multiple machine learning algorithms when possible because no machine learning algorithm is consistently the best.

```
# create Naive Bayes model
nb <- naiveBayes(as.factor(y) ~., data=data[sample,])
pr <- predict(nb, newdata=data[test, ])
# Generate the confusion matrix showing counts.
tab<-table(na.omit(data[test, ])$y, pr,
           dnn=c("Actual", "Predicted"))
if (verbose) print (tab)
nb_acc <- 100*sum(diag(tab))/length(test)
if (verbose) print(sprintf("Naive Bayes accuracy = %1.2f%%",nb_acc))
# create SVM model
if (verbose) print ("SVM")
if (verbose) print (Sys.time())
ksvm <- ksvm(as.factor(y) ~ .,
             data=data[sample,],
             kernel="rbfdot",
             prob.model=TRUE)
if (verbose) print (Sys.time())
```

```
pr <- predict(ksvm, newdata=na.omit(data[test, ]))
# Generate the confusion matrix showing counts.
tab<-table(na.omit(data[test, ])$y, pr,
           dnn=c("Actual", "Predicted"))
if (verbose) print (tab)
svm_acc <- 100*sum(diag(tab))/length(test)
if (verbose) print(sprintf("SVM accuracy = %1.2f%%",svm_acc))
# create Neural Network model
rm(pr,tab)
set.seed(199)
if (verbose) print ("Neural Network")
if (verbose) print (Sys.time())
nnet <- nnet(as.factor(y) ~ .,
             data=data[sample,],
             size=10, skip=TRUE, MaxNWts=10000, trace=FALSE, maxit=100)
if (verbose) print (Sys.time())
pr <- predict(nnet, newdata=data[test, ], type="class")
# Generate the confusion matrix showing counts.
tab<-table(data[test, ]$y, pr,
           dnn=c("Actual", "Predicted"))
if (verbose) print (tab)
nn_acc <- 100*sum(diag(tab))/length(test)
if (verbose) print(sprintf("Neural Network accuracy = %1.2f%%",nn_acc))
# create Random Forest model
rm(pr,tab)
if (verbose) print ("Random Forest")
if (verbose) print (Sys.time())
rf_model<-randomForest(as.factor(y) ~., data=data[sample,])
if (verbose) print (Sys.time())
pr <- predict(rf_model, newdata=data[test, ], type="class")
# Generate the confusion matrix showing counts.
tab<-table(data[test, ]$y, pr,
           dnn=c("Actual", "Predicted"))
if (verbose) print (tab)
rf_acc <- 100*sum(diag(tab))/length(test)
if (verbose) print(sprintf("Random Forest accuracy = %1.2f%%",rf_acc))
dfParams <- data.frame(w,stem,stop)
dfParams$nb_acc <- nb_acc
dfParams$svm_acc <- svm_acc
dfParams$nn_acc <- nn_acc
dfParams$rf_acc <- rf_acc
return(dfParams)
}
```

We now call the function with different hyperparameters in the following code:

```r
dfResults <- TextClassification("tfidf",verbose=1) # tf-idf, no stemming
dfResults<-rbind(dfResults,TextClassification("tf",verbose=1)) # tf, no
stemming
dfResults<-rbind(dfResults,TextClassification("binary",verbose=1)) #
binary, no stemming

dfResults<-rbind(dfResults,TextClassification("tfidf",1,verbose=1)) # tf-
idf, stemming
dfResults<-rbind(dfResults,TextClassification("tf",1,verbose=1)) # tf,
stemming
dfResults<-rbind(dfResults,TextClassification("binary",1,verbose=1)) #
binary, stemming

dfResults<-rbind(dfResults,TextClassification("tfidf",0,1,verbose=1)) # tf-
idf, no stemming, remove stopwords
dfResults<-rbind(dfResults,TextClassification("tf",0,1,verbose=1)) # tf, no
stemming, remove stopwords
dfResults<-rbind(dfResults,TextClassification("binary",0,1,verbose=1)) #
binary, no stemming, remove stopwords

dfResults<-rbind(dfResults,TextClassification("tfidf",1,1,verbose=1)) # tf-
idf, stemming, remove stopwords
dfResults<-rbind(dfResults,TextClassification("tf",1,1,verbose=1)) # tf,
stemming, remove stopwords
dfResults<-rbind(dfResults,TextClassification("binary",1,1,verbose=1)) #
binary, stemming, remove stopwords

dfResults[, "best_acc"] <- apply(dfResults[,
c("nb_acc","svm_acc","nn_acc","rf_acc")], 1, max)
dfResults <- dfResults[order(-dfResults$best_acc),]
dfResults

strResult <- sprintf("Best accuracy score was %1.2f%%. Hyper-parameters:
",dfResults[1,"best_acc"])
strResult <- paste(strResult,dfResults[1,"w"],",",sep="")
strResult <- paste(strResult,
                    ifelse(dfResults[1,"stem"] == 0,"no
stemming,","stemming,"))
strResult <- paste(strResult,
                    ifelse(dfResults[1,"stop"] == 0,"no stop word
processing,","removed stop words,"))
if (dfResults[1,"best_acc"] == dfResults[1,"nb_acc"]){
  strResult <- paste(strResult,"Naive Bayes model")
} else if (dfResults[1,"best_acc"] == dfResults[1,"svm_acc"]){
  strResult <- paste(strResult,"SVM model")
} else if (dfResults[1,"best_acc"] == dfResults[1,"nn_acc"]){
```

```
      strResult <- paste(strResult,"Neural Network model")
    }else if (dfResults[1,"best_acc"] == dfResults[1,"rf_acc"]){
      strResult <- paste(strResult,"Random Forest model")
    }

    print (strResult)
```

For each combination of hyperparameters, the script saves the best score from the four machine learning algorithms in the `best_acc` field. Once the training is complete, we can look at the results:

```
> dfResults
   w stem stop nb_acc svm_acc nn_acc rf_acc best_acc
12 binary   1    1   86.06  95.24  90.52  94.26   95.24
9  binary   0    1   87.71  95.15  90.52  93.72   95.15
10 tfidf    1    1   91.99  95.15  91.05  94.17   95.15
3  binary   0    0   85.98  95.01  90.29  93.99   95.01
6  binary   1    0   84.59  95.01  90.34  93.63   95.01
7  tfidf    0    1   91.27  94.43  94.79  93.54   94.79
11 tf       1    1   77.47  94.61  92.30  94.08   94.61
4  tfidf    1    0   92.25  94.57  90.96  93.99   94.57
5  tf       1    0   75.11  94.52  93.46  93.90   94.52
1  tfidf    0    0   91.54  94.26  91.59  93.23   94.26
2  tf       0    0   75.82  94.03  91.54  93.59   94.03
8  tf       0    1   78.14  94.03  91.63  93.68   94.03

> print (strResult)
[1] "Best accuracy score was 95.24%. Hyper-parameters: binary, stemming,
removed stop words, SVM model"
```

The results are ordered by best results, so here we can can see that our best accuracy overall was `95.24%`. The reason for training so many models is that there is no right formula for traditional NLP tasks that's work for most cases, so you should try multiple combinations of preprocessing and different algorithms, as we have done here. For example, if you searched for an example online on text classification, you could find an example that would suggest to use tf-idf and naive bayes. Here, we can see that it is one of the worst performers.

Deep learning text classification

The previous code ran 48 traditional machine learning algorithms over the data across a number of different hyperparameters. Now, it is time to see if we can find a deep learning model that outperforms them. The first deep learning model is in `Chapter7/classify_keras1.R`. The first part of the code loads the data. The tokens in the reuters dataset are ranked by how often they occur (in the training set) and the `max_features` parameter controls how many distinct tokens will be used in the model. We will use all the tokens by setting this to the number of entries in the word index. The maxlen parameter controls the length of the input sequences to the model, they must all be the same length. If the sequences are longer than the maxlen variable, they are truncated, if they are shorter, then padding is added to make the length=maxlen. We set this to 250, which means our deep learning model expects 250 tokens as input per instance:

```
library(keras)

set.seed(42)
word_index <- dataset_reuters_word_index()
max_features <- length(word_index)
maxlen <- 250
skip_top = 0

reuters <- dataset_reuters(num_words = max_features,skip_top = skip_top)
c(c(x_train, y_train), c(x_test, y_test)) %<-% reuters
x_train <- pad_sequences(x_train, maxlen = maxlen)
x_test <- pad_sequences(x_test, maxlen = maxlen)
x_train <- rbind(x_train,x_test)
y_train <- c(y_train,y_test)
table(y_train)

y_train[y_train!=3] <- 0
y_train[y_train==3] <- 1
table(y_train)
```

The next section of code builds the model:

```
model <- keras_model_sequential() %>%
  layer_embedding(input_dim = max_features, output_dim = 16,input_length =
maxlen) %>%
  layer_flatten() %>%
  layer_dropout(rate = 0.25) %>%
  layer_dense(units = 16, activation = 'relu') %>%
  layer_dropout(rate = 0.5) %>%
  layer_dense(units = 16, activation = 'relu') %>%
  layer_dropout(rate = 0.5) %>%
  layer_dense(units = 1, activation = "sigmoid")
```

```
model %>% compile(
  optimizer = "rmsprop",
  loss = "binary_crossentropy",
  metrics = c("acc")
)
summary(model)
history <- model %>% fit(
  x_train, y_train,
  epochs = 5,
  batch_size = 32,
  validation_split = 0.2
)
```

The only thing in this code that we have not seen before is `layer_embedding`. This takes the input and creates an embedding layer, which is a vector of numbers for each input token. We will describe word vectors in more detail in the next section. Another thing to note is that we don't preprocess the text or create any features – we just feed in the word indices and let the deep learning algorithm make sense of it. Here is the output of the script as the model is trained:

```
Train on 8982 samples, validate on 2246 samples
Epoch 1/5
8982/8982 [==============================] - 3s 325us/step - loss: 0.4953 -
acc: 0.7674 - val_loss: 0.2332 - val_acc: 0.9274
Epoch 2/5
8982/8982 [==============================] - 3s 294us/step - loss: 0.2771 -
acc: 0.9235 - val_loss: 0.1990 - val_acc: 0.9394
Epoch 3/5
8982/8982 [==============================] - 3s 297us/step - loss: 0.2150 -
acc: 0.9414 - val_loss: 0.1975 - val_acc: 0.9497
Epoch 4/5
8982/8982 [==============================] - 3s 282us/step - loss: 0.1912 -
acc: 0.9515 - val_loss: 0.2118 - val_acc: 0.9461
Epoch 5/5
8982/8982 [==============================] - 3s 280us/step - loss: 0.1703 -
acc: 0.9584 - val_loss: 0.2490 - val_acc: 0.9466
```

Despite the simplicity of the code, we get 94.97% accuracy on the validation set after just three epochs, which is only 0.27% less than the best traditional NLP approach. Now, it is time to discuss word vectors in more detail.

Word vectors

Instead of representing our text data as a bag of words, deep learning represents them as word vectors or embeddings. A vector/embedding is nothing more than a series of numbers that represent a word. You may have already heard of popular word vectors such as Word2Vec and GloVe. The Word2vec model was invented by Google (*Mikolov, Tomas, et al. Efficient estimation of word representations in vector space. arXiv preprint arXiv:1301.3781 (2013)*). In their paper, they provide examples of how these word vectors have somewhat mysterious and magical properties. If you take the vector of the word "*King*", subtract the vector of the word "*Man*", add the vector of the word "*Man*", then you get a value close to the vector of the word "*Queen*". Other similarities also exist, for example:

- *vector('King') - vector('Man') + vector('Woman') = vector('Queen')*
- *vector('Paris') - vector('France') + vector('Italy') = vector('Rome')*

If this is the first time you have seen Word2Vec, then you are probably somewhat amazed by this. I know I was! These examples imply that word vectors *understand* language, so have we solved natural language processing? The answer is no – we are very far away from this. Vectors are learned from collections of text documents. In fact, the very first layer in our deep learning model is an embedding layer which creates a vector space for the words. Let's look at some of the code from `Chapter7/classify_keras.R` again:

```
library(keras)

word_index <- dataset_reuters_word_index()
max_features <- length(word_index)
max_features
[1] 30979
.......

model <- keras_model_sequential() %>%
  layer_embedding(input_dim = max_features, output_dim = 16,input_length =
maxlen) %>%
.......

summary(model)
```

Layer (type)	Output Shape	Param #
embedding_1 (Embedding)	(None, 150, 16)	495664

`.......`

The value for `max_features` is `30979`, that is, we have `30979` unique features. These features are **tokens**, or words. In the traditional text classification, we had almost the same number of unique tokens (`30538`). The difference between these two numbers is not important; it is due to the different tokenization processes used between the two approaches, that is, how the documents were split into tokens. The embedding layer has `495664` parameters, which is *30,979 x 16*, that is, each unique feature/token is represented by a vector of `16` numbers. The word vectors or embeddings learned by deep learning algorithms will have some of the characteristics described earlier, for example:

- Synonyms (two words that have the same meaning) will have very similar word vectors
- Words from the same semantic collection will be clustered (for example, colors, days of the week, makes of cars, and so on)
- The vector space between related words can signify the relationship between those words (for example, gender for w(King) – w(Queen))

The embedding layer creates word vectors/embeddings based on words and their surrounding words. The word vectors end up having these characteristics because of a simple fact, which can be summarized by a quote from John Firth, an English linguist in 1957:

> *"You shall know a word by the company it keeps."*

The deep learning algorithm learns the vectors for each word by looking at surrounding words and therefore learns some of the context. When it sees the word *King*, some words near this word may indicate gender, for example, The *King* picked up *his* sword. Another sentence could be The *Queen* looked in *her* mirror. The word vectors for *King* and *Queen* have a latent gender component that is learned from the words surrounding *King* and *Queen* in the data. But it is important to realize that the deep learning algorithm has no concept of what gender is, or what type of entities it applies to. Even so, word vectors are a huge improvement over bag-of-word approaches which have no way of identifying relationships between different tokens. Using word vectors also means that we do not have to discard sparse terms. Finally, as the number of unique tokens increases, they are much more efficient to process than bag-of-words approaches.

We will look at embeddings again in `Chapter 9`, *Anomaly Detection and Recommendation Systems*, when we use them in auto-encoders. Now that we have seen some traditional machine learning and deep learning approaches for solving this problem, it is time to compare them in more detail.

Comparing traditional text classification and deep learning

The traditional text classification performed a number of preprocessing steps, including word stemming, stop-word processing, and feature generation (tf-idf, tf or binary). The deep learning text classification did not need this preprocessing. You may have heard various reasons for this previously:

- Deep learning can learn features automatically, so feature creation is not needed
- Deep learning algorithms for NLP tasks requires far less preprocessing than traditional text classification

There is some truth to this, but this does not answer why we need complex feature generation in traditional text classification. A big reason that preprocessing is needed in traditional text classification is to overcome a fundamental problem.

For some traditional NLP approaches (for example, classification), text preprocessing is not just about creating better features. It is also necessary because the bag-of-words representation creates a sparse high-dimensional dataset. Most machine learning algorithms have problems with such datasets, meaning that we have to reduce the dimensionality before applying machine learning algorithms. Proper preprocessing of the text is an essential part of this to ensure that relevant data is not thrown away.

For traditional text classification, we used an approach called **bag-of-words**. This is essentially one-hot encoding each *token* (word). Each column represents a single token, and the value of each cell is one of the following:

- A **tf-idf** (**term frequency, inverse document frequency**) for that token
- The term frequency, that is, the count of how many times that token occurs for that document/instance
- A binary flag, that is, one if the token is in that document/instance; otherwise, it is zero

You may not have heard of *tf-idf* before. It measures the importance of a token by calculating the term frequency (*tf*) of the token in the document (such as how many times it occurs in the document) divided by the log of how many times it appears in the entire corpus (*idf*). The **corpus** is the entire collection of documents. The *tf* part measures how important the token is within a single document, and the *idf* measures how unique the token is among all the documents. If the token appears many times in the document, but also many times in other documents, then it is unlikely to be useful for categorizing documents. If the token appears in only a few documents, then it is a potentially valuable feature for the classification task.

Our traditional text classification approach also used *stemming* and processed *stop-words*. Indeed, our best result in traditional text classification used both approaches. Stemming tries to reduce words to their word stem or root form, which reduces the vocabulary size. It also means that words with the same meaning but with different verb tenses or noun forms are standardized to the same token. Here is an example of stemming. Note that 6/7 of the input words have the same output value:

```
library(corpus)
text <- "love loving lovingly loved lover lovely love"
text_tokens(text, stemmer = "en") # english stemmer
[[1]]
[1] "love" "love" "love" "love" "lover" "love" "love"
```

Stop-words are common words that appear in most documents for a language. They occur so frequently in most documents that they are almost never useful for machine learning. The following example shows the list of stop-words for the English language:

```
library(tm)
> stopwords()
 [1] "i" "me" "my" "myself" "we" "our"
 [7] "ours" "ourselves" "you" "your" "yours" "yourself"
[13] "yourselves" "he" "him" "his" "himself" "she"
[19] "her" "hers" "herself" "it" "its" "itself"
[25] "they" "them" "their" "theirs" "themselves" "what"
.........
```

The final piece we want to cover in traditional NLP is how it deals with sparse terms. Recall from earlier that traditional NLP uses a bag-of-words approach, where each unique token gets an individual column. For a large collection of documents, there will be thousands of unique tokens, and since most tokens will not appear in an individual document, this a very sparse representation, that is, most cells are empty. We can check this by looking at taking some of the code from `classify_text.R`, modifying it slightly, and looking at the `dtm` and `dtm2` variables:

```
library(tm)
df <- read.csv("../data/reuters.train.tab", sep="\t", stringsAsFactors =
FALSE)
df2 <- read.csv("../data/reuters.test.tab", sep="\t", stringsAsFactors =
FALSE)
df <- rbind(df,df2)

df[df$y!=3,]$y<-0
df[df$y==3,]$y<-1
rm(df2)

corpus <- Corpus(DataframeSource(data.frame(df[, 2])))
```

```
corpus <- tm_map(corpus, content_transformer(tolower))

dtm <- DocumentTermMatrix(corpus,control=list(weighting=weightBin))

# keep terms that cover 95% of the data
dtm2<-removeSparseTerms(dtm, 0.95)

dtm
<<DocumentTermMatrix (documents: 11228, terms: 30538)>>
Non-/sparse entries: 768265/342112399
Sparsity : 100%
Maximal term length: 24
Weighting : binary (bin)

dtm2
<<DocumentTermMatrix (documents: 11228, terms: 230)>>
Non-/sparse entries: 310275/2272165
Sparsity : 88%
Maximal term length: 13
Weighting : binary (bin)
```

We can see that our first document-term matrix (dtm) has 11,228 documents and 30,538 unique tokens. In this document-term matrix, only 768,265 (0.22%) cells have values. Most machine learning algorithms would struggle with such a high-dimensionality sparse data frame. If you tried using these machine learning algorithms (for example, SVM, random forest, naive bayes) on a data frame with 30,538 dimensions, they would fail to run in R (I tried!). This is a known problem in traditional NLP, so there is a function (removeSparseTerms) in the NLP libraries to remove sparse terms from the document-term matrix. This removes columns that have the most empty cells. We can see the effect of this, as the second document-term matrix has only 230 unique tokens and 310,275 (12%) cells have values. This dataset is still relatively sparse, but it is in a usable format for machine learning.

This highlights the problem with traditional NLP approaches: the *bag-of-words* approach creates a very sparse high-dimensional dataset which is not usable by machine learning algorithms. Therefore, you need to remove some of the dimensions, and this results in a number of cells with values going from 768,265 to 310,275 in our example. We threw away almost 60% of the data before applying any machine learning! This also explains why text preprocessing, such as stemming and stop-word removal, is used in traditional NLP. Stemming helps to reduce the vocabulary and standardize terms by combining variations of many words into one form.

By combining variations, it means they are more likely to survive the culling of data. We process stop-words for the opposite reason: if we don't remove stop-words, these terms will probably be kept after removing sparse terms. There are 174 terms in the `stopwords()` function in the `tm` package. If the reduced dataset had many of these terms, then they would probably not be useful as predictor variables due to their commonality throughout the documents.

It is also worth noting that this is a very small dataset in NLP terms. We only have 11,228 documents and 30,538 unique tokens. A larger *corpus* (collection of text documents) could have half a million unique tokens. In order to reduce the number of tokens to something that could be processed in R, we would have to throw away a lot more data.

When we use a deep learning approach for NLP, we represent the data as word vectors/embeddings rather than using the bag-of-words approach in traditional NLP. This is much more efficient, so do not have to preprocess data to remove common words, reduce words to a simpler form, or reduce the number of terms before applying the deep learning algorithm. The only thing we do have to do is pick an embedding size and a max length size for the number of tokens we process for each instance. This is needed because deep learning algorithms cannot use variable length sequences as inputs to a layer. When instances have more tokens than the max length, they are truncated and when instances have less tokens than the max length, they are padded.

After all of this, you may be wondering why the deep learning algorithm did not outperform the traditional NLP approach significantly, if the traditional NLP approach throws away 60% of the data. There are a few reasons for this:

- The dataset is small. If we had more data, the deep learning approach would improve at a faster rate than the traditional NLP approach.
- Certain NLP tasks such as document classification and sentiment analysis depend on a very small set of terms. For example, to differentiate between sports news and financial news, maybe 50 selected terms would be sufficient to get over 90% accuracy. Recall that the function to remove sparse terms in the traditional text classification approach – this works because it assumes (correctly) that non-sparse terms will be useful features for the machine learning algorithms.
- We ran 48 machine learning algorithms and only one deep learning approach, which was relatively simple! We will soon come across approaches that beat the traditional NLP approach.

This book has really only touched the surface of traditional NLP approaches. Entire books have been written on the subject. The purpose of looking at these approaches is to show how brittle these approaches can be. The deep learning approach is much simpler to understand and has far fewer settings. It does not involve preprocessing the text or creating features based on weightings such as tf-idf. Even so, our first deep learning approach is not very far away from the best model out of 48 models in traditional text classification.

Advanced deep learning text classification

Our basic deep learning model is much less complex than the traditional machine learning approach, but its performance is not quite as good. This section looks at some advanced techniques for text classification in deep learning. The following sections explain a number of different approaches and focus on code examples rather than heavy deep explanations. If you are interested in more detail, then look at the book *Deep Learning* by Goodfellow, Bengio, and Courville (*Goodfellow, Ian, et al. Deep learning. Vol. 1. Cambridge: MIT Press, 2016.*). Another good reference that covers NLP in deep learning is a book by Yoav Goldberg (*Goldberg, Yoav. Neural network methods for natural language processing*).

1D convolutional neural network model

We have seen that the bag-of-words approach in traditional NLP approaches ignores sentence structure. Consider applying a sentiment analysis task on the four movie reviews in the following table:

Id	sentence	Rating (1=recommended, 0=not recommended)
1	this movie is very good	1
2	this movie is not good	0
3	this movie is not very good	0
4	this movie is not bad	1

If we represent this as a bag of words with term frequency, we will get the following output:

Id	bad	good	is	movie	not	this	very
1	0	1	1	1	0	1	1
2	0	1	1	1	1	1	0
3	0	1	1	1	1	1	1
4	1	0	1	1	1	1	0

In this simple example, we can see some of the problems with a bag-of-words approach, we have lost the relationship between the negation (**not**) and the adjectives (**good, bad**). To work around this problem, traditional NLP could use bigrams, so instead of using single words as tokens, use two words as tokens. Now, for the second example, **not good** is a single token, which makes it more likely that the machine learning algorithm will pick it up. However, we still have a problem with the third example (**not very good**), where we will have tokens for **not very** and **very good**. These are still ambiguous, as **not very** implies negative sentiment, while **very good** implies positive sentiment. We could try higher order n-grams, but this further exacerbates the sparsity problem we saw in the previous section.

Word vectors or embeddings have the same problem. We need some method to handle word sequences. Fortunately, there are types of layers in deep learning algorithms that can handle sequential data. One that we have already seen is convolutional neural networks in Chapter 5, *Image Classification Using Convolutional Neural Networks*. Recall that these are 2D patches that are moved across the image to identify patterns such as a diagonal line or an edge. In a similar manner, we can apply a 1D convolutional neural network across the word vectors. Here is an example of using a 1D convolutional neural network layer for the same text classification problem. The code is in Chapter7/classify_keras2.R. We are only showing the code for the model architecture, because that is the only change from the code in Chapter7/classify_keras1.R:

```
model <- keras_model_sequential() %>%
  layer_embedding(input_dim = max_features, output_dim = 16,input_length =
maxlen) %>%
  layer_dropout(rate = 0.25) %>%
  layer_conv_1d(64,5, activation = "relu") %>%
  layer_dropout(rate = 0.25) %>%
  layer_max_pooling_1d() %>%
  layer_flatten() %>%
  layer_dense(units = 50, activation = 'relu') %>%
  layer_dropout(rate = 0.6) %>%
  layer_dense(units = 1, activation = "sigmoid")
```

We can see that this follows the same pattern that we saw in the image data; we have a convolutional layer followed by a max pooling layer. There are 64 convolutional layers with a length=5, and so these *learn* local patterns in the data. Here is the output from the model's training:

```
Train on 8982 samples, validate on 2246 samples
Epoch 1/5
8982/8982 [==============================] - 13s 1ms/step - loss: 0.3020 -
acc: 0.8965 - val_loss: 0.1909 - val_acc: 0.9470
Epoch 2/5
8982/8982 [==============================] - 13s 1ms/step - loss: 0.1980 -
acc: 0.9498 - val_loss: 0.1816 - val_acc: 0.9537
```

```
Epoch 3/5
8982/8982 [==============================] - 12s 1ms/step - loss: 0.1674 -
acc: 0.9575 - val_loss: 0.2233 - val_acc: 0.9368
Epoch 4/5
8982/8982 [==============================] - 12s 1ms/step - loss: 0.1587 -
acc: 0.9606 - val_loss: 0.1787 - val_acc: 0.9573
Epoch 5/5
8982/8982 [==============================] - 12s 1ms/step - loss: 0.1513 -
acc: 0.9628 - val_loss: 0.2186 - val_acc: 0.9408
```

This model is an improvement on our previous deep learning model; it gets 95.73% accuracy on the fourth epoch. This beats the traditional NLP approach by 0.49%, which is a significant improvement. Let's move on to other methods that also look to matching sequences. We will start with **recurrent neural networks (RNNs)**.

Recurrent neural network model

The deep learning networks we have seen so far have no concept of memory. Every new piece of information is treated as atomic and has no relation to what has already occurred. But, sequences are important in time series and text classification, especially sentiment analysis. In the previous section, we saw how word structure and order matters, and we used CNNs to resolve this. While this approach worked, it does not resolve the problem completely as we still must pick a filter size, which limits the range of the layer. Recurrent neural networks are deep learning layers which are used to solve this problem. They are networks with feedback loops that allow information to flow and therefore are able to *remember* important features:

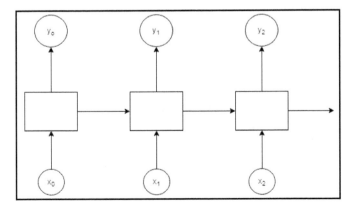

Figure 7.1: A recurrent neural network

In the preceding diagram, we can see an example of a recurrent neural network. Each piece of information (X_0, X_1, X_2) is fed into a node which predicts y variables. The predicted value is also passed to the next node as input, thus preserving some sequence information.

Our first RNN model is in `Chapter7/classify_keras3.R`. We have to change some of the parameters for the model: we must decrease the number of features used to 4,000, our max length to 100, and drop the most common 100 tokens. We must also increase the size of the embedding layer to 32 and run it for 10 epochs:

```
word_index <- dataset_reuters_word_index()
max_features <- length(word_index)
max_features <- 4000
maxlen <- 100
skip_top = 100


........

model <- keras_model_sequential() %>%
  layer_embedding(input_dim = max_features, output_dim = 32,input_length =
maxlen) %>%
  layer_spatial_dropout_1d(rate = 0.25) %>%
  layer_simple_rnn(64,activation = "relu", dropout=0.2) %>%
  layer_dense(units = 1, activation = "sigmoid")


........

history <- model %>% fit(
  x_train, y_train,
  epochs = 10,
  batch_size = 32,
  validation_split = 0.2
)
```

Here is the output from the model's training:

```
Train on 8982 samples, validate on 2246 samples
Epoch 1/10
8982/8982 [==============================] - 4s 409us/step - loss: 0.5289 -
acc: 0.7848 - val_loss: 0.3162 - val_acc: 0.9078
Epoch 2/10
8982/8982 [==============================] - 4s 391us/step - loss: 0.2875 -
acc: 0.9098 - val_loss: 0.2962 - val_acc: 0.9305
Epoch 3/10
8982/8982 [==============================] - 3s 386us/step - loss: 0.2496 -
acc: 0.9267 - val_loss: 0.2487 - val_acc: 0.9234
Epoch 4/10
8982/8982 [==============================] - 3s 386us/step - loss: 0.2395 -
```

```
acc: 0.9312 - val_loss: 0.2709 - val_acc: 0.9332
Epoch 5/10
8982/8982 [==============================] - 3s 381us/step - loss: 0.2259 -
acc: 0.9336 - val_loss: 0.2360 - val_acc: 0.9270
Epoch 6/10
8982/8982 [==============================] - 3s 381us/step - loss: 0.2182 -
acc: 0.9348 - val_loss: 0.2298 - val_acc: 0.9341
Epoch 7/10
8982/8982 [==============================] - 3s 383us/step - loss: 0.2129 -
acc: 0.9380 - val_loss: 0.2114 - val_acc: 0.9390
Epoch 8/10
8982/8982 [==============================] - 3s 382us/step - loss: 0.2128 -
acc: 0.9341 - val_loss: 0.2306 - val_acc: 0.9359
Epoch 9/10
8982/8982 [==============================] - 3s 378us/step - loss: 0.2053 -
acc: 0.9382 - val_loss: 0.2267 - val_acc: 0.9368
Epoch 10/10
8982/8982 [==============================] - 3s 385us/step - loss: 0.2031 -
acc: 0.9389 - val_loss: 0.2204 - val_acc: 0.9368
```

The best validation accuracy was after epoch 7, where we got 93.90% accuracy, which is not as good as the CNN model. One of the problems with simple RNN models is that it is difficult to maintain context as the gap grows between the different pieces of information. Let's move onto a more complex model, that is, the LSTM model.

Long short term memory model

LSTMs are designed to learn long-term dependencies. Similar to RNNs, they are chained and have four internal neural network layers. They split the state into two parts, where one part manages short-term state and the other adds long-term state. LSTMs have *gates* which control how *memories* are stored. The input gate controls which part of the input should be added to the long-term memory. The forget gate controls the part of long-term memory that should be forgotten. The final gate, the output gate, controls which part of the long-term memory should be in the output. This is a brief description of LSTMs – a good reference for more details is http://colah.github.io/posts/2015-08-Understanding-LSTMs/.

The code for our LSTM model is in Chapter7/classify_keras4.R. The parameters for the model are max length=150, the size of the embedding layer=32, and the model was trained for 10 epochs:

```
word_index <- dataset_reuters_word_index()
max_features <- length(word_index)
maxlen <- 150
```

```
skip_top = 0

.........

model <- keras_model_sequential() %>%
  layer_embedding(input_dim = max_features, output_dim = 32,input_length =
maxlen) %>%
  layer_dropout(rate = 0.25) %>%
  layer_lstm(128,dropout=0.2) %>%
  layer_dense(units = 1, activation = "sigmoid")

.........

history <- model %>% fit(
  x_train, y_train,
  epochs = 10,
  batch_size = 32,
  validation_split = 0.2
)
```

Here is the output from the model's training:

```
Train on 8982 samples, validate on 2246 samples
Epoch 1/10
8982/8982 [==============================] - 25s 3ms/step - loss: 0.3238 -
acc: 0.8917 - val_loss: 0.2135 - val_acc: 0.9394
Epoch 2/10
8982/8982 [==============================] - 26s 3ms/step - loss: 0.2465 -
acc: 0.9206 - val_loss: 0.1875 - val_acc: 0.9470
Epoch 3/10
8982/8982 [==============================] - 26s 3ms/step - loss: 0.1815 -
acc: 0.9493 - val_loss: 0.2577 - val_acc: 0.9408
Epoch 4/10
8982/8982 [==============================] - 26s 3ms/step - loss: 0.1691 -
acc: 0.9521 - val_loss: 0.1956 - val_acc: 0.9501
Epoch 5/10
8982/8982 [==============================] - 25s 3ms/step - loss: 0.1658 -
acc: 0.9507 - val_loss: 0.1850 - val_acc: 0.9537
Epoch 6/10
8982/8982 [==============================] - 25s 3ms/step - loss: 0.1658 -
acc: 0.9508 - val_loss: 0.1764 - val_acc: 0.9510
Epoch 7/10
8982/8982 [==============================] - 26s 3ms/step - loss: 0.1659 -
acc: 0.9522 - val_loss: 0.1884 - val_acc: 0.9466
Epoch 8/10
8982/8982 [==============================] - 26s 3ms/step - loss: 0.1548 -
acc: 0.9556 - val_loss: 0.1900 - val_acc: 0.9479
Epoch 9/10
```

```
8982/8982 [==============================] - 26s 3ms/step - loss: 0.1562 -
acc: 0.9548 - val_loss: 0.2035 - val_acc: 0.9461
Epoch 10/10
8982/8982 [==============================] - 26s 3ms/step - loss: 0.1508 -
acc: 0.9567 - val_loss: 0.2052 - val_acc: 0.9470
```

The best validation accuracy was after epoch 5, when we got 95.37% accuracy, which is a big improvement on the simple RNN model, although still not as good as the CNN model. We will cover GRU cells next, which are a similar concept to LSTM.

Gated Recurrent Units model

Gated recurrent units (GRUs) are similar to LSTM cells but simpler. They have one gate that combines the forget and input gates in LSTM, and there is no output gate. While GRUs are simpler than LSTMs and therefore quicker to train, it is a matter of debate on whether they are better than LSTMs, as the research is inconclusive. Therefore, it is recommended to try both, as the results of your task may vary. The code for our GRU model is in `Chapter7/classify_keras5.R`. The parameters for the model are max length=150, the size of the embedding layer=32, and the model was trained for 10 epochs:

```
word_index <- dataset_reuters_word_index()
max_features <- length(word_index)
maxlen <- 250
skip_top = 0

. . . . . . . . . .

model <- keras_model_sequential() %>%
  layer_embedding(input_dim = max_features, output_dim = 32,input_length =
maxlen) %>%
  layer_dropout(rate = 0.25) %>%
  layer_gru(128,dropout=0.2) %>%
  layer_dense(units = 1, activation = "sigmoid")

. . . . . . . . . .
history <- model %>% fit(
  x_train, y_train,
  epochs = 10,
  batch_size = 32,
  validation_split = 0.2
)
```

Here is the output from the model's training:

```
Train on 8982 samples, validate on 2246 samples
Epoch 1/10
8982/8982 [==============================] - 35s 4ms/step - loss: 0.3231 -
acc: 0.8867 - val_loss: 0.2068 - val_acc: 0.9372
Epoch 2/10
8982/8982 [==============================] - 35s 4ms/step - loss: 0.2084 -
acc: 0.9381 - val_loss: 0.2065 - val_acc: 0.9421
Epoch 3/10
8982/8982 [==============================] - 35s 4ms/step - loss: 0.1824 -
acc: 0.9454 - val_loss: 0.1711 - val_acc: 0.9501
Epoch 4/10
8982/8982 [==============================] - 35s 4ms/step - loss: 0.1656 -
acc: 0.9515 - val_loss: 0.1719 - val_acc: 0.9550
Epoch 5/10
8982/8982 [==============================] - 35s 4ms/step - loss: 0.1569 -
acc: 0.9551 - val_loss: 0.1668 - val_acc: 0.9541
Epoch 6/10
8982/8982 [==============================] - 35s 4ms/step - loss: 0.1477 -
acc: 0.9570 - val_loss: 0.1667 - val_acc: 0.9555
Epoch 7/10
8982/8982 [==============================] - 35s 4ms/step - loss: 0.1441 -
acc: 0.9605 - val_loss: 0.1612 - val_acc: 0.9581
Epoch 8/10
8982/8982 [==============================] - 36s 4ms/step - loss: 0.1361 -
acc: 0.9611 - val_loss: 0.1593 - val_acc: 0.9590
Epoch 9/10
8982/8982 [==============================] - 35s 4ms/step - loss: 0.1361 -
acc: 0.9620 - val_loss: 0.1646 - val_acc: 0.9568
Epoch 10/10
8982/8982 [==============================] - 35s 4ms/step - loss: 0.1306 -
acc: 0.9634 - val_loss: 0.1660 - val_acc: 0.9559
```

The best validation accuracy was after epoch 5, when we got 95.90% accuracy, which is an improvement on the 95.37% we got with LSTM. In fact, this is the best result we have seen so far. In the next section, we will look at bidirectional architectures.

Bidirectional LSTM model

We saw in *Figure 7.1* that RNNs (as well as LSTMs and GRUs) are useful because they can pass information forwards. But in NLP tasks, it is also useful to look backwards. For example, the following two strings have the same meaning:

- I went to Berlin in spring
- In spring I went to Berlin

Bidirectional LSTMs can pass information backwards as well as forwards. The code for our bidirectional LSTM model is in `Chapter7/classify_keras6.R`. The parameters for the model are max length=150, the size of the embedding layer=32, and the model was trained for 10 epochs:

```
word_index <- dataset_reuters_word_index()
max_features <- length(word_index)
maxlen <- 250
skip_top = 0

. . . . . . . . . . . . . . . . .

model <- keras_model_sequential() %>%
  layer_embedding(input_dim = max_features, output_dim = 32,input_length =
maxlen) %>%
  layer_dropout(rate = 0.25) %>%
  bidirectional(layer_lstm(units=128,dropout=0.2)) %>%
  layer_dense(units = 1, activation = "sigmoid")

. . . . . . . . . . . . . . . . .
history <- model %>% fit(
  x_train, y_train,
  epochs = 10,
  batch_size = 32,
  validation_split = 0.2
)
```

Here is the output from the model's training:

```
Train on 8982 samples, validate on 2246 samples
Epoch 1/10
8982/8982 [==============================] - 82s 9ms/step - loss: 0.3312 -
acc: 0.8834 - val_loss: 0.2166 - val_acc: 0.9377
Epoch 2/10
8982/8982 [==============================] - 87s 10ms/step - loss: 0.2487 -
acc: 0.9243 - val_loss: 0.1889 - val_acc: 0.9457
Epoch 3/10
8982/8982 [==============================] - 86s 10ms/step - loss: 0.1873 -
```

```
acc: 0.9464 - val_loss: 0.1708 - val_acc: 0.9519
Epoch 4/10
8982/8982 [==============================] - 82s 9ms/step - loss: 0.1685 -
acc: 0.9537 - val_loss: 0.1786 - val_acc: 0.9577
Epoch 5/10
8982/8982 [==============================] - 83s 9ms/step - loss: 0.1634 -
acc: 0.9531 - val_loss: 0.2094 - val_acc: 0.9310
Epoch 6/10
8982/8982 [==============================] - 82s 9ms/step - loss: 0.1567 -
acc: 0.9571 - val_loss: 0.1809 - val_acc: 0.9475
Epoch 7/10
8982/8982 [==============================] - 83s 9ms/step - loss: 0.1499 -
acc: 0.9575 - val_loss: 0.1652 - val_acc: 0.9555
Epoch 8/10
8982/8982 [==============================] - 83s 9ms/step - loss: 0.1488 -
acc: 0.9586 - val_loss: 0.1795 - val_acc: 0.9510
Epoch 9/10
8982/8982 [==============================] - 83s 9ms/step - loss: 0.1513 -
acc: 0.9567 - val_loss: 0.1758 - val_acc: 0.9555
Epoch 10/10
8982/8982 [==============================] - 83s 9ms/step - loss: 0.1463 -
acc: 0.9571 - val_loss: 0.1731 - val_acc: 0.9550
```

The best validation accuracy was after epoch 4, when we got 95.77% accuracy.

Stacked bidirectional model

Bidirectional models are good at picking up information from future states that can affect the current state. Stacked bidirectional models allow us to stack multiple LSTM/GRU layers in a similar manner to how we stack multiple convolutional layers in computer vision tasks. The code for our bidirectional LSTM model is in `Chapter7/classify_keras7.R`. The parameters for the model are max length=150, the size of the embedding layer=32, and the model was trained for 10 epochs:

```
word_index <- dataset_reuters_word_index()
max_features <- length(word_index)
maxlen <- 250
skip_top = 0

.................

model <- keras_model_sequential() %>%
  layer_embedding(input_dim = max_features, output_dim = 32, input_length =
maxlen) %>%
  layer_dropout(rate = 0.25) %>%
  bidirectional(layer_lstm(units=32, dropout=0.2, return_sequences = TRUE))
```

```
%>%
  bidirectional(layer_lstm(units=32,dropout=0.2)) %>%
  layer_dense(units = 1, activation = "sigmoid")

................
history <- model %>% fit(
  x_train, y_train,
  epochs = 10,
  batch_size = 32,
  validation_split = 0.2
)
```

Here is the output from the model's training:

```
Train on 8982 samples, validate on 2246 samples
Epoch 1/10
8982/8982 [==============================] - 70s 8ms/step - loss: 0.2854 -
acc: 0.9006 - val_loss: 0.1945 - val_acc: 0.9372
Epoch 2/10
8982/8982 [==============================] - 66s 7ms/step - loss: 0.1795 -
acc: 0.9511 - val_loss: 0.1791 - val_acc: 0.9484
Epoch 3/10
8982/8982 [==============================] - 69s 8ms/step - loss: 0.1586 -
acc: 0.9557 - val_loss: 0.1756 - val_acc: 0.9492
Epoch 4/10
8982/8982 [==============================] - 70s 8ms/step - loss: 0.1467 -
acc: 0.9607 - val_loss: 0.1664 - val_acc: 0.9559
Epoch 5/10
8982/8982 [==============================] - 70s 8ms/step - loss: 0.1394 -
acc: 0.9614 - val_loss: 0.1775 - val_acc: 0.9533
Epoch 6/10
8982/8982 [==============================] - 70s 8ms/step - loss: 0.1347 -
acc: 0.9636 - val_loss: 0.1667 - val_acc: 0.9519
Epoch 7/10
8982/8982 [==============================] - 70s 8ms/step - loss: 0.1344 -
acc: 0.9618 - val_loss: 0.2101 - val_acc: 0.9332
Epoch 8/10
8982/8982 [==============================] - 70s 8ms/step - loss: 0.1306 -
acc: 0.9647 - val_loss: 0.1893 - val_acc: 0.9479
Epoch 9/10
8982/8982 [==============================] - 70s 8ms/step - loss: 0.1286 -
acc: 0.9646 - val_loss: 0.1663 - val_acc: 0.9550
Epoch 10/10
8982/8982 [==============================] - 70s 8ms/step - loss: 0.1254 -
acc: 0.9669 - val_loss: 0.1687 - val_acc: 0.9492
```

The best validation accuracy was after epoch 4, when we got 95.59% accuracy, which is worse than our bidirectional model, which got 95.77% accuracy.

Bidirectional with 1D convolutional neural network model

So far, the best approaches we have seen are from the 1D convolutional neural network model which got 95.73%, and the gated recurrent units model which got 95.90% accuracy. The following code combines them! The code for our bidirectional with 1D convolutional neural network model is in `Chapter7/classify_keras8.R`.

The parameters for the model are max length=150, the size of the embedding layer=32, and the model was trained for 10 epochs:

```
word_index <- dataset_reuters_word_index()
max_features <- length(word_index)
maxlen <- 250
skip_top = 0

. . . . . . . . . . . . . . . . .

model <- keras_model_sequential() %>%
  layer_embedding(input_dim = max_features, output_dim = 32,input_length =
maxlen) %>%
  layer_spatial_dropout_1d(rate = 0.25) %>%
  layer_conv_1d(64,3, activation = "relu") %>%
  layer_max_pooling_1d() %>%
  bidirectional(layer_gru(units=64,dropout=0.2)) %>%
  layer_dense(units = 1, activation = "sigmoid")

. . . . . . . . . . . . . . . . .
history <- model %>% fit(
  x_train, y_train,
  epochs = 10,
  batch_size = 32,
  validation_split = 0.2
)
```

Here is the output from the model's training:

```
Train on 8982 samples, validate on 2246 samples
Epoch 1/10
8982/8982 [==============================] - 26s 3ms/step - loss: 0.2891 -
acc: 0.8952 - val_loss: 0.2226 - val_acc: 0.9319
Epoch 2/10
```

```
8982/8982 [==============================] - 25s 3ms/step - loss: 0.1712 -
acc: 0.9505 - val_loss: 0.1601 - val_acc: 0.9586
Epoch 3/10
8982/8982 [==============================] - 26s 3ms/step - loss: 0.1651 -
acc: 0.9548 - val_loss: 0.1639 - val_acc: 0.9541
Epoch 4/10
8982/8982 [==============================] - 26s 3ms/step - loss: 0.1466 -
acc: 0.9582 - val_loss: 0.1699 - val_acc: 0.9550
Epoch 5/10
8982/8982 [==============================] - 26s 3ms/step - loss: 0.1391 -
acc: 0.9606 - val_loss: 0.1520 - val_acc: 0.9586
Epoch 6/10
8982/8982 [==============================] - 26s 3ms/step - loss: 0.1347 -
acc: 0.9626 - val_loss: 0.1626 - val_acc: 0.9550
Epoch 7/10
8982/8982 [==============================] - 27s 3ms/step - loss: 0.1332 -
acc: 0.9638 - val_loss: 0.1572 - val_acc: 0.9604
Epoch 8/10
8982/8982 [==============================] - 26s 3ms/step - loss: 0.1317 -
acc: 0.9629 - val_loss: 0.1693 - val_acc: 0.9470
Epoch 9/10
8982/8982 [==============================] - 26s 3ms/step - loss: 0.1259 -
acc: 0.9654 - val_loss: 0.1531 - val_acc: 0.9599
Epoch 10/10
8982/8982 [==============================] - 28s 3ms/step - loss: 0.1233 -
acc: 0.9665 - val_loss: 0.1653 - val_acc: 0.9573
```

The best validation accuracy was after epoch 6, when we got 96.04% accuracy, which beats all of the previous models.

Comparing the deep learning NLP architectures

Here is a summary of all of the models in this chapter, ordered by their sequence in this chapter. We can see that the best traditional machine learning approach got 95.24%, which was beaten by many of the deep learning approaches. While the incremental changes from the best traditional machine learning to the best deep learning model may seem small at 0.80%, it reduces our misclassified examples by 17%, which is a significant relative change:

Model	Accuracy
Best traditional machine learning approach	95.24%
Simple deep learning approach	94.97%
1D convolutional neural network model	95.73%
Recurrent neural network model	93.90%

Long short term memory model	95.37%
Gated recurrent units model	95.90%
Bidirectional LSTM model	95.77%
Stacked bidirectional model	95.59%
Bidirectional with 1D convolutional neural network	96.04%

Summary

We really covered a lot in this chapter! We built a fairly complex traditional NLP example that had many hyperparameters, as well as training it on several machine learning algorithms. It achieved a reputable result of getting 95.24% accuracy. However, when we looked into traditional NLP in more detail, we found that it had some major problems: it requires non-trivial feature engineering, it creates sparse high-dimensional data frames, and it may require discarding a substantial amount of data before machine learning.

In comparison, the deep learning approach uses word vectors or embeddings, which are much more efficient and do not require preprocessing. We ran through a number of deep learning approaches, including 1D convolutional layers, Recurrent Neural Networks, GRUs, and LSTM. We finally combined the two best previous approaches into one approach in our final model to get 96.08% accuracy, compared to 95.24% by using traditional NLP.

In the next chapter, we will develop models using TensorFlow. We will look at TensorBoard, which allows us to visualize and debug complex deep learning models. We will also look at using TensorFlow estimators, an alternative option for using TensorFlow. Then, we will also look at TensorFlow Runs, which automates a lot of the steps for hyperparameter tuning. Finally, we will look at options for deploying deep learning models.

8
Deep Learning Models Using TensorFlow in R

This chapter is about using TensorFlow in R. We have already used TensorFlow quite a lot, as Keras is a high-level neural network API that uses either TensorFlow, CNTK, or Theano. In R, Keras uses TensorFlow in the background. TensorFlow is more difficult to develop deep learning models in. However, there are two interesting packages in TensorFlow that could be overlooked: TensorFlow estimators and TensorFlow runs. We will cover both of these packages in this chapter.

In this chapter, we will cover the following topics:

- Introduction to TensorFlow
- Building models using TensorFlow
- TensorFlow estimators
- TensorFlow runs packages

Introduction to the TensorFlow library

TensorFlow is not just a deep learning library, but an expressive programming language that can implement various optimization and mathematical transformations on data. While it is mainly used to implement deep learning algorithms, it can perform much more. In TensorFlow, programs are represented as computational graphs, and data in TensorFlow is stored in `tensors`. A **tensor** is an array of data that has the same data type, and the rank of a tensor is the number of dimensions. Because all the data in a tensor must have the same type, they are more similar to R matrices than data frames.

Here is an example of tensors of various ranks:

```
library(tensorflow)

> # tensor of rank-0
> var1 <- tf$constant(0.1)
> print(var1)
Tensor("Const:0", shape=(), dtype=float32)

> sess <- tf$InteractiveSession()
T:\src\github\tensorflow\tensorflow\core\common_runtime\gpu\gpu_device.cc:1
084] Created TensorFlow device
(/job:localhost/replica:0/task:0/device:GPU:0 with 3019 MB memory) ->
physical GPU (device: 0, name: GeForce GTX 1050 Ti, pci bus id:
0000:01:00.0, compute capability: 6.1)

> sess$run(tf$global_variables_initializer())
> var2 <- tf$constant(2.3)
> var3 = var1 + var2
> print(var1)
Tensor("Const:0", shape=(), dtype=float32)
 num 0.1

> print(var2)
Tensor("Const_1:0", shape=(), dtype=float32)
 num 2.3

> print(var3)
Tensor("Add:0", shape=(), dtype=float32)
 num 2.4

> # tensor of rank-1
> var4 <- tf$constant(4.5,shape=shape(5L))
> print(var4)
Tensor("Const_2:0", shape=(5,), dtype=float32)
 num [1:5(1d)] 4.5 4.5 4.5 4.5 4.5

> # tensor of rank-2
> var5 <- tf$constant(6.7,shape=shape(3L,3L))
> print(var5)
Tensor("Const_3:0", shape=(3, 3), dtype=float32)
 num [1:3, 1:3] 6.7 6.7 6.7 6.7 6.7 ...
```

A TensorFlow program has two parts. First, you have to build the computational graph, which contains the tensors and the operations on those tensors. When they have defined the graph, the second part is to create a TensorFlow session to run the graph. In the previous example, the first time we print out the value for the tensor, a, we only get the tensor definition and not the value. All we have done is define part of the computation graph. It is only when we call tf$InteractiveSession that we tell TensorFlow to run the operations on the tensors. A session is responsible for running the computational graph.

The TensorFlow program is referred to as a graph because the code can be structured as a graph. This might not be obvious to us as most of the deep learning models that we have built in this book have consisted of sequential operations on layers. In TensorFlow (and Keras and MXNet), it is possible to use the output of an operation multiple times and to combine inputs in one operation.

As deep learning models get larger, it is increasingly difficult to visualize and debug them. In some code blocks, we have printed a summary of the model showing the layers, or we have plotted the network. However, neither of these tools would be helpful for debugging problems in a model with 10 million+ parameters! Fortunately, there is a visualization tool included with TensorFlow to help summarize, debug, and fix TensorFlow programs. This is called TensorBoard, and we will cover this next.

Using TensorBoard to visualize deep learning networks

Computation graphs in TensorFlow can be very complex, so there is a visualization tool called **TensorBoard** to visualize these graphs and assist in debugging. TensorBoard can plot a computation graph, display metrics from training, and so on. Since Keras uses TensorFlow in the backend, it too can use TensorBoard. Here is the MNIST example from Keras with TensorBoard logging enabled. This code can be found in the Chapter8/mnist_keras.R folder. The first part of the code loads the data, pre-processes it, and defines the model architecture. Hopefully, this should be familiar to you at this stage:

```
library(keras)

mnist_data <- dataset_mnist()
xtrain <-
array_reshape(mnist_data$train$x,c(nrow(mnist_data$train$x),28,28,1))
ytrain <- to_categorical(mnist_data$train$y,10)
xtrain <- xtrain / 255.0
```

```
model <- keras_model_sequential()
model %>%
  layer_conv_2d(filters=32,kernel_size=c(5,5),activation='relu',
                input_shape=c(28,28,1)) %>%
  layer_max_pooling_2d(pool_size=c(2,2)) %>%
  layer_dropout(rate=0.25) %>%
  layer_conv_2d(filters=32,kernel_size=c(5,5),activation='relu') %>%
  layer_max_pooling_2d(pool_size=c(2,2)) %>%
  layer_dropout(rate=0.25) %>%
  layer_flatten() %>%
  layer_dense(units=256,activation='relu') %>%
  layer_dropout(rate=0.4) %>%
  layer_dense(units=10,activation='softmax')

model %>% compile(
  loss=loss_categorical_crossentropy,
  optimizer="rmsprop",metrics="accuracy"
)
```

To enable logging, add a `callbacks` parameter to the `model.fit` function to tell Keras/TensorFlow to log events to a directory. The following code will output log data to the `/tensorflow_logs` directory:

```
model %>% fit(
  xtrain,ytrain,
  batch_size=128,epochs=10,
  callbacks=callback_tensorboard("/tensorflow_logs",
                                 histogram_freq=1,write_images=0),
  validation_split=0.2
)
# from cmd line,run 'tensorboard --logdir /tensorflow_logs'
```

Warning: The event logs can take up a lot of space. For 5 epochs on the MNIST dataset, 1.75 GB of information was created. Most of this was because of the image data that was included, so you may consider setting `write_images=0` to reduce the size of the logs.

TensorBoard is a web application, and you must start the TensorBoard program for it to run. When the model has finished training, follow these steps to start the TensorBoard web application:

1. Open up Command Prompt and enter the following:

    ```
    $ tensorboard --logdir /tensorflow_logs
    ```

2. If TensorBoard starts successfully, you should get a message similar to the following at Command Prompt:

    ```
    TensorBoard 0.4.0rc2 at http://xxxxxx:6006 (Press CTRL+C to quit)
    ```

3. Open a web browser to the link that was provided. The web page should be similar to the following:

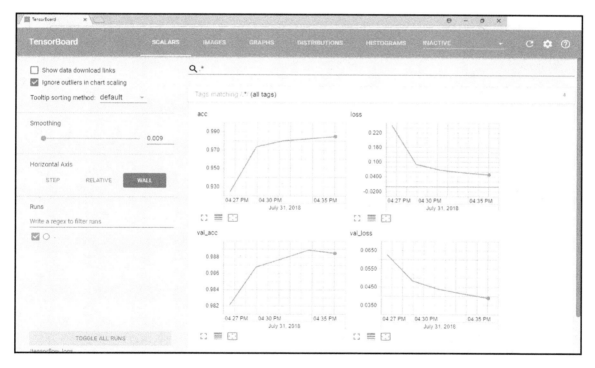

Figure 8.1: TensorBoard – model metrics

4. The preceding screenshot shows us the model metrics on the training and validation test sets – these are similar to the metrics shown in RStudio during training:

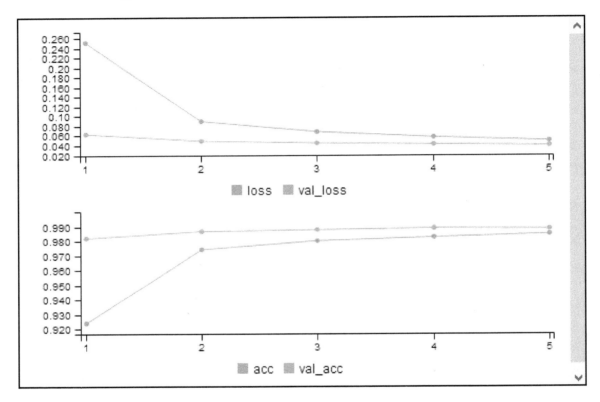

Figure 8.2: RStudio – model metrics

5. If you click on the **Images** option, you will be able to visualize the layers in the model and see how they change over epochs:

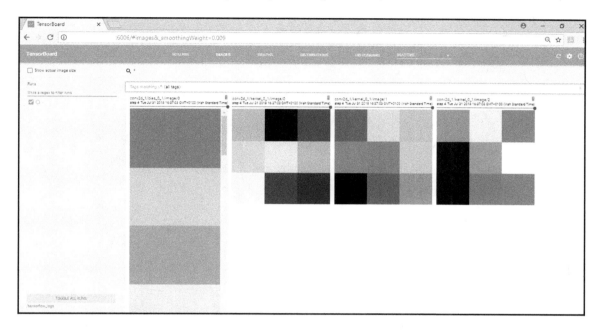

Figure 8.3: TensorBoard – visualizing the model layers

6. If you click on the **Graphs** option, it will show the computation graph for the model. You can also download it as an image file. Here is the computation graph for this model:

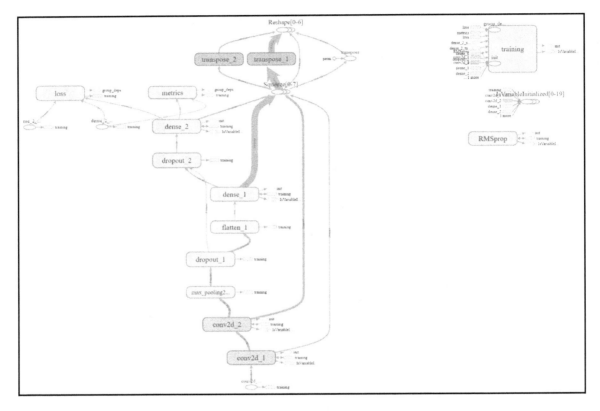

Figure 8.4: TensorBoard – computation graph

Some of this will seem familiar. We can see our convolutional, max pooling, flatten, dense, and dropout layers. The rest are not as obvious. As a higher-level abstraction, Keras takes care of a lot of the complexities in creating the computation graph.

7. By clicking on the **Histogram** option, you can see how the distribution of tensors changes over time:

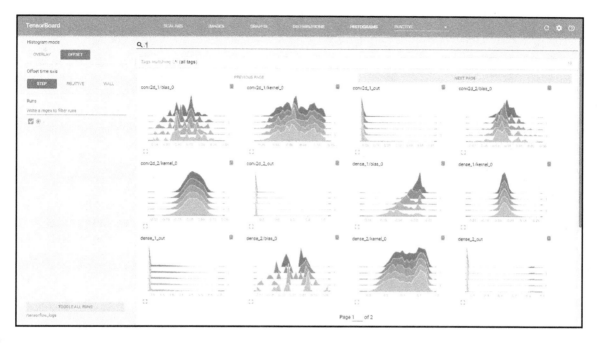

Figure 8.5: TensorBoard – histograms

It is possible to use TensorBoard to debug a model. For example, it would be possible to investigate a vanishing gradient or an exploding gradient problem to see where the weights of the model were either vanishing to zero or exploding to infinity. There is a lot more to TensorBoard, so if you are curious you can follow the online documentation on it.

In the next section, we will use TensorFlow to build a regression model and a convolutional neural network.

TensorFlow models

In this section, we will use TensorFlow to build some machine learning models. First, we will build a simple linear regression model and then a convolutional neural network model, similar to what we have seen in Chapter 5, *Image Classification Using Convolutional Neural Networks*.

The following code loads the TensorFlow library. We can confirm it loaded successfully by setting and accessing a constant string value:

```
> library(tensorflow)

# confirm that TensorFlow library has loaded
> sess=tf$Session()
> hello_world <- tf$constant('Hello world from TensorFlow')
> sess$run(hello_world)
b'Hello world from TensorFlow'
```

Linear regression using TensorFlow

In this first Tensorflow example, we will look at regression. The code for this section is in the `Chapter8/regression_tf.R` folder:

1. First, we create some fake data for an an input value, *x*, and an output value, *y*. We set *y* to be approximately equal to `0.8 + x * 1.3`. We want the application to discover the `beta0` and `beta1` values, which are `0.8` and `1.3`, respectively:

```
library(tensorflow)

set.seed(42)
# create 50000 x variable between 0 and 100
x_var <- runif(50000,min=0,max=1)
#y = approx(1.3x + 0.8)
y_var <- rnorm(50000,0.8,0.04) + x_var * rnorm(50000,1.3,0.05)

# y_pred = beta0 + beta1 * x
beta0 <- tf$Variable(tf$zeros(shape(1L)))
beta1 <- tf$Variable(tf$random_uniform(shape(1L), -1.0, 1.0))
y_pred <- beta0 + beta1*x_var
```

2. Now, we set up our `loss` function so that the gradient descent algorithm can work:

```
# create our loss value which we want to minimize
loss <- tf$reduce_mean((y_pred-y_var)^2)
# create optimizer
optimizer <- tf$train$GradientDescentOptimizer(0.6)
train <- optimizer$minimize(loss)
```

3. We then set up a TensorFlow session and initialize the variables. Finally, we can run the graph:

```
# create TensorFlow session and initialize variables
sess = tf$Session()
sess$run(tf$global_variables_initializer())

# solve the regression
for (step in 0:80) {
  if (step %% 10 == 0)
    print(sprintf("Step %1.0f:beta0=%1.4f,
beta1=%1.4f",step,sess$run(beta0), sess$run(beta1)))
  sess$run(train)
}
[1] "Step 0:beta0=0.0000, beta1=-0.3244"
[1] "Step 10:beta0=1.0146, beta1=0.8944"
[1] "Step 20:beta0=0.8942, beta1=1.1236"
[1] "Step 30:beta0=0.8410, beta1=1.2229"
[1] "Step 40:beta0=0.8178, beta1=1.2662"
[1] "Step 50:beta0=0.8077, beta1=1.2850"
[1] "Step 60:beta0=0.8033, beta1=1.2932"
[1] "Step 70:beta0=0.8014, beta1=1.2967"
[1] "Step 80:beta0=0.8006, beta1=1.2983"
```

We can see that the model manages to find the values for `beta0` and `beta1` that solve the function `y=beta0 + beta1*x`. The next section is a more more complex example, where we will build a TensorFlow model for image classification.

Convolutional neural networks using TensorFlow

In this section, we will build a TensorFlow model on the MNIST dataset. The code has similar layers and parameters to the Lenet model that we saw in `Chapter 5`, *Image Classification Using Convolutional Neural Networks*. However, the code to build the model in TensorFlow is more complicated than the code to build the model in Keras or in MXNet. One reason for this is that it is the programmer's job to ensure that the sizes of the layers are correctly aligned. In the Keras/MXNet models, we can just change the number of nodes in a layer in one statement. In TensorFlow, if we change the number of nodes in a layer, we must ensure that we also change the inputs in the next layer.

In some ways, programming in TensorFlow is closer to the hand-written neural network code we wrote in Chapter 3, *Deep Learning Fundamentals*. Another difference from Keras/MXNet in the training loop is that we need to manage the batches rather than just call, asking to iterate over all the data x times (where x is an epoch). The code for this example is in the Chapter8/mnist_tf.R folder. First, we load the Keras package to get the MNIST data, but we train the model using TensorFlow. Here is the first part of the code:

```
library(RSNNS) # for decodeClassLabels
library(tensorflow)
library(keras)

mnist <- dataset_mnist()
set.seed(42)

xtrain <- array_reshape(mnist$train$x,c(nrow(mnist$train$x),28*28))
ytrain <- decodeClassLabels(mnist$train$y)
xtest <- array_reshape(mnist$test$x,c(nrow(mnist$test$x),28*28))
ytest <- decodeClassLabels(mnist$test$y)
xtrain <- xtrain / 255.0
xtest <- xtest / 255.0
head(ytrain)
      0 1 2 3 4 5 6 7 8 9
[1,] 0 0 0 0 0 1 0 0 0 0
[2,] 1 0 0 0 0 0 0 0 0 0
[3,] 0 0 0 0 1 0 0 0 0 0
[4,] 0 1 0 0 0 0 0 0 0 0
[5,] 0 0 0 0 0 0 0 0 0 1
[6,] 0 0 1 0 0 0 0 0 0 0
```

We use the decodeClassLabels function from the RSNNS library because TensorFlow requires a dummy coded matrix, so each possible class is represented as a column coded as 0/1, as shown in the preceding code output.

In the next code block, we create some placeholders for our input and output values in the model. We also reshape the input data into a rank-4 tensor, that is, a 4 dimensional data structure. The first dimension (-1L) is for the records that will be processed in a batch. The next two dimensions are the dimensions of the image files, and the final dimension is the channels, which is the number of colors. Since our images are greyscale, there is only 1 channel. If the images were color images, there would be 3 channels. The following code block creates the placeholders and reshapes the data:

```
# placeholders
x <- tf$placeholder(tf$float32, shape(NULL,28L*28L))
y <- tf$placeholder(tf$float32, shape(NULL,10L))
x_image <- tf$reshape(x; shape(-1L,28L,28L,1L))
```

Next, we will define the model architecture. We will create convolution blocks, just like we did previously. However, there are a lot more values that need to be set. For example, in the first convolutional layer, we must define the shape, initialize the weights, and take care of the bias variable. Here is the code for the TensorFlow model:

```
# first convolution layer
conv_weights1 <- tf$Variable(tf$random_uniform(shape(5L,5L,1L,16L), -0.4,
0.4))
conv_bias1 <- tf$constant(0.0, shape=shape(16L))
conv_activ1 <- tf$nn$tanh(tf$nn$conv2d(x_image, conv_weights1,
strides=c(1L,1L,1L,1L), padding='SAME') + conv_bias1)
pool1 <- tf$nn$max_pool(conv_activ1,
ksize=c(1L,2L,2L,1L),strides=c(1L,2L,2L,1L), padding='SAME')

# second convolution layer
conv_weights2 <- tf$Variable(tf$random_uniform(shape(5L,5L,16L,32L), -0.4,
0.4))
conv_bias2 <- tf$constant(0.0, shape=shape(32L))
conv_activ2 <- tf$nn$relu(tf$nn$conv2d(pool1, conv_weights2,
strides=c(1L,1L,1L,1L), padding='SAME') + conv_bias2)
pool2 <- tf$nn$max_pool(conv_activ2,
ksize=c(1L,2L,2L,1L),strides=c(1L,2L,2L,1L), padding='SAME')

# densely connected layer
dense_weights1 <- tf$Variable(tf$truncated_normal(shape(7L*7L*32L,512L),
stddev=0.1))
dense_bias1 <- tf$constant(0.0, shape=shape(512L))
pool2_flat <- tf$reshape(pool2, shape(-1L,7L*7L*32L))
dense1 <- tf$nn$relu(tf$matmul(pool2_flat, dense_weights1) + dense_bias1)

# dropout
keep_prob <- tf$placeholder(tf$float32)
dense1_drop <- tf$nn$dropout(dense1, keep_prob)

# softmax layer
dense_weights2 <- tf$Variable(tf$truncated_normal(shape(512L,10L),
stddev=0.1))
dense_bias2 <- tf$constant(0.0, shape=shape(10L))

yconv <- tf$nn$softmax(tf$matmul(dense1_drop, dense_weights2) +
dense_bias2)
```

Now, we have to define the loss equation, define the optimizer to use (Adam), and define the accuracy metric:

```
cross_entropy <- tf$reduce_mean(-tf$reduce_sum(y * tf$log(yconv),
reduction_indices=1L))
train_step <- tf$train$AdamOptimizer(0.0001)$minimize(cross_entropy)
correct_prediction <- tf$equal(tf$argmax(yconv, 1L), tf$argmax(y, 1L))
accuracy <- tf$reduce_mean(tf$cast(correct_prediction, tf$float32))
```

Finally, we can train the model over 10 epochs. However, one complication still exists, so we must manually manage the batches. We get the number of batches to train for and load them in turn. If we have 60,000 images in our train dataset, we have 469 batches (60,000/128 = 468.75 and round up to 469) per epoch. We feed in every batch and output metrics every 100 batches:

```
sess <- tf$InteractiveSession()
sess$run(tf$global_variables_initializer())

# if you get out of memory errors when running on gpu
# then lower the batch_size
batch_size <- 128
batches_per_epoch <- 1+nrow(xtrain) %/% batch_size
for (epoch in 1:10)
{
  for (batch_no in 0:(-1+batches_per_epoch))
  {
    nStartIndex <- 1 + batch_no*batch_size
    nEndIndex <- nStartIndex + batch_size-1
    if (nEndIndex > nrow(xtrain))
      nEndIndex <- nrow(xtrain)
    xvalues <- xtrain[nStartIndex:nEndIndex,]
    yvalues <- ytrain[nStartIndex:nEndIndex,]
    if (batch_no %% 100 == 0) {
      batch_acc <-
accuracy$eval(feed_dict=dict(x=xvalues,y=yvalues,keep_prob=1.0))
      print(sprintf("Epoch %1.0f, step %1.0f: training
accuracy=%1.4f",epoch, batch_no, batch_acc))
    }
    sess$run(train_step,feed_dict=dict(x=xvalues,y=yvalues,keep_prob=0.5))
  }
  cat("\n")
}
```

Here is the output for the first epoch:

```
[1] "Epoch 1, step 0: training accuracy=0.0625"
[1] "Epoch 1, step 100: training accuracy=0.8438"
[1] "Epoch 1, step 200: training accuracy=0.8984"
[1] "Epoch 1, step 300: training accuracy=0.9531"
[1] "Epoch 1, step 400: training accuracy=0.8750"
```

When training is complete, we can evaluate the model by calculating the accuracy on the test set. Again, we have to do this in batches to prevent out-of-memory errors:

```
# calculate test accuracy
# have to run in batches to prevent out of memory errors
batches_per_epoch <- 1+nrow(xtest) %/% batch_size
test_acc <- vector(mode="numeric", length=batches_per_epoch)
for (batch_no in 0:(-1+batches_per_epoch))
{
  nStartIndex <- 1 + batch_no*batch_size
  nEndIndex <- nStartIndex + batch_size-1
  if (nEndIndex > nrow(xtest))
    nEndIndex <- nrow(xtest)
  xvalues <- xtest[nStartIndex:nEndIndex,]
  yvalues <- ytest[nStartIndex:nEndIndex,]
  batch_acc <-
accuracy$eval(feed_dict=dict(x=xvalues,y=yvalues,keep_prob=1.0))
  test_acc[batch_no+1] <- batch_acc
}
# using the mean is not totally accurate as last batch is not a complete
batch
print(sprintf("Test accuracy=%1.4f",mean(test_acc)))
[1] "Test accuracy=0.9802"
```

We get a final accuracy of 0.9802. If we compare this code to the MNIST example in Chapter 5, *Image Classification Using Convolutional Neural Networks*, the TensorFlow code is more verbose and it is easier to make mistakes. We can really see the benefit of using a higher, level abstraction, such as MXNet or Keras (which can use TensorFlow as a backend). For most deep learning use cases, especially for building deep learning models using existing layers as building blocks, there is little to be gained in developing code in TensorFlow. For these use cases, it is simpler and more efficient to use Keras or MXNet.

After seeing this code, you may want to go back to something more familiar in Keras and MXNet. However, the next section looks at TensorFlow estimators and TensorFlow runs, which are two useful packages that you should be aware of.

TensorFlow estimators and TensorFlow runs packages

TensorFlow estimators and the TensorFlow runs packages are great packages to use for deep learning. In this section, we will use both to train a model based on our churn prediction data from Chapter 4, *Training Deep Prediction Models*.

TensorFlow estimators

TensorFlow estimators allow you to build TensorFlow models using a simpler API interface. In R, the tfestimators package allows you to call this API. There are different model types, including linear models and neural networks. The following estimators are available:

- linear_regressor() for linear regression
- linear_classifier() for linear classification
- dnn_regressor() for deep neural network regression
- dnn_classifier() for deep neural network classification
- dnn_linear_combined_regressor() for deep neural network linear combined regression
- dnn_linear_combined_classifier() for deep neural network linear combined classification

Estimators hide a lot of the detail in creating a deep learning model, including building the graph, initializing variables and layers, and they can also integrate with TensorBoard. More details are available at https://tensorflow.rstudio.com/tfestimators/. We will use dnn_classifier with the data from the binary classification task from Chapter 4, *Training Deep Prediction Models*. The following code in the Chapter8/tf_estimators.R folder demonstrates TensorFlow estimators.

1. We only include the code that is specific to TensorFlow estimators and omit the code at the start of the file that loads the data and splits it into train and test data:

```r
response <- function() "Y_categ"
features <- function() predictorCols

FLAGS <- flags(
  flag_numeric("layer1", 256),
  flag_numeric("layer2", 128),
  flag_numeric("layer3", 64),
  flag_numeric("layer4", 32),
  flag_numeric("dropout", 0.2)
)
num_hidden <-
c(FLAGS$layer1,FLAGS$layer2,FLAGS$layer3,FLAGS$layer4)

classifier <- dnn_classifier(
  feature_columns = feature_columns(column_numeric(predictorCols)),
  hidden_units = num_hidden,
  activation_fn = "relu",
  dropout = FLAGS$dropout,
  n_classes = 2
)

bin_input_fn <- function(data)
{
 input_fn(data, features = features(), response = response())
}
tr <- train(classifier, input_fn = bin_input_fn(trainData))
[\] Training -- loss: 22.96, step: 2742

tr
Trained for 2,740 steps.
Final step (plot to see history):
 mean_losses: 61.91
total_losses: 61.91
```

2. Once the model is trained, the following code plots the training and validation metrics:

```
plot(tr)
```

3. This produces the following plot:

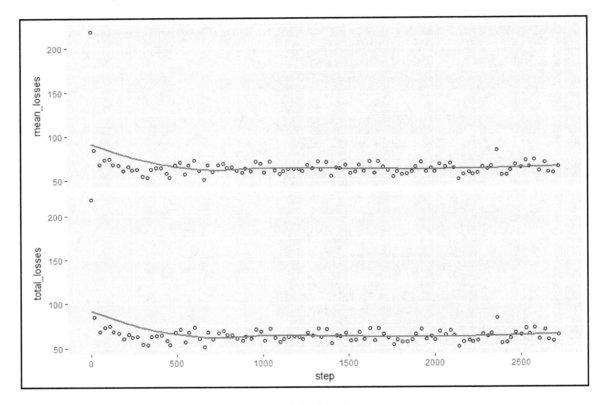

Figure 8.6: Training a loss plot for a TensorFlow estimator model

4. The next part of the code calls the `evaluate` function to produce metrics for the model:

```
# predictions <- predict(classifier, input_fn =
bin_input_fn(testData))
evaluation <- evaluate(classifier, input_fn =
bin_input_fn(testData))
[-] Evaluating -- loss: 37.77, step: 305

for (c in 1:ncol(evaluation))
 print(paste(colnames(evaluation)[c]," = ",evaluation[c],sep=""))
[1] "accuracy = 0.77573162317276"
[1] "accuracy_baseline = 0.603221416473389"
[1] "auc = 0.842994153499603"
[1] "auc_precision_recall = 0.887594640254974"
[1] "average_loss = 0.501933991909027"
[1] "label/mean = 0.603221416473389"
[1] "loss = 64.1636199951172"
[1] "precision = 0.803375601768494"
[1] "prediction/mean = 0.562777876853943"
[1] "recall = 0.831795573234558"
[1] "global_step = 2742"
```

We can see that we got an accuracy of `77.57%`, which is actually almost identical to the accuracy we got on the MXNet model in `Chapter 4`, *Training Deep Prediction Models*, which had a similar architecture. The `dnn_classifier()` function hides a lot of the detail, so Tensorflow estimators are a good way to use the power of TensorFlow for tasks with structured data.

Models created using TensorFlow estimators can be saved onto disk and loaded later. The `model_dir()` function shows the location of where the model artifacts were saved (usually in a `temp` directory, but it can be copied elsewhere):

```
model_dir(classifier)
"C:\\Users\\xxxxxx\\AppData\\Local\\Temp\\tmpv1e_ri23"
# dnn_classifier has a model_dir parameter to load an existing model
?dnn_classifier
```

Included in the model artifacts are the event logs that can be used by TensorBoard. For example, when I load TensorBoard up and point it to the logs directory in the `temp` directory, I can see the TensorFlow graph that was created:

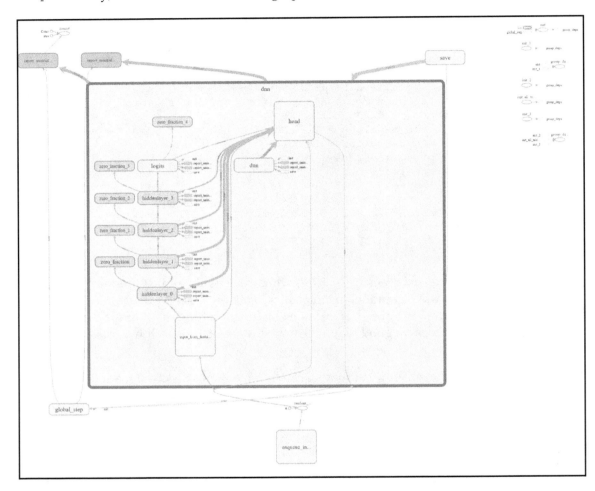

Figure 8.7: Graph using TensorBoard for a TensorFlow estimator model

TensorFlow runs package

The tfruns package is a set of utilities for managing different training runs for deep learning models. It can be used as a framework to build multiple deep learning models using different hyper-parameters. It can track the hyper-parameters, metrics, output, and source code for every training run and allows you to compare the best models so that you can see the differences between the training runs. This makes hyper-parameter tuning much easier and can be used with any tfestimator model or Keras model. For more details, go to https://tensorflow.rstudio.com/tools/tfruns/articles/overview.html.

The following code is in the Chapter8/hyperparams.R folder and also uses the script we used in the *TensorFlow estimators* section (Chapter8/tf_estimators.R):

```
library(tfruns)
# FLAGS <- flags(
# flag_numeric("layer1", 256),
# flag_numeric("layer2", 128),
# flag_numeric("layer3", 64),
# flag_numeric("layer4", 32),
# flag_numeric("dropout", 0.2),
# flag_string("activ","relu")
# )

training_run('tf_estimators.R')
training_run('tf_estimators.R', flags =
list(layer1=128,layer2=64,layer3=32,layer4=16))
training_run('tf_estimators.R', flags = list(dropout=0.1,activ="tanh"))
```

This will run the Chapter8/tf_estimators.R script with different hyper-parameters. The first time, we don't change any hyper-parameters, so it uses the defaults included in Chapter8/tf_estimators.R. Each time a new model is trained using the classification script, it is called a **training run**, and the details of the training run is stored in the runs folder in the current working directory.

For each training run, a new website will pop up with details on the run, as shown in the following screenshot:

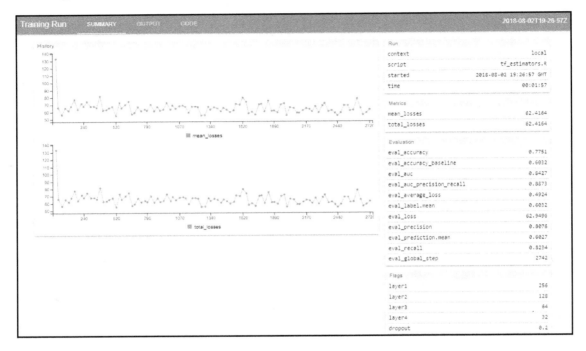

Figure 8.8: TensorFlow training run – Summary screen

We can see the progress of the training in the plots, along with the details of when the training run occurred and the evaluation metrics. We can also see in the bottom right that the **flags** (that is, hyper-parameters) used in the training run are also shown. There is another tab for the R code output, which includes all of the output from the R code in the inner file (`Chapter8/tf_estimators.R`), including plots.

Once all of the training runs are complete, the following code shows a summary of all the training runs:

```
ls_runs(order=eval_accuracy)
ls_runs(order=eval_accuracy)[,1:5]
Data frame: 3 x 5
                  run_dir eval_accuracy eval_accuracy_baseline eval_auc
eval_auc_precision_recall
3 runs/2018-08-02T19-50-17Z         0.7746                 0.6032   0.8431
0.8874
2 runs/2018-08-02T19-52-04Z         0.7724                 0.6032   0.8425
```

```
0.8873
1 runs/2018-08-02T19-53-39Z          0.7711            0.6032    0.8360
0.8878
```

Here, we have ordered the results by the column `eval_accuracy`. If you close the window showing the summary for the training run, you can display it again by calling the `view_run` function and passing in the folder name. For example, to show the summary for the best training run, use the following code:

```
dir1 <- ls_runs(order=eval_accuracy)[1,1]
view_run(dir1)
```

Finally, you can also compare two runs. Here, we are comparing the two best models:

```
dir1 <- ls_runs(order=eval_accuracy)[1,1]
dir2 <- ls_runs(order=eval_accuracy)[2,1]
compare_runs(runs=c(dir1,dir2))
```

This brings up a page similar to the following:

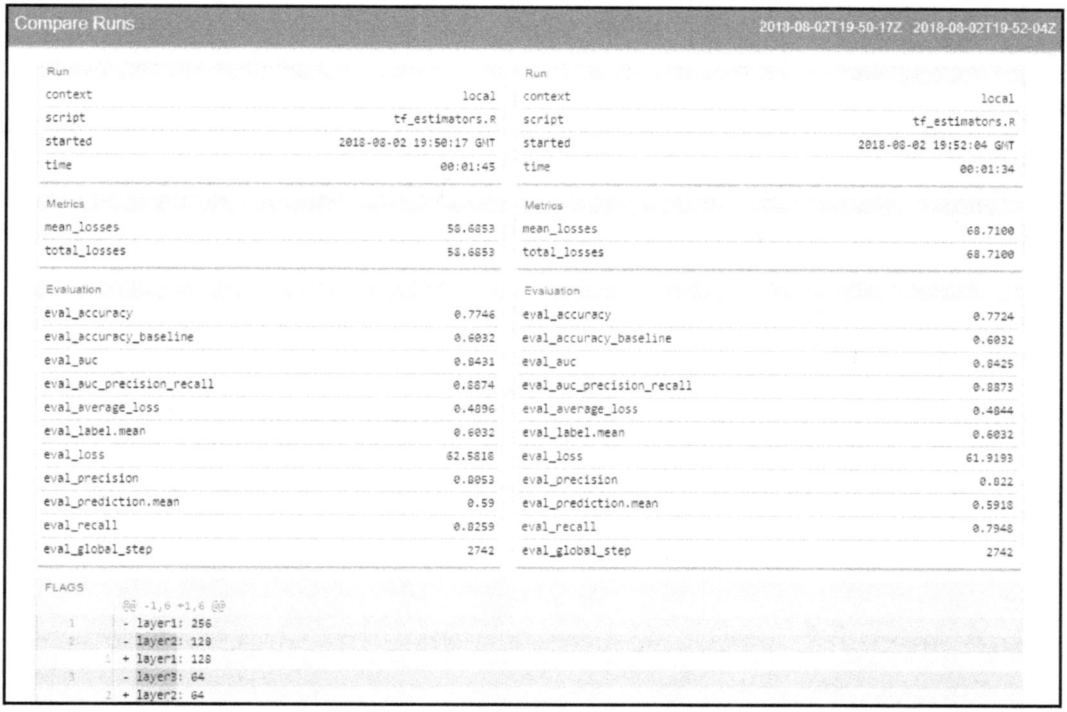

Figure 8.9: Comparing two TensorFlow runs

This page shows the evaluation metrics for both training runs and also displays the hyper-parameters that were used. As we can see, this makes managing the process of tuning deep learning models much easier. This approach to hyper-parameter tuning has automatic logging, traceability, and it is easy to compare different sets of hyper-parameters. You can see the metrics and the different hyper-parameters used for the training runs. There's no more comparing configuration files to try and match hyper-parameter settings to output logs! In comparison, the code I wrote for hyper-parameter selection for the NLP example in Chapter 7, *Natural Language Processing Using Deep Learning*, seems crude in comparison

Summary

In this chapter, we developed some TensorFlow models. We looked at TensorBoard, which is a great tool for visualizing and debugging deep learning models. We built a couple of models using TensorFlow, including a basic regression model and a Lenet model for computer vision models. From these examples, we saw that programming in TensorFlow was more complicated and error-prone than using the higher-level APIs (MXNet and Keras) that we used elsewhere in this book.

We then moved onto using TensorFlow estimators, which is a much easier interface than using TensorFlow. We then used that script in another package called **tfruns**, which stands for TensorFlow runs. This package allows us to call a TensorFlow estimators or Keras script with different flags each time. We used this for hyper-parameter selection, running, and evaluating multiple models. The TensorFlow runs have excellent integration with RStudio and we were able to view summaries for each run and compare runs to see the difference in the metrics and hyper-parameters that were used.

In the next chapter, we we will look at embeddings and auto-encoders. We have already seen embeddings in Chapter 7, *Natural Language Processing Using Deep Learning*, so in the next chapter we will see how embeddings can create a lower level encoding of data. We will also use train auto-encoders, which create these embeddings. We will use auto-encoders for anomaly detection and also for collaborative filtering (recommender system).

Anomaly Detection and Recommendation Systems

9

This chapter will look at auto-encoder models and recommendation systems. Although these two use cases may seem very different, they both rely on finding different representations of data. These representations are similar to the embeddings we saw in Chapter 7, *Natural Language Processing Using Deep Learning*. The first part of this chapter introduces unsupervised learning where there is no specific outcome to be predicted. The next section provides a conceptual overview of auto-encoder models in a machine learning and deep neural network context in particular. We will show you how to build and apply an auto-encoder model to identify anomalous data. Such atypical data may be bad data or outliers, but could also be instances that require further investigation, for example, fraud detection. An example of applying anomaly detection is detecting when an individual's credit card spending pattern differs from their usual behavior. Finally, this chapter closes with a use case on how to apply recommendation systems for cross-sell and up-sell opportunities using the retail dataset that was introduced in Chapter 4, *Training Deep Prediction Models*.

This chapter will cover the following topics:

- What is unsupervised learning?
- How do auto-encoders work?
- Training an auto-encoder in R
- Using auto-encoders for anomaly detection
- Use case – collaborative filtering

What is unsupervised learning?

So far, we have focused on models and techniques that broadly fall under the category of supervised learning. Supervised learning is supervised because the task is for the machine to learn the relationship between a set of variables or features and one or more outcomes. For example, in `Chapter 4`, *Training Deep Prediction Models*, we wanted to predict whether someone would visit a store in the next 14 days. In this chapter, we will delve into methods of unsupervised learning. In contrast with supervised learning, where there is an outcome variable(s) or labeled data is being used, unsupervised learning does not use any outcomes or labeled data. Unsupervised learning uses only input features for learning. A common example of unsupervised learning is cluster analysis, such as k-means clustering, where the machine learns hidden or latent clusters in the data to minimize a criterion (for example, the smallest variance within a cluster).

Another unsupervised learning method is to find another representation of the data, or to reduce the input data into a smaller dataset without losing too much information in the process, this is known as dimensionality reduction. The goal of dimensionality reduction is for a set of p features to find a set of latent variables, k, so that $k < p$. However, with k latent variables, p raw variables can be reasonably reproduced. We used **principal component analysis (PCA)** in the neural networks example from `Chapter 2`, *Training a Prediction Model*. In that example, we saw that there is a trade-off between the number of dimensions and the information loss, as shown in *Figure 2.1*. Principal component analysis uses an orthogonal transformation to go from the raw data to the principal components. In addition to being uncorrelated, the principal components are ordered from the component that explains the most variance to that which explains the least. Although all principal components can be used (in which case the dimensionality of the data is not reduced), only components that explain a sufficiently large amount of variance (for example, based on high eigenvalues) are included and components that account for relatively little variance are dropped as noise or unnecessary. In the neural networks example in `Chapter 2`, *Training a Prediction Model*, we had 624 inputs after eliminating the features with zero variance. When we applied PCA, we found that 50% of our variance (information) by our data could be represented in just 23 principal components.

How do auto-encoders work?

Auto-encoders are a form of dimensionality reduction technique. When they are used in this manner, they mathematically and conceptually have similarities to other dimensionality reduction techniques such as PCA. Auto-encoders consist of two parts: an encoder which creates a representation of the data, and a decoder which tries to reproduce or predict the inputs. Thus, the hidden layers and neurons are not maps between an input and some other outcome, but are self (auto)-encoding. Given sufficient complexity, auto-encoders can simply learn the identity function, and the hidden neurons will exactly mirror the raw data, resulting in no meaningful benefit. Similarly, in PCA, using all the principal components also provides no benefit. Therefore, the best auto-encoder is not necessarily the most accurate one, but one that reveals some meaningful structure or architecture in the data or one that reduces noise, identifies outliers, or anomalous data, or some other useful side-effect that is not necessarily directly related to accurate predictions of the model inputs.

Auto-encoders with a lower dimensionality than the raw data are called **undercomplete**; by using an undercomplete auto-encoder, one can force the auto-encoder to learn the most important features of the data. One common application of auto-encoders is to pre-train deep neural networks or other supervised learning models. In addition, it is possible to use the hidden features themselves. We will see this later on for anomaly detection. Using an undercomplete model is effectively a way to regularize the model. However, it is also possible to train overcomplete auto-encoders where the hidden dimensionality is greater than the raw data, so long as some other form of regularization is used.

There are broadly two parts to auto-encoders:

- First, an encoding function, $f()$, encodes the raw data, x, to the hidden neurons, H
- Second, a decoding function, $g()$, decodes H back to x

The following diagram shows an undercomplete encoder, where we have fewer nodes in the hidden layer. The output layer on the right is the decoded version of the input layer on the left. The task of the hidden layer is to store as much information as possible about the input layer (encode the input layer) so that the input layer can be re-constructed (or decoded):

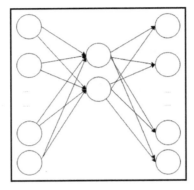

Figure 9.1: An example of an auto-encoder

Regularized auto-encoders

An undercomplete auto-encoder is a form of a regularized auto-encoder, where the regularization occurs through using a shallower (or in some other way lower) dimensional representation than the data. However, regularization can be accomplished through other means as well. These are penalized auto-encoders.

Penalized auto-encoders

As we have seen in previous chapters, one approach to preventing overfitting is to use penalties, that is, regularization. In general, our goal is to minimize the reconstruction error. If we have an objective function, F, we may optimize $F(y, f(x))$, where $f()$ encodes the raw data inputs to generate predicted or expected y values. For auto-encoders, we have $F(x, g(f(x)))$, so that the machine learns the weights and functional form of $f()$ and $g()$ to minimize the discrepancy between x and the reconstruction of x, namely $g(f(x))$. If we want to use an overcomplete auto-encoder, we need to introduce some form of regularization to force the machine to learn a representation that does not simply mirror the input. For example, we might add a function that penalizes based on complexity, so that instead of optimizing $F(x, g(f(x)))$, we optimize $F(x, g(f(x))) + P(f(x))$, where the penalty function, P, depends on the encoding or the raw inputs, $f()$.

Such penalties differ somewhat from those we have seen before, in that the penalty is designed to induce sparseness, not of the parameters but rather of the latent variables, *H*, which are the encoded representations of the raw data. The goal is to learn a latent representation that captures the essential features of the data.

Another type of penalty that can be used to provide regularization is one based on the derivative. Whereas sparse auto-encoders have a penalty that induces sparseness of the latent variables, penalizing the derivatives results in the model learning a form of *f()* that is relatively insensitive to minor perturbations of the raw input data, *x*. What we mean by this is that it forces a penalty on functions where the encoding varies greatly for changes in *x*, preferring regions where the gradient is relatively flat.

Denoising auto-encoders

Denoising auto-encoders remove noise or denoise data, and are a useful technique for learning a latent representation of raw data (*Vincent, P., Larochelle, H., Bengio, Y., and Manzagol, P. A. (2008, July); Bengio, Y.,Courville, A., and Vincent, P. (2013)*). We said that the general task of an auto-encoder was to optimize: *F(x, g(f(x)))*. However, for a denoising auto-encoder, the task is to recover *x* from a noisy or corrupted version of *x*. One application of denoising auto-encoders is to restore old images that may be blurred or corrupted.

Although denoising auto-encoders are used to try and recover the true representation from corrupted data or data with noise, this technique can also be used as a regularization tool. As a method of regularization, rather than having noisy or corrupted data and attempting to recover the truth, the raw data is purposefully corrupted. This forces the auto-encoder to do more than merely learn the identity function, as the raw inputs are no longer identical to the output. This process is shown in the following diagram:

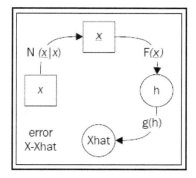

Figure 9.2: Denoising auto-encoders

The remaining choice is what the function, *N()*, which adds the noise or corrupts *x*, should be. Two choices are to add noise through a stochastic process or for any given training iteration to only include a subset of the raw *x* inputs. In the next section, we will explore how to actually train auto-encoder models in R.

Training an auto-encoder in R

In this section, we are going to train an auto-encoder in R and show you that it can be used as a dimensionality reduction technique. We will compare it with the approach we took in Chapter 2, *Training a Prediction Model*, where we used PCA to find the principal components in the image data. In that example, we used PCA and found that 23 factors was sufficient to explain 50% of the variance in the data. We built a neural network model using just these 23 factors to classify a dataset with either 5 or 6. We got 97.86% accuracy in that example.

We are going to follow a similar process in this example, and we will use the MINST dataset again. The following code from Chapter8/encoder.R loads the data. We will use half the data for training an auto-encoder and the other half will be used to build a classification model to evaluate how good the auto-encoder is at dimensionality reduction. The first part of the code is similar to what we have seen in previous examples; it loads and normalizes the data so that the values are between 0.0 and 1.0:

```
library(keras)
library(corrplot)
library(neuralnet)
options(width = 70, digits = 2)
options(scipen=999)
dataDirectory <- "../data"
if (!file.exists(paste(dataDirectory,'/train.csv',sep="")))
{
  link <-
'https://apache-mxnet.s3-accelerate.dualstack.amazonaws.com/R/data/mnist_cs
v.zip'
  if (!file.exists(paste(dataDirectory,'/mnist_csv.zip',sep="")))
  download.file(link, destfile =
paste(dataDirectory,'/mnist_csv.zip',sep=""))
  unzip(paste(dataDirectory,'/mnist_csv.zip',sep=""), exdir = dataDirectory)
  if (file.exists(paste(dataDirectory,'/test.csv',sep="")))
  file.remove(paste(dataDirectory,'/test.csv',sep=""))
}

data <- read.csv("../data/train.csv", header=TRUE)
set.seed(42)
```

```
sample<-sample(nrow(data),0.5*nrow(data))
test <- setdiff(seq_len(nrow(data)),sample)
train.x <- data[sample,-1]
test.x <- data[test,-1]
train.y <- data[sample,1]
test.y <- data[test,1]
rm(data)
train.x <- train.x/255
test.x <- test.x/255
train.x <- data.matrix(train.x)
test.x <- data.matrix(test.x)
input_dim <- 28*28 #784
```

Now, we will move on to our first auto-encoder. We will use 16 hidden neurons in our auto-encoder and use tanh as the activation function. We use 20% of our data as validation to provide an unbiased estimate of how the auto-encoder performs. Here is the code. To keep it concise, we are only showing part of the output:

```
# model 1
inner_layer_dim <- 16
input_layer <- layer_input(shape=c(input_dim))
encoder <- layer_dense(units=inner_layer_dim,
activation='tanh')(input_layer)
decoder <- layer_dense(units=784)(encoder)
autoencoder <- keras_model(inputs=input_layer, outputs = decoder)
autoencoder %>% compile(optimizer='adam',
loss='mean_squared_error',metrics='accuracy')
history <- autoencoder %>% fit(train.x,train.x,
 epochs=40, batch_size=128,validation_split=0.2)

Train on 16800 samples, validate on 4200 samples
Epoch 1/40
16800/16800 [==============================] - 1s 36us/step - loss: 0.0683
- acc: 0.0065 - val_loss: 0.0536 - val_acc: 0.0052
Epoch 2/40
16800/16800 [==============================] - 1s 30us/step - loss: 0.0457
- acc: 0.0082 - val_loss: 0.0400 - val_acc: 0.0081
Epoch 3/40
16800/16800 [==============================] - 0s 29us/step - loss: 0.0367
- acc: 0.0101 - val_loss: 0.0344 - val_acc: 0.0121
...
...
Epoch 38/40
16800/16800 [==============================] - 0s 29us/step - loss: 0.0274
- acc: 0.0107 - val_loss: 0.0275 - val_acc: 0.0098
Epoch 39/40
```

```
16800/16800 [==============================] - 1s 31us/step - loss: 0.0274
- acc: 0.0111 - val_loss: 0.0275 - val_acc: 0.0093
Epoch 40/40
16800/16800 [==============================] - 1s 32us/step - loss: 0.0274
- acc: 0.0120 - val_loss: 0.0275 - val_acc: 0.0095
```

The validation loss is 0.0275, which shows that the model is performing quite well. Another nice feature is that if you run the code in RStudio, it will show the training metrics in graphs, which will automatically update as the model is trained. This is shown in the following screenshot:

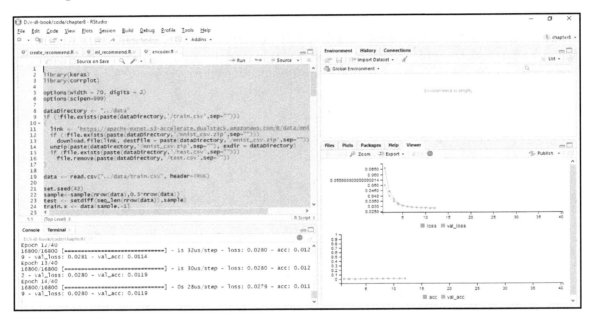

Figure 9.3: Model metrics showing in the Viewer pane in RStudio

Once the model has completed training, you can also plot the model architecture and model metrics using the following code (the output is also included). By calling the plot function, you can see the plots for the accuracy and the loss on the training and validation datasets:

```
summary(autoencoder)
```

Layer (type)	Output Shape	Param #
input_1 (InputLayer)	(None, 784)	0

```
dense_1 (Dense)                 (None, 16)                  12560

dense_2 (Dense)                 (None, 784)                 13328
=============================================================
Total params: 25,888
Trainable params: 25,888
Non-trainable params: 0
```

```
plot(history)
```

This code produces the following plot:

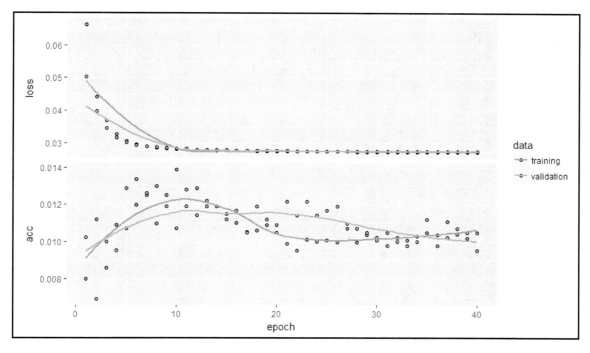

Figure 9.4: Auto-encoder model metrics

The preceding plots shows that the validation accuracy is relatively stable, but it probably peaked after epoch 20. We will now train a second model with 32 hidden nodes instead in the following code:

```
# model 2
inner_layer_dim <- 32
input_layer <- layer_input(shape=c(input_dim))
encoder <- layer_dense(units=inner_layer_dim,
```

```
activation='tanh')(input_layer)
decoder <- layer_dense(units=784)(encoder)
autoencoder <- keras_model(inputs=input_layer, outputs = decoder)
autoencoder %>% compile(optimizer='adam',
 loss='mean_squared_error',metrics='accuracy')
history <- autoencoder %>% fit(train.x,train.x,
 epochs=40, batch_size=128,validation_split=0.2)

Train on 16800 samples, validate on 4200 samples
Epoch 1/40
16800/16800 [==============================] - 1s 41us/step - loss: 0.0591
- acc: 0.0104 - val_loss: 0.0406 - val_acc: 0.0131
Epoch 2/40
16800/16800 [==============================] - 1s 34us/step - loss: 0.0339
- acc: 0.0111 - val_loss: 0.0291 - val_acc: 0.0093
Epoch 3/40
16800/16800 [==============================] - 1s 33us/step - loss: 0.0262
- acc: 0.0108 - val_loss: 0.0239 - val_acc: 0.0100
...
...
Epoch 38/40
16800/16800 [==============================] - 1s 33us/step - loss: 0.0174
- acc: 0.0130 - val_loss: 0.0175 - val_acc: 0.0095
Epoch 39/40
16800/16800 [==============================] - 1s 31us/step - loss: 0.0174
- acc: 0.0132 - val_loss: 0.0175 - val_acc: 0.0098
Epoch 40/40
16800/16800 [==============================] - 1s 34us/step - loss: 0.0174
- acc: 0.0126 - val_loss: 0.0175 - val_acc: 0.0100
```

Our validation loss has improved to 0.0175, so let's try 64 hidden nodes:

```
# model 3
inner_layer_dim <- 64
input_layer <- layer_input(shape=c(input_dim))
encoder <- layer_dense(units=inner_layer_dim,
activation='tanh')(input_layer)
decoder <- layer_dense(units=784)(encoder)
autoencoder <- keras_model(inputs=input_layer, outputs = decoder)
autoencoder %>% compile(optimizer='adam',
 loss='mean_squared_error',metrics='accuracy')
history <- autoencoder %>% fit(train.x,train.x,
 epochs=40, batch_size=128,validation_split=0.2)

Train on 16800 samples, validate on 4200 samples
Epoch 1/40
16800/16800 [==============================] - 1s 50us/step - loss: 0.0505
- acc: 0.0085 - val_loss: 0.0300 - val_acc: 0.0138
```

```
Epoch 2/40
16800/16800 [==============================] - 1s 39us/step - loss: 0.0239
- acc: 0.0110 - val_loss: 0.0197 - val_acc: 0.0090
Epoch 3/40
16800/16800 [==============================] - 1s 41us/step - loss: 0.0173
- acc: 0.0115 - val_loss: 0.0156 - val_acc: 0.0117
...
...
Epoch 38/40
16800/16800 [==============================] - 1s 41us/step - loss: 0.0094
- acc: 0.0124 - val_loss: 0.0096 - val_acc: 0.0131
Epoch 39/40
16800/16800 [==============================] - 1s 39us/step - loss: 0.0095
- acc: 0.0128 - val_loss: 0.0095 - val_acc: 0.0121
Epoch 40/40
16800/16800 [==============================] - 1s 37us/step - loss: 0.0094
- acc: 0.0126 - val_loss: 0.0098 - val_acc: 0.0133
```

Our validation loss here is 0.0098, which again is an improvement. We have probably got to the stage where adding more hidden nodes will cause the model to overfit because we are only using 16800 rows to train the autoencoder. We could look at applying regularization, but since our first models have an accuracy of 0.01, we are doing well enough.

Accessing the features of the auto-encoder model

We can extract the deep features from the model, that is, the values for the hidden neurons in the model. For this, we will use the model with 16 hidden nodes. We will examine the distribution of correlations using the ggplot2 package, as shown in the following code. The results are shown in *Figure 9.5*. The deep features have small correlations, that is, usually with an absolute value of <.20. This is what we expect in order for the auto-encoder to work. This means that the features should not duplicate information between them:

```
encoder <- keras_model(inputs=input_layer, outputs=encoder)
encodings <- encoder %>% predict(test.x)
encodings<-as.data.frame(encodings)
M <- cor(encodings)
corrplot(M, method = "circle", sig.level = 0.1)
```

The preceding code produces the following plot:

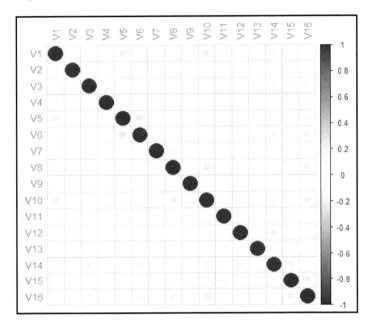

Figure 9.5: Correlation between weights in the hidden layer of the auto-encoder

In Chapter 2, *Training a Prediction Model*, we used PCA for dimensionality reduction and found that for a binary classification task of telling the difference between 5 and 6, we could still get 97.86% accuracy, even if we only used 23 features as input. These 23 features were the 23 **principal components** and accounted for 50% of the variance in our dataset. We will use the weights in the auto-encoder to perform the same experiment. Note that we trained the auto-encoder on 50% of the data, and that we are using the other 50% of the data for the binary classification task, that is, we do not want to try and build a classification task on data that was used to build the auto-encoder:

```
encodings$y <- test.y
encodings <- encodings[encodings$y==5 | encodings$y==6,]
encodings[encodings$y==5,]$y <- 0
encodings[encodings$y==6,]$y <- 1
table(encodings$y)
    0    1
1852 2075
nobs <- nrow(encodings)
train <- sample(nobs, 0.9*nobs)
test <- setdiff(seq_len(nobs), train)
trainData <- encodings[train,]
```

```
testData <- encodings[test,]
col_names <- names(trainData)
f <- as.formula(paste("y ~", paste(col_names[!col_names
%in%"y"],collapse="+")))
nn <- neuralnet(f,data=trainData,hidden=c(4,2),linear.output = FALSE)
preds_nn <- compute(nn,testData[,1:(-1+ncol(testData))])
preds_nn <- ifelse(preds_nn$net.result > 0.5, "1", "0")
t<-table(testData$y, preds_nn,dnn=c("Actual", "Predicted"))
acc<-round(100.0*sum(diag(t))/sum(t),2)
print(t)
       Predicted
Actual 0 1
     0 182 5
     1 3 203
print(sprintf(" accuracy = %1.2f%%",acc))
[1] " accuracy = 97.96%"
```

Our model gets 97.96% accuracy, which is a slight improvement on the 97.86% accuracy we achieved in Chapter 2, *Training a Prediction Model*. It is not really a surprise that the two models are very similar as the mathematical foundations for PCA involves matrix decomposition, while the auto-encoder uses back-propagation to set the matrix weights for the hidden layer. In fact, if we dropped the non-linear activation function, our encodings would be very similar to PCA. This demonstrates that auto-encoder models can be used effectively as a dimensionality reduction technique.

Using auto-encoders for anomaly detection

Now that we have built an auto-encoder and accessed the features of the inner layers, we will move on to an example of how auto-encoders can be used for anomaly detection. The premise here is quite simple: we take the reconstructed outputs from the decoder and see which instances have the most error, that is, which instances are the most difficult for the decoder to reconstruct. The code that is used here is in Chapter9/anomaly.R, and we will be using the UCI HAR dataset that we have already been introduced to in Chapter 2, *Training a Prediction Model*. If you have not already downloaded the data, go back to that chapter for instructions on how to do so.. The first part of the code loads the data, and we subset the features to only use the ones with mean, sd, and skewness in the feature names:

```
library(keras)
library(ggplot2)
train.x <- read.table("UCI HAR Dataset/train/X_train.txt")
train.y <- read.table("UCI HAR Dataset/train/y_train.txt")[[1]]
test.x <- read.table("UCI HAR Dataset/test/X_test.txt")
test.y <- read.table("UCI HAR Dataset/test/y_test.txt")[[1]]
```

```
use.labels <- read.table("UCI HAR Dataset/activity_labels.txt")
colnames(use.labels) <-c("y","label")

features <- read.table("UCI HAR Dataset/features.txt")
meanSD <- grep("mean\\(\\)|std\\(\\)|max\\(\\)|min\\(\\)|skewness\\(\\)",
features[, 2])

train.x <- data.matrix(train.x[,meanSD])
test.x <- data.matrix(test.x[,meanSD])
input_dim <- ncol(train.x)
```

Now, we can build our auto-encoder model. This is going to be a stacked auto-encoder with two 40 neuron hidden encoder layers and two 40-neuron hidden decoder layers. For conciseness, we have removed some of the output:

```
# model
inner_layer_dim <- 40
input_layer <- layer_input(shape=c(input_dim))
encoder <- layer_dense(units=inner_layer_dim,
activation='tanh')(input_layer)
encoder <- layer_dense(units=inner_layer_dim, activation='tanh')(encoder)
decoder <- layer_dense(units=inner_layer_dim)(encoder)
decoder <- layer_dense(units=inner_layer_dim)(decoder)
decoder <- layer_dense(units=input_dim)(decoder)

autoencoder <- keras_model(inputs=input_layer, outputs = decoder)
autoencoder %>% compile(optimizer='adam',
 loss='mean_squared_error',metrics='accuracy')
history <- autoencoder %>% fit(train.x,train.x,
 epochs=30, batch_size=128,validation_split=0.2)
Train on 5881 samples, validate on 1471 samples
Epoch 1/30
5881/5881 [==============================] - 1s 95us/step - loss: 0.2342 -
acc: 0.1047 - val_loss: 0.0500 - val_acc: 0.1013
Epoch 2/30
5881/5881 [==============================] - 0s 53us/step - loss: 0.0447 -
acc: 0.2151 - val_loss: 0.0324 - val_acc: 0.2536
Epoch 3/30
5881/5881 [==============================] - 0s 44us/step - loss: 0.0324 -
acc: 0.2772 - val_loss: 0.0261 - val_acc: 0.3413
...
...

Epoch 27/30
5881/5881 [==============================] - 0s 45us/step - loss: 0.0098 -
acc: 0.2935 - val_loss: 0.0094 - val_acc: 0.3379
Epoch 28/30
5881/5881 [==============================] - 0s 44us/step - loss: 0.0096 -
```

```
acc: 0.2908 - val_loss: 0.0092 - val_acc: 0.3215
Epoch 29/30
5881/5881 [==============================] - 0s 44us/step - loss: 0.0094 -
acc: 0.2984 - val_loss: 0.0090 - val_acc: 0.3209
Epoch 30/30
5881/5881 [==============================] - 0s 44us/step - loss: 0.0092 -
acc: 0.2955 - val_loss: 0.0088 - val_acc: 0.3209
```

We can see the layers and number of parameters for the model by calling the summary function, like so:

```
summary(autoencoder)
```

Layer (type)	Output Shape	Param #
input_4 (InputLayer)	(None, 145)	0
dense_16 (Dense)	(None, 40)	5840
dense_17 (Dense)	(None, 40)	1640
dense_18 (Dense)	(None, 40)	1640
dense_19 (Dense)	(None, 40)	1640
dense_20 (Dense)	(None, 145)	5945

```
Total params: 16,705
Trainable params: 16,705
Non-trainable params: 0
```

Our validation loss is 0.0088, which means that our model is good at encoding the data. Now, we will use the test set on the auto-encoder and get the reconstructed data. This will create a dataset with the same size as the test set. We will then select any instance where the sum of the squared error (se) between the predicted values and the test set is greater than 4.

These are the instances that the auto-encoder had the most trouble in reconstructing, and therefore they are potential anomalies. The limit value of 4 is a hyperparameter; if it is set higher, fewer potential anomalies are detected and if it is set lower, more potential anomalies are detected. This value would be different according to the dataset used.

There are 6 classes in this dataset. We want to analyze if the anomalies are spread over all of our classes or if they are specific to some classes. We will print out a table of the frequencies of our classes in our test set, and we will see that the distribution of our classes is fairly even. When printing out a table of the frequencies of our classes of our potential anomalies, we can see that most of them are in the WALKING_DOWNSTAIRS class. The potential anomalies are shown in *Figure 9.6:*

```
# anomaly detection
preds <- autoencoder %>% predict(test.x)
preds <- as.data.frame(preds)
limit <- 4
preds$se_test <- apply((test.x - preds)^2, 1, sum)
preds$y_preds <- ifelse(preds$se_test>limit,1,0)
preds$y <- test.y
preds <- merge(preds,use.labels)
table(preds$label)
    LAYING  SITTING  STANDING  WALKING  WALKING_DOWNSTAIRS  WALKING_UPSTAIRS
       537      491       532      496                 420               471

table(preds[preds$y_preds==1,]$label)
    LAYING  SITTING  STANDING  WALKING  WALKING_DOWNSTAIRS  WALKING_UPSTAIRS
        18        7         1       17                  45                11
```

We can plot this with the following code:

```
ggplot(as.data.frame(table(preds[preds$y_preds==1,]$label)),aes(Var1,
Freq)) +
  ggtitle("Potential anomalies by activity") +
  geom_bar(stat = "identity") +
  xlab("") + ylab("Frequency") +
  theme_classic() +
  theme(plot.title = element_text(hjust = 0.5)) +
  theme(axis.text.x = element_text(angle = 45, hjust = 1, vjust = 1))
```

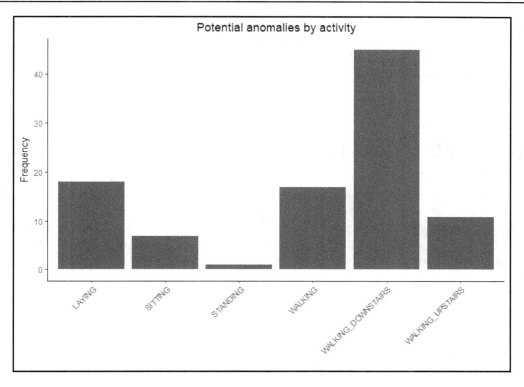

Figure 9.6: Distribution of the anomalies

In this example, we used a deep auto-encoder model to learn the features of actimetry data from smartphones. Such work can be useful for excluding unknown or unusual activities, rather than incorrectly classifying them. For example, as part of an app that classifies what activity you engaged in for how many minutes, it may be better to simply leave out a few minutes where the model is uncertain or the hidden features do not adequately reconstruct the inputs, rather than to aberrantly call an activity walking or sitting when it was actually walking downstairs.

Such work can also help to identify where the model tends to have more issues. Perhaps further sensors and additional data are needed to represent walking downstairs or more could be done to understand why walking downstairs tends to produce relatively high error rates.

These deep auto-encoders are also useful in other contexts where identifying anomalies is important, such as with financial data or credit card usage patterns. Anomalous spending patterns may indicate fraud or that a credit card has been stolen. Rather than attempt to manually search through millions of credit card transactions, one could train an auto-encoder model and use it to identify anomalies for further investigation.

Use case – collaborative filtering

This use-case is about collaborative filtering. We are going to build a recommendation system based on embeddings created from a deep learning model. To do this, we are going to use the same dataset we used in `Chapter 4`, *Training Deep Prediction Models*, which is the retail transactional database. If you have not already downloaded the database, then go to the following link, `https://www.dunnhumby.com/sourcefiles`, and select *Let's Get Sort-of-Real*. Select the option for the smallest dataset, titled *All transactions for a randomly selected sample of 5,000 customers*. Once you have read the terms and conditions and downloaded the dataset to your computer, unzip it into a directory called `dunnhumby/in` under the code folder. Ensure that the files are unzipped directly under this folder, and not a subdirectory, as you may have to copy them after unzipping the data.

The data contains details of retail transactions linked by basket IDs. Each transaction has a date and a store code, and some are also linked to customers. Here are the fields that we will use in this analysis:

Field-name	Description	Format
CUST_CODE	Customer Code. This links the transactions/visits to a customer.	Char
SPEND	Spend associated to the items bought.	Numeric
PROD_CODE	Product Code.	Char
PROD_CODE_10	Product Hierarchy Level 10 Code.	Char
PROD_CODE_20	Product Hierarchy Level 20 Code.	Char
PROD_CODE_30	Product Hierarchy Level 30 Code.	Char
PROD_CODE_40	Product Hierarchy Level 40 Code.	Char

If you want more details on the structure of the files, you can go back and re-read the use case in `Chapter 4`, *Training Deep Prediction Models*. We are going to use this dataset to create a recommendation engine. There are a family of machine learning algorithms called **Market Basket Analysis** that can be used with transactional data, but this use case is based on collaborative filtering. Collaborative filtering are recommendations based on the ratings people give to products. They are commonly used for music and film recommendations, where people rate the items, usually on a scale of 1-5. Perhaps the best known recommendation system is Netflix because of the Netflix prize (`https://en.wikipedia.org/wiki/Netflix_Prize`).

We are going to use our dataset to create implicit rankings of how much a customer *rates* an item. If you are not familiar with implicit rankings, then they are rankings that are derived from data rather than explicitly assigned by the user. We will use one of the product codes, PROD_CODE_40, and calculate the quantiles of the spend for that product code. The quantiles will divide the fields into 5 roughly equally sized groups. We will use these to assign a rating to each customer for that product based on how much they spent on that product code. The top 20% of customers will get a rating of 5, the next 20% will get a rating of 4, and so on. Each customer/product code combination that exists will have a rating from 1-5:

There is a rich history of using quantiles in retail loyalty systems. One of the earliest segmentation approaches for retail loyalty data was called **RFM analysis**. RFM is an acronym for Recency, Frequency, and Monetary spend. It gives each customer a ranking 1 (lowest) – 5 (highest) on each of these categories, with an equal number of customers in each ranking. For *Recency*, the 20% of the customers that visited most recently would be given a 5, the next 20% would be given a 4, and so on. For *Frequency*, the top 20% of customers with the most transactions would be given a 5, the next 20% would be given a 4, and so on. Similarly for *Monetary* spend, the top 20% of the customers by revenue would be given a 5, the next 20% would be given a 4, and so on. The numbers would then be concatenated, so a customer with an RFM of 453 would be 4 for Recency, 5 for Frequency, and 3 for Monetary spend. Once the score has been calculated, it can be used for many purposes, for example, cross-sell, churn analysis, and so on. RFM analysis was very popular in the late 1990's / early 2000's with many marketing managers because it is easily implemented and well-understood. However, it is not flexible and is being replaced with machine learning techniques.

Preparing the data

The code to create our ratings is in Chapter9/create_recommend.R. The first part of the code runs through the raw transactional data. The data is in separate CSV files, so it processes each file, selects the records that have a customer linked (that is, CUST_CODE!="") to them, and then groups the sales by CUST_CODE and PROD_CODE_40. It then appends the results to a temporary file and moves on to the next input file:

```
library(magrittr)
library(dplyr)
library(readr)
library(broom)
```

```
set.seed(42)
file_list <- list.files("../dunnhumby/in/", "trans*")
temp_file <- "../dunnhumby/temp.csv"
out_file <- "../dunnhumby/recommend.csv"
if (file.exists(temp_file)) file.remove(temp_file)
if (file.exists(out_file)) file.remove(out_file)
options(readr.show_progress=FALSE)

i <- 1
for (file_name in file_list)
{
  file_name<-paste("../dunnhumby/in/",file_name,sep="")
  df<-suppressMessages(read_csv(file_name))

  df2 <- df %>%
    filter(CUST_CODE!="") %>%
    group_by(CUST_CODE,PROD_CODE_40) %>%
    summarise(sales=sum(SPEND))

  colnames(df2)<-c("cust_id","prod_id","sales")
  if (i ==1)
    write_csv(df2,temp_file)
  else
    write_csv(df2,temp_file,append=TRUE)
  print (paste("File",i,"/",length(file_list),"processed"))
  i <- i+1
}
[1] "File 1 / 117 processed"
[1] "File 2 / 117 processed"
[1] "File 3 / 117 processed"
...
...
...
[1] "File 115 / 117 processed"
[1] "File 116 / 117 processed"
[1] "File 117 / 117 processed"
rm(df,df2)
```

This section groups by customer and product code for the 117 input files. As we process each file, we rename the customer code to cust_id and the product department code to prod_id. Once we are done, the combined file will obviously have duplicate customer-product code combinations; that is, we need to group again over the combined data. We do that by opening up the temporary file and grouping over the fields again:

```
df_processed<-read_csv(temp_file)
if (file.exists(temp_file)) file.remove(temp_file)
```

```
df2 <- df_processed %>%
  group_by(cust_id,prod_id) %>%
  summarise(sales=sum(sales))
```

We could have tried to load all of the transactional data and run a group on that data, but that would have been memory and computationally expensive. By running it in two steps, we reduce the amount of data we need to process at each stage, which means it is more likely to run on machines with limited memory.

Once we have the total spend for each customer and product department code combination, we can create the ratings. Thanks to the excellent `tidyr` packages, it only takes a few lines to assign a rating to each row. First, we group by the `prod_id` field, and use the quantile function to return quantiles for the sales for each product code. These quantiles will return the sales ranges that correspond to splitting the customers into 5 equal sized groups. We then use these quantiles to assign rankings:

```
# create quantiles
dfProds <- df2 %>%
  group_by(prod_id) %>%
  do( tidy(t(quantile(.$sales, probs = seq(0, 1, 0.2)))) )
colnames(dfProds)<-c("prod_id","X0","X20","X40","X60","X80","X100")
df2<-merge(df2,dfProds)
df2$rating<-0
df2[df2$sales<=df2$X20,"rating"] <- 1
df2[(df2$sales>df2$X20) & (df2$sales<=df2$X40),"rating"] <- 2
df2[(df2$sales>df2$X40) & (df2$sales<=df2$X60),"rating"] <- 3
df2[(df2$sales>df2$X60) & (df2$sales<=df2$X80),"rating"] <- 4
df2[(df2$sales>df2$X80) & (df2$sales<=df2$X100),"rating"] <- 5
```

The only thing remaining is to save the results. Before we do, we do a couple of sanity checks to ensure that our ratings are evenly distributed from 1-5 overall. We then select a random product code and check that our ratings are evenly distributed from 1-5 for those products:

```
# sanity check, are our ratings spread out relatively evenly
df2 %>%
  group_by(rating) %>%
  summarise(recs=n())
  rating  recs
1      1 68246
2      2 62592
3      3 62162
4      4 63488
5      5 63682
df2 %>%
  filter(prod_id==df2[sample(1:nrow(df2), 1),]$prod_id) %>%
```

```
  group_by(prod_id,rating) %>%
  summarise(recs=n())
  prod_id rating recs
1 D00008      1  597
2 D00008      2  596
3 D00008      3  596
4 D00008      4  596
5 D00008      5  596

df2 <- df2[,c("cust_id","prod_id","rating")]
write_csv(df2,out_file)
```

Everything looks good here: the count for `rating=1` is higher at 68246 against 62162 to 63682 for ratings 2 to 5, but that is not really a concern as collaborative filtering models do not expect an even distribution of ratings. For the individual item (D00008), the distribution is even at 596 or 597 for each rating.

Building a collaborative filtering model

Before we jump into applying a deep learning model, we should follow the same practice as we have done in previous chapters and create a benchmark accuracy score using a standard machine learning algorithm. It is quick, easy, and will give us confidence that our deep learning model is working better than just using *normal* machine learning. Here are the 20 lines of code to do collaborative filtering in R. This code can be found in `Chapter8/ml_recommend.R`:

```
library(readr)
library(recommenderlab)
library(reshape2)

set.seed(42)
in_file <- "../dunnhumby/recommend.csv"
df <- read_csv(in_file)
dfPivot <-dcast(df, cust_id ~ prod_id)
m <- as.matrix(dfPivot[,2:ncol(dfPivot)])

recommend <- as(m,"realRatingMatrix")
e <- evaluationScheme(recommend,method="split",
 train=0.9,given=-1, goodRating=5)
e
Evaluation scheme using all-but-1 items
Method: 'split' with 1 run(s).
Training set proportion: 0.900
Good ratings: >=5.000000
Data set: 5000 x 9 rating matrix of class 'realRatingMatrix' with 25688
```

```
ratings.

r1 <- Recommender(getData(e,"train"),"UBCF")
r1
Recommender of type 'UBCF' for 'realRatingMatrix'
learned using 4500 users.

p1 <- predict(r1,getData(e,"known"),type="ratings")
err1<-calcPredictionAccuracy(p1,getData(e,"unknown"))
print(sprintf(" User based collaborative filtering model MSE =
%1.4f",err1[2]))
[1] " User based collaborative filtering model MSE = 0.9748"
```

This code creates a collaborative filtering model, and the MSE for the model is `0.9748`. As before, we do this because most of the work for this sample is in data preparation and not model building, so it is relatively easy to use a base machine learning algorithm to compare the performance against a deep learning model. The code here uses standard R libraries to create a recommendation system, and as you can see, it is relatively simple because the data is already in the expected format. If you want more information on this collaborative filtering algorithm, then search for `user based collaborative filtering in r`, or go through the doc pages.

Now lets focus on creating a deep learning model.

Building a deep learning collaborative filtering model

Here, we will see if we can build a deep learning model to beat the previous approach! The following code is in `Chapter9/keras_recommend.R`. The first part loads the dataset and creates new IDs for the customer and product codes. This is because Keras expects the indexes to be sequential, starting at zero, and unique:

```
library(readr)
library(keras)

set.seed(42)
use_session_with_seed(42, disable_gpu = FALSE, disable_parallel_cpu =
FALSE)

df<-read_csv("recommend.csv")
custs <- as.data.frame(unique(df$cust_id))
custs$cust_id2 <- as.numeric(row.names(custs))
colnames(custs) <- c("cust_id","cust_id2")
custs$cust_id2 <- custs$cust_id2 - 1
```

```
prods <- as.data.frame(unique(df$prod_id))
prods$prod_id2 <- as.numeric(row.names(prods))
colnames(prods) <- c("prod_id","prod_id2")
prods$prod_id2 <- prods$prod_id2 - 1
df<-merge(df,custs)
df<-merge(df,prods)
n_custs = length(unique(df$cust_id2))
n_prods = length(unique(df$prod_id2))

# shuffle the data
trainData <- df[sample(nrow(df)),]
```

We have 5,000 unique customers and 9 unique product codes. This is not typical of most collaborative filtering examples; usually, the number of products is much higher than the number of customers. The next part creates the model. We will create embedding layers for the customer and the products and then calculate the dot product of those embedding layers. An embedding layer is a lower-order representation of the data and is exactly the same as the encoders in the auto-encoder examples we saw earlier. We will also have a bias term for each customer and product – this performs a sort of normalization on the data. If a particular product is very popular, or a customer has a lot of high ratings, this accounts for this. We will use 10 factors in our embedding layer for both customers and products. We will use some L2 regularization in our embeddings to prevent overfitting. The following code defines the model architecture:

```
n_factors<-10
# define the model
cust_in <- layer_input(shape = 1)
cust_embed <- layer_embedding(
  input_dim = n_custs
  ,output_dim = n_factors
  ,input_length = 1
  ,embeddings_regularizer=regularizer_l2(0.0001)
  ,name = "cust_embed"
  )(cust_in)
prod_in <- layer_input(shape = 1)
prod_embed <- layer_embedding(
  input_dim = n_prods
  ,output_dim = n_factors
  ,input_length = 1
  ,embeddings_regularizer=regularizer_l2(0.0001)
  ,name = "prod_embed"
  )(prod_in)

ub = layer_embedding(
  input_dim = n_custs,
  output_dim = 1,
```

```
  input_length = 1,
  name = "custb_embed"
  )(cust_in)
ub_flat <- layer_flatten()(ub)

mb = layer_embedding(
  input_dim = n_prods,
  output_dim = 1,
  input_length = 1,
  name = "prodb_embed"
  )(prod_in)
mb_flat <- layer_flatten()(mb)

cust_flat <- layer_flatten()(cust_embed)
prod_flat <- layer_flatten()(prod_embed)

x <- layer_dot(list(cust_flat, prod_flat), axes = 1)
x <- layer_add(list(x, ub_flat))
x <- layer_add(list(x, mb_flat))
```

Now, we are ready to build the model. We are going to hold out 10% of our data for validation:

```
model <- keras_model(list(cust_in, prod_in), x)
compile(model,optimizer="adam", loss='mse')

model.optimizer.lr=0.001
fit(model,list(trainData$cust_id2,trainData$prod_id2),trainData$rating,
  batch_size=128,epochs=40,validation_split = 0.1 )
Train on 23119 samples, validate on 2569 samples
Epoch 1/40
23119/23119 [==============================] - 1s 31us/step - loss: 10.3551
- val_loss: 9.9817
Epoch 2/40
23119/23119 [==============================] - 0s 21us/step - loss: 8.6549
- val_loss: 7.7826
Epoch 3/40
23119/23119 [==============================] - 0s 20us/step - loss: 6.0651
- val_loss: 5.2164
...
...
...
Epoch 37/40
23119/23119 [==============================] - 0s 19us/step - loss: 0.6674
- val_loss: 0.9575
Epoch 38/40
23119/23119 [==============================] - 0s 18us/step - loss: 0.6486
- val_loss: 0.9555
```

```
Epoch 39/40
23119/23119 [==============================] - 0s 19us/step - loss: 0.6271
- val_loss: 0.9547
Epoch 40/40
23119/23119 [==============================] - 0s 20us/step - loss: 0.6023
- val_loss: 0.9508
```

Our model achieved an MSE of 0.9508, which is an improvement on the MSE of 0.9748 that we got on our machine learning model. Our deep learning model is overfitting, but one reason for this is because we have a relatively small database. I tried increasing the regularization, but this did not improve the model.

Applying the deep learning model to a business problem

Now that we have a model, how can we use it? The most typical example of using a collaborative filtering model is to recommend items to people they have not rated yet. That concept works well in domains such as music and movie recommendations where collaborative filtering models are often applied. However, we are going to use it for a different purpose. One concern of marketing managers is the **Share of wallet** they get from a customer. The definition of this (from https://en.wikipedia.org/wiki/Share_of_ wallet) is the *percentage ('share') of a customer's expenses ('of wallet') for a product that goes to the firm selling the product*. It basically measures the value of a customer on the percentage of the potential spend they could have with us. As an example, we may have customers who visit our shop regularly and spend a considerable amount. But are they buying all of their goods from us? Maybe they buy their fresh food elsewhere, that is, they purchase their meat, fruit, vegetables, and so on, at other stores. We can use collaborative filtering to find customers where the collaborative filtering model predicts that they purchase certain products in our store, but in fact they do not. Remember that collaborative filtering works on the basis of making recommendations based on what other similar customers do. So, if customer A does not purchase meat, fruit, vegetables, and so on, at our store when other similar customers do, then we could try and entice them to spend more at our stores by sending them offers for these products.

We will look for customer-product department codes where the prediction is greater than 4, but the actual value is less than 2. These customers should be purchasing these goods from us (according to the model), so by sending them vouchers for items in these departments, we can capture a greater amount of their spending.

A collaborative filtering model should work well for this type of analysis. The basis of this algorithm is to find the recommend products based on the activity of similar customers, so it already adjusts for the scale of spend. For example, if the prediction for a customer is that their spend on fresh fruit and vegetables should be 5, that is based on the comparison with other similar customers. Here is the evaluation code, which is also in `Chapter8/kerarecommend.R`. The first part of the code generates the predictions and links it back. We output a few metrics, which look impressive, but note that they are run on all the data, including the data that the model was trained on, so these metrics are overly optimistic. We make one adjustment to the predictions – some of these values are greater than 5 or less than 1, so we change them back to valid values. This produces a very small improvement on our metrics:

```
##### model use-case, find products that customers 'should' be purchasing
######
df$preds<-predict(model,list(df$cust_id2,df$prod_id2))
# remove index variables, do not need them anymore
df$cust_id2 <- NULL
df$prod_id2 <- NULL
mse<-mean((df$rating-df$preds)^2)
rmse<-sqrt(mse)
mae<-mean(abs(df$rating-df$preds))
print (sprintf("DL Collaborative filtering model: MSE=%1.3f, RMSE=%1.3f,
MAE=%1.3f",mse,rmse,mae))
[1] "DL Collaborative filtering model: MSE=0.478, RMSE=0.691, MAE=0.501"

df <- df[order(-df$preds),]
head(df)
      prod_id        cust_id rating      preds
10017 D00003 CUST0000283274      5   5.519783
4490  D00002 CUST0000283274      5   5.476133
9060  D00002 CUST0000084449      5   5.452055
6536  D00002 CUST0000848462      5   5.447111
10294 D00003 CUST0000578851      5   5.446453
7318  D00002 CUST0000578851      5   5.442836

df[df$preds>5,]$preds <- 5
df[df$preds<1,]$preds <- 1
mse<-mean((df$rating-df$preds)^2)
rmse<-sqrt(mse)
mae<-mean(abs(df$rating-df$preds))
print (sprintf("DL Collaborative filtering model (adjusted): MSE=%1.3f,
RMSE=%1.3f, MAE=%1.3f",mse,rmse,mae))
[1] "DL Collaborative filtering model (adjusted): MSE=0.476, RMSE=0.690,
MAE=0.493"
```

Now, we can look at the customer-product department codes that have the biggest difference between predicted ratings and actual ratings:

```
df$diff <- df$preds - df$rating
df <- df[order(-df$diff),]
head(df,20)
        prod_id        cust_id rating     preds      diff
3259    D00001 CUST0000375633      1  5.000000  4.000000
12325   D00003 CUST0000038166      1  4.306837  3.306837
14859   D00004 CUST0000817991      1  4.025836  3.025836
15279   D00004 CUST0000620867      1  4.016025  3.016025
22039   D00008 CUST0000588390      1  3.989520  2.989520
3370    D00001 CUST0000530875      1  3.969685  2.969685
22470   D00008 CUST0000209037      1  3.927513  2.927513
22777   D00008 CUST0000873432      1  3.905162  2.905162
13905   D00004 CUST0000456347      1  3.877517  2.877517
18123   D00005 CUST0000026547      1  3.853488  2.853488
24208   D00008 CUST0000732836      1  3.810606  2.810606
22723   D00008 CUST0000872856      1  3.746022  2.746022
22696   D00008 CUST0000549120      1  3.718482  2.718482
15463   D00004 CUST0000035935      1  3.714494  2.714494
24090   D00008 CUST0000643072      1  3.679629  2.679629
21167   D00006 CUST0000454947      1  3.651651  2.651651
23769   D00008 CUST0000314496      1  3.649187  2.649187
14294   D00004 CUST0000127124      1  3.625893  2.625893
22534   D00008 CUST0000556279      1  3.578591  2.578591
22201   D00008 CUST0000453430      1  3.576008  2.576008
```

This gives us a list of customers and the products we should send them offers for. For example, for the second row, the actual rating is 1 and the predicted rating is 4.306837. This customer is not purchasing the items for this product code and our model *predicts* he should be purchasing these items.

We can also look at cases where the actual rating is much higher than the predicted value. These are customers who are over-spending in that department compared to other similar customers:

```
df <- df[order(df$diff),]
head(df,20)
        prod_id        cust_id rating     preds      diff
21307   D00006 CUST0000555858      5  1.318784 -3.681216
15353   D00004 CUST0000640069      5  1.324661 -3.675339
21114   D00006 CUST0000397007      5  1.729860 -3.270140
23097   D00008 CUST0000388652      5  1.771072 -3.228928
21551   D00006 CUST0000084985      5  1.804969 -3.195031
21649   D00007 CUST0000083736      5  1.979534 -3.020466
23231   D00008 CUST0000917696      5  2.036216 -2.963784
```

```
21606  D00007  CUST0000899988      5  2.050258  -2.949742
21134  D00006  CUST0000373894      5  2.071380  -2.928620
14224  D00004  CUST0000541731      5  2.081161  -2.918839
15191  D00004  CUST0000106540      5  2.162569  -2.837431
13976  D00004  CUST0000952727      5  2.174777  -2.825223
21851  D00008  CUST0000077294      5  2.202812  -2.797188
16545  D00004  CUST0000945695      5  2.209504  -2.790496
23941  D00008  CUST0000109728      5  2.224301  -2.775699
24031  D00008  CUST0000701483      5  2.239778  -2.760222
21300  D00006  CUST0000752292      5  2.240073  -2.759927
21467  D00006  CUST0000754753      5  2.240705  -2.759295
15821  D00004  CUST0000006239      5  2.264089  -2.735911
15534  D00004  CUST0000586590      5  2.272885  -2.727115
```

What can we do with these recommendations? Our model assigns a score of 1-5 based on a customers' spend in each product department, so if a customer has a high actual rating compared to the predicted value in general, they are over-spending in these departments compared to similar customers. These people are probably not spending in other departments, so they should be targeted as part of a cross-sell campaign; that is, they should be sent offers for products in other departments to tempt them to purchase there.

Summary

I hope that this chapter has shown you that deep learning is not just about computer vision and NLP problems! In this chapter, we covered using Keras to build auto-encoders and recommendation systems. We saw that auto-encoders can be used as a form of dimensionality reduction and, in their simplest forms with only one layer, they are similar to PCA. We used an auto-encoder model to create an anomaly detection system. If the reconstruction error in the auto-encoder model was over a threshold, then we marked that instance as a potential anomaly. Our second major example in this chapter built a recommendation system using Keras. We constructed a dataset of implicit ratings from transactional data and built a recommendation system. We demonstrated the practical application of this model by showing you how it could be used for cross-sell purposes.

In the next chapter, we will look at various options for training your deep learning model in the cloud. If you do not have a GPU on your local machine, cloud providers such as AWS, Azure, Google Cloud, and Paperspace allow you to access GPU instances cheaply. We will cover all of these options in the next chapter.

Running Deep Learning Models in the Cloud

10

Up till now, we have only briefly discussed the hardware requirements for training deep learning models, as almost all of the examples in this book run on any modern computer. While you do not need a **GPU** (**Graphical Processing Unit**) based computer to run the examples in this book, there is no getting away from the fact that training complicated deep learning models requires a computer with a GPU. Even if you have a suitable GPU on your machine, installing the necessary software to train deep learning models using GPUs is not a trivial task. This section will briefly discuss how to install the necessary software to run deep learning models on GPUs and also discusses the advantages and disadvantages of using cloud computing for deep learning. We will use various cloud providers to create virtual instances or access services that will allow us to train deep learning models in the cloud.

This chapter covers the following topics:

- Setting up a local computer for deep learning
- Using Amazon Web Services (AWS) for deep learning
- Using Azure for deep learning
- Using Google Cloud for deep learning
- Using Paperspace for deep learning

Setting up a local computer for deep learning

At the time of writing this book, it is possible to purchase a computer with a GPU card suitable for deep learning for under $1,000. The current on-demand cost of the cheapest GPU computer on AWS is $0.90 per hour, which is equivalent to using the machine constantly for 46 days. So, if you are just starting with deep learning, cloud resources are the cheapest way to begin. Once you have learned the basics, then you may decide to get a GPU-based computer, but even then you may continue using cloud resources for deep learning. You have much more flexibility in the cloud. For example, in AWS, you can get a p3.16xlarge machine with 8 Tesla V100 GPU cards for an on-demand price of $24.48 per hour. An equivalent box is the DGX-1 from NVIDIA (`https://www.nvidia.com/en-us/data-center/dgx-1/`), which has 8 Tesla V100 GPU cards and costs $149,000!

If you are considering using your own computer for deep learning, then one of the following applies to you:

- You already have a computer that you can use with a suitable GPU processor
- You will buy a computer to build deep learning models
- You will build a computer to build deep learning models

If you want to use your local computer for deep learning, you need a suitable GPU card, which must be from NVIDIA. The best way to check this is to go to the NVIDIA site and check if your graphics card is compatible with CUDA. CUDA is an application programming interface (API) that allows programs to use GPU for computing. You need to install CUDA to be able to use the GPU for deep learning. The current link to check if your graphics card is compatible with CUDA is `https://developer.nvidia.com/cuda-gpus`.

While some companies sell machines that are designed specifically for deep learning, they are very expensive. I would not advise getting one of them if you are just beginning to, learn deep learning. Instead, I would recommend looking at buying a computer that is for high-end computer games. This computer should have an appropriate GPU card for deep learning. Again, check that the card is compatible with CUDA (`https://developer.nvidia.com/cuda-gpus`) first.

A gaming computer for deep learning? It is not as strange as it seems. GPUs were developed to play high-end games on computers, not for deep learning. But a machine that is designed for games is likely to have a higher than usual specification, for example, an SSD drive, lots of (fast) RAM, and most importantly a GPU card. Early deep learning practitioners realized that the matrix operations involved in calculating 3D spaces were very similar to the matrix operations used in neural networks. NVIDIA released CUDA as an API so that other applications could use the GPU as a co-processor. Whether it was luck or foresight, NVIDIA became the de facto standard for GPU cards for deep learning and has seen its share price grow by 10 times in the past 3 years, largely because of the huge demand for GPU cards for artificial intelligence.

The third option is to build your own deep learning computer. If you are considering this option, then other than the GPU card, memory, and an SSD drive, you will also need to consider the power supply and the motherboard. You may need a bigger capacity power supply than what is in a standard computer because of the GPU card and fans. For the motherboard, you need to consider if the hardware interface between the motherboard and the GPU card may limit the data transfer – these are PCIe lanes. A GPU can use 16 PCIe lanes at full capacity. For expansion purposes, you may want a motherboard that supports 40 PCIe lanes so that you can support two GPU cards and an SSD drive simultaneously.

Before we move on to the rest of this chapter which discusses using cloud computing for deep learning, we should briefly discuss the performance of GPU cards in the cloud against what was used for this book. For this book, I used a GTX 1050 Ti which has 768 cores and 4 GB RAM. In my experience, the performance of this card is about the same as a **p2.xlarge** instance on AWS. I checked this by running two models on a local CPU (i5 processor), local GPU (GTX 1050 Ti), and AWS GPU (**p2.xlarge**). I ran the test on two models: the binary prediction task from Chapter 4, *Training Deep Prediction Models,* and the LeNet convolutional neural network from Chapter 5, *Image Classification Using Convolutional Neural Networks.* Both of these models were built using MXNet, and ran for 50 epochs:

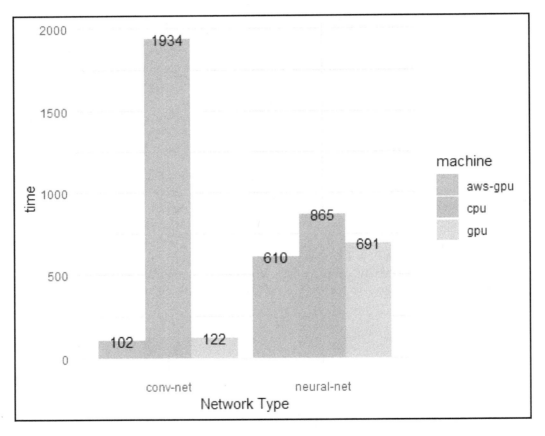

Figure 10.1: Execution time in seconds for two deep learning networks on CPU, local GPU, and AWS GPU

On my local machine, running the deep learning model for the binary prediction task on the GPU is about 20% faster than running on the CPU, and the AWS GPU machine is approximately 13% faster than the local GPU. However, there is a much bigger difference when running convolutional neural networks, training it on the local CPU is almost 16 times slower than training it on the local GPU. In turn, the AWS GPU is approximately 16% faster than the local GPU. These results are expected and mirror what I have seen in practice and other benchmarks on the web and show conclusively that for deep learning computer vision tasks, a GPU is a necessity. The GPU card on my local machine (GTX 1050 Ti) is probably the lowest specification GPU card you should use for deep learning. It currently costs under $200. As a comparison, a high-end GPU card (GTX 1080 Ti) has 3,584 cores and 11 GB of RAM, and currently costs approx $700. The GTX 1080 Ti is approximately 4-5 times faster than the GTX 1050 Ti.

Why does the previous graph just look at AWS and not Azure, Google Cloud, and Paperspace? Why did I not benchmark all of them on performance and/or cost? I decided not to do so for a few reasons. Firstly, and most importantly, any recommendation would have been out of date after a few months—deep learning is very popular and the various cloud providers are changing their offerings and prices constantly. Another reason is that the examples in this book are relatively small and we are using the cheapest GPU instances. Therefore, any comparisons to production use cases would be misleading. Finally, when you are starting out, ease of use is probably more important than raw cost. All the examples in this book should run in under 1 hour in the cloud regardless of which provider you use, so arguing that one provider costs $0.55/hour and another costs $0.45/hour is not important.

How do I know if my model is training on a GPU?

One question that many people starting in deep learning ask is, *how do I know if my model is training on a GPU?* Fortunately, whether you are using a cloud instance or your local machine, you can check if the deep learning model is being trained on the GPU or the CPU. There is a utility on the instance that shows the GPU's activity. In Linux, you can type in the following command:

```
watch -n0.5 nvidia-smi
```

In Windows, you can use the following command from a command prompt:

```
nvidia-smi -l 1
```

This will run a script that outputs diagnostic messages about the GPU on the computer. If your model is currently training on the GPU, the GPU utility will be high. In the following example, we can see that it is 75-78%. We can also see that the file called `rsession.exe` is using GPU memory. This confirms that the model is being trained on the GPU:

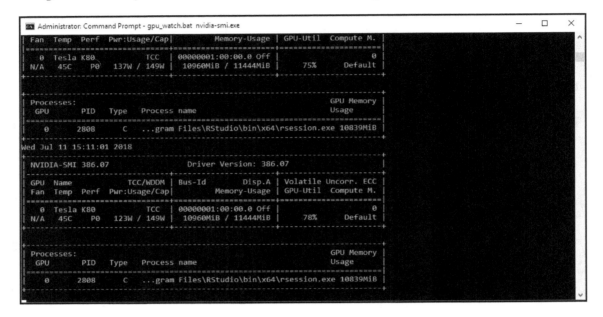

Figure 10.2: nvidia-smi utility showing that the GPU card is at 75-85% utilization

Using AWS for deep learning

AWS is the biggest cloud provider, and so it deserves our attention. If you know how to use AWS and especially if you are familiar with spot requests, it can be a very cost-effective method to train complex deep learning models.

A brief introduction to AWS

This section gives you a brief introduction to how AWS works. It describes EC2, AMIs, and how to create a virtual machine in the cloud. This will not be an exhaustive introduction to AWS – there are plenty of tutorials online that will guide you.

AWS is a suite of cloud resources. Another term for it is **Infrastructure as a Service (IaaS)**, as opposed to **Software as a Service (SaaS)** or **Platform as a Service (PaaS)**. In IaaS, as opposed to SaaS or PaaS, you are supplied with infrastructure (hardware), and it is up to you to use it as you wish. This includes installing software and managing security and networking, although AWS take care of some aspects of security and networking. AWS has many services, but for deep learning, the one you will use is EC2, which is a virtual computing environment so that you can launch instances (virtual computers). You can control these virtual computers either through web interfaces or by remote logging into them to run commands from the shell. When you launch an EC2 instance, you can select the operating system (Ubuntu, Linux, Windows, and so on) and the type of machine you want.

You can also select to use an **Amazon Machine Image (AMI)**, which has software applications and libraries pre-installed on it. This is a good choice for deep learning as it means that you can start an EC2 instance with the deep learning libraries already installed and jump straight into deep learning.

One other service you should be familiar with is S3, which is a form of persistent storage. A very useful practice that I suggest you to adopt is to consider your virtual machines as temporary resources and to keep your data and interim results in S3. We will not discuss this in this chapter because it is an advanced topic.

In the previous section, we stated that the current on-demand cost of the cheapest GPU computer on AWS is $0.90 per hour. *On-demand* is one way to use a virtual machine in AWS, but there are three different ways to rent a virtual machine in AWS:

- **On-demand instances**: When you rent an instance as needed.
- **Reserved instances**: When you commit to renting the machine for a certain period of time (usually 1-3 years). This is about 50% cheaper than on-demand instances. However you are committed to paying for the resource for the period of time.
- **Spot instances**: In order to deal with fluctuating demand, Amazon has spare computing capacity most of the time. You can bid for this unused capacity and, depending on the demand for that type of machine, you can usually get it cheaper than on-demand and reserved instances. However, once you have the machine, it is not guaranteed that you will keep it as long as you need – if the demand for the computer goes up, your computer may be terminated.

Reserve instances are not useful for deep learning. The cost of renting the cheapest GPU machine for 1 year would be over $5,000, and you can buy a deep learning machine with better performance for much less. On-demand instances guarantee that you will have the resource as long as needed, but are expensive. Spot instances are an interesting and cost-effective method to use if you know how to use them correctly and plan for the chance that your computer will be terminated.

Typically, the spot price is about 30% of the on-demand price, so the savings are significant. Your bid is the maximum amount that you are willing to pay for the spot instances, the actual price depends on the market price, which is based on the demand.

Therefore, you should set your bid price higher; I recommend to set it at either 51%, 76%, or 101% of the on-demand price. The extra 1% from 50%, 75%, and 100% is because, similar to any bidding market, humans anchor their bids to round numbers, so by avoiding this with an extra 1%, it can make a difference.

The original use case for spot instances was for low-priority batch jobs. Companies used spot instances to the avail of themselves cheaper computing resources for long-running jobs that could be restarted in the event that they did not finish. An example might be running a secondary data ingestion process on data that was not critical to operations. However, the demand pattern for GPU based instances is different, possibly because of online data mining competitions such as Kaggle. Because GPU instances are not very common, demand spikes much more for GPU instances. This has led to some strange behavior in spot pricing, where the price that people bid for a spot instance can be 10x that of the on-demand price. People do this because they believe that this makes it unlikely that they will be outbid. There are cases where a p2.16xlarge has had a spot price of $144 per hour while the on-demand price is $14.40. The people who set these bids do not want their machines to be terminated and believe that they will still pay less on average for spot instances than on-demand instances. This is not something I would encourage if you use spot instances as you can get a very nasty surprise if demand goes up! However, you should be aware of this pricing quirk – do not think that setting the bid price to just above the on-demand price guarantees that your machine will not be terminated.

AWS provides you help in setting up your spot request bid by providing pricing history charts that advise you on the on-demand price and the bid prices. In the following screenshot, we can see how the price has changed over the past 3 months for a particular region (us-east). There are 6 availability zones (us-east-1a to us-east-1f) and the current spot price of this instance type (**p2.16xlarge**) varies from $4.32-$14.40, while the on-demand price is $14.40:

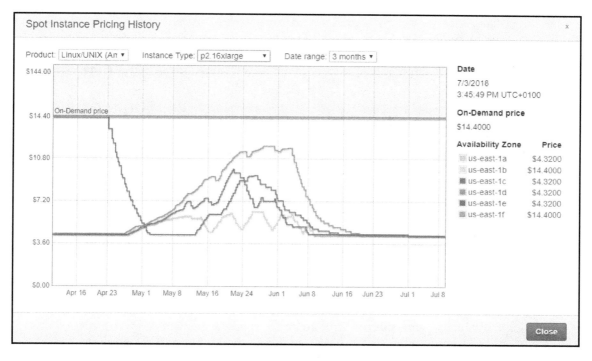

Figure 10.3: Pricing history for spot bids for p2.16xlarge instance type

Looking at the preceding graph for this resource, I would consider the following:

- I would use the availability zone **us-east-1a** if possible, as it has the lowest price volatility.
- I would set the price to $7.21 per hour, which is just over 50% of the on-demand price. I would probably only pay $4.32 per hour as it has been 1 month since the bid price in us-east-1a has gone over $4.32 per hour. Setting it at the higher price would make it less likely that my spot instance would be terminated.

Regions and availability zones: AWS arranges its services in regions (**us-east1**, **eu-west1**, and so on). Currently, there are 18 different regions and in each region, there are multiple availability zones, which you can consider as physical data centers. For some use cases (for example, websites, disaster recovery, and so on) and regulatory requirements, regions and availability zones are important. For deep learning, they are not so important, as you can usually run your deep learning models at any location. The bid price for spot instances is different for regions/availability zones, and some resources are more expensive in some regions. You also need to be aware that there is a cost in transferring data between regions, so keep your data and instances in the same region.

Creating a deep learning GPU instance in AWS

This section will use AWS to train a deep learning model from Chapter 9, *Anomaly Detection and Recommendation Systems*. This will include setting up the machine, accessing the machine, downloading the data, and running the model. We are going to use a pre-built AWS AMI from RStudio that has TensorFlow and Keras already installed. For details on this AMI, go to this link: https://aws.amazon.com/marketplace/pp/B0785SXYB2. You will need to sign up for an AWS account if you do not already have one at https://portal.aws.amazon.com/billing/signup. Once you have signed up, follow these steps to create a virtual machine that has a GPU on AWS:

Note that when you set up an instance in AWS, you will be billed for as long as it is running! Always ensure that you shut down your instances, otherwise you will continue to be charged. Check the AWS console to ensure you have no running instances when you are finished using the virtual instance.

1. Log in to the AWS console and select EC2. You should see a screen similar to the following. This is the web interface for creating new virtual machines:

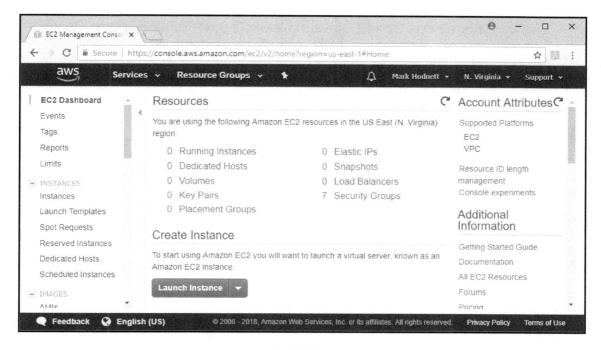

Figure 10.4: AWS EC2 dashboard

2. Click on the launch instance button and the following page will load.

3. Click **AWS Marketplace** on the left and in the search box type `rstudio` (see the following screenshot).

4. Select **RStudio Server with Tensorflow-GPU for AWS**. Be aware that there is another option with the word **Pro** – this is a paid subscription with additional costs, so do not select this AMI:

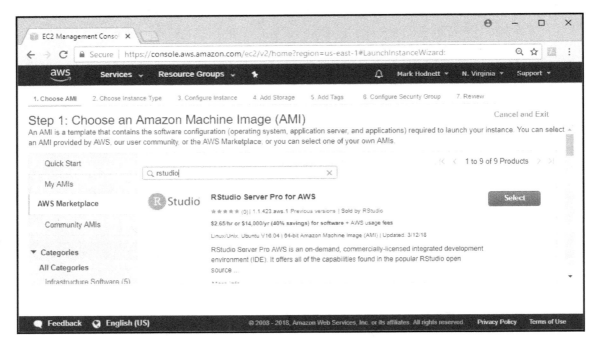

Figure 10.5: AWS launch instance wizard, Step 1

5. Once you click **Select**, the following screen may appear with some additional information on accessing the instance. Read the instructions carefully, as they may have changed from what's shown in the screenshot that follows:

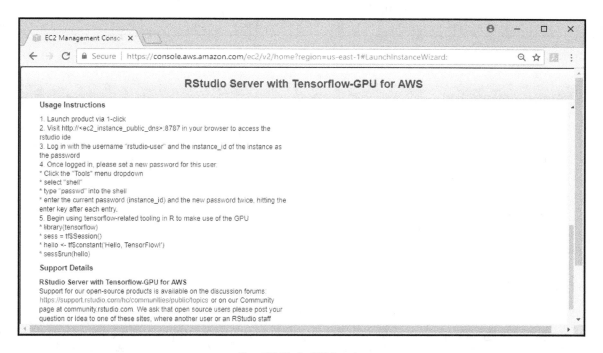

Figure 10.6: RStudio AMI information

6. When you click **Continue**, the following screen will appear for the machine type. It is vital to select a machine that has a GPU, so from the **Filter by:** option, select GPU compute and then select **p2.xlarge** from the list. Your options should look similar to the following screenshot:

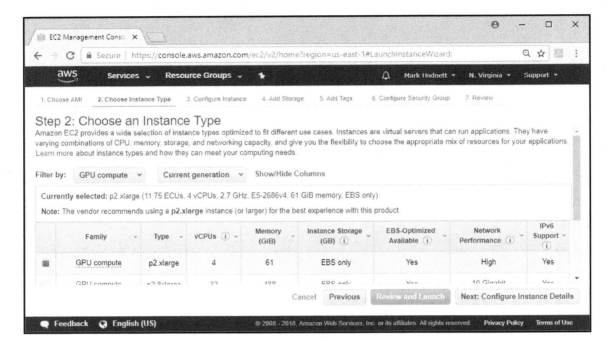

Figure 10.7: AWS launch instance wizard, Step 2

7. When you click **Next**, you will get to the following screen with various configuration options. The default options are OK, so just press **Next** again:

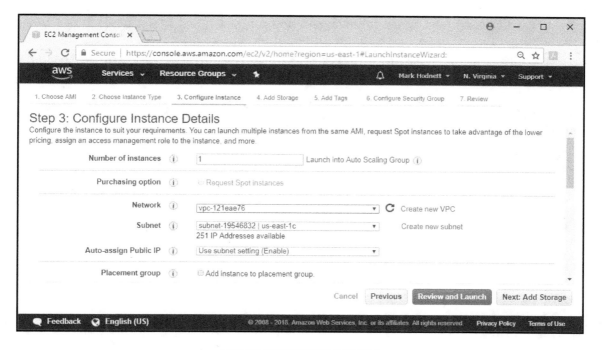

Figure 10.8: AWS launch instance wizard, Step 3

8. This screen allows you to change the storage options. You may need to add additional storage depending on the size of the data. Storage is relatively cheap, so I recommend going with 3x-5x the size of the input data.

9. Click **Next** to go to the following screenshot:

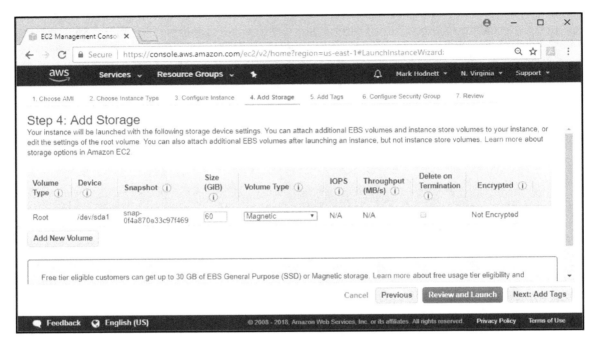

Figure 10.9: AWS launch instance wizard, Step 4

10. The following screen is not important – tags are used to keep track of resources in AWS, but we do not need them. Click Next to go to the following screenshot:

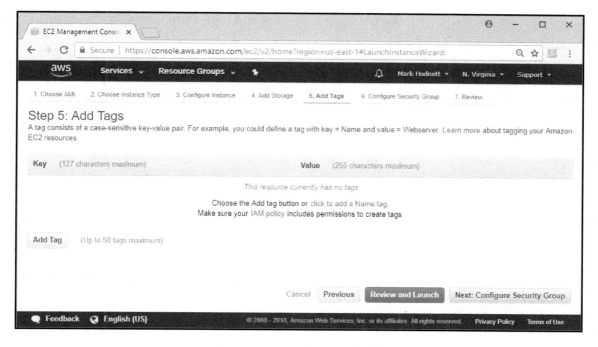

Figure 10.10: AWS launch instance wizard, step 5

11. The following screenshot shows security options. AWS restricts access to instances, so you must open any needed ports. The defaults provided here allow access to port 22 (SSH) to access the shell and also for port 8787, which is the web port that RStudio uses. Click **Review and Launch** to continue:

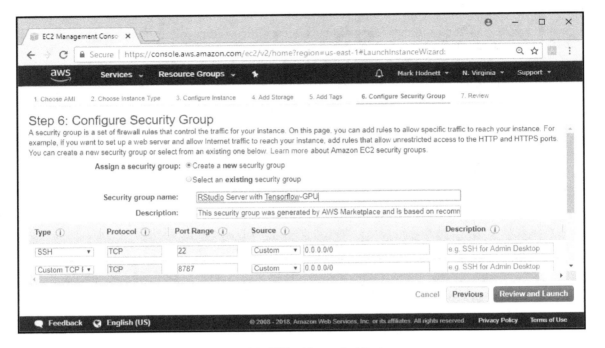

Figure 10.11: AWS launch instance wizard, Step 6

The following screenshot will appear. Note the warning messages regarding security – in a production environment, you would probably want to address these.

12. Click the **Launch** button to continue:

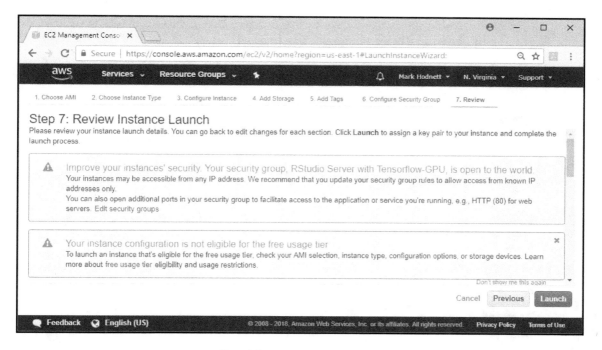

Figure 10.12: AWS launch instance wizard, Step 7

13. You will be asked for a key pair. If you have not already created a key pair, then select the option to do so. Give it a descriptive name and press the **Download Key Pair** button. Then, click on **Launch Instances**:

A key pair is used to access the instance using SSH. You should guard this very carefully, as if someone manages to get your private key, then they will be able to log in to any of your instances. You should delete your key pair occasionally and create a new one.

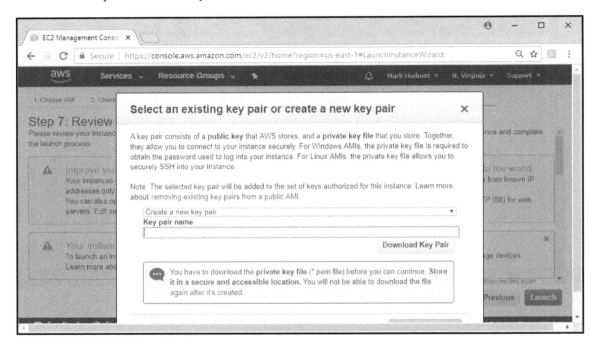

Figure 10.13: AWS launch instance wizard, select key pair

14. Once you have completed this, you can go back to the EC2 dashboard and you will see that you have **1 Running Instances**. Click on that link to move on to the details of the instance:

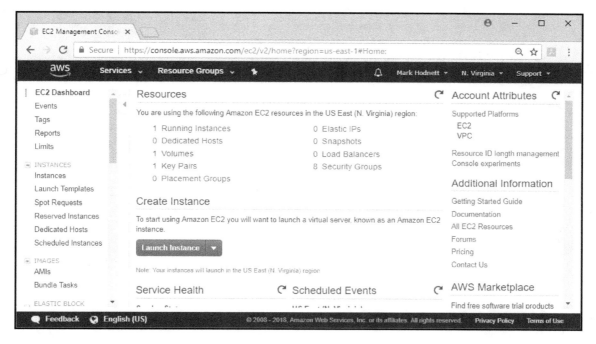

Figure 10.14: AWS EC2 dashboard

15. Here, you will see the details of the instance. In this case, the IP address is 34.227.109.123. Also note down the instance ID that is highlighted, as this is the password that is used to connect to the RStudio instance:

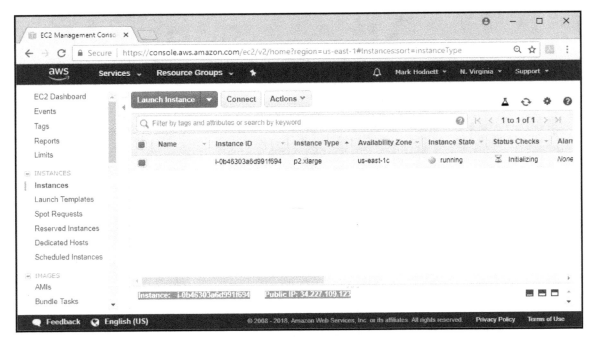

Figure 10.15: AWS EC2 dashboard, instance details

16. Open another web page and browse to the IP address of your machine and add :8787 to access the link. In my example, the link is http://34.227.109.123:8787/. Instructions for logging in are in *Figure 10.6*, that is, use rstudio-user as the username and the instance ID as the password. You should also consider changing the password as per the instructions.

17. When you log in, you will see a familiar interface – it is similar to the RStudio desktop program. One difference you have is the **Upload** button on the bottom-right pane, which allows you to upload files. In the following example, I have uploaded the data and the script from Chapter 9, *Anomaly Detection and Recommendation Systems*, for the Keras recommender example and ran it successfully:

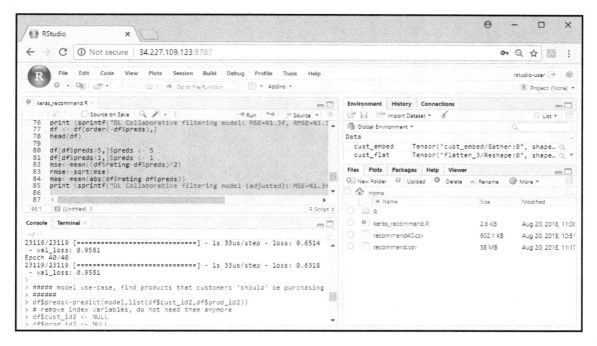

Figure 10.16: Accessing deep learning instance in the cloud using RStudio Server

The web interface in RStudio is similar to using RStudio on your local computer. In *Figure 10.16*, you can see data files that I have uploaded (recomend.csv, recomend40.csv) and the R script in the **Files** in the bottom-left window. We can also see the code that was executed in the Console window in the bottom-left.

This finishes our example on how to set up a deep learning machine in AWS. Again, remember that you will be billed for as long as the computer is running. Ensure that your instances are terminated, otherwise you will continue to be charged. To do so, go back to the EC2 dashboard, find the instance, and click on the **Actions** button. A pop-up menu will appear, where you can select **Instance State** and then select **Terminate**:

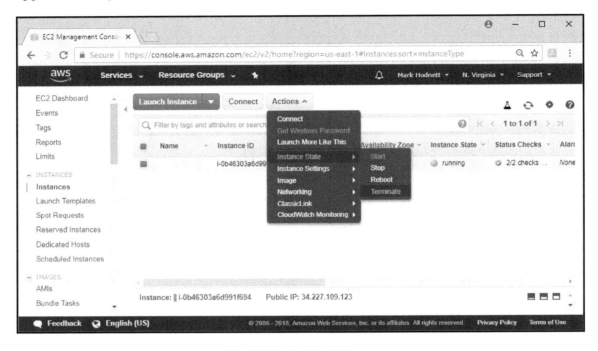

Figure 10.17: Terminating the AWS instance

Creating a deep learning AMI in AWS

In the previous example, we used an **Amazon Machine Image** (**AMI**) that was built by RStudio. In AWS, you can also create your own AMI's. When you create an AMI, you can install the software you want, load data onto it, and set it up as you wish. This section will show you how to use an AMI to use MXNet on AWS.

1. The first step in creating an AMI is to select the base image that you are going to use. We could start with a base image that just has the operating system installed, but instead we are going to use the **RStudio Server with Tensorflow-GPU for AWS** that we used previously and add the MXNet package to it.

2. The instructions to install MXNet were adapted from https://mxnet.incubator. apache.org/install/index.html. The first step is to create the instance from the **RStudio Server with Tensorflow-GPU for AWS** AMI as per the previous section.

3. Once you have done this, you need to SSH into the machine. How you do this depends on the operating system on your own computer. For Linux and macOS, you can execute a local command on the shell, and in Windows you can use Putty.

4. Once you have logged in to the machine, run the following command:

   ```
   vi ~/.profile
   ```

5. Add the following line to the end of this file and save the file:

   ```
   export CUDA_HOME=/usr/local/cuda
   ```

6. Once you are back at the shell, run the following lines one by one:

   ```
   sudo apt-get update
   sudo dpkg --configure -a
   sudo apt-get install -y build-essential git
   export CUDA_HOME=/usr/local/cuda
   git clone --recursive https://github.com/apache/incubator-mxnet
   cd incubator-mxnet
   make -j $(nproc) USE_OPENCV=1 USE_CUDA=1
   USE_CUDA_PATH=/usr/local/cuda USE_CUDNN=1
   ```

7. The last command could take up to 2 hours to complete. Once it is done, run the last few lines:

   ```
   sudo ldconfig /usr/local/cuda/lib64
   sudo make rpkg
   sudo R CMD INSTALL mxnet_current_r.tar.gz
   ```

The second line may take up to 30 minutes. The final line may return a warning about a missing file, which can be ignored.

8. To test if everything installed correctly, go to the RStudio page for the instance and type in the following code:

```
library(mxnet)
a <- mx.nd.ones(c(2,3), ctx = mx.gpu())
b <- a * 2 + 1
b
```

9. You should get the following output:

```
      [,1] [,2] [,3]
[1,]     3    3    3
[2,]     3    3    3
```

10. Now go back to the EC2 dashboard, click on **Running Instances**, and select the machine in the list. Click on the **Action** button, select **Image** from the drop-down menu, and select **Create Image**. This is shown in the following screenshot:

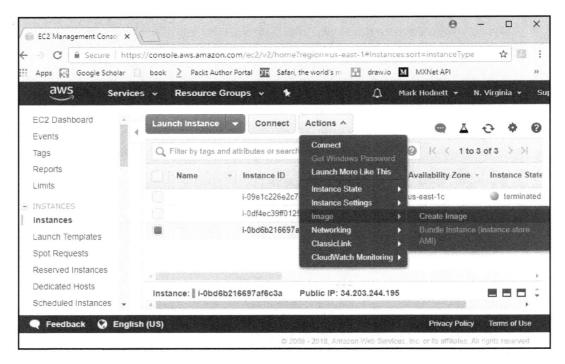

Figure 10.18: Creating an AMI

11. The image may take 15-20 minutes to complete. When it is done, click on AMIs on the left menu selection to show the list of AMIs associated with your account. You should see the AMI you just created. This AMI can then be used to create a new on-demand instance or a new spot instance. The following screenshot shows the menu option to create a spot instance for the AMI:

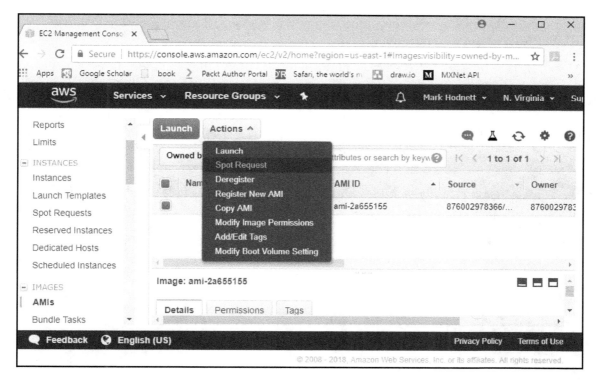

Figure 10.19: Using an existing AMI for a spot request

This AMI is now available so that you can create new deep learning instances. You should be aware that there is an ongoing cost in storing the AMI, even if you do not use it.

Using Azure for deep learning

Azure is the brand name for Microsoft's cloud services. You can use Azure for deep learning and, similar to AWS, it provides deep learning virtual machines that is pre-configured with deep learning libraries installed. In this example, we are going to create a Windows instance that can be used for Keras or MXNet. This assumes that your local computer is also a Windows computer, as you will be using **Remote Desktop Protocol (RDP)** to access the cloud instance.

1. The first step is to create an account in Azure and then log in to Azure at `https://portal.azure.com`. You will see a screenshot similar to the following. Click **Create a resource** and search for **Deep Learning Virtual Machine**:

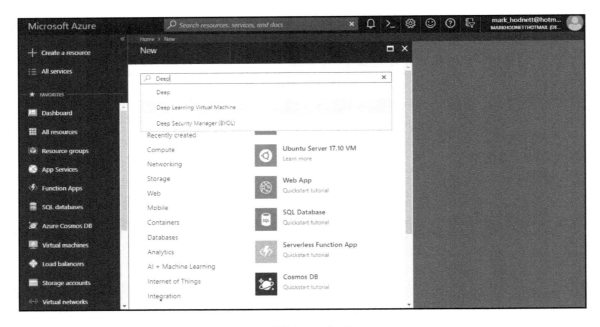

Figure 10.20: Azure portal website

2. When you select **Deep Learning Virtual Machine**, the following screen will appear. Click **Create**:

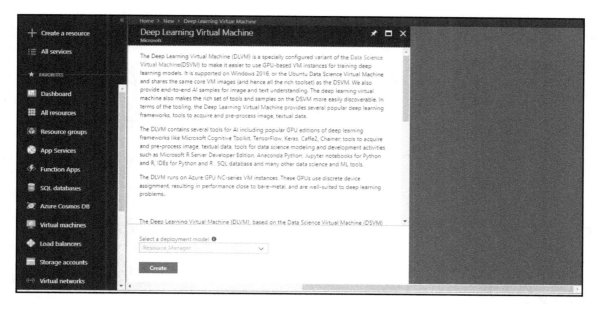

Figure 10.21: Provisioning a deep learning instance on Azure, step 0

3. You will now start a 4-step wizard to create the new instance.

    The first step (Basics), asks for some basic details. It is OK to enter the same values as I have done, but fill in the username and password carefully as you will need them later:

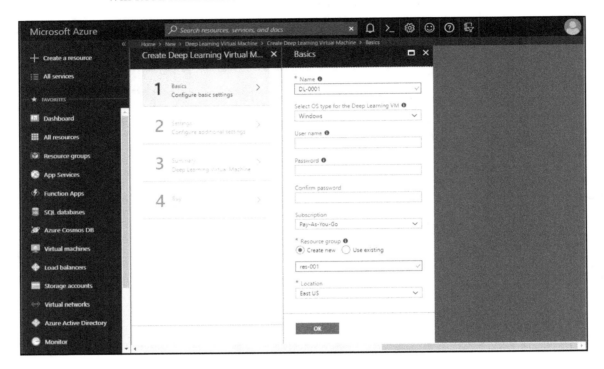

Figure 10.22: Provisioning a deep learning instance on Azure, step 1

For Step 2 (Settings), ensure that the virtual machine size is 1 x Standard NC6 (1 GPU), and click **OK** to continue:

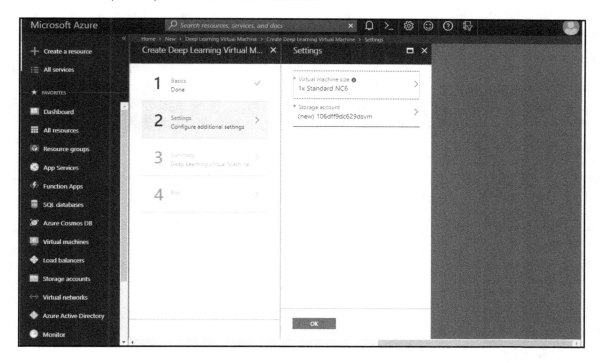

Figure 10.23: Provisioning a deep learning instance on Azure, step 2

For Step 3 (Summary), there is a brief validation check. You may be told that your account does not have sufficient Compute/VM (cores/vCPUs) resources available, which is because Microsoft may have restricted your account when it was first created. Create a support ticket to increase your resources and try again. If you have passed this step, click **OK** to continue. You are now on the final step, so just click **Create**:

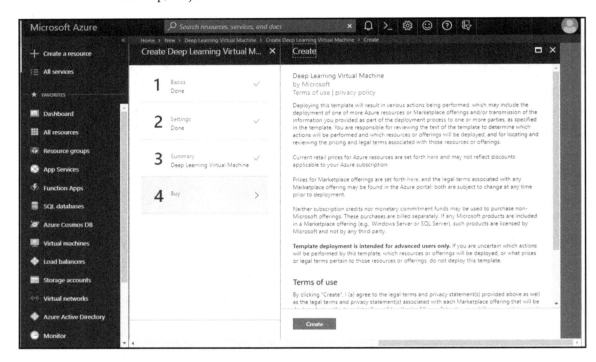

Figure 10.24: Provisioning a deep learning instance on Azure, Step 4

You may have to wait 30-40 minutes until the resources are created. When this is complete, select **All resources** on the left and you will see that all of the objects have been created. The following screenshot shows an example of this. Click on the one where the type is **Virtual Machine**:

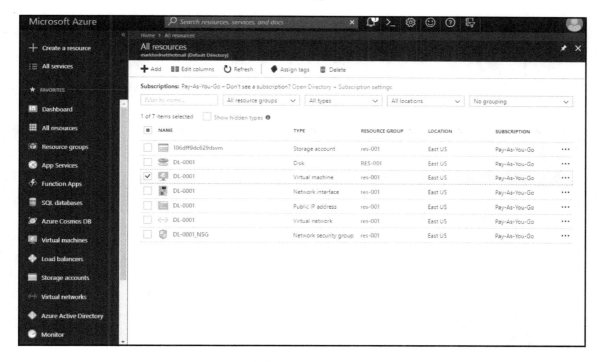

Figure 10.25: List of currently provisioned resources on Azure

4. You will then see the following screenshot. Click on the **Connect** button on the top of the screen.

5. A pane will open up on the right and give you an option to **Download RDP File**. Click on that, and when the file is downloaded, double-click on it:

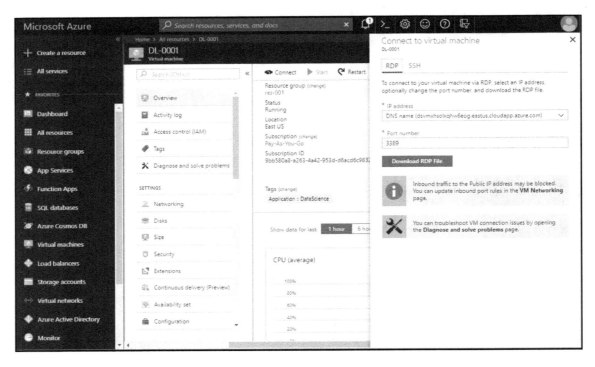

Figure 10.26: Downloading the RDP file to connect to the cloud instance in Azure

6. This should bring up a login window to connect to the cloud instance. Enter the username and password that you created in step 1 to connect to the instance. When you connect, you will see a desktop similar to the following screenshot:

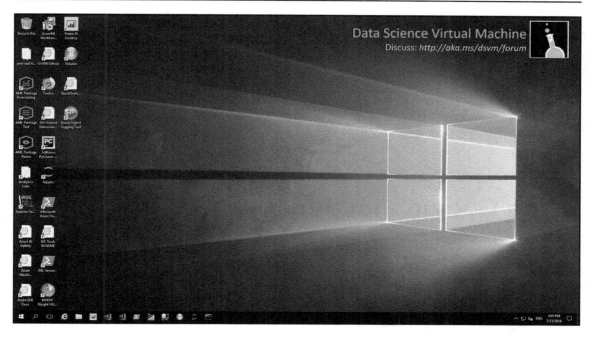

Figure 10.27: The remote desktop of the deep learning instance (Azure)

Great! RStudio is already installed. Keras is already installed, so any Keras deep learning code you have will run. Let's try and run some MXNet code. Open RStudio and run the following commands to install MXNet:

```
cran <- getOption("repos")
cran["dmlc"] <-
"https://apache-mxnet.s3-accelerate.dualstack.amazonaws.com/R/CRAN/GPU/cu90
"
options(repos = cran)
install.packages("mxnet")

# validate install
library(mxnet)
a <- mx.nd.ones(c(2,3), ctx = mx.gpu())
b <- a * 2 + 1
b
```

This will not work on the version of R installed. If you want to use MXNet, you must download the latest version of R (3.5.1 at the time of writing) and install it. Unfortunately, this will disable Keras, so only do this if you want to use MXNet instead of Keras. Once you download R from https://cran.r-project.org/, then re-run the code above to install MXNet.

 Note: The software installed on these AMI's change very frequently. Before installing any deep learning library, check the version of CUDA that is installed. You need to ensure that they deep learning library is compatible with the version of CUDA installed on the machine.

Using Google Cloud for deep learning

Google Cloud also has GPU instances. At the time of writing this book, the price of an instance with an NVIDIA Tesla K80 GPU card (which is also the GPU card in an AWS p2.xlarge instance) is $0.45 per hour on-demand. This is significantly cheaper than the AWS on-demand price. Further details of Google Cloud's GPU instances are at `https://cloud.google.com/gpu/`. However, for Google Cloud, we are not going to use instances. Instead, we are going to use the Google Cloud Machine Learning Engine API to submit machine learning jobs to the cloud. One big advantage of this approach over provisioning virtual machines is that you only pay for the hardware resources that you use and do not have to worry about setting up and terminating instances. More details and pricing can be found at `https://cloud.google.com/ml-engine/pricing`.

Go through the following steps to sign up for Google Cloud and enable the API:

1. Sign up for an account with Google Cloud.
2. You need to login to the portal at `https://console.cloud.google.com` and enable the **Cloud Machine Learning Engine** API.
3. Select **APIs & Services** from the main menu and click on the **Enable APIs and services** button.
4. The APIs are contained in groups. Select **View All** for the **Machine Learning** group, then select **Cloud Machine Learning Engine** and ensure that the API is enabled.

Once the API is enabled, execute the following code from RStudio:

```
devtools::install_github("rstudio/cloudml")
library(cloudml)
gcloud_init()
```

This should install the Google Cloud SDK, and you will asked to connect your Google account to the SDK. Then, you will be taken through a menu of options in the Terminal window. The first option is as follows:

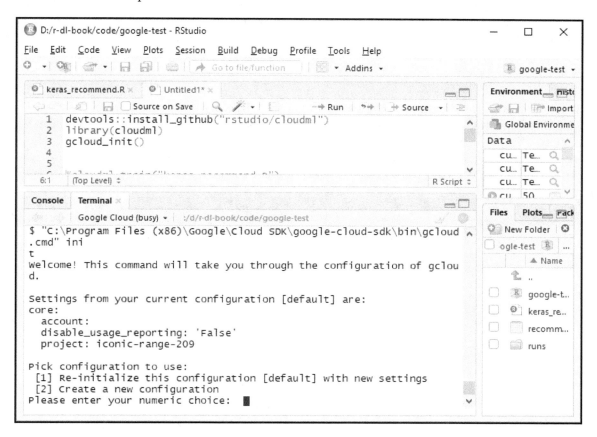

Figure 10.28: Accessing Google Cloud SDK from RStudio

For now, do not create any new projects or configurations, just select the ones that already exist. Once you have linked your Google account to the Google SDK on your machine and enabled the services, you are ready to go. The Cloud Machine Learning Engine allows you to submit a job to Google Cloud without having to create any instances. All the files in the working folder (R scripts and data) will be zipped up and sent to Google Cloud as a package.

For this example, I took a the recommendation file from the project in Chapter 8, *Deep Learning models using TensorFlow in R*. I copied this file and the `keras_recommend.R` script into a new directory and created a new RStudio project in that directory. I then opened the project in RStudio. You can see these two files and the RStudio project file in the previous screenshot. Then, I executed the following line in RStudio to submit the deep learning job:

```
cloudml_train("keras_recommend.R", master_type = "standard_gpu")
```

This will collect the files within the current working directory and send them to the Cloud Machine Learning Engine. As the job is executed, some progress information will be sent back to RStudio. You can also monitor the activity on the console page on `https://console.cloud.google.com` by selecting **ML Engine** | **Jobs**. Here is a screenshot of this web page showing two finished jobs and one that was canceled:

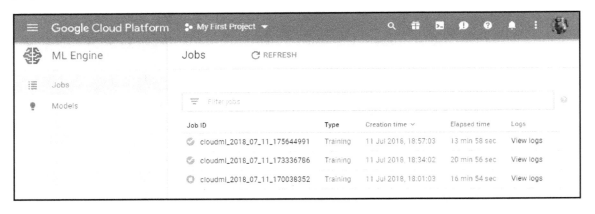

Figure 10.29: The ML Engine/Jobs page on the Google Cloud Platform web page

When the job is finished, the logs will be downloaded to your local machine. A nice summary web page is automatically created showing statistics for the job, as shown in the following screenshot:

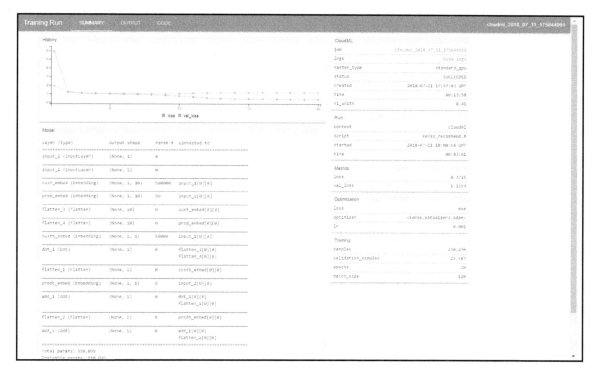

Figure 10.30: Web summary page from the machine learning job

We can see the graph showing the progress of the model during training, the model summary, some hyperparameters (**epochs**, **batch_size**, and so on), as well as the cost (**ml_units**). The web page also contains the output from the R script. Select **Output** from the menu to see it. In the following screenshot, we can see the R code and the output from that code:

```
Training Run        SUMMARY        OUTPUT        CODE                                    cloudml_2018_07_11_175644991

> mae <- mean(abs(df$rating - df$preds))

> print(sprintf("DL Collaborative filtering model: MSE=%1.3f, RMSE=%1.3f, MAE=%1.3f",
+     mse, rmse, mae))
[1] "DL Collaborative filtering model: MSE=0.163, RMSE=0.403, MAE=0.281"

> df <- df[order(-df$preds), ]

> head(df)
        prod_id        cust_id rating     preds
193512  D00005 CUST0000991836      5  5.842071
54820   D00002 CUST0000485110      5  5.836084
17735   D00001 CUST0000299527      5  5.806091
37823   D00001 CUST0000448940      5  5.796087
97862   D00003 CUST0000264553      5  5.785829
61905   D00002 CUST0000124725      5  5.783827

> df[df$preds > 5, ]$preds <- 5

> df[df$preds < 1, ]$preds <- 1

> mse <- mean((df$rating - df$preds)^2)

> rmse <- sqrt(mse)

> mae <- mean(abs(df$rating - df$preds))

> print(sprintf("DL Collaborative filtering model (adjusted): MSE=%1.3f, RMSE=%1.3f, MAE=%1.3f",
+     mse, rmse, mae))
[1] "DL Collaborative filtering model (adjusted): MSE=0.150, RMSE=0.387, MAE=0.242"

> df$diff <- df$preds - df$rating

> df <- df[order(-df$diff), ]

> head(df, 20)
        prod_id        cust_id rating     preds      diff
```

Figure 10.31: Web summary page from the machine learning job showing the R code and output

This is only a brief introduction to using the Google Cloud Machine Learning Engine. There is an excellent tutorial at `https://tensorflow.rstudio.com/tools/cloudml/articles/tuning.html` that explains how you can use this service for hyperparameter training. Using this service rather than cloud instances for hyperparameter training is simpler and probably cheaper than trying to manage it yourself using virtual instances. You do not have to monitor it and coordinate the different runs of the model training. More information on using this service is available at `https://tensorflow.rstudio.com/tools/cloudml/articles/getting_started.html`.

Using Paperspace for deep learning

Paperspace is another interesting way to perform deep learning in the cloud. It might be the easiest way to train deep learning models in the cloud. To set up a cloud instance with Paperspace, you can log in to their console, provision a new machine, and connect to it from your web browser:

1. Start by signing up for a Paperspace account, log in to the console, and go into the Virtual Machine section by selecting Core or Compute. Paperspace has an RStudio TensorFlow template with NVIDIA GPU libraries (CUDA 8.0 and cuDNN 6.0) already installed, along with the GPU version of TensorFlow and Keras for R. You will see this machine type when you select **Public Templates**, as shown in the following screenshot:

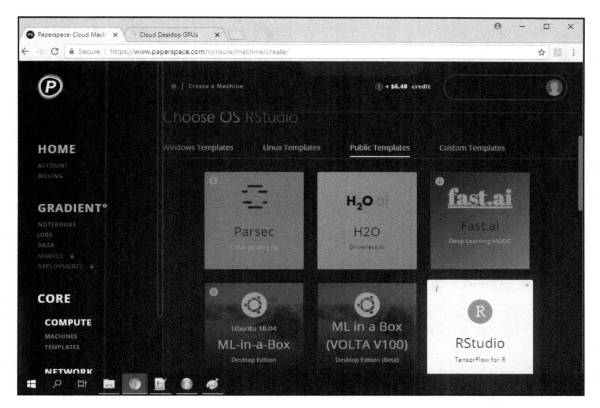

Figure 10.32: Paperspace portal

2. You will be given a choice of three GPU instances and the choice of pay by the hour or monthly. Select the cheapest option (currently P4000 at $0.40 per hour) and the hourly pricing. Scroll down to the bottom of the page and press the **Create** button. After a few minutes, your machine will be provisioned and you will be able to access it through your browser. An example of an RStudio Paperspace instance is shown as follows:

Figure 10.33: Accessing the virtual machine's desktop from a web page and running RStudio for a Paperspace instance

By default, Keras is already installed, so you can go ahead and train deep learning models using Keras. However, we are also going to install MXNet on our instance:

1. The first step is to open RStudio and install a few packages. Execute the following commands from RStudio:

```
install.packages("devtools")
install.packages(c("imager","DiagrammeR","influenceR","rgexf"))
```

2. The next step is to access the Terminal (or shell) for the instance you just created. You can go back to the console page and do it from there. Alternatively, click on the circle target in the top right corner of the desktop (see the previous screenshot). This also gives you other options such as synchronizing copy-and-paste between your local computer and the VM.

3. Once you have logged in to the Terminal for the instance, running the following commands will install MXNet:

```
sudo apt-get update
sudo dpkg --configure -a
sudo apt-get install -y build-essential git
export CUDA_HOME=/usr/local/cuda
git clone --recursive https://github.com/apache/incubator-mxnet
cd incubator-mxnet
make -j $(nproc) USE_OPENCV=1 USE_BLAS=blas USE_CUDA=1
USE_CUDA_PATH=/usr/local/cuda USE_CUDNN=1

sudo ldconfig /usr/local/cuda/lib64
sudo make rpkg
```

4. You also need to add the following line to the end of the .profile file:

```
export CUDA_HOME=/usr/local/cuda
```

When you are done, restart the instance. You now have a machine that can train Keras and MXNet deep learning models in the cloud. For more details on using RStudio in Paperspace, see https://tensorflow.rstudio.com/tools/cloud_desktop_gpu.html.

Summary

We have covered a lot of options for training deep learning models in this chapter! We discussed options for running it locally and showed the importance of having a GPU card. We used the three main cloud providers to train deep learning models in R on the cloud. Cloud computing is a fantastic resource – we gave an example of a super-computer costing $149,000. A few years ago, such a resource would have been out of reach for practically everyone, but now thanks to cloud computing, you can rent a machine like this on an hourly basis.

For AWS, Azure, and Paperspace, we installed MXNet on the cloud resources, giving us the option of which deep learning library to use. I encourage you to use the examples in the other chapters in this book and try all the different cloud providers here. It is amazing to think that you could do so and your total cost could be less than $10!

In the next chapter, we build an image classification solution from image files. We will demonstrate how to apply transfer learning, which allows you to adapt an existing model to a new dataset. We will show how to deploy a model to production using a REST API and briefly discuss Generative Adversarial Networks, reinforcement learning.

The Next Level in Deep Learning **11**

We will begin this chapter by revisiting an image classification task and building a complete image classification solution image files rather than tabular data. We will then move on to explaining transfer learning, where you can use an existing model on a new dataset. Next we discuss an important consideration in any machine learning project - how will your model be used in deployment, that is, production? We will show how to create a REST API that allows any programming language to call a deep learning model in R to predict on new data. We will then move on to briefly discussing two other deep learning topics: Generative Adversarial Networks and reinforcement learning.

In this chapter, we will cover the following topics:

- Building a complete image classification solution
- The ImageNet dataset
- Transfer learning
- Deploying TensorFlow models
- Generative adversarial networks
- Reinforcement learning
- Additional deep learning resources

Image classification models

We covered image classification in Chapter 5, *Image Classification Using Convolutional Neural Networks*. In that chapter, we described convolutional and pooling layers that are essential for deep learning tasks involving images. We also built a number of models on a simple dataset, the MNIST dataset. Here, we are going to look at some advanced topics in image classification. First, we will build a complete image classification model using image files as input. We will look at callbacks, which are a great aid in building complex deep learning models. A call-back function will be used to persist (save) a model to file, which will be loaded back later. We then use this model in our next example, which is transfer learning. This is where you use some of the layers in a pre-trained model on new data.

Building a complete image classification solution

We have built a few image classification models, but they used the MNIST dataset that was loaded from Keras or from CSV files. The data was always in tabular format. Obviously that is not how images are stored in most situations. This section looks at how to build an image classification model using a collection of image files. The first task is to acquire a set of image files. We are going to load the CIFAR10 data that is included in Keras and save the data as image files. We will then use those files to build a deep learning model. After this exercise, you will know how to create a deep learning image classification task with your own image files.

The deep learning model in this chapter is not a complex model. The focus is to show how the data pipeline for an image classification task is structured. We look at how to arrange the image files, how to use data augmentation and how callbacks can be used during training.

Creating the image data

The first step is to create the image files. The code for this section is in the Chapter11/gen_cifar10_data.R folder. We will load the CIFAR10 data and save the image files in the data directory. The first step is to create the directory structure. There are 10 classes in the CIFAR10 dataset: we will save 8 classes for building a model and we will use 2 classes in a later section (*Transfer learning*). The following code creates the following directories under data:

- cifar_10_images
- cifar_10_images/data1

- cifar_10_images/data2
- cifar_10_images/data1/train
- cifar_10_images/data1/valid
- cifar_10_images/data2/train
- cifar_10_images/data2/valid

This is the structure that Keras expects image data to be stored in. If you use this structure, then the images can be used to train a model in Keras. In the first part of the code, we create these directories:

```
library(keras)
library(imager)
# this script loads the cifar_10 data from Keras
# and saves the data as individual images

# create directories,
# we will save 8 classes in the data1 folder for model building
# and use 2 classes for transfer learning
data_dir <- "../data/cifar_10_images/"
if (!dir.exists(data_dir))
  dir.create(data_dir)
if (!dir.exists(paste(data_dir,"data1/",sep="")))
  dir.create(paste(data_dir,"data1/",sep=""))
if (!dir.exists(paste(data_dir,"data2/",sep="")))
  dir.create(paste(data_dir,"data2/",sep=""))
train_dir1 <- paste(data_dir,"data1/train/",sep="")
valid_dir1 <- paste(data_dir,"data1/valid/",sep="")
train_dir2 <- paste(data_dir,"data2/train/",sep="")
valid_dir2 <- paste(data_dir,"data2/valid/",sep="")

if (!dir.exists(train_dir1))
  dir.create(train_dir1)
if (!dir.exists(valid_dir1))
  dir.create(valid_dir1)
if (!dir.exists(train_dir2))
  dir.create(train_dir2)
if (!dir.exists(valid_dir2))
  dir.create(valid_dir2)
```

Under each of the train and valid directories, a separate directory is used for each category. We save the images for 8 classes under the data1 folder, and save the images for 2 classes under the data2 folder:

```
# load CIFAR10 dataset
c(c(x_train,y_train),c(x_test,y_test)) %<-% dataset_cifar10()
# get the unique categories,
```

```
# note that unique does not mean ordered!
# save 8 classes in data1 folder
categories <- unique(y_train)
for (i in categories[1:8])
{
  label_dir <- paste(train_dir1,i,sep="")
  if (!dir.exists(label_dir))
    dir.create(label_dir)
  label_dir <- paste(valid_dir1,i,sep="")
  if (!dir.exists(label_dir))
    dir.create(label_dir)
}
# save 2 classes in data2 folder
for (i in categories[9:10])
{
  label_dir <- paste(train_dir2,i,sep="")
  if (!dir.exists(label_dir))
    dir.create(label_dir)
  label_dir <- paste(valid_dir2,i,sep="")
  if (!dir.exists(label_dir))
    dir.create(label_dir)
}
```

Once we have created the directories, the next step is to save the images in the correct directories, which we will do in the following code:

```
# loop through train images and save in the correct folder
for (i in 1:dim(x_train)[1])
{
  img <- x_train[i,,,]
  label <- y_train[i,1]
  if (label %in% categories[1:8])
    image_array_save(img,paste(train_dir1,label,"/",i,".png",sep=""))
  else
    image_array_save(img,paste(train_dir2,label,"/",i,".png",sep=""))
  if ((i %% 500)==0)
    print(i)
}

# loop through test images and save in the correct folder
for (i in 1:dim(x_test)[1])
{
  img <- x_test[i,,,]
  label <- y_test[i,1]
  if (label %in% categories[1:8])
    image_array_save(img,paste(valid_dir1,label,"/",i,".png",sep=""))
  else
    image_array_save(img,paste(valid_dir2,label,"/",i,".png",sep=""))
```

```
  if ((i %% 500)==0)
    print(i)
}
```

Finally, as we have done previously, we will do a validation check to ensure that our images are correct. Let's load in 9 images from one category. We want to check that the images display correctly and that they are from the same class:

```
# plot some images to verify process
image_dir <- list.dirs(valid_dir1, full.names=FALSE, recursive=FALSE)[1]
image_dir <- paste(valid_dir1,image_dir,sep="")
img_paths <- paste(image_dir,list.files(image_dir),sep="/")

par(mfrow = c(3, 3))
par(mar=c(2,2,2,2))
for (i in 1:9)
{
  im <- load.image(img_paths[i])
  plot(im)
}
```

This produces the following plot:

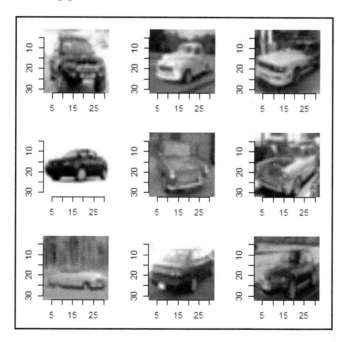

Figure 11.1: Sample CIFAR10 images

This looks good! The images display correctly and we can see that these images all appear to be of the same class, which is cars. The images are out of focus, but that is because they are only thumbnail images of size 32 x 32.

Building the deep learning model

Once you have run the script from the preceding section, you should have 40,000 images for training in the cifar_10_images/data1/train directory and 8,000 images for validation in the cifar_10_images/data1/valid directory. We will train a model with this data. The code for this section is in the Chapter11/build_cifar10_model.R folder. The first section creates the model definition, which should be familiar to you:

```r
library(keras)

# train a model from a set of images
# note: you need to run gen_cifar10_data.R first to create the images!
model <- keras_model_sequential()
model %>%
  layer_conv_2d(name="conv1", input_shape=c(32, 32, 3),
    filter=32, kernel_size=c(3,3), padding="same"
  ) %>%
  layer_activation("relu") %>%
  layer_conv_2d(name="conv2",filter=32, kernel_size=c(3,3),
            padding="same") %>%
  layer_activation("relu") %>%
  layer_max_pooling_2d(pool_size=c(2,2)) %>%
  layer_dropout(0.25,name="drop1") %>%
  layer_conv_2d(name="conv3",filter=64, kernel_size=c(3,3),
            padding="same") %>%
  layer_activation("relu") %>%
  layer_conv_2d(name="conv4",filter=64, kernel_size=c(3,3),
            padding="same") %>%
  layer_activation("relu") %>%
  layer_max_pooling_2d(pool_size=c(2,2)) %>%
  layer_dropout(0.25,name="drop2") %>%
  layer_flatten() %>%
  layer_dense(256) %>%
  layer_activation("relu") %>%
  layer_dropout(0.5) %>%
  layer_dense(256) %>%
  layer_activation("relu") %>%
  layer_dropout(0.5) %>%
  layer_dense(8) %>%
  layer_activation("softmax")

model %>% compile(
```

```
        loss="categorical_crossentropy",
        optimizer="adam",
        metrics="accuracy"
)
```

The model definition was adapted from the VGG16 architecture, which we will see later. I used a smaller number of blocks and fewer nodes. Note that the final dense layer must have 8 nodes, because there are only 8, not 10 classes in the `data1` folder.

The next part sets up a data generator; the purpose of this is to load batches of image files into the model as it is being trained. We can also apply data augmentation to the train dataset in the data generator. We will select to create artificial data by randomly flipping the images horizontally, shifting images horizontally/vertically, and rotating the images by up to 15 degrees. We saw in Chapter 6, *Tuning and Optimizing Models,* that data augmentation can significantly improve existing models:

```
# set up data generators to stream images to the train function
data_dir <- "../data/cifar_10_images/"
train_dir <- paste(data_dir,"data1/train/",sep="")
valid_dir <- paste(data_dir,"data1/valid/",sep="")

# in CIFAR10
# there are 50000 images in training set
# and 10000 images in test set
# but we are only using 8/10 classes,
# so its 40000 train and 8000 validation
num_train <- 40000
num_valid <- 8000
flow_batch_size <- 50
# data augmentation
train_gen <- image_data_generator(
  rotation_range=15,
  width_shift_range=0.2,
  height_shift_range=0.2,
  horizontal_flip=TRUE,
  rescale=1.0/255)
# get images from directory
train_flow <- flow_images_from_directory(
  train_dir,
  train_gen,
  target_size=c(32,32),
  batch_size=flow_batch_size,
  class_mode="categorical"
)

# no augmentation on validation data
valid_gen <- image_data_generator(rescale=1.0/255)
```

```
valid_flow <- flow_images_from_directory(
  valid_dir,
  valid_gen,
  target_size=c(32,32),
  batch_size=flow_batch_size,
  class_mode="categorical"
)
```

Once the data generators have been set up, we will also use two callback functions. Callback functions allow you to run custom code after a specific number of batches / epochs have executed. You can write your own callbacks or use some predefined callback functions. Previously, we used callbacks for logging metrics, but here the callbacks will implement model checkpointing and early stopping, which are are often used when building complex deep learning models.

Model checkpointing is used to save the model weights to disk. You can then load the model from disk into memory and use it for predicting new data, or you can continue training the model from the point it was saved to disk. You can save the weights after every epoch, this might be useful if you are using cloud resources and are worried about the machine terminating suddenly. Here, we use it to keep the best model we have seen so far in training. After every epoch, it checks the validation loss, and if it is lower than the validation loss in the existing file, it saves the model.

Early stopping allows you to stop training a model when the performance no longer improves. Some people refer to it as a form of regularization because early stopping can prevent a model from overfitting. While it can avoid overfitting, it works very differently to the regularization techniques, such as L1, L2, weight decay, and dropout, that we saw in Chapter 3, *Deep Learning Fundamentals*. When using early stopping, you usually would allow the model to continue for a few epochs even if performance is no longer improving, the number of epochs allowed before stopping training is known as *patience* in Keras. Here we set it to 10, that is, if we have 10 epochs where the model has failed to improve, we stop training. Here is the code to create the callbacks that we will use in our model:

```
# call-backs
callbacks <- list(
  callback_early_stopping(monitor="val_acc",patience=10,mode="auto"),
  callback_model_checkpoint(filepath="cifar_model.h5",mode="auto",
                            monitor="val_loss",save_best_only=TRUE)
)
```

Here is the code to train the model:

```
# train the model using the data generators and call-backs defined above
history <- model %>% fit_generator(
  train_flow,
```

```
    steps_per_epoch=as.integer(num_train/flow_batch_size),
    epochs=100,
    callbacks=callbacks,
    validation_data=valid_flow,
    validation_steps=as.integer(num_valid/flow_batch_size)
)
```

One thing to note here is that we have to manage the steps per epoch for the train and validation generators. When you set up a generator, you don't know how much data is actually there, so we need to set the number of steps for each epoch. This is simply the number of records divided by the batch size.

This model should take less than an hour to train on a GPU and significantly longer if training on a CPU. As the model is training, the best model is saved in `cifar_model.h5`. The best result on my machine was after epoch 64, when the validation accuracy was about 0.80. The model continued to train for another 10 epochs after this but failed to improve. Here is a plot of the training metrics:

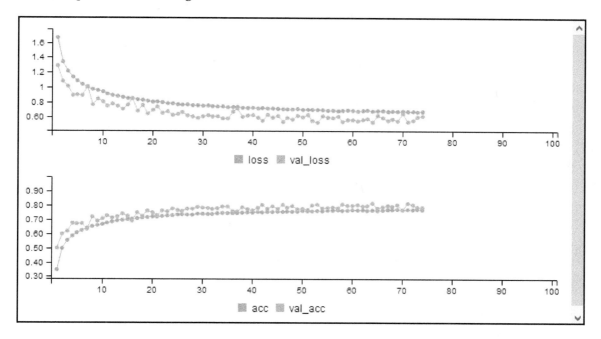

Figure 11.2: Output metrics during model training

Using the saved deep learning model

Now that we have built our deep learning model, we can restart R and reload the model from disk. The code for this section is in the `Chapter11/use_cifar10_model.R` folder. We will load the model that was created in the previous section by using the following code:

```
library(keras)

# load model trained in build_cifar10_model.R
model <- load_model_hdf5("cifar_model.h5")
```

We will use this model to generate a prediction for an image file from the validation set. We will pick the first directory in the validation folder and then pick the 7th file from that folder. We load the image and apply the same preprocessing to it as we did when preprocessing the images during training, which is to normalize the data by dividing the pixel values by 255.0. Here is the code that loads the image and generates the prediction:

```
> valid_dir <-"../data/cifar_10_images/data1/valid/"
> first_dir <- list.dirs(valid_dir, full.names=FALSE, recursive=FALSE)[1]
> valid_dir <- paste(valid_dir,first_dir,sep="")
> img_path <- paste(valid_dir,list.files(valid_dir)[7],sep="/")

# load image and convert to shape we can use for prediction
> img <- image_load(img_path, target_size = c(32,32))
> x <- image_to_array(img)
> x <- array_reshape(x, c(1, dim(x)))
> x <- x / 255.0
> preds <- model %>% predict(x)
> preds <- round(preds,3)
> preds
       [,1] [,2] [,3] [,4] [,5] [,6] [,7]  [,8]
[1,] 0.997    0    0    0    0    0    0 0.003
```

The model predicts that the input is from the first class with 99.7% certainty. Since we chose the first directory in the validation set, the prediction is correct.

The final thing we will do with our model is to evaluate it on a directory of image files. We will also show how to generate predictions for an entire directory of image files. This code loads the images from the directories using data generators, similar to how we trained the model. Here is the code that evaluates and predicts categories by using the model for the validation images we saved to disk:

```
> valid_dir <-"../data/cifar_10_images/data1/valid/"
> flow_batch_size <- 50
> num_valid <- 8000
>
> valid_gen <- image_data_generator(rescale=1.0/255)
> valid_flow <- flow_images_from_directory(
  valid_dir,
  valid_gen,
  target_size=c(32,32),
  batch_size=flow_batch_size,
  class_mode="categorical"
)
>
> evaluate_generator(model,valid_flow,
  steps=as.integer(num_valid/flow_batch_size))
$`loss`
[1] 0.5331386

$acc
[1] 0.808625
```

The validation accuracy is 80.86%, which is similar to what we observed during model training, this confirms that the model was saved correctly to disk. Here is the code that generates predictions for all 8,000 validation images:

```
> preds <- predict_generator(model,valid_flow,
    steps=as.integer(num_valid/flow_batch_size))
> dim(preds)
[1] 8000 8

> # view the predictions,
> preds <- round(preds,3)
> head(preds)
        [,1]  [,2]  [,3]  [,4]  [,5]  [,6]  [,7]  [,8]
[1,] 0.000 0.000 0.000 0.000 0.000 0.000 0.999 0.001
[2,] 0.000 0.007 0.001 0.002 0.990 0.000 0.000 0.000
[3,] 0.000 0.855 0.069 0.032 0.021 0.017 0.002 0.002
[4,] 0.134 0.001 0.000 0.000 0.000 0.000 0.001 0.864
[5,] 0.011 0.064 0.057 0.226 0.051 0.515 0.004 0.073
[6,] 0.108 0.277 0.135 0.066 0.094 0.091 0.052 0.179
```

We can see that our prediction output has 8,000 rows and 8 columns, so for each validation image, there is a probability for each category. We can see that the sum for each row is 1.0 and that there is usually one class that has a significant probability. For example, the model is predicting that the first image is in class 7 with a probability of 99.9%.

We have now built a complete image classification solution using image files. This template can be reused for other tasks once the image data is stored in the same directory structure. If the new task had a different number of categories, then all you would need to change is the number of nodes in the last dense layer and possibly the softmax activation. However, if you did have a new image classification task that involved real-life images, then you probably would get better results by using an existing model and using transfer learning. Before I explain how to do that, I will provide some background on the ImageNet dataset, which is often used to train complex models which are then used in transfer learning.

The ImageNet dataset

From 2010, an annual image classification competition has been run called the **ImageNet Large Scale Visual Recognition Challenge** (**ILSVRC**). The image set consists of over 14 million images that have been labelled with over 1,000 categories. Without this dataset, there would not be the huge interest in deep learning that there is today. It has provided the stimulus for research in deep learning through the competition. The models and weights learnt on the Imagenet dataset have then been used in thousands of other deep learning models through transfer learning. The actual history of ImageNet is an interesting story. The following link (`https://qz.com/1034972/the-data-that-changed-the-direction-of-ai-research-and-possibly-the-world/`) explains how the project originally got little attention, but that changed with a number of linked events:

- The ILSVRC became the benchmark for image classification for researchers.
- NVIDIA had released libraries that allowed access to **graphical processing units** (**GPUs**). GPUs are designed to do massive parallel matrix operations, which is exactly what is needed to create deep neural networks.
- Geoffrey Hinton, Ilya Sutskever, and Alex Krizhevsky from the University of Toronto created a deep convolutional neural network architecture called **AlexNet** that won the competition in 2012. Although this was not the first use of convolutional neural networks, their submission beat the next approach by a huge margin.
- Researchers noticed that when they trained models using the ImageNet dataset, they could use them on other classification tasks. They almost always got much better performance from using the ImageNet model and then using transfer learning than just training a model from scratch on the original dataset.

The advances in image classification can be tracked with some notable entries in the ILSVRC competition:

Team	Year	Error rate
2011 ILSVRC winner (not deep learning)	2011	25.8%
AlexNet (7 layers)	2012	15.3%
VGG Net (16 layers)	2014	7.32%
GoogLeNet / Inception (19 layers)	2014	6.67%
ResNet (152 layers)	2015	3.57%

VGGNet, Inception, and Resnet are all available in Keras. A complete list of available networks can be found at `https://keras.rstudio.com/reference/index.html#section-applications`.

The models for these networks can be loaded in Keras and used to classify a new image into one of the 1,000 categories in ImageNet. We will look at this next. If you have a new classification task with a different set of images, then you can also use these networks and then use transfer learning, which we will look at later in this chapter. The number of categories can be different; you do not need to have 1,000 categories for your task.

Perhaps the simplest model to begin with is VGGNet, as it is not that different to what we saw in `Chapter 5`, *Image Classification Using Convolutional Neural Networks*.

Loading an existing model

In this section, we will load an existing model (VGGNet) in Keras and use it to classify a new image. The code for this section can be found in the `Chapter11/vgg_model.R`. We will begin by loading the model and looking at its architecture:

```
> library(keras)
> model <- application_vgg16(weights = 'imagenet', include_top = TRUE)

> summary(model)
```

Layer (type)	Output Shape	Param #
input_1 (InputLayer)	(None, 224, 224, 3)	0
block1_conv1 (Conv2D)	(None, 224, 224, 64)	1792
block1_conv2 (Conv2D)	(None, 224, 224, 64)	36928

block1_pool (MaxPooling2D)	(None, 112, 112, 64)	0
block2_conv1 (Conv2D)	(None, 112, 112, 128)	73856
block2_conv2 (Conv2D)	(None, 112, 112, 128)	147584
block2_pool (MaxPooling2D)	(None, 56, 56, 128)	0
block3_conv1 (Conv2D)	(None, 56, 56, 256)	295168
block3_conv2 (Conv2D)	(None, 56, 56, 256)	590080
block3_conv3 (Conv2D)	(None, 56, 56, 256)	590080
block3_pool (MaxPooling2D)	(None, 28, 28, 256)	0
block4_conv1 (Conv2D)	(None, 28, 28, 512)	1180160
block4_conv2 (Conv2D)	(None, 28, 28, 512)	2359808
block4_conv3 (Conv2D)	(None, 28, 28, 512)	2359808
block4_pool (MaxPooling2D)	(None, 14, 14, 512)	0
block5_conv1 (Conv2D)	(None, 14, 14, 512)	2359808
block5_conv2 (Conv2D)	(None, 14, 14, 512)	2359808
block5_conv3 (Conv2D)	(None, 14, 14, 512)	2359808
block5_pool (MaxPooling2D)	(None, 7, 7, 512)	0
flatten (Flatten)	(None, 25088)	0
fc1 (Dense)	(None, 4096)	102764544
fc2 (Dense)	(None, 4096)	16781312
predictions (Dense)	(None, 1000)	4097000

```
=================================================================
Total params: 138,357,544
Trainable params: 138,357,544
Non-trainable params: 0
```

This model looks complicated, but when you look at it in detail, there is nothing that we haven't seen before. There are two blocks with two convolutional layers, which are then followed by a max pooling layer. These are followed by three blocks with three convolutional layers, which are then followed by a max pooling layer. Finally, we have a flatten layer and three dense layers. The last dense layer has 1,000 nodes, which is the number of categories in the ImageNet dataset.

Let's use this model to make a prediction for a new image. This image is a bicycle, albeit an unusual one – it is a time trial bicycle:

Figure 11.3: Test image for classification

The following code block processes the image into a suitable format to use in the VGG model. It loads the image and resizes it to the dimensions of the images used to train the model (224, 224). We then have to preprocess the image data before calling the `predict` function. Finally, there is a helper function in Keras called `imagenet_decode_predictions` that we can use to get the prediction categories and the probabilities:

```
> img_path <- "image1.jpg"
> img <- image_load(img_path, target_size = c(224,224))
```

```
> x <- image_to_array(img)
> x <- array_reshape(x, c(1, dim(x)))
> x <- imagenet_preprocess_input(x)

> preds <- model %>% predict(x)
> imagenet_decode_predictions(preds, top = 5)
[[1]]
  class_name      class_description      score
1 n02835271       bicycle-built-for-two  0.31723219
2 n03792782       mountain_bike          0.16578741
3 n03891332       parking_meter          0.12548350
4 n04485082       tripod                 0.06399463
5 n09193705       alp                    0.04852912
```

The top prediction is `bicycle-built-for-two` at just over 30%, and the second best prediction is `mountain_bike` at 16.5%. ImageNet has a category for a tricycle and unicycle (and even a `Model_T` car!), but does not seem to have a category for a bicycle, so this prediction is a not a bad result. However, `mountain_bike` is probably a more accurate category for this image as it definitely is not a bicycle for two people!

Transfer learning

One of the few disadvantages deep learning has over traditional machine learning is that it requires lots of data. Transfer learning is one way to overcome this, by using the weights of a previously trained model (usually trained on ImageNet data) and then applying them to a new problem set.

The ImageNet dataset consists of 15 million images in 1,000 classes. Since we can reuse parts of a model that has been trained on this amount of data, it may be possible to train the new model with just a few hundred images per category. This would depend on the images being somewhat related to the data used in the original model. For example, trying to use transfer learning from ImageNet models (which is trained on photographs) on data from other domains (for example, satellite or medical scans), would be more difficult and would require much more data. Some of the concerns we raised in Chapter 6, *Tuning and Optimizing Models*, about different data sources also applies. If the data is from a different type of data distribution, for example, mobile images, off-center photos, different lighting conditions, and so on, this will also matter. This is where creating more synthetic data through data augmentation can make a big difference.

We will now apply transfer learning using the model we built in the *Building the deep learning model* section. Recall that we only used 8/10 of the classes in building and evaluating this model. We will now build a new model using transfer learning that will differentiate between the 2 remaining classes. The code for this section can be found in the `Chapter11/cifar_txr.R` folder:

1. We will use the model we built in the previous section and load it using the following code:

```
library(keras)

# load model trained in build_cifar10_model.R
model <- load_model_hdf5("cifar_model.h5")
```

2. Next, we will call `trainable_weights` on the model object to get the number of trainable layers. This will count all the non-activation layers in our model.

```
> length(model$trainable_weights)
[1] 14
```

3. Next, we freeze the early layers in our model. Freezing the layers in a model means that the weights will not be updated during back-propagation. We freeze the convolutional blocks, but do not freeze the dense layers at the end of the model. We use the names we set in the model definition to set the first and last layers to freeze.

4. We then call `trainable_weights` on the model once more to confirm that the number changed from the preceding value, `14`, to `6`. Here is the code for freezing the layers:

```
freeze_weights(model,from="conv1", to="drop2")
length(model$trainable_weights)
[1] 6
```

5. Next, we will remove the last dense layer and last activation layer from our model by calling the `pop_layer` function twice in the following code. We need to do this because our new task has 2 classes and not 8:

```
# remove the softmax layer
pop_layer(model)
pop_layer(model)
```

6. Now, we can add a new layer with 2 nodes (because we have 2 classes in the new task) by using the following code:

```
# add a new layer that has the correct number of nodes for the new
task
model %>%
   layer_dense(name="new_dense",units=2, activation='softmax')
summary(model)
```

7. The following code block compiles the model again and sets up the generators to load the data. This is similar to what we saw when we built the model. One difference is that we do not use data augmentation here:

```
# compile the model again
model %>% compile(
   loss = "binary_crossentropy",
   optimizer="adam",
   metrics=c('accuracy')
)

# set up data generators to stream images to the train function
data_dir <- "../data/cifar_10_images/"
train_dir <- paste(data_dir,"data2/train/",sep="")
valid_dir <- paste(data_dir,"data2/valid/",sep="")

# in CIFAR10, # there are 50000 images in training set
# and 10000 images in test set
# but we are only using 2/10 classes,
# so its 10000 train and 2000 validation
num_train <- 10000
num_valid <- 2000
flow_batch_size <- 50
# no data augmentation
train_gen <- image_data_generator(rescale=1.0/255)
# get images from directory
train_flow <- flow_images_from_directory(
   train_dir,
   train_gen,
   target_size=c(32,32),
   batch_size=flow_batch_size,
   class_mode="categorical"
)

# no augmentation on validation data
valid_gen <- image_data_generator(rescale=1.0/255)
valid_flow <- flow_images_from_directory(
   valid_dir,
   valid_gen,
```

```
    target_size=c(32,32),
    batch_size=flow_batch_size,
    class_mode="categorical"
)
```

8. Finally, we can train the model by using the following code:

```
> history <- model %>% fit_generator(
+ train_flow,
+ steps_per_epoch=as.integer(num_train/flow_batch_size),
+ epochs=10,
+ validation_data=valid_flow,
+ validation_steps=as.integer(num_valid/flow_batch_size)
+ )
Found 10000 images belonging to 2 classes.
Found 2000 images belonging to 2 classes.
Epoch 1/10
200/200 [==============================] - 5s 27ms/step - loss:
0.3115 - acc: 0.8811 - val_loss: 0.1529 - val_acc: 0.9425
Epoch 2/10
200/200 [==============================] - 4s 20ms/step - loss:
0.1971 - acc: 0.9293 - val_loss: 0.1316 - val_acc: 0.9550
Epoch 3/10
200/200 [==============================] - 4s 20ms/step - loss:
0.1637 - acc: 0.9382 - val_loss: 0.1248 - val_acc: 0.9540
Epoch 4/10
200/200 [==============================] - 4s 20ms/step - loss:
0.1367 - acc: 0.9497 - val_loss: 0.1200 - val_acc: 0.9575
Epoch 5/10
200/200 [==============================] - 4s 20ms/step - loss:
0.1227 - acc: 0.9543 - val_loss: 0.1148 - val_acc: 0.9605
Epoch 6/10
200/200 [==============================] - 4s 20ms/step - loss:
0.1161 - acc: 0.9559 - val_loss: 0.1110 - val_acc: 0.9625
Epoch 7/10
200/200 [==============================] - 4s 20ms/step - loss:
0.1022 - acc: 0.9622 - val_loss: 0.1118 - val_acc: 0.9620
Epoch 8/10
200/200 [==============================] - 4s 20ms/step - loss:
0.0996 - acc: 0.9655 - val_loss: 0.1068 - val_acc: 0.9645
Epoch 9/10
200/200 [==============================] - 4s 20ms/step - loss:
0.0861 - acc: 0.9687 - val_loss: 0.1095 - val_acc: 0.9655
Epoch 10/10
200/200 [==============================] - 4s 20ms/step - loss:
0.0849 - acc: 0.9696 - val_loss: 0.1189 - val_acc: 0.9620
```

The best accuracy was on epoch 9 when we got 96.55% accuracy. This is significantly better than what we got on the multi-classification model (approximately 81%), but binary classification tasks are much easier than multi-classification tasks. We can also see that the model was very quick to train, because it only had to update the weights in the last few layers.

Deploying TensorFlow models

Historically, one of the perceived disadvantages of using R for data science projects was the difficulty in deploying machine learning models built in R. This often meant that companies used R mainly as a prototyping tool to build models which were then rewritten in another language, such as Java and .NET. It is also one of the main reasons cited for companies switching to Python for data science as Python has more *glue code*, which allows it to interface with other programming languages.

Thankfully, this is changing. One interesting new product from RStudio, called RStudio Connect, allows companies to create a platform for sharing R-Shiny applications, reports in R Markdown, dashboards, and models. This allows companies to serve machine learning models using a REST interface.

The TensorFlow (and Keras) models we have created in this book can be deployed without any runtime dependency on either R or Python. One way of doing this is TensorFlow Serving, which is an open source software library for serving TensorFlow models. Another option is to use the Google CloudML interface that we saw in Chapter 10, *Running Deep Learning Models in the Cloud*. This allows you to create a publicly available REST API that can be called from your applications. TensorFlow models can also be deployed to iPhones and Android mobile phones.

There are two basic options for scoring models in production:

- **Batch mode**: In batch mode, a set of data is scored offline and the prediction results are stored and used elsewhere
- **Real-time mode**: In real-time mode, the data is scored immediately, usually a record at a time, and the results are immediately used.

For a lot of applications, batch mode is more than adequate. You should carefully consider if you really need a real-time prediction system as it is requires more resources and needs constant monitoring. It is much more efficient to score records in a batch rather than individually. Another advantage of batch mode is that you know the demand on the application beforehand and can plan resources accordingly. With real-time systems, a spike in demand or a denial of service attack can cause problems with your prediction model.

We have already seen batch mode for a saved model in the *Using the saved deep learning model* section in this chapter. So, let's look at how we can build a REST interface to get a prediction on new data from a deep learning model in real-time. This will use the tfdeploy package. The code for this section can be found in the Chapter11/deploy_model.R. We are going to build a simple model based on the MNIST dataset and then create a web interface where we can submit a new image for classification. Here is the first part of the code that builds the model and prints out the predictions for the first 5 rows in the test set:

```
library(keras)
#devtools::install_github("rstudio/tfdeploy")
library(tfdeploy)

# load data
c(c(x_train, y_train), c(x_test, y_test)) %<-% dataset_mnist()

# reshape and rescale
x_train <- array_reshape(x_train, dim=c(nrow(x_train), 784)) / 255
x_test <- array_reshape(x_test, dim=c(nrow(x_test), 784)) / 255

# one-hot encode response
y_train <- to_categorical(y_train, 10)
y_test <- to_categorical(y_test, 10)

# define and compile model
model <- keras_model_sequential()
model %>%
  layer_dense(units=256, activation='relu',
input_shape=c(784),name="image") %>%
  layer_dense(units=128, activation='relu') %>%
  layer_dense(units=10, activation='softmax',name="prediction") %>%
  compile(
    loss='categorical_crossentropy',
    optimizer=optimizer_rmsprop(),
    metrics=c('accuracy')
  )

# train model
history <- model %>% fit(
```

```
    x_train, y_train,
    epochs=10, batch_size=128,
    validation_split=0.2
)
preds <- round(predict(model, x_test[1:5,]),0)
head(preds)
      [,1] [,2] [,3] [,4] [,5] [,6] [,7] [,8] [,9] [,10]
[1,]    0    0    0    0    0    0    0    1    0     0
[2,]    0    0    1    0    0    0    0    0    0     0
[3,]    0    1    0    0    0    0    0    0    0     0
[4,]    1    0    0    0    0    0    0    0    0     0
[5,]    0    0    0    0    1    0    0    0    0     0
```

There is nothing new about this code. Next, we will create a JSON file for one image file in the test set. JSON stands for JavaScript Object Notation, and is the accepted standard for serializing and sending data over a network connection. If HTML is the language for computers-to-human web communication, JSON is the language for computers-to-computers web communication. It is heavily used in microservice architecture, which is a framework for building a complex web ecosystem from lots of small web services. The data in the JSON file must have the same preprocessing applied as what was done during training – since we normalized the training data, we must also normalize the test data. The following code creates a JSON file with the values for the first instance in the testset and saves the file to `json_image.json`:

```
# create a json file for an image from the test set
json <- "{\"instances\": [{\"image_input\": ["
json <- paste(json,paste(x_test[1,],collapse=","),sep="")
json <- paste(json,"]}]}",sep="")
write.table(json,"json_image.json",row.names=FALSE,col.names=FALSE,quote=FA
LSE)
```

Now that we have a JSON file, let's create a REST web interface for our model:

```
export_savedmodel(model, "savedmodel")
serve_savedmodel('savedmodel', browse=TRUE)
```

Once you do this, a new web page should pop up that is similar to the following:

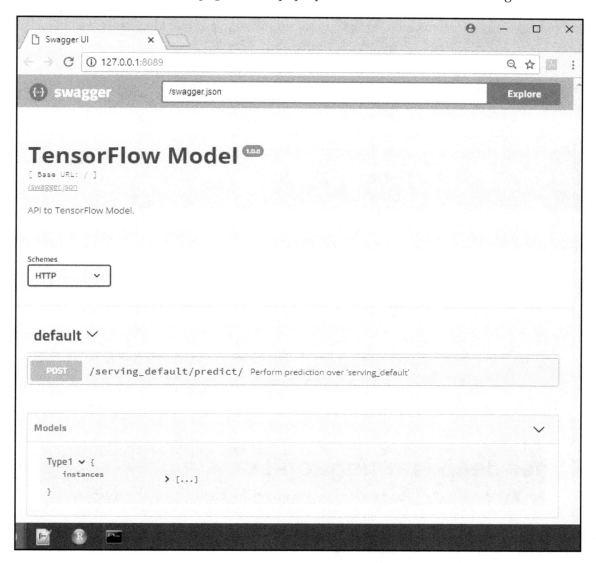

Figure 11.4: Swagger UI for the TensorFlow model REST web service

This is a Swagger UI page showing the RESTful web services for the TensorFlow model. This allows us to test our API. While we could try to use this interface, it is easier to use the JSON file we just created. Open up Command Prompt on your machine, browse to the `Chapter11` code directory, and run the following command:

```
curl -X POST -H "Content-Type: application/json" -d @json_image.json
http://localhost:8089/serving_default/predict
```

You should get the following response:

The REST web interface returns another JSON string with these results. We can see that the 8th entry in the list is 1.0 and that all the other numbers are extremely small. This matches the prediction for the first row that we saw in the code at the start of this section.

I imagine that half of the people reading this are very excited about this and the other half couldn't care less! The half that really like this can see how R can be used to serve model predictions that interface with web applications. This opens up huge possibilities for using R, where beforehand it was believed that you either had to use Python or you had to redevelop models in other languages. The half that couldn't care less probably never had to deal with these issues with R, but in time they will see how important this is as well!

Other deep learning topics

Two topics that get a lot of attention in deep learning are **Generative Adversarial Networks (GANs)** and reinforcement learning. We only briefly introduce both topics, there is no code for this section for a couple of reasons. Firstly both topics are very advanced and trying to create a use-case that is non-trivial would require a few chapters for each topic. Secondly, reinforcement learning is not well supported in R, so creating an example would be difficult. Despite this, I include both of these topics in the book because I believe they are important emerging areas in deep learning that you should definitely be aware of.

Generative adversarial networks

Generative Adversarial Networks have been called *the coolest thing since sliced bread* by Yann LeCunn, one of the most prominent people in deep learning. If he believes that, then we should all take notice!

Most of our models in this book have been discriminative models, that is, we try to differentiate one class from another. However in Chapter 9, *Anomaly Detection and Recommendation Systems* we created a generative model in the anomaly detection use-case. This model could create new data, albeit a different representation of the input data. Creating complex generative models is a very hot research topic in deep learning. Many believe that generative models can solve many problems in deep learning, including one of the biggest, which is the lack of correctly labelled data. However before GANs, it was difficult to judge how good a generative model actually was. A group of researchers led by Ian Goodfellow proposed Generative Adversarial Networks (GANs) (Goodfellow, Ian, et al. *Generative adversarial nets.* Advances in neural information processing systems. 2014) that could be used to create realistic artificial data.

In GANs, two models are trained together, the first is a generative model G that creates new data. The second model is a discriminative model D that tries to predict if an example is from the real dataset, or has been created by the generative model G. The basic GAN idea is for the generative model to try to fool the discriminative model, while the discriminative model must try to tell the differences from fake data and real data. The generator keeps creating new data and refining its process until the discriminative model can no longer tell the difference between the generated data and the real training data.

In the paper, the process is compared to a team of counterfeiters creating fake currency (the generative model) and the police who are trying to detect the counterfeit currency (the discriminative model). Both models improve incrementally until it is impossible to differentiate between the counterfeit currency and the real currency.

GANs are notoriously hard to train. One paper that documented a working approach to training GANs on image data called their approach deep convolutional generative adversarial networks (Radford, Alec, Luke Metz, and Soumith Chintala. *Unsupervised representation learning with deep convolutional generative adversarial networks.* arXiv preprint arXiv:1511.06434 (2015)). In this paper, they recommended a number of guidelines to train stable deep convolutional generative adversarial networks (DCGANs):

- Replace any pooling layers with strided convolutions (discriminator) and fractional-strided convolutions (generator).
- Use batchnorm for both models.
- Remove fully connected hidden layers for deep architectures.

- For the generator, use tanh activation in the output layer and ReLU elsewhere.
- For the discriminator, use LeakyReLU activation for all layers.

Training DCGANs is an iterative process, the following steps are repeated:

- First the generator creates some new examples.
- The discriminator is trained using real data and generated data.
- After the discriminator has been trained, both models are trained together. The discriminator's weights are frozen, but its gradients are used in the generator model so that the generator can update it's weights.

During this loop, it is vital that one model does not dominate the other model, they should both improve together. If the discriminator is too smart and is very confident that the instances from the generator are fakes, then there is no signal passed back to the generator and it can no longer improve. Similarly, if the generator finds a clever trick to fool the discriminator, it may generate images that are too similar, or of only one input category and the GAN again fails to improve. This shows the difficulty in training any GAN's, you have to find a set of parameters that works for the data and keeps two models synchronized. A good reference from one of the authors of the DCGAN paper on advice to make GANs work is `https://github.com/soumith/ganhacks`.

GANs have many potential use-cases including being able to train with less data. They also could be used to predict missing data, e.g. add definition to blurred images / videos. They in reinforcement learning, which we discuss in the next section.

Reinforcement learning

Reinforcement learning has a deceptively simple definition: an agent interacts with its environment and changes its behaviors based on the the consequences of its actions. This is actually how humans and animals behave in the real world and is why many people believe that reinforcement learning is the key to achieving artificial general intelligence (AGI).

Artificial general intelligence (AGI) will be achieved if and when computers can perform complex tasks as well as people. This also requires that computers be able to adapt their current knowledge to new problems, just as humans do. Experts disagree on whether AGI is even possible. If we take the very first image from Chapter 1, *Getting Started with Deep Learning*, we can see that the definition of artificial intelligence (... *performing functions that require intelligence when performed by people*) closely resembles the definition of reinforcement learning:

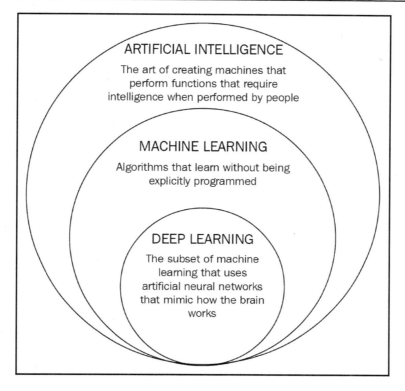

Figure 11.5: The relationship between artificial intelligence, machine learning, and deep learning

David Silver, one of the most prominent people in reinforcement learning and one of the main people involved in AlphaGo, coined the following formula:

Artificial intelligence = Reinforcement learning + Deep learning

One well-known example of reinforcement learning is an algorithm that can play a number of Atari 2600 video games better than most people by just using image pixels as input to the algorithm. The reinforcement learning algorithm learns by playing the game thousands, maybe millions of times, and learns what actions it needs to take to achieve rewards, which could be to collect points or to keep its avatar alive as long as possible. Perhaps the best known example in reinforcement learning is AlphaGo, which defeated one of the best players in the world in Go. AlphaGo is a hybrid artificial system that was composed of neural networks, reinforcement learning, and heuristic search algorithms. It is much harder to program a computer to win in a game of Go than other games, such as chess, because brute-force approaches are not feasible. An additional problem in Go is the difficulty in evaluating the current position.

A formal definition of reinforcement learning is where an agent observes a state s_t at timestep t. When in state s_t, the agent interacts with its environment by taking action, which means that the agent transitions to the new state s_{t+1}. The movement into a new state is linked with a reward, and the goal of the agent is to learn a policy that maximizes the expected rewards. The rewards could be cumulative and/or discounted; for example, near-time rewards are worth more than far-off returns. The value function is the prediction of the future reward. If the new state s_{t+1} is dependent only on the previous state s_t and the action a_t, then it becomes a Markov process. However, one of the major problems in reinforcement learning is that rewards may be sparse and that there may a long delay between an action and achieving the reward. There is also the problem where an immediate reward might cause the agent to go down a path that could ultimately be destructive. For example, in a computer game, the agent could take an immediate step of trying to maximize a score, but this ultimately means that the character *dies* sooner. In a more real-life scenario, for example, a self-driving car, if the goal is to get to a location quickly, then the agent might decide to drive dangerously, putting passengers and other road users at risk.

The core elements in reinforcement learning include the following:

- Rewards are the gains that an agent can achieve in the near-term.
- A value function is the expected reward an agent can expect to achieve from the current state. The value function looks at the long-term rewards / goals, so this may mean taking actions that do not maximize rewards in the short-term.
- A policy guides the actions that an agent can take, it maps the states to possible actions from that state.
- The model is encapsulation of the environment that the agent interacts with. As such it is an incomplete representation of the physical world, but as long as it can accurately simulate the next step given an action, and calculate the reward, then it is an adequate representation that can be used for reinforcement learning.

Other important mechanisms in reinforcement learning include multi-label classification, memory, unsupervised learning, knowledge transfer (using knowledge learned from one problem to solve related problems), search (to select the next best action by looking at all possible permutations x moves ahead), multi-agent RL, and learning to learn. We will not go into detail on these tasks, some may already be familiar to you. However, this list does highlight the complexity involved in reinforcement learning.

Deep learning can be used as a component in reinforcement learning to work on subtasks, such as object detection, speech recognition, NLP, and so on. Deep learning can also be an integral part of reinforcement learning when it is used in the key components of reinforcement learning, which are the value function, policy, and the environmental model. This is called deep reinforcement learning (deep RL). For example, by using recurrent connections between hidden units, Hausknecht and Stone built a deep recurrent Q-network (DRQN) that could predict the speed of the ball in the computer game **Pong**. Another research area in linking deep learning with RL is for imitation learning. In imitation learning, an agent learns by observing an *expert*. It is especially useful where there are delayed rewards and evaluating the current position is hard. But imitation learning can be costly, so one approach is to use GANs to produce artificial data to be used in reinforcement learning.

Even though AlphaGo managed to beat the world champion in Go, it is nowhere near solving the problem of artificial general intelligence. DeepMind are a dedicated artificial intelligence company who combined experts in reinforcement learning, supervised learning and tree search functions and huge hardware resources to solve a single problem. AlphaGo was trained on a dataset of 30 million game states and simulated millions of games. The version that beat one of the best players in the world in Go used almost 2,000 CPUs and 300 GPUs. Before it could beat the world champion, it was coached by the European champion, although the early version did beat him first. However, AlphaGo solves only one problem, it cannot even generalize to other board games. Therefore, it does not come anywhere near solving artificial general intelligence.

One of the more honest appraisals of AlphaGo is from Andrej Karpathy, who is a distinguished researcher in deep learning and currently is director of artificial intelligence at Tesla. He posted a blog called **AlphaGo, in context** (https://medium.com/@karpathy/alphago-in-context-c47718cb95a5) after AlphaGo defeated the number one ranked player in 2017. Karpathy listed the following limitations of Go compared to other artificial intelligence tasks:

- The game is fully deterministic, that is, rules are fixed and fully known beforehand. In comparison, most real-world problems are not
- The game is fully observable, that is, complete information is known to all parties, there are no hidden variables or states.
- The games has a discrete action space, that is, there is a fixed number of allowable actions
- A perfect simulator exists, that is, you can model millions of examples in a safe space. Real-life artificial intelligence does not have this.
- The game is relatively short.
- There are historical datasets from previous games

If we consider self-driving cars as an artificial intelligence task, it probably does not match any of these properties.

One unusual quirk in AlphaGo games with the world champion is that it sometimes passed on moves that would have captured board space. As humans, when we play games, we sometimes crave immediate feedback and therefore make moves to achieve short-term rewards. AlphaGo was programmed to win the game, regardless of the margin, so was quite content to pass on making such moves during the games. It is interesting that some expert Go players believe that they can improve by studying the strategies of AlphaGo. We have come full circle – humans trying to imitate the actions of computers, which in turn are modeled on the actions of humans.

Summary

In this chapter, you have seen some advanced deep learning techniques. First, we looked at some image classification models and looked at some historical models. Next, we loaded an existing model with pre-trained weights into R and used it to classify a new image. We looked at transfer learning, which allows us to reuse an existing model as a base on which to build a deep learning model for new data. We built an image classifier model that could train on image files. This model also showed us how to use data augmentation and callbacks, which are used in many deep learning models. Finally, we demonstrated how we can build a model in R and create a REST endpoint for a prediction API that can be used from other applications or across the web.

R is a great language for data science and I believe it is easier to use and allows you to develop machine learning prototypes faster than the main alternative, Python. Now that it has support for some excellent deep learning frameworks in MXNet, Keras and TensorFlow. In the next chapter we would be looking at the uses of deep learning using R with practical examples.

12
Handwritten Digit Recognition using Convolutional Neural Networks

Now we dive deep into our R deep learning journey with the fundamental and core concepts of deep learning, and a deep learning 101 project—handwritten digit recognition. We will start with what deep learning is about, why we need it, and its evolution in recent years. We will also discuss why deep learning stands out and several typical deep learning applications. With the important deep learning concepts in mind, we get it started with our image classification project where we first conduct exploratory analysis on the data and make an initial attempt using shallow single-layer neural networks. Then we move on with deeper neural networks and achieve better results. However, we argue that chaining more hidden layers does not necessarily improve classification performance. The key is to extract richer representation and more informative features. And **convolutional neural networks** (**CNNs**) are the way to go! We will be demonstrating how we boost the digit recognition accuracy to nearly 99% with CNNs, which are well suited to exploiting strong and unique features that differentiate between images. We finally wrap up the chapter after several more experiments and validations.

We will look into these topics in detail:

- What is deep learning and what is special about it
- Applications of deep learning
- Exploratory analysis on MNIST handwritten digit data
- Handwritten digit recognition using logistic regression and single-layer neural networks with the `nnet` package
- Handwritten digit recognition using deep neural networks with the `MXNet` package
- Rectified linear unit
- The mechanics and structure of convolutional neural networks
- Handwritten digit recognition using convolutional neural networks with the `MXNet` package
- Visualization of outputs of convolutional layers
- Early stopping in deep neural networks

What is deep learning and why do we need it?

Deep learning is an emerging subfield of machine learning. It employs **artificial neural network (ANN)** algorithms to process data, derive patterns or to develop abstractions, simulating the thinking process of a biological brain. And those ANNs usually contain more than one **hidden layer**, which is how deep learning got its name—machine learning with *stacked* neural networks. Going beyond shallow ANNs (usually with only one hidden layer), a deep learning model with the right architectures and parameters can better represent complex non-linear relationships.

Here is an example of a shallow ANN:

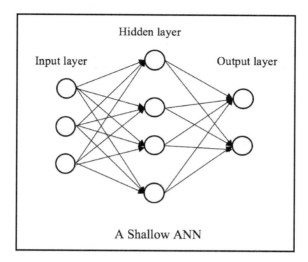

A Shallow ANN

And an example of a deep learning model:

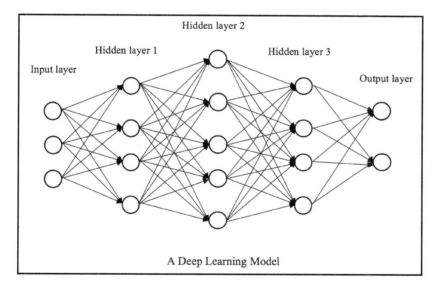

A Deep Learning Model

Don't feel scared, regardless of how complicated it might sound or look. We will be going from shallow to deep dives into deep learning throughout five projects in this book.

First of all, as a part of the broad family of machine learning, deep learning can be used in supervised learning, semi-supervised learning, as well as unsupervised learning tasks, even reinforcement learning tasks. So what sets it apart from traditional machine learning algorithms?

What makes deep learning special?

Deep learning employs a stack of multiple hidden layers of non-linear processing units. The input of a hidden layer is the output of its previous layer. This can be easily observed from the examples of a shallow neural network and a deep neural network shown previously.

Features are extracted from each hidden layer. Features from different layers represent abstracts or patterns of different levels. Hence, higher-level features are derived from lower-level features, which are extracted from previous layers. All these together form a hierarchical representation learned from the data.

Take the cats and dogs image classification as an example, in traditional machine learning solutions, the classification step follows a feature extraction process, which is often based on:

- Domain knowledge, such as color, shape, color of the animals, shape of the ears in this case, which are usually hand-crafted
- Dimensionality reduction, such as **principal component analysis (PCA)**, **Latent Dirichlet Allocation (LDA)**
- Feature engineering techniques, such as **histogram of oriented gradients transformation (HOG)**, **Scale Invariant Feature Transform (SIFT)**, and **Speeded up Robust Features (SURF)**

The workflow of traditional machine learning solution to cats and dogs classification is displayed as follows:

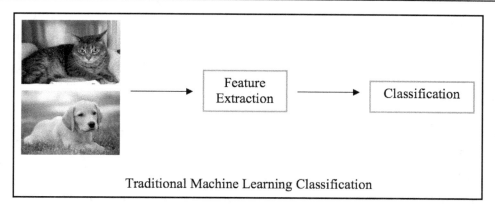

Traditional Machine Learning Classification

However, in deep learning based solutions (such as CNNs, which we will be learning shortly), hierarchical representations are derived throughout the latent learning process and features of the highest level are then fed into the final classification step. These features capture the important and distinguishable details in the cat and dog images. Depending on the magic worked in hidden layers:

- The low-level features can be edges, lines or dots of whiskers, nose or eyes, ears and so on
- The higher-level features can be outlines or contours of the animals

The entire workflow of deep learning solution is shown as follows:

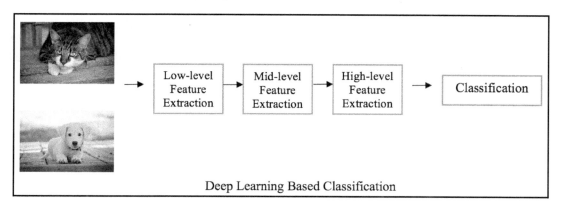

Deep Learning Based Classification

Deep learning removes those manual or explicit feature extraction steps, and instead relies on the training process to automatically discover useful patterns underneath the input data. And through tweaking the layout (number of layers, number of hidden units for a layer, activation function, and so on) of the networks, we can find the most efficient sets of features.

Recall the example of the shallow ANN and that of the deep learning model in the last section, data flow one-way from the input layer to the output. Besides feedforward architectures, deep learning models allow data to proceed in any direction, even to circle back to the input layer. Data looping back from the previous output becomes part of the next input data. **Recurrent neural networks (RNNs)** are great examples. We will be working on projects using RNNs later in this book. For now, we can still get a sense of what the recurrent or cycle-like architecture looks like from the diagram of RNNs as follows:

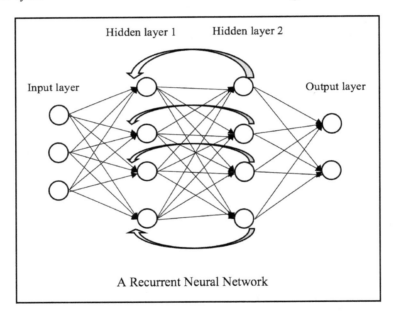

A Recurrent Neural Network

The recurrent architecture makes the models applicable to time series data and sequences of inputs. As data from previous time points goes into the training of the current time point, the deep learning recurrent model effectively solves a time series or sequence learning problem in a feedforward manner. In traditional machine learning solutions (read more in *Machine Learning for Sequential Data: A Review* by T. Dietterich) to time series problems, sliding windows of previous lags are usually provided as current inputs. This can be ineffective as the size of the sliding windows needs to be decided and so does the number of windows, while the recurrent models figure out timely or sequential relationships themselves.

 Although we are discussing here all the advantages about deep learning over the other machine learning techniques, we did not make any claim or statement that the *modern* deep learning is superior to the *traditional* machine learning. That's right, there is *no free lunch* in this field, which was also emphasized in my last book, *Python Machine Learning By Example*. There is no single algorithm that can solve all machine learning problems more efficiently than others. It all depends on specific use cases - in some applications, the "traditional" ones are a better fit, or a deep learning setting makes no difference; in some cases, the "modern" ones yield better performance.

Next, we will see some typical applications of deep learning that will better motivate us to get started in deep learning projects.

What are the applications of deep learning?

Computer vision and image recognition is often considered the first area where breakthroughs of deep learning occurred. Handwritten digit recognition has become a Hello World in this field, and a common evaluation set for image classification algorithms and techniques is the scanned document dataset constructed from the **National Institute of Standards and Technology** (NIST), called **MNIST** (M stands for **modified**, which means data is pre-processed for the ease of machine learning processes).

Some examples from MNIST are shown as follows:

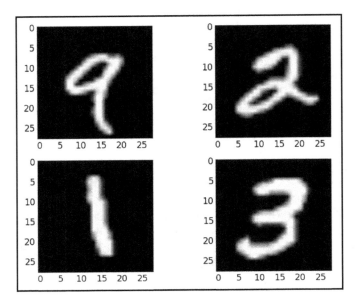

Some researchers have so far achieved the best performance 0.21% error rate on the MNIST dataset using CNNs. Details can be found in the paper, *Regularization of Neural Networks using DropConnect*, published in the **International Conference on Machine Learning (ICML)** in 2013. Other comparable results, for example 0.23%, 0.27% and 0.31%, are also yielded by CNNs and deep neural networks. However, traditional machine learning algorithms with sophisticated feature engineering techniques could only yield error rates ranging from 0.52% to 7.6%, which were achieved by using **Support Vector Machine (SVMs)** and pairwise linear classifiers respectively.

Besides image recognition (such as the well known face recognition), the applications of deep learning are extended to more challenging tasks including:

- Image-based search engines, which cover image classification and image similarity encoding, heavily utilizing deep learning techniques.
- Machine vision, with self-driving cars as an example, which interprets 360° camera views to make decisions in real time.

- Color restoration from black and white photos—the examples after color recovery from `http://hi.cs.waseda.ac.jp/~iizuka/projects/colorization/extra.html` are impressive.
- Image generation, including handwriting, cat images, and even video game images, or whatever image you name it. For example, we use an interesting playground, `https://www.cs.toronto.edu/~graves/handwriting.html` (developed by Alex Graves from the University of Toronto), to create handwritings of the title of this book in three different styles:

Natural language processing (**NLP**) is another field where deep learning is dominant in modern solutions. Recall we described deep learning models with recurrent architecture are appropriate for sequences of inputs, such as natural language and text. In recent years, deep learning has greatly helped to improve:

- Machine translation, for example the sentence-based **Google Neural Machine Translation system** (**GNMT**) which utilizes deep RNNs to improve accuracy and fluency
- Sentiment analysis, information retrieval, theme detection and many other common NLP applications, where deep learning models have achieved state-of-the-art performance thanks to word embedding techniques
- Text generation, where RNNs learn the intricate relationship between words (including punctuation) in sentences and to *write* text, to become an author or a virtual Shakespeare

Image captioning generation, also known as image to text, couples recent breakthroughs in computer vision and NLP. It leverages CNNs to detect and classify objects in images, and assigns labels to those objects. It then applies RNNs to describe those labels in a comprehensible sentence. The following examples are captured from the web demo from `http://cs.stanford.edu/people/karpathy/deepimagesent/generationdemo/` (developed by Andrej Karpathy from Stanford University):

a train is traveling down the tracks near a building

a train traveling down tracks next to a forest

Similarly, sound and speech is also a field of sequential learning, where machine learning algorithms are applied to predict time series or label sequence data. Speech recognition has been greatly revolutionized by deep learning. And now, deep learning based products like Apple's Siri, Amazon's Alexa, Google Home, Skype Translator and many others are "invading" our lives, in a good way for sure. Besides an author writing text, deep learning models can also be a music composer. For example, Francesco Marchesani from the Polytechnic University of Milan was able to train RNNs to produce Chopin's music.

Additionally, deep learning also excels in many use cases in video. It makes significant contributions to the boost of virtual reality with its capability of accurate motion detection, and to the advance of real-time behavior analysis in surveillance videos. Scientists from Google, DeepMind, and Oxford even built a computer lip reader called LipNet, achieving a success rate of 93%.

Besides supervised and unsupervised learning cases, deep learning is heavily used in reinforcement learning. Robots who can handle objects, climb stairs, operate in kitchens are not new to us. Recently, Google's AlphaGo beating the world's elite *Go* players received widespread media coverage. Nowadays, everybody looks forward to seeing self-driving cars being out in the market in just one or two years. These have all benefited from the advance of deep learning in reinforcement learning. Oh, and don't forget computers are taught to play the game, FlappyBird!

We did not even mention bioinformatics, drug discovery, recommendation systems in e-commerce, finance, especially the stock market, insurance and the **Internet of Things** (**IoT**). In fact, the list of deep learning applications is already long, and only gets longer and longer.

I hope this section excited you about deep learning and its power of providing better solutions to many machine learning problems we are facing. Artificial intelligence has a brighter future thanks to the advance of deep learning.

So what are we waiting for? Let's get started with handwritten digit recognition!

Handwritten digit recognition using CNNs

For sure, we begin with exploration of the handwritten digit dataset.

Get started with exploring MNIST

The MNIST dataset from http://yann.lecun.com/exdb/mnist/ consists of a training set of 60,000 samples, and a testing set of 10,000 samples. As said previously, images were originally taken from the NIST, and then centered and resized to the same height and width (28 * 28).

Rather than handling the ubyte files, train-images-idx3-ubyte.gz and train-labels-idx1-ubyte.gz in the preceding website and merge them, we use a dataset that is well-formatted from the Kaggle competition Digit Recognizer, https://www.kaggle.com/c/digit-recognizer/. We can download the training dataset, train.csv directly from https://www.kaggle.com/c/digit-recognizer/data. It is the only labeled dataset provided in the site, and we will use it to train classification models, evaluate models and do predictions. Now let's load it up:

```
> data <- read.csv ("train.csv")
> dim(data)
[1] 42000 785
```

We have 42,000 labeled samples available, and each sample has 784 features, which means each digit image has 784 (28 * 28) pixels. Take a look at the label and the first 5 features (pixels) for each of the first 6 data samples:

```
> head(data[1:6])
label pixel0 pixel1 pixel2 pixel3 pixel4
1 1 0 0 0 0 0
2 0 0 0 0 0 0
3 1 0 0 0 0 0
4 4 0 0 0 0 0
5 0 0 0 0 0 0
6 0 0 0 0 0 0
```

The target label ranging from 0 to 9 denotes 10 digits:

```
> unique(unlist(data[1]))
[1] 1 0 4 7 3 5 8 9 2 6
```

The pixel variable ranges from 0 to 255, representing the brightness of the pixel, for example 0 means black and 255 stands for white:

```
> min(data[2:785])
[1] 0
> max(data[2:785])
[1] 255
```

Now let's take a look at two samples, first, the fourth image:

```
> sample_4 <- matrix(as.numeric(data[4,-1]), nrow = 28, byrow = TRUE)
> image(sample_4, col = grey.colors(255))
```

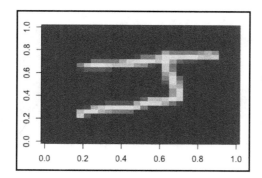

Where we reshaped the feature vector of length 784 into a matrix of 28 * 28.

Second, the 7th image:

```
> sample_7 <- matrix(as.numeric(data[7,-1]), nrow = 28, byrow = TRUE)
> image(sample_7, col = grey.colors(255))
```

The result is as follows:

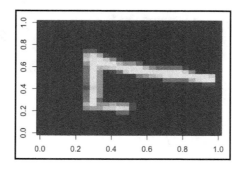

We noticed that the images are rotated 90 degrees to the left. To better view the images, a rotation of 90 degrees clockwise is required. We simply need to reserve elements in each column of an image matrix:

```
> # Rotate the matrix by reversing elements in each column
> rotate <- function(x) t(apply(x, 2, rev))
```

Now visualize the rotated images:

```
> image(rotate(sample_4), col = grey.colors(255))
```

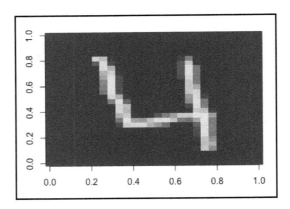

```
> image(rotate(sample_7), col = grey.colors(255))
```

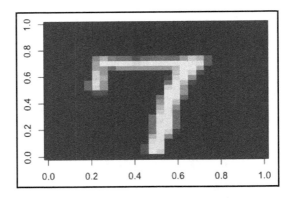

After viewing what the data and images behind look like, we do more exploratory analysis on the labels and features. Firstly, because it is a classification problem, we inspect whether the classes from the data are balanced or unbalanced as a good practice. But before doing so, we should transform the label from integer to factor:

```
> # Transform target variable "label" from integer to factor, in order to
perform classification
> is.factor(data$label)
[1] FALSE
> data$label <- as.factor(data$label)
> is.factor(data$label)
[1] TRUE
```

Now, we can summarize the label distribution in counts:

```
> summary(data$label)
0  1  2  3  4  5  6  7  8  9
4132 4684 4177 4351 4072 3795 4137 4401 4063 4188
```

Or combined with proportion (%):

```
> proportion <- prop.table(table(data$label)) * 100
> cbind(count=table(data$label), proportion=proportion)
count proportion
0  4132  9.838095
1  4684  11.152381
2  4177  9.945238
3  4351  10.359524
4  4072  9.695238
5  3795  9.035714
6  4137  9.850000
7  4401  10.478571
8  4063  9.673810
9  4188  9.971429
```

Classes are balanced.

Now, we explore the distribution of features, the pixels. As an example, we take the 4 pixels from the central 2*2 block (that is, `pixel376`, `pixel377`, `pixel404`, and `pixel405`) in each image and display the histogram for each of the 9 digits:

```
> central_block <- c("pixel376", "pixel377", "pixel404", "pixel405")
> par(mfrow=c(2, 2))
> for(i in 1:9) {
+ hist(c(as.matrix(data[data$label==i, central_block])),
+ main=sprintf("Histogram for digit %d", i),
+ xlab="Pixel value")
+ }
```

The resulting pixel brightness histograms for digit 1 to 4 are displayed respectively, as follows:

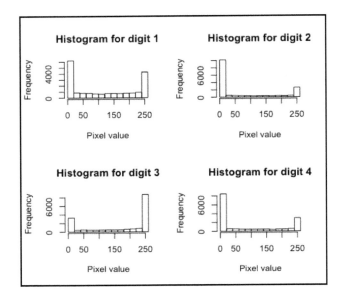

Histograms for digits 5 to 9:

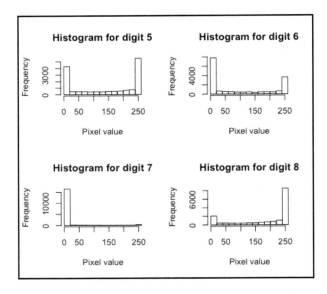

And that for digit 9:

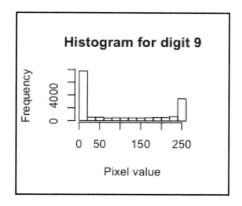

The brightness of central pixels is distributed differently among 9 digits. For instance, the majority of the central pixels are bright, as digit 8 is usually written in a way that strokes go through the center; while digit 7 is not written in this way, hence most of the central pixels are dark. Pixels taken from other positions can also be distinctly distributed among different digits.

The exploratory analysis we just conducted helps move us forward with building classification models based on pixels.

First attempt – logistic regression

We start off with probably the most basic classifier, the logistic regression, to be specific multinomial logistic regression as it is a multiclass case. It is a probabilistic linear classifier parameterized by a weight matrix W (also called coefficient matrix) and a bias (also called intercept) vector b. And it maps an input vector x to a set of probabilities $P(y=1)$, $P(y=2)$,. . ., $P(y-K)$ for K possible classes.

A multinomial logistic regression for two possible classes can be represented graphically as follows:

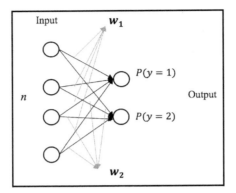

Suppose x is n-dimension, then the weight matrix W is of size n by K with each column W_k representing the coefficients associated with class k; similarly, the bias vector b is of length K, with each element b_k served as the bias for class k. For simplicity, the bias b can be viewed as an additional row in the weight matrix W. So the probability of x being class k can be expressed mathematically as:

$$P(y = k|x, W) = softmax_k(Wx)$$

$$= \frac{exp(w_k x)}{\sum_{j=1}^{j=k} exp(w_j x)}$$

Where *softmax()* denotes the softmax function and that is why multinomial logistic regression is often called softmax regression.

Given a set of training samples $(x^{(1)}, y^{(1)}), (x^{(2)}, y^{(2)}), \ldots (x^{(i)}, y^{(i)}) \ldots, (x^{(m)}, y^{(m)})$ where $y \in 1, 2, \ldots, K$, the optimal model w is obtained by minimizing the cost (also called log loss), which is defined as:

$$J(W) = -\left[\sum_{i=1}^{m} \sum_{k=1}^{k} 1\{y^{(i)} = k\} log \frac{exp(w_k x)}{\sum_{j=1}^{j=k} exp(w_j x)} \right]$$

$$\text{where} \quad 1\{y^{(i)} = k\} = \begin{cases} 1, & if \ y^{(i)} = k \\ 0, & otherwise \end{cases}$$

As usual we resort to gradient descent, an iterative optimization algorithm, to solve for the optimal w. In each iteration, w moves a step that is proportional to the negative derivative Δw of the objective function at the current point. That is, $w := w - \eta \Delta w$, where η is the learning rate. Each column Δw_k of Δw can be computed as:

$$\triangle w_k = \frac{\partial}{\partial w_j} J(w) = -\sum_{i=1}^{m} [x^{(i)} (1\{y^{(i)} = k\} - P(y^{(i)} = k \mid x^{(i)}, W))]$$

The well trained model, the optimal w will be used to classify a new sample x' by:

$$y' = \underset{k}{\text{argmax}} \frac{\exp\left(w_k x'\right)}{\sum_{j=1}^{j=K} \exp\left(w_j x'\right)} = \underset{k}{\text{argmax}} \left(w_k x'\right)$$

Armed with the mechanics of the multinomial logistic regression we just reviewed, we can then apply it as the first solution to our digit classification project.

We first split the dataset into two subsets for training and testing respectively using the `caret` package.

 caret stands for **classification and regression training**. The package is designed to facilitate the process for training and evaluating models. It contains tools and methods for data splitting, data pre-processing, feature selection and model tuning. Documentation and a full list of functions can be found in

https://cran.r-project.org/web/packages/caret/caret.pdf.

Install and import package `caret`:

```
> if (!require("caret"))
+ install.packages("caret")
> library (caret)
Loading required package: lattice
Loading required package: ggplot2
```

We first split the data into two partitions, 75% for training and 25% for testing, using the `createDataPartition` function:

```
> set.seed(42)
> train_perc = 0.75
> train_index <- createDataPartition(data$label, p=train_perc, list=FALSE)

> data_train <- data[train_index,]
> data_test <- data[-train_index,]
```

To ensure the experiments are reproducible, it is always a good practice to pick a seed from the random number generator.

Then, we implement the multinomial logistic regression model using the nnet package. The package contains functions for feed-forward single-layer neural networks as well as multinomial logistic regression models. More details can be found in https://cran.r-project.org/web/packages/nnet/nnet.pdf:

```
> library(nnet)
> # Multinomial logistic regression
> model_lr <- multinom(label ~ ., data=data_train, MaxNWts=10000,
decay=5e-3, maxit=100)
# weights: 7860 (7065 variable)
initial value 72538.338185
iter 10 value 17046.804658
iter 20 value 11166.225504
iter 30 value 9514.340319
iter 40 value 8819.724147
iter 50 value 8405.001712
iter 60 value 8164.997939
iter 70 value 7983.427139
iter 80 value 7897.005940
iter 90 value 7831.663204
iter 100 value 7730.047242
final value 7730.047242
stopped after 100 iterations
```

We fit a multinomial logistic regression model on the training subset, with parameters which include:

- MaxNWts=10000: It allows, at most, 10,000 weights. In our case, there are (784 dimensions + 1 bias) * 10 classes = 7850 elements in the weight matrix w
- decay=5e-3: The regularization strength, the weight decay is 0.005
- maxit=100: The maximum number of iterations is set to be 100

The error value is printed for every 10 iterations, and it is decreasing. The model converges as the maximum number of iterations is reached. Then we use the trained model to predict the classes of the testing samples:

```
> prediction_lr <- predict(model_lr, data_test, type = "class")
```

Take a look at the prediction results of the first five samples:

```
> prediction_lr[1:5]
[1] 1 0 7 5 8
Levels: 0 1 2 3 4 5 6 7 8 9
```

And their true values are:

```
> data_test$label[1:5]
[1] 1 0 7 5 8
Levels: 0 1 2 3 4 5 6 7 8 9
```

We can also obtain the confusion matrix by:

```
> cm_lr = table(data_test$label, prediction_lr)
> cm_lr
```

```
   prediction_lr
      0    1    2    3    4    5    6    7    8    9
0   965    0   11    4    1   12   23    6    7    4
1     0 1126    8    7    0    2    2    3   17    6
2     5   16  899   24   18    6   24   15   29    8
3     5    4   37  921    1   47    9   10   33   20
4     6   10    4    2  903    1   14    6   12   60
5    12    6    9   27    6  770   23    8   75   12
6     5    4   13    0   11    8  981    3    9    0
7     6    3   20    1    6    3    3  995    6   57
8     7   20    6   25    5   31    5    4  892   20
9     6    4    2   15   37    3    0   41   11  928
```

And the classification accuracy:

```
> accuracy_lr = mean(prediction_lr == data_test$label)
> accuracy_lr
[1] 0.8935886
```

89.4% for the first try. Not bad! We could definitely do better by tweaking the model parameters, such as `decay` and `maxit`. But our focus is for a more advanced model that learns the underneath patterns better. So we move on with the second solution, the feed-forward neural networks with a single hidden layer.

Going from logistic regression to single-layer neural networks

Basically, logistic regression is a feed-forward neural network without a hidden layer, where the output layer directly connects with the input layer. In other words, logistic regression is a single neuron that maps the input to the output layer. Theoretically, the neural networks with an additional hidden layer between the input and output layer should be able to learn more about the relationship underneath.

A single-layer neural network for two possible classes can be represented graphically as follows:

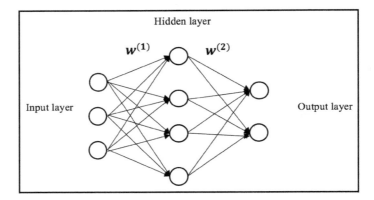

Suppose x is n-dimension, and there are H hidden units in the hidden layer, then the weight matrix $w^{(1)}$ connecting the input layer to the hidden layer is of size n by H with each column $w_h^{(1)}$ representing the coefficients associated with the h-th hidden unit. So, the output (also called **activation**) of the h-th hidden unit $a_h^{(2)}$ can be expressed mathematically as:

$$a_h^{(2)} = f(z^{(2)}) = f(w_h^{(1)}x)$$

For example, for the outputs of the first, second and the last hidden unit:

$$a_1^{(2)} = f(w_1^{(1)}x)$$

$$a_H^{(2)} = f(w_H^{(1)}x)$$

$$a_H^{(2)} = f(w_H^{(1)}x)$$

where $f(z)$ is an activation function. Typical choices for the activation function in simple networks include logistic function (more often called sigmoid function) and `tanh` function (which can be considered a re-scaled version of logistic function):

$$sigmoid(z) = \frac{1}{1 + e^{-z}}$$

$$tanh(z) = \frac{e^{-z} - e^{-z}}{e^{z} + e^{-z}} = \frac{2}{1 + e^{-2z}} - 1$$

Plots of these two functions are as follows:

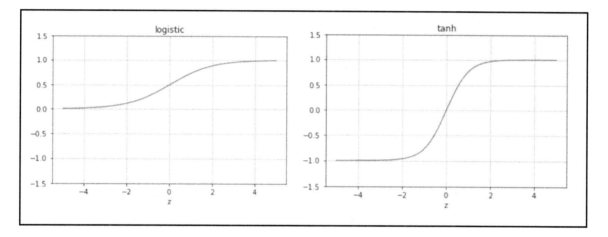

We will be using the logistic function in our single-layered networks for now.

For a case of K possible classes, the weight matrix $w^{(2)}$ connecting the hidden layer to the output layer is of size H by K. Each column $w_k^{(2)}$ represents the coefficients associated with class k. The input to the output layer is the output of the hidden layer $a^{(2)} = \{a_1^{(2)}, a_2^{(2)}, ..., a_I^{(2)}\}$, the probability of x being class k can be expressed mathematically as (for consistency, we denote it as $a_k^{(3)}$):

$$a_k^{(3)} = f(z^{(3)}) = softmax_k(W^{(2)} a^{(2)})$$

Similarly, given m training samples, to train the neural network, we learn all weights $w = \{w^{(1)}, w^{(2)}\}$ using gradient descent with the goal of minimizing the mean squared error cost $J(w)$.

Computation of the gradients Δw can be realized through the **backpropagation algorithm**. The idea of the backpropagation algorithm is the following, we first travel through the network and compute all outputs of the hidden layers and output layer; then moving backward from the last layer, we calculate how much each node contributed to the error in the final output and propagate it back to the previous layers. In our single-layer network, the detailed steps are:

1. Compute $a^{(2)}$ for the hidden layer and feed them to the output layer to compute the outputs $a^{(3)}$

2. For the output layer, compute the derivative of the cost function of one sample

$$\delta_k^{(3)} = \frac{\delta}{\delta z_k^{(3)}} j(W) = -(y_k - a_k^{(3)}) \cdot f'(z_k^{(3)})$$

$j(W)$ with regards to each unit, , or

$\delta^{(3)} = -(y - a^{(3)}) \cdot f'(z^{(3)})$, rewritten for the entire layer

3. For the hidden layer, we compute the error term $\delta^{(2)}$ based on a weighted average of $\delta^{(3)} : \delta^{(2)} = ((W^{(2)})^T \delta^{(3)}) \cdot f'^{(2)})$

4. Compute the gradients applying the chain rule:

$$\Delta W^{(2)} = \frac{\partial J(W)}{\partial z_k^{(3)}} \frac{\partial z_k^{(3)}}{\partial W^{(2)}} = \delta^{(3)} (a^{(2)})^T$$

$$\Delta W^{(1)} = \frac{\partial J(W)}{\partial z_k^{(2)}} \frac{\partial z_k^{(2)}}{\partial W^{(1)}} = \delta^{(2)} (x)^T$$

We repeatedly update all weights by taking these steps until the cost function converges.

After a brief review of the single-layer network, we can then apply it as the second solution to our digit classification project.

Again, we use the nnet package to implement our single-layer network:

```
> model_nn <- nnet(label ~ ., data=data_train, size=50, maxit=300,
MaxNWts=100000, decay=1e-4)
# weights: 39760
initial value 108597.598656
iter 10 value 27708.286001
iter 20 value 16027.005297
iter 30 value 14058.141050
iter 40 value 12615.442747
iter 50 value 11793.700937
iter 60 value 11026.672273
```

```
iter  70 value 10654.855058
iter  80 value 10193.580947
iter  90 value 9854.836168
iter 100 value 9544.973159
iter 110 value 9307.192737
iter 120 value 9043.028253
iter 130 value 8845.069307
iter 140 value 8686.707561
iter 150 value 8525.104362
iter 160 value 8281.609223
iter 170 value 8140.051273
iter 180 value 7998.721024
iter 190 value 7854.388240
iter 200 value 7712.459027
iter 210 value 7636.945553
iter 220 value 7557.675909
iter 230 value 7449.854506
iter 240 value 7355.021651
iter 250 value 7259.186906
iter 260 value 7192.798089
iter 270 value 7055.027833
iter 280 value 6957.926522
iter 290 value 6866.641511
iter 300 value 6778.342997
final value 6778.342997
stopped after 300 iterations
```

We fit the model with parameters including:

- `size=50`: There are 50 hidden units in the hidden layer.
- `MaxNWts=100000`: It allows at most 100,000 weights. In our case, there are (784 input dimensions + 1 bias) * 50 hidden units = 39,250 elements in the weight matrix $w^{(1)}$ and (50 hidden units + 1 bias) * 10 output units = 510 elements in the weight matrix $w^{(1)}$. So there are 39,760 weights in total.
- `decay=1e-4`: The regularization strength, the weight decay is `0.0001`.
- `maxit=300`: The maximum number of iterations is set to be 300.

We apply the trained network model on the testing set:

```
> prediction_nn <- predict(model_nn, data_test, type = "class")
> cm_nn = table(data_test$label, prediction_nn)
> cm_nn
prediction_nn
  0   1   2  3  4  5   6   7  8  9
0 987   0   3  3  2 11  10   7  5  5
1   0 1134   9  6  0  2   0   5 11  4
```

```
2  14  9  918 31  11  11  7  15  22  6
3  3   1  17  966 0   41  3  14  24  18
4  4   3  8   2   929 4   11 11  5   41
5  12  2  6   17  5   851 15 9   26  5
6  10  1  14  0   9   14  970 0  15  1
7  4   4  23  6   5   2   0  1010 7  39
8  5   15 9   18  5   31  9  4   912 7
9  11  2  1   20  52  4   0  36  8   913
> accuracy_nn = mean(prediction_nn == data_test$label)
> accuracy_nn
[1]  0.9135944
```

Better than our first attempt! Can we do better with deep learning models, say intuitively more hidden layers? Sure.

Adding more hidden layers to the networks

We have just achieved 91.3% accuracy with a single-layer neural network model. Theoretically, we can obtain a better one with more than one hidden layer. As an example, we provide a solution of a deep neural network model with two hidden layers:

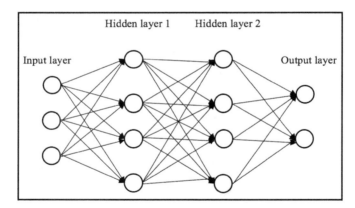

Weight optimization in feed-forward deep neural networks is also realized through the backpropagation algorithm, which is identical to single-layer networks. However, the more layers, the higher the computation complexity, and the slower the model convergence. One way to accelerate the weight optimization, is to use a more computational efficient activation function. The most popular one in recent years is the **rectified linear unit (ReLU)**:

$$relu(z) = z^+ = max(0, z)$$

A plot of the ReLU function is as follows:

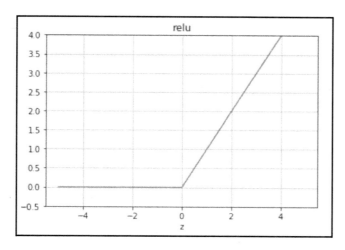

Thanks to the properties of its derivative, which is $relu'(z) = \begin{cases} 0, z < 0 \\ 1, z \geq 0 \end{cases}$, there are two main advantages of using the ReLU activation function over sigmoid:

- Faster learning because of constant value of *relu'(z)*, compared to that of the logistic function $sigmoid'(z) = sigmoid(z) * (1 - sigmoid(z))$.
- Less likely to have the vanishing gradient problem, exponential decrease of gradient, which can be found in networks with multiple stacked sigmoid layers. As we multiply the derivative of the activation function when calculating errors δ for each layer, and the maximal value of *sigmoid'(z)* is ¼, the gradients will decrease exponentially as we stack more and more sigmoid layers.

The `nnet` package we used in previous sections is (by now) only capable of modeling a single-layer network. In this chapter, we use the `MXNet` package to implement deep neural networks with multiple hidden layers. `MXNet` (`https://mxnet.incubator.apache.org/`) is a deep learning framework that supports programming languages include R, Scala, Python, Julia, C++, and Perl. It is developed by the DMLC (`http://dmlc.ml/`) team, a group of experts collaborating on open-source machine learning projects. It is portable and can scale to multiple CPUs, multiple GPUs and multiple machines, for example, in the cloud. Most importantly, it allows us to flexibly and efficiently construct state-of-the-art deep learning models, including deep neural networks, CNNs and RNNs.

Let's install MXNet first:

```
> cran <- getOption("repos")
> cran["dmlc"] <- "https://s3-us-west-2.amazonaws.com/apache-mxnet/R/CRAN/"
> options(repos = cran)
> if (!require("mxnet"))
install.packages("mxnet")
```

Now we can import MXNet and convert the data into the format preferred by the neural network models in MXNet:

```
> require(mxnet)
> data_train <- data.matrix(data_train)
> data_train.x <- data_train[,-1]
> data_train.x <- t(data_train.x/255)
> data_train.y <- data_train[,1]
```

Note we scale the input features to a range from 0 to 1, by dividing the maximal possible value 255. Otherwise, the deep neural networks may be skewed towards some features and such skewness will accumulate over layers.

Now that the training dataset is ready, we can start constructing the network by defining its architecture as follows:

```
> data <- mx.symbol.Variable("data")
> fc1 <- mx.symbol.FullyConnected(data, name="fc1", num_hidden=128)
> act1 <- mx.symbol.Activation(fc1, name="relu1", act_type="relu")
> fc2 <- mx.symbol.FullyConnected(act1, name="fc2", num_hidden=64)
> act2 <- mx.symbol.Activation(fc2, name="relu2", act_type="relu")
> fc3 <- mx.symbol.FullyConnected(act2, name="fc3", num_hidden=10)
> softmax <- mx.symbol.SoftmaxOutput(fc3, name="sm")
```

In the MXNet's Symbol API, we represent the network in the data type symbol. We begin with the input layer data, the input data, and follow up with the first hidden layer fc1 with 128 nodes, which fully connects with the input layer. We then attach the ReLU function to fc1 and output the activations act1 for this layer. Similarly, we chain another hidden layer fc2, with 64 nodes this time, and output ReLU-based activates act2. Finally, we end up with the output layer with a softmax function, generating 10 probabilities corresponding to 10 classes. The overall structure looks like this:

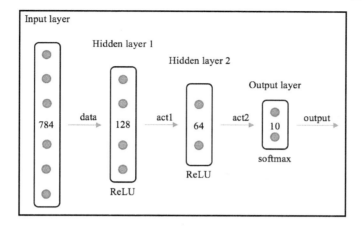

After building the bone, it is time to train the model. We can choose our computation device, CPU and/or GPU—here is a CPU example:

```
> devices <- mx.cpu()
```

Before training, don't forget to set the random seed to make the modeling process reproducible:

```
> mx.set.seed(42)
> model_dnn <- mx.model.FeedForward.create(softmax, X=data_train.x,
y=data_train.y, ctx=devices, num.round=30, array.batch.size=100,
learning.rate=0.01, momentum=0.9, eval.metric=mx.metric.accuracy,
initializer=mx.init.uniform(0.1),
epoch.end.callback=mx.callback.log.train.metric(100))
Start training with 1 devices
[1] Train-accuracy=0.724793650793651
[2] Train-accuracy=0.904715189873417
[3] Train-accuracy=0.925537974683544
[4] Train-accuracy=0.939936708860759
[5] Train-accuracy=0.950379746835443
[6] Train-accuracy=0.95873417721519
[7] Train-accuracy=0.96509493670886
[8] Train-accuracy=0.969905063291139
[9] Train-accuracy=0.974303797468355
[10] Train-accuracy=0.977784810126584
[11] Train-accuracy=0.980696202531648
[12] Train-accuracy=0.983164556962027
[13] Train-accuracy=0.985284810126584
[14] Train-accuracy=0.987405063291141
[15] Train-accuracy=0.988924050632913
[16] Train-accuracy=0.990727848101267
[17] Train-accuracy=0.992088607594938
```

```
[18] Train-accuracy=0.993227848101268
[19] Train-accuracy=0.994398734177217
[20] Train-accuracy=0.995284810126584
[21] Train-accuracy=0.995854430379748
[22] Train-accuracy=0.996835443037975
[23] Train-accuracy=0.997183544303798
[24] Train-accuracy=0.997848101265823
[25] Train-accuracy=0.998164556962026
[26] Train-accuracy=0.998575949367089
[27] Train-accuracy=0.998924050632912
[28] Train-accuracy=0.999177215189874
[29] Train-accuracy=0.999367088607595
[30] Train-accuracy=0.999525316455696
```

We just fit the model with hyperparameters including:

- `num.round = 30`: The maximum number of iterations is set to be `30`.
- `array.batch.size = 100`: The batch size of the mini-batch gradient descent is 100. As a variation of a stochastic gradient descent, the mini-batch gradient descent algorithm calculates costs and gradients by small batches, instead of individual training samples. Hence, it is computationally more efficient and allows faster model convergence. As a result, the mini-batch gradient descent is more commonly used in training deep neural networks.
- `learning.rate = 0.01`: The learning rate is `0.01`.
- `momentum=0.9`: In general, the cost function of deep architectures has the form of one or more shallow ravines (local minima) leading to the global optimum. **Momentum** as seen in the physical law of motion is employed to avoid getting stuck in sub-optimum and make the convergence faster. With momentum, weights are updated as follows:

$$\nu = \gamma \nu - \eta \triangle W$$

$$W = W + \nu$$

where the left and right v is the previous and current velocity respectively, and $\gamma \in (0,1]$ is the momentum factor determining how much of the previous velocity is incorporated into the current one.

- `eval.metric=mx.metric.accuracy`: It uses classification accuracy as the evaluation metric

- `initializer=mx.init.uniform(0.1)`: Initial weights are randomly generated from the uniform distribution ranging from 0 to 1, so as to lower the chances of the weight exploding and vanishing in the deep network

After the model is trained, let's see how it performs on the testing set. First, remember to conduct the same pre-processing on the test dataset:

```
> data_test.x <- data_test[,-1]
> data_test.x <- t(data_test.x/255)
```

Then, predict the testing cases and evaluate the performance:

```
> prob_dnn <- predict(model_dnn, data_test.x)
> prediction_dnn <- max.col(t(prob_dnn)) - 1
> cm_dnn = table(data_test$label, prediction_dnn)

> cm_dnn
   prediction_dnn
       0    1    2    3    4    5    6    7    8    9
  0 1041    0    2    0    0    1    3    0    8    1
  1    0 1157    3    1    1    0    1    3    1    0
  2    2    1  993    3    3    1    2   13    5    2
  3    1    3   14 1033    1   13    0    5   14    6
  4    0    2    1    0  991    0    4    4    1   12
  5    4    2    3   12    3  892    4    3    6    8
  6   10    0    1    0    3    4  988    0    4    0
  7    0    5    9    1    2    0    0 1116    2    1
  8    4    8    3    5    0    8    3    2 1020   12
  9    1    1    0    4   13    3    0   16    2  957
> accuracy_dnn = mean(prediction_dnn == data_test$label)
> accuracy_dnn
[1] 0.9704706
```

By adding one more hidden layer, accuracy is improved from 91.4% to 97.0%! Since each hidden layer in a deep neural network provides representations of the data at a certain level, can we simply conclude that the more hidden layers (such as 100, 1,000, 10,000...), the more underneath patterns are discovered, the better the classification accuracy? It might be true if we have plentiful resources and time to enable computation and to make sure overfitting does not occur with such complex networks. Is there any way where we can extract richer and more informative representations than by simply chaining more hidden layers, and at the same time, not excessively grow our networks? The answer is CNNs.

Extracting richer representation with CNNs

Although regular hidden layers (we also call them fully connected layers) do the job of obtaining representations at certain levels, these representations might be able to help us differentiate between images of different classes. We need to extract richer and distinguishable representations that, for example, make a "9" a "9", a "4" a "4", or a cat a cat, a dog a dog. We resort to CNNs as variants of multi-layered neural networks which are biologically inspired by the human visual cortex. Basically, CNNs take inspiration from the following two neuroscience findings:

- The visual cortex has a complex system of neuronal cells that are sensitive to specific sub-regions of the visual field, called the **receptive field**. For instance, some cells respond only in the presence of vertical edges; some cells fire only when exposed to horizontal edges; and some react more strongly when shown edges of a certain orientation. The cells are organized together to produce the entire visual perception, while each individual cell is specialized in a specific component.
- Simple cells respond only when those edge-like patterns are presented within their receptive sub-regions. More complex cells are sensitive to larger sub-regions, and as a result, are less variant to the local position of those edge-like patterns in the entire visual field.

Similarly, CNNs classify images by first deriving low-level representations, local edges and curves, then by composing higher-level representations, overall shape and contour, through a series of low-level representations. CNNs are well suited to exploiting strong and unique features that differentiate between images.

In general, CNNs take in an image, pass it through a sequence of convolutional layers, non-linear layers, pooling layers and fully connected layers, and finally output the probabilities of each possible class. We now look at each type of layer individually, in detail.

The **convolutional layer** is the first layer in a CNN. It simulates the way neuronal cells respond to receptive fields by applying a convolutional operation to the input. To be specific, it computes the dot product between the weights of the convolutional layer and a small region they are connected to in the input layer. The small region is the receptive field, and the weights can be viewed as the values on a filter. As the filter slides from the beginning to the end of the input layer, the dot product between the weights and current receptive field is computed. A new layer called **feature map** is obtained after convolving over all sub-regions. Take a look at the following example:

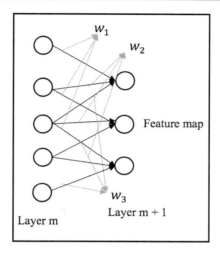

Layer *m* has five nodes and the filter has three units [w_1, w_2, w_3]. We compute the dot product between the filter and the first three nodes in layer *m* and obtain the first node in the feature map; then, we compute the dot product between the filter and the middle three nodes and generate the second node; finally, we obtain the third node resulting from the last three nodes in layer *m*.

Another example that helps us better understand how the convolutional layer works on images is as follows:

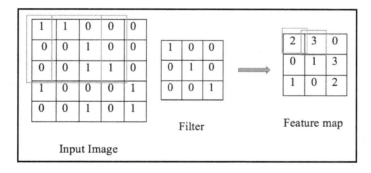

A 3*3 filter is sliding around a 5*5 image from the top left sub-region to the bottom right. For every sub-region, the dot product is computed with the filter. A 3*3 feature map is generated as a result.

Convolutional layers are actually used to extract features, such as edges and curves. The output pixel in the feature map will be of high value, if the corresponding receptive field contains an edge or curve specified by the filter. For instance, in the preceding example, the filter portrays a backslash-shape diagonal edge, the receptive field in the blue rectangle contains a similar curve and hence, the highest intensity *3 (1*1 + 1* 1 + 1*1 = 3)* is produced; however, the receptive field in the bottom left corner does not contain such a shape, which results in a pixel of value 1. The convolutional layer acts as a curve detector, mimicking the way our visual cells work.

Remember in the preceding case, we only applied one filter and generated one feature map, which indicates how well the shape in the input image resembles the curve represented in the filter. To achieve a richer representation of the data, we can employ more filters, such as horizontal, vertical curve, 30-degree, or right-angle shape, so that the hidden layer composed of feature maps can detect more patterns. Additionally, stacking many convolutional layers can produce higher-level representations, such as overall shape and contour. To ensure the strong spatially local patterns are caught, each filter in a layer is only responsive to the corresponding receptive fields. Chaining more layers results in larger receptive fields which capture more global patterns.

Right after each convolutional layer, we often apply a **non-linear layer** (also called **activation layer**, as we mentioned), in order to introduce non-linearity, obviously. This is because only linear operations (multiplication and addition) are conducted in the convolutional layer. And a neural network with only linear hidden layers would behave just like a single-layer perceptron, regardless of how many layers. Again, ReLu is the most popular candidate for the non-linear layer in deep neural networks.

Normally, after obtaining features via one or more pairs of convolutional layers and non-linear layers, we can use the output for classification, for example applying a softmax layer in our multiclass case. Let's do some math, suppose we apply 20 5*5 filters in the first convolutional layer, then the output of this layer will be of size *20 * (28 - 5 + 1) * (28 - 5 + 1) = 20 * 24 * 24 = 11520*, which means the number of features as inputs for the next layer becomes 11,520 from 784; we then apply 50 5*5 filters in the second convolutional layer, the size of the output grows to 50 * 20 * (24 - 5 + 1) * (24 - 5 + 1) = 400,000, which is high-dimensional compared to our initial size of 784. We can see that the dimension increases dramatically with each convolutional layer before the softmax layer for classification. This can easily lead to overfitting, not to mention the large number of weights to be trained in the corresponding non-linear layer.

To address the dimension growth issue, we often employ a **pooling layer** (also called **downsampling layer**) after a pair of convolutional and non-linear layers. As its name implies, it aggregates statistics of features by sub-regions to generate much lower dimensional features. Typical pooling methods include max pooling and mean pooling, which take the max values and mean values over all non-overlapping sub-regions, respectively. For example, we apply a 2*2 max pooling filter on a 4*4 feature map and output a 2*2 one:

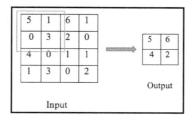

Besides reducing overfitting with lower dimensional output, the pooling layer aggregating statistics over regions has another advantage—translation invariant. It means the output does not change, if the input image undergoes a small amount of translation. For example, suppose we shift the input image to a couple of pixels left or right, up or down, as long as the highest pixels remain the same in sub-regions, the output of the max pooling layer is still the same. In another words, the prediction becomes less position-sensitive with pooling layers.

Putting these three types of convolutional-related layers together, along with fully connected layers, we can structure our CNN model as follows:

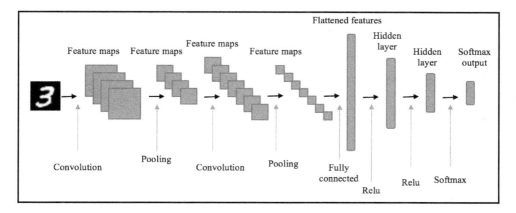

It starts with the first convolutional layer, ReLu non-linear layer and pooling layer. Here, we use 20 5*5 convolutional filters, and a 2*2 max pooling filter:

```
> # first convolution
> conv1 <- mx.symbol.Convolution(data=data, kernel=c(5,5),
num_filter=20)
> act1 <- mx.symbol.Activation(data=conv1, act_type="relu")
> pool1 <- mx.symbol.Pooling(data=act1, pool_type="max",
+ kernel=c(2,2), stride=c(2,2))
```

It follows with the second convolutional, ReLu non-linear and pooling layer, where 50 5*5 convolutional filters and a 2*2 max pooling filter are used:

```
> # second convolution
> conv2 <- mx.symbol.Convolution(data=pool1, kernel=c(5,5),
num_filter=50)
> act2 <- mx.symbol.Activation(data=conv2, act_type="relu")
> pool2 <- mx.symbol.Pooling(data=act2, pool_type="max",
+ kernel=c(2,2), stride=c(2,2))
```

Now that we extract rich representations of the input images by detecting edges, curves and shapes, we move on with the fully connected layers. But before doing so, we need to flatten the resulting feature maps from previous convolution layers:

```
> flatten <- mx.symbol.Flatten(data=pool2)
```

In the fully connected section, we apply two ReLu hidden layers with 500 and 10 units respectively:

```
> # first fully connected layer
> fc1 <- mx.symbol.FullyConnected(data=flatten, num_hidden=500)
> act3 <- mx.symbol.Activation(data=fc1, act_type="relu")
> # second fully connected layer
> fc2 <- mx.symbol.FullyConnected(data=act3, num_hidden=10)
```

Finally, the softmax layer producing outputs for 10 classes:

```
> # softmax output
> softmax <- mx.symbol.SoftmaxOutput(data=fc2, name="sm")
```

Now, the bone is constructed. Time to set a random seed and start training the model:

We need to first reshape the matrix, `data_train.x` into an array as required by the convolutional layer in MXNet:

```
> train.array <- data_train.x
> dim(train.array) <- c(28, 28, 1, ncol(data_train.x))
> mx.set.seed(42)
> model_cnn <- mx.model.FeedForward.create(softmax, X=train.array,
y=data_train.y, ctx=devices, num.round=30,
array.batch.size=100, learning.rate=0.05,
momentum=0.9, wd=0.00001,
eval.metric=mx.metric.accuracy,
epoch.end.callback=mx.callback.log.train.metric(100))
Start training with 1 devices
[1] Train-accuracy=0.306984126984127
[2] Train-accuracy=0.961898734177216
[3] Train-accuracy=0.981139240506331
[4] Train-accuracy=0.987151898734179
[5] Train-accuracy=0.990348101265825
[6] Train-accuracy=0.992689873417723
[7] Train-accuracy=0.994493670886077
[8] Train-accuracy=0.995822784810128
[9] Train-accuracy=0.995601265822786
[10] Train-accuracy=0.997246835443039
[11] Train-accuracy=0.997341772151899
[12] Train-accuracy=0.998006329113925
[13] Train-accuracy=0.997626582278482
[14] Train-accuracy=0.998069620253165
[15] Train-accuracy=0.998765822784811
[16] Train-accuracy=0.998449367088608
[17] Train-accuracy=0.998765822784811
[18] Train-accuracy=0.998955696202532
[19] Train-accuracy=0.999746835443038
[20] Train-accuracy=0.999841772151899
[21] Train-accuracy=0.999905063291139
[22] Train-accuracy=1
[23] Train-accuracy=1
[24] Train-accuracy=1
[25] Train-accuracy=1
[26] Train-accuracy=1
[27] Train-accuracy=1
[28] Train-accuracy=1
[29] Train-accuracy=1
[30] Train-accuracy=1
```

Besides those hyperparameters we used in the previous deep neural network model, we fit the CNN model with L2 regularization weight decay wd = 0.00001, which adds penalties for large weights in order to avoid overfitting.

Again, training of the CNN model is no different to other networks. Optimal weights are obtained through a backpropagation algorithm.

After the model is trained, let's see how it performs on the testing set. First, remember to conduct the same pre-processing on the test dataset:

```
> test.array <- data_test.x
> dim(test.array) <- c(28, 28, 1, ncol(data_test.x))
```

Predict the testing cases and evaluate the performance:

```
> prob_cnn <- predict(model_cnn, test.array)
> prediction_cnn <- max.col(t(prob_cnn)) - 1
> cm_cnn = table(data_test$label, prediction_cnn)
> cm_cnn
prediction_cnn
  0    1    2    3    4    5    6    7    8    9
0 1051 0    1    0    0    1    1    0    2    0
1 0    1161 0    0    0    1    1    3    1    0
2 0    0    1014 4    0    0    0    7    0    0
3 0    0    2    1075 0    6    0    2    3    2
4 0    0    0    0    1000 0    4    2    2    7
5 1    0    0    4    0    923  3    0    3    3
6 3    0    0    0    0    0    1006 0    1    0
7 0    1    2    0    3    0    0    1129 1    0
8 3    3    1    1    2    5    1    0    1043 6
9 2    0    2    0    3    3    1    2    0    984
> accuracy_cnn = mean(prediction_cnn == data_test$label)
> accuracy_cnn
[1] 0.9893313
```

Our CNN model further boosts the accuracy to close to 99%!

We can also view the network structure by:

```
> graph.viz(model_cnn$symbol)
```

Let's do some more inspection to make sure we get things right. We start with the learning curving, for example the classification performance of the model on both the training set and testing set over the number of training iterations. In general, *it is a good practice to plot the learning curve where we can visualize whether overfitting or underfitting issues occur*:

```
> data_test.y <- data_test[,1]
> logger <- mx.metric.logger$new()
> model_cnn <- mx.model.FeedForward.create(softmax, X=train.array,
y=data_train.y,eval.data=list(data=test.array,
label=data_test.y), ctx=devices, num.round=30,
array.batch.size=100, learning.rate=0.05,
momentum=0.9, wd=0.00001,eval.metric=
mx.metric.accuracy, epoch.end.callback =
mx.callback.log.train.metric(1, logger))
Start training with 1 devices
[1] Train-accuracy=0.279936507936508
[1] Validation-accuracy=0.912857142857143
[2] Train-accuracy=0.959462025316456
[2] Validation-accuracy=0.973523809523809
[3] Train-accuracy=0.979841772151899
[3] Validation-accuracy=0.980666666666666
[4] Train-accuracy=0.986677215189875
[4] Validation-accuracy=0.983428571428571
[5] Train-accuracy=0.990822784810129
[5] Validation-accuracy=0.981809523809523
[6] Train-accuracy=0.992626582278482
[6] Validation-accuracy=0.983904761904761
[7] Train-accuracy=0.993322784810128
[7] Validation-accuracy=0.986
[8] Train-accuracy=0.995474683544305
[8] Validation-accuracy=0.987619047619047
[9] Train-accuracy=0.996487341772153
[9] Validation-accuracy=0.983904761904762
[10] Train-accuracy=0.995949367088608
[10] Validation-accuracy=0.984761904761904
[11] Train-accuracy=0.997310126582279
[11] Validation-accuracy=0.985142857142856
[12] Train-accuracy=0.997658227848102
[12] Validation-accuracy=0.986857142857142
[13] Train-accuracy=0.997848101265824
[13] Validation-accuracy=0.984095238095238
[14] Train-accuracy=0.998006329113924
[14] Validation-accuracy=0.985238095238094
[15] Train-accuracy=0.998607594936709
[15] Validation-accuracy=0.987619047619047
[16] Train-accuracy=0.99863924050633
[16] Validation-accuracy=0.987428571428571
[17] Train-accuracy=0.998987341772152
```

```
[17] Validation-accuracy=0.985142857142857
[18] Train-accuracy=0.998765822784811
[18] Validation-accuracy=0.986285714285713
[19] Train-accuracy=0.999240506329114
[19] Validation-accuracy=0.988761904761905
[20] Train-accuracy=0.999335443037975
[20] Validation-accuracy=0.98847619047619
[21] Train-accuracy=0.999841772151899
[21] Validation-accuracy=0.987809523809523
[22] Train-accuracy=0.99993670886076
[22] Validation-accuracy=0.990095238095237
[23] Train-accuracy=1
[23] Validation-accuracy=0.989999999999999
[24] Train-accuracy=1
[24] Validation-accuracy=0.989999999999999
[25] Train-accuracy=1
[25] Validation-accuracy=0.990190476190476
[26] Train-accuracy=1
[26] Validation-accuracy=0.990190476190476
[27] Train-accuracy=1
[27] Validation-accuracy=0.990095238095237
[28] Train-accuracy=1
[28] Validation-accuracy=0.990095238095237
[29] Train-accuracy=1
[29] Validation-accuracy=0.990095238095237
[30] Train-accuracy=1
[30] Validation-accuracy=0.990190476190475
```

We can get the performance on the training set after each round of training:

```
> logger$train
 [1] 0.2799365 0.9594620 0.9798418 0.9866772 0.9908228 0.9926266 0.9933228
 0.9954747 0.9964873 0.9959494 0.9973101
[12] 0.9976582 0.9978481 0.9980063 0.9986076 0.9986392 0.9989873 0.9987658
 0.9992405 0.9993354 0.9998418 0.9999367
[23] 1.0000000 1.0000000 1.0000000 1.0000000 1.0000000 1.0000000 1.0000000
 1.0000000
```

As well as the performance on the testing set after each round of training:

```
> logger$eval
 [1] 0.9128571 0.9735238 0.9806667 0.9834286 0.9818095 0.9839048 0.9860000
 0.9876190 0.9839048 0.9847619 0.9851429
[12] 0.9868571 0.9840952 0.9852381 0.9876190 0.9874286 0.9851429 0.9862857
 0.9887619 0.9884762 0.9878095 0.9900952
[23] 0.9900000 0.9900000 0.9901905 0.9901905 0.9900952 0.9900952 0.9900952
 0.9901905
```

The learning curve can be visualized by the following codes:

```
> plot(logger$train,type="l",col="red", ann=FALSE)
> lines(logger$eval,type="l", col="blue")
> title(main="Learning curve")
> title(xlab="Iterations")
> title(ylab="Accuary")
> legend(20, 0.5, c("training","testing"), cex=0.8,
col=c("red","blue"), pch=21:22, lty=1:2);
```

And we will get:

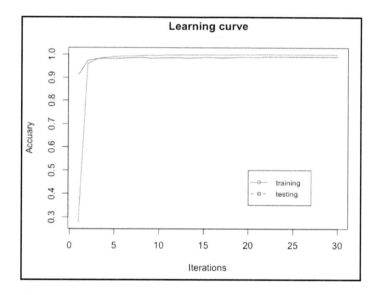

The learning curve indicates little chance of overfitting or underfitting.

Since the model works great, why don't we visualize the output of the convolutional layers of the trained model so that we can get a better understanding of CNNs. Let's use the first two samples in the testing set as an example. They are 1 and 0:

```
> par(mfrow=c(1,2))
> test_1 <- matrix(as.numeric(data_test[1,-1]), nrow = 28,
byrow = TRUE)
> image(rotate(test_1), col = grey.colors(255))
> test_2 <- matrix(as.numeric(data_test[2,-1]), nrow = 28,
byrow = TRUE)
> image(rotate(test_2), col = grey.colors(255))
```

For our reference, they are displayed as:

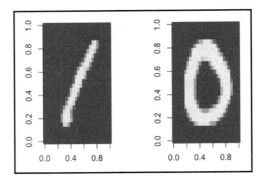

To visualize the activation of the convolutional layers, we first create an executor (can be loosely viewed as a copy of our trained CNN model) by grouping all of the layers with activations:

```
> layerss_for_viz <- mx.symbol.Group(mx.symbol.Group(c(conv1, act1, pool1,
conv2, act2, pool2, fc1, fc2)))
> executor <- mx.simple.bind(symbol=layerss_for_viz,
data=dim(test.array), ctx=mx.cpu())
```

Now, update the weights in the executor with those in the trained model:

```
> mx.exec.update.arg.arrays(executor, model_cnn$arg.params,
match.name=TRUE)
> mx.exec.update.aux.arrays(executor, model_cnn$aux.params,
match.name=TRUE)
```

And apply the executor on the testing set by making a feed-forward pass:

```
> mx.exec.update.arg.arrays(executor,
list(data=mx.nd.array(test.array)), match.name=TRUE)
> mx.exec.forward(executor, is.train=FALSE)
```

We can see the names of the layers recorded in the executor, as we will be extracting the activation of a layer by its name (note the names can be different, we should use the corresponding ones):

```
> names(executor$ref.outputs)
[1] "convolution10_output" "activation15_output"
"pooling10_output" "convolution11_output"
[5] "activation16_output" "pooling11_output"
"fullyconnected10_output" "fullyconnected11_output"
```

Now, we can visualize the activations for the first and second convolutional layer and ReLu layer, as well as the first pooling layer.

Let's start with the ReLu activations for the first 16 filters in the first convolutional layer, which are called `activation15_output` in our case (again, the name may vary). For the first sample, (a "1"), we run the following scripts:

```
> par(mfrow=c(4,4), mar=c(0.1,0.1,0.1,0.1))
> for (i in 1:16) {
+ outputData <- as.array
(executor$ref.outputs$activation15_output)[,,i,1]
+ image(outputData, xaxt='n', yaxt='n',
col=grey.colors(255)
+ )
+ }
```

Similarly, for the second sample, (a "0"), we run:

```
> par(mfrow=c(4,4), mar=c(0.1,0.1,0.1,0.1))
> for (i in 1:16) {
+ outputData <- as.array
(executor$ref.outputs$activation15_output)[,,i,2]
+ image(outputData, xaxt='n', yaxt='n',
col=grey.colors(255)
+ )
+ }
```

We plot the activations of the first convolutional layer for a 1 (left) and a 0 (right) input image, respectively:

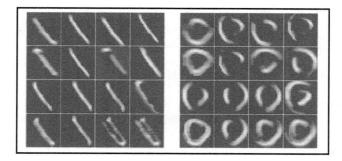

We can observe that each feature map effectively extracts the edges, curves and strikes of the digits.

We continue with the corresponding outputs of the first pooling layer called `pooling10_output`:

```
> par(mfrow=c(4,4), mar=c(0.1,0.1,0.1,0.1))
> for (i in 1:16) {
+ outputData <-as.array
(executor$ref.outputs$pooling10_output)[,,i,1]
+ image(outputData, xaxt='n', yaxt='n',
col=grey.colors(255)
+ )
+ }
> par(mfrow=c(4,4), mar=c(0.1,0.1,0.1,0.1))
> for (i in 1:16) {
+ outputData <- as.array
(executor$ref.outputs$pooling10_output)[,,i,2]
+ image(outputData, xaxt='n', yaxt='n',
col=grey.colors(255)
+ )
+ }
```

We plot the outputs of the first max pooling layer:

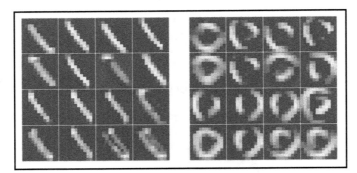

As we can easily tell, they are the downsampled versions of the convolution outputs.

Finally, we visualize one more layer, the second convolutional layer, which is labeled as `convolution11_output`. Take the first 16 feature maps as an example:

```
> par(mfrow=c(4,4), mar=c(0.1,0.1,0.1,0.1))
> for (i in 1:16) {
+ outputData <- as.array
(executor$ref.outputs$convolution11_output)[,,i,1]
+ image(outputData, xaxt='n', yaxt='n',
col=grey.colors(255)
+ )
+ }
```

```
> par(mfrow=c(4,4), mar=c(0.1,0.1,0.1,0.1))
> for (i in 1:16) {
+ outputData <- as.array
(executor$ref.outputs$convolution11_output)[,,i,2]
+ image(outputData, xaxt='n', yaxt='n',
col=grey.colors(255)
+ )
+ }
```

We plot the outputs of the second convolutional layer for two images, respectively:

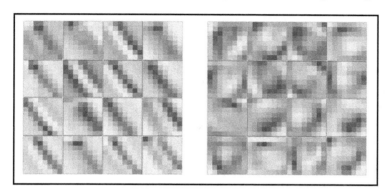

The second convolutional layer extracts higher-level features of the input images, such as shape and contour. All these 50 feature maps combined together, provide rich representations which are then fed into the fully connected layers. Therefore, classification performance is increased thanks to the convolution operations.

So far, we have examined the effectiveness of our CNN model by plotting the learning curve and visualizing the convolution extracted features. We can do one more inspection on the generalization of our model. For instance, we can take out a subset of data from the testing set to simulate a validation set, and use the remainder as the new testing set. We perform **early stopping** based on the validation set, which provides instruction on how many iterations is good enough and does not overfit the model. Finally, we employ the trained model with early stopping on the testing set and see how well the model is able to generalize to unseen data.

We first split the testing set into validation (40%) and final testing set (60%):

```
> validation_perc = 0.4
> validation_index <- createDataPartition(data_test.y, p=validation_perc,
list=FALSE)
>
> validation.array <- test.array[, , , validation_index]
> dim(validation.array) <- c(28, 28, 1,
```

```
length(validation.array[1,1,]))
> data_validation.y <- data_test.y[validation_index]
> final_test.array <- test.array[, , , -validation_index]
> dim(final_test.array) <- c(28, 28, 1,
length(final_test.array[1,1,]))
> data_final_test.y <- data_test.y[-validation_index]
```

To conduct early stopping, we write our custom callback function and will assign it to the parameter, `epoch.end.callback`. The callback function checks the classification performance on the validation set, and if it is greater than the threshold we set, the training stops:

```
> mx.callback.early.stop <- function(eval.metric) {
+ function(iteration, nbatch, env, verbose) {
+ if (!is.null(env$metric)) {
+ if (!is.null(eval.metric)) {
+ result <- env$metric$get(env$eval.metric)
+ if (result$value >= eval.metric) {
+ return(FALSE)
+ }
+ }
+ }
+ return(TRUE)
+ }
+ }
```

Now, we train the CNN model with early stopping based on the validation set where we set the stopping criteria as a validation accuracy greater than `0.985`:

```
> model_cnn_earlystop <- mx.model.FeedForward.create(softmax,
X=train.array, y=data_train.y,
eval.data=list(data=validation.array, label=data_validation.y),
+ ctx=devices, num.round=30, array.batch.size=100,
+ learning.rate=0.05, momentum=0.9, wd=0.00001,
eval.metric=mx.metric.accuracy,
+ epoch.end.callback = mx.callback.early.stop(0.985))
Start training with 1 devices
[1] Train-accuracy=0.284571428571429
[1] Validation-accuracy=0.921395348837209
[2] Train-accuracy=0.959145569620254
[2] Validation-accuracy=0.972325581395349
[3] Train-accuracy=0.980221518987343
[3] Validation-accuracy=0.97906976744186
[4] Train-accuracy=0.986613924050634
[4] Validation-accuracy=0.982790697674419
```

```
[5]  Train-accuracy=0.990537974683546
[5]  Validation-accuracy=0.981627906976744
[6]  Train-accuracy=0.992848101265824
[6]  Validation-accuracy=0.985348837209302
```

Training stops after the sixth iteration as the criteria is met. Finally, the performance on the new testing set is examined:

```
> prob_cnn <- predict(model_cnn_earlystop, final_test.array)
> prediction_cnn <- max.col(t(prob_cnn)) - 1
> cm_cnn = table(data_final_test.y, prediction_cnn)
> cm_cnn
                 prediction_cnn
data_final_test.y  0   1   2   3   4   5   6   7   8   9
               0 626   0   0   0   0   0   0   0   1   0
               1   0 701   1   0   0   2   1   3   4   0
               2   1   0 598   4   0   0   0   6   0   0
               3   0   0   0 658   0   5   0   0   2   1
               4   0   0   0   0 585   1   3   3   1   4
               5   1   0   1   3   0 558   5   0   0   2
               6   4   0   0   0   0   0 595   0   0   0
               7   0   1   3   0   1   0   0 675   0   0
               8   4   0   1   1   1   7   3   0 621   2
               9   1   0   0   0   2   1   0   4   0 589
> accuracy_cnn = mean(prediction_cnn == data_final_test.y)
> accuracy_cnn
[1] 0.9855487
```

Our CNN model is able to generalize decently.

Summary

We have just finished our first mile in the R and deep learning journey! Through this chapter, we got more familiar with the important concepts of deep learning. We started with what deep learning is all about, why it is important and the recent success of applications, as well. After we were well equipped, we solved the handwritten digit using shallow neural networks, deep neural networks and CNNs in sequence, and proved that CNNs are the best suited to exploiting strong and unique features that differentiate images of different classes.

Inspired by the human visual cortex, CNNs classify images by first deriving rich representations such as edges, curves and shapes, which was demonstrated in the visualization of the outputs of convolutional layers. In addition, we verified the performance and generalization of the CNN model using early stopping as a technique to avoid overfitting. Overall, we not only covered the mechanics of CNNs, including the concepts of convolution and pooling, but also implemented a CNN model with `MXNet`, as one of the most popular deep learning packages in R.

13
Traffic Signs Recognition for Intelligent Vehicles

Convolutional neural networks (**CNNs**) are so useful in computer vision that we are going to use one for another application, traffic sign detection for intelligent vehicles. We will also cover several important concepts of deep learning in this chapter and will get readers exposed to other popular frameworks and libraries for deep learning.

We continue our R deep learning journey with one of the core problems in self-driving cars, object recognition, and to be specific, traffic sign classification. To avoid accidents and ensure safety, robust traffic sign classification is critical to realizing driving autonomy. We will start with what self-driving cars are and what aspects deep learning is applied to. We will also discuss how deep learning stands out and becomes the state-of-the-art solution for object recognition in intelligent vehicles. With the background knowledge in mind, we'll get started with our project when we first conduct an exploratory analysis of the data and performance data preprocessing, including Y'UV color encoding conversion. We'll make our first attempt at using CNNs with MXNet and achieve more than 99% accuracy. Then we'll move on to another powerful deep learning framework called TensorFlow and an API built on top of it called Keras.

We'll also introduce the dropout technique as a regularization approach similar to Lasso (L1) / Ridge (L2) regularization. Besides overfitting, we'll demonstrate how to deal with a lack of training data, utilizing data augmentation techniques. We'll wrap up the chapter by summarizing approaches to prevent overfitting in CNN models. Once again, we will prove that deep learning models remove manual or explicit feature extraction steps that are taken in traditional approaches, and they instead automatically discover useful patterns underneath input data during the training process.

We will get into the details of the topics mentioned here:

- What self-driving cars are
- How deep learning is applied in self-driving cars
- How deep learning becomes a state-of-the-art solution for object recognition in intelligent vehicles
- Exploratory analysis on the German Traffic Sign Recognition Benchmark dataset's data
- Traffic sign recognition using convolutional neural networks with the MXNet package
- Keras and TensorFlow
- Traffic sign recognition using convolutional neural networks with the `keras` package
- Reducing overfitting with dropout
- Data augmentation and common augmentation methods
- Using data augmentation for a small training set
- Summarizing approaches to prevent overfitting in CNN models

How is deep learning applied in self-driving cars?

A self-driving car (also called an autonomous/automated vehicle or driverless car) is a robotic vehicle that is capable of traveling between destinations and navigating without human intervention. To enable autonomy, self-driving cars detect and interpret environments using a variety of techniques such as radar, GPS and computer vision; and they then plan appropriate navigational paths to the desired destination.

In more detail, the following is how self-driving cars work in general:

- The software plans the routes based on the destination, traffic, and road information and starts the car
- A **Light Detection and Ranging** (**LiDAR**) sensor captures the surroundings in real time and creates a dynamic 3D map
- Sensors monitor lateral movement to calculate the car's position on the 3D map

- Radar systems exploit information on distances from other traffic participants, pedestrians, or obstacles
- Computer vision algorithms recognize traffic signs, traffic lights, and other landmarks from a camera and provide advance notices
- The algorithm-driven software analyzes all sensory data, combines inputs from other sources, and controls actions such as steering and braking, simulating the way humans perceive the surroundings and make decisions

How does deep learning become a state-of-the-art solution?

As we can see, robust object recognition is critical to realizing driving autonomy. To avoid accidents and ensure safety, it is necessary to be attentive to the surrounding environment, traffic signs, and lights. Generally speaking, object recognition in self-driving cars can be summarized into four tasks:

- Object detection, such as obstacles, pedestrians, traffic signs, and lights.
- Object identification and classification. An example is of labeling traffic lights (red, yellow, green, and off) if detected in the images captured by the frontal camera. Then we have categorizing of traffic participants into bicycle, motorcycle, car, truck and bus, and of course classifying traffic signs (our main talking point in this chapter).
- Object localization, which maps ground-level images to aerial imagery.
- Movement prediction, for example, understanding the speed of an object or estimating the behavior and intention of a pedestrian based on his/her pose.

Since the past two decades, a variety of machine learning algorithms have been applied to solve object recognition problems in intelligent vehicles.

For example, in *Detecting Pedestrians Using Patterns of Motion and Appearance* (Viola et al., published in the International Journal of Computer Vision, 63(2)), the **AdaBoost** (short for **Adaptive Boosting**, which corrects classification errors sequentially) classifier was employed to detect walking pedestrians.

In *Histograms of Oriented Gradients for Human Detection* (Dalal and Triggs, published in the IEEE Conference on Computer Vision and Pattern Recognition (CVPR) in 2005), efficient features were extracted using the **histogram of orientation (HOG)** technique, and fed into a **support vector machine (SVM)** classifier for human detection. Since then, more sophisticated variants such as gradient field HOG (GF-HOG) and other more complex feature extraction methods were developed. To name some, we have zoning + projection, projection + HOG, and so on.

Conventional object recognition approaches (explicit feature extraction + machine learning classification) rely heavily on hand-crafted features, such as gradient orientation histogram with HOG, local keypoints with **Sped-Up Robust Features (SURF)**, or **Scale Invariant Feature Transform (SIFT)**. Although they perform well in certain tasks, designing these feature descriptors is difficult and requires lots of manual tweaks and experiments.

Recall that in the previous chapter on classifying handwritten digits, we resorted to a CNN. It first derives low-level representations, local edges and curves, and then composes higher level representations such as overall shape and contour through a series of low-level representations. We also concluded that CNNs are well suited to exploit strong and unique features.

In fact, it has been proven in many solutions that CNNs are able to efficiently automate feature extraction while allowing a significant boost in performance. For example, in *Pedestrian Detection with Unsupervised Multi-Stage Feature Learning* (Sermanet et al., published in the IEEE Conference on **Computer Vision and Pattern Recognition (CVPR)** in 2013), CNNs were first introduced into the pedestrian detection problem. In *Rich feature hierarchies for accurate object detection and semantic segmentation* (Girshick et al., published in the IEEE Conference on CVPR in 2014), a variant region-based CNN model was proposed to improve performance. Nowadays, a number of state-of-the-art object recognition approaches involve deep learning techniques, CNNs specifically. A good testimony would be their prevalence in top positions in the leaderboard of the KITTI Vision Benchmark for autonomous cars (http://www.cvlibs.net/datasets/kitti/eval_object.php?obj_benchmark=2d).

I hope all of these cases have excited you about CNNs and their power of providing better object recognition solutions to intelligent vehicles.

So what are we waiting for? Let's proceed with our project, traffic signs recognition, as it is one of the most important topics in autonomous cars!

Traffic sign recognition using CNN

As always, we begin by exploring the **German Traffic Sign Recognition Benchmark** (**GTSRB**) dataset at `http://benchmark.ini.rub.de/?section=gtsrb&subsection=dataset`.

Getting started with exploring GTSRB

The GTSRB dataset, compiled and generously published by the real-time computer vision research group in Institut für Neuroinformatik, was originally used for a competition of classifying single images of traffic signs. It consists of a training set of 39,209 labeled images and a testing test of 12,630 unlabeled images. The training dataset contains 43 classes—43 types of traffic signs. We will go through all classes and exhibit several samples for each class.

The dataset can be downloaded via `http://benchmark.ini.rub.de/Dataset/GTSRB_Final_Training_Images.zip` (located in the **Downloads | Training dataset** section on the page). Unzip the downloaded file and there will be a folder called `Images` containing 43 folders (`00000`, `00001`... up to `00042`); they represent 43 classes of images. These images are in the following form:

- The image files are in **PPM** (short for **portable pixmap**) format.
- The number of images from each class ranges from 210 to 2250. So it is an unbalanced multi-class classification problem.
- Each image contains one traffic sign.
- The sizes of the images are not uniform, ranging from 15*15 to 250*250 pixels, and images are not necessarily square.
- Images contain a border of up to 10% around the actual sign. Thus the sign is not necessarily centered with the image.

Let's start by plotting a sample, `00000_00002.ppm`, in the `00000` folder.

We use the `pixmap` package (`https://cran.r-project.org/web/packages/pixmap`) to read the PPM file:

```
> library('pixmap')
> image <-
read.pnm('GTSRB/Final_Training/Images/00000/00000_00002.ppm',cellres=1)
```

Now we obtain a `pixmapRGB` object with attributes `red`, `green`, and `blue` (which are the pixels for each of the three channels), as well as `size`, which is the width and height of the image. And we can access the red, green, and blue channel as follows:

```
> red_matrix <- matrix(image@red, nrow = image@size[1], ncol =
image@size[2])
> green_matrix <- matrix(image@green, nrow = image@size[1], ncol =
image@size[2])
> blue_matrix <- matrix(image@blue, nrow = image@size[1], ncol =
image@size[2])
```

We visualize the original image and its three channels individually:

```
> plot(image, main=sprintf("Original"))
> rotate <- function(x) t(apply(x, 2, rev))
> par(mfrow=c(1, 3))
> image(rotate(red_matrix), col = grey.colors(255), main=sprintf("Red"))
> image(rotate(green_matrix), col = grey.colors(255),
main=sprintf("Green"))
> image(rotate(blue_matrix), col = grey.colors(255), main=sprintf("Blue"))
```

Note that here we reuse the rotate function we defined in the last chapter to better view the images. This is an original image:

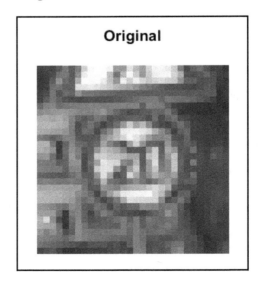

The following images show the output for the red, blue, and green channel, respectively:

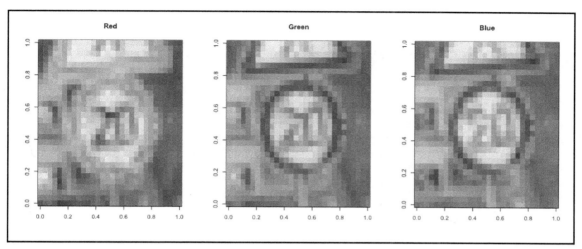

It is a 20 km/h speed limit sign.

We can now go through 43 classes of signs and display three samples for each type by defining the following function:

```
> plot_samples <- function(training_path, class, num_sample){
+       classes <- c("Speed limit (20km/h)", "Speed limit (30km/h)",
                     "Speed limit (50km/h)", "Speed limit (60km/h)",
+                    "Speed limit (70km/h)", "Speed limit (80km/h)",
                     "End of speed limit (80km/h)",
+                    "Speed limit (100km/h)", "Speed limit (120km/h)",
                     "No passing",
+                    "No passing for vehicles over 3.5 metric tons",
                     "Right-of-way at the next intersection",
+                    "Priority road", "Yield", "Stop", "No vehicles",
                     "Vehicles over 3.5 metric tons prohibited",
+                    "No entry", "General caution", "Dangerous curve to
                     the left", "Dangerous curve to the right",
+                    "Double curve", " Bumpy road", "Slippery road",
                     "Road narrows on the right", "Road work",
+                    "Traffic signals", "Pedestrians", "Children
                     crossing", "Bicycles crossing",
                     "Beware of ice/snow",
+                    "Wild animals crossing",
                     "End of all speed and passing limits",
                     "Turn right ahead",
+                    "Turn left ahead", "Ahead only",
                     "Go straight or right", "Go straight or left",
```

```
                        "Keep right", "Keep left", "Roundabout mandatory",
                        "End of no passing",
   +                    "End of no passing by vehicles over 3.5 metric
                        tons")
   +    if (class<10) {
   +      path <- paste(training_path, "0000", class, "/", sep="")
   +    } else {
   +      path <- paste(training_path, "000", class, "/", sep="")
   +    }
   +    par(mfrow=c(1, num_sample))
   +    # Randomly display num_sample samples
   +    all_files <- list.files(path = path)
   +    title <- paste('Class', class, ':', classes[class+1])
   +    print(paste(title, "              (", length(all_files),
                    " samples)", sep=""))
   +    files <- sample(all_files, num_sample)
   +    for (file in files) {
   +      image <- read.pnm(paste(path, file, sep=""), cellres=1)
   +      plot(image)
   +    }
   +    mtext(title, side = 3, line = -23, outer = TRUE)
   + }
```

Call the function with `class=0`:

```
> training_path <- "GTSRB/Final_Training/Images/"
> plot_samples(training_path, 0, 3)
[1] "Class 0 : Speed limit (20km/h)              (211 samples)"
```

Three samples are displayed:

Class 0 : Speed limit (20km/h)

Repeat this function call with a different class (or use a loop) to go through the remaining 42 types:

```
> plot_samples(training_path, 1, 3)
[1] "Class 1 : Speed limit (30km/h)        (2221 samples)"
```

Three samples from class 1 are displayed as follows:

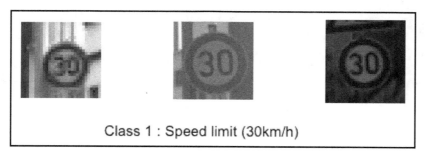

Class 1 : Speed limit (30km/h)

```
> plot_samples(training_path, 2, 3)
[1] "Class 2 : Speed limit (50km/h)        (2251 samples)"
```

Three images from class 2 are shown here:

Class 2 : Speed limit (50km/h)

```
> plot_samples(training_path, 3, 3)
[1] "Class 3 : Speed limit (60km/h)        (1411 samples)"
```

Here is the result for class 3:

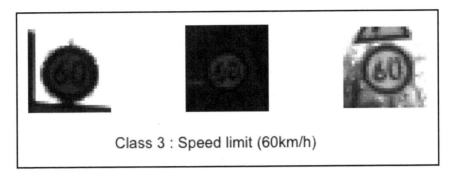

Class 3 : Speed limit (60km/h)

```
> plot_samples(training_path, 4, 3)
[1] "Class 4 : Speed limit (70km/h)          (1981 samples)"
```

We plot three images from class 4:

Class 4 : Speed limit (70km/h)

Here we skip the remainder, but it is clear that the images were captured under various conditions, including weather, illumination, occlusion, rotations, and so on. Instead, we list all types of sample sizes for easy reference:

ID	Type	Number of samples
0	Speed limit (20km/h)	211
1	Speed limit (30km/h)	2221
2	Speed limit (50km/h)	2251
3	Speed limit (60km/h)	1411
4	Speed limit (70km/h)	1981
5	Speed limit (80km/h)	1861
6	End of speed limit (80km/h)	421
7	Speed limit (100km/h)	1441
8	Speed limit (120km/h)	1411
9	No passing	1471
10	No passing for vehicles over 3.5 metric tons	2011
11	Right-of-way at the next intersection	1321
12	Priority road	2101
13	Yield	2161
14	Stop	781
15	No vehicles	631
16	Vehicles over 3.5 metric tons prohibited	421
17	No entry	1111
18	General caution	1201
19	Dangerous curve to the left	211
20	Dangerous curve to the right	361
21	Double curve	331
22	Bumpy road	391
23	Slippery road	511
24	Road narrows on the right	271
25	Road work	1501
26	Traffic signals	601
27	Pedestrians	241
28	Children crossing	541
29	Bicycles crossing	271

30	Beware of ice/snow	451
31	Wild animals crossing	781
32	End of all speed and passing limits	241
33	Turn right ahead	690
34	Turn left ahead	421
35	Ahead only	1201
36	Go straight or right	391
37	Go straight or left	211
38	Keep right	2071
39	Keep left	301
40	Roundabout mandatory	361
41	End of no passing	241
42	End of no passing by vehicles over 3.5 metric tons	241

Obviously, the signs, our **regions of interest (ROI)**, are not centered within the images, whose sizes unfortunately vary. As a result, we need to separate the ROI from the image and standardize its size (resizing it to 32*32 as most researchers have done) before we can analyze and classify the data. We resort to the annotations provided along with the images. Each class folder contains an annotation file, for example, GT-00000.csv located at 00000. Each annotation file contains the following useful fields:

- Filename: The filename of the image
- ROI.X1: The x coordinate of the top-left corner of the ROI bounding box
- ROI.Y1: The y coordinate of the top-left corner of the ROI bounding box
- ROI.X2: The x coordinate of the bottom-right corner of the ROI bounding box
- ROI.Y2: The y coordinate of the bottom-right corner of the ROI bounding box

Here is an example of the ROI in a sample:

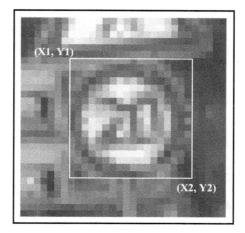

Now we define the preprocessing function for a raw image, which includes separating the ROI and resizing it to 32*32:

```
> source("http://bioconductor.org/biocLite.R")
> biocLite("EBImage")
> library("EBImage")
> roi_resize <- function(input_matrix, roi){
+      roi_matrix <- input_matrix[roi[1, 'Roi.Y1']:roi[1, 'Roi.Y2'],
                        roi[1, 'Roi.X1']:roi[1, 'Roi.X2']]
+      return(resize(roi_matrix, 32, 32))
+ }
```

Note that the resize function is from the EBImage package:

```
https://bioconductor.org/packages/release/bioc/html/EBImage.html
```

We try it out on our first sample (red channel only):

```
> # read annotation csv file
> annotation <-
read.csv(file="GTSRB/Final_Training/Images/00000/GT-00000.csv",
header=TRUE, sep=";")
> roi = annotation[3, ]
> red_matrix_cropped <- roi_resize(red_matrix, roi)
> par(mfrow=c(1, 2))
> image(rotate(red_matrix), col = grey.colors(255) ,
main=sprintf("Original"))
> image(rotate(red_matrix_cropped), col = grey.colors(255) ,
main=sprintf("Preprocessed"))
```

We get the preprocessed red channel on the right:

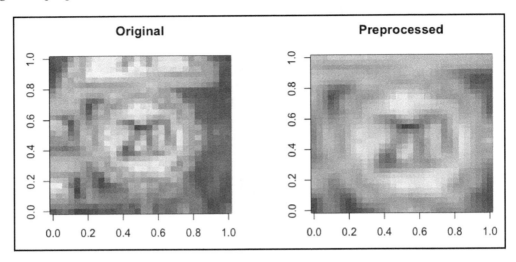

Similarly, we can process the other two channels. Based on these three channels, how can we construct the feature space? Discarding any channel might result in loss of information. Simply stacking them up could lead to redundancy. So, combining three channels into one would be a better solution. In the color world, Y'UV is an encoding system that encrypts brightness information separately from color information. It is typically used as part of a color image pipeline and computer graphics hardware. Y'UV represents human perception of color in terms of three components: Y' as the luminance (brightness), and U and V as the chrominance (color). Y'UV can be converted from RGB using:

- $Y' = 0.299R + 0.587G + 0.114B$
- $U = 0.492(B - Y')$
- $V = 0.877(R - Y')$

For our feature space, we can only take the brightness channel Y'.

Now that we have the last piece of the whole preprocessing ready, let's put them together, load, and process (ROI + resize + conversion to Y') the entire labeled dataset:

```
> load_labeled_data <- function(training_path, classes){
+    # Initialize the pixel features X and target y
+    X <- matrix(, nrow = 0, ncol = 32*32)
+    y <- vector()
+    # Load images from each of the 43 classes
+    for(i in classes) {
+       print(paste('Loading images from class', i))
+       if (i<10) {
```

```
+           annotation_path <- paste(training_path, "0000", i, "/GT-0000",
+                               i, ".csv", sep="")
+           path <- paste(training_path, "0000", i, "/", sep="")
+       } else {
+           annotation_path <- paste(training_path, "000", i, "/GT-000",
+                               i, ".csv", sep="")
+           path <- paste(training_path, "000", i, "/", sep="")
+       }
+       annotation <- read.csv(file=annotation_path, header=TRUE,
+                               sep=";")
+
+       for (row in 1:nrow(annotation)) {
+         # Read each image
+         image_path <- paste(path, annotation[row, "Filename"], sep="")
+         image <- read.pnm(image_path, cellres=1)
+         # Parse RGB color space
+         red_matrix <- matrix(image@red, nrow = image@size[1],
+                               ncol = image@size[2])
+         green_matrix <- matrix(image@green, nrow = image@size[1],
+                               ncol = image@size[2])
+         blue_matrix <- matrix(image@blue, nrow = image@size[1],
+                               ncol = image@size[2])
+         # Crop ROI and resize
+         red_matrix_cropped <- roi_resize(red_matrix,
+                               annotation[row, ])
+         green_matrix_cropped <- roi_resize(green_matrix,
+                               annotation[row, ])
+         blue_matrix_cropped <- roi_resize(blue_matrix,
+                               annotation[row, ])
+         # Convert to brightness, e.g. Y' channel
+         x <- 0.299 * red_matrix_cropped + 0.587 *
+               green_matrix_cropped + 0.114 * blue_matrix_cropped
+         X <- rbind(X, matrix(x, 1, 32*32))
+         y <- c(y, i)
+       }
+
+   }
+
+   return(list("x" = X, "y" = y))
+ }
```

After defining the data loading function as shown previously, we apply it to the entire raw dataset:

```
> classes <- 0:42
> data <- load_labeled_data(training_path, classes)
```

Be patient as it might take a couple of hours to read and process 39,209 images. Just in case anything unexpected happens, a good practice is to save the data object so that we can restore it anytime later:

```
> # Save the data object to a file
> saveRDS(data, file = "43 classes.rds")
> # Restore the data object
> data <- readRDS(file = "43 classes.rds")
```

Just do a quick check on the ready-to-use data:

```
> data.x <- data$x
> data.y <- data$y
> dim(data.x)
[1] 39209   1024
```

Correct dimension!

```
> summary(as.factor(data.y))
    0    1    2    3    4    5    6    7    8    9   10   11   12   13   14
   15   16   17   18   19   20   21   22
  210 2220 2250 1410 1980 1860  420 1440 1410 1470 2010 1320 2100 2160  780
  630  420 1110 1200  210  360  330  390
   23   24   25   26   27   28   29   30   31   32   33   34   35   36   37
   38   39   40   41   42
  510  270 1500  600  240  540  270  450  780  240  689  420 1200  390  210
 2070  300  360  240  240
```

Correct class sizes, and again they are rather unbalanced!

 Never skip checking the class balance for classification.

After ensuring that the data is loaded and processed properly, we do more exploratory analysis on the distribution of features, that is, the pixels. As an example, we take the 16 pixels from the central 4*4 block (222nd to 225th, 254th to 257th, 286th to 289th, and 318th to 321st) in each image from class 1 (Speed limit=30km/h), 14 (Stop), 20 (Dangerous curve to the right), and 27 (Pedestrians). We display their histograms:

```
> central_block <- c(222:225, 254:257, 286:289, 318:321)
> par(mfrow=c(2, 2))
> for(i in c(1, 14, 20, 27)) {
+   hist(c(as.matrix(data.x[data.y==i, central_block])),
```

```
+         main=sprintf("Histogram for class %d", i),
+         xlab="Pixel brightness")
+ }
```

The resulting pixel brightness histograms are displayed as follows:

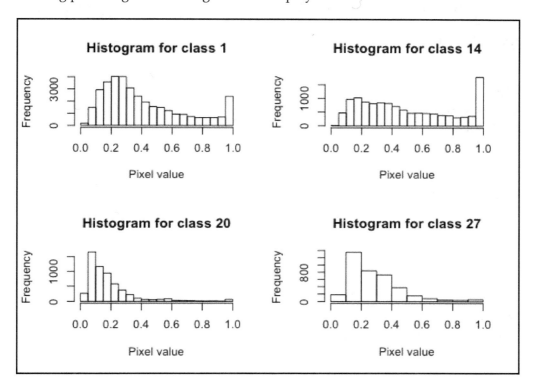

The brightness of the central pixels is distributed differently among these four classes. For instance, the majority of the central pixels from class 20 are dark, as the sign (Dangerous curve to the right) has a thick black stroke through the center; while in class 14, the stop sign has a white stroke (the left part of the **O**) near the central area. Pixels taken from other positions can also be distinctly distributed among different classes.

The exploratory analysis we just conducted helps us to move forward with building classification models based on pixels.

First solution – convolutional neural networks using MXNet

We start off with a solution similar to the one we developed at the end of the previous chapter, with CNNs using MXNet.

Again, we first split the dataset into two subsets for training (75%) and testing (25%) using the `caret` package:

```
> if (!require("caret"))
+       install.packages("caret")
> library (caret)
> set.seed(42)
> train_perc = 0.75
> train_index <- createDataPartition(data.y, p=train_perc, list=FALSE)
> train_index <- train_index[sample(nrow(train_index)),]
> data_train.x <- data.x[train_index,]
> data_train.y <- data.y[train_index]
> data_test.x <- data.x[-train_index,]
> data_test.y <- data.y[-train_index]
```

Don't forget to specify a particular random seed for reproducible work. We normally do data normalization before applying CNNs. In our case, the raw pixels loaded are already in the range of 0 to 1; after Y' brightness conversion, the resulting pixels are still in the range of 0 to 1.

In general, normalizing our data is necessary before putting it into a CNN or in fact any neural network or gradient-descent-based model. As for image inputs, we usually scale the pixels in the range of 0 to 1.

After preparing the training and testing set, we structure our CNN model as follows:

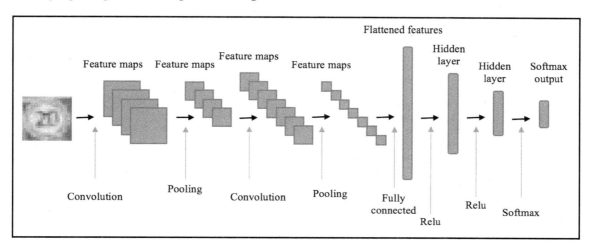

The network starts with the first set of convolutional layers, the ReLu nonlinear layer and the pooling layer. Here we use 32 5*5 convolutional filters and a 2*2 max pooling filter:

```
> require(mxnet)
> data <- mx.symbol.Variable("data")
> # first convolution
> conv1 <- mx.symbol.Convolution(data=data, kernel=c(5,5),
                                 num_filter=32)
> act1 <- mx.symbol.Activation(data=conv1, act_type="relu")
> pool1 <- mx.symbol.Pooling(data=act1, pool_type="max",
+                            kernel=c(2,2), stride=c(2,2))
```

It follows with the second set of convolutional, ReLu nonlinear and pooling layer, where 64 5*5 convolutional filters and 2*2 max pooling filter are used:

```
> # second convolution
> conv2 <- mx.symbol.Convolution(data=pool1, kernel=c(5,5),
                                 num_filter=64)
> act2 <- mx.symbol.Activation(data=conv2, act_type="relu")
> pool2 <- mx.symbol.Pooling(data=act2, pool_type="max",
+                            kernel=c(2,2), stride=c(2,2))
```

Now that we've extracted rich representations of the input images by detecting edges, curves, and shapes, we move on to the fully connected layers. But before doing so, we need to flatten the resulting feature maps from the previous convolution layers:

```
> flatten <- mx.symbol.Flatten(data=pool2)
```

In the fully connected section, we apply a ReLu hidden layer with 1,000 units and a softmax layer with 43 units:

```
> # first fully connected layer
> fc1 <- mx.symbol.FullyConnected(data=flatten, num_hidden=1000)
> act3 <- mx.symbol.Activation(data=fc1, act_type="relu")
> # second fully connected layer
> fc2 <- mx.symbol.FullyConnected(data=act3, num_hidden=43)
```

Finally, the softmax layer, producing outputs for each of the 43 classes:

```
> # softmax output
> softmax <- mx.symbol.SoftmaxOutput(data=fc2, name="sm")
```

All pieces of the network are now assembled. Before we start training the model, we specify the random seed and training devices and reshape the matrix `data_train.x` into an array as required by the convolutional layer in MXNet:

```
> devices <- mx.cpu()
> train.array <- t(data_train.x)
> dim(train.array) <- c(32, 32, 1, nrow(data_train.x))
> mx.set.seed(42)
```

Time for model training:

```
> model_cnn <- mx.model.FeedForward.create(softmax, X=train.array,
y=data_train.y, ctx=devices, num.round=30,
array.batch.size=100,learning.rate=0.05, momentum=0.9,
wd=0.00001, eval.metric=mx.metric.accuracy,
            epoch.end.callback=mx.callback.log.train.metric(100))
```

Start training with one device:

```
[1]  Train-accuracy=0.184965986394558
[2]  Train-accuracy=0.824610169491525
[3]  Train-accuracy=0.949389830508475
[4]  Train-accuracy=0.968305084745763
[5]  Train-accuracy=0.983050847457628
[6]  Train-accuracy=0.988372881355934
[7]  Train-accuracy=0.990745762711866
[8]  Train-accuracy=0.993152542372882
[9]  Train-accuracy=0.992576271186442
[10] Train-accuracy=0.994372881355933
[11] Train-accuracy=0.99542372881356
[12] Train-accuracy=0.995118644067798
[13] Train-accuracy=0.99671186440678
[14] Train-accuracy=0.999830508474576
[15] Train-accuracy=0.999932203389831
```

```
[16] Train-accuracy=1
[17] Train-accuracy=1
[18] Train-accuracy=1
[19] Train-accuracy=1
[20] Train-accuracy=1
[21] Train-accuracy=1
[22] Train-accuracy=1
[23] Train-accuracy=1
[24] Train-accuracy=1
[25] Train-accuracy=1
[26] Train-accuracy=1
[27] Train-accuracy=1
[28] Train-accuracy=1
[29] Train-accuracy=1
[30] Train-accuracy=1
```

We just fit our model with hyperparameters:

- `num.round =30`: The maximum number of iterations
- `array.batch.size = 100`: The batch size of mini-batch gradient descent
- `learning.rate = 0.05`: The learning rate
- `momentum=0.9`: The momentum factor that determines how much of the previous velocity is incorporated into the current one
- `eval.metric=mx.metric.accuracy`: This uses classification accuracy as the evaluation metric
- `initializer=mx.init.uniform(0.1)`: Initial weights are randomly generated from the uniform distribution between -0.1 and 0.1 so as to lower the chances of weights exploding and vanishing in the deep network
- `wd = 0.00001`: The weight decay for L2 regularization, which adds penalties for large weights in order to avoid overfitting

We can view the structure of the model by:

```
> graph.viz(model_cnn$symbol)
```

The trained model is then applied to the testing set:

```
> test.array <- t(data_test.x)
> dim(test.array) <- c(32, 32, 1, nrow(data_test.x))
> prob_cnn <- predict(model_cnn, test.array)
> prediction_cnn <- max.col(t(prob_cnn)) - 1
```

We compute the confusion matrix and classification accuracy as follows:

```
> cm_cnn = table(data_test.y, prediction_cnn)
> cm_cnn
```

The first half of the resulting confusion matrix:

prediction_cnn

data_test.y	0	1	2	3	4	5	6	7	8	9	10	11	12	13	14	15	16	17	18	19	20	21	22	23	24
0	39	0	0	0	0	0	0	0	0	0	0	0	0	0	0	0	0	0	0	0	0	0	0	0	0
1	0	551	1	0	0	0	0	0	0	0	0	0	1	0	0	0	0	0	0	0	0	0	0	0	0
2	0	0	589	0	1	0	0	1	0	0	0	0	0	0	0	0	0	0	0	0	0	0	0	0	0
3	0	0	0	336	0	1	0	0	0	0	0	0	0	0	0	0	0	0	0	0	0	0	0	1	0
4	0	0	0	0	505	0	0	0	0	0	0	0	0	0	0	0	0	0	0	0	0	0	0	0	0
5	0	0	0	0	0	453	0	0	0	0	0	0	0	0	0	0	0	1	0	0	0	0	0	0	0
6	0	0	0	0	0	0	95	1	0	0	0	0	0	0	0	0	0	0	0	0	0	0	0	0	0
7	0	0	1	1	0	2	0	362	0	0	0	0	0	0	0	0	0	0	0	0	0	0	0	0	0
8	0	0	0	0	0	0	0	0	356	0	1	0	0	0	1	0	0	0	0	0	0	0	0	0	0
9	0	0	0	0	0	0	0	0	0	357	0	0	0	0	1	0	0	0	0	0	0	0	0	0	0
10	0	0	0	0	0	0	1	0	0	1	505	0	0	0	0	0	0	0	0	0	0	0	0	0	0
11	0	0	0	0	0	0	0	0	0	0	0	311	0	0	0	0	0	0	0	0	0	0	0	0	0
12	0	0	0	0	0	0	0	0	0	0	0	0	539	0	0	2	0	0	0	0	0	0	0	0	0
13	0	1	1	0	0	0	0	0	0	1	1	1	1	513	0	0	0	0	1	0	0	0	0	0	0
14	0	0	0	1	0	0	0	0	0	0	0	0	0	0	194	0	0	0	0	0	0	0	0	0	0
15	0	1	0	0	0	0	0	0	0	0	0	0	2	0	0	170	0	0	0	0	0	0	0	0	0
16	0	0	0	0	0	0	0	0	0	0	0	0	0	0	0	0	113	0	0	0	0	0	0	0	0
17	0	0	0	0	0	0	0	0	0	0	0	0	0	0	0	0	0	285	0	0	0	0	0	0	0
18	0	0	0	0	0	0	0	0	0	0	0	1	0	0	0	0	0	0	308	0	0	0	0	0	0
19	0	0	0	0	0	0	0	0	0	0	0	0	0	0	0	0	0	0	0	57	0	0	0	0	0
20	0	0	0	0	0	0	0	0	0	0	0	0	0	0	0	0	0	0	1	3	77	0	0	0	0
21	0	0	0	0	0	0	0	0	0	0	0	0	0	0	0	0	0	0	0	0	0	82	0	0	0
22	0	0	0	0	0	0	0	0	0	0	0	0	0	0	0	0	0	0	0	0	0	0	79	0	0
23	0	0	0	0	0	0	0	0	0	0	0	0	0	0	0	0	0	0	0	0	0	0	1	135	0
24	0	0	0	0	0	0	0	0	0	0	0	0	0	0	0	0	0	1	0	0	0	0	0	0	66
25	0	0	0	0	0	0	0	0	0	0	0	0	0	0	0	0	0	0	0	0	0	0	0	0	0
26	0	0	0	0	0	0	0	0	0	1	0	0	0	0	0	0	0	0	1	0	1	0	0	0	0
27	0	0	0	0	0	0	0	0	0	0	0	0	0	0	0	0	0	0	0	0	0	0	0	0	1
28	0	0	0	0	0	0	0	0	0	0	0	0	0	0	0	0	0	0	1	0	0	0	0	0	0
29	0	0	0	0	0	0	0	0	0	0	0	0	0	0	0	0	0	0	0	0	0	0	0	0	1
30	0	0	0	0	0	1	0	0	0	0	0	0	0	0	0	0	0	0	0	0	0	0	0	0	0
31	0	0	0	0	0	0	0	0	0	0	0	0	0	0	0	0	0	0	0	0	0	0	0	0	0
32	0	0	0	0	0	0	0	0	0	0	0	0	0	0	0	0	0	0	0	0	0	0	0	0	0
33	0	0	0	0	0	0	0	0	0	0	0	0	0	0	0	0	0	0	0	0	0	0	0	0	0
34	0	0	1	0	0	0	0	0	0	0	0	0	0	0	0	0	0	0	0	0	0	0	0	0	0
35	0	0	0	0	0	0	0	0	0	0	0	0	0	0	0	0	0	0	0	0	0	0	0	0	0
36	0	0	0	0	0	0	0	0	0	0	0	0	0	0	0	0	0	0	0	1	0	0	0	0	0
37	0	0	0	0	0	0	0	0	0	1	0	0	0	0	0	0	0	0	0	0	0	0	0	0	0
38	0	0	0	0	0	0	0	0	0	0	0	0	0	0	0	0	0	0	0	0	0	0	0	0	0
39	0	0	0	0	0	0	0	0	0	0	0	0	0	0	0	0	0	0	0	0	0	0	0	0	0
40	0	0	0	0	0	0	0	0	0	0	0	0	0	0	0	0	0	0	0	0	0	0	0	0	0
41	0	0	0	0	0	0	0	0	0	0	0	0	0	0	0	0	0	0	0	0	0	0	0	0	0
42	0	0	0	1	0	0	0	0	0	0	0	0	0	0	0	0	0	0	0	0	0	0	0	0	0

The second half:

data_test.y	prediction_cnn																	
	25	26	27	28	29	30	31	32	33	34	35	36	37	38	39	40	41	42
0	0	0	0	0	0	0	0	0	0	0	0	0	0	0	0	0	0	0
1	0	0	0	0	0	0	0	0	0	0	0	0	0	0	0	0	0	0
2	0	0	0	0	0	0	0	0	0	0	0	0	0	0	0	0	0	0
3	0	0	0	0	0	0	0	0	0	0	0	0	0	0	0	0	0	0
4	0	0	0	0	0	0	0	0	0	0	0	0	0	0	0	0	0	0
5	0	0	0	0	0	0	0	0	0	0	0	0	1	1	0	0	0	0
6	0	0	0	0	0	0	0	0	0	0	0	0	0	0	0	0	0	0
7	0	0	0	0	0	0	0	0	0	0	0	0	0	0	0	1	0	0
8	0	0	0	0	0	0	0	0	0	0	0	0	0	0	0	0	0	0
9	0	0	0	0	0	0	0	0	0	0	0	0	0	0	0	1	0	0
10	0	1	0	0	0	0	0	0	0	0	0	0	0	0	0	0	0	0
11	0	0	0	0	0	1	0	0	0	0	0	0	0	0	0	0	0	0
12	0	0	0	0	0	0	0	0	0	0	1	0	0	0	0	0	0	0
13	0	0	0	0	0	0	0	0	0	0	0	0	0	0	0	0	0	0
14	0	0	0	0	0	0	0	0	0	0	0	0	0	0	0	0	0	0
15	0	0	0	0	0	0	0	0	0	0	0	0	0	0	0	0	0	0
16	0	0	0	0	0	0	0	0	0	0	0	0	0	0	0	0	0	0
17	0	0	0	0	0	0	0	0	0	0	0	0	0	0	0	0	0	0
18	1	0	0	0	0	0	0	0	0	0	0	0	0	0	0	0	0	0
19	0	0	0	0	0	0	0	0	0	0	0	0	0	0	0	0	0	0
20	0	0	0	2	0	0	0	0	0	0	0	0	0	0	0	0	0	0
21	1	0	0	0	0	0	0	0	0	0	0	0	0	0	0	0	0	0
22	0	0	0	0	0	0	0	0	0	0	0	0	0	0	0	0	0	0
23	0	0	0	0	1	0	0	0	0	0	0	0	0	0	0	0	0	0
24	0	0	0	0	1	0	0	0	0	0	0	0	0	0	1	0	0	0
25	363	0	0	0	0	0	0	0	0	0	0	0	0	0	0	0	0	0
26	0	150	0	0	0	0	0	0	0	0	0	0	0	0	0	0	0	0
27	0	0	57	0	0	0	0	0	0	0	0	0	0	0	0	0	0	0
28	0	0	0	131	0	0	0	0	0	0	0	0	0	0	0	0	0	0
29	0	0	0	0	65	0	0	0	0	0	0	0	0	0	0	0	0	0
30	0	0	0	0	0	122	0	0	0	0	0	0	0	0	0	0	0	0
31	0	0	0	0	0	0	198	0	0	0	0	0	0	0	0	0	0	0
32	0	0	0	0	0	0	0	47	0	0	0	0	0	0	0	0	0	0
33	0	0	0	0	0	0	0	0	181	1	0	0	0	0	0	0	0	0
34	0	0	0	0	0	0	0	0	0	110	0	0	0	0	0	0	0	0
35	1	0	0	0	0	0	0	0	0	0	288	1	0	0	0	0	0	0
36	1	0	0	1	0	0	0	0	0	0	0	95	0	0	0	0	0	0
37	0	0	0	0	0	0	0	0	0	0	0	0	40	0	0	0	0	0
38	0	0	0	0	0	0	0	0	0	0	0	0	0	499	0	0	0	0
39	0	0	0	0	0	0	0	0	0	0	0	0	0	0	74	0	0	0
40	0	0	0	0	0	0	0	0	0	0	0	0	0	0	0	94	0	0
41	0	0	0	0	0	0	0	1	0	0	0	0	0	0	0	0	71	0
42	0	0	0	0	0	0	0	0	0	0	0	0	0	0	0	0	0	70

Misclassification occurs only in several rare cases regardless of large variations in appearances of images due to illumination changes, partial occlusions, rotations, weather conditions, and so on:

```
> accuracy_cnn = mean(prediction_cnn == data_test.y)
> accuracy_cnn
[1] 0.9930612
```

We just built a robust CNN model that correctly classifies more than 99.30% of the testing signs. The CNN model efficiently learns the representations by deriving low-level and high-level features. It makes those hand-crafted features obsolete, as it captures important and distinguishable features by itself from the sign images.

Now that we have achieved great success using our favorite (so far) deep learning tool MXNet, why don't we explore other tools that are also powerful? In fact, another deep learning API called Keras has been gaining popularity recently; its backend, TensorFlow, is probably the best known deep learning framework.

Trying something new – CNNs using Keras with TensorFlow

Keras (https://keras.io/) is a high-level deep learning API written in Python that can run on top of any of these three deep learning frameworks: TensorFlow (from Google), CNTK (from Microsoft), and Theano (from the Montreal Institute for Learning Algorithms, Université de Montréal, Canada). To solve a machine learning problem efficiently, being able to quickly prototype ideas is the key. And this is why Keras was developed initially, to facilitate fast experimentation in the following key aspects:

- User-friendly API built on top of multiple powerful backends, including TensorFlow, CNTK, and Theano.
- Built-in CNN, RNN, and autoencoder models as well as support classes and methods (metrics, optimizers, regularizers, visualization, and so on), which enable easy and fast prototyping.
- Excellent modularity and extensibility. These allow for customized network architectures: Multiple input, multiple output, layer sharing, model sharing, memory-based network, and so on.
- Allowing the same code to run seamlessly on CPU and GPU.

For R users, the R interface to Keras (`https://keras.rstudio.com/`) was developed in 2017, and its adoption by the community has gradually grown. Let's first install the `keras` R package from GitHub as follows:

```
> if (!require("keras"))
+     devtools::install_github("rstudio/keras")
> library(keras)
```

This is not finished yet. We need to install the underlying backend(s) that Keras connects to. By default, it uses TensorFlow as the backend engine. We can use the following function to install the TensorFlow backend:

```
> install_keras()
Using existing virtualenv at  ~/.virtualenvs/r-tensorflow
Upgrading pip ...
......
Installation complete.
```

While we are waiting for the installation, let's learn a bit more about TensorFlow.

TensorFlow (`https://www.tensorflow.org/`) is an open source machine learning framework created by Google. It is well known for being used to design, build, and train deep learning models, but it can also be used for general numerical computation. In TensorFlow, computation is described using data flow graphs, where each node in a graph represents an instance of a mathematical operation and each edge represents a multidimensional data array (the so-called tensor, which can hold a matrix, vector, or scalar) on which the operations are performed. Such flexible architecture allows us to efficiently perform data-crunching machine learning operations, such as derivatives on huge matrices. Here is an example of a data flow graph:

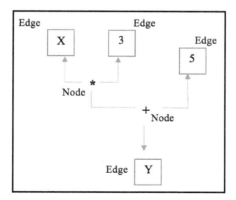

Now we see where its name TensorFlow is derived from: Tensors flowing in networks.

By now, the installation of the core Keras library as well as the TensorFlow backend is done. We continue our Keras-based solution for traffic signs classification.

First, prepare the input data for Keras modeling by reshaping the training and testing feature matrix:

```
> x_train <- data_train.x
> dim(x_train) <- c(nrow(data_train.x), 32, 32, 1)
> x_test <- data_test.x
> dim(x_test) <- c(nrow(data_test.x), 32, 32, 1)
```

Again, the input pixels are already of values ranging from 0 to 1, so we do not need to perform any rescaling.

We also convert training and testing target vectors (integers from 0 to 42) into a binary class matrix (one-hot encoded) as required by the Keras classification models:

```
> y_train <- to_categorical(data_train.y, num_classes = 43)
> y_test <- to_categorical(data_test.y, num_classes = 43)
```

Before we start modeling, there is a trick for obtaining reproducible results in Keras in R. It is specifying a random seed before development of a model using the following function:

```
> use_session_with_seed(42)
```

It takes all measures known to ensure reproducible results from Keras sessions.

Time to define the model after data preparation!

We begin by initializing the Keras sequential model as follows:

```
> model <- keras_model_sequential()
```

Then we add the first set of convolutional layers, the ReLu nonlinear layer and the pooling layer, with the same parameters used in the previous MXNet solution (same parameters are used for rest of the network):

```
> model %>%
```

Start with a hidden 2D convolutional layer being fed 32*32 pixel images:

```
+   layer_conv_2d(
+     filter = 32, kernel_size = c(5,5),
+     input_shape = c(32, 32, 1)
+   ) %>%
+   layer_activation("relu") %>%
+   layer_max_pooling_2d(pool_size = c(2,2)) %>%
```

Note that we use the pipe (%>%) operator to add layers to the Keras sequential model.

It follows with the second set of convolutional, ReLu nonlinear, and pooling layer:

```
+   # Second hidden convolutional layer layer
+   layer_conv_2d(filter = 64, kernel_size = c(5,5)) %>%
+   layer_activation("relu") %>%
+   layer_max_pooling_2d(pool_size = c(2,2)) %>%
```

Flatten the resulting feature maps from the previous convolution layers:

```
+   layer_flatten() %>%
```

And feed into a dense layer:

```
+   layer_dense(1000) %>%
+   layer_activation("relu") %>%
```

Finally, connect to a softmax layer containing 43 output units:

```
+   layer_dense(43) %>%
+   layer_activation("softmax")
```

We can use the `summary()` function to view the details of the model:

```
> summary(model)
```

Layer (type)	Output Shape	Param #
conv2d_1 (Conv2D)	(None, 28, 28, 32)	832
activation_1 (Activation)	(None, 28, 28, 32)	0
max_pooling2d_1 (MaxPooling2D)	(None, 14, 14, 32)	0
conv2d_2 (Conv2D)	(None, 10, 10, 64)	51264
activation_2 (Activation)	(None, 10, 10, 64)	0
max_pooling2d_2 (MaxPooling2D)	(None, 5, 5, 64)	0
flatten_1 (Flatten)	(None, 1600)	0
dense_1 (Dense)	(None, 1000)	1601000
activation_3 (Activation)	(None, 1000)	0
dense_2 (Dense)	(None, 43)	43043
activation_4 (Activation)	(None, 43)	0

```
Total params: 1,696,139
Trainable params: 1,696,139
Non-trainable params: 0
```

Depending on when the model is constructed, the names of the layers may have different suffixes (_1, _2 for example).

All the pieces of the CNN model are now assembled. Before compiling the model, we need to explicitly specify its optimizer. In MXNet, the optimizer is a parameter in the `mx.model.FeedForward.create` method with **stochastic gradient descent** (**SGD**) as the default value. In Keras, we use the same optimizer with the same learning rate and momentum:

```
> opt <- optimizer_sgd(lr = 0.005, momentum = 0.9)
```

Along with the optimizer we just defined, cross entropy as the loss function, and classification accuracy as the metric, we compile the CNN model:

```
> model %>% compile(
+     loss = "categorical_crossentropy",
+     optimizer = opt,
+     metrics = "accuracy"
+ )
```

We can now safely kick off our model training. Again, the same hyperparameters are used, including batch size and number of iterations. Note that the testing dataset is used for model validation, where the classification performance of the current CNN model is computed for each training iteration. Last but not least, shuffle is not necessary in our case as the training data is already shuffled after raw data splits:

```
> model %>% fit(
+     x_train, y_train,
+     batch_size = 100,
+     epochs = 30,
+     validation_data = list(x_test, y_test),
+     shuffle = FALSE
+ )
Train on 29409 samples, validate on 9800 samples
Epoch 1/30
29409/29409 [==============================] - 109s 4ms/step - loss: 2.8031
- acc: 0.2823 - val_loss: 1.1719 - val_acc: 0.6733
Epoch 2/30
29409/29409 [==============================] - 109s 4ms/step - loss: 0.6438
- acc: 0.8372 - val_loss: 0.4079 - val_acc: 0.8891
Epoch 3/30
29409/29409 [==============================] - 110s 4ms/step - loss: 0.3154
- acc: 0.9217 - val_loss: 0.2623 - val_acc: 0.9336
Epoch 4/30
29409/29409 [==============================] - 109s 4ms/step - loss: 0.1969
- acc: 0.9533 - val_loss: 0.2096 - val_acc: 0.9483
Epoch 5/30
29409/29409 [==============================] - 24703s 840ms/step - loss:
0.1410 - acc: 0.9682 - val_loss: 0.1715 - val_acc: 0.9604
Epoch 6/30
29409/29409 [==============================] - 1076s 37ms/step - loss:
0.1055 - acc: 0.9761 - val_loss: 0.1363 - val_acc: 0.9690
Epoch 7/30
29409/29409 [==============================] - 34344s 1s/step - loss:
0.0860 - acc: 0.9806 - val_loss: 0.1147 - val_acc: 0.9742
Epoch 8/30
29409/29409 [==============================] - 104s 4ms/step - loss: 0.0698
- acc: 0.9841 - val_loss: 0.1065 - val_acc: 0.9756
```

```
Epoch 9/30
29409/29409 [==============================] - 108s 4ms/step - loss: 0.0535
- acc: 0.9874 - val_loss: 0.1015 - val_acc: 0.9780
Epoch 10/30
29409/29409 [==============================] - 109s 4ms/step - loss: 0.0414
- acc: 0.9913 - val_loss: 0.0927 - val_acc: 0.9801
Epoch 11/30
29409/29409 [==============================] - 108s 4ms/step - loss: 0.0415
- acc: 0.9917 - val_loss: 0.0912 - val_acc: 0.9807
Epoch 12/30
29409/29409 [==============================] - 106s 4ms/step - loss: 0.0341
- acc: 0.9933 - val_loss: 0.1054 - val_acc: 0.9769
Epoch 13/30
29409/29409 [==============================] - 108s 4ms/step - loss: 0.0266
- acc: 0.9946 - val_loss: 0.0811 - val_acc: 0.9842
Epoch 14/30
29409/29409 [==============================] - 106s 4ms/step - loss: 0.0207
- acc: 0.9965 - val_loss: 0.0790 - val_acc: 0.9845
Epoch 15/30
29409/29409 [==============================] - 106s 4ms/step - loss: 0.0221
- acc: 0.9955 - val_loss: 0.0780 - val_acc: 0.9841
Epoch 16/30
29409/29409 [==============================] - 109s 4ms/step - loss: 0.0169
- acc: 0.9974 - val_loss: 0.0753 - val_acc: 0.9854
Epoch 17/30
29409/29409 [==============================] - 109s 4ms/step - loss: 0.0137
- acc: 0.9982 - val_loss: 0.0777 - val_acc: 0.9863
Epoch 18/30
29409/29409 [==============================] - 109s 4ms/step - loss: 0.0114
- acc: 0.9986 - val_loss: 0.0757 - val_acc: 0.9863
Epoch 19/30
29409/29409 [==============================] - 109s 4ms/step - loss: 0.0101
- acc: 0.9990 - val_loss: 0.0775 - val_acc: 0.9867
Epoch 20/30
29409/29409 [==============================] - 108s 4ms/step - loss: 0.0086
- acc: 0.9993 - val_loss: 0.0786 - val_acc: 0.9862
Epoch 21/30
29409/29409 [==============================] - 110s 4ms/step - loss: 0.0077
- acc: 0.9994 - val_loss: 0.0776 - val_acc: 0.9859
Epoch 22/30
29409/29409 [==============================] - 110s 4ms/step - loss: 0.0071
- acc: 0.9995 - val_loss: 0.0774 - val_acc: 0.9862
Epoch 23/30
29409/29409 [==============================] - 109s 4ms/step - loss: 0.0066
- acc: 0.9996 - val_loss: 0.0779 - val_acc: 0.9862
Epoch 24/30
29409/29409 [==============================] - 110s 4ms/step - loss: 0.0062
- acc: 0.9997 - val_loss: 0.0783 - val_acc: 0.9860
```

```
Epoch 25/30
29409/29409 [==============================] - 114s 4ms/step - loss: 0.0059
- acc: 0.9997 - val_loss: 0.0786 - val_acc: 0.9859
Epoch 26/30
29409/29409 [==============================] - 115s 4ms/step - loss: 0.0056
- acc: 0.9998 - val_loss: 0.0791 - val_acc: 0.9861
Epoch 27/30
29409/29409 [==============================] - 117s 4ms/step - loss: 0.0053
- acc: 0.9998 - val_loss: 0.0793 - val_acc: 0.9860
Epoch 28/30
29409/29409 [==============================] - 115s 4ms/step - loss: 0.0051
- acc: 0.9998 - val_loss: 0.0794 - val_acc: 0.9862
Epoch 29/30
29409/29409 [==============================] - 114s 4ms/step - loss: 0.0050
- acc: 0.9998 - val_loss: 0.0795 - val_acc: 0.9864
Epoch 30/30
29409/29409 [==============================] - 113s 4ms/step - loss: 0.0048
- acc: 0.9998 - val_loss: 0.0796 - val_acc: 0.9865
```

After 30 epochs, the model is well trained, with 98.65% accuracy achieved on the testing set. In the RStudio viewer pane, we can also see the classification performance for each epoch in real time:

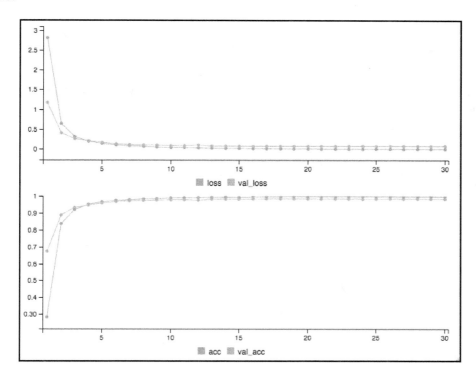

Reducing overfitting with dropout

You may notice that we had employed L2 regularization in the MXNet solution, which adds penalties for large weights in order to avoid overfitting; but we did not do so in this Keras solution. This results in a slight difference in classification accuracy on the testing set (99.30% versus 98.65%). We are going to employ regularization in our Keras solution, specifically **dropout** this time.

Dropout is a regularization technique in neural networks initially proposed by Geoffrey Hinton et. al. in 2012 (*Improving Neural Networks by Preventing Co-adaptation of Feature Detectors* in *Neural and Evolutionary Computing*). As the name implies, it ignores a small subset of neurons (can be hidden or visible) that are randomly selected in a neural network during training. The *dropped-out* neurons temporarily make no contribution to the activation of downstream neurons or the weight updates to neurons on backward pass. So how is the dropout technique able to prevent overfitting?

Recall that in a standard neural network, neurons are co-dependent among neighboring neurons during training. And weights of neurons are tuned for a particular context within the network, which restricts the individual power of each neuron. Such reliance on context may cause the model to be too specialized to training data. When some neurons in the network are not considered, the weights of neurons become less sensitive to those of other neurons. Neurons are forces to learn useful information more independently. Co-adaptation on training data is penalized.

Employing dropout is simple. During the training phase and in a layer with dropout rate p, for each iteration, we randomly switch off a fraction p of neurons. In the testing phase, we use all neurons but scale their activations by a factor of $q = 1 - p$, in order to account for the dropped-out activations in the training phase.

Here is a standard neural network (first image) and the same network with dropout (second image):

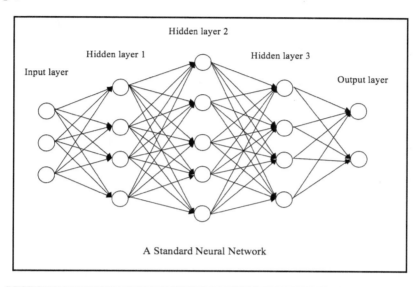

A Standard Neural Network

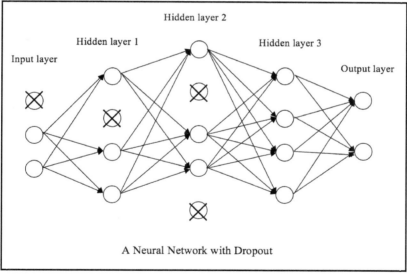

A Neural Network with Dropout

In this example, dropout is applied to a visible layer, the input layer, besides the hidden layers.

In practice, the dropout rate is usually set from 20% to 50%. A layer with a too low dropout rate makes little difference whereas a too high rate causes underfitting.

Now let's apply dropout to our Keras solution by using the function `layer_dropout(p)`. We define a function that initializes and compiles a CNN model with dropout (for reuse purposes):

```
> init_cnn_dropout <- function(){
+     model_dropout <- keras_model_sequential()
+     model_dropout %>%
+         layer_conv_2d(
+             filter = 32, kernel_size = c(5,5),
+             input_shape = c(32, 32, 1)
+         ) %>%
+         layer_activation("relu") %>%
+         layer_max_pooling_2d(pool_size = c(2,2)) %>%
+
+         # Second hidden convolutional layer layer
+         layer_conv_2d(filter = 64, kernel_size = c(5,5)) %>%
+         layer_activation("relu") %>%
+         # Use max pooling
+         layer_max_pooling_2d(pool_size = c(2,2)) %>%
+         layer_dropout(0.25) %>%
+
+         # Flatten and feed into dense layer
+         layer_flatten() %>%
+         layer_dense(1000) %>%
+         layer_activation("relu") %>%
+         layer_dropout(0.25) %>%
+
+         # Outputs from dense layer
+         layer_dense(43) %>%
+         layer_activation("softmax")
+
+     opt <- optimizer_sgd(lr = 0.005, momentum = 0.9)
+
+     model_dropout %>% compile(
+         loss = "categorical_crossentropy",
+         optimizer = opt,
+         metrics = "accuracy"
+     )
+     return(model_dropout)
+ }
```

Obtain a new model:

```
> model_dropout <- init_cnn_dropout()
```

We just employ 25% dropout in the second max pooling layer and 25% dropout in the fully connected hidden layer. By calling `summary(model_dropout)`, we can see two dropout layers right below the second MaxPooling2D layer and the first dense and activation layer respectively.

Continue with the model training:

```
> model_dropout %>% fit(
+    x_train, y_train,
+    batch_size = 100,
+    epochs = 30,
+    validation_data = list(x_test, y_test),
+    shuffle = FALSE
+ )
Train on 29409 samples, validate on 9800 samples
Epoch 1/30
29409/29409 [==============================] - 108s 4ms/step - loss: 3.1078
- acc: 0.1987 - val_loss: 1.4475 - val_acc: 0.6487
Epoch 2/30
29409/29409 [==============================] - 106s 4ms/step - loss: 0.9772
- acc: 0.7337 - val_loss: 0.4570 - val_acc: 0.8934
Epoch 3/30
29409/29409 [==============================] - 106s 4ms/step - loss: 0.5194
- acc: 0.8598 - val_loss: 0.3043 - val_acc: 0.9310
Epoch 4/30
29409/29409 [==============================] - 106s 4ms/step - loss: 0.3606
- acc: 0.9037 - val_loss: 0.2058 - val_acc: 0.9529
Epoch 5/30
29409/29409 [==============================] - 106s 4ms/step - loss: 0.2828
- acc: 0.9250 - val_loss: 0.1677 - val_acc: 0.9640
Epoch 6/30
29409/29409 [==============================] - 106s 4ms/step - loss: 0.2272
- acc: 0.9406 - val_loss: 0.1424 - val_acc: 0.9707
Epoch 7/30
29409/29409 [==============================] - 106s 4ms/step - loss: 0.1910
- acc: 0.9494 - val_loss: 0.1138 - val_acc: 0.9793
Epoch 8/30
29409/29409 [==============================] - 106s 4ms/step - loss: 0.1560
- acc: 0.9602 - val_loss: 0.0986 - val_acc: 0.9797
Epoch 9/30
29409/29409 [==============================] - 106s 4ms/step - loss: 0.1423
- acc: 0.9621 - val_loss: 0.0956 - val_acc: 0.9804
Epoch 10/30
29409/29409 [==============================] - 106s 4ms/step - loss: 0.1256
```

```
- acc: 0.9663 - val_loss: 0.0814 - val_acc: 0.9841
Epoch 11/30
29409/29409 [==============================] - 106s 4ms/step - loss: 0.1111
- acc: 0.9708 - val_loss: 0.0760 - val_acc: 0.9847
Epoch 12/30
29409/29409 [==============================] - 106s 4ms/step - loss: 0.0987
- acc: 0.9735 - val_loss: 0.0795 - val_acc: 0.9824
Epoch 13/30
29409/29409 [==============================] - 106s 4ms/step - loss: 0.0899
- acc: 0.9752 - val_loss: 0.0626 - val_acc: 0.9876
Epoch 14/30
29409/29409 [==============================] - 106s 4ms/step - loss: 0.0799
- acc: 0.9787 - val_loss: 0.0665 - val_acc: 0.9868
Epoch 15/30
29409/29409 [==============================] - 106s 4ms/step - loss: 0.0794
- acc: 0.9792 - val_loss: 0.0571 - val_acc: 0.9887
Epoch 16/30
29409/29409 [==============================] - 106s 4ms/step - loss: 0.0691
- acc: 0.9817 - val_loss: 0.0534 - val_acc: 0.9898
Epoch 17/30
29409/29409 [==============================] - 106s 4ms/step - loss: 0.0668
- acc: 0.9817 - val_loss: 0.0560 - val_acc: 0.9892
Epoch 18/30
29409/29409 [==============================] - 106s 4ms/step - loss: 0.0583
- acc: 0.9846 - val_loss: 0.0486 - val_acc: 0.9916
Epoch 19/30
29409/29409 [==============================] - 106s 4ms/step - loss: 0.0541
- acc: 0.9861 - val_loss: 0.0484 - val_acc: 0.9914
Epoch 20/30
29409/29409 [==============================] - 106s 4ms/step - loss: 0.0529
- acc: 0.9858 - val_loss: 0.0494 - val_acc: 0.9906
Epoch 21/30
29409/29409 [==============================] - 106s 4ms/step - loss: 0.0500
- acc: 0.9864 - val_loss: 0.0449 - val_acc: 0.9909
Epoch 22/30
29409/29409 [==============================] - 106s 4ms/step - loss: 0.0469
- acc: 0.9872 - val_loss: 0.0414 - val_acc: 0.9926
Epoch 23/30
29409/29409 [==============================] - 106s 4ms/step - loss: 0.0473
- acc: 0.9863 - val_loss: 0.0415 - val_acc: 0.9917
Epoch 24/30
29409/29409 [==============================] - 107s 4ms/step - loss: 0.0406
- acc: 0.9894 - val_loss: 0.0416 - val_acc: 0.9916
Epoch 25/30
29409/29409 [==============================] - 108s 4ms/step - loss: 0.0413
- acc: 0.9888 - val_loss: 0.0445 - val_acc: 0.9909
Epoch 26/30
29409/29409 [==============================] - 108s 4ms/step - loss: 0.0337
```

```
- acc: 0.9906 - val_loss: 0.0412 - val_acc: 0.9922
Epoch 27/30
29409/29409 [==============================] - 108s 4ms/step - loss: 0.0333
- acc: 0.9911 - val_loss: 0.0388 - val_acc: 0.9928
Epoch 28/30
29409/29409 [==============================] - 108s 4ms/step - loss: 0.0332
- acc: 0.9905 - val_loss: 0.0395 - val_acc: 0.9933
Epoch 29/30
29409/29409 [==============================] - 108s 4ms/step - loss: 0.0312
- acc: 0.9910 - val_loss: 0.0371 - val_acc: 0.9937
Epoch 30/30
29409/29409 [==============================] - 108s 4ms/step - loss: 0.0305
- acc: 0.9917 - val_loss: 0.0383 - val_acc: 0.9940
```

With dropout, the prediction accuracy on the testing set is increased to 99.40%.

Dealing with a small training set – data augmentation

We have been very fortunate so far to possess a large-enough training dataset with 75% of 39,209 samples. This is one of the reasons why we are able to achieve a 99.3% to 99.4% classification accuracy. However, in reality, obtaining a large training set is not easy in most supervised learning cases, where manual work is necessary or the cost of data collection and labeling is high. In our traffic signs classification project, can we still achieve the same performance if we are given a lot less training samples to begin with? Let's give it a shot.

We simulate a small training set with only 10% of the 39,209 samples and a testing set with the rest 90%:

```
> train_perc_1 = 0.1
> train_index_1 <- createDataPartition(data.y, p=train_perc_1, list=FALSE)
> train_index_1 <- train_index_1[sample(nrow(train_index_1)),]
> data_train_1.x <- data.x[train_index_1,]
> data_train_1.y <- data.y[train_index_1]
> data_test_1.x <- data.x[-train_index_1,]
> data_test_1.y <- data.y[-train_index_1]
> x_train_1 <- data_train_1.x
> dim(x_train_1) <- c(nrow(data_train_1.x), 32, 32, 1)
> x_test_1 <- data_test_1.x
> dim(x_test_1) <- c(nrow(data_test_1.x), 32, 32, 1)
> y_train_1 <- to_categorical(data_train_1.y, num_classes = 43)
> y_test_1 <- to_categorical(data_test_1.y, num_classes = 43)
```

Initialize a new model and fit it with the new training set:

```
> model_1 <- init_cnn_dropout()
> model_1 %>% fit(
+    x_train_1, y_train_1,
+    batch_size = 100,
+    epochs = 1,
+    validation_data = list(x_test_1, y_test_1),
+    shuffle = FALSE
+ )
```

Train on 3,921 samples; validate on 35,288 samples:

```
Epoch 1/30
3921/3921 [==============================] - 19s 5ms/step - loss: 3.6705 -
acc: 0.0594 - val_loss: 3.5191 - val_acc: 0.0592
Epoch 2/30
3921/3921 [==============================] - 17s 4ms/step - loss: 3.5079 -
acc: 0.0681 - val_loss: 3.4663 - val_acc: 0.0529
......
......
Epoch 29/30
3921/3921 [==============================] - 17s 4ms/step - loss: 0.1935 -
acc: 0.9462 - val_loss: 0.2760 - val_acc: 0.9381
Epoch 30/30
3921/3921 [==============================] - 17s 4ms/step - loss: 0.1962 -
acc: 0.9431 - val_loss: 0.2772 - val_acc: 0.9393
```

It is not bad to achieve 93.93% accuracy by a model trained with only 3,921 samples. But can we do better, at least close to 99% as we accomplished with sufficient training data? Yes! One solution is data augmentation.

Data augmentation simply means expanding the size of the existing data that we feed to the supervised learning models in order to compensate for the cost of further data collection and labeling.

There are many ways to augment data in computer vision. The simplest one is probably flipping an image horizontally or vertically. Take the General caution sign as an example; we implement flipping using the function flow_images_from_data() in Keras as follows.

Load the General caution sample:

```
> img<-image_load(paste(training_path, "00018/00001_00004.ppm", sep=""))
> img1<-image_to_array(img)
> dim(img1)<-c(1,dim(img1))
```

We generate a horizontally flipped image and save the resulting image in the `augmented` directory we created:

```
> images_iter  <- flow_images_from_data(img1, , generator =
                   image_data_generator(horizontal_flip = TRUE),
+                  save_to_dir = 'augmented',
+                  save_prefix = "horizontal", save_format = "png")
> reticulate::iter_next(images_iter)
```

The flipped sign (right) along with the original image (left) is displayed as follows:

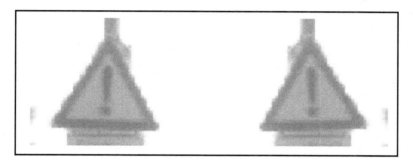

The horizontally flipped sign image conveys the same message as the original one. It should be noted that flipping works only in orientation-insensitive cases, such as a classification between cats and dogs, or our recognition of traffic lights. However, in cases where orientation matters, such as a classification between right turn and left turn, a small to medium degree rotation can still be applied. For instance, flipping the *Dangerous curve to the right* sign is absolutely dangerous, but rotating it by at most 20 degrees is harmless and even helpful, as we can see in the following example:

```
> img<-image_load(paste(training_path, "00020/00002_00017.ppm", sep=""))
> img1<-image_to_array(img)
> dim(img1)<-c(1,dim(img1))
> images_iter  <- flow_images_from_data(img1, , generator =
                   image_data_generator(rotation_range = 20),
+                  save_to_dir = 'augmented',
+                  save_prefix = "rotation", save_format = "png")
> reticulate::iter_next(images_iter)
```

The rotated sign (right) and the original image (left) contain identical information:

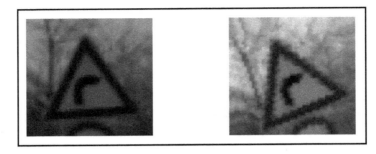

Shifting is perhaps the most common augmentation method. Moving the image horizontally and/or vertically by a small number of pixels generates an identically functioning image. Using the same example as before, we shift it horizontally and vertically by at most 20% of the width and height:

```
> images_iter   <- flow_images_from_data(img1,
                generator=image_data_generator(width_shift_range=0.2,
                height_shift_range=0.2), save_to_dir = 'augmented',
+               save_prefix = "shift", save_format = "png")
> reticulate::iter_next(images_iter)
```

This results in a shifted image in the right half here:

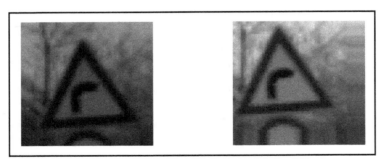

Armed with common augmentation approaches, let's augment our small training dataset by at most 20 degrees' rotation and at most 20% shifting (note that we cannot apply flipping as some signs, such as class 19, 20, 21, 33, and 34, are not semantically symmetric):

```
> datagen <- image_data_generator(
+    rotation_range = 20,
+    width_shift_range = 0.2,
+    height_shift_range = 0.2,
+    horizontal_flip = FALSE
+ )
>
> datagen %>% fit_image_data_generator(x_train_1)
Augmented data generator is defined and now being applied to a CNN model
with function fit_generator:
> model_2 <- init_cnn_dropout()
> model_2 %>% fit_generator(
+    flow_images_from_data(x_train_1, y_train_1,
                           datagen, batch_size = 100),
+    steps_per_epoch = as.integer(50000/100),
+    epochs = 30,
+    validation_data = list(x_test_1, y_test_1)
+ )
Epoch 1/30
500/500 [==============================] - 74s 149ms/step - loss: 3.4566 -
acc: 0.0798 - val_loss: 3.2963 - val_acc: 0.1322
Epoch 2/30
500/500 [==============================] - 77s 153ms/step - loss: 3.0920 -
acc: 0.1666 - val_loss: 2.1010 - val_acc: 0.4249
......
......
Epoch 25/30
500/500 [==============================] - 83s 166ms/step - loss: 0.1396 -
acc: 0.9584 - val_loss: 0.0636 - val_acc: 0.9860
Epoch 26/30
500/500 [==============================] - 79s 158ms/step - loss: 0.1359 -
acc: 0.9592 - val_loss: 0.0672 - val_acc: 0.9859
Epoch 27/30
500/500 [==============================] - 80s 160ms/step - loss: 0.1344 -
acc: 0.9600 - val_loss: 0.0727 - val_acc: 0.9843
Epoch 28/30
500/500 [==============================] - 81s 163ms/step - loss: 0.1227 -
acc: 0.9628 - val_loss: 0.0647 - val_acc: 0.9862
Epoch 29/30
500/500 [==============================] - 79s 158ms/step - loss:
```

```
0.1222 - acc: 0.9627 - val_loss: 0.0668 - val_acc: 0.9858
Epoch 30/30
500/500 [==============================] - 80s 160ms/step - loss: 0.1220 -
acc: 0.9636 - val_loss: 0.0614 - val_acc: 0.9870
```

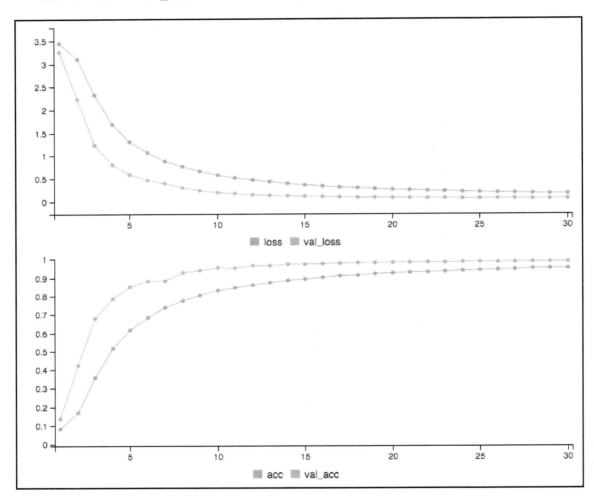

With data augmentation, we can get excellent results of 98.70% accuracy with a small training set.

Besides the 4.77% (93.93% to 98.70%) performance increase compared to no data augmentation, we observe that each iteration takes a longer time than before (around 20 s to around 80 s). This is because `image_data_generator()` generates mini-batches of augmented image data in real time for each iteration. So, even if the same set of samples is used in two iterations, the augmented data can be very different. Such setting adds more variation to the training set, which in turn makes the model more robust. And that is why data augmentation is considered an approach to reduce overfitting.

Another particularly useful application of data augmentation is balancing a dataset. In most unbalanced classification cases (such as online ads click-through prediction, or banking fraud detection), we usually down-sample the dominant class. However, this can be counterproductive for small datasets. The alternative solution is to augment data from the minor class.

Last but not least, there are other approaches not mentioned previously to augment image data. For example, rescaling multiplies pixel values by a factor and, as a result, changes the lighting condition. Shearing and zooming are useful data augmentation transformations as well. They can be specified in `image_data_generator()`. If interested, you can try applying any of these approaches and see whether you can beat 98.70%.

Reviewing methods to prevent overfitting in CNNs

Overfitting occurs when the model fits too well to the training set but is not able to generalize to unseen cases. For example, a CNN model recognizes specific traffic sign images in the training set instead of general patterns. It can be very dangerous if a self-driving car is not able to recognize sign images in ever-changing conditions, such as different weather, lighting, and angles different from what are presented in the training set. To recap, here's what we can do to reduce overfitting:

- Collecting more training data (if possible and feasible) in order to account for various input data.
- Using data augmentation, wherein we *invent* data in a smart way if time or cost does not allow us to collect more data.
- Employing dropout, which diminishes complex co-adaptations among neighboring neurons.

- Adding Lasso (L1) or/and Ridge (L2) penalty, which prevents model coefficients from fitting so perfectly that overfitting arises.
- Reducing the complexity of network architecture. Recall that in the last chapter, we mentioned that adding hidden layers will not help boost the model performance but increase chances of overfitting.

Summary

We just accomplished our second computer vision project in this R and deep learning journey! Through this chapter, we got more familiar with convolutional neural networks and their implementation in MXNet, and another powerful deep learning tool: Keras with TensorFlow.

We started with what self-driving cars are and how deep learning techniques are making self-driving cars feasible and more reliable. We also discussed how deep learning stands out and becomes the state-of-the-art solution for object recognition in intelligent vehicles. After exploring the traffic sign dataset, we developed our first CNN model using MXNet and achieved more than 99% accuracy. Then we moved on to another powerful deep learning framework, Keras + TensorFlow, and obtained comparable results.

We introduced the dropout technique to reduce overfitting. We also learned how to deal with lack of training data and utilize data augmentation techniques, including flipping, shifting, and rotation. We finally wrapped up the chapter by summarizing some approaches to prevent overfitting in CNN models. That was the second example where we observed how deep learning removes manual or explicit feature extraction steps taken in traditional approaches, and instead efficiently finds the best sets of features.

We have practiced CNNs in these two computer vision projects. In the next project, we will be working with totally different types of deep neural networks—autoencoders.

14
Fraud Detection with Autoencoders

In this chapter, we continue our journey into deep learning with R with **autoencoders**.

A classical autoencoder consists of three parts:

- **An encoding function**, which compresses your data
- **A decoding function**, which reconstructs data from a compressed version
- **A metric or distance**, which calculates the difference between the information lost by compression on your data

We typically assume that all these involved functions are smooth enough to be able to use backpropagation or other gradient-based methods, although they need not be and we could use derivative-free methods to train them.

 Autoencoding is the process of summarizing information from a potentially large feature set into a smaller feature set.

Although the compression bit might remind you of algorithms, such as the MP3 compression algorithm, an important difference is that autoencoders are data specific. An autoencoder trained in pictures of cats and dogs will likely perform poorly in pictures of buildings. In contrast, the MP3 compression algorithm uses assumptions of sound in general and can work regardless of the sound data. The data-specific bit is a serious caveat for widespread application which makes autoencoders rarely used for compression tasks.

One reason autoencoders have attracted so much attention in recent years is because many people believe that they might be the key for **unsupervised learning,** although strictly speaking, they are a **self-supervised** learning algorithm.

Sometimes the features abstracted from autoencoders can be fed into supervised learning algorithms, making them somewhat comparable to **principal component analysis (PCA)** as a dimensionality reduction technique.

Autoencoders are typically used in computer vision problems such as image denoising or for picking up features such as colors, light and edges. They are also used for data visualization of large dimensional datasets, as they can find more interesting features than PCA. Other recent applications include fraud and intrusion detection.

For our purposes, an autoencoder neural network is simply an algorithm for unsupervised learning that applies backpropagation by setting the target values equal to the inputs, if $x_1, x_2, \ldots x_m$ are the training examples and $y_1, y_2, \ldots y_m$ are the labels, then we will do backpropagation by setting $x_i = y_i$ for all values of i.

From your previous experience with machine learning, you might be familiar with PCA. Don't worry if you are not familiar with it, this is not strictly required for our purposes. PCA is a **dimensionality reduction** technique, which means, given a set of training examples, a suitable transformation is applied (for math geeks, this is just a projection into the vector space generated by the eigenvectors of the covariance matrix). The goal of this projection is to find the most relevant features of the input data, so that in the end we get a simplified representation of it.

Autoencoders work in a similar vein, except that the transformation involved is not a projection, but rather a non-linear function f. Given a training example x, an autoencoder encodes x using a neural network into a hidden state $h:=f(x)$, and decodes h using a function g, which brings an overall transformation of $x => g(f(x))$. If the result of this process would be simply $g(f(x))=x$, we would not have a very useful transformation. The idea is illustrated in the following diagram:

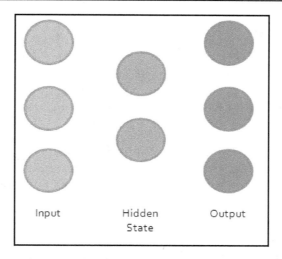

A simple autoencoder in action: Encoding a three-dimensional vector into a two-dimensional hidden state, and then back to a three-dimensional space.

On the left part, a three-dimensional input vector is transformed into a two-dimensional encoded state (this is the action of f) and then transformed back into a three-dimensional vector (by the action of g).

Why do we take the trouble of encoding and decoding? This has two purposes. On one hand, autoencoders provide, as PCA, a way to automatically generate features in a lower dimensional space. This is useful as part of a machine learning pipeline for **feature extraction**, in the same way PCA is also useful. Synthesizing the data and automatically generating features (instead of relying on domain expertise and feature handcrafting) to improve the accuracy of a supervised learning algorithm, be it for classification or regression tasks. For our purposes, it is also useful for outlier detection. As the computer is forced to understand the essential features of the data, anything that jumps out as odd will be thrown away during the reconstruction process (that is, the full encoding–decoding cycle), and the outliers will be easily identifiable.

Before jumping into the fraud example for this chapter, let's get our feet wet looking at a simpler example, and at the same time getting our tools ready.

Getting ready

In this chapter, we will introduce `keras` and `tensorflow` for R. `keras` is a model-level building, in that it provides a high-level interface to quickly develop deep learning models. Instead of implementing low-level operations such as convolutions and tensor products, it relies on Theano, TensorFlow or CNTK in the backend, and according to the development team, more backends would be supported in the future.

Why do you need a backend? Well, if the computation becomes more complicated, which is often the case in deep learning, you need to use different computation methods (known as computation graphs) and hardware (GPUs). For instructional purposes, all our sample codes run without GPU.

Installing Keras and TensorFlow for R

As per the official documentation, you can install Keras simply with:

```
devtools::install_github("rstudio/keras")
```

The Keras R interface uses `tensorflow` as a backend engine by default. To install both the core `keras` library and `tensorflow`, then do:

```
library(keras)
install_keras()
```

However smooth this might seem, we have seen this setup fail a number of times. Our recommended plan B is:

- Download and install the Anaconda distribution for Python. This is the standard data science stack, with the most popular Python libraries for data scientists.
- Install your Keras backend, for instance, Tensorflow.
- Install Keras (within Python).

After this, you should be ready to install Keras in R.

To be sure that you are working with the most recent version of R, you can update it from R GUI (not from RStudio) using the `installr` package:

```
### Run these from RGUi
install.packages("installr")
installr::updateR()
```

Once you are done, you can install `keras` with `devtools`:

```
install.packages("devtools")
devtools::install_github("rstudio/keras")
```

Finally, check that everything is correct by importing the library:

```
library(keras)
```

The preceding instructions worked well for a laptop with Windows 10, running R version 3.4. If you have an older version and you do not want to update, you need to install the dependencies specified as follows (I tried this with R version 3.3):

```
install.packages("Rcpp")
install.packages("devtools")
devtools::install_github("rstudio/reticulate", force=TRUE)
devtools::install_github("r-lib/debugme")
devtools::install_github("r-lib/processx")
devtools::install_github("tidyverse/rlang")
devtools::install_github("tidyverse/glue")
devtools::install_github("tidyverse/tidyselect")
devtools::install_github("rstudio/tfruns")
devtools::install_github("rstudio/tensorflow")
devtools::install_github("rstudio/keras")
devtools::install_github("jeroen/jsonlite")
```

Installing H2O

We will also show you how to use H2O for some of the exercises. The easiest way to install H2O is to get it from CRAN.

It has a few dependencies, notably the packages:

- `RCurl`
- `bitops`
- `rjson`
- `statmod`
- `tools`

If you run into trouble, chances are that there is some dependency missing. Re-read the error message and install any missing packages.

If it all goes smoothly, import the library and initialize the service to check that everything works:

```
install.packages("h2o")
library(h2o)
h2o.init()
```

Our first examples

Let's begin with a few simple examples to understand what is going on.

For some of us, it's very easy to get tempted to try the shiniest algorithms and do hyper-parameter optimization instead of the less glamorous step-by-step understanding.

A simple 2D example

Let's develop our intuition of how the autoencoder works with a simple two-dimensional example.

We first generate 10,000 points coming from a normal distribution with mean 0 and variance 1:

```
library(MASS)
library(keras)
Sigma <- matrix(c(1,0,0,1),2,2)
n_points <- 10000
df <- mvrnorm(n=n_points, rep(0,2), Sigma)
df <- as.data.frame(df)
```

The distribution of the values should look as follows:

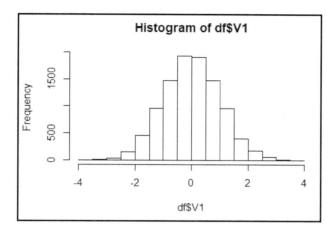

Distribution of the variable V1 we just generated; the variable V2 looks fairly similar.

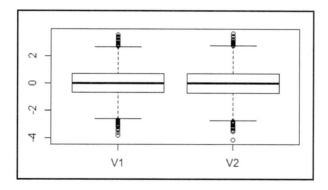

Distribution of the variables V1 and V2 we generated.

Let's spice things up a bit and add some outliers to the mixture. In many fraud applications, the fraud rate is about 1–5%, so we generate 1% of our samples as coming from a normal distribution, with mean 5 and standard deviation 1:

```
# Set the outliers
n_outliers <- as.integer(0.01*n_points)
idxs <- sample(n_points, size = n_outliers)
outliers <- mvrnorm(n=n_outliers, rep(5,2), Sigma)
df[idxs,] <- outliers
```

The new distribution of points looks like this now:

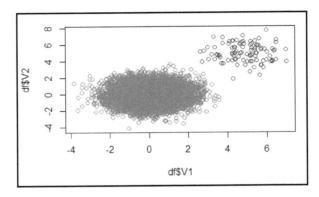

New distribution of points after adding the outliers.

We will use an autoencoder with a single neural network in the hidden layer. Why not add more? The problem is that if the hidden state has equal or higher dimensions than the input state, we risk that our model might learn the identity function, that is, that the model learns $g(f(x))=x$ everywhere. This is clearly not a very useful outlier identification method. We need to capture the essential features of the data, so that those unusual features would be highlighted later on, hence allowing to detect outliers.

With `keras`, it is really easy to set up the model, we need an input layer of shape 2, for our two-dimensional example. This is passed to our one-dimensional encoder, using a ReLU activation function and then decoded back into a two-dimensional space:

```
input_layer <- layer_input(shape=c(2))
 encoder <- layer_dense(units=1, activation='relu')(input_layer)
 decoder <- layer_dense(units=2)(encoder)
 autoencoder <- keras_model(inputs=input_layer, outputs = decoder)
```

Before using the model, we need to compile it. We need to specify a loss functional, a metric to optimize and an algorithm to perform the gradient descent updates. We will go for the Adam solver, optimizing the classical mean squared error (that works in this problem, but we might need to change it for our particular application) and choose accuracy as the metric to optimize:

```
autoencoder %>% compile(optimizer='adam',
loss='mean_squared_error',
metrics=c('accuracy'))
```

Once this is set up, we are ready for training:

```
# Coerce the dataframe to matrix to perform the training
df <- as.matrix(df)
history <- autoencoder %>% fit(
df,df,
epochs = 30, batch_size = 128,
validation_split = 0.2
)
```

Using the command, `plot(history)`, we can see how the training went for this example:

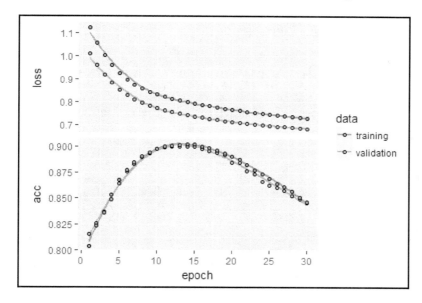

Training of our autoencoder.

So we see that, while the accuracy remains fairly high, there is a mysterious drop during the training. We should not worry too much about it for now, we will come to this issue later. As for the loss, it keeps decreasing as we add more data, which is expected.

Finally, Let's look at the reconstruction. We first generate the predictions from our trained autoencoder:

```
preds <- autoencoder %>% predict(df)
colnames(preds) <- c("V1", "V2")
preds <- as.data.frame(preds)
```

This is the reconstruction of the points, as per our autoencoder. We will color red those points whose reconstruction is at a (Euclidean) distance larger than three from the original images, and leave the others blue. Why those points? Our autoencoder learned that our dataset had some intrinsic properties (it learned the distribution of the average point), so in those points where the reconstruction error is anomalously large, there might be something worth looking at:

```
# Coerce back the matrix to data frame to use ggplot later
df <- as.data.frame(df)
# Euclidean distance larger than 3 = sum of squares larger than 9
df$color <- ifelse((df$V1-preds$V1)**2+(df$V2-preds$V2)**2>9,"red","blue")
```

Finally, we can look at the results with `ggplot`:

```
library(ggplot2)
  df %>% ggplot(aes(V1,V2),col=df$color)+geom_point(color = df$color,
position="jitter")
```

The following screenshot shows how well we did identifying unusual points:

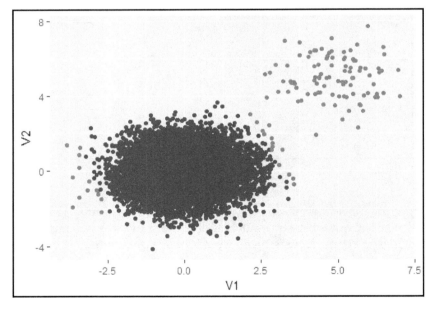

Output of the autoencoder. In blue, the reconstructed points by our autoencoder. In red, the original points in the dataset. We see that there is a cloud of red points that thanks to our autoencoder we can identify as unusual.

In the preceding screenshot, the blue points are the reconstructed images from the autoencoder. We see that it learned correctly that most of the points come from a normal distribution centered at *(0,0)*, as expected. However there are still some points which are *normal* on the original dataset and where pointed out as unusual. No need to get discouraged from learning autoencoders that soon, the reason for this is that the autoencoder we used is rather simple. We will look at more sophisticated ways to tackle the outlier detection problem with autoencoders.

Autoencoders and MNIST

Many examples of deep learning algorithms in either research papers, blog posts or books deal with the MNIST dataset. We should not be the exception and introduce a small use case for autoencoders using MNIST.

The motivation is the following, suppose you want to detect fake banknotes automatically. Then you would need to teach the computer what the representation of the *average banknote* is to be able to detect those that have significant differences. Due to the large volume of cash transactions happening every day worldwide, and to the increasing sophistication of fraudsters, it would be unthinkable to do this process manually. One way to do this is to use sophisticated imaging software, which is how counterfeit banknote detectors, such as D40 or D50, work.

Another reason for using MNIST is obviously practical. At the time of writing I was unable to find a nice training dataset with counterfeit banknotes, and MNIST comes already preinstalled in `keras`.

We start with loading the dataset:

```
library(keras)
mnist <- dataset_mnist()
X_train <- mnist$train$x
y_train <- mnist$train$y
X_test <- mnist$test$x
y_test <- mnist$test$y
```

Let's take a closer look at the dataset:

```
image(X_train[1,,], col=gray.colors(3))
y_train[1]
```

If everything works correctly, you should see the image of the number five.

We need to do a bit of preprocessing before training our autoencoder. The X_train data is a three-dimensional array (images, width, height) of grayscale values. We need to first convert these arrays into matrices by reshaping the height and width into a single vector, so that instead of dealing with 28 x 28 squares we have a *28*28=784* vector. Then, we convert the grayscale values from integers ranging between 0 to 255 into floating point values, ranging between 0 and 1:

```
# reshape
dim(X_train) <- c(nrow(X_train), 784)
dim(X_test) <- c(nrow(X_test), 784)
# rescale
X_train <- X_train / 255
X_test <- X_test / 255
```

Once the initial preprocessing is done, we define the topology of our autoencoder. Let's use an encoding layer with 32 neurons, to achieve a compression ratio of *784/32 = 24.5:*

```
input_dim <- 28*28 #784
inner_layer_dim <- 32
input_layer <- layer_input(shape=c(input_dim))
encoder <- layer_dense(units=inner_layer_dim,
activation='relu')(input_layer)
decoder <- layer_dense(units=784)(encoder)
autoencoder <- keras_model(inputs=input_layer, outputs = decoder)
```

We are ready to compile and train the model:

```
autoencoder %>% compile(optimizer='adam',
 loss='mean_squared_error',
 metrics=c('accuracy'))
history <- autoencoder %>% fit(
 X_train,X_train,
 epochs = 50, batch_size = 256,
 validation_split=0.2
)
```

Using the `plot` command, we can see the performance of our model during the training and validation as follows:

```
plot(history)
```

Even better, if you are using RStudio as your IDE, there is a real-time view in the **Viewer** panel. With this command you should see two plots, showing the accuracy and loss as a function of the epoch number:

Use the **Viewer** panel to see the training in real time. Click on the **Open in New Window** button:

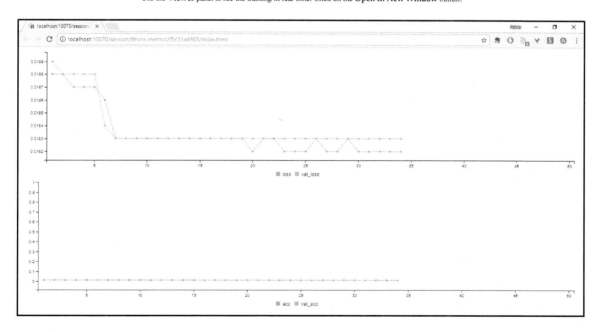

Real time training. On the horizontal axis, the epoch number. Loss and accuracy are shown in the vertical axes.

Using the `predict` method, we reconstruct the digits and compute the reconstruction errors:

```
# Reconstruct on the test set
preds <- autoencoder %>% predict(X_test)
error <- rowSums((preds-X_test)**2)
error
```

Intuitively, some classes might be harder to predict, because some people write numbers in slightly different ways. Which classes have a higher reconstruction error?

```
# Which were more problematic to reconstruct?
eval <- data.frame(error=error, class=as.factor(y_test))
library(dplyr)
eval %>% group_by(class) %>% summarise(avg_error=mean(error))

## OUTPUT
# A tibble: 10 x 2
  class avg_error
  <fctr> <dbl>
  1 0 14.091963
  2 1 6.126858
  3 2 17.245944
  4 3 14.138960
  5 4 13.189842
  6 5 15.170581
  7 6 14.570642
  8 7 11.778826
  9 8 16.120203
 10 9 11.645038
```

Note that, some small variations are expected, since there is, for instance, a random component involved in the shuffling of the data. However, the general trends should be similar.

An image says more than a thousand words, so even better than summarizing our data with `dplyr`, we can use `ggplot2` to visualize this information:

```
library(ggplot2)
eval %>%
  group_by(class) %>%
  summarise(avg_error=mean(error)) %>%
  ggplot(aes(x=class,fill=class,y=avg_error))+geom_col()
```

We can see, as follows, how our reconstruction error performed per class. This is important as it will let's know if our classifier is biased in some way, or if it finds some classes harder to train than others:

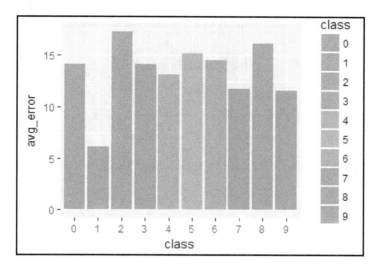

Reconstruction error in the MNIST dataset. 2 and 8 seem to be the most problematic classes, and 1 seems the most straight forward to recognize.

Well, that is certainly useful and interesting to see, we see that **2** is somewhat harder to reconstruct, which might be due to the fact that it looks like a **7** sometimes. Intuitively, **8** could be easily confused with **9** or with **0**, so the results somehow make sense.

An even better way to look at how our reconstruction autoencoder is performing, is to look directly at the reconstructed examples. For this, we need first to reshape back our original data and the reconstruction:

```
# Reshape original and reconstructed
dim(X_test) <- c(nrow(X_test),28,28)
dim(preds) <- c(nrow(preds),28,28)
```

And now let's look at the reconstructed image:

```
image(255*preds[1,,], col=gray.colors(3))
```

Let's look at the reconstructed image of a typical element of the test set:

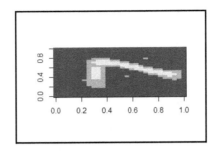

Reconstructed image by our autoencoder.

How does it compare to the original image, before reconstruction? Let's take a look:

```
y_test[1]
  image(255*X_test[1,,], col=gray.colors(3))
```

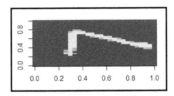

Original image.

Overall, not bad for a 24.5 compression! Clearly there is a lot to be improved, but we can already see the potential of autoencoders to learn intrinsic features of the data.

Outlier detection in MNIST

All right, so admittedly our previous application has nothing to do with fraud or outlier detection so far. We can do a small modification on the previous setup to show how a similar framework works. For this, let's assume that the number 7 is an outlier class and we will try to identify it from the result of our *normal* numbers: 0, 1, 2 , 3, 4, 5, 6, 8, 9.

We will train the autoencoder on the *normal* dataset and then apply it to the test set. The aim will be to abstract as many features of the *normal* situation as possible. This requires knowledge of the *normal* situation, which translates into availability of labelled data and hence, it is an ideal scenario, for many practical applications, for instance credit card fraud or intrusion detection, we sometimes (or rather often) lack such labeled data.

We begin as before:

```
library(keras)
mnist <- dataset_mnist()
X_train <- mnist$train$x
y_train <- mnist$train$y
X_test <- mnist$test$x
y_test <- mnist$test$y
```

But now we will exclude 7 from the training set, as it will be the outlier in our example.

```
## Exclude "7" from the training set. "7" will be the outlier
outlier_idxs <- which(y_train!=7, arr.ind = T)
X_train <- X_train[outlier_idxs,,]
y_test <- sapply(y_test, function(x){ ifelse(x==7,"outlier","normal")})
```

We continue as before, with re-scaling and reshaping before defining our autoencoder:

```
# reshape
dim(X_train) <- c(nrow(X_train), 784)
dim(X_test) <- c(nrow(X_test), 784)
# rescale
X_train <- X_train / 255
X_test <- X_test / 255
input_dim <- 28*28 #784
inner_layer_dim <- 32
# Create the autoencoder
input_layer <- layer_input(shape=c(input_dim))
encoder <- layer_dense(units=inner_layer_dim,
activation='relu')(input_layer)
decoder <- layer_dense(units=784)(encoder)
autoencoder <- keras_model(inputs=input_layer, outputs = decoder)
autoencoder %>% compile(optimizer='adam',
                        loss='mean_squared_error',
                        metrics=c('accuracy'))
history <- autoencoder %>% fit(
 X_train,X_train,
 epochs = 50, batch_size = 256,
 validation_split=0.2
)
plot(history)
```

Once the autoencoder is trained, we can start looking at the performance, using the reconstruction of the test set:

```
# Reconstruct on the test set
preds <- autoencoder %>% predict(X_test)
error <- rowSums((preds-X_test)**2)
eval <- data.frame(error=error, class=as.factor(y_test))
library(ggplot2)
library(dplyr)
eval %>%
  group_by(class) %>%
  summarise(avg_error=mean(error)) %>%
  ggplot(aes(x=class,fill=class,y=avg_error))+geom_boxplot()
```

Let's look at the reconstruction error in our different classes:

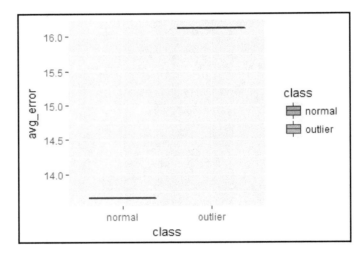

Distribution of reconstruction error in the test set

From the plot, we see that we can set up the threshold value at 15, that is, observations with a reconstruction error above 15 would be marked as outliers:

```
threshold <- 15
y_preds <- sapply(error, function(x)
ifelse(x>threshold, "outlier", "normal")})
```

Once this is done, we can calculate the confusion matrix. This is a useful way of visualizing what the model is doing:

```
# Confusion matrix
table(y_preds,y_test)
```

This gives us the following:

```
         y_test
y_preds   normal  outlier
  normal    5707      496
  outlier   3265      532
```

So clearly we could do better. Perhaps the vertical stroke shared by digits 1 and 7 contributes to the huge error rate. We caught, however, a bit over 50% of the outlier cases with this simple architecture. One way to improve this would be to add more hidden layers. We will use this trick later in this chapter.

Credit card fraud detection with autoencoders

Fraud is a multi-billion dollar industry, with credit card fraud being probably the closest to our daily lives. Fraud begins with the theft of the physical credit card or with data that could compromise the security of the account, such as the credit card number, expiration date and security codes. A stolen card can be reported directly, if the victim knows that their card has been stolen, however, when the data is stolen, a compromised account can take weeks or even months to be used, and the victim then only knows from their bank statement that the card has been used.

Traditionally, fraud detection systems rely on the creation of manually engineered features by subject matter experts, working either directly with financial institutions or with specialized software vendors.

One of the biggest challenges in fraud detection is the availability of labelled datasets, which are often hard or even impossible to come by.

Our first fraud example comes from a dataset made public in Kaggle, (`https://www.kaggle.com/dalpozz/creditcardfraud`), by researchers from the Université Libre de Bruxelles in Belgium (for the full work, you can read their paper: Andrea Dal Pozzolo, Olivier Caelen, Reid A. Johnson and Gianluca Bontempi, *Calibrating Probability with Undersampling for Unbalanced Classification. In Symposium on Computational Intelligence and Data Mining (CIDM), IEEE, 2015)*.

The datasets contain transactions made by credit cards in two days in September 2013 by European cardholders. We have 492 frauds out of 284,807 transactions. Unlike toy datasets (I am looking at you, Iris), real-life datasets are highly unbalanced. In this example, the positive class (frauds) account for 0.172% of all transactions.

It contains just numerical information factors which are the aftereffect of a PCA change. Because of classification issues, the creators can't give the first highlights and more foundation data about the information. Features V1, V2, ... V28 are the chief segments got with PCA, the main features which have not been changed with PCA are `Time` and `Amount`.

The feature, `Time` contains the seconds elapsed between each transaction and the first transaction in the dataset. The feature, `Amount` is the transaction's amount, this feature can be used for example-dependent, cost-sensitive learning. The feature, `Class` is the response variable and it takes value 1 in case of fraud and 0 otherwise. Given the class imbalance ratio, the authors recommend measuring the area under the **precision-recall curve (AUC)**, instead of the confusion matrix. The precision-recall curve is also called **ROC** (receiver-operator characteristic).

At this point you might be thinking: well, why should I bother with autoencoders since this is clearly a binary classification problem, and we already have the labeled data? Sure, you can go the traditional way and try to do standard supervised learning algorithms, such as random forests or support vector machines, just be careful to either oversample the fraud class or undersample the normal class, so that these methods can perform well. However, in many real-life instances we do not have the labeled data beforehand, and in complex fraud scenarios it might be very tricky to get an accurate label. Suppose you are a criminal willing to commit fraud.

Previous to the fraud (or even after) you may have completely normal activity in your account. So shall we flag all of your transactions as rogue? Or only a certain subset? Some people in the business may argue that, after all, the transactions were committed by a criminal, so they are tainted somehow and we should flag all your activity, introducing bias into the model. Instead of relying on the label, we will treat the problem as an *anomaly detection* or *outlier detection* problem and use autoencoders, as before.

Exploratory data analysis

An often overlooked step is exploratory data analysis. Before jumping straight into the data and trying to do fancy deep learning architectures, let's step back and look at what we have around.

Let's begin by downloading the dataset from Kaggle: (`https://www.kaggle.com/dalpozz/creditcardfraud`) and importing it into R:

```
df <- read.csv("./data/creditcard.csv", stringsAsFactors = F)
head(df)
```

Before moving on, we should do a basic sanity check. Some of the things we should look for are:

- Verify that there are indeed only two classes (0 for normal transactions, 1 for fraudulent)
- Verify that the timestamp corresponds to two days
- Check that there are no missing values

Once this is done, we can perform two quick checks, an idea would be to see if there is an obvious pattern between the time of day and the amount. Perhaps fraudulent transactions happen at a certain time, when our system is vulnerable? We should check this first:

```
library(ggplot2)
library(dplyr)
 df %>% ggplot(aes(Time,Amount))+geom_point()+facet_grid(Class~.)
```

First, let's see if there is some seasonality pattern. We just plot the time variable against the amount, per class:

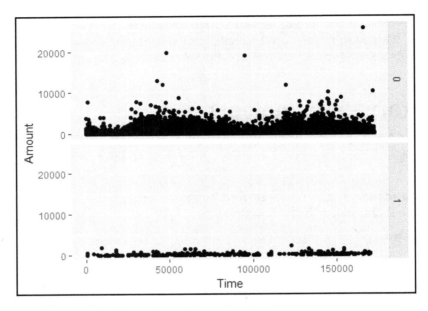

Quick inspection for fraud: the class 0 corresponds to normal transactions and the class 1 to fraudulent transactions.

So nothing jumps out. Interestingly, the amount involved in fraud transactions is much lower than in normal transactions. This suggests we should filter out the transactions and look at them on the right scale. For this, let's use the `dplyr` and filter out the transactions above 300 and look at smaller transactions:

```
df$Class <- as.factor(df$Class)
df %>%filter(Amount<300) %>%ggplot(aes(Class,Amount))+geom_violin()
```

How does the distribution look by class? The following plot tells us something:

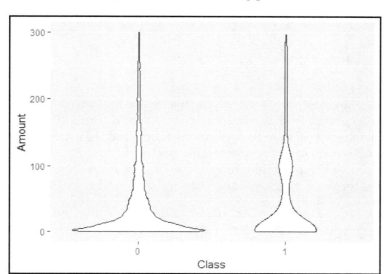

First insight on the data: The amount involved in fraudulent transactions seems more likely to be around 100 than in non-fraudulent transactions.

Aha! So we get our first insight on the data! Fraudulent transactions, although much smaller, are anomalously centered around 100. This might be part of the fraudster's strategy, instead of having large amounts at regular times, they hide small amounts more or less uniformly in time.

Sure, this was fun to find out, but it is definitely not a scalable approach and requires domain knowledge and intuition. It is time to try something more sophisticated.

The autoencoder approach – Keras

OK, time to get into Keras. We should leave apart a small fraction of the data to use as a validation or test set, and develop the model on the remaining. There is no golden standard as to how this should be done. For this example, we will use a 10% test set and a 90% training set:

```
# Remove the time and class column
idxs <- sample(nrow(df), size=0.1*nrow(df))
train <- df[-idxs,]
test <- df[idxs,]
y_train <- train$Class
```

```
y_test <- test$Class
X_train <- train %>% select(-one_of(c("Time","Class")))
X_test <- test %>% select(-one_of(c("Time","Class")))
# Coerce the data frame to matrix to perform the training
X_train <- as.matrix(X_train)
X_test <- as.matrix(X_test)
```

Notice that we also excluded the `Class` and `Time` columns. We are ignoring the label and treating our fraud detection problem as an unsupervised learning problem, hence we need to remove the label column from the training data. As for the temporal information, as we saw before, there does not seem to be an obvious time trend. Furthermore, in real-life fraud detection scenarios, we are rather concerned about the intrinsic properties of the fraudster, for instance, device used, geolocation information or data from the CRM system, as well as account properties (balance, average transaction volume, and so on).

For the architecture of the autoencoder, instead of using one intermediate layer as before, we will now use a **stacked autoencoder**. A stacked autoencoder is nothing more than several layers of encoders, followed by layers of decoders. In this case, we will use a network with outer encoder-decoder layers of 14 fully connected neurons, two inner layers of 7 neurons and yet another inner layer of 7 neurons. You can experiment with different architectures and compare results with ours, there is no universally correct architecture for autoencoders, it relies merely on experience and on diagnosing your model via validation plots and other metrics.

Our input (and output) dimension is 29 in each case. The code to construct the autoencoder is:

```
library(keras)
input_dim <- 29
outer_layer_dim <- 14
inner_layer_dim <- 7
input_layer <- layer_input(shape=c(input_dim))
encoder <- layer_dense(units=outer_layer_dim,
activation='relu')(input_layer)
encoder <- layer_dense(units=inner_layer_dim, activation='relu')(encoder)
decoder <- layer_dense(units=inner_layer_dim)(encoder)
decoder <- layer_dense(units=outer_layer_dim)(decoder)
decoder <- layer_dense(units=input_dim)(decoder)
autoencoder <- keras_model(inputs=input_layer, outputs = decoder)
```

We can look at our work to check everything is correct:

```
autoencoder
 Model
```

Layer (type) Output Shape Param #
input_5 (InputLayer) (None, 29) 0
dense_17 (Dense) (None, 14) 420
dense_18 (Dense) (None, 7) 105
dense_22 (Dense) (None, 7) 56
dense_23 (Dense) (None, 7) 56
dense_24 (Dense) (None, 14) 112
dense_25 (Dense) (None, 29) 435

```
Total params: 1,184
Trainable params: 1,184
Non-trainable params: 0
```

We are now ready to begin our training. We should first compile the model and then fit it:

```
autoencoder %>% compile(optimizer='adam',
                        loss='mean_squared_error',
                        metrics=c('accuracy'))

history <- autoencoder %>% fit(
 X_train,X_train,
 epochs = 10, batch_size = 32,
 validation_split=0.2
 )

plot(history)
```

Our results are shown as follows. You can see that there is an increase in accuracy as the number of epochs increases:

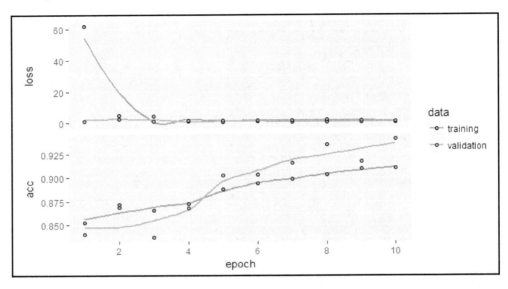

Diagnostic plots for our 14-7-7-7-14 architecture.

Once we have the autoencoder ready, we use it to reconstruct the test set:

```
# Reconstruct on the test set
preds <- autoencoder %>% predict(X_test)
preds <- as.data.frame(preds)
```

We will look for anomalously large reconstruction errors, as before, to be labelled as unusual. For instance, we can look at those points whose reconstruction error is larger than 30 and declare them as unusual:

```
y_preds <- ifelse(rowSums((preds-X_test)**2)/30<1, rowSums((preds-
X_test)**2)/30,1)
```

Again, this threshold is not set in stone, and using your test set in your particular application you can fine-tune it and find the most suitable threshold for your problem.

Finally, let's generate the ROC curve to see if our model is performing correctly using:

```
library(ROCR)
pred <- prediction(y_preds, y_test)
perf <- performance(pred, measure = "tpr", x.measure = "fpr")
plot(perf, col=rainbow(10))
```

We see that the results are satisfactory. Our curve looks quite straight, and the reason for that is that the output of our model is just binary, as well as our original labels. When your model inputs class probabilities, or a proxy for it, then the curve would be smoother:

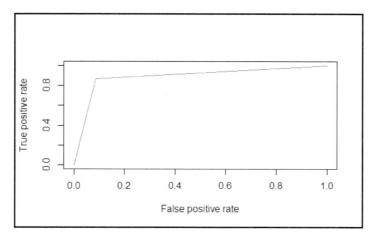

ROC curve: It looks quite straight since the outputs of the model are not class probabilities, but binary.

Fraud detection with H2O

Let's try a slightly different tool, that might help us in real-life deployments. It is often useful to try different tools in the ever-growing data science landscape, if only for sanity0-check purposes.

H2O is an open source software for doing big data analytics. The young start-up (founded in 2016) counts with top researchers in mathematical optimization and statistical learning theory on their advisory board. It runs in standard environments (Linux/Mac/Windows) as well as big data systems and cloud computing environments.

You can run H2O in R, but you need to install the package first:

```
install.packages("h2o")
```

Once this is done, you can load the library:

```
library(h2o)
```

You will then see a welcome message, among some warnings (objects that are masked from other packages):

```
Your next step is to start H2O:
  > h2o.init()
For H2O package documentation, ask for help:
  > ??h2o
After starting H2O, you can use the Web UI at http://localhost:54321
  For more information visit http://docs.h2o.ai
```

So let's do that, and then we will be ready for work:

```
h2o.init()
```

Now we need to read our data into H2O. As the computations work somehow differently, we can not use the vanilla dataframe structure from R, so we either read the file as usual and then coerce it:

```
df <- read.csv("./data/creditcard.csv", stringsAsFactors = F)
  df <- as.h2o(df)
```

Or we read it with the `h2o.uploadFile` function:

```
df2 <- h2o.uploadFile("./data/creditcard.csv")
```

Either way, the resulting structure type is no longer a dataframe, but an environment.

Let's leave aside one portion of the data for training and one for testing, as usual. In `h2o`, we can use the `h2o.splitFrame` function:

```
splits <- h2o.splitFrame(df, ratios=c(0.8), seed=1)
  train <- splits[[1]]
  test <- splits[[2]]
```

Now let's identify between features and label, which will be useful in a minute:

```
label <- "Class"
  features <- setdiff(colnames(train), label)
```

We are ready to start the training of our autoencoder:

```
autoencoder <- h2o.deeplearning(x=features,
  training_frame = train,
  autoencoder = TRUE,
  seed = 1,
  hidden=c(10,2,10),
  epochs = 10,
  activation = "Tanh")
```

Some comments are in order. The autoencoder parameter is set to true, as you would expect. We will use a slightly different architecture this time, just for illustration purposes. You can see in the `hidden` parameter, the structure of the layers. We will also use a different activation function. In practice, it is sometimes useful to use bounded activation functions, such as tanh instead of ReLu, which can be numerically unstable.

We can generate the reconstructions in a similar way as we did with `keras`:

```
# Use the predict function as before
preds <- h2o.predict(autoencoder, test)
```

We get something like this:

```
> head(preds)
  reconstr_Time reconstr_V1 reconstr_V2 reconstr_V3 reconstr_V4 reconstr_V5
reconstr_V6 reconstr_V7
1 380.1466 -0.3041237 0.2373746 1.617792 0.1876353 -0.7355559 0.3570959
-0.1331038
2 1446.0211 -0.2568674 0.2218221 1.581772 0.2254702 -0.6452812 0.4204379
-0.1337738
3 1912.0357 -0.2589679 0.2212748 1.578886 0.2171786 -0.6604871 0.4070894
-0.1352975
4 1134.1723 -0.3319681 0.2431342 1.626862 0.1473913 -0.8192215 0.2911475
-0.1369512
5 1123.6757 -0.3194054 0.2397288 1.619868 0.1612631 -0.7887480 0.3140728
-0.1362253
6 1004.4545 -0.3589335 0.2508191 1.643208 0.1196120 -0.8811920 0.2451117
-0.1380364
```

And from here on, we can proceed as before. However, h2o has a built-in function, `h2o.anomaly`, that simplifies part of our work.

Another simplification we can do is instead of importing `ggplot2` and `dplyr` separately, we can import the `tidyverse` package, that brings these (and other) packages useful for data manipulation into our environment:

We call this function and do a bit of formatting to make the row names a column itself, as well as adding the label for the real class:

```
library(tidyverse)
anomaly <- h2o.anomaly(autoencoder, test) %>%
as.data.frame() %>%
tibble::rownames_to_column() %>%
mutate(Class = as.vector(test[, 31]))
```

Let's calculate the average mean square error:

```
# Type coercion useful for plotting later
anomaly$Class <- as.factor(anomaly$Class)
mean_mse <- anomaly %>%
 group_by(Class) %>%
 summarise(mean = mean(Reconstruction.MSE))
```

And finally, visualize our test data as per the reconstruction error:

```
anomaly$Class <- as.factor(anomaly$Class)
mean_mse <- anomaly %>%
    group_by(Class) %>%
    summarise(mean = mean(Reconstruction.MSE))
```

We see that the autoencoder does a not too terrible job. A good proportion of the fraud cases have a relatively high reconstruction error, although it is far from perfect. How could you improve it?:

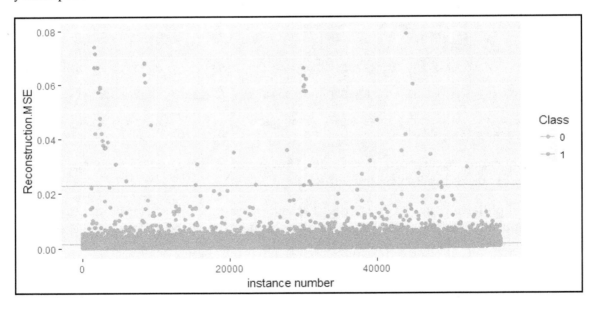

Results from our architecture using H2O, we see that the autoencoder does a good job flagging the fraud cases, but it could still be improved.

Exercises

- We used a mixture of fraud and non-fraud cases in our credit card fraud example. In this case, we are lucky enough to have the correct label for each case. So perhaps in this case, it makes more sense to do the reconstruction of the normal transactions only. Would the detection rate improve if we only used non-fraud cases? Run the same experiment but use only the non-fraud cases for the training set.

- Using the Credit Card dataset, use the reconstructions from the autoencoder as inputs for a classification model, pretty much in the same way you would use PCA. Does this improve the accuracy of the classification? Note that you can do this in this particular dataset, because you have information about the class of the transaction (fraud/non-fraud) which might not be available in other data.

Variational Autoencoders

Variational Autoencoders (**VAE**) are a more recent take on the autoencoding problem. Unlike autoencoders, which learn a compressed representation of the data, Variational Autoencoders learn the random process that generates such data, instead of learning an essentially arbitrary function as we previously did with our neural networks.

VAEs have also an encoder and decoder part. The encoder learns the mean and standard deviation of a normal distribution that is assumed to have generated the data. The mean and standard deviation are called **latent variables** because they are not observed explicitly, rather inferred from the data.

The decoder part of VAEs maps back these latent space points into the data. As before, we need a loss function to measure the difference between the original inputs and their reconstruction. Sometimes an extra term is added, called the **Kullback-Leibler divergence,** or simply KL divergence. The KL divergence computes, roughly, how much a probability distribution differs from another. Adding the KL divergence, forces the posterior distribution to be similar to the prior. This, in turn, helps to both learn better representations of the data and to reduce overfitting.

Unlike autoencoders, VAEs have a solid probabilistic foundation, so the score you get is indeed the probability of an observation being an outlier. In autoencoders, the score we get has no such interpretation, therefore the choice of the cutoff or threshold value is entirely reliant on the input of a human expert, and is strictly data specific.

Image reconstruction using VAEs

Our first example will use the MNIST data to illustrate the use of Variational Autoencoders.

The development strategy is as follows:

- First, an encoder network turns the input samples x, into two parameters in a latent space, which will be denoted *z_mean* and *z_log_sigma*
- Then, we randomly sample similar points z from the latent normal distribution which we assumed is used to generate the data, as *z ~ z_mean + exp(z_log_sigma)*epsilon* where epsilon is a random normal tensor
- Once this is done, a decoder network maps these latent space points z back to the original input data

We begin as usual, getting and preprocessing the data:

```
library(keras)
# Switch to the 1-based indexing from R
options(tensorflow.one_based_extract = FALSE)
K <- keras::backend()
mnist <- dataset_mnist()
X_train <- mnist$train$x
y_train <- mnist$train$y
X_test <- mnist$test$x
y_test <- mnist$test$y
# reshape
dim(X_train) <- c(nrow(X_train), 784)
dim(X_test) <- c(nrow(X_test), 784)
# rescale
X_train <- X_train / 255
X_test <- X_test / 255
```

Note the additional line:

```
K <- keras::backend()
```

This gets us a reference to the tensor backend where Keras will perform the tensor operations.

Now we turn to the VAE. It will consist of a latent dimension of size 2 and a hidden layer of 256 neurons:

```
orig_dim <- 784
latent_dim <- 2
inner_dim <- 256
X <- layer_input(shape = c(original_dim))
hidden_state <- layer_dense(X, intermediate_dim, activation = "relu")
z_mean <- layer_dense(hidden_state, latent_dim)
z_log_sigma <- layer_dense(hidden_state, latent_dim)
```

Next, with the help of our Keras backend, we define the sampling function that will generate the data from the latent variables:

```
sample_z<- function(params){
 z_mean <- params[,0:1]
 z_log_sigma <- params[,2:3]
 epsilon <- K$random_normal(
 shape = c(K$shape(z_mean)[[1]]),
 mean=0.,
 stddev=1
 )
 z_mean + K$exp(z_log_sigma/2)*epsilon
}
```

We now define the sampled points:

```
z <- layer_concatenate(list(z_mean, z_log_sigma)) %>%
  layer_lambda(sample_z)
```

Time to define the decoder. We create separate instances of these layers to be able to reuse them later:

```
decoder_hidden_state <- layer_dense(units = intermediate_dim, activation =
"relu")
decoder_mean <- layer_dense(units = original_dim, activation = "sigmoid")
hidden_state_decoded <- decoder_hidden_state(z)
X_decoded_mean <- decoder_mean(hidden_state_decoded)
```

We are ready! Our VAE is specified by the following encoder and decoder components:

```
# end-to-end autoencoder
variational_autoencoder <- keras_model(X, X_decoded_mean)

encoder <- keras_model(X, z_mean)
decoder_input <- layer_input(shape = latent_dim)
```

```
decoded_hidden_state_2 <- decoder_hidden_state(decoder_input)
decoded_X_mean_2 <- decoder_mean(decoded_hidden_state_2)
generator <- keras_model(decoder_input, decoded_X_mean_2)
```

It remains to specify the custom loss function, since we are adding the KL-divergence penalization:

```
loss_function <- function(X, decoded_X_mean){
  cross_entropy_loss <- loss_binary_crossentropy(X, decoded_X_mean)
  kl_loss <- -0.5*K$mean(1 + z_log_sigma - K$square(z_mean) -
K$exp(z_log_sigma), axis = -1L)
  cross_entropy_loss + kl_loss
}
```

We compile and run our algorithm, as usual:

```
variational_autoencoder %>% compile(optimizer = "rmsprop", loss =
loss_function)
history <- variational_autoencoder %>% fit(
  X_train, X_train,
  shuffle = TRUE,
  epochs = 10,
  batch_size = 256,
  validation_data = list(X_test, X_test)
)
plot(history)
```

After the training is done, we can see the performance (or, follow it in real time using the **Viewer** in RStudio):

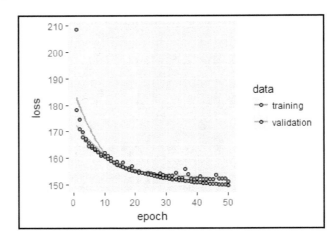

Performance of our for reconstruction in the MNIST data.

We can examine the performance of our algorithm with the following snippet:

```
library(ggplot2)
preds <- variational_autoencoder %>% predict(X_test)
error <- rowSums((preds-X_test)**2)
eval <- data.frame(error=error, class=as.factor(y_test))
eval %>%
  group_by(class) %>%
  summarise(avg_error=mean(error)) %>%
  ggplot(aes(x=class,fill=class,y=avg_error))+geom_col()
```

The results are shown here:

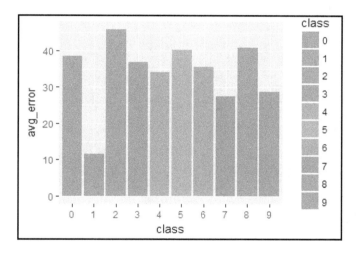

The reconstruction error looks rather discouraging, because we were clearly better off with autoencoders. How could we improve this? One way is to improve the dimension of the latent space. In our current setup, our latent space is only two dimensional. However, note that there is not much lost in terms of quality:

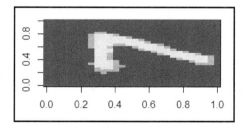

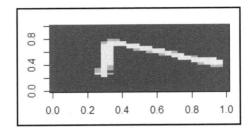

Reconstructed image by our VAE on the left, and the original image on the right (on screen).

Moreover, we now have a generative process! That means that we can create our digits ourselves. Let's loop over the latent space and use the probability distribution to generate our own digits:

```
# Reshape original and reconstructed
dim(X_test) <- c(nrow(X_test),28,28)
dim(preds) <- c(nrow(preds),28,28)
image(255*preds[1,,], col=gray.colors(3))
y_test[1]
image(255*X_test[1,,], col=gray.colors(3))

grid_x <- seq(-4, 4, length.out = 3)
grid_y <- seq(-4, 4, length.out = 3)

rows <- NULL
for(i in 1:length(grid_x)){
  column <- NULL
  for(j in 1:length(grid_y)){
    z_sample <- matrix(c(grid_x[i], grid_y[j]), ncol = 2)
    column <- rbind(column, predict(generator, z_sample) %>% matrix(ncol =
28) )
  }
  rows <- cbind(rows, column)
}
rows %>% as.raster() %>% plot()
```

Let's look at a few digits generated by our VAE:

Digits generated by the VAE.

Outlier detection in MNIST

Let's look again at the outlier detection problem in MNIST. As before, let's say that the digit 0 is our outlier this time, and we would like to be able to detect it.

We go as before, reading and preprocessing the data:

```
library(keras)
# Switch to the 1-based indexing from R
options(tensorflow.one_based_extract = FALSE)
K <- keras::backend()
mnist <- dataset_mnist()
X_train <- mnist$train$x
y_train <- mnist$train$y
X_test <- mnist$test$x
y_test <- mnist$test$y
## Exclude "0" from the training set. "0" will be the outlier
outlier_idxs <- which(y_train!=0, arr.ind = T)
X_train <- X_train[outlier_idxs,,]
y_test <- sapply(y_test, function(x){ ifelse(x==0,"outlier","normal")})
# reshape
dim(X_train) <- c(nrow(X_train), 784)
dim(X_test) <- c(nrow(X_test), 784)
# rescale
X_train <- X_train / 255
X_test <- X_test / 255
```

Then we define our encoder structure. Note that we will use a different structure of 128 dimensional latent space and 256 neurons in the intermediate layer:

```
original_dim <- 784
latent_dim <- 2
intermediate_dim <- 256
X <- layer_input(shape = c(original_dim))
hidden_state <- layer_dense(X, intermediate_dim, activation = "relu")
z_mean <- layer_dense(hidden_state, latent_dim)
z_log_sigma <- layer_dense(hidden_state, latent_dim)
```

And rewrite our `sample_z` function to make it easier to customize:

```
sample_z<- function(params){
  z_mean <- params[,0:1]
  z_log_sigma <- params[,2:3]
  epsilon <- K$random_normal(
    shape = c(K$shape(z_mean)[[1]]),
    mean=0.,
    stddev=1
  )
```

```
    z_mean + K$exp(z_log_sigma/2)*epsilon
}
```

Then we go for the decoder part:

```
z <- layer_concatenate(list(z_mean, z_log_sigma)) %>%
  layer_lambda(sample_z)
decoder_hidden_state <- layer_dense(units = intermediate_dim, activation =
"relu")
decoder_mean <- layer_dense(units = original_dim, activation = "sigmoid")
hidden_state_decoded <- decoder_hidden_state(z)
X_decoded_mean <- decoder_mean(hidden_state_decoded)
```

And finally, the full autoencoder:

```
variational_autoencoder <- keras_model(X, decoded_X_mean)
encoder <- keras_model(X, z_mean)
decoder_input <- layer_input(shape = latent_dim)
decoded_hidden_state_2 <- decoder_hidden_state(decoder_input)
decoded_X_mean_2 <- decoder_mean(decoded_hidden_state_2)
generator <- keras_model(decoder_input, decoded_X_mean_2)
```

We define loss function with:

```
loss_function <- function(X, decoded_X_mean){
  cross_entropy_loss <- loss_binary_crossentropy(X, decoded_X_mean)
  kl_loss <- -0.5*K$mean(1 + z_log_sigma - K$square(z_mean) -
K$exp(z_log_sigma), axis = -1L)
  cross_entropy_loss + kl_loss
}
```

We use the same function as before and train the model:

```
variational_autoencoder %>% compile(optimizer = "rmsprop", loss =
loss_function)
history <- variational_autoencoder %>% fit(
  X_train, X_train,
  shuffle = TRUE,
  epochs = 10,
  batch_size = 256,
  validation_data = list(X_test, X_test)
)
plot(history)
```

Once the training is done, we look at the performance:

```
preds <- variational_autoencoder %>% predict(X_test)
error <- rowSums((preds-X_test)**2)
eval <- data.frame(error=error, class=as.factor(y_test))
library(dplyr)
library(ggplot2)
eval %>%
  ggplot(aes(x=class,fill=class,y=error))+geom_boxplot()
```

Let's look at the reconstruction error per class:

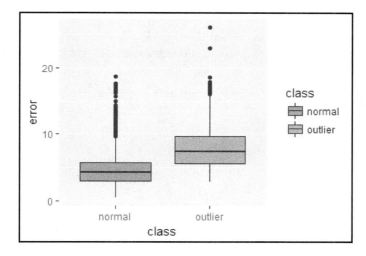

Reconstruction error using the VAE.

The plot suggests you set a reconstruction error for the threshold as 5:

```
threshold <- 5
y_preds <- sapply(error,
function(x){ifelse(x>threshold,"outlier","normal")})
```

And we now look at the confusion matrix:

```
table(y_preds,y_test)
         y_test
y_preds normal outlier
  outlier 9020      980
```

Which suggests that we are on the right track! But before celebrating, we should look at the other classification metrics, the ROC curve and the area under this curve (AUC):

```
library(ROCR)
 pred <- prediction(error, y_test)
 perf <- performance(pred, measure = "tpr", x.measure = "fpr")
 auc <- unlist(performance(pred, measure = "auc")@y.values)
 auc
 plot(perf, col=rainbow(10))
```

We get an AUC of 0.8473375 and a reasonable ROC plot shown as follows, which tells us that our VAE did a good job distinguishing the outlier 0.

Note that this was much better than when the digit 7 was the outlier. This tells us that we need to put in extra effort when an abnormal observation resembles the usual observations too much:

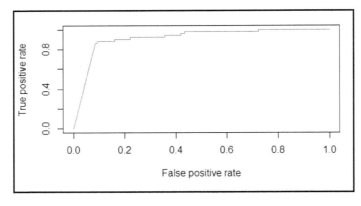

ROC curve for our variational autoencoder.

Text fraud detection

Fraud has become an issue beyond the traditional transaction fraud. Many websites, for instance, rely on user reviews about services, such as restaurants, hotels or tourist attractions, that are monetized in different ways. If the users lose trust in those reviews, for example, by a business owner deliberately messing with the good reviews for his or her own business, then the website will find it hard to regain that trust and to remain profitable. Hence, it is important to detect such potential issues.

How can autoencoders help us with this? As before, the idea is to learn the representation of a *normal* review on a website, and then find those that do not fit the *normal* review. The issue with text data is that there is some processing to be done before. We will illustrate this with an example, which will also serve as a motivation for the different ways of modelling text that will be discussed in the next chapters.

From unstructured text data to a matrix

An issue with text data is that words and sentences are messy, and algorithms for data mining usually do not work out of the box, as they are designed to operate on abstractions of the data, usually in matrix form. So we need to find a way to represent our messy text data as a matrix.

One of the most commonly used matrix representations in practice is the *bag of words* model. This is a very simple and intuitive way of extracting information from text. There are some caveats to it, which will be discussed later.

A bag of words representation of a text consists of:

- A vocabulary of known words
- A numerical measure associated to the presence of such words

For example, suppose we have a *corpus* (a collection of documents) consisting of three sentences:

- `"My sentence"`
- `"Your sentence"`
- `"My sentence, your sentence, our sentences"`

The vocabulary (ignoring the comma) is the collection
(`"My"`, `"sentence"`, `"sentences"`, `"Your"`, `"your"`, `"our"`). As for the numerical measure, a natural option would be the count function. So the matrix representation would be:

My	Your	sentence	sentences	your	our
1	0	1	0	0	0
0	1	1	0	0	0
1	0	2	1	1	1

This is now something we can operate with. Note that a few comments are in order. We ignored the comma, which does not seem like a big deal, but it is, and we will come back to it. Second, we are including "Your" and "your" as different words, which is probably not desirable. Note that also "sentence" and "sentences" are similar from the information point of view. If we want to infer the content of a document, it might suffice to keep just one of them.

To deal with the capitalization issue, we can simply convert all the words to lower case first, before passing to the matrix form. Dealing with plurals or other derived words from a *root* word is done through different algorithms, called **stemmers**. The most common choice is Porter's stemming algorithm. Sometimes it is not a good idea to do stemming, it might depend on the language and the context of your problem.

Depending on the context, sometimes common words such as pronouns are better omitted. There are lists of such words, called **stop words** readily available on the internet. So before creating the matrix representation, you filter those words, which also reduces the dimension of the problem.

A problem with scoring word frequency is that we will have highly frequent words dominating the matrix representation, but this domination might be useless from the information point of view. Instead, what is done often is to use alternative representations such as TF–IDF, which stands for text document-inverse document frequency. There are different ways to calculate it, roughly equivalent, if w is a word, D is the set of documents and d is a document there (in the preceding example, one of the sentences), then:

$$tfidf(w, d, D) = \frac{\text{frequency of w in d}}{\text{number of documents in D that have w in them}}$$

You can play around with these, for example, instead of frequency of word in the numerator, you can use the characteristic function (0 if the word is not there, 1 if it is), or the logarithm of that. Similarly, you can consider different possibilities for the denominator.

The issue with removing the punctuation is a bit more subtle, and it has to do with the main disadvantage of the bag of words approach, meaning is completely lost. Even without considering punctuation, sentences like `Alice loves pizza` and `Pizza loves Alice` would be represented identically, but they have different meanings. With punctuation, we can get completely opposite meanings, the sentences `Pardon, impossible execution` and `Pardon impossible, execution` mean opposite things.

Context is also lost, and relations within words might be lost. For instance, the documents `I was in Paris` and `I saw the Eiffel tower` are clearly related, but they would appear as orthogonal documents in a bag of words representation. We will address some of these issues in later chapters.

From text to matrix representation — the Enron dataset

The Enron email dataset contains approximately 500,000 emails generated by employees of the Enron Corporation. It was obtained by the Federal Energy Regulatory Commission of the United States during its investigation of Enron's collapse. The Enron corporation was an American energy company based in Houston, Texas, that was involved in an accountant fraud scandal that eventually led to its bankruptcy. We will use a subset as an example, but you can access the full dataset (500,000 emails) from Kaggle, (`https://www.kaggle.com/wcukierski/enron-email-dataset`) or from the Computer Science school in Carnegie Mellon University (`https://www.cs.cmu.edu/~./enron/`).

For text mining, we will use the packages, `tm` (`https://cran.r-project.org/web/packages/tm/index.html`) and `SnowballC` (`https://cran.r-project.org/web/packages/SnowballC/index.html`). Be sure to install them before:

```
install.packages("tm")
install.packages("SnowballC")
```

We start by loading the dataframe in our workspace. We will omit some of the preprocessing stems and assume that your dataframe has two columns, email and responsive. We hand-label the responsive column for our small sample, if not available from the original data (not all versions have it). Responsive means, in legal terms, whether the email is relevant to the fraud investigation:

```
df <- read.csv("./data/enron.csv")
names(df)
[1] "email"      "responsive"
```

We load the `tm` library and create a corpus object from the email column:

```
library(tm)
corpus <- Corpus(VectorSource(df$email))
```

We can access each email with the `inspect` command, as follows:

```
inspect(corpus[[1]])
```

A series of transformations are applied to our data before modeling: converting to lower case, remove punctuation, stop words and stemming:

```
corpus <- tm_map(corpus,tolower)
corpus <- tm_map(corpus, removePunctuation)
corpus <- tm_map(corpus, removeWords, stopwords("english"))
corpus <- tm_map(corpus, stemDocument)
```

Once this is done, we are ready to obtain a matrix representation of the documents, as follows:

```
dtm <- DocumentTermMatrix(corpus)
dtm <-   removeSparseTerms(dtm, 0.97)
X <- as.data.frame(as.matrix(dtm))
X$responsive <- df$responsive
```

We create the train/test split. For this, we can use the library `caTools`:

```
# Train, test, split
library(caTools)
set.seed(42)
spl <- sample.split(X$responsive, 0.7)
train <- subset(X, spl == TRUE)
test <- subset(X, spl == FALSE)
train <- subset(train, responsive==0)
```

Autoencoder on the matrix representation

Once we put the text in matrix form, we can continue the training of the autoencoder, as in the previous sections.

Note that our autoencoder will have only non-responsive emails on the training part. This turns out to be quite helpful in this dataset, which has only a few hundred samples.

Once this is done, we create our training and testing sets, splitting in x and y components as before:

```
X_train <- subset(train,select=-responsive)
y_train <- train$responsive
X_test <- subset(test,select=-responsive)
y_test <- test$responsive
```

Now, we are ready to define our autoencoder. We will use only an inner layer with size 32:

```
library(keras)
input_dim <- ncol(X_train)
inner_layer_dim <- 32
input_layer <- layer_input(shape=c(input_dim))
encoder <- layer_dense(units=inner_layer_dim,
activation='relu')(input_layer)
decoder <- layer_dense(units=input_dim)(encoder)
autoencoder <- keras_model(inputs=input_layer, outputs = decoder)
autoencoder %>% compile(optimizer='adam',
                        loss='mean_squared_error',
                        metrics=c('accuracy'))
```

Then, for the training:

```
X_train <- as.matrix(X_train)
X_test <- as.matrix(X_test)
history <- autoencoder %>% fit(
 X_train,X_train,
 epochs = 100, batch_size = 32,
 validation_data = list(X_test, X_test)
)
plot(history)
```

We look at the reconstruction on the test set and look at the distribution of errors across both classes:

```
# Reconstruct on the test set
preds <- autoencoder %>% predict(X_test)
error <- rowSums((preds-X_test)**2)
library(tidyverse)
eval %>%
 filter(error < 1000) %>%
 ggplot(aes(x=error,color=class))+geom_density()
```

As usual, let's take a look at the distribution of error per class, this time with a density plot:

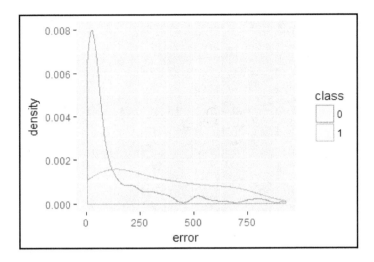

Distribution of the reconstruction error per class.

Note that we filtered on the reconstruction error, As before, this helps us look at the scale on where the majority of the observations are. Our goal is to set a threshold for the reconstruction error, to flag as outlier (which in this context means that the email is not an ordinary email communication). Visually, it seems that 100 is a reasonable threshold, although we will get a high number of false positives:

```
threshold <- 100
y_preds <- sapply(error,
function(x){ifelse(x>threshold,"outlier","normal")})
# Confusion matrix
table(y_preds,y_test)
          y_test
y_preds    0 1
 normal   142 7
 outlier  73 35
```

We do a reasonably good job catching the suspicious emails, at the cost of 73 false positives. There is always a trade off between catching a high number of false positives and ignoring true positives. The model could be improved by adding more data, we used only around 800 emails from 500,000 available, so clearly there is room for improvement. The model works reasonably well, nonetheless, as confirmed by the AUC value of 0.79 and the ROC plot:

```
library(ROCR)
pred <- prediction(error, y_test)
perf <- performance(pred, measure = "tpr", x.measure = "fpr")
auc <- unlist(performance(pred, measure = "auc")@y.values)
plot(perf, col=rainbow(10))
auc
[1] 0.7951274
plot(perf, col=rainbow(10))
```

We see the ROC curve for the Enron dataset, as follows. This allows us to diagnose our model for binary classifiers in general, not only in this case:

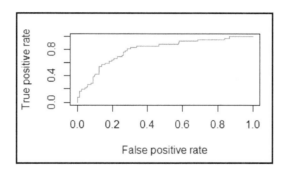

ROC curve for the Enron dataset.

Exercises

- Use the original Enron dataset to create an autoencoder that would identify suspicious from non-suspicious emails.
- Instead of an autoencoder, you can try with Variational Autoencoders. Compare the performance of both approaches.

Summary

In this chapter, we learned that autoencoders are a technique used mainly in image reconstruction and denoising, to obtain compressed and summarized representations of the data. We saw that they are also used sometimes for fraud detection tasks. The outlier identification comes from measuring the reconstruction error, observing the distribution of the reconstruction error, we can set up thresholds for identifying the outliers and learn the probabilistic process that generates the data. Hence, Variational Autoencoders are also able to generate new data.

15
Text Generation using Recurrent Neural Networks

In this chapter, we will describe some of the most exciting techniques in modern (at the time of writing—late 2017) machine learning, recurrent neural networks. They are, however, not new; they have been around since the 1980s, but they have become popular due to the numerous records in language-related tasks in recent years.

Why do we need a different type of architecture for text? Consider the following example:

"I live in Prague since 2015"

and

"Since 2015 I live in Prague"

If we would like to teach a traditional feed-forward network such as a perceptron or a multi-layer perceptron to identify the date I moved to Prague, then this network would have to learn separate parameters for each input feature, which in particular implies that it would have to learn grammar to answer this simple question! This is undesirable in many applications. Similar issues motivated machine learning researchers and statisticians in the 1980s to introduce the idea of sharing parameters across different parts of the model. This idea is the secret sauce of recurrent neural networks, our next deep learning architecture.

By design, recurrent neural networks are well-suited for processing sequential data. In general, machine learning applied to sequential data can be roughly divided into four main areas:

- Sequence prediction: Given $[x_{t-2}, x_{t-1}, x_t]$, predict the next element of the sequence, x_{t+1}

- Sequence classification: Given $[x_{t-2}, x_{t-1}, x_t]$, predict a category or label for it

- Sequence generation: Given $[x_{t-2}, x_{t-1}, x_t]$, generate a new element of the sequence, x_{t+1}

- Sequence to sequence prediction: Given $[x_{t-2}, x_{t-1}, x_t]$, generate an equivalent sequence, $[y_{t-1}, y_t, y_{t+1}]$

Applications of sequence prediction include weather forecasting and stock market prediction. For classification, we can think, for example, of sentiment analysis and document classification. Automatic image captioning or text generation are part of the sequence generation family of problems, whereas machine translation might be the most familiar example of sequence to sequence prediction we see in our everyday lives.

Our focus for this chapter is on applications of recurrent neural networks for text generation. Since, as we saw previously, text generation is part of a much larger set of problems, many of our algorithms are portable to other contexts.

Training deep learning models is often time-consuming, and recurrent neural networks are not the exception. Our focus is on the ideas over the data, which we will illustrate with smaller datasets than those that you might encounter later on in the wild. This is for the purpose of clarity: We want to make it easier for you to get started on any standard laptop. Once you grasp the basics, you can spin off your own cluster in your favorite cloud provider.

What is so exciting about recurrent neural networks?

Coming from a mathematics background, in my rather hectic career I have seen many different trends, particularly during the last few years, which all sound very similar to me: *"you have a problem? wavelets can save you!"*, *"finite elements are the solution to everything"*, and similar over-enthusiastic claims.

Of course, each tool has its time and place and, more importantly, an application domain where it excels. I find recurrent neural networks quite interesting for the many features they can achieve:

- Produce consistent markup text (opening and closing tags, recognizing timestamp-like data)
- Write Wikipedia articles with references, and create URLs from non-existing addresses, by learning what a URL should look like
- Create credible-looking scientific papers from LaTeX

All these amazing features are possible without the network having any context information or metadata. In particular, without knowing English, nor what a URL or a bit of LaTeX syntax looks like.

These and even more interesting capabilities of neural networks are superbly described by Andrej Karpathy in *The Unreasonable Effectiveness of Recurrent Neural Networks:* `http://karpathy.github.io/2015/05/21/rnn-effectiveness/`.

> What makes recurrent neural networks exciting? Instead of a constrained fixed-input size to fixed-output size, we can operate over sequences of vectors instead.

A limitation of many machine learning algorithms, including standard feed-forward neural networks, is that they accept a fixed size vector as input and produce a fixed size vector as output. For instance, if we want to classify text, we receive a corpus of documents from which we create a vocabulary to vectorize each document and the output is a vector with class probabilities. Recurrent neural networks instead allow us to take sequences of vectors as input. So, from a one-to-one correspondence between fixed input size and fixed output size, we have a much richer landscape, one-to-one, one-to-many, many-to-one, many-to-many.

Why is that desirable? Let's look at a few examples:

- **One-to-one**: Supervised learning, for instance, text classification
- **One-to-many**: Given an input text, generate a summary (a sequence of words with important information)
- **Many-to-one**: Sentiment analysis in text
- **Many-to-many**: Machine translation

Moreover, as recurrent neural networks maintain an internal state which gets updated according to new information, we can view RNNs as a description of a program. In fact, a paper by Siegelman in 1995 shows that recurrent neural networks are Turing complete, they can simulate arbitrary programs.

But what is a recurrent neural network, really?

How does the network keep track of the previous states? To put it in the context of text generation, think of our training data as a list of character sequences (tokenized words). For each word, from the first character, we will predict the following:

Formally, let's denote a sequence of $t+1$ characters as $x = [x_0, x_1, x_2, ... , x_t]$. Let $s_{-1} = 0$.

For $k=0,2,...t$, we construct the following sequence:

$$s_k = \tanh(Ux_k + Ws_{k-1})$$
$$o_k = \text{softmax}(Vs_k)$$

This is summarized in the following diagram, when input x is received, the internal state, s, of the network is modified, and then used to generate an output, o:

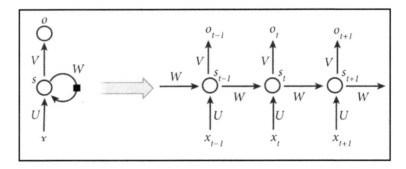

Figure 1: Information flow for an RNN. The representations are equivalent; the unfolded representation hints at how backpropagation could work in this setup.

The hidden state, s, need not be one-dimensional, as you might have imagined. Of course, it should not be too big, otherwise you might experience overfitting. A good way to start is to choose a hidden layer one order of magnitude smaller than the input space, so that if your input vector has lives in a thousand-dimensional space (not uncommon in text problems), then your hidden state should be in the hundreds.

A traditional deep neural network uses different parameters at each layer. In a recurrent neural network, the parameters are shared across all time steps (see preceding *Figure 1*) across all steps. This reflects the fact that the task is the same (in this case, *reading*), just with different inputs. It also helps to reduce the number of parameters we need to learn.

We choose the `tanh` function because it puts the inputs in the range [-1,1]. Later, we will want to use the outputs of the network as probabilities; the output layer is the *softmax* function.

The diagram shown in *Figure 1* fully describes the **forward propagation** of our network, given the weight matrices, we can calculate the output of the network. But how should we train the network to find those weights?

As usual in neural networks, the idea is to use the difference between the predictions of the network and the training labels to adjust the weights in the right direction. For this, we need to specify a loss function. A common choice is the cross-entropy loss function:

$$L(y, o) := -\frac{1}{N} \sum_{n \in N} y_n \log o_n$$

Where N denotes the number of training examples. This function measures a weighted score on the predicted class times the log probability of that class. Note that we get a loss of zero if we have probability of 1 for the correct class, and a positive loss otherwise. This means that the cross entropy punishes us for not being confident. Notice that it also punishes us for being confident and incorrect (why is that?).

To update the weights, we need to compute the derivatives:

$$\frac{\partial L}{\partial U}, \frac{\partial L}{\partial V}, \frac{\partial L}{\partial W}$$

We also need to update the weights in the direction that reduces the error, that is, the opposite direction of the gradient. This sounds no more complicated than vanilla backpropagation in standard neural networks. The situation is a bit more complicated in recurrent neural networks because of the hidden state, which links the current time step with the previous history. To see this, let's say that we want to compute the partial derivative of the loss function with respect to W. We need to calculate:

$$\frac{\partial L}{\partial W} := \frac{\partial L}{\partial o_t} \cdot \frac{\partial o_t}{\partial s_t} \cdot \frac{\partial s_t}{\partial W}$$

Nothing strange here, simply using the chain rule. What's the trick? The catch is in the second and third term in the preceding expression. The internal state at time t depends on the internal state at the previous time. Hence, our computation is actually:

$$\frac{\partial L}{\partial W} = \frac{\partial L}{\partial o_t} \cdot \frac{\partial o_t}{\partial s_t} \cdot \frac{\partial s_t}{\partial s_{t-1}} \cdot \frac{\partial s_{t-1}}{\partial s_{t-2}} \cdots \frac{\partial s_1}{\partial W}$$

You can see how this computation should be done from the preceding diagram, showing the unfolded version of the network. The preceding computation is a different form of the backpropagation algorithm, called **backpropagation through time**.

An important consequence of the preceding is that recurrent neural networks are hard to train. Since the derivative of the `tanh` function is bounded by 1, in the preceding computation, we see a lot of terms multiplying each other between 0 and 1. So the resulting gradient will be small, and it might become numerically zero early on in the training. This is quite bad, because this prevents from learning long-term dependencies. This is because the gradient contributions from *far away* steps become zero because, in line with the chain rule, they are the product of many numbers less than 1. This problem is known as the vanishing gradient problem and was first discovered by Sepp Hochreiter in 1991. It is by no means exclusive of recurrent neural networks. Standard feed-forward neural networks have the same issue when you have many layers (we say they are deep when they have four or more layers), it is just that recurrent neural networks tend to be very deep; as deep as the sentence length, in our case.

There are a few ways to address the vanishing gradient problem, you can use the ReLU function, which in R notation is:

```
ifelse(x>0,x,0)
```

This function has a gradient of 0 or 1, hence it helps us to avoid the vanishing gradient issue. Relevant sections of the parameter space will be explored, even if they correspond to changes in the *far-away* history. Another possibility is to use different mechanisms, such as LSTM networks, proposed by Hochreiter and Schmidhuber in 1997, or GRU networks, by Cho and coauthors in 2014. We will describe these networks briefly in the next section.

Besides the vanishing gradient problem, you can imagine that, depending on the structure of the network and the activation functions you choose, you can have the opposite situation, exploding gradients. This can happen, for instance, if the Jacobian has very small values. This is somehow less serious because you will get a `NaN` error on your code. One way around it is to clip the gradients, this simply means that you should add a condition that filters out values above a certain threshold. Of course, this will depend on your particular application and you might want to take a look at different values in certain cases.

The main complication for implementing different types of neural networks is the computation of the gradients. In simple cases, this can be done by hand, but, as you can see, things quickly get out of control.

Once the gradients are obtained, there are different methods we can use, perhaps the most popular being stochastic gradient descent. Unfortunately, stochastic gradient descent is not *plug and play*. You need to spend some time messing with the step size hyperparameter to get it to work properly. This is quite bad for working with neural networks. Other solutions, such as **Adagrad**, are used in practice. Adagrad is particularly simple to implement, and we will do so later in this chapter. The learning rate is adapted component-wise, and is given by the square root of the sum of squares of the historical, component-wise gradient. Other optimizers include RMSProp and Adam. An advantage, or at least a theoretical guarantee of Adagrad, is that it has a sound theory behind it, rather than being heuristic.

It is possible to optimize a recurrent neural network without relying on gradient methods. For instance, by using genetic or evolutionary algorithms. Evolutionary algorithms are good for finding global minima in some cases, as by avoiding the direction of the gradient, they can find better solutions. A drawback of such algorithms is that they can be quite computing-intensive.

LSTM and GRU networks

As we saw, the recursive structure of RNN and LSTM networks have problems with gradients, either the gradients vanish or explode. One workaround is to introduce forget gates, which will delete some of the old information. This helps to keep track of relevant information without destroying the gradients, and to better preserve important data observed a long time ago.

Both LSTM and GRU share the same design principle with recurrent neural networks, give an input, compute an output, and then a black box updates the internal state. This is crucial in order to understand the bigger picture.

LSTM

For an LSTM, we compute a number of things:

- An input gate, i
- A forget gate, f
- An output gate, o

- A candidate internal state, g
- An internal memory of the unit, c
- A final internal state, s

These are defined by the following recursive equations:

$$
\begin{aligned}
i &= \sigma(U^i x_t + W^i s_{t-1}) \\
f &= \sigma(U^f x_t + W^f s_{t-1}) \\
o &= \sigma(U^o x_t + W^o s_{t-1}) \\
g &= \tanh(U^g x_t + W^g s_{t-1}) \\
c_t &= c_{t-1} \cdot f + g \cdot i \\
s_t &= \tanh(c_t) \cdot o
\end{aligned}
$$

Where:

$$
\sigma(x) := \frac{1}{1 + e^{-x}}
$$

The first three equations describe the input, forget, and output gates. They are called **gates** because they decide which fraction of the newly computed candidate state will be allowed through, and which fraction will be forgotten. Given the new observations, we might want to keep something from the old memories and delete other things, or decide how much of the new information to take into account. This is computed in the memory variable, c. Finally, given this memory update, we keep a fraction of it that will be used by other parts of the network. If the weights in the input gate are all set to 1, the weights in the forget gate are all set to 0 and the weights of the output gate are all set to 1. We almost recover standard recurrent neural networks, except that the activation layer will have an extra `tanh`.

There are many variations of LSTM architectures, building on this basic model. Examples include convolutional, bi-directional, peephole, and LSTM with a forget gate. A great resource is Chris Olah's blog post on the topic: `http://colah.github.io/posts/2015-08-Understanding-LSTMs/`.

GRU

Gated recurrent units (**GRUs**) share a similar design philosophy to LSTM layers. They consist of:

- A hidden state, h
- An internal state, s

- An update gate, z
- A reset gate, r

The updates are given by the following recurrence relations:

$$z = \sigma(U^z x_t + W^z s_{t-1})$$
$$r = \sigma(U^r x_t + W^r s_{t-1})$$
$$h = \tanh(U^h x_t + W^h(s_{t-1} r))$$
$$s_t = (1 - z) \cdot h + z \cdot s_{t-1}$$

The reset gate tells us how to put together the input with the previous memory. The update gate defines how much of the previous memory we should keep for the next iteration. This helps the network to forget useless things, and create connections with newer evidence. The resulting network has no hidden memory (c) which is independent of the internal state, as in the case with LSTMs. They also have input and forget gates merged into the update gate. One more key difference is that there is no second non-linearity (the second call to `tanh` in LSTMs) when computing the final output.

So, which one to use? The jury is still out on that one. There is no conclusive evidence to use one network over another. GRUs have fewer parameters and may be a bit faster to train. They also might need less data to generalize well (as it is easier to estimate the weights accurately). GRUs are quite new, from 2014, so they have not been very well-explored.

RNNs from scratch in R

The purpose of this section is to show you how you can implement recurrent neural networks from bare bones in R. This is perhaps not the optimal solution for a number of reasons, but it is a great way to get started in deep learning.

There are many *plug and play* frameworks like H2O, MXNet, TensorFlow, or Keras, that have compatibility with R. Our goal is to focus on the understanding of the algorithm rather than a particular API, although we will include an example using Keras. This is for two reasons, at the time of writing, the compatibility with R suffers from growing pains and we encountered many errors and issues with the different packages. On the other hand, even the stable versions of such packages have ever-changing APIs. We will focus on this section in building a very simple recurrent neural network from scratch, using simple tools from R.

We will start from the beginning, with a super-quick introduction to R6 classes in R using the example of the perceptron, and incrementally build from there.

Classes in R with R6

The R language supports object oriented programming, although there is no universal standard for class definition. R has different class systems, S3, S4, R5, and R6. Since R is, in its origins, a statistics playground software, some features from modern general purpose programming languages are not present there. Complex projects are a bit harder to write, as a result, but not impossible, and the situation keeps improving thanks to the community support.

Why the name R6? As per the official R documentation (https://cran.r-project.org/web/packages/R6/vignettes/Introduction.html), R6 is the successor of the package R5, whose development was halted. R6 is an attempt to improve some deficiencies in S3 and S4. It is also the recommended method to implement self-modifying objects, as is the case here. We need to change the weights of the network as the training progresses.

How do we define an R6 class? Let's show you this with an example in the next section.

Perceptron as an R6 class

The perceptron is the simplest neural network. It consists of an input and an output (no hidden layers), and the activation function is just the Heaviside function (step function at the origin), when the bias term is included.

This is the skeleton of the class:

```
library(R6)
Perceptron <- R6Class("Perceptron",
 public = list(
      threshold = NULL,
      dim = NULL,
      n_iter = NULL,
      learning_rate = NULL,
      w = NULL,
  initialize = function(threshold = 0, learning_rate = 0.25, n_iter=100,
dim=2) {
      self$n_iter <- n_iter
      self$threshold <- threshold
      self$learning_rate <- learning_rate
  }
  , forward = function(x) {
      }
  , backward = function(t,y,x) {
      }

  }
```

```
    ,   train = function(X,t){
        }
    }
    }
    }
    ,   predict = function(X){
        X <- cbind(-1,X)  #add bias
        preds <- c()
        for(i in 1:nrow(X)){
        preds[i] <- self$forward(X[i,])
    }
    return(preds)
    }
    )
)
```

Although R6 supports private methods, we do not really need them at this point; we can live with public methods, which are specified previously. Note that you do need to initialize with NULL all the objects you plan to use; failing to do so will result in errors.

Now we can implement the perceptron, filling in the blanks in the preceding function:

```
library(R6)
Perceptron <- R6Class("Perceptron",
 public = list(
     threshold = NULL,
     dim = NULL,
     n_iter = NULL,
     learning_rate = NULL,
     w = NULL,
     initialize = function(threshold = 0,
                           learning_rate = 0.25,
                           n_iter=100, dim=2)
                       {
                       self$n_iter <- n_iter
                       self$threshold <- threshold
                       self$learning_rate <- learning_rate
                       self$dim <- dim
                       self$w <- matrix(runif(self$dim+1), ncol = self$dim+1)
                       }
    ,   forward = function(x){
                       dot_product <- sum(x*self$w)
                       y <- ifelse(dot_product>self$threshold,1,0)
                       return(y)
        }
    ,   backward = function(t,y,x){
                       for(j in 1:ncol(x)){
                       self$w[j] <- self$w[j]+self$learning_rate*(t-y)*x[j]
```

```
                }
    }
    , train = function(X,t){
                X <- cbind(-1,X) #add bias term
                n_examples <- nrow(X)

                for(iter in 1:self$n_iter){
                    for(i in 1:nrow(X)){
                        y_i <- self$forward(X[i,])
                        self$backward(t[i],y_i, X[i,])
                        }
                    if(iter %% 20 == 0){
                        cat("Iteration: ", iter)
                        print("Weights: ")
                        print(unlist(self$w))
                        }
                    }
        }
    , predict = function(X){
                X <- cbind(-1,X) #add bias
                preds <- c()
                for(i in 1:nrow(X)){
                    preds[i] <- self$forward(X[i,])
                    }
            return(preds)
        }
    )
)
```

How can you test that your implementation is correct? Well, your network should be able to predict correctly the labels of the following data (the OR function) after a few iterations:

x1	x2	t
0	0	0
1	0	1
0	1	1
1	1	1

To test your implementation, you need first to create a data frame with this dataset:

```
x1 <- c(0,0,1,1)
x2 <- c(0,1,0,1)
t <- c(0,1,1,1)
X <- data.frame(x1=x1, x2=x2)
```

Now, let's initialize:

```
lr <- LR$new(n_iter=100, dim=ncol(X))
lr
```

Next, we call the `train` method:

```
lr$train(X,t)
lr$w
```

And, finally, `predict`:

```
lr$predict(X)
```

To get an insight into what the perceptron is doing, we will draw the decision boundary, that is, the criteria the algorithm is using for classification.

First, we coerce to a data frame, as we will use the `ggplot2` library:

```
df <- as.data.frame(X)
df$t <- as.factor(t)
```

Then, we get the coefficients:

```
# Get the line
w0 <- as.numeric(lr$w[1])
w1 <- as.numeric(lr$w[2])
w2 <- as.numeric(lr$w[3])
```

And finally, we create the line:

```
x1_vals <- seq(-0.15,1,0.1)
x2_vals <- (w0-w1*x1_vals)/w2
boundary <- data.frame(x1_vals=x1_vals, x2_vals=x2_vals)

#Plot decision boundary
library(ggplot2)
ggplot()+
    geom_point(data=df, aes(x=x1,y=x2, color=t, size=2))+
    geom_line(data=boundary, aes(x=x1_vals, y=x2_vals, size=1))+
    theme_bw()
```

This gives us the following output:

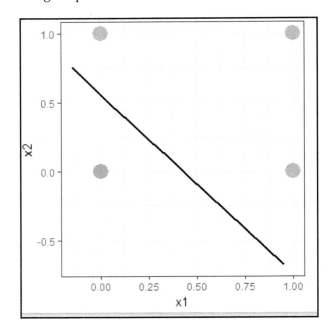

The OR function and the decision boundary

This shows us that the perceptron can separate this dataset in a non-unique way.

The functionality of the perceptron is quite limited, and it is only shown here to illustrate the way to implement classes in R. For instance, the perceptron is unable to separate simple examples as the one shown as follows:

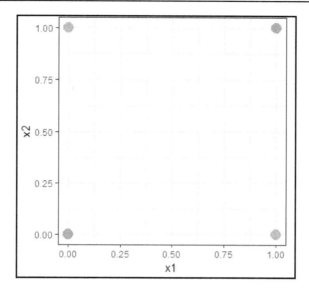

The XOR function

As you can see, there is no way to draw a line that separates both classes, hence showing the limitations of the perceptron.

There are two ways around this. One is to create additional features, like *x1*x2*, which would indeed make the data separable. The other way is to create a more complicated decision mechanism (a non-linear decision boundary). We will, in some sense, show you how to do the second.

Logistic regression

We can, in a very similar way, implement logistic regression as an R6 class. The code is included just for intellectual curiosity, as it is closely related.

There is not a lot of difference between the perceptron and logistic regression. They share a lot in common, the main difference being the activation function (logit instead of the Heaviside step function), which also changes the update rule for the weights. For convenience, we highlight in bold the more relevant differences:

```
library(R6)
logit <- function(x){
  1/(1+exp(-x))
}
LR <- R6Class("LR",
```

```
            public = list(
            dim = NULL,
            n_iter = NULL,
            learning_rate = NULL,
            w = NULL,
            initialize = function(learning_rate = 0.25, n_iter=100, dim=2){
                self$n_iter <- n_iter
                self$learning_rate <- learning_rate
                self$dim <- dim
                self$w <- matrix(runif(self$dim+1), ncol = self$dim+1)
    }
    , forward = function(x){
                dot_product <- sum(x*self$w)
                y <- logit(dot_product)
                return(y)
        }
    , backward = function(t,y,x){
                for(j in 1:ncol(x)){
                self$w[j] <- self$w[j]+self$learning_rate*(t-
y)*x[j]*logit(x[j])*(1-logit(x[j]))
    }

    }
    , train = function(X,t){
                X <- cbind(-1,X) #add bias term
                n_examples <- nrow(X)

    for(iter in 1:self$n_iter){
        for(i in 1:nrow(X)){
        y_i <- self$forward(X[i,])
        self$backward(t[i],y_i, X[i,])
    }
    if(iter %% 20 == 0){
        cat("Iteration: ", iter)
        print("Weights: ")
        print(unlist(self$w))
    }

    }
    }
    , predict = function(X){
        X <- cbind(-1,X) #add bias
        preds <- c()
        for(i in 1:nrow(X)){
            preds[i] <- self$forward(X[i,])
        }
    return(preds)
    }
```

```
    )
  )
```

As we can see, there are not a lot of changes with respect to the previous code, the main action happening on the backward step.

Multi-layer perceptron

Like pancakes, neural networks are made to be stacked with each other. We can make the output of a layer the input of the next layer, called a **hidden layer**. This hidden layer consists of a linear combination of the inputs to which an activation function is applied. This creates a new hidden vector which we can take as an input for the following hidden layer, on each step recombining the outputs from the previous layer by some weights and applying an activation function.

Let's start by introducing the sigmoid function, which will be useful later:

```
library(R6)

sigmoid <- function(x){
  1/(1+exp(-x))
}
```

The skeleton of the class is now:

```
MLP <- R6Class("MLP",
                    public = list(
                      dim = NULL,
                      n_iter = NULL,
                      learning_rate = NULL,
                      hidden_layer_size=NULL,
                      Wih = NULL,
                      Who = NULL,
                      a = NULL,
                      initialize = function(learning_rate = 0.3,
                                            n_iter=NA,
                                            dim=NA,
                                            hidden_layer_size=NA){
                        #INITIALIZATION CODE
                      }
                      , forward = function(x){
                        #Input: training vector
                        #Output: Class
                      }
                      , backward = function(t,y,X){
                        # Input: Target, prediction and matrix of
```

```
training examples
                                # No output, gradients are modified in the class
`
               }
    , train = function(X,t){
               # Run the training loop: forward and backward
propagation for n_iter
               }
    , predict = function(X){
               # Call to the forward function for all training
examples
               }
        )
    )
```

The forward step is usually the simplest, which in our case is:

```
    , forward = function(x){
                        h <- as.matrix(x)%*%self$Wih
                        self$a <- sigmoid(h)
                        y <- sigmoid(self$a %*% self$Who) #Output of the
network
                        return(y)
                    }
```

The backward step is the tricky part here. We have one error component, coming from the derivative of the loss function with respect to the last component. This is called `layer2_delta` in the code. The other component comes from the derivative with respect to the weights on the first layer, called `layer1_delta`. These are the derivatives that need to be evaluated in the corresponding points, namely X for the case of `layer1_delta` and the output a of the activation function for `layer2_delta`.

```
    , backward = function(t,y,X){
                        # Compute the error in the output layer
                        layer2_error <- t-y
                        layer2_delta <- (layer2_error)*(y*(1-y))

                        #Compute the error in the input layer
                        layer1_error <- layer2_delta %*% t(self$Who)
                        layer1_delta <- layer1_error*self$a*(1-self$a)
                        # Adjustments of the weights
                        layer1_adjustment <- t(X) %*% layer1_delta
                        layer2_adjustment <- t(self$a) %*% layer2_delta
                        self$Wih <-
self$Wih+self$learning_rate*layer1_adjustment
                        self$Who <-
```

```
self$Who+self$learning_rate*layer2_adjustment
                              }
```

The other functions are easier to complete. For completeness, the full code is included here:

```
MLP <- R6Class("MLP",
                        public = list(
                            dim = NULL,
                            n_iter = NULL,
                            learning_rate = NULL,
                            hidden_layer_size=NULL,
                            Wih = NULL,
                            Who = NULL,
                            a = NULL,
                            initialize = function(learning_rate = 0.3,
                                                  n_iter=NA,
                                                  dim=NA,
                                                  hidden_layer_size=NA){
                            self$dim <- dim
                            self$n_iter <- n_iter
                            self$learning_rate <- learning_rate
                            self$hidden_layer_size <- hidden_layer_size
                            self$Wih <-
matrix(runif(self$hidden_layer_size*self$dim),
                                                  ncol =
self$hidden_layer_size)
                            self$Who <-
matrix(runif((self$hidden_layer_size)), ncol = 1)
                            self$a <-
matrix(runif(self$hidden_layer_size*self$dim), ncol = self$dim)
                            }
                        , forward = function(x){
                            h <- as.matrix(x)%*%self$Wih
                            self$a <- sigmoid(h)
                            y <- sigmoid(self$a %*% self$Who) #Output of the
network
                            return(y)
                        }
                        , backward = function(t,y,X){
                            # Compute the error in the output layer
                            layer2_error <- t-y
                            layer2_delta <- (layer2_error)*(y*(1-y))

                            #Compute the error in the input layer
                            layer1_error <- layer2_delta %*% t(self$Who)
                            layer1_delta <- layer1_error*self$a*(1-self$a)
                            # Adjustments of the weights
```

```
                            layer1_adjustment <- t(X) %*% layer1_delta
                            layer2_adjustment <- t(self$a) %*% layer2_delta
                            self$Wih <-
self$Wih+self$learning_rate*layer1_adjustment
                            self$Who <-
self$Who+self$learning_rate*layer2_adjustment

            }
            , train = function(X,t){
                n_examples <- nrow(X)
                for(iter in 1:self$n_iter){
                    preds <- self$forward(X)
                    self$backward(t,preds, X)
                    if(iter %% 1000 == 0){
                        cat("Iteration: ", iter,"\n")
                    }
                }
            }
            , predict = function(X){
                preds <- self$forward(X)
                return(preds)
            }
        )
    )
```

Let's try our network in the OR function, which as we saw, is linearly separable:

```
x1 <- c(0,0,1,1)
x2 <- c(0,1,0,1)
t <- c(0,1,1,1)
X <- as.matrix(data.frame(x1=x1, x2=x2))
```

Now, let's generate the predicted labels:

```
clf <- MLP$new(n_iter=5000,dim=ncol(X), hidden_layer_size=4)
clf$train(X,t)
clf$predict(X)
```

Well, that's all very nice, but certainly not much of an advantage, right? We already knew that this simple training example was correctly solved by the perceptron.

To really go one step further, let's consider the following data (the xor) function:

```
xor <- data.frame(x1=c(0,0,1,1), x2=c(0,1,0,1), t = c(0,1,1,0))
clf$train(xor[,1:2],xor[,3])
clf$predict(xor[,1:2])
```

We know that this is not linearly separable:

```
library(ggplot2)
grid_size <- 1e2
grid <- data.frame(V1=0,V2=0)
base <- seq(0,1,1/grid_size)
```

Let's generate a grid to which we will apply the decision function:

```
for(j in 1:grid_size){
 V1 <- rep(base[j],grid_size+1)
 V2 <- base
 tmp <- data.frame(V1=V1,V2=V2)
 grid <- rbind(tmp,grid)
}
```

Now, let's finally plot the evaluation of this function on the grid:

```
grid$z <- with(grid,clf$predict(cbind(V1,V2)))
ggplot(grid,aes(x=V1,y=V2))+geom_tile(aes(fill=z))+theme_bw()
```

We see that the multi-layer perceptron does a better job on this data, and is able to correctly guess the separation boundary between these two regions:

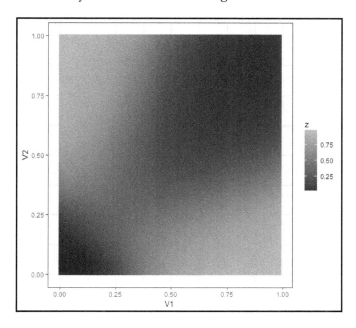

Implementing a RNN

Let's go to the most important part of this chapter. Implementing our recurrent neural network with our bare hands. We show two different implementations, the first one using R6 classes, which we find could be more useful for using in your projects, since it is more portable. The second implementation we show closely follows sample code used in Andrej Karpathy's blog post for a minimal character-level recurrent neural network cited previously.

Implementation as an R6 class

First, let's show the skeleton of this class. We need a number of functions here. First, we need to import the R6 package and create two auxiliary functions:

```
library(R6)
set.seed(1234)
softmax <- function(x){
 xt <- exp(x-max(x))
 return(xt/sum(xt))
}
zeros_like <- function(M){
 return(matrix(0,dim(as.matrix(M))[1],dim(as.matrix(M))[2]))
}
```

This will come in handy during the code to calculate the *softmax* and initialize matrices with the correct sizes. As before, our program needs the following basic functions:

- Forward propagation
- Backward propagation
- A sample from the obtained probability distribution
- Train the model

The structure of the class should look like:

```
RNN <- R6Class("RNN",
          public = list(
          hidden_size = NULL,
          vocab_size = NULL,
          learning_rate = NULL,
          U = NULL,
          V = NULL,
          W = NULL,
          seq_length = NULL,
          chars = NULL,
```

```
        n_iter = NULL,
        initialize = function(hidden_size = NA, vocab_size = NA,
                    chars=NA, n_iter=100, seq_length=NA,
learning_rate=0.01){
        }
        , forward_step = function(input_sample){
            ## Takes one column vector and returns the softmax output
        }
        , bptt = function(inputs,targets,s_prev){
            seq_size <- length(inputs) #total length of the sequence
            loss <- 0
            for(idx in 1:seq_size){
             # Forward pass: Update the hidden state and predict
               # Backward pass: updates using the gradient
                  for(j in length(inputs):1){
                      ## derivatives of error vs output
                      }
            }
            return(list("loss"=loss, "dU"=dU, "dW"=dW, "dV"=dV,
"hs"=hs[length(inputs)-1]))
        }
        ,   sample_char <- function(h, seed_ix, n){
        ## generate a sample from the model
        ## given a hidden state and an initial seed
            }
        , train = function(text){
            ## Main training loop with Adagrad updates
            }
    )
  )
```

The most interesting is the `bptt` function, so let us describe it in more detail. When the inputs from the environment are received, in this case, a chunk of text, we will loop through every character of this chunk and generate predictions for the following states given the present state and the value of the hidden state from the previous iteration. Once we traverse the input chunk, we need to calculate the updates for the gradients in reverse order. This is done in the back propagation part of this function.

We observed better performance with Adagrad instead of stochastic gradient descent, which should be implemented on the final part, in the `train` function.

The full code is:

```
library(R6)
set.seed(1234)
softmax <- function(x){
  xt <- exp(x-max(x))
```

```
    return(xt/sum(xt))
}
zeros_like <- function(M){
    return(matrix(0,dim(as.matrix(M))[1],dim(as.matrix(M))[2]))
}
RNN <- R6Class("RNN",
                public = list(
                    hidden_size = NULL,
                    vocab_size = NULL,
                    learning_rate = NULL,
                    U = NULL,
                    V = NULL,
                    W = NULL,
                    seq_length = NULL,
                    chars = NULL,
                    n_iter = NULL,
                    initialize = function(hidden_size = NA, vocab_size = NA,
chars=NA, n_iter=100, seq_length=NA, learning_rate=0.01){
                        self$hidden_size <- hidden_size
                        self$n_iter <- n_iter
                        self$learning_rate <- learning_rate
                        self$seq_length <- seq_length
                        self$vocab_size <- as.numeric(vocab_size)
                        self$chars <- chars
                        self$U <- matrix(rnorm(hidden_size*vocab_size)*0.01,
nrow=self$hidden_size) # input to hidden
                        self$W <- matrix(rnorm(hidden_size*hidden_size)*0.01,
nrow=self$hidden_size) # hidden to hidden
                        self$V <- matrix(rnorm(vocab_size*hidden_size)*0.01,
nrow=self$vocab_size) # hidden to output
                    }
                    , forward_step = function(input_sample){
                        ## Takes one column vector and returns probabilities
                        x <- input_sample
                        s <- tanh(self$U%*%x+self$W%*%self$s)
                        o <- softmax(self$V%*%self$s)
                        return(list("pred"=o,"state"=s))
                    }
                    , bptt = function(inputs,targets,s_prev){
                        seq_size <- length(inputs) #total length of the sequence
                        xs <- lapply(vector('list',seq_size), function(i)
matrix(0,self$vocab_size, 1))
                        hs <- lapply(vector('list',seq_size), function(i)
matrix(0,self$hidden_size, 1))
                        ys <- lapply(vector('list',seq_size), function(i)
matrix(0,self$vocab_size, 1))
                        ps <- lapply(vector('list',seq_size), function(i)
matrix(0,self$vocab_size,1))
```

```r
                loss <- 0
                for(idx in 1:seq_size){
                  xs[[idx]] <- matrix(0,self$vocab_size,1)
                  xs[[idx]][inputs[[idx]]] = 1
                  ## Update the hidden state
                  if(idx==1){
                    hs[[idx]] <-
tanh(self$U%*%xs[[idx]]+self$W%*%s_prev)
                  }
                  else{
                    hs[[idx]] <-
tanh(self$U%*%xs[[idx]]+self$W%*%hs[[(idx-1)]])
                  }
                  ## calculate the probabilities for the next character
                  ys[[idx]] <- self$V%*%hs[[idx]]
                  ps[[idx]] <- softmax(ys[[idx]])
                  ## Cross-entropy loss
                  loss <- loss-log(ps[[idx]][targets[idx], 1])
                  # Calculate gradients
                  dU <- zeros_like(self$U)
                  dW <- zeros_like(self$W)
                  dV <- zeros_like(self$V)
                  dhnext <- zeros_like(s_prev)
                  for(j in length(inputs):1){
                    ## Gradient of the error vs output
                    dy <- ps[[j]]
                    dy[targets[j]] <- dy[targets[j]]-1
                    dV <- dV+dy%*%t(hs[[j]])
                    dh <- t(self$V)%*%dy + dhnext
                    ## backprop through the tanh
                    dhraw <- (1 - hs[[j]] * hs[[j]]) * dh
                    ## derivative of the error between input and hidden
layer
                    dU <- dU+dhraw%*%t(xs[[j]])
                    if(j==1){
                      dW <- dW+dhraw%*%t(s_prev)
                    }
                    else{
                      dW <- dW+dhraw%*%t(hs[[(j-1)]])
                    }
                    dhnext <- t(self$W)%*%dhraw
                  }
                }
                return(list("loss"=loss, "dU"=dU, "dW"=dW, "dV"=dV,
"hs"=hs[length(inputs)-1]))
              }
              ,
              sample_char = function(h, seed_ix, n){
```

```
# Generate a sequence of characters given a seed and a
hidden state
x <- matrix(0,self$vocab_size, 1)
x[seed_ix] <- 1
ixes <- c()
for(t in 1:n){
  h <- tanh(self$U%*%x+self$W%*%h)
  y <- self$V%*%h
  p <- exp(y)/sum(exp(y)) #softmax
  ix <- sample(self$chars,size=1, replace=T, prob=p)
  x <- matrix(0,self$vocab_size,1)
  x[which(chars==ix)] <- 1
  ixes[t] <- ix
}
return(ixes)
}
, train = function(text){
  n <- 1
  p <- 1
  mU <- zeros_like(self$U)
  mW <- zeros_like(self$W)
  mV <- zeros_like(self$V)
# memory variables for Adagrad
smooth_loss = -log(1.0/self$vocab_size)*self$seq_length
# loss at iteration 0
for(n in 1:self$n_iter){
  #
  if(p + self$seq_length + 1 >= length(text) || n == 1){
    # reset RNN memory
    ## h_old is the previous hidden state of RNN
    h_old <- matrix(0,self$hidden_size, 1)
    # go from start of data
    p <- 1
  }
  inputs <-
unlist(lapply(text[p:(p+self$seq_length)],function(c){which(self$chars==c)}
))
  targets <-
unlist(lapply(text[(p+1):(p+self$seq_length+1)],function(c){which(self$char
s==c)}))
  # See what the model is doing from time to time
  if(n %% 100 == 0){
    txt <- self$sample_char(h_old, inputs[[1]], 200)
    ## Find the line breaks
    line_breaks <- which(txt=="\n")
    if(length(line_breaks)<2){
      print(txt)
    }
```

```
                              else{
                                for(ix in 2:(length(line_breaks-1))){
                                  first_ix <- line_breaks[ix-1]+1
                                  last_ix <- line_breaks[ix]-1
                                  print(paste(txt[first_ix:last_ix], collapse=""))
                                }
                              }
                              smooth_loss = smooth_loss*0.99+loss*0.01
                              print('---- sample -----')
                              cat("Iteration number: ",n, "\n")
                              cat("Loss: ", smooth_loss)
                           }
                           tmp <- self$bptt(inputs, targets, h_old)
                           loss <- unlist(tmp$loss)
                           dU <- unlist(tmp$dU)
                           dW <- unlist(tmp$dW)
                           dV <- unlist(tmp$dV)
                           h_old <- unlist(tmp$hs)
                           ## Time to update the Adagrad weights
                           mU <- mU+dU**2
                           self$U <- self$U-self$learning_rate * dU / sqrt(mU +
1e-8)

                           mW <- mW+dW**2
                           self$W <- self$W-self$learning_rate * dW / sqrt(mW +
1e-8)

                           mV <- mV+dV**2
                           self$V <- self$V-self$learning_rate * dV / sqrt(mV +
1e-8)

                           p <- p+self$seq_length
                           n <- n+1
                        }
                        return(1)
                     }
                  )
               )
```

There is certainly some work to be done here. For instance, you can refactor the part of the forward pass to use the `forward_step` function explicitly. We leave that as an exercise.

To test your code, you can use the list of male and female names (see the *Exercises* section). We show how to do this if we use the list for female names (after removing the header information manually):

```
library(readr)
library(stringr)
library(purrr)
library(tokenizers)
data <- read_lines("./data/female.txt")
```

```
text <- data %>%
    str_to_lower() %>%
    str_c(collapse = "\n") %>%
    tokenize_characters(strip_non_alphanum = FALSE, simplify = TRUE)
chars <- text %>% unique
test <- RNN$new(hidden_size = 100,
                vocab_size = length(chars),
                chars=chars,
                n_iter=100,
                seq_length=25,
                learning_rate=0.01)
test$train(text)
```

You can use your own data; it simply needs to be a text file.

> While training your models with your own data, be careful with what you are passing as input, always remember, *garbage in, garbage out*. Insert some logs or print statements here and there, so that you can see what your network doing.

Implementation without R6

In this section, we include the implementation of the same basic recurrent neural network without using R6 classes. First, some imports and setting the seed:

```
library(readr)
library(stringr)
library(purrr)
library(tokenizers)
set.seed(1234)
```

We introduce an auxiliary function to initialize to zeros a matrix with the shape of a matrix, M:

```
zeros_like <- function(M){
  return(matrix(0,dim(as.matrix(M))[1],dim(as.matrix(M))[2]))
}
```

We also need the softmax function:

```
softmax <- function(x){
  xt <- exp(x-max(x))
  return(xt/sum(xt))
}
```

We will use this for testing the female names data (see the *Exercises* section):

```
data <- read_lines("./data/female.txt")
```

And do some preprocessing:

```
text <- data %>%
  str_to_lower() %>%
  str_c(collapse = "\n") %>%
  tokenize_characters(strip_non_alphanum = FALSE, simplify = TRUE)
```

We set up the characters of our vocabulary. This is required to do the one-hot encoding of each input data:

```
chars <- text %>% unique
chars
```

Now, we go to the main part of the program. Besides the initializations, notice that we define a `lossFun` which includes the forward steps and backpropagation through time:

```
library(readr)
library(stringr)
library(purrr)
library(tokenizers)

set.seed(1234)

zeros_like <- function(M){
  return(matrix(0,dim(as.matrix(M))[1],dim(as.matrix(M))[2]))
}


softmax <- function(x){
  xt <- exp(x-max(x))
  return(xt/sum(xt))
}
data <- read_lines("./data/female.txt")
head(data)


text <- data %>%
  str_to_lower() %>%
  str_c(collapse = "\n") %>%
  tokenize_characters(strip_non_alphanum = FALSE, simplify = TRUE)


chars <- text %>% unique
chars
```

```
# hyperparameters
hidden_size = 100 # size of hidden layer of neurons
seq_length = 10 # number of steps to unroll the RNN for
learning_rate = 1e-1
vocab_size = length(chars)


U <- matrix(rnorm(hidden_size*vocab_size)*0.01, nrow=hidden_size) # input
to hidden
W <- matrix(rnorm(hidden_size*hidden_size)*0.01, nrow=hidden_size) # hidden
to hidden
V <- matrix(rnorm(vocab_size*hidden_size)*0.01, nrow=vocab_size) # hidden
to output
bh <- matrix(0,hidden_size, 1) # hidden bias
by <- matrix(0,vocab_size, 1) # output bias


lossFun <- function(inputs,targets,prev_hidden){
  tot <- length(inputs) #total sequence length
  xs <- lapply(vector('list',tot), function(i) matrix(0,vocab_size, 1))
  hs <- lapply(vector('list',tot), function(i) matrix(0,hidden_size, 1))
  ys <- lapply(vector('list',tot), function(i) matrix(0,vocab_size, 1))
  ps <- lapply(vector('list',tot), function(i) matrix(0,vocab_size,1))
  loss <- 0
  for(idx in 1:tot){
    xs[[idx]] <- matrix(0,vocab_size,1)
    xs[[idx]][inputs[[idx]]] = 1

    ## update the hidden state
    if(idx==1){
      hs[[idx]] <- tanh(U%*%xs[[idx]]+W%*%h_old+bh)
    }
    else{
      hs[[idx]] <- tanh(U%*%xs[[idx]]+W%*%hs[[(idx-1)]]+bh)
    }
    ## Get char probabilities
    ys[[idx]] <- V%*%hs[[idx]] + by
    ps[[idx]] <- softmax(ys[[idx]])
    ## Loss function (cross-entropy here)
    loss <- loss-log(ps[[idx]][targets[idx], 1])
    # Initialize the gradients
    dU <- zeros_like(U)
    dW <- zeros_like(W)
    dV <- zeros_like(V)
    dbh <- zeros_like(bh)
    dby <- zeros_like(by)
    dhnext <- zeros_like(h_old)
    # Here comes the backprop loop
```

```
  for(j in length(inputs):1){
    # Output vs loss
    dy <- ps[[j]]
    dy[targets[j]] <- dy[targets[j]]-1
    dV <- dV+dy%*%t(hs[[j]])
    dby <- dby+dy
    ## Hidden layer
    dh <- t(V)%*%dy + dhnext
    dh_raw <- (1 - hs[[j]] * hs[[j]]) * dh
    dbh <- dbh+dh_raw
    dU <- dU+dh_raw%*%t(xs[[j]])
    if(j==1){
      dW <- dW+dh_raw%*%t(h_old)
    }
    else{
      dW <- dW+dh_raw%*%t(hs[[(j-1)]])
    }
    dhnext <- t(W)%*%dh_raw
  }
}
  return(list("loss"=loss, "dU"=dU, "dW"=dW, "dV"=dV, "dbh"=dbh, "dby"=dby,
"hs"=hs[length(inputs)-1]))
}


## Sample a few chars given a hidden state and a seed
sample_char <- function(h, seed_ix, n){
  x <- matrix(0,vocab_size, 1)
  x[seed_ix] <- 1
  ixes <- c()
  for(t in 1:n){
    h <- tanh(U%*%x+W%*%h+bh)
    y <- V%*%h+by
    p <- exp(y)/sum(exp(y)) #softmax
    ix <- sample(chars,size=1, replace=T, prob=p)
    x <- matrix(0,vocab_size,1)
    x[which(chars==ix)] <- 1
    ixes[t] <- ix
  }
  return(ixes)
}


n <- 1
p <- 1

mU <- zeros_like(U)
mW <- zeros_like(W)
```

```
mV <- zeros_like(V)
mbh <- zeros_like(bh)
mby <- zeros_like(by) # memory variables for Adagrad
smooth_loss = -log(1.0/vocab_size)*seq_length # loss at iteration 0

while(T){
  if(p + seq_length + 1 >= length(data) || n == 1){
    # reset RNN memory
    ## h_old is the hidden state of RNN
    h_old <- matrix(0,hidden_size, 1)
    # go from the start of the data
    p <- 1
  }
  inputs <-
unlist(sapply(text[p:(p+seq_length)],function(c){which(chars==c)}))
  targets <-
unlist(sapply(text[(p+1):(p+seq_length+1)],function(c){which(chars==c)}))
  # Check what the model is doing from time to time
  if(n %% 100 == 0){
    txt <- sample_char(h_old, inputs[[1]], 200)
    ## Find line breaks
    line_breaks <- which(txt=="\n")
    if(length(line_breaks)<2){
      print(txt)
    }
    else{
      for(ix in 2:(length(line_breaks-1))){
        first_ix <- line_breaks[ix-1]+1
        last_ix <- line_breaks[ix]-1
        print(paste(txt[first_ix:last_ix], collapse=""))
      }
    }
    smooth_loss = smooth_loss*0.99+loss*0.01
    print('---- sample -----')
    cat("Iteration number: ",n, "\n")
    cat("Loss: ", smooth_loss)
  }
  tmp <- lossFun(inputs, targets, h_old)
  loss <- unlist(tmp$loss)
  dU <- unlist(tmp$dU)
  dW <- unlist(tmp$dW)
  dV <- unlist(tmp$dV)
  dbh <- unlist(tmp$dbh)
  dby <- unlist(tmp$dby)
  h_old <- unlist(tmp$hs)
  ## Weight updates for Adagrad

  mU <- mU+dU**2
```

```
U <- U-learning_rate * dU / sqrt(mU + 1e-8)
mW <- mW+dW**2
W <- W-learning_rate * dW / sqrt(mW + 1e-8)
mV <- mV+dV**2
V <- V-learning_rate * dV / sqrt(mV + 1e-8)
mbh <- mbh+mbh**2
bh <- bh-learning_rate * dbh / sqrt(mbh + 1e-8)
mby <- mby+dby**2
by <- by-learning_rate * dby / sqrt(mby + 1e-8)

p <- p+seq_length
n <- n+1
}
```

What does this recurrent neural network produce? In the beginning, we get the following female names:

```
[1] "iaiaaan"
[1] "aannaeinraaniaraeinareanaeaaraana"
[1] "iainii"
[1] "laeoda"
[1] "arineaeia"
[1] "rdiiaai"
[1] "eiaa"
[1] "irineaaasrnaaaaaalaiiaaiaiiaranaxiaaaannnaiiorieiida"
[1] "naiiaaiaaialiaraaaaannaian"
[1] "aaaaieaiaain"
[1] "nad"
[1] "iiaaeaeaianiaa"
[1] "---- sample -----"
Iteration number: 100
```

After some time, the network starts to make sense of the data:

```
[1] "anna"
[1] "annanianinbnatarmadnanannannnablantd"
[1] "antsnamannd"
[1] "iniaina"
[1] "anta"
[1] "alnaenalnalna"
[1] "annilinnina"
[1] "anma"
[1] "bna"
[1] "anganna"
[1] "alnaniannnnna"
[1] "iriannannennandana"
[1] "anyoa"
[1] "annannllynaenpanda"
```

```
[1]  "anedaannna"
[1]  "anna"
[1]  "---- sample -----"
Iteration number: 700
```

Note how really amazing this is. After only 700 iterations, you start rediscovering female names, and generate a few real-sounding names (like `anyoa`). All this is achieved from the character level. The network has no idea about words, nor language. It is able to create those names from statistical dependencies on the input data only.

What else can we do? I tried the same code on the LaTeX version of my PhD thesis. After a few thousand iterations, it learns to do the imports of the packages correctly. A bit further ahead, it starts to write small words in English. You can try it with other data; see the *Exercises* section for some suggestions.

RNN without derivatives — the cross-entropy method

We will replace the backward propagation part on the preceding neural network with a Monte Carlo algorithm, called the **cross-entropy method**. This is a general-purpose algorithm introduced by Reuven Rubinstein which is quite helpful in many cases, especially for rare event simulation. It has been proven efficient for many reinforcement learning tasks, so why not give it a try?

The method consists of two parts:

1. Generate a random data sample (trajectories, vectors) according to a specified mechanism.
2. Update the parameters of the random mechanism based on the data to produce a *better* sample in the next iteration. This step involves minimizing the cross-entropy or Kullback–Leibler divergence.

Let's first illustrate the situation with a small sample code. Suppose we want to minimize the function:

```
# the function we need to maximize
f <- function(theta){
  reward = -sum((solution - theta)**2)
  return(reward)
}
```

The maximum of this function, as a function of `theta`, is reached when `theta==solution`.

Let's fix a value for `solution` as the vector:

```
solution <- c(0.5, 0.1, -0.3)
```

And set up some initial parameters:

```
dim_theta <- 3
theta_mean <- matrix(0,dim_theta,1)
theta_std <- diag(dim_theta)
```

The cross-entropy method we will use works as follows:

- Generate some sample solutions using an initial estimate for mean and standard deviation of the parameters.
- Calculate as many as `batch_size` of those (where `batch_size` is a hyper-parameter).
- Consider only a fraction of them, called the elite fraction (`elite_frac`). This is another hyper-parameter.
- Get the top `elite_frac` of those, that means, those generated sample solutions that gave the highest reward in terms of the function we want to maximize.
- Find the mean and covariance of those parameters to generate new candidate solutions.

The following code example shows how to implement the logic described previously:

```
cem <- function(f, n_iter, theta_mean, theta_std, batch_size=25,
elite_frac=0.2){
 for(it in 1:n_iter){
 # Get a sample using the previous parameters
 thetas <- matrix(mvrnorm(n=batch_size*dim_theta, mu= theta_mean,
Sigma=theta_std), ncol = dim_theta)
 rewards <- apply(thetas,1,f)
 # Now choose the best
 n_elite <- as.integer(batch_size * elite_frac)
 elite_inds <- sort(rewards, decreasing = T, index.return=T)$ix[1:n_elite]
 elite_thetas <- thetas[elite_inds,]
 # Update theta_mean, theta_std
 theta_mean <- apply(elite_thetas, 2,mean)
 theta_std <- 0.01*diag(dim_theta)+0.99*cov(elite_thetas)
 }
 return(theta_mean)
}
```

We call our function:

```
cem(f,300, theta_mean, theta_std)
```

And we get a very reasonable approximation of those values, in only a few iterations.

For the text generation problem, we need to gather together our matrices, `self$U`, `self$V`, `self$W`, into a big vector, `theta`, run the forward pass of the network, and calculate the negative of the log loss. So, we have a function that maps our vector into a scalar value, which is the same situation as shown prior. The `train` function is the only one that gets modified, and will look as follows:

```
train = function(text){
                    n <- 1
                    p <- 1
                    smooth_loss = -log(1.0/self$vocab_size)*self$seq_length
# loss at iteration 0
                    for(n in 1:self$n_iter){
                      if(p + self$seq_length + 1 >= length(text) || n == 1){
                        # reset RNN memory
                        ## s_prev is the hidden state of RNN
                        s_prev <- matrix(0,self$hidden_size, 1)
                        # go from start of data
                        p <- 1
                      }
                      inputs <-
unlist(lapply(text[p:(p+self$seq_length)],function(c){which(self$chars==c)}
))
                      targets <-
unlist(lapply(text[(p+1):(p+self$seq_length+1)],function(c){which(self$char
s==c)}))
                      if(n %% 100 == 0){
                        txt <- self$sample_char(s_prev, inputs[[1]], 200)
                        ## Find the \n in the string
                        line_breaks <- which(txt=="\n")
                        if(length(line_breaks)<2){
                          print(txt)
                        }
                        else{
                          for(ix in 2:(length(line_breaks-1))){
                            first_ix <- line_breaks[ix-1]+1
                            last_ix <- line_breaks[ix]-1
                            print(paste(txt[first_ix:last_ix], collapse=""))
                          }
                        }
                        print('---- sample -----')
                        cat("Iteration number: ",n, "\n")
```

```
                    cat("Loss: ", smooth_loss)
                }
                ## UPDATES
                theta_m <- c(as.vector(self$U), as.vector(self$V),
as.vector(self$W))
                new_m <- cem(-self$forward, theta_m,
diag(length(theta_m))*0.01)
                self$U <-
as.matrix(theta_m[1:hidden_size*vocab_size],nrow=self$hidden_size)
                self$W <-
as.matrix(theta_m[(hidden_size*vocab_size+1):(hidden_size*(vocab_size+hidde
n_size)+1)],
                                        nrow=self$hidden_size)
                self$V <-
as.matrix(theta_m[(hidden_size*(vocab_size+hidden_size)+1):length(theta_m)]
, nrow=self$vocab_size) # hidden to output
                loss <- self$forward(inputs,targets,s_prev)
                p <- p+self$seq_length
                n <- n+1
            }
            return(1)
        }
```

You can try this on your own! The results are comparable, although note that it takes much longer to run! This is, unfortunately, the situation with many of the algorithms relying on stochastic optimization, whether Monte Carlo or evolutionary algorithms. However, often the waiting time is worth it, because they are able to avoid local extrema and have at least a high probability of reaching the optimum.

With the preceding code, you have a good template to start trying different evolutionary algorithms.

RNN using Keras

In this section, we introduce an example using Keras. Keras is possibly the highest-level API for deep learning (again, at the time of writing, in this rapidly changing world of deep learning). This is very useful when you need to do production-ready models quite quickly, but is unfortunately sometimes not that great for learning, as everything is hidden away from you. Since, ideally, by the time you reach this section, an expert in recurrent neural networks, we can present you how to create a similar model.

Before that, let's introduce a simple benchmark model. Something that comes to mind when we speak about the memory of a neural network is the following, well, what if I had sufficient storage to calculate the conditional probabilities and simulate text generation as a Markov process, where the state variable is the observed text? We will implement this benchmark model to see how it compares in text generation quality with recurrent neural networks.

A simple benchmark implementation

Let's create a simple benchmark implementation and simulate text generation as a Markov chain. The idea is the following, we will estimate the probability of character c appearing after history h has been observed, where h has a fixed length. This length is called **memory**. For example, if we have a tiny corpus consisting of:

```
"My name is Pablo"
```

And we fix a memory length of 4, we get a training set that looks like this:

h	c
My n	a
y na	m
nam	e

Our task is to estimate the conditional probability distribution:

$$\mathbb{P}(c \mid h)$$

This conditional probability is obtained simply by estimating the number of times c appears after h, divided by the number of times history h appears.

The goal of this chapter is to build a benchmark model. We should clarify what we mean, as there is no *golden standard* for assessing performance in generative models. The way we will evaluate the model is by looking at the quality of the text generated, for which we need information about the context of the problem, namely, the corpus we want to learn to generate text from.

For this example, we will use the text of *Alice in Wonderland,* the book by Lewis Carroll, which is available online thanks to Project Gutenberg. You can find it on their website: `https://www.gutenberg.org/`.

We start by loading some libraries:

```
library(readr)
library(stringr)
library(purrr)
library(tokenizers)
library(dplyr)
```

Now, we load the data (available on the book's website), and set up a memory length of 5:

```
orig <- read_lines("./data/alice.txt")
maxlen <- 2
```

Next, we should clean our text from newlines and convert everything to lowercase for simplicity:

```
text <- orig %>%
  str_to_lower() %>%
  str_c(collapse = "\n") %>%
  tokenize_characters(strip_non_alphanum = FALSE, simplify = TRUE)
```

We set the variable `chars` as our set of tokens:

```
chars <- text %>% unique %>% sort
```

We now initialize an empty data frame and define a function to convert the tokenized vector input into a string:

```
records <- data.frame()
vec2str <- function(history){
 history <- toString(history)
 history <- str_replace_all(history,",","")
 history <- str_replace_all(history," ","")
 history <- str_replace_all(history,"\n"," ")
 history
 }
```

Now, we need to loop through the history and store in the records data frame:

```
idxs <- seq(1, length(text) - max_length - 1, by=3)
for(i in idxs){
 history <- text[i:(i+max_length-1)]
 next_char <- text[i+max_length]
 history <- vec2str(history)
 records <- rbind(data.frame(history=history, next_char=next_char),
records)
 tot_rows <- length(idxs)
}
```

Finally, we calculate the conditional probabilities:

$$\mathbb{P}(c \mid h)$$

Introduced previously. This can be done very easily using the `dplyr` package, as follows:

```
library(dplyr)
tot_histories <- records %>%
                  group_by(history) %>%
                  summarize(total_h=n())
tot_histories_char <- records %>%
                       group_by(history, next_char) %>%
                       summarize(total_h_c=n())
probas <- left_join(tot_histories, tot_histories_char)
probas$prob <- probas$total_h_c/probas$total_h
```

Now, we are ready to start generating text! We define a text generating function that will sample the next character conditional on the history:

```
generate_next <- function(h){
  sub_df <- probas%>%filter(history==h)
  if(nrow(sub_df)>0){
    prob_vector <- sub_df %>% select(prob)%>%as.matrix %>%c()
    char_vector <- sub_df %>% select(next_char)%>%as.matrix %>%c()
    char_vector <- as.vector(char_vector)
    sample(char_vector,size=1,prob=prob_vector)
  }
}
```

The preceding function helps us sample characters from the distribution we estimated.

With the following code, we can generate words of different lengths, to make it more interesting:

```
n_iter <- 100
for(iter in 1:n_iter){
  # Generate random initialization
  generated <- " "
  start_index <- sample(1:(length(text) - maxlen), size = 1)
  h <- text[start_index:(start_index + maxlen - 1)]
  h <- vec2str(h)
  random_len <- sample(5:10,1)
  for(i in 1:random_len){
    c <- generate_next(h)
    h <- paste0(h,c)
    generated <- str_c(generated,c)
    h <- substr(h,i,i+maxlen)
  }
  cat(generated)
  cat("\n")
}
```

Generating new text from old

Let's compare our simple, Markov chain model benchmark against LSTM networks. You can use the implementation we used earlier in this chapter. We will show how to use the Keras API for this task, as we did in the previous chapter.

We will illustrate this with an example close to one of the authors' hearts, generating names in Spanish.

First, we should load the required libraries:

```
library(keras)
library(readr)
library(stringr)
library(purrr)
library(tokenizers)
```

Then, define a sampling function based on the probabilities we will estimate:

```
sample_mod <- function(preds, temperature = 0.8){
 preds <- log(preds)/temperature
 exp_preds <- exp(preds)
 preds <- exp_preds/sum(exp(preds))
 rmultinom(1, 1, preds) %>%
 as.integer() %>%
```

```
which.max()
}
```

Strictly speaking, we do not estimate probabilities, rather some score between 0 and 1 which we can understand as such. The point is that this score will help us generate text, and the score has the same order as the real probabilities. A higher score equates to higher probability.

Now, we read the file and do some parsing. This is very similar to before:

```
orig <- read_lines("./data/Spanish.txt")
text <- orig %>%
    str_to_lower() %>%
    str_c(collapse = "\n") %>%
    tokenize_characters(strip_non_alphanum = FALSE, simplify = TRUE)
```

We define the vocabulary, that is, the collection of tokens in our text:

```
chars <- text %>%
    str_c(collapse="\n")%>%
    tokenize_characters(simplify=TRUE) %>%
    unique %>% sort
chars
 [1] "a" "á" "à" "b" "c" "d" "e" "é" "f" "g" "h" "i" "í" "j" "l" "m" "n" "ñ"
"o" "ó" "p" "q" "r" "s" "t" "u"
[27] "ú" "v" "x" "y" "z"
```

We keep the accentuated vowels, as they are part of the language. Next, we set up the window size and cut the text into overlapping sequences of that size:

```
max_length <- 5
dataset <- map(
  seq(1, length(text) - max_length - 1, by = 3),
  ~list(name = text[.x:(.x + max_length - 1)], next_char = text[.x +
max_length])
)
dataset <- transpose(dataset)
```

We use one-hot vectorization to encode our data into numerical inputs for the neural network that we will build using the `keras` library:

```
# One-hot vectorization
X <- array(0, dim = c(length(dataset$name), max_length, length(chars)))
y <- array(0, dim = c(length(dataset$name), length(chars)))
```

Finally, we set up the training set:

```
for(i in 1:length(dataset$name)){
    X[i,,] <- sapply(chars, function(x){
    as.integer(x == dataset$name[[i]])
    })
 y[i,] <- as.integer(chars == dataset$next_char[[i]])
 }
```

Then, we define the architecture of our network:

```
model <- keras_model_sequential()
model %>%
  layer_lstm(128, input_shape = c(max_length, length(chars))) %>%
  layer_dense(length(chars)) %>%
  layer_dropout(0.1)%>%
  layer_activation("softmax")
```

We require a *softmax* activation in the end, as we would like to interpret the final scores as probabilities; hence, it will be useful to have them between 0 and 1.

We now call the optimizer and compile our model:

```
optimizer <- optimizer_rmsprop(lr = 0.01)
model %>% compile(
 loss = "categorical_crossentropy",
 optimizer = optimizer
 )
```

We have to specify a sampling function, which is a version of *softmax:*

```
sample_mod <- function(preds, temperature = 0.8){
 preds <- log(preds)/temperature
 exp_preds <- exp(preds)
 preds <- exp_preds/sum(exp(preds))
 rmultinom(1, 1, preds) %>%
 as.integer() %>%
 which.max()
 }
```

Finally, we train our model:

```
history <- model %>% fit(
 X, y,
 batch_size = 128,
 epochs = 20
 )
plot(history)
```

If everything went well, the history plot will show us a learning curve that looks like the following. This suggests that our model is training correctly:

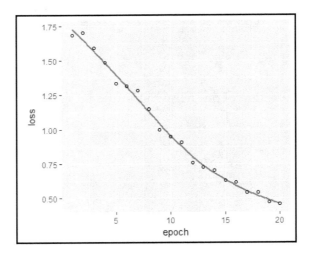

Training of our model in Keras

Perhaps we could increase the number of epochs? That's something you can try as an exercise!

It is now time to generate some of the samples:

```
start_idx <- sample(1:(length(text) - max_length), size = 1)
name <- text[start_idx:(start_idx + max_length - 1)]
generated <- ""
for(i in 1:10){
 x <- sapply(chars, function(x){
 as.integer(x == name)
 })
 dim(x) <- c(1, dim(x))
 preds <- predict(model, x)
 next_idx <- sample_mod(preds, 0.3)
 next_char <- chars[next_idx]

 generated <- str_c(generated, next_char, collapse = "")
 name <- c(name[-1], next_char)
 cat(generated)
 cat("\n\n")
}
```

With a simple modification of the preceding code you can generate names of different lengths. For this, we need to replace our preceding fixed length with a randomly sampled length, noted `random_len` in the following code snippet:

```
n_iter <- 100
for(iter in 1:n_iter){
  start_idx <- sample(1:(length(text) - max_length), size = 1)
  name <- text[start_idx:(start_idx + max_length - 1)]
  generated <- " "
  random_len <- sample(5:10,1)
  for(i in 1:random_len){
    x <- sapply(chars, function(x){
      as.integer(x == name)
    })
    dim(x) <- c(1, dim(x))
    preds <- predict(model, x)
    next_idx <- sample_mod(preds, 0.1)
    next_char <- chars[next_idx]
    generated <- str_c(generated, next_char)
    name <- c(name[-1], next_char)
    # cat(generated)
    # cat("\n\n")
  }
  cat(generated)
}
```

Among the generated samples (which might be different in your computer) are:

`Asarara, Laralaso`

Which sound rather convincingly like Spanish last names.

Of course, you can adapt the preceding model to any other text, perhaps including text like HTML or LaTeX.

A subtlety here is that we used character-level prediction. You can try to adapt the text to word-level prediction, to make it work like the auto-complete function of a smartphone.

Exercises

- Try the LSTM example for `Alice in Wonderland` to generate baby names using the datasets compiled by Mark Kantrowitz, available at: `https://www.cs.cmu.edu/Groups/AI/areas/nlp/corpora/names/0.html`.
- Music generation is also a sequential prediction problem, as we mentioned. You can take a look at the version of the Nottingham Music Database written in ABC notation at `http://abc.sourceforge.net/NMD/` to teach the computer to write music, using a similar recurrent neural network.
- Refactor the code on our recurrent neural network from scratch (the R6 implementation) so that it uses the `forward_step` function within the `bptt` function.
- We ignored bias terms in our recurrent neural network implementations. How will that affect the performance, if at all? Try to modify the code to include bias terms.
- Modify the code for the network using the cross-entropy method to use natural evolution strategies: `https://blog.openai.com/evolution-strategies/`.

Summary

In this chapter, we introduced different architectures for recurrent neural networks, and pointed out some of their limitations and capabilities. By introducing a naive Markovian model, we compared the efficiency of introducing such complicated architectures. When applied to the text generation problem, we saw that these different architectures had a noticeable improvement in the quality of the predictions. For training networks, we introduced different methods. The classical backpropagation algorithm and other gradient-free methods that are useful to solve black-box optimization problems.

Sentiment Analysis with Word Embedding

16

In this chapter, we turn to the problem of sentiment analysis. Sentiment analysis is an umbrella term for a number of techniques to figure out how a speaker feels about a certain topic or piece of content.

A vanilla case study of sentiment analysis is **polarity**. Given a document or text string (for instance, a Tweet, a review, or a comment on a social network), the aim is to determine whether the author feels good, bad, or neutral about the item or topic in question.

At first look, this problem might seem trivial: A lookup table with positive and negative words, and simply counting the word frequencies should do, right? Not so fast. Here are a few examples of why this is tricky:

- Their decadent desserts made me hate myself
- You should try this place if you love cold food
- Disliking cake is not really my thing

What can we see in these examples?

- Negative terms used in a possibly positive sense
- Positive terms used sarcastically
- Two negative terms that imply something positive

 Note that we have not dealt with spelling mistakes, neologisms and use of multiple languages, just to name a few potential issues in real-life situations.

As you can see, sentiment analysis is a very complicated task, and we will merely scratch the surface.

The human element is the most important element in sentiment analysis. The accuracy of a sentiment analysis system depends on how much it agrees with human judgement. And how accurate could that be? Unfortunately not that much. Some researchers report disagreement rates as high as 20%. This means that if your sentiment analysis system has an accuracy of 70%, although seemingly unimpressive, it will still be good, since humans would agree on 80% of the classifications of a perfect sentiment analysis system. But, beware!

These figures are not exactly comparable, since the computer will have issues identifying subtleties that are best guessed by humans, such as sarcasm, jokes, or the subtle differences in meaning from the examples shown previously.

Nonetheless, there seems to be an increasing awareness from individuals and organizations about the importance of their presence online. We can measure that impact by the mushrooming of agencies and professionals specializing in social media monitoring. This has contributed to increased attention in the field from researchers (both in universities and industries), and we believe that it is likely that we will see significant advances in the area.

Our focus, as stated elsewhere in the book, is to introduce you to the algorithms in the simplest way possible. We will use a well-known dataset, which shares many of the properties of *real-life* datasets that you will find out there.

Warm-up – data exploration

Let's get things moving with a tiny example. Let's look at this tiny reviews corpus:

```
text <- c("The food is typical Czech, and the beer is good. The service is
quick, if short and blunt, and the waiting on staff could do with a bit of
customer service training",
          "The food was okay. Really not bad, but we had better",
          "A venue full of locals. No nonsense, no gimmicks. Only went for
drinks which were good and cheap. People friendly enough.",
          "Great food, lovely staff, very reasonable prices considering the
location!")
```

We will do some simple analysis here, which will help us appreciate some of the subtleties of sentiment analysis.

Working with tidy text

For this, we will use the `tidytext` package. This package is built on the philosophy of tidy data, introduced by Hadley Wickham in his 2014 paper (`https://www.jstatsoft.org/article/view/v059i10`). A dataset is tidy if the following three conditions are satisfied:

- Each variable is a column
- Each observation is a row
- Each type of observational unit is a table

The `tidytext` package helps us turn our text into tidy form, by putting one token per row. Let's start by loading `dplyr` and `tidytext`. If you don't have `tidytext`, install it first using `install.packages("tidytext")`.

Load the packages and let's transform our text into a data frame:

```
library(tidytext)
library(dplyr)
text_df <- data_frame(line = 1:4, text = text)
```

The `unnest_tokens` function is where the magic of `tidytext` begins:

```
text_df <- text_df %>%
 unnest_tokens(word, text)
head(text_df)
# A tibble: 6 x 2
   line word
  <int> <chr>
1 1 the
2 1 food
3 1 is
4 1 typical
5 1 czech
6 1 and
```

As you can see, our text was transformed as one token (the default is one word = one token) per row. First, let's get rid of stop words:

```
data(stop_words)
head(stop_words)
text_df <- text_df %>% anti_join(stop_words)
```

Our goal is to determine, at least visually by now, the sentiment of the preceding reviews. Let's begin with a quick summary of the word count:

```
library(ggplot2)
text_df %>%
    count(word, sort=T) %>%
    mutate(word = reorder(word, n)) %>%
    ggplot(aes(word, n)) +
    geom_col() +
    xlab(NULL) +
    coord_flip()+
    theme_bw()
```

We get a nice bar chart like this:

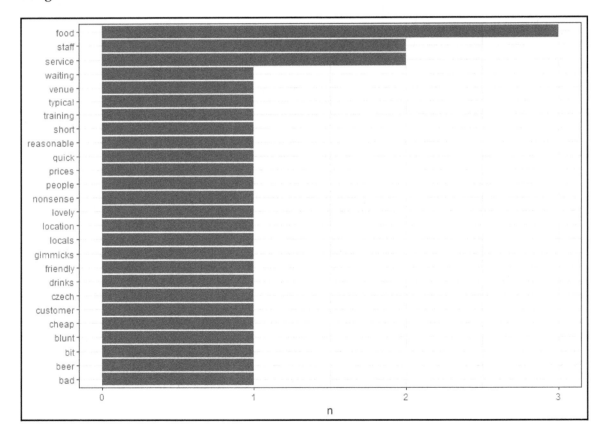

Basic word count in our toy review dataset

The `tidytext` package includes three lexicons (collection of words) annotated by sentiment:

- AFINN from Finn Årup Nielsen (http://www2.imm.dtu.dk/pubdb/views/publication_details.php?id=6010)
- bing from Bing Liu and collaborators (https://www.cs.uic.edu/~liub/FBS/sentiment-analysis.html)
- nrc from Saif Mohammad and Peter Turney (http://saifmohammad.com/WebPages/NRC-Emotion-Lexicon.htm)

The AFINN lexicon gives a numeric value between -5 and 5 to common words in English, with negative values being negative words. For instance:

```
get_sentiments("afinn") %>%
  filter(score==-5) %>%
  head
```

Gives (sensitive readers should skip the next snippet):

```
# A tibble: 6 x 2
        word score
       <chr> <int>
1 bastard -5
2 bastards -5
```

Whereas, the following:

```
get_sentiments("afinn") %>%
 filter(score==0) %>%
 head
```

Is simply:

```
# A tibble: 1 x 2
 word score
 <chr> <int>
1 some kind 0
```

And the following:

```
get_sentiments("afinn") %>%
 filter(score==5) %>%
 head
```

Returns:

```
# A tibble: 5 x 2
  word score
  <chr> <int>
1 breathtaking 5
2 hurrah 5
3 outstanding 5
4 superb 5
5 thrilled 5
```

The `bing` lexicon has only positive and negative words:

```
> get_sentiments("bing") %>% head
# A tibble: 6 x 2
  word sentiment
  <chr> <chr>
1 2-faced negative
2 2-faces negative
3 a+ positive
4 abnormal negative
5 abolish negative
6 abominable negative
```

Whereas, the `nrc` has different categories:

```
> get_sentiments("nrc") %>% head
# A tibble: 6 x 2
  word sentiment
  <chr> <chr>
1 abacus trust
2 abandon fear
3 abandon negative
4 abandon sadness
5 abandoned anger
6 abandoned fear
```

How can we use these word lists? Well, once our data is tidy, we can join them and create different aggregations to try to get a feeling of what is going on. Let's start by storing the `bing` lexicon somewhere:

```
bing <- get_sentiments("bing")
```

And joining it with our data:

```
> text_df %>% inner_join(bing) %>% count(line,sentiment)
Joining, by = "word"
# A tibble: 5 x 3
```

```
line sentiment n
<int> <chr> <int>
1 1 negative 1
2 2 negative 1
3 3 negative 3
4 3 positive 1
5 4 positive 2
```

Not bad, but we can always do better with a plot:

```
# Plot
text_df %>%
  inner_join(bing) %>%
  count(line, sentiment) %>%
  ggplot(aes(line, n, fill=sentiment))+
  geom_col()+
  coord_flip()+
  theme_bw()
```

The results are shown as follows. Not bad. We see that a simple join and a summary aggregation already gives a basic insight into how to classify the reviews by sentiment:

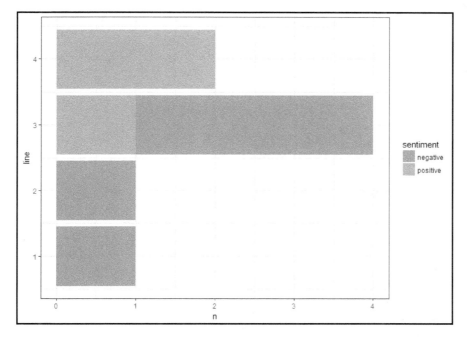

Aggregate statistics using the bing lexicon

This is already valuable, but in some cases we would like to know how positive or negative a review is; for instance, to redirect the issue to the proper customer service representative. In this case, it might be useful to use the AFINN lexicon instead:

```
afinn <- get_sentiments("afinn")
```

Now, we join the review data as before:

```
text_df %>% inner_join(afinn)
```

And look at the total score per review:

```
# Group
text_df %>%
  inner_join(afinn) %>%
  group_by(line) %>%
  summarize(total_score = sum(score))
```

Not bad; but again, it's better to make a plot:

```
# Plot
text_df %>%
  inner_join(afinn) %>%
  group_by(line) %>%
  summarize(total_score = sum(score)) %>%
  mutate(sentiment=ifelse(total_score>0,"positive","negative")) %>%
  ggplot(aes(line, total_score, fill=sentiment))+
  geom_col()+
  coord_flip()+
  theme_bw()
```

Which is shown here:

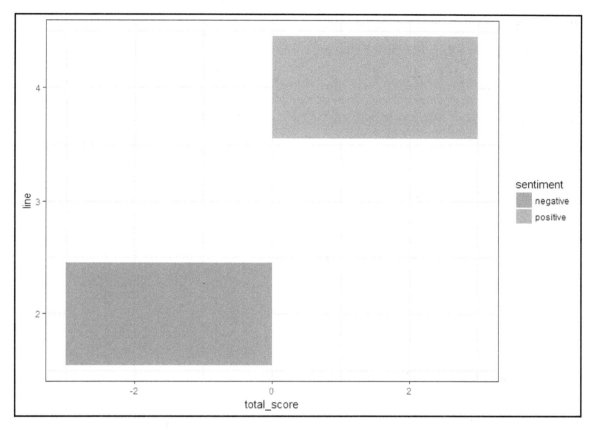

Aggregate statistics using the AFINN lexicon

Wow, what happened here? The situation looks a bit weird. First, note that one review has disappeared. This is because there are no common words with the AFINN lexicon for the first review (recall that we had an inner join). A bit more worrying is what has happened to the third review. The score is zero, which comes from summing the positive and negative scores of each word in the review, as per the AFINN lexicon. However, note that review 3 is mostly positive. What happened then?

The more, the merrier – calculating n-grams instead of single words

The reason for such an odd result in the previous section can be traced back to the context. Notice that review 3 had the phrase `No nonsense, no gimmicks`, which is largely positive, but has two negative words attached to it. How can we take context into account? Enter n-grams. An n-gram is a sequence of *n* consecutive items (words, or in the case of speech, phonemes) from a given sequence of text or speech. Let's make this clear with an example and use 2-grams, or bigrams:

```
text_df <- data_frame(line = 1:4, text = text)
text_df <- text_df %>%
  unnest_tokens(bigram, text, token="ngrams", n=2)
text_df
```

This gives us the following:

```
# A tibble: 70 x 2
  line bigram
  <int> <chr>
1 1 the food
2 1 food is
3 1 is typical
4 1 typical czech
5 1 czech and
6 1 and the
7 1 the beer
8 1 beer is
9 1 is good
10 1 good the
# ... with 60 more rows
```

So, we now see that consecutive words are put together. Already, this can be helpful enough to determine the negations of negative words that are actually positive, as in our preceding review 3. Let's find out which negative words are negated. First, we split the two words of the bigram into two columns:

```
library(tidyr)
text_df <- text_df %>% separate(bigram, c("w1","w2"), sep=" ")
text_df
```

Which gives us:

```
# A tibble: 70 x 3
   line w1      w2
 * <int> <chr>   <chr>
 1   1   the     food
 2   1   food    is
 3   1   is      typical
 4   1   typical czech
 5   1   czech   and
 6   1   and     the
 7   1   the     beer
 8   1   beer    is
 9   1   is      good
10   1   good    the
# ... with 60 more rows
```

A bit of `dplyr` magic brings the offending part of the sentence to question:

```
text_df %>%
  filter(w1=="no") %>%
  inner_join(afinn, by=c(w2="word"))
```

Which is:

```
# A tibble: 1 x 4
   line w1    w2       score
  <int> <chr> <chr>    <int>
1     3 no    nonsense    -2
```

We could now use this information to override the score of our third review. However, note how involved a process it might be. Sure, in many cases it would work well, but we should find more systematic ways of dealing with context.

 n-grams are important to keep track of the context of a word, and use it correctly for classification.

Bag of words benchmark

We came across one-hot embeddings while identifying fraudulent emails in `Chapter 14`, *Fraud Detection with Autoencoders*. The idea is to represent each word as a basis vector; that is, a vector with zeros except one coordinate. Hence, each document (a review in this case) is represented as a vector with ones and zeros. We went a bit further from that and used different weighting (tf-idf).

Let's revisit this model once again, but include n-grams instead of single words. This will be our benchmark for the more sophisticated word embeddings we will do later.

Preparing the data

The data is a subset of the Stanford Large Movie Review dataset, originally published in:

Andrew L. Maas, Raymond E. Daly, Peter T. Pham, Dan Huang, Andrew Y. Ng, and Christopher Potts. (2011). *Learning Word Vectors for Sentiment Analysis*. The 49th Annual Meeting of the Association for Computational Linguistics (ACL 2011).

This data is available to download at `http://ai.stanford.edu/~amaas/data/sentiment/`, provided proper credit is given to the original paper. This is the raw data, but you can find a preprocessed version in Kaggle, `https://www.kaggle.com/c/word2vec-nlp-tutorial/data`.

Let's begin with loading the data:

```
df <- read.csv("./data/labeledTrainData.tsv", encoding = "utf-8", quote =
"", sep="\t", stringsAsFactors = F)
text <- df$review
```

We revisit the `tm` library. Note that the code is a bit different, since we are loading the text as `VCorpus` instead of `Corpus` as before:

```
library(tm)
corpus <- VCorpus(VectorSource(text))
inspect(corpus[[1]])
```

Which yields the first review in this data:

```
> inspect(corpus[[1]])
<<PlainTextDocument>>
Metadata: 7
Content: chars: 1681

  stuff going moment mj ive started listening music watching odd documentary
watched wiz watched moonwalker maybe just want get certain insight guy
thought really cool eighties just maybe make mind whether guilty innocent
moonwalker part biography part feature film remember going see cinema
originally released subtle messages mjs feeling towards press also obvious
message drugs bad mkaybr br visually impressive course michael jackson
unless remotely like mj anyway going hate find boring may call mj egotist
consenting making movie mj fans say made fans true really nice himbr br
actual feature film bit finally starts 20 minutes excluding smooth criminal
sequence joe pesci convincing psychopathic powerful drug lord wants mj dead
bad beyond mj overheard plans nah joe pescis character ranted wanted people
know supplying drugs etc dunno maybe just hates mjs musicbr br lots ...
<truncated>
```

First, some preprocessing:

```
corpus <- tm_map(corpus,content_transformer(tolower))
corpus <- tm_map(corpus, content_transformer(removePunctuation))
corpus <- tm_map(corpus, content_transformer(removeWords),
stopwords("english"))
```

The next step is to create bigrams. We saw that this is important:

```
BigramTokenizer <- function(x){ unlist(lapply(ngrams(words(x), 2), paste,
collapse = " "), use.names = FALSE)}
dtm <- DocumentTermMatrix(corpus, control = list(tokenize =
BigramTokenizer))
dtm <- removeSparseTerms(dtm, 0.995)
X <- as.data.frame(as.matrix(dtm))
X$sentiment <- df$sentiment
X$sentiment <- ifelse(X$sentiment<0.5,0,1)
```

We are now ready to apply this data to a classification model; for instance, logistic regression.

Implementing a benchmark – logistic regression

Logistic regression might not be the fanciest algorithm in town, but for sure, it is one of the most commonly used. It is quite robust and powerful, yet simple to interpret. Unlike other methods, it is easy to look under the hood and see what it is doing.

First, we choose some indices for the training and testing set:

```
# Train, test, split
library(caTools)
set.seed(42)
spl <- sample.split(X$sentiment, 0.7)
train <- subset(X, spl == TRUE)
test <- subset(X, spl == FALSE)
```

And now we split into train and test sets:

```
X_train <- subset(train,select=-sentiment)
y_train <- train$sentiment
X_test <- subset(test,select=-sentiment)
y_test <- test$sentiment
```

Now let's look at the model and the coefficients:

```
model <- glm(y_train ~ ., data = X_train, family = "binomial")
coefs <- as.data.frame(model$coefficients)
names(coefs) <- c("value")
coefs$token <- row.names(coefs)
```

And see how the model is using each feature:

```
library(ggplot2)
library(dplyr)
coefs %>%
 arrange(desc(value)) %>%
 head %>%
 ggplot(aes(x=token, y=value))+
 geom_col()+
 coord_flip()+
 theme_bw()
```

This gives us the following chart:

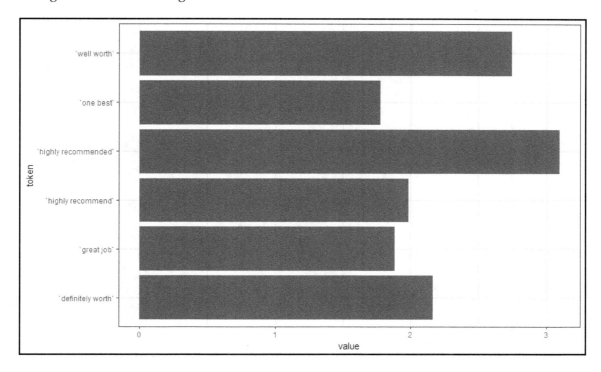

Features correlated with positive sentiment

Now let's take a look at the features correlated with a negative sentiment (try to do it yourself before looking at the code!):

```
coefs %>%
 arrange(value) %>%
 head %>%
 ggplot(aes(x=token, y=value))+
 geom_col()+
 coord_flip()+
 theme_bw()
```

This looks like:

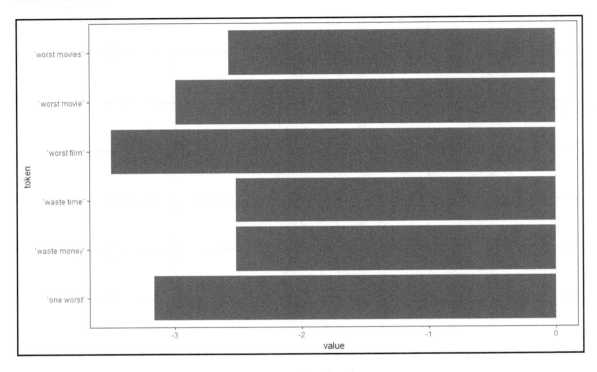

Features correlated with negative sentiment

Now let's take a closer look at the performance using the ROC curve. We can write our own function instead of using an extra package:

```
roc <- function(y_test, y_preds){
  y_test <- y_test[order(y_preds, decreasing = T)]
  return(data.frame(fpr=cumsum(!y_test)/sum(!y_test),
                    tpr=cumsum(y_test)/sum(y_test)) )
}
```

We can now generate predictions and plot the curve using the base R graphics:

```
y_preds <- predict(model, X_test, type="response")
plot(roc(y_test,y_preds), xlim=c(0,1), ylim=c(0,1))
```

Or store them on a data frame and use `ggplot2`:

```
roc_df <- roc(y_test,y_preds)
ggplot(roc_df, aes(x=fpr,y=tpr))+geom_point(color="red")+theme_bw()
```

The ROC curve looks like this:

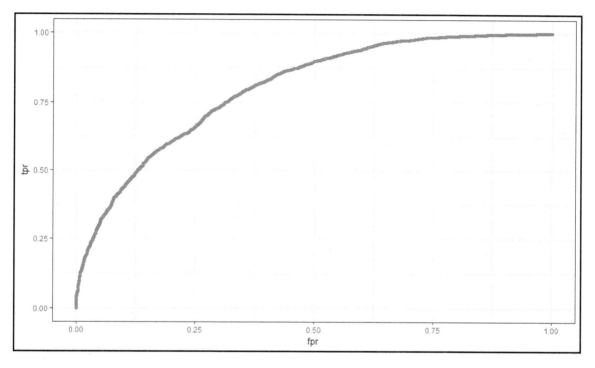

ROC curve for logistic regression with bigrams

We could quantify the AUC, but this is a bit more involved using base R code. You can try using the ROCR or pROC packages. We will simply set up a threshold of 0.5 and compute the precision for the positive class for that threshold, just to get a feel for what's going on:

```
labels <- ifelse(y_preds<0.5,0,1)
table(labels,y_test)
```

This gives:

```
table(labels,y_test)
  y_test
labels   0     1
  0    2536   896
  1    1214  2854
```

So we get a precision of:

```
2536/(2536+896)
[1] 0.7389277
```

For the positive class. Not bad, in practice; 80% would be a good classifier, since this is roughly the agreement rate among humans. You can try to improve this benchmark in a few different ways, suggested in the *Exercises* section.

Exercises

1. Explore the performance of your classifier for different values of *n* in n-grams. Does it change significantly?
2. The charts in the previous section suggest that some stemming might be needed, as some of the top features are quite similar in meaning. Apply stemming and look at the shape of the ROC curve.
3. Experiment with other classifiers, for instance, random forests or support vector machines, and different kinds of n-grams. Can you improve the performance?

Word embeddings

The field of **natural language processing (NLP)** is advancing pretty quickly these days, as much as modern data science and artificial intelligence.

Algorithms such as word2vec (Mikolov and others, 2013) and GloVe (Pennington and others, 2014) have been pioneers in the field, and although strictly neither of them is related to deep learning, the models trained with them are used as input data in many applications of deep learning to NLP.

We will briefly describe word2vec and GloVe, which are perhaps the most commonly used algorithms for word embedding, although research in the intersection of neural networks and language goes back to at least Jeff Elman in the 1990s.

word2vec

The word2vec algorithm (or, rather, family of algorithms) takes a text corpus as input and produces the word vectors as output. It first constructs a vocabulary from the training text data and then learns vector representation of words. Then we use those vectors as features for machine learning algorithms.

Word vectors are able to catch some intuitive regularities in the language, for instance:

vector('Paris') - vector('France') + vector('Italy')

Results in a vector that is very close to:

vector('Rome'),

And,

vector('king') - vector('man') + vector('woman')

Is close to:

vector('queen').

What does word2vec do behind the scenes? word2vec arrives at word vectors by training a neural network to predict:

- A word in the center from its surroundings (continuous bag of words, CBOW)
- A word's surroundings from the center word (skip-gram model)

Why is that useful? According to the distributional hypothesis, words occurring together tend to convey similar meanings. Researchers Goldberg and Levy point out (https://arxiv.org/abs/1402.3722) that the word2vec objective function causes words that occur in similar contexts to have similar embeddings, which is in line with the distributional hypothesis. However, they also point out that a better explanation is required.

> The distributional hypothesis states that words that are used in the same contexts are related. This is an underlying assumption of vector embedding algorithms such as GloVe or word2vec.

GloVe

About a year after word2vec, researchers at Stanford published a paper (`http://web.stanford.edu/~jpennin/papers/glove.pdf`) that explicitly identifies the objective that word2vec optimizes under the hood. Their method, **GloVe**, (**global vectors**) explicitly names the objective matrix, identifies the factorization, and provides some intuitive justification as to why this should give us working similarities.

 This section describes, at a high level, the inner workings of the GloVe algorithm. As such, it is a bit more math-heavy than we would have wanted. If you are not familiar with linear algebra and calculus, you can safely skip it.

How does GloVe work?

1. Create a word **co-occurrence matrix** where each entry represents how often word *i* appears in the context of word *j*. This matrix is clearly symmetric. Moreover, for each term, we look for words co-occurring on certain windows, and give less weight to more distant words.
2. Define soft constraints for each word pair.
3. Finally, introduce a cost function that penalizes learning from very common word pairs.
   For the soft constraints, we mean:

$$w_i^T w_j + b_i + b_j = log(X_{ij})$$

Where the w_i and w_j denote the main and context embedded vectors, respectively, with biases b_i and b_j, and X_{ij} is the co-occurrence of word *j* in the context of word *i*.

The cost function is defined by:

$$\sum_{i,j}^{V} f(X_{i,j}) \cdot (w_i^T w_j - b_i - b_j - log(Xij))^2$$

Where *V* is the vocabulary and *f* is defined by:

$$f(X_{ij}) = \begin{cases} (\frac{X_{ij}}{X_{max}})^\alpha & , \quad X_{ij} < X_{max} \\ 1 & , \quad X_{ij} \geq X_{max} \end{cases}$$

Where *alpha* and X_{max} are hyperparameters that you can choose.

Sentiment analysis from movie reviews

Let's continue with the IMDb data and put into practice the ideas from the previous sections. In this section, we will use a few familiar packages, like `tidytext`, `plyr` and `dplyr`, as well as the excellent `text2vec` by Dimitriy Selivanov, which was released in 2017, and the well-known `caret` package by Max Kuhn.

Data preprocessing

We need to prepare our data for the algorithm.

First, a few imports that will be necessary:

```
library(plyr)
library(dplyr)
library(text2vec)
library(tidytext)
library(caret)
```

We will use the IMDb data as before:

```
imdb <- read.csv("./data/labeledTrainData.tsv", encoding = "utf-8", quote =
"", sep="\t", stringsAsFactors = F)
```

And create an iterator over the tokens:

```
tokens <- space_tokenizer(imdb$review)
token_iterator <- itoken(tokens)
```

The tokens are simple words, also known as **unigrams**. This constitutes our vocabulary:

```
vocab <- create_vocabulary(token_iterator)
```

It's important for the co-occurrence matrix to include only words that appear frequently together a significant amount of times. We will set this threshold to 5:

```
vocab <- prune_vocabulary(vocab, term_count_min = 5)
```

We use our filtered vocabulary:

```
vectorizer <- vocab_vectorizer(vocab)
```

And set up a window of size 5 for context words:

```
tcm <- create_tcm(token_iterator, vectorizer, skip_grams_window = 5)
```

Now that we have the co-occurrence matrix, let's continue with the vector embedding.

From words to vectors

We are ready to create the word embedding using GloVe. First, let's initialize an instance of the GlobalVectors class:

```
glove <- GlobalVectors$new(word_vectors_size = 50,
                           vocabulary = vocab,
                           x_max = 10)
```

We now apply the `fit_transform` method (scikit learn users might be familiar with it):

```
wv_main <- glove$fit_transform(tcm,
                               n_iter = 10,
                               convergence_tol = 0.01)
```

And once this is done, we have our vectorizer ready. We now need to parse our text:

```
text <- unlist(imdb$review)
length(text)
# 25000
text_df <- data_frame(line = 1:25000, text = text)
```

And apply the `unnest_tokens` functions from `tidytext` to turn our data in a tidy format:

```
text_df <- text_df %>%
  unnest_tokens(word, text)
head(text_df)
```

This gives a familiar output:

```
  head(text_df)
# A tibble: 6 x 2
  line word
  <int> <chr>
1 1 with
2 1 all
3 1 this
4 1 stuff
5 1 going
6 1 down
```

But wait, what about the GloVe? Let's take a look:

```
head(wv_main[,1:3])
            [,1]   [,2]   [,3]
overpowered 0.03408282 -0.225022092 0.077734992
nears 0.65971708 -0.005281781 -0.100175403
producers) 0.46528772 0.063937798 -0.165794402
Daddy, 0.06035958 -0.076200403 0.008196513
rhetoric, -0.05500082 0.149410397 -0.314875215
Johnsons' 0.43385875 0.078220785 -0.177165091
```

Actually the `text2vec` package returns two objects:

```
wv_context <- glove$components
```

We can use either `wv_main` or `wv_context` as our vector embedding, but it sometimes helps (according to the GloVe paper) to put them together. So, you can create a `wv` object as the sum or average of these two vectors, for instance:

```
wv <- wv_main + t(wv_context).
```

Let's use only the `wv_main` for now. We need to coerce the matrix to a data frame format and add `row.names` as a column, to join it with our text, in tidy format:

```
wv <- as.data.frame(wv_main)
wv$word <- row.names(wv)
```

And finally, put these two together:

```
df <- wv%>% inner_join(text_df)
```

This is still not ready to use as we need to aggregate the vectors as they appear in the review. One possibility is to just take the average vector as representative; the vector of the review would be the average vector of all the words that compose the review. We will take this approach here and suggest some other possibilities in the exercises:

```
df <- df %>%
        group_by(line) %>%
        summarize_all(mean) %>%
        select(1:50)
df$label <- as.factor(imdb$sentiment)
```

This data is now ready for passing through different classifiers, from which we can predict the sentiment polarity (positive/negative).

Sentiment extraction

We will use `caret` to try different classifiers at once:

```
library(caret)
```

We first need to prepare the training scheme:

```
control <- trainControl(method="cv", repeats=5)
```

And we will set up the different models to try:

- Random forest
- Gradient boosting machines
- Logit boost
- Naive Bayes

Do not forget to set the seed for the random number generator, to make the results repeatable:

```
set.seed(7)
 modelRF <- train(
                label~.,
                data=df,
                method="rf",
                trControl=control
               )

    modelGbm <- train(
                label~.,
                data=df,
                method="gbm",
                trControl=control,
                verbose=FALSE
               )

 modelLogitBoost <- train(
                label~.,
                data=df,
                method="LogitBoost",
                trControl=control
```

```
                                )
modelNaiveBayes <- train(
                        label~.,
                        data=df,
                        method="nb",
                        trControl=control
                        )
```

The training will take some time, but once this is done, we can collect the results in a data frame for later exploration:

```
results <- resamples(
                    list(
                        RF=modelRF,
                        GBM=modelGbm,
                        LB=modelLogitBoost,
                        NB=modelNaiveBayes
                        )
                    )
```

We can easily get a summary of the results, with the familiar summary function:

```
> summary(results)

Call:
summary.resamples(object = results)

Models: RF, GBM, LB, NB
Number of resamples: 10

Accuracy
      Min. 1st Qu. Median Mean 3rd Qu. Max. NA's
RF 0.7116 0.7189 0.7284 0.72732 0.7363 0.7412 0
GBM 0.7168 0.7199 0.7352 0.73228 0.7410 0.7496 0
LB 0.5680 0.5933 0.6124 0.60656 0.6184 0.6420 0
NB 0.6244 0.6291 0.6374 0.63992 0.6510 0.6588 0

Kappa
      Min. 1st Qu. Median Mean 3rd Qu. Max. NA's
RF 0.4232 0.4378 0.4568 0.45464 0.4726 0.4824 0
GBM 0.4336 0.4398 0.4704 0.46456 0.4820 0.4992 0
LB 0.1360 0.1866 0.2248 0.21312 0.2368 0.2840 0
NB 0.2488 0.2582 0.2748 0.27984 0.3020 0.3176 0
```

Or more detailed visualizations with:

```
bwplot(results)
```

The preceding code produces the following metrics:

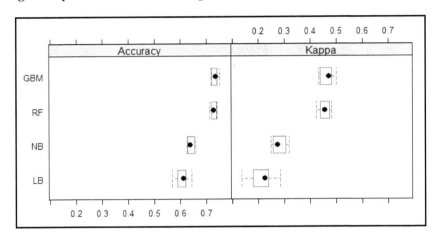

Boxplot comparing the performance of different classifiers on top of GloVe

You can also do it with:

```
dotplot(results)
```

Anyhow, time to look at the performance metrics!

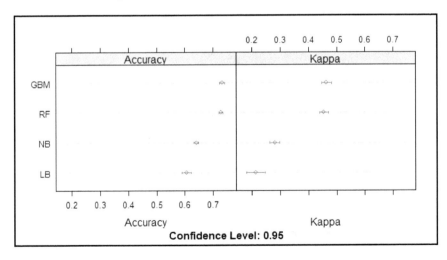

Dotplot comparing the performance of different classifiers on top of GloVe

On the plots and the preceding summary results shown, the **accuracy** is the percentage of correctly classified instances out of all instances, whereas the **kappa** metric (or Cohen's kappa statistic) is the accuracy normalized with the baseline random classification for your data, as if every observation were classified according to the probability distribution given by the frequency of each class.

 A kappa of zero means that the model is useless (kappa is between 0 and 1) and the higher the kappa, the more likely your model is useful, although there is no unified interpretation of this statistic.

So we see that tree-based methods tend to do quite well. This is somehow in contrast to one-hot encoding models. It is usually not recommended to use tree-based methods in data with a large number of sparse features, which would be the case if we had one-hot encoded models as before. Since we are instead embedding into dense vectors, trees are welcome again and they do perform well, even without tweaking hyperparameters.

The importance of data cleansing

If you follow the preceding workflow, and stop from time to time to see the results (which you absolutely should, by the way) you will notice that there is a lot of garbage around—words with upper and lower case, punctuation and so on. What happens if you improve this workflow by properly parsing the words? You can use the tokenizers library instead of the `space_tokenizer` function from text2vec to remove stopwords and punctuation in a single line:

```
library(tokenizers)
tokens <- tokenize_words(imdb$review, stopwords = stopwords())
```

The full code is now:

```
library(plyr)
library(dplyr)
library(text2vec)
library(tidytext)
library(caret)

imdb <- read.csv("./data/labeledTrainData.tsv"
                , encoding = "utf-8"
                , quote = ""
                , sep="\t"
                , stringsAsFactors = F)
# Standard preprocessing: change to lowercase, remove english stopwords and
punctuation
```

```
library(tokenizers)
tokens <- tokenize_words(imdb$review, stopwords = stopwords())


# Create vocabulary. The tokens are simple words here.
token_iterator <- itoken(tokens)
vocab <- create_vocabulary(token_iterator)

# Kill sparse terms
vocab <- prune_vocabulary(vocab, term_count_min = 5L)

vectorizer <- vocab_vectorizer(vocab)

# use window of 5 for context words
 tcm <- create_tcm(token_iterator, vectorizer, skip_grams_window = 5L)

glove <- GlobalVectors$new(word_vectors_size = 50,
                           vocabulary = vocab,
                           x_max = 10)
wv_main <- glove$fit_transform(tcm,
                               n_iter = 10,
                               convergence_tol = 0.05)

text <- unlist(imdb$review)

text_df <- data_frame(line = 1:25000, text = text)

text_df <- text_df %>%
        unnest_tokens(word, text)

wv <- as.data.frame(wv_main)

wv$word <- row.names(wv)

df <- wv%>% inner_join(text_df)

# Now we need to create the trained matrix
df <- df %>% group_by(line) %>% summarize_all(mean) %>% select(1:51)
df$label <- as.factor(imdb$sentiment)

library(caret)

control <- trainControl(method="cv", repeats=5)
```

```
# Train the different models
set.seed(7)
modelRF <- train(label~., data=df, method="rf", trControl=control)

set.seed(7)
modelGbm <- train(label~., data=df, method="gbm", trControl=control,
verbose=FALSE)

set.seed(7)
modelLogitBoost <- train(label~., data=df, method="LogitBoost",
trControl=control)

set.seed(7)
modelNaiveBayes <- train(label~., data=df, method="nb", trControl=control)

# collect resamples: this is useful for the plots
results <- resamples(
                list(RF=modelRF,
                GBM=modelGbm,
                LB=modelLogitBoost,
                NB=modelNaiveBayes))


# summarize and check the model performance
summary(results)
bwplot(results)
dotplot(results)
```

We can see a significant improvement in the results!

```
> summary(results)
Call:
summary.resamples(object = results)
Models: RF, GBM, LB, NB
Number of resamples: 10
Accuracy
 Min. 1st Qu. Median Mean 3rd Qu. Max. NA's
RF 0.7820 0.7892 0.7946 0.79340 0.7972 0.8012 0
GBM 0.7904 0.7952 0.7978 0.79732 0.7996 0.8036 0
LB 0.6904 0.6978 0.7040 0.70388 0.7098 0.7176 0
NB 0.6728 0.6810 0.6900 0.68824 0.6957 0.7008 0
```

The dotplot and boxplot here are shown as follows:

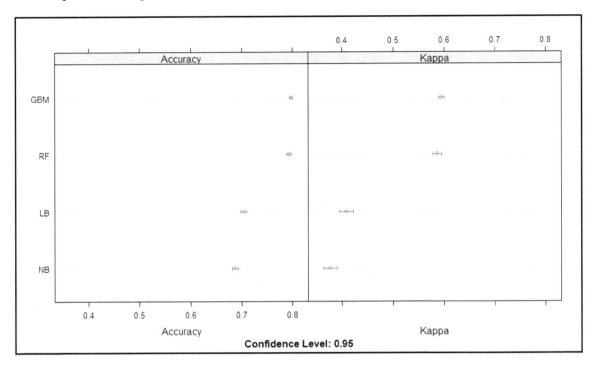

Dotplot showing the different classifiers after proper preprocessing

And the boxplot:

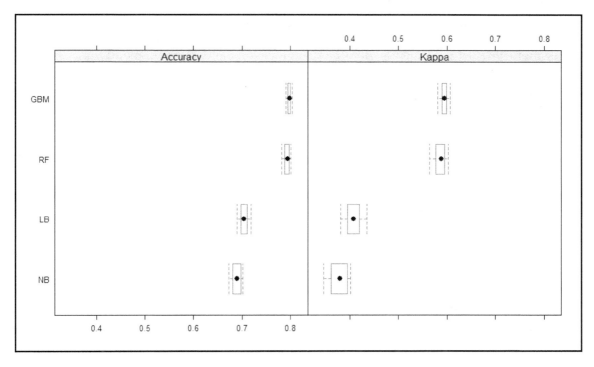

Boxplot showing the different classifiers after proper preprocessing

Remember, when it comes to software in general, and data science is not the exception:

Garbage in, garbage out: Always pay attention to the data you are feeding to the models! The most powerful models available will produce unsatisfactory results when feeding them with the wrong data! It's important to log, or at least print, to the console, any preprocessing steps you are doing. Treating models as a magic black box is a very dangerous thing, and unfortunately too common.

As we mentioned earlier, vector embeddings is not proper deep learning, rather a feature representation method. However, we can combine vector embeddings with deep neural networks and, hopefully, get better results.

Vector embeddings and neural networks

It's time to combine vector embeddings and neural networks to, hopefully, create more robust models. Let's do a simple extension to our workflow by training a neural network as a classifier. We start with the now familiar preprocessing and vector embedding:

```
library(plyr)
library(dplyr)
library(text2vec)
library(tidytext)
library(caret)
library(tokenizers)

imdb <- read.csv("./data/labeledTrainData.tsv"
                 , encoding = "utf-8"
                 , quote = ""
                 , sep="\t"
                 , stringsAsFactors = F)

tokens <- tokenize_words(imdb$review, stopwords = stopwords())

# Boring boilerplate preprocessing
token_iterator <- itoken(tokens)
vocab <- create_vocabulary(token_iterator)
vocab <- prune_vocabulary(vocab, term_count_min = 5L)
vectorizer <- vocab_vectorizer(vocab)

# Create context and embedding
tcm <- create_tcm(token_iterator, vectorizer, skip_grams_window = 5L)
glove <- GlobalVectors$new(word_vectors_size = 50,
 vocabulary = vocab,
 x_max = 10)
wv_main = glove$fit_transform(tcm,
 n_iter = 10,
 convergence_tol = 0.01)
text <- unlist(imdb$review)
text_df <- data_frame(line = 1:length(text), text = text)
text_df <- text_df %>%
 unnest_tokens(word, text)
```

Let's try now with the context vector as well, instead of the main word vector:

```
wv_context <- glove$components
wv <- as.data.frame(wv_main+t(wv_context))
wv$word <- row.names(wv)
df <- wv%>% inner_join(text_df)
```

To then finally create the trained matrix:

```
df <- df %>% group_by(line) %>% summarize_all(mean) %>% select(1:51)
df$label <- as.factor(imdb$sentiment)
```

And finally, create a baseline neural network model with a single layer:

```
library(keras)

X <- df[,2:51]
y <- df[,52]

y <- to_categorical(y[["label"]])
y <- y[,2:3]

model <- keras_model_sequential()
model %>%
  layer_dense(activation='relu', units =20, input_shape=c(50))%>%
  layer_dense(units=2, activation = 'softmax')

model %>% compile(
  loss = 'categorical_crossentropy',
  optimizer = optimizer_rmsprop(),
  metrics = c('accuracy')
  )

history <- model %>% keras::fit(
as.matrix(X), y,
epochs = 30, batch_size = 128,
validation_split = 0.2
  )
```

Calling the fit method triggers the training procedure. Once the training is done, we can see how it went by using the `plot` function:

```
plot(history)
```

Which gives us some slightly disappointing results:

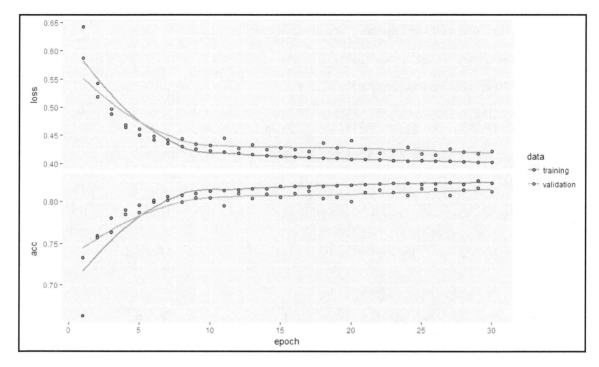

Performance of our single layer neural network with 20 neurons

Why is that disappointing? Well, our mighty neural network with 20 neurons did not improve upon, say, random forests. How can we improve this result?

It seems to be that neural networks in this case, or at least feed-forward neural networks might not be of much help here, or at least we were not able to find significant improvements by adding more layers. Actually it seemed to worsen results with three or more layers, and we even observed over-fitting.

 Occam's razor should prevail. The model you keep should be as simple as possible. A complicated model might be of little use in production because of the technical complications needed to deploy it. Furthermore, when we have no way of interpreting the model, unexpected results might happen when the model is applied to slightly different data from that used for training and testing.

We can save both our vector embedding and model for later use:

```
write.csv(wv,"./data/wv.csv", row.names = F)
save_model_hdf5(model,"glove_nn.hdf5")
```

Bi-directional LSTM networks

Well, our model did not quite work before with simple feed-forward networks. In this section, we will try a different model: Bi-directional LSTM networks.

Recall that LSTM networks preserve parts of the previous information via the hidden state. However, this information is only about the **past**.

Bidirectional LSTM run both ways—from past to future and back! The LSTM that runs backwards preserves information from the **future**. Using the two hidden states combined, you are able to keep the context of both past and future. Clearly this would not make sense for stock price prediction! Their use was initially justified in the domain of speech recognition because, as you might know from experience, the context of the full phrase is often needed to understand the meaning of a word. This happens, for instance, when you are trying to simultaneously translate from one language to another.

Ok, so how do we do this? Let's come back to `keras`. This will make the experience rather smooth, as we have seen before.

For the bidirectional LSTM API, keras expects, per row, one document with a list of words, which are passed over sequentially.

Let's begin with some familiar preprocessing steps:

```
library(purrr)
library(stringr)
library(tm)
library(keras)

df <- read.csv("./data/labeledTrainData.tsv", encoding = "utf-8", quote =
"", sep="\t", stringsAsFactors = F)

text <- df$review

corpus <- VCorpus(VectorSource(text))
corpus <- tm_map(corpus,content_transformer(tolower))
corpus <- tm_map(corpus, content_transformer(removePunctuation))
corpus <- tm_map(corpus, content_transformer(removeNumbers))
corpus <- tm_map(corpus, content_transformer(removeWords),
stopwords("english"))
```

```
dtm <- DocumentTermMatrix(corpus)
dtm <- removeSparseTerms(dtm, sparse=0.99)

X <- as.data.frame(as.matrix(dtm))
```

This returns a huge document-term matrix that has a lot of zeros. Now, we need to parse it to keep only the indices of the words that have non-zero values:

```
vocab <- names(X)
maxlen <- 100
dataset <- map(
 1:nrow(X),
 ~list(review = which(X[.x,]!=0))
)
dataset <- transpose(dataset)
```

And finally vectorize this in a usable way:

```
X <- array(0, dim = c(length(dataset$review), maxlen))
y <- array(0, dim = c(length(dataset$review)))
for(i in 1:length(dataset$review)){
  for(j in 1:maxlen){
    if(length(dataset$review[[i]])>j){
      X[i,j] <- dataset$review[[i]][j]
    }
    else{
      X[i,j] <- 0
    }
  }
  y[i] <- df[i,"sentiment"]
}

X <- as.matrix(X)
```

Which gives us:

```
> X[1,]
 [1] 23 46 49 65 71 100 109 115 137 144 149 161 165 185 188 190 193 196 210
217 235 271
 [23] 286 287 295 308 317 326 359 365 366 376 380 390 407 436 441 464 469
483 494 498 511 514
 [45] 520 521 571 580 585 588 595 603 613 628 662 693 705 726 734 742 749
760 776 795 797 803
 [67] 808 828 832 843 848 852 871 872 890 892 897 900 908 922 929 931 955
973 975 983 994 1008
 [89] 1019 1044 1072 1127 1140 1144 1184 1205 1217 1315 1317 1321
```

On each row, we have the first 100 words of the review, and we added zeros to the end if the review was shorter than 100 words. Now, we are ready to define our network:

```
# Initialize model
model <- keras_model_sequential()
model %>%
  # Creates dense embedding layer; outputs 3D tensor
  # with shape (batch_size, sequence_length, output_dim)
                layer_embedding(input_dim = length(vocab),
                output_dim = 128,
                input_length = maxlen) %>%
  bidirectional(layer_lstm(units = 64)) %>%
  layer_dropout(rate = 0.5) %>%
  layer_dense(units = 1, activation = 'sigmoid')
```

A few comments are in order here: First, note that the output layer is one-dimensional instead of two-dimensional, as before. This is purely for pedagogic purposes, and in the multi-class setup you would prefer to use similar code as before. Next, observe that there is a `layer_embedding` function, which is used for passing sequential data. Finally, the layer corresponding to the bidirectional LSTM comes, followed by a dropout.

Wait, what is dropout? **Dropout** is a technique introduced recently that simply *forgets* to train some neurons. This might seem weird, but in reality it is a very efficient way of performing model averaging with neural networks. In a similar way that averaging trees produces better models (less prone to over-fitting), averaging weaker neural networks results in a more robust model.

Now, we compile the model (note the different loss function, due to the different output):

```
# Compile: you can try different compilers
model %>% compile(
 loss = 'binary_crossentropy',
 optimizer = 'adam',
 metrics = c('accuracy')
)
```

And we are now ready to call the `fit` method:

```
> history <- model %>% fit(
  X, y,
  batch_size = 128,
  epochs = 4,
  validation_size = 0.2
  )
Epoch 1/4
25000/25000 [==============================] - 155s - loss: 0.4428 - acc:
0.7886
```

```
Epoch 2/4
25000/25000 [==============================] - 161s - loss: 0.3162 - acc:
0.8714
Epoch 3/4
25000/25000 [==============================] - 166s - loss: 0.2983 - acc:
0.8770
Epoch 4/4
25000/25000 [==============================] - 176s - loss: 0.2855 - acc:
0.8825

# Train model over four epochs
history <- model %>% fit(
  X, y,
  batch_size = 128,
  epochs = 4,
  validation_size = 0.2
)

> plot(history)
```

Not bad, we reach very good accuracy with LSTMs, significantly above feed-forward networks.

Other LSTM architectures

Bidirectional LSTM seemed to be a good idea, right? What about a simpler network architecture?

Instead of a bidirectional LSTM, we can consider a simple LSTM. To do this, we can replace the preceding model (after doing the same preprocessing; that is, feeding the data in the same format) with a simple LSTM:

```
model <- keras_model_sequential()
model %>%
 layer_embedding(input_dim = length(vocab),
 output_dim = 128,
 input_length = 100) %>%
 layer_lstm(units = 64, dropout = 0.2, recurrent_dropout = 0.2) %>%
 layer_dense(units = 1, activation = 'sigmoid')

model %>% compile(
    loss = "binary_crossentropy",
    optimizer = "adam",
```

```
    metrics = "accuracy"
  )
```

After training, we get the following results:

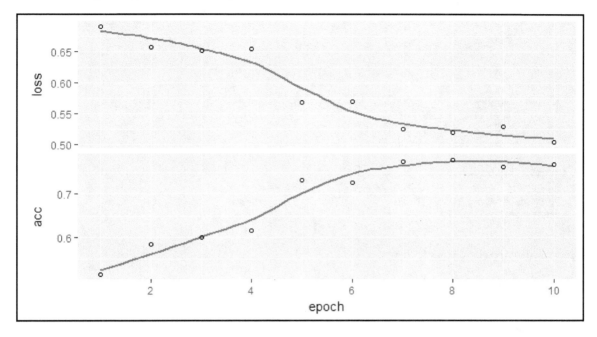

Training an LSTM in the IMDb data

So, as you can see, we experienced a significant loss in quality. This dataset is unfortunately too small for vanilla LSTMs to beat simpler configurations, such as tf-idf and logistic regression, or our GloVe + random forest experiment.

Notice also the different shape of the loss. An interesting, if not completely clear (at least to us), issue that calls our attention is the difference in shape—a small bump instead of exponential decay. This is not unusual to see in LSTMs, as opposed to other architectures, such as feed-forward networks or convolutional neural networks.

Actually, now that we mention CNNs, they can be used in language, too!:

```
# Initialize model
model <- keras_model_sequential()

model %>%
  layer_embedding(
                  input_dim = length(vocab),
```

```
                output_dim = 128,
                input_length = 100
                ) %>%
layer_dropout(0.25) %>%
layer_conv_1d(
                filters=64,
                kernel_size=5,
                padding = "valid",
                activation = "relu",
                strides = 1
            ) %>%
layer_max_pooling_1d(pool_size=4) %>%
layer_lstm(70) %>%
layer_dense(1) %>%
layer_activation("sigmoid")

model %>% compile(
 loss = "binary_crossentropy",
 optimizer = "adam",
 metrics = "accuracy"
)
```

The results are shown as follows:

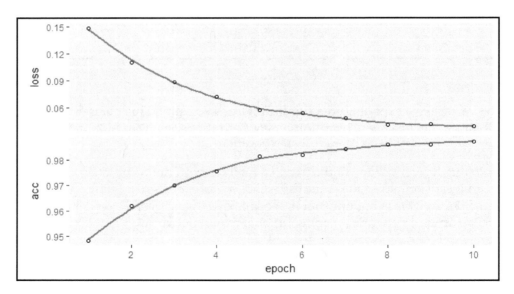

Results for a combination of a CNN and an LSTM network

We get an almost too impressive performance. How do CNNs work in text? In a similar way as they work in pictures, one-dimensional convolutional neural networks are convolved with the input layer over a spatial window length (five in our example). It is certainly easier to imagine *average of colors/intensity* on a certain window in an image, and we would not like to push an analogy that makes no sense. As the field is evolving so fast, perhaps soon we would have a more satisfactory explanation of the effectiveness of CNN in sentiment analysis tasks. For the time being, let's be glad that they work fine and can be trained reasonably fast.

> Beware that, for the sake of brevity, in most of the examples in this chapter we have omitted the verification of the results on the validation set (which is still the right thing to do, even if we rely on Keras' validation mechanism). So do not take the scores presented at face value.

Exercises

- Use the *context vector*, or a combination of the context vector and the main vector from GloVe. How do the results change? You can also build a meta-model that calculates the appropriate weight you should give to each vector.
- Do the results improve significantly if we use stemming?
- Can you improve the results by playing with the parameters of GloVe? You can tweak `skip_grams_window` for instance, or the number of iterations.
- You can also try to implement `fastText` (https://keras.rstudio.com/articles/examples/imdb_fasttext.html) using `keras`.

Mining sentiment from Twitter

It's time to put our knowledge of different sentiment classification models in a more realistic scenario—Twitter sentiment analysis.

As we mentioned in the introduction, sentiment analysis is of great interest for all companies that have a presence online (which is, well, lots of companies in many countries). It is also relevant for politicians, researchers, stock traders and others.

Before using any service or API, be sure to review their *terms of service* and follow them! We do not encourage unlawful behavior in any way.

Connecting to the Twitter API

Luckily for us, there is a nice package in R to retrieve our Tweets: The library `twitteR`. First, there are a number of steps you need to follow:

1. If you do not have one, create a Twitter account to be able to access their API.
2. Go to `https://dev.twitter.com/apps` and log in with your credentials.
3. Once logged in, click on **Create New App**.
4. Put this as callback URL `http://localhost:1410`.
5. Now go to **Keys and Access Tokens** and then **Create my access token**.
6. You should have a screen showing you four things:
   - **Consumer key**
   - **Consumer secret**
   - **Access token**
   - **Access secret**

Use them in the following snippet to gather some Tweets:

```
#install.packages("twitteR")
library(twitteR)

# Change the next four lines based on your own consumer_key,
consume_secret, access_token, and access_secret.
consumer_key <- "YOUR CONSUMER KEY"
consumer_secret <- "YOUR CONSUMER SECRET"
access_token <- "YOUR ACCESS TOKEN"
access_secret <- "YOUR ACCESS SECRET"

setup_twitter_oauth(consumer_key, consumer_secret, access_token,
access_secret)
tw = twitteR::searchTwitter('#something'
                            , n = 1e4
                            , since = '2017-12-08'
                            , retryOnRateLimit = 1e3)
d = twitteR::twListToDF(tw)
```

Note that this is merely for demonstration purposes, but remember, you should use the APIs responsibly and at your own risk and responsibility.

Building our model

If you have a Twitter account and you would like to analyze your own history, you can follow the official instructions on their website (`https://help.twitter.com/en/managing-your-account/how-to-download-your-twitter-archive`) and you will receive a ZIP file with your own Tweet history.

We will use Pablo's Twitter data for demonstration.

Exploratory data analysis

As explained earlier in this chapter, one thing you can do is to look for an annotated lexicon per sentiment and try to do some basic analysis there, thanks to the package `tidytext`.

First, we import a few libraries that would come handy and load our Twitter history:

```
library(plyr)
library(dplyr)
library(tidytext)
library(ggplot2)
df <- read.csv("./data/Tweets.csv", stringsAsFactors = F)
text_df <- data_frame(tweet_id=df$tweet_id, tweet=df$text)
```

Now, we use the `unnest_tokens` function to bring the data into tidy format:

```
text_df <- text_df %>%
  unnest_tokens(word, tweet)
```

And remove the stop words:

```
data(stop_words)
head(stop_words)
text_df <- text_df %>% anti_join(stop_words)
```

Once this is done, we join it with, for instance, the `bing` lexicon:

```
bing <- get_sentiments("bing")
text_df %>% inner_join(bing)
```

And we are ready!

```
# Plot
text_df %>%
  inner_join(bing) %>%
  count(sentiment) %>%
  ggplot(aes(sentiment, n, fill=sentiment))+
  geom_col()+
  theme_bw()
```

What do we learn from this? Well, that Pablo is a bit more of a negative person on Twitter, as the data shows. Unfortunately, it is our duty as data scientists to present the facts, even when they are not favorable to us.

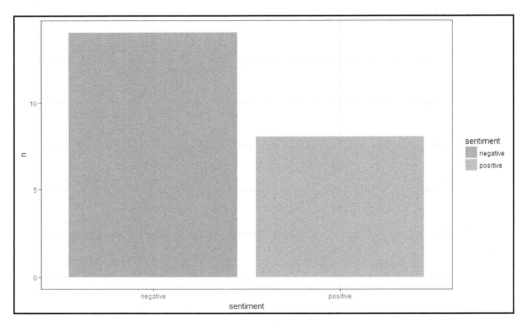

Pablo is slightly more negative in Twitter than in person

Using a trained model

Alternatively, and perhaps more interestingly, we can use a trained model to predict sentiment. We can train our model in a larger corpus and then simply apply it online to the new examples that come.

First, let's load our model and the vector embedding that we trained before for the movie reviews:

```
wv <- read.csv("./data/wv.csv")
model <- load_model_hdf5("glove_nn.hdf5")
```

As before, we join the vector representations with the data in tidy form:

```
df <- wv%>% inner_join(text_df)
```

And take the average of those vectors per Tweet as the embedded representation of our Tweet:

```
df <- df %>% group_by(tweet_id) %>% summarize_all(mean) %>% select(1:51)
preds <- model %>% predict(as.matrix(df[,2:51]))
hist(preds[,1])
```

As we structured our model, we will get predicted probabilities for each class. This is shown in the histogram as follows:

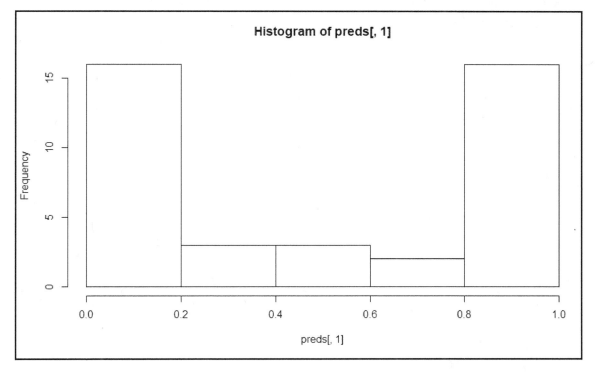

Distribution of predicted class (i.e. sentiment) probabilities

So, this is roughly the same distribution as before (recall that before we had no probabilities, but we inferred the sentiment directly). This is a good sign that the model might be doing the right things, but as always, it is better to take a look directly at the data.

Summary

In this chapter, we covered a lot! We learned how to use dense instead of sparse vectors to represent words, using word2vec or GloVe, although we only used GloVe. We worked with an annotated lexicon; tidy data can already bring a lot of insight! No need to bring in the heavy artillery in many cases. We saw that slightly more complicated models may not perform well (adding layers to the feed-forward neural network); surprisingly, much more complicated models can (using bidirectional LSTMs)! After that, we provided a reference for connecting to Twitter, while keeping in mind that terms of service should be respected. For this, we used previously calculated vector embeddings and models to evaluate the sentiment of new data. And, don't forget, a key point—always check your data! Remember, garbage in, garbage out. Even the best models will provide useless results if the wrong data is used.

Other Books You May Enjoy

If you enjoyed this book, you may be interested in these other books by Packt:

Machine Learning with R - Second Edition
Brett Lantz

ISBN: 978-1-78439-390-8

- Harness the power of R to build common machine learning algorithms with real-world data science applications
- Get to grips with R techniques to clean and prepare your data for analysis, and visualize your results
- Discover the different types of machine learning models and learn which is best to meet your data needs and solve your analysis problems
- Classify your data with Bayesian and nearest neighbor methods
- Predict values by using R to build decision trees, rules, and support vector machines
- Forecast numeric values with linear regression, and model your data with neural networks
- Evaluate and improve the performance of machine learning models
- Learn specialized machine learning techniques for text mining, social network data, big data, and more

R Deep Learning Cookbook
Dr. PKS Prakash, Achyutuni Sri Krishna Rao

ISBN: 9781787121089

- Build deep learning models in different application areas using TensorFlow, H2O, and MXnet.
- Analyzing a Deep boltzmann machine
- Setting up and Analyzing Deep belief networks
- Building supervised model using various machine learning algorithms
- Set up variants of basic convolution function
- Represent data using Autoencoders.
- Explore generative models available in Deep Learning.
- Discover sequence modeling using Recurrent nets
- Learn fundamentals of Reinforcement Leaning
- Learn the steps involved in applying Deep Learning in text mining
- Explore application of deep learning in signal processing
- Utilize Transfer learning for utilizing pre-trained model
- Train a deep learning model on a GPU

Leave a review - let other readers know what you think

Please share your thoughts on this book with others by leaving a review on the site that you bought it from. If you purchased the book from Amazon, please leave us an honest review on this book's Amazon page. This is vital so that other potential readers can see and use your unbiased opinion to make purchasing decisions, we can understand what our customers think about our products, and our authors can see your feedback on the title that they have worked with Packt to create. It will only take a few minutes of your time, but is valuable to other potential customers, our authors, and Packt. Thank you!

Index